DISCARD

ROOSEVELT
AND
MORGENTHAU

Also by John Morton Blum

ROOSEVELT

AND

MORGENTHAU

A Revision and Condensation of

FROM THE MORGENTHAU DIARIES

John Morton Blum

Boston

HOUGHTON MIFFLIN COMPANY

1970

First Printing w

CONTENTS

Book Two. *Years of Urgency, 1938–1941*

*To those who tried and
those who still attempt to effect
that rendezvous with destiny.*

INTRODUCTION

"I WANT SOMEONE," Mr. Morgenthau said to me at luncheon one day in 1954, "who will work with me on my biography. I want an historian to go through my Diaries* and write an account of my years with Franklin Roosevelt. . . . I want him to tell the whole story." That statement provided the chart and compass for the three volumes, *From the Morgenthau Diaries*, on which this book is based. Those three volumes, endeavoring to tell "the whole story," contain rather elaborate accounts of Morgenthau's major activities as Secretary of the Treasury, of his discharge of his official duties and of the special missions the President continually assigned to him. Much of the material pertinent to those ventures is of a somewhat technical nature; much of it focuses on ventures in government only remotely related to the President. This single volume attempts to concentrate the account, within the limits of the historically possible, on its two central protagonists — Roosevelt and Morgenthau, and in so doing to emphasize the most significant episodes in their long relationship.

As with the three-volume study, so with this book, the text is not autobiographical. I wrote all of it, but Mr. Morgenthau, who

* See "A Note on Sources," p. 653.

participated intimately in the process, gave the longer work much of its flavor and that flavor imbues the shorter, too. We had from the first an easy method of collaboration: I prepared a draft based upon the Morgenthau Diaries and other materials; he reviewed the draft and made suggestions for revisions, none of which ever violated the integrity of the historical data which I had explored and selected for use. We employed no intermediaries, we had no staff except for a succession of assiduous and amiable typists, but we did value the historical and literary advice of Arthur Schlesinger, Jr., who had introduced us. Still, the product, including this one volume, represents exactly what Mr. Morgenthau initially asked for, a book by an historian working with him, a book about his years with Roosevelt, a kind of authorized biography tempered by his reflections and organized according to my own sense of historical and biographical relevance.

As Mr. Morgenthau had intended, the product of our collaboration left the ultimate assessment of his career, both of his policies and of his relationship with President Roosevelt, primarily to the reader. Some readers, especially since Mr. Morgenthau's death in 1967, have urged me not only to prepare this book but also to step aside from the material and express assessments of my own. Stepping aside raises some difficult problems. Mr. Morgenthau did not expect me to sit in judgment on him, though he was prepared to accept the judgments, however adverse, that others reached after examination of the record. Further, over a period of a dozen years, years of continual research in the Morgenthau Diaries and of continual visits with their creator, I grew fond of my older collaborator, who was generous and sympathetic in his friendship for me. I do not in this book intend a eulogy by any means, but I do not pretend to a distant objectivity about an avuncular man whom I liked and respected.

Still, within the limits I have described, I see no objection to stepping aside as I often did in my private conversations with Mr. Morgenthau. To cite two major examples: as I often told him, it seemed to me that the unsophisticated economics of the early 1930's left public policy makers for several crucial years without the intelligence by which they might otherwise have prevented the tragic prolongation of depression. When at last the insights of Keynesian theory did penetrate both the academic world and some councils of government, most responsible men in Washington, both in Congress and within the Executive Branch, continued to question the new economics. Secretary Morgenthau was one such influential skeptic. As this book indicates, he never embraced the idea of deliberate countercyclical fiscal policy. Like most historians and economists, I believe he was wrong. To the day he died, however, he argued that a balanced budget had never been tried and might have worked. We simply agreed to disagree. Similarly Mr. Morgenthau knew that, in retrospect, I shared the criticisms of the Morgenthau Plan for Germany that his own staff advanced at the time he was developing that plan. Nevertheless he was confident in 1967, as he had been in 1945, that a renascent Germany constituted the single, greatest potential threat to peace in Europe. In discussing that issue, as in discussing others, I learned what the Treasury staff had learned, that Mr. Morgenthau welcomed, indeed invited, the honest opinion of those to whom he had assigned responsibility, but that he also reserved his right as an individual to make up his own mind.

During a sunny luncheon at his farm in 1966, Mr. Morgenthau reflected about his years in government and what they had meant to him. Those reflections appear, essentially unedited, in the last pages of this book. The weight of current historical opinion does not, of course, wholly concur in his emphases and conclusions. But historical judgments have themselves a continuing flux, and today's critics of Roosevelt and the New Dealers will doubtless soon have successors of still different casts of mind. Against that day, some further assessment here of parts of the record of the team of Roosevelt and Morgenthau may be in order.

To many of his colleagues during the New Deal, Henry Morgenthau, Jr., seemed too conservative, for in their view his orthodox fiscal policies impeded spending programs they wanted to undertake. Yet Harry Hopkins, whom Morgenthau trusted, was always able in the end to enlist the Treasury in spending to assist the unemployed. Further, at least until 1938 and in some measure thereafter, Roosevelt shared Morgenthau's hesitancies about massive spending, and even after 1938 the Congress remained dubious about the new economics. The fiscal preferences of the Treasury did not, in and of themselves, significantly delay federal public policy from following the implications of Keynesian thought.

More important, Morgenthau, by the standards of the 1960's, was distinctly liberal in other facets of political economy. Without success, but in contrast to the President's most influential counsellors on agriculture, Morgenthau opposed the effort to help farmers by limiting production as a device to raise commodity prices. His continuing objective was to distribute rather than to curtail abundance. So it was that he sponsored the food stamp program which had as one purpose assuring a properly balanced diet for the indigent. To men like Henry Wallace and Rex Tugwell, Morgenthau seemed impractical at best, but however impractical at the time, his intention has come to command the enthusiasm of a self-conscious "left" in this day.

So, too, the continuing reliance of Morgenthau and the Treasury on monetary policy, the concern of the Secretary and his associates for low interest rates as one tool for regulating the economy and for helping Americans on farms and in small businesses, have their latter-day advocates. The techniques that the Treasury employed, with Roosevelt's support, appear now unsophisticated, even crude. But the 1960's have witnessed a renewed interest among professional economists in monetary policy, and a renewed concern among liberals for a monetary policy that helps, rather than hindering, the small operator or entrepreneur.

In the same vein, Morgenthau's purpose, which became in a degree the purpose of the New Deal for a few years after 1935, to attack the power of incorporated bigness in the United States, has won new adherents in the 1960's. Morgenthau's suspicions of Wall Street, which were Roosevelt's too, did not seem quaint in 1933 and do not seem quaint in 1969, though Wall Street had its season in the sun in some intervening years. Further, Morgenthau's restlessness after 1940 with the influence of Manhattan lawyers, investment brokers and their friends within the War and Navy Departments, his restlessness, that is, with what has lately on occasion been called the Establishment, marks him by today's standard neither as a conservative nor as a populist obstructionist, which Henry Stimson sometimes thought he was.

Most significantly, perhaps, the Treasury and its Secretary stood, to a degree no one of Morgenthau's successors has yet matched, for the kind of redistributive taxation, and for the elimination of tax loopholes for the wealthy, during peace and war alike, that Congress rejected to the continuing detriment of social justice in the United States. As Morgenthau put it himself, he was a New Dealer, so was Roosevelt, and there were never enough of them. They believed in the people and in their future, and their liberal aspirations still speak to liberal men.

Like other liberals of his time, Roosevelt in particular, Morgenthau has been criticized by the New Left for his effective opposition to German and Japanese aggression, an opposition which the New Left has interpreted as American imperialism. So, too, he has been criticized from the right for his allegedly soft attitude toward the Soviet Union. Along the spectrum of attitudes toward foreign policy, Morgenthau was, in his time, ordinarily more "left" than "right," but he always stood for what he conceived to be the national interest. On that basis he recognized the threat of Nazi Germany and her allies, and he concluded, as most of his generation and their children came also to conclude, that the defeat of the Axis constituted the essential prerequisite for democracy anywhere. At the appropriate hour, like Roosevelt and Churchill, he welcomed the Soviet Union as an ally in that objective. Further, he believed that Russian-American friendship, like Anglo-American friendship, was necessary for a true postwar peace. He cultivated that friendship, even sponsored without success a proposal for a large postwar credit for Russia, not without some suspicions about Russian intentions, but always with patience and hope. Those qualities today commend themselves again in the structuring of American foreign policy.

Morgenthau's further conviction that ideals lay at the root of the conflict during World War II led him to doubt the value of Chiang Kai-shek as an ally and to question the wisdom of American arrangements of expediency with men like Darlan and Badoglio. Unhappy with those compromises of American purpose, he appeared naïve to advocates of *real politik* — often to Henry Stimson, sometimes to Roosevelt himself. But the legacies of wartime *real politik* do not after a quarter of a century seem demonstrably brighter than might have been the ultimate consequences of Morgenthau's idealism. As he feared, the habit of compromise with unattractive allies has clouded the reputation of the United States as a true champion of the high principles which Roosevelt defined during World War II for American policy then and later.

Henry Morgenthau never thought of himself as a great man. Rather, he was a man of influence who served a great President. As he constantly said, he could have done nothing without Roosevelt's confidence and support. Those who disliked Morgenthau considered him contentious, irritable, and unyielding. As they saw it, he was either a puppet or a scold within the President's official household. But in the view of Eleanor Roosevelt, Morgenthau above all was "Franklin's conscience." She described their relationship exactly:

> For . . . many years, both as friends and as workers, my husband and I were closely associated with Mr. and Mrs. Henry Morgenthau, Jr. They were much younger than we were but the difference in age seemed to matter very little. They were our neighbors in the country and we enjoyed them as neighbors and friends before politics and work for different social aims came into our friendship. . . . My husband never held a political office from the time of his governorship . . . without having Henry Morgenthau, Jr., in some way in his official family. My husband no doubt often treated Henry as a younger brother, they differed and were annoyed with each other and probably said things neither of them meant on occasion, but there was an underlying deep devotion and trust which never really wavered.

That, again in Mrs. Roosevelt's words, is what this book is about: "the existence of basic trust and respect between two men who lived in strenuous and exciting times which required great qualities and . . . fostered great friendships."

JOHN MORTON BLUM

BOOK ONE

YEARS OF CRISIS

1928–1938

I

ONE OF TWO OF A KIND

1891–1932

1. The Land and the People

THE SOURCE of the good life was the land. The purpose of the good life was helping those who needed help. The land and the people were the important things, the things the young man cared about. He was a sensitive young man who wanted to strike out on his own. He had grown up with wealth but he had no interest in a career of making money. He had attended an excellent school and college but he had no interest in the professions of law or medicine or management for which excellent schools and colleges train most of their alumni. He found his satisfactions instead in his family, in the bounty and the beauty of the land, and in striving to bring something of the bountiful and the beautiful to the thousands of Americans whose existence was meager and drab. He did not think he knew the secrets of the universe, but he did think he knew good from evil, and he believed the land and people good.

He was a farmer, a reformer, a democrat, one of the children of American plenty whose spirits have transcended the material advantages of their personal inheritances. This transcendence and his independence gave him the equipment for disinterested public service. Friendship with another young man of wealth and independence and high purpose gave him in time the opportunity for public service.

As the close associate of Franklin Delano Roosevelt, Henry Morgenthau, Jr., made his contributions to America. For Morgenthau the young man, the desire to contribute grew out of the definitions of the good life he made in his youth.

Henry Morgenthau, Jr., was born in New York City on May 11, 1891, the only son and the third of four children of Henry and Josephine Sykes Morgenthau. His forebears were German Jews. The senior Henry Morgenthau, starting with little, had become rich by 1891 and was to become increasingly so thereafter. A self-made, self-confident, restless, and forceful man, one of New York's shrewdest investors in real estate, the elder Morgenthau was also a generous and conscientious steward of his wealth who was involved emotionally as well as financially in supporting the Ethical Culture church, the Henry Street Settlement, and the movement "to clear up the slums and the fire traps" that followed the death of over a hundred girls in the Triangle fire of 1911. In the same year he joined the campaign to make Woodrow Wilson President. "Mother felt weak," Morgenthau, Jr., recalled, "when father walked into the room. He was electric, a bundle of nerves and ambition."

Josephine Morgenthau, a woman almost as ambitious and as energetic as her husband, brought to her home warmth, volatility, and a love of beautiful things. For many years she was absorbed by social work, particularly the development of Bronx House and the school of music there. She wanted young Henry, who had a fine deep voice, to learn to sing, but her husband considered singing "sissy," so the boy was taught instead to play the cello, which he never much enjoyed. Characteristically, the senior Morgenthau exercised a kind of exclusive proprietorship over the upbringing of his son, who found the restrictive intimacy of this relationship at times oppressive.

"Henry Morgenthau, Jr.," his wife Elinor later recalled, "was an average, sturdy, fun-loving youngster, not particularly given to intellectual study. He loved riding, golf, swimming, driving a car, sailing, puttering with a motor boat, rowing and canoeing. For all these things he had a natural aptitude." But, she went on, he was "an only son with a father who adored him, who made him his constant companion. He adored his father. This undoubtedly had both its good and bad sides. . . . Things his father did and told him come back to him — never to drive such a hard bargain that your customer wouldn't return, never to go on a note, never to become director of a bank controlled by politicians, never to accept a business favor for which you were not able to pay in full. . . . On the other hand, his father tried to regulate his life and to dominate his thoughts — he kept him too much with him and away from companions his own age."

At thirteen Morgenthau entered Phillips Exeter Academy, where he began to keep a diary, a practice which he continued intermittently the rest of his life. On September 19, 1904, "the first check I ever drew from a bank" was to the order of "cash" for $2; on February 9, 1905, "it snowed all day. . . . We had an English Exam and I received B as a mark." Morgenthau's grades were ordinarily less than B. He continually fell asleep over his work, not from lack of interest, but from the fatigue of his adolescent growth. "He had been robust," Elinor Morgenthau pointed out, "but in one year before he was 14 he grew about 9 inches so that at 14 he had his present height of 6′ 1½″. This handicapped him all through school and college. A great big gawk, loving sports and naturally good at them, yet in decidedly delicate health, never being allowed to join in organized athletics, and always being so tired that he couldn't quite keep up with his work."

After two years at Exeter, Morgenthau returned home to finish preparing for college, first at Sachs Collegiate Institute in New York City and then with a Mr. Kramer in Ithaca. In January 1909 he matriculated at Cornell to study architecture, not because he had any real interest in the subject, but because his father thought it relevant to the future he planned for his son in real estate. Three semesters were enough for Morgenthau, who left Cornell in 1911.

During the following year, he tried various ventures his father selected, but none suited him. In contrast, at the Henry Street Settlement, New York's equivalent of Hull House in Chicago, he gained genuine satisfactions. There during the hot weeks of the summer, he nightly pulled his mattress to the roof, daily presided over the boys' table and saw how the indigent lived. It was an awakening apprenticeship. Years later, Lillian D. Wald, the head of the settlement, wrote to Josephine Roche, a new Assistant Secretary of the Treasury: "You are associated with my dear friend Secretary Morgenthau. . . . He will understand and appreciate your simplicity and sincerity."

There was much to learn. To convalesce from typhoid fever, Morgenthau in 1911 went to Texas, where he had the leisure to find out something about farming and ranching and a lot about himself. In 1912 he told his father that he had decided to become a farmer. Above all he was determined to be in a business about which his father knew nothing, to stand on his own feet and make his own mistakes. "Pop started from the bottom," Morgenthau later said, "when he was nine years old. From then on his whole life he had all of his family on his neck. He was the only one who was a financial success. Every penny meant something to him. He had to fight every inch of the way. His theory for me was you can start at the top and save all that. That was his philosophy. I had to overcome that. He was crazy to have me in business with him. He would say to my poor mother, 'Josy, you can have the girls, let me have the boy.' In a desperate move to get out from under I moved to the country."

First he enrolled again at Cornell, this time to study agriculture. Impatient as always with books and lectures, he left the college after a few months to see for himself what the farmer's opportunities were. With Carl Schurz Scofield, a young expert from the Department of Agriculture, he set out on a trip to the west coast. He and Scofield investigated farms producing wheat, potatoes, alfalfa, milk and cream, cattle, sugar, rice, and citrus fruits. He gave special attention to the mechanization of agriculture, to scientific farming, to canning for home consumption, and to rural schools. He returned to New York with new enthusiasm for agriculture as a calling, convinced that better management could result in increased production, wider consumption, and an improved standard of living not for farmers only but for the entire country. He was persuaded also that his own best opportunity lay close to home in Dutchess County. There, in the area of East Fishkill, where the foothills of the Berkshires come within an easy ride of the Hudson River, in 1913 he purchased several hundred acres, many of them orchard, the core of the farm that was thereafter his home and his vocation.

2. New Vistas

Morgenthau's first years as a farmer were interrupted by journeys to Turkey, where his father was the American ambassador. On his second visit the young man arrived soon after the Turks entered World War I as allies of the Germans. He left the day before the British and French began to bombard the Dardanelles — the first stage of a military plan of the *enfant terrible* of the British Admiralty, Winston Churchill — and returned home via London where, as private secretary to his father, he delivered a message about conditions in Constantinople to Sir Edward Grey, the distinguished British Foreign Secretary. In London again in November 1915 he received from Grey for communication to the Turks an official proposal for an exchange of prisoners. After reaching Constantinople, he inspected the tough Turkish lines at Gallipoli, where a "perfectly gorgeous" view contrasted with the land pocked while he watched by shells of the British artillery.

At the American embassy German officials disturbed Morgenthau by their outspoken intention to resort to brutality to win the war. They also impressed him in other ways. The new German ambassador had been to luncheon, he wrote home: "It was most interesting. . . . The German is very shrewd, of the old school of diplomacy, by which I mean he always flatters by suggestion and is very suave, etc. . . . it will not be long before he will have great influence here." Like his father, Morgenthau deplored that influence, sympathized with France and England,

and hoped and expected that the United States would get into the war on their side.

"I was a little office boy," he recalled. "I never did anything, but it was a thrilling experience. I was there because my father wanted company. What the Turks did to the Armenians made a terrific impact on me. Later on when the Germans did the same things to the Jews, I remembered the feelings I had had in Turkey during World War I. And I also always remembered one Christmas Eve at the Dardanelles. There was a German officer there sitting and talking who didn't know that I understood German. I heard him damning Americans in foul language. This made a great impression on me."

He witnessed some great events and met some famous men, but Morgenthau remained committed to his farm and to Dutchess County. There he took his bride of April 1916, Elinor Fatman, whom he had known since their childhood when they met at play in Central Park. Her father was the chairman of the Raritan Woolen Mills of New Jersey; her mother, a Lehman. She graduated in 1913 from Vassar College, where she was a competent and popular student and the president of the dramatic society. Her dark, poised intensity, her quick intelligence, her extraordinary warmth made an immediate and persisting impression upon those who knew her. She had an energetic and informed interest both in creative arts and in social work, a suppressed ambition and a latent talent for a career in the law, a selfless zeal for community service.

Like her husband city-born and city-bred, she nevertheless found, as he did, large satisfactions in country life. From the time they were married it was as a team that they made plans for their farm and their future, made friends, and made a mark in their adopted new home. Thinking back to the beginning of their happy life together and forward across the whole range of his career, Morgenthau without hesitation attributed to her the principal credit for anything worthwhile that he had done. After brief service in the Navy during World War I, Morgenthau tried his hand at potatoes and cabbages, squash and rye, corn and beef cattle. At last he settled on a dairy herd over which one profit-sharing employee presided, and an apple orchard, which became his own special enthusiasm. "Mr. Morgenthau," the manager of the herd once remarked, "knows his cows." He knew his apples, too; he had to. Apples demand courageous care, being subject to more blights and bugs than children, and enormous patience, for some kinds of trees do not bear commercially useful crops for years. But pain and patience made them pay, and Morgenthau liked to attribute his lasting financial conservatism to his difficult times with a dozen breeds of apples.

The visitor to his farm was sure to be invited to join its owner for an hour or so in the orchards, to learn from him the name and history and bearing habits of each variety of tree, to hear him discuss with his superintendent the latest spray, the irrigation ditches, the machinery, the possible patterns for new planting or annual picking, the condition of the market, the prospects for rain or frost. So it was for twenty years after 1913 — a tall man, heavy but not stout, squinting a little behind pince-nez, seeming therefore to frown, but given sporadically to a wide, slow smile, dressed for his task in soft shoes or rubber boots, a white shirt open at the collar, an old brown hat to cover a hairline completely receded, in some seasons a tweed jacket and in others sun glasses — a man at home on his farm and in the green, rolling cultivated hills in which it sat, not very far from Manhattan Island, but of another world.

The farm during the 1920's had to compete for Morgenthau's time. He had repeatedly to consider, though he usually declined, his father's importunities to join in some business venture. He had continually to advise his much traveled parent about their large and complex portfolio of investments. He also gave constant attention to, and found great joy in, his three children, Henry III, Robert, and Joan, their education and their play. He went occasionally to Europe. He and his wife, moreover, were involved more and more deeply in the life of the county. They served on the boards of rural schools and state fairs, established for Dutchess County a visiting nurse service and a mobile library, worked with the dairymen's cooperative and the Grange. Besides all this, Morgenthau published the *American Agricul-*

turist. This weekly, one of two farm papers in New York, had a full-time editor, but Morgenthau guided its policies, deliberately concentrating on the education and protection of its increasing number of subscribers. It warned its readers, as in their isolation they had to be warned, against the schemes of fraudulent promoters who traded on their gullibility, who proposed, for example, that the propensity of rabbits to multiply guaranteed an eternal bonanza to purchasers of a pair of bunnies. The paper's honesty cost it advertising and led to several libel suits, no one of which Morgenthau lost. It also earned him the confidence of farmers. Using the *A.A.* as his platform, he drew attention to the questions that seemed to him most important for the welfare of the farmers of the state. With their growing support, he advocated inexpensive rural credit, lighter rural taxes, rural electrification, reforestation, reclamation, and more efficient utilization of land, construction with state aid of more rural schools, more farm markets, more farm-to-market roads.

Partly to further this program Morgenthau developed an active interest in Democratic party politics. He had had a first taste of politics in company with his father in 1912. It fell to him that summer to serve one afternoon as the unofficial chauffeur for Speaker of the House Champ Clark when that "ol' hound dawg" of the Missouri Democracy visited Woodrow Wilson, who had bested him for the presidential nomination. At headquarters in New York City Morgenthau also met the managers of Wilson's campaign and the candidate himself. Two years later, as his father's representative, he attended a Democratic conference at Saratoga to discuss the possibility of nominating a progressive ticket. "The whole conference," he reported sadly, "was a cooked up . . . performance." Boss Charlie Murphy of Tammany Hall had things his own way. One of those who suffered on that account was the former state senator from Dutchess County, then Assistant Secretary of the Navy, Franklin D. Roosevelt, who in 1914 aspired to the senatorial nomination.

Then in his early thirties, Roosevelt was already something of a celebrity. A tall, slight, handsome young man, a graduate of Groton and Harvard, he had managed his family estate in Hyde

Park while practicing law in New York City. In 1910 and again in 1912 he had been elected to the state senate as a Democrat by a constituency previously Republican for twenty-eight years. To politics he brought not only his vibrant voice but also a patrician sense of obligation comparable to that of his distant cousin, Theodore Roosevelt, the uncle of his wife and the hero, in or out of office, of America. Young Roosevelt had won the confidence of the farmers of Dutchess by talking their language, which he understood, and by pleading their cause, in which he believed, against city bossism, Democratic or Republican. The example of his cousin Ted's career and his own enthusiasm for the sea, which he loved as he loved the land, made him welcome his appointment as Assistant Secretary of the Navy. From that post he hoped to move on, as his distinguished cousin had before him, to higher office. Endowed both with an extra nerve of energy common to the Roosevelts and with a special nerve for politics, he was happily active simultaneously within the Navy Department, among the young liberals around Wilson in Washington, in the New York Democracy, and in the affairs of Dutchess County.

Though his father had worked with Roosevelt on behalf of Wilson in 1912, Morgenthau did not meet his Dutchess neighbor until 1915, when Roosevelt at luncheon at Hyde Park tried without success to persuade him to run for sheriff. "He is an awfully nice fellow," Roosevelt judged after this first meeting, "and one who will be a tremendous asset to us in the county. . . . Certainly we ought to do everything possible to keep him interested."

Morgenthau, who was flattered by the offer he declined, had also thoroughly enjoyed his luncheon companion. During the next few years, he warmed to the friendship Roosevelt offered. Even Roosevelt's exacting and commanding mother seemed to approve. "Young Mr. Morgenthau and his wife called this P.M.," Sarah Roosevelt wrote her son from Hyde Park. ". . . We had a pleasant tea, young Morgenthau was easy and yet modest and so nice and intelligent. The wife . . . appeared very well." From Europe later that year Roosevelt instructed

Louis Howe — his homely, perspicacious, dedicated political and personal secretary — to ask after the welfare of "Morgenthau, Jr." "I was apparently solicitous about you," he recalled jokingly twenty years later, "but I do not know why!"

When Roosevelt received the Democratic vice-presidential nomination in 1920, Morgenthau served as chairman of the notification ceremonies at Hyde Park. He also helped to direct the unsuccessful Democratic campaign in Dutchess. He attributed its failure there and elsewhere in upstate New York largely to excessive urban influence in the party, an opinion Roosevelt shared.

It was their mutual intention to redress this political imbalance; it was Roosevelt's purpose thereby to enhance his political future; and to his friend's ambition, even when it wandered beyond rural reformism, Morgenthau gave his fond loyalty. This increased during the dreary months when poliomyelitis seemed to have undone Roosevelt's hopes. The Morgenthaus in those years on occasion joined Roosevelt aboard the houseboat *Narooco*, on which he sailed in the winter through the Florida Keys. There and at Hyde Park Morgenthau drank without relish or complaint the gin and orange juice his host insisted upon serving and played parcheesi with him hour after hour.

He was much less involved in Roosevelt's politics than was Louis Howe, but he did occasionally see influential Democrats like Senator Carter Glass of Virginia, and he brought to them a point of view about the party in New York that worked to Roosevelt's advantage. The *American Agriculturist*, furthermore, advocated precisely those agricultural policies that Roosevelt held most necessary. Meanwhile, Elinor Morgenthau was busy with Eleanor Roosevelt, organizing women voters for social reform and for the Democratic party, keeping the Roosevelt name in that way before potential constituents.

In 1924 and again in 1928 Roosevelt and Morgenthau both supported the Presidential candidacy of the Governor of New York, Alfred E. Smith, Tammany's finest flower, a child of the Lower East Side, a Catholic, a "wet," and a reformer. Roosevelt, while he convalesced, needed his identification with Smith, the

strongest Democrat in America, and Morgenthau had considerable enthusiasm for many of the governor's policies. The *American Agriculturist* consistently supported Smith, and in return the
governor in 1924 conferred about agricultural matters with upstate publishers and farm leaders selected by Morgenthau. Both
Morgenthau and his wife were in Houston at the Democratic
Convention that nominated Smith for President in 1928.

"Franklin," Morgenthau reported in the same year, guessing
incorrectly as did most observers, "will definitely not run for
Governor. . . . There is quite a little talk about running Senator Wagner. . . . There is also some talk of putting me on the
state ticket with Wagner. Elinor and I are not getting excited
over the prospect as there is only about one chance in fifty of
this coming about."

While Smith, the victim of Coolidge prosperity and corrosive
anti-Catholicism, was becoming one of the worst-beaten
Democratic nominees in history, Roosevelt, initially a reluctant
but already an accomplished campaigner, was carrying New
York. Morgenthau contributed both funds and energy to this
victory. He helped to plan his friend's tour of upstate cities, and
he helped to muster among farmers an extraordinary Democratic
vote. It was natural, then, for political as well as for personal
reasons, that Roosevelt after the election should invite Morgenthau to Warm Springs to discuss New York's agricultural problems. Then and later, when conferring upon Morgenthau some
new trust, Roosevelt was wont to explain that he was the only
man he knew who had made a profit farming. It was equally
natural for Morgenthau to hurry south. There, at his urging,
Roosevelt agreed to appoint an Agricultural Advisory Commission, and decided to make Morgenthau its chairman.

3. *A Program for Agriculture*

The studies of Morgenthau's commission led to a series of recommendations to the New York legislature which, with no significant exception, became law. The state relieved the rural counties, and therefore rural taxpayers, of almost all their previous expenses for the construction of highways, for snow removal, and for the elimination of grade crossings; the state doubled its appropriation for rural roads, a long step toward Morgenthau's announced goal of "a hard road to every farm." County taxes for rural schools were reduced, but the rural school program was expanded. The budget for research on fruit and potato blights was trebled. Other appropriations permitted a rigorous inspection of dairy products, accelerated reforestation, and underwrote surveys of soil, weather, and agricultural possibilities throughout the state. These were impressive accomplishments, especially for a party which in New York had ordinarily directed its energies to satisfying the needs of the cities. On the manuscript copy of a speech reviewing the record, so much the fulfillment of Morgenthau's purpose, Roosevelt gratefully wrote: "For Henry himself."

While they worked together, Roosevelt and Morgenthau grew constantly closer. They embarked upon a neighborly rivalry in the cultivation of squash. "Please write me any further directions as to how the common stock should be planted," Roosevelt asked in one characteristic squash-letter, "whether it should be watered, whether the distribution should be wide or closely harrowed, whether it carries any bonus (beside bugs)."

"Why don't you take a shot at forecasting the price of squash and pickles next fall," Morgenthau asked at a time when official Washington was blinking away the implications of panic on Wall Street. "I am sure you will come just as close to it as Hoover."

"A little birdie told me that you lost the raincoat we gave you last year," Morgenthau wrote in 1930. "Elinor and I sent you another . . . and we hope that this will prove to be storm relief against all farm relief."

"You and Elinor are angels," Roosevelt replied. "I have told William that if this raincoat is stolen out of the car, he will never have a chance to lose another!"

There were, as Morgenthau's Diary showed, other, less bantering, exchanges. "Elinor and I," read the entry for June 4, 1930, "arrived in Boston . . . to attend James Roosevelt's wedding. I went up to Franklin's room at nine o'clock and spent one and a half hours with him. . . . He told me in the strictest confidence that . . . he was beginning to be suspicious of the fact that Alfred E. Smith was working for the nomination for President in 1932."

Roosevelt wanted that nomination for himself, but first he had convincingly to win reelection as governor. Morgenthau accompanied him on one major campaign trip. On October 18, 1930, the governor's party set out from Albany in two cars and two buses, almost "froze to death" at a picnic lunch, and in the afternoon drove on to Binghamton while Roosevelt, Samuel I. Rosenman, Morgenthau, and Basil O'Connor, the governor's law partner, "had a lot of fun joking and teasing one another." As he had two years earlier, Morgenthau that night led the governor onto the stage. The next day they went on to Elmira, where Eleanor Roosevelt joined them temporarily for dinner and went walking with Morgenthau before departing for New York City. Morgenthau then "matched Sam Rosenman to see who would sleep with the Governor and . . . won. Before retiring we had a grand rough house." They all enjoyed the ride to Buffalo for "the Governor was in an excellent mood and made up silly songs." The caravan covered over a thousand miles in the tier of counties north of the Pennsylvania border. Before it disbanded on its eighth day, Roosevelt stopped "at the Poughkeepsie bridge . . . and we said goodbye to him and he turned and said to me — this is the only day that you did not arrange and it is the only one we were late at every meeting."

As a reward for services rendered, Roosevelt after his reelection appointed Morgenthau to the office he most desired. "I just want to tell you," Elinor Morgenthau wrote him, "that I feel a tremendous joy and pride in your giving Henry the important post of 'Conservation Commissioner,' for I think that Henry always goes about his work with a real feeling of consecration, but the fact that he is working under you and for you, fills him with . . . enthusiasm. . . . The part which pleases me the most is that while you are moving on in your own work . . . it also gives Henry a chance to grow, so that your friendship can continue to be cemented by a community of interest as well as by the deep affection with which he holds you."

That was also the governor's intention, for he told Morgenthau that he wanted him to gain experience in running a department that would be useful someday in Washington. Roosevelt was "getting ready to be President," and he expected Morgenthau to "get ready" to accompany him. The governor instructed his friend, whose sentiments he knew so well, to shake hands with the head of Tammany Hall. "This was very repulsive to me," Morgenthau remembered years later, "but F.D.R. was insistent."

In his new office Morgenthau had jurisdiction over lands and forests, water power, fish, and game. He also controlled patronage that Democratic leaders hoped would "prove useful in the building up of the . . . party." He was conscious, as he went to work, that his job, like those of the rest of the governor's cabinet, was complicated by two new situations: the depression that engulfed New York and the rest of the nation, intensifying the difficulties of farmers, adding each day to the appalling numbers of unemployed workers and bankrupt firms; and the candidacy of Franklin Roosevelt for the Presidency, which demanded of his associates political and administrative behavior that would persuade Democrats the country over to support him.

As his wife put it, Morgenthau had a clear public "philosophy": "if you care enough about seeing a thing go through, work out a plan, get the best people to help you (here again real ability to know who the best people are) then present it to whomever you think has the best chance of putting it through, and forget about yourself. This scheme worked perfectly in New York state." His reorganization of his department revealed his talent in selecting expert advisers, his ability to take their advice, and his willingness to delegate the authority they needed to do their jobs. He began characteristically by appointing an advisory council of distingushed conservationists, of whom Dr. George F. Warren was one.

Warren made a pilot study of Tompkins County, investigating there the interdependent factors of soil, climate, population, the potential demand for various products, and the potential availability of hydroelectric power. His conclusions confirmed Morgenthau's personal enthusiasm for retimbering, for withdrawing marginal land from production, and for developing a long-range, regional program for the use of land in New York. To those ends Morgenthau's advisory council worked out a program of reclamation and reforestation which Roosevelt supported as an amendment to the state's constitution. The council also helped Morgenthau bring order to his department. Acting partly on its suggestions, he established an independent bureau to employ scientific techniques for the protection and propagation of fish and game, and he introduced a system for the distribution of game on an ecological basis. Within the department he established a management section to improve administrative techniques and a bureau of law enforcement under a chief inspector whose staff made life as grim as possible for poachers, previously little policed. He also created a division of finance that replaced the haphazard accounting of earlier years with a tightly controlled budget.

If those who valued efficiency were pleased, Democratic politicians were not. "We had," Boss Edward J. Flynn of the Bronx recalled, "some difficulty with Morgenthau." The commissioner chose as his deputy a newspaperman, Herbert Gaston, formerly a member of the staff of the New York *World*. A quiet, serious, fearless westerner who was for many years to be a loyal and unselfish member of Morgenthau's staff, Gaston had been the chief of publications of the radical farmers' Nonpartisan League. He had crusaded against gambling and the political protection of gamblers in Minneapolis; he had further alienated regular Democrats by moving successively from the Bull Moose to the Socialist to the La Follette Progressive parties before coming to the support of Smith in 1928. The regulars were equally annoyed by Morgenthau's appointments to lesser offices, for he ignored party lines so consistently that one Republican subordinate concluded he was "probably the world's worst politician."

That kind of behavior by Roosevelt's friends provoked Smith to complain to a newspaperman: "Do you know, by God, that he has never consulted me about a damn thing since he has been Governor? He has taken bad advice. . . . He has ignored me!" Even if he had not felt that way, Smith would have coveted the Democratic nomination for himself, for as 1931 wore on and the depression deepened, it became clearer and clearer that almost any Democrat would defeat President Hoover. Though he denied that he was an active candidate, Smith opened his campaign at Tammany Hall by attacking a proposed amendment to the New York constitution which Morgenthau's group of experts had recommended and Roosevelt had approved. The amendment was, he suggested, unnecessary, expensive, and contrary to the principles of good government.

In fact, the amendment simply provided for a schedule of mandatory appropriations for twenty years, in all for $20,000,000, for reforestation in certain areas outside the Adirondack's forest preserve, areas where abandoned or submarginal farms could be purchased by the state for planting designed both for the conservation of land and water and for the development of recreational facilities. "The human species," Morgenthau told one audience during the fight over the amendment, "requires for a proper habitat something more than farming land, factory locations and urban areas. We need . . . common public playgrounds of wide extent to give us a place fit to live in and to live a healthy, balanced life. The waste spaces of today, the uncultivated areas which we plan to reforest and the existing woodlands form such a natural playground."

The voters approved the amendment, Roosevelt's political

stock rose, and New York embarked upon a larger forestry operation than any state had previously attempted. During 1931 and 1932 that planting provided an opportunity for the useful employment of young men unable to find work with private industry. Charity might keep them alive, but they needed desperately to feel wanted and productive. No one understood this better than did Morgenthau and Harry Hopkins, the director of the state's Temporary Emergency Relief Administration. A veteran social worker who had been in charge of fresh-air work and unemployment relief for the New York Association for Improving the Condition of the Poor, Hopkins first met Roosevelt in 1928. As Secretary of the Temporary Emergency Relief Administration, he impressed Morgenthau who, when the agency's first chairman retired, urged the governor to name Hopkins as his successor. Fond of playing at being a man-about-town, extroverted, exuberant, sometimes even profligate, Hopkins was in personality Morgenthau's opposite, but they had a common background in social work, a common dedication to improving the lot of the poor, and a common loyalty to Roosevelt. Morgenthau, furthermore, from the beginning of their relationship, found to his gratification that Hopkins, when he gave his word, always followed through.

Working together, in the spring of 1932 they directed the state's employment on reforestation projects of ten thousand men. This was the genesis of the New Deal's Civilian Conservation Corps, the federal agency that was to put young men to work on reforestation and related projects. Morgenthau had earlier experimented by using the unemployed to thin out a hundred acres as a wood lot. On the basis of that experience, he calculated how many could be employed on each hundred acres to be reforested, and he accumulated data on how their work assignments could be organized. Because he alone had a plan for assigning labor to worthwhile projects, he was given three-quarters of the state's appropriation for work relief.

Soliciting lists of young men from social workers in New York City, Morgenthau also personally organized a precursor of the New Deal's National Youth Administration, the federal agency that was to provide work relief for young people. "We took the gas house gang," he recalled, "the bad boys who were loafing on the streets and getting into trouble, and we put them on the 4 A.M. train that ran up to the Bear Mountain area where they worked all day. Then because there was no housing for them we took them back at night. F.D.R. was much interested in this conservation of human resources, as in all conservation work."

The planting program was only one facet of the total experience of Roosevelt and his associates in Albany. There the governor assembled part of his future Washington team and gave them a first assignment in reconstruction and reform. There, in programs like that over which Morgenthau presided, this team was bound together by a creative approach to problems of government and by humanitarian ideals.

4. Roosevelt and Morgenthau

Outside his department, Morgenthau, like the others, was an avid partisan, anxiously watching Roosevelt's campaign for the Presidential nomination. As trouble developed in New York City, where the chicanery of several of the grandest tigers in Tammany posed a problem for the governor, Morgenthau urged him to prosecute the corrupt even at the risk of alienating the faithful. Because he understood his friend, he understood why Roosevelt proceeded more cautiously than he advised.

Some of the candidate's maneuvering was good for a chuckle. "I was greatly amused," Morgenthau wrote his father, ". . . to see that there apparently had been a leak in Franklin's plans to meet with Governor Gifford Pinchot [the celebrated Pennsylvania progressive]. I would be willing to bet dollars to doughnuts that the leak was from the Chief Executive himself. . . . He finds it very difficult to keep as good a story as this."

At Roosevelt's request Morgenthau undertook one especially sensitive assignment in the preconvention campaign. Early in May 1932 he set out on a trip through the Middle West and South to survey the opinions of farmers, editors of farm newspapers, and agricultural experts about the continuing agricultural depression and about Roosevelt as a candidate. There was little disagreement about the need for federal action, but there was wide difference of opinion about the forms it should take. Many of those whom Morgenthau saw gave first priority to the establishment of federal agencies to refinance the agricultural debt. Others favored, as farmers had for generations in times of depression, currency inflation of one kind or another. Still others, confusing their situation with that of industrialists who had benefited from high Republican tariffs, thought that tariff protection for agriculture would help them. Perhaps the most controversial issue was the Domestic Allotment Plan, which called for government intervention to control production as a means of raising prices and liquidating surpluses.

Speaking to that point, Henry A. Wallace of Iowa, agricultural economist and editor of the influential *Wallace's Farmer*, told Morgenthau at their first meeting that if low prices persisted he expected either revolution or state socialism in the near future. Only by limiting domestic production and insulating the national market, Wallace argued, could prices be raised. He was therefore an advocate of Domestic Allotment, as were other advisers who in 1932 had Roosevelt's ear. The governor had decided by June 1932 to make some version of the Domestic Allotment Plan his own, but Morgenthau, even after hearing Wallace's case, had reservations about any device that put an artificial ceiling on production. Prices, he agreed, had to be raised, but he accepted only reluctantly and tentatively the theory that this could best be accomplished by growing less. He had always believed that the solution had to lie in distributing more.

Yet what he heard and what he saw enlightened Morgenthau. Though the situation was even worse than he had feared, a new and bold administration would have available various correctives. Farmers, moreover, were "numb," as Morgenthau put it publicly. They wanted "a change" and would "leave the Republican fold." "My trip is going fine," he wrote Roosevelt. "I am meeting a lot of very interesting farm leaders. Most of them are Republicans but are ready to vote for you, if given the opportunity. Our New York story on agriculture has reached them and they all admit New York has done more for the farmer than any other state."

After Roosevelt's nomination, Morgenthau contributed a summary of the New York record to the text of the candidate's major address on agriculture. He was at the Biltmore Hotel in New York with Roosevelt, his family, and some of his closest associates while the returns came in during the evening of November 8, 1932. Like the governor, he was supremely happy as bulletin after bulletin fulfilled the hopes for victory so long nourished. As he left for home at 1:40 A.M., the President-elect said to his mother: "This is the greatest night of my life." Those who had been working intimately with him felt the same way.

To continue to work with Franklin Roosevelt was Morgenthau's only ambition. He was therefore pleased that recognition of his achievements brought him, though he was an easterner, many endorsements for the position of Secretary of Agriculture. But the appointment was not to be Morgenthau's. On several counts Roosevelt decided to give it to Henry Wallace. Wallace was a western man, identified as had been his father and grandfather before him with the western farmer, well-known in the corn and wheat country, a progressive Republican with Bull Moose blood in his veins. It was politically important to have such a man in the Cabinet and especially in the Department of Agriculture. Wallace, furthermore, was in favor of Domestic Allotment. Like-minded men, aware of Morgenthau's hesitation, urged the Iowan upon Roosevelt, causing unnecessary "bad blood," as one observer interpreted it, about the possibilities of Morgenthau's getting the office.

Morgenthau had difficulty, as Roosevelt prepared to leave Albany, in reading his intentions. "I cannot make this a formal letter," the governor wrote him, "but before I go out I want you to know how very grateful I am to you for all the splendid work you have done for the people of this State . . . also for the splendid loyalty you have given me." But Morgenthau, sensing his friend's inclination toward Wallace, came to suspect that he had no future in Washington. About a month before his inauguration Roosevelt gave him vague reassurance. He wanted him, he said, "very close." As the senior Morgenthau then remarked, "If F.D.R. wants you 'very close' the only way he can do so is to put you in." Roosevelt did.

"F.D.R. first offered to make me the head of an agency for the unemployed," Morgenthau remembered. "He said it would be the most powerful agency in Washington. He said I would have the Army and Navy working for me. He had thought this out almost to the last detail. But I could not grasp the possibilities and refused it. Later . . . I had the pleasure of telephoning Hopkins that he would get this job." To Morgenthau Roosevelt offered instead the governorship of Herbert Hoover's Federal Farm Board with a broad mandate in the field of farm credit. Morgenthau happily accepted.

The two men had come to mean much to each other. "Slowly," Eleanor Roosevelt wrote, recalling her life before she was mistress of the White House, "a friendship grew . . . with . . . Mr. and Mrs. Henry Morgenthau, Jr. . . . We had many interests in common in the county, and Mr. Morgenthau and my husband were thrown more and more together. Mrs. Morgenthau . . . and I grew gradually to have a warm affection for each other." Morgenthau and a few others, she said, were men whose "interest was in my husband and in the work to be done. . . . They could be very objective even when their own work was involved." She once commented that Louis Howe and Morgenthau alone dared tell her husband categorically that he was wrong, but to this short list Morgenthau prefixed her name. She was, he knew, the incomparable force for good in Franklin Roosevelt's life.

Morgenthau's bond with her husband was firm. They had, to begin with, the same sense of adventure and of fun. They both delighted in finding simple and direct devices to resolve complex problems. They hugely enjoyed practical jokes, especially at each other's expense. They found the same stories funny, particularly each other's. They liked their reciprocal banter. It was unrecorded in the '20's, but the documents of the '30's revealed the spirit of both decades. So, for example, at a Cabinet meeting in 1935 Roosevelt passed Morgenthau a note chiding him for sailing home from Europe on a French rather than an American liner. "I paid my own expenses . . . and therefore could choose the fastest ship," Morgenthau scribbled back, differentiating his trip from that of a colleague who had traveled on public funds.

"So glad," the President retorted, "you are so rich and seek speed — more speed."

Or once while Morgenthau was taking a brief vacation from monetary problems, Roosevelt sent him a turgid book on currency, "to read while in swimming," with the comment that "this inspiring detective story will probably cause you to commit suicide."

Roosevelt and Morgenthau had in common also similar backgrounds and habits of mind. Both were the sons of wealthy fathers, both were comfortable, both enjoyed a degree of easy elegance, yet neither really cared for the toys and games of the adult rich. Both loved the land, the trees, the soil itself, all the things that conservation was intended to protect and to develop. Both, in the best sense of the word, were gentlemen, considerate, civilized, decent men who avoided displays of wealth or emotion. Both, furthermore, took their problems one by one, looking for practical solutions rather than for broad concepts about government, society or man. Theirs was a kind of patrician instinct for public service and social welfare, theirs also an inbred attachment to country, to family, to neighborhood, and to private property. Neither was a radical, neither an intellectual, but both had a respect for intellectuals and an openminded zest for new ideas.

They complemented each other. Morgenthau's diffidence with strangers, his seeming suspiciousness and brusqueness, shielded the warmth and generosity that Roosevelt's way brought out. Those qualities Roosevelt had to have in a man who took him for himself, not for what was his to dispense. The celebrated smile, the great "hello" that Winston Churchill somewhere called the most wonderful word in the English language, the spontaneous, contagious laugh — those were also shields of a kind. Franklin Roosevelt revealed to most men very little of himself. But he could and did trust Morgenthau with personal matters of which few others were aware. Morgenthau was never a rival or a sycophant or a scold. He had a quick sympathy for Roosevelt's moods. His worries and his migraine Roosevelt could help him laugh away. His understanding and his dedication helped Roosevelt in those private hours when he did not want to laugh, helped him to bear the lonely responsibilities of high office.

"To Henry," Franklin Roosevelt once wrote across a photograph of himself and Morgenthau riding side by side in an automobile, "from one of two of a kind."

II

"THE COURAGE TO EXPERIMENT"

1932-1933

1. The Agricultural Crisis

FOR THOSE who were part of it, the New Deal was a great adventure, "unforgettably thrilling," as Morgenthau attested. The New Dealers were mostly young, many of them in their late thirties or early forties. Though they came into office in a time of trouble, they brought with them a zest for their work, a willingness to share the spirit of their leader, whose confidence in himself and in his country was an indispensable qualification for the Presidency. The despondency that attended depression, the terror that accompanied the paralysis of the banking system in the early months of 1933, produced a state of mind in the United States that needed most of all to be told that the only thing to fear was fear itself. What Franklin Roosevelt and his associates intended to do was for many months less important than their determination to do something. They had plans, of course, but none of them proved to be as significant as the underlying belief in the social responsibility of the federal government, or as the commitment to experimentation. The crisis of 1933 was very much a crisis of morale.

It was also a time of want and despair. Long lines of brooding, hungry men formed in front of soup kitchens and employment agencies. Failing businesses and closing banks threatened the sav-

ings and the position of the comfortable, introducing them to a
new insecurity, a new experience of fear. Need and hopelessness
and lost status bewildered urban man.

For rural America the depression was as terrifying. Most
farmers, even in the worst of times, could ordinarily produce
food enough to prevent hunger, though not necessarily malnu-
trition. But agriculture had long since ceased to be a self-
sufficient occupation. The farmer had to have cash for a multitude of personal essentials — shoes, clothing, fuel, medicine. He
needed cash more urgently for his business. The capital equipment vital for an increasingly mechanized agriculture was
expensive to buy and to maintain. The fixed costs of the
mortgages on this equipment and on land and improvements,
moreover, had to be met in bad years as well as in good. Failure
to meet them meant foreclosure followed at best by tenancy and
dead hopes, at worst by dispossession, migrancy, and abject unemployment.

The depression, furthermore, had come to agriculture first.
Throughout the 1920's the farmers' share of the national income
decreased. With the onset of general depression, agricultural
prices fell further and faster than did the average price level. In
1932 Morgenthau, on his trip through the country for Roosevelt, had seen corn, shelled and delivered in Illinois, selling at
twenty-three cents a bushel; milk sold in Wisconsin at about a
cent and a half a quart; eggs in Oklahoma at five cents a dozen.
Men whose incomes depended upon those prices simply could
not pay off debts they had contracted during relatively prosperous years. In 1932 it took roughly three times as much farm
produce to earn a dollar as it had in 1921; by 1932 some twenty
thousand farms were being foreclosed each month.

The decline in farm income had for several years been a drag
on the whole economy. It damaged not only investors in farm
mortgages but also, more generally, all producers of manufactured goods. The average city dweller was no more than
vaguely aware of the significance for his own life of the increasing inability of the farmer to buy, but urban representatives in
Washington, exposed for a decade to the demands of their rural

colleagues for federal aid, were coming to see the connection. Republican policies had afforded insufficient remedy. The Agricultural Marketing Act of 1929 created the Federal Farm Board principally to direct the lending of a $500,000,000 fund to cooperative associations and to supervise the activities of stabilization corporations which were attempting by their purchases to promote an orderly market. The framers of this act intended it for normal times. They expected the Farm Board to sustain farmer-controlled cooperatives and through them to level off fluctuations in the market occasioned by good or bad crops, seasonal variations in deliveries and other such conditions. The crash of 1929, however, altered dramatically the environment which the Farm Board was supposed to control. The remedies it had in hand could not halt the precipitate and continuing decline of agricultural prices. The board did make its resources available to corporations founded to stabilize grain and cotton prices by buying crops and holding them for sale until prices improved. But in the disastrous years after the crash prices did not improve.

The high Republican tariff of 1930, erecting new obstacles to the sale of European products in the United States, intensified the difficulties of marketing crops in Europe, while at home the production of staple crops was inadvertently stimulated by the Farm Board's purchases. In mid-1931, its funds exhausted, the board began to liquidate its holdings. Wheat then fell below forty cents a bushel. A year later, though the government owned three and a half million bales of cotton, the price of that staple had reached the historic low of four and six-tenths cents a pound. Farmers generally valued federal assistance to marketing cooperatives, but the Farm Board was thoroughly discredited by the patent inadequacy of its techniques for combatting depression. Indeed, its own economists were among the vast majority of agricultural experts who were fully persuaded that some device to curtail production had to accompany any successful stabilization operation.

The collapse of agricultural prices and income, moreover, so exhausted the savings and the credit of farmers that by 1933 some immediate financial aid had become urgent. Federal agricultural credit agencies established in 1916 and 1923 had not been organized to cope with the conditions of depression, with potential borrowers who neither had assets nor the prospect of profits. The Hoover Administration scarcely touched this problem. While the resources for agricultural credit remained inadequate, interest rates were often inordinately high, especially in districts remote from money centers. From 1929 on the pace of foreclosures and dispossessions quickened. By 1933, loans that banks had made on crops and farm mortgages had lost much of their face value and almost all of their liquidity. Directly in the South and West, indirectly elsewhere, this contributed to the spate of bank failures and, at the time of Roosevelt's inauguration, to the enforced bank holiday.

By that time rural newspapers were seriously advocating a moratorium on mortgage payments. Some also favored nationalization of the banking system, and many proposed that the federal government print paper money to lend to farmers for paying their debts. In Iowa, Minnesota, and elsewhere, farmers were attempting to prevent foreclosures by brandishing shotguns or threatening lynchings. In order to raise prices, farmers almost universally urged immediate inflation of the currency. To keep prices from falling any further, some burned their crops; others responded eagerly to the campaign of the National Farmers' Holiday Association for the organization of farmers' strikes. In this, probably the most harassed hour in the whole history of American agriculture, Roosevelt and his advisers had to fashion policy.

Among them, they settled upon three separate but interdependent thrusts, each of which Congress approved. Henry A. Wallace, the new Secretary of Agriculture, sponsored the program for reducing production, primarily by retiring land under cultivation. Farmers cooperating in that program were to receive cash benefits, and in theory to profit also as diminishing supplies raised the market prices of basic staple crops. The objective was to restore the purchasing power of those producing the agriculture commodities affected to the level of the golden years just before World War I — the level defined as "parity."

Morgenthau, who believed fervently in improving the distribution of crops rather than in reducing production, trusted neither Wallace, nor his plan, nor the Agriculture Adjustment Administration which was created to administer it. For his part, Morgenthau had a growing interest in a second policy, increasingly popular with farmers, a policy of deliberate currency inflation, to which the President was not ready to subscribe at the time of his inauguration. More immediately, Morgenthau, by virtue of his office, had responsibility for the third facet of the New Deal's effort for agriculture — the reorganization and enlargement of the federal government's system for providing inexpensive credit to farmers.

To that end, Morgenthau supervised the liquidation of the Federal Farm Board, and the creation of a new, successor agency, the Farm Credit Administration, of which he became governor. As its primary task, the FCA undertook to refinance farm mortgages, in the process reducing the average interest they carried from 6 per cent to 4½ per cent. It also facilitated applications for intermediate and short-term agricultural credit. "Get results," was Morgenthau's central message to his staff, "or give way to someone who will." They got results. In the first year of its life, FCA approved over 540,000 loans aggregating $1,356,000,000. In its first year and a half, it refinanced about 20 per cent of the total farm mortgage debt in the United States. By 1937 there were some 300,000 more owner-operators of American farms than there had been in 1933. The crisis in farm credit had passed.

"I could write you a book," one loan recipient said in a letter to Morgenthau, "on how your loan has helped me but you wouldn't have time to read this from way down in Arkansas." Another recipient wrote: "I would be without a roof over my head if it hadn't been for the government loan . . . God bless Mr. Roosevelt and the Democratic party who saves thousands of poor people from all over this country from starvation." Vice President John N. Garner assessed the results in still another way. "Damn you old money-bags," Garner told Morgenthau at one Cabinet meeting. "Until you came along Mrs. Garner and I averaged 16 per cent a year on our money, and now we can't get better than 5 per cent."

2. Prescriptions for "Galloping Palsy"

As governor of the Farm Credit Administration, just as in every administrative post he held, Morgenthau depended upon two basic personal relationships. First, he could do nothing, as he often said, without the confidence and support of Franklin Roosevelt, who often gave him assignments that fell outside his official domain. Second, he could not carry out those assignments nor discharge his official duties without appointing first-rate subordinates and giving them large responsibility and authority. His staff and stay within the FCA were William I. Myers, formerly a professor of agricultural finance at Cornell, and Herman Oliphant, an expert on the statistical and quantitative aspects of law. A shy man, tireless, acid, one of the keenest and most unselfish New Dealers, Oliphant brought to government his broad learning, his imagination, and his unshakable faith in the potentialities of progressive democracy.

That was also Morgenthau's faith, and it persuaded him of the immorality of a reduction of agricultural abundance at a time when millions of men throughout the world were hungry. In an effort to find a substitute for Wallace's policy of curtailing production, Morgenthau, at Roosevelt's direction, helped to negotiate a $50 million credit for China with which that country would purchase American wheat and cotton. But the Chinese expended only a small fraction of that sum.

More important, Roosevelt had asked Morgenthau to help conduct conversations looking toward the recognition of Soviet Russia. The President considered the policy of nonrecognition futile, for whether or not the Soviet government was democratic, it had been for over a decade the established government of Russia, recognized by the major powers except the United States. Roosevelt also felt that continued isolation of Russia would impede his purpose of preventing war in Europe or Asia by organizing the collective moral sense of the nations of the world. He therefore included the President of the Soviet Union among the heads of state to whom he sent a cable in May calling for military and economic disarmament. He viewed Russia, moreover, as a potential ally against Japanese aggression in the Orient or German resurgence in Europe.

Because the Department of State was unfriendly to the idea of opening negotiations with the Russians, Roosevelt turned for assistance to Morgenthau. In and out of government, advocates of recognition expected the Soviet Union to absorb some of the American surpluses of manufactured goods and raw materials, and Morgenthau, engaged in liquidating the holdings of the Farm Board, was especially well placed to discuss the disposition of cotton stocks in which the Russian trading corporation, Amtorg, was interested.

Morgenthau approached Amtorg through two intermediaries, whose first reports revealed the delicacy and the risk of any negotiation with the Russians. If the deal worked out well, he remarked to Roosevelt one day at luncheon, he would be a hero, but if it flopped, he would have to leave Washington. "Well, of course, you know that I stand back of you in these negotiations," Roosevelt replied, "and if you have to leave Washington I will leave with you."

Conversations moved slowly partly because the Russians tried to play off against each other the various Americans who represented Morgenthau, the Treasury Department, and the Reconstruction Finance Corporation, partly because no individual Russian was willing to assume authority or make a commitment. "Gosh," Roosevelt told Morgenthau, "If I could only, myself, talk to some one man representing the Russians, I could straighten out this whole question. If you get the opportunity, Henry, you could say that you believe but have no authority to say so, that the President would like to send some person to Moscow . . . in order to break the ice between the two countries and in that way gradually get the people of the United States used to doing business with the Russians."

The scheme failed, and Roosevelt had to continue to work through agents whose activities he supervised. When Morgenthau reported in August that the Soviet Union wanted to buy $75,000,000 worth of raw materials, the President informed him that through other channels, they were seeking $50,000,000 worth of machine goods. Instructing Morgenthau to set an overall limit of $100,000,000 on sales to the Russians during the next few months, he suggested making half the sales raw materials, half machinery, all on the basis of a down payment of 15 to 20 per cent.

Such purchases depended upon large loans to the Russians which would have involved considerable publicity. That had to await a decision about recognition. "What would you think," Roosevelt asked Morgenthau late in September 1933, "of bringing this whole Russian question into our front parlor instead of back in the kitchen?" He had in mind writing a letter to the President of the Soviet Union suggesting formal negotiations to lead to diplomatic relations, but he wanted first to be certain that the Russians would welcome the gesture.

Morgenthau learned about the details of the President's plan the next day at luncheon with William C. Bullitt, who was handling Soviet affairs for the State Department and was later to become the first American ambassador to the Soviet Union. Bullitt, a man of "great charm" and "violent" loves and hatreds, had gone to Russia on a mission for Woodrow Wilson during the Paris conference after World War I. He returned convinced that the Western democracies had to overcome their antipathies to Bolshevism and work with the Soviet government. Persisting in this attitude, Bullitt now saw in American aid "the means by which the Soviet Union could break away from its dependence on Germany and could become a bulwark against the aggressive tendencies . . . developing in Japan."

Bullitt ascribed the bias of the State Department against recognition to the concern of Secretary of State Cordell Hull about the religious issue. Hull, a Tennessee Democrat who had been in Congress for many years, brought to his office a controlled and quiet manner that ordinarily hid his large personal ambitions and his jealousy of his prerogatives. He had a veteran politican's educated sense about how to treat senators and about inveterate Democratic sensibilities, and he placed his unshakable faith in the ability of free trade to cure almost all the ills of the world. He believed that Americans in Russia should be allowed to worship as they pleased. He was perhaps also convinced that American Catholics, most of them Democrats, would resent the recognition of a notoriously anti-Christian government. But the Secretary of State also had larger reservations about the recognition of the Soviet Union which he had communicated directly to the President. These pertained to the settlement of the war debt owed the United States by the pre-Soviet government and more significantly, to interference in American affairs by Soviet-sponsored Communist organizations.

During the last stage of the conflict over recognition, Morgenthau was an informed and sometimes an involved observer. "Bullitt began walking me to work in the mornings," he recollected, "in order to pump me about the latest developments. At first this annoyed the President, on the ground that Bullitt was going over Hull's head. . . . But, as affairs developed, he entrusted the negotiations more and more to Bullitt." Morgenthau helped to bring Bullitt together with the Soviet representative, Boris Skvirsky, in order to arrange the exchange of letters Roosevelt desired. "I have a piece of paper in my hand," Bullitt told the Russian at one point. "It is unsigned. It can be made into an invitation for you to send representatives here to discuss diplomatic relations. We wish you to telegraph it by your most confidential code and learn if it is acceptable. . . . If not, will you give me your word of honor that there never will be any publicity about this proposed exchange of letters and that the whole matter will be kept secret?"

Skvirsky gave his word, the exchange was arranged as Roosevelt had proposed, and in November Maxim Litvinov arrived in Washington to begin the talks that resulted on the 16th of that month in American recognition of the Soviet Union. Morgenthau took part in the early discussions with Litvinov who impressed him then "as a warm, friendly man, sparkling in conversation, abundant in hospitality." But the little Russian, whatever his personal charm, could not depart from his orders from Moscow. These permitted him to give Hull plausible assurances about the religious freedom of Americans in Russia and about the activities of Communists in the United States, but the question of the Russian debt had to be postponed until after the two countries exchanged ambassadors. Discussions of the debt dragged on for years. While they continued, never to be settled, the government-owned Export-Import Bank of Washington would not give the Soviets credits for purchasing raw materials or machinery from the United States.

As in the case of China, so in the case of Russia, Morgenthau's first ventures in foreign policy did not get rid of the cotton glutting the American market. He nevertheless counted the Russian negotiation a success. "Recognition," he observed years later when the memory of Russian-American cooperation to defeat Hitler was fresh, "was one of Roosevelt's first attempts to create a community of good neighbors as the best security against the depredations of the neighborhood roughnecks."

The diplomatic success left commodity prices untouched. Increasingly worried about them, Morgenthau urged Roosevelt to emphasize the distribution instead of the destruction of surpluses. The government, he suggested, could combat falling prices and urban destitution by purchasing 1,000,000 bales of cotton and 100,000,000 bushels of wheat to distribute to the unemployed. Roosevelt declined, answering rather sharply that the machinery for plowing crops under had already been set up. But as the price of wheat dropped to 90 cents at the end of September and then skidded below 70 cents during the next twelve days, even the proponents of plowing under were alarmed.

The President, Morgenthau later noted, "was gravely concerned. The malady threatened much more than just the farm belt: the whole recovery program was jeopardized by this galloping palsy." Roosevelt therefore gave to Morgenthau and

Jesse Jones a chance to experiment with the resources of their credit agencies. Jones, a big, breezy, genial man, one of the many Texans in the New Deal, had for many years been a banker in Houston and a money-raiser for the Democratic party. On the recommendation of Jack Garner, Jones's old friend and companion in matters political and spiritual, Hoover had appointed Jones a director of the Reconstruction Finance Corporation in 1932. In 1933 Roosevelt made him chairman.

Partly because of their common objections to Wallace's program, Jones and Morgenthau had worked together on the loan for China. They were allied again in attempting to lift agricultural prices. Jones's RFC in October underwrote the Commodity Credit Corporation, established to prop up prices by offering cotton growers a loan of ten cents for every pound they kept from market, a loan larger than the price they could realize by selling. This induced them not to dump their cotton and push prices still lower, but it also involved the government in the kind of operation which Hoover's Farm Board had tried without success, and it did not help to clothe the urban unemployed. Morgenthau hoped, therefore, to handle wheat a different way. On the night of October 16, a telephone call from Roosevelt gave him his chance.

"We have got to do something about the price of wheat," the President said, his voice registering worry and fatigue. "I can't take it any longer. . . . Can't you buy 25,000,000 bushels for Harry Hopkins and see if you can't put the price up?"

Hopkins was then head of the Federal Emergency Relief Administration, established by an act of Congress of May 12, 1933. The first of the New Deal's relief agencies, it operated largely by providing the states with funds, food, and clothing for the needy unemployed. With Wallace, Hopkins drove over to Morgenthau's, where he agreed to take 30,000,000 bushels of wheat. Farm Credit was to lend the money with which to buy it to the Farmers' National Grain Corporation, a private organization that had worked closely with the Farm Board, but Morgenthau "was certain not to get stuck with loads of surplus" because Hopkins's FERA would undertake to process and distribute the wheat.

After checking with Roosevelt, Morgenthau started buying the first thing the following morning. Wheat opened at 64⅞, but his first order for 1,000,000 bushels at 72 to 74 held the market up above 70 for about half an hour. In spite of his second order for another 1,000,000 at 74⅛, the market "busted" down to 68. "I was a pretty sick boy when this happened," Morgenthau confided to his Diary. "It seemed to me that I was trying to hold up not only the commodity markets of the world but also the stock market as everything was sagging."

He fought on, placing a standing order to buy all cash wheat offered that day and reporting this news to the *Wall Street Journal* and the press services. In the end he bought 103 carloads. His purchase, along with the publicity he planted, helped the price of wheat to hit a ceiling for the day of 74⅛, up almost ten cents from the opening. The stock market also rallied, and Morgenthau felt he had accomplished what the President wanted. Late in the afternoon he called Roosevelt to say that the firm of Hopkins and Morgenthau was in the wheat business, and to offer him one-quarter interest in the company. "Make it one third," the President said, with the old fight in his voice. "Squeeze the life out of the shorts and put the price up just as far as you can."

As the purchasing program continued there were some frantic days. On November 4 an early order of 500,000 bushels of corn for Harry Hopkins's account raised the price less than a cent. When the price sagged again in the afternoon, Morgenthau ordered another 500,000 bushels. In the last five minutes before closing, this order put corn up two cents and delighted the President.

The last Saturday in October had been even more worrisome. Roosevelt, learning that wheat was off three cents, told Morgenthau to try to make it recover before the market closed. The effort might involve purchasing two or three million bushels, the President warned, but he wanted to attempt to boost prices in order to lend cheer to the weekend and to the Sunday newspapers' financial sections. Morgenthau began to buy, but, he noted, "evidently the crowd in the wheat pit was laying for me because I made very little headway." About six minutes before

closing, he told his agent "to give them the gun and to buy
everything that they offered in order to try and reach our objective. When the smoke cleared away we had bought four million
four hundred thousand bushels. . . . I felt literally dizzy while
the thing was going on. I went home and went to bed for two
hours after lunch."

As both Roosevelt and Morgenthau knew, not even forays
conducted on a grand scale could sustain commodity prices. Just
as the huge purchases of the Farm Board had failed to stabilize
the market, so Morgenthau's purchases, even though they were
not held for resale, could provide only transitory remedy. He
could and did on occasion outwit the bears in the wheat pit, but
his operations did not touch the basic problem. Nor was the distribution of surpluses to families on relief a promising long-range
solution. It was, in Morgenthau's opinion, vastly preferable to
destroying existing crops, but there was too much cotton, too
much wheat, and too little machinery for its disposal to permit
domestic consumption to bring demand up to supply. Furthermore, whatever the remote possibilities of "bridging the gap between domestic surpluses and world hunger," for the immediate
future, markets in Europe were closed by a complex of trade
barriers, and markets in Russia and China could not quickly be
opened. Nevertheless, except as a temporary and, indeed, a sin-
ful expedient, Morgenthau could not accept Wallace's formula.
He was therefore especially responsive to the possibility of de-
valuing the dollar by raising the price of gold, a prospect increasingly attractive after prices broke in June 1933.

3. The Price of Gold

Probably the foremost exponent of devaluation, and certainly
the man who most influenced Morgenthau's thinking about it,
was Dr. George Warren, who maintained that reducing the gold

value of the dollar would have two sure, salubrious results. It would raise the level of prices and restore the balance between the prices of raw materials and consumers' goods. The price of raw materials, he argued, moved faster and further than other prices in times of inflation and deflation. By 1933, he went on, deflation had produced a serious distortion in the price structure, with basic commodity prices relatively lower than industrial prices. Increasing the price of gold, he concluded, would rapidly and directly reinflate commodity prices and thus correct the abnormality of the price structure. He also contended that no effort to restore prices to pre-depression levels could succeed unless the price of gold were first increased. As one of Warren's associates put it succinctly to Morgenthau: "Only as the amount of gold in the dollar is reduced can commodity prices be raised and held. . . . In no case has any country been able to change the course of wholesale commodity prices . . . except by changing the gold content of its money."

Not laymen and politicians only, but many businessmen and professional economists believed in 1933 that depressions were simply the result of a collapse in prices. Given the insistence of Warren's theory that prices varied directly with the price of gold, the conclusion was inevitably suggested that recovery would follow an increase in the price of gold. In the temper of 1933 that was not a radical idea. Farmers and other debtors, the most ardent of American inflationists, endorsed all kinds of inflationary devices, including the printing of billions of dollars of paper money, which in recent memory had led Germany down a path of disaster, and the extensive use of silver as a base for currency, a panacea that had frightened most of the business community for half a century. Increasing the price of gold seemed relatively conservative. Gold had long been the only measure of value generally accepted by most Americans and Europeans. To abandon the existing, orthodox gold standard that set the value of gold at $20.67 an ounce was, to be sure, an adventurous proposal, for that ratio had existed unchallenged since 1900, but 1879 Warren's theory, even though it involved establishing a new and flexible ratio, did not substitute for gold either silver or paper.

Various European nations, furthermore, including Great Britain, had already abandoned orthodoxy, shifting to a managed currency that left gold at a modified ratio which could be manipulated. Those nations had neither resorted to the printing press nor been swept away by uncontrolled inflation. By devaluation they had obtained some temporary advantage in competing for trade with the United States and other countries still wedded to orthodoxy. The physical movement of gold from the United States during 1931-32 represented in part American payments in an unfavorable balance of trade. The outflow of gold had serious domestic repercussions, for by depleting the monetary base, it contributed to deflation.

At the time of Roosevelt's inauguration, orthodoxy still had its illustrious champions, among them Hoover and most Republicans of stature, Al Smith, Lewis Douglas, the Director of the Budget, and other right-wing Democrats. There were also impressive proponents of change. The Committee for the Nation to Rebuild Prices and Purchasing Power, for example, numbered among its devotees scores of business executives, and among its leaders J. H. Rand, Jr., of Remington, Rand; General Robert E. Wood of Sears, Roebuck; and Frank A. Vanderlip, president of the National City Bank of New York, all of whom pretty much subscribed to Warren's theory. The new President was under such great pressure that his real problem was not whether there should be inflation but whether he could control the direction it was to take and the dimensions it was to reach.

Roosevelt's initial moves were heterodox but not directly inflationary. To stop the accelerating flow of gold to Europe and to combat the hoarding of gold domestically, both of which helped to bring on the banking crisis and were in turn accentuated by the panic accompanying that crisis, the President in March 1933 suspended the export of gold except by license from the Treasury. In April he forbade the hoarding of gold and required the delivery of all gold held domestically to the Federal Reserve Banks. Those orders were essential preliminaries for currency management or reinflation, but for the time being the United States remained on the rigid gold standard, for the Treasury did license the export of gold to support the dollar in foreign exchange, and the dollar did not immediately depreciate abroad.

Late in April the President went further. The dollar was beginning to sag abroad, and New York bankers were applying for licenses to export gold in large quantities. In Congress, where the farm bill was being debated, senators from agricultural states insisted upon inflationary policies. Only by a close vote did the Administration defeat a proposal for the mandatory coinage of silver at a ratio to gold of sixteen to one, the magical formula of the silver crusade of the 1890's. There were still pending proposals to force the printing of greenbacks in large quantity. The Administration had either to take charge of inflation and manage it or permit Congress to impose by statute an uncontrolled and possibly uncontrollable inflation.

The threat from Congress, coupled as it was with pressure on the dollar, forced Roosevelt's hand. On April 19 he announced his willingness to accept the discretionary powers which Senator Thomas's amendment to the farm bill invested in him. Those powers permitted but did not compel him to issue paper money, to provide for the unlimited coinage of silver, to force the Federal Reserve System to expand the credit base, or to reduce the gold content of the dollar. Roosevelt was not ready to use any of the powers, but he did renounce a rigid gold standard. His Executive Orders on April 19 and 20 prohibited the export of gold. At once the value of the dollar in terms of other currencies fell off. Concurrently the prices of commodities and securities in the United States rose, and there began a period of speculative increases in prices that lasted until almost the end of June.

To some, like Lewis Douglas, the abandonment of the gold standard seemed to portend an end to Western civilization, but more perceptive men were less deluded than he was by monetary orthodoxy. J. Pierpont Morgan welcomed the President's action. Efforts to maintain the exchange value of the dollar, he commented, were having a deflationary effect upon already deflated American prices, wages and employment. "The way out of the depression," Morgan said, "is to combat and overcome the deflationary forces." Conservative economists considered the embargo on gold temporarily essential to permit the Administration to initiate measures for domestic recovery, whether by monetary action or by deficit expenditures to stimulate business activity. But in April 1933, even as Roosevelt applied the embargo, there was no certainty that it would continue, and even less certainty about what action would accompany it.

Morgenthau was much concerned about both of these questions. Although he had played no significant part in the decisions already made, he was, as he intermittently indicated to the President, an advocate not only of what had been done but also of supplementing it as soon as possible by reducing the gold content of the dollar.

The test of Roosevelt's intentions came toward the end of June, just before prices began their downward plunge. There was then meeting in London the World Economic Conference. One of its crucial problems was currency. Most of the nations of Europe had left the gold standard, but France, Holland, Belgium, Italy, and Switzerland had not, and they wanted the conference to stabilize the gold value of currencies. Great Britain, after depreciating the pound sterling in 1931, was prepared to stabilize at 1933 levels advantageous to her.

For the United States the problem was different. The gold content of the dollar had not been changed. Had the dollar been fixed at the existing level, at its existing gold value and its existing ratio to European currencies, it would have been difficult, if not impossible, to raise domestic prices. On June 17 Roosevelt therefore rejected a stabilization agreement that would have committed him not to use the inflationary powers of the Thomas Amendment. On June 29, at his summer home at Campobello Island, where Morgenthau was visiting, he received a compromise proposal that endorsed the principle of stabilization but did not bind countries not then on the gold standard to work toward stabilization immediately. Those in London who had arranged the compromise fully expected the President to accept it; those at home who favored inflation opposed any international limitation on domestic monetary policy.

After hearing about the compromise proposal from Louis

Howe, who was adamantly against it, Morgenthau with his usual candor noted in his Diary that he knew little about the issue, but on principle agreed with Howe. The compromise, Morgenthau felt, would have impeded or even prevented the devaluation he considered necessary. He had, moreover, received gloomy reports about London from his father, a technical expert at the conference, who observed that the prospects were "not at all hopeful . . . unless F.D.R. is very positive and takes leadership in his own hands."

The President had kept his own counsel, but on June 30 he gave Morgenthau the impression that he wanted first and foremost to raise prices, especially commodity prices, in the United States. Two days later he read to Morgenthau and Howe a message he had drafted for London. It chastised the conference for considering stabilization ahead of "larger purposes" and asserted that "the sound internal economic system of a Nation is a greater factor in its well-being than the price of its currency." The content and tone of the message dispelled any hope for agreement on stabilization at London. Morgenthau was delighted. "We were tied up hand and fist at the London Conference," he later recalled. "We had to break it. He broke it. I really had nothing to do with it."

The continuing decline in prices during the following month persuaded Roosevelt that he had to make some monetary change. At luncheon on August 16, he told Morgenthau that he would like to buy gold in the open market at more than the prevailing price, but he did not know how he could do so. Late in September Morgenthau learned that the Attorney General believed the President did not have the power to buy gold. Morgenthau immediately told Roosevelt that the lawyers in Farm Credit disagreed. At Roosevelt's request, he obtained a fuller statement about the issue. Herman Oliphant had already defined a legal basis for action. His fertile intelligence found various sources for the necessary authority, including, among others, two forgotten statutes of 1862 and 1864. After reading the memorandum Oliphant had prepared, Roosevelt commented, in great good spirits: "I have a method of my own to break the law which I think is much simpler." He proposed setting up a corporation under RFC to buy gold. Following his instructions, Morgenthau discussed that possibility with Jesse Jones, and together they suggested forming a new federal corporation to purchase gold, silver, cotton, and other commodities. The Attorney General tentatively endorsed the scheme, but Roosevelt, still uncertain, referred it to a group of lawyers from the Treasury and Justice Departments for further consideration. While their inconclusive discussions rambled on through the middle of October, prices fell and the sentiment for inflation mounted.

Among Roosevelt's advisers the outstanding opponent of Oliphant's memorandum on gold was Dean Acheson, the Under Secretary of the Treasury, whose chief, William Woodin, was seriously ill. Acheson, a dedicated and brilliant public servant, had an impeccable legal and liberal pedigree. A graduate of Yale and of the Harvard Law School, he had been private secretary to Associate Justice Louis D. Brandeis, and he had also been a junior member of the law firm of George Rublee, a prominent T.R. Progressive. But Acheson, like his friend Lewis Douglas, was never comfortable with the pace and the tumult of the early New Deal. Opposed in any case to manipulating the currency, Acheson worried especially about what he considered the ethical implications of embarking upon a policy of devaluation at just the time he was completing the sale of a series of federal securities to the public. If the dollar were devalued, the value of those securities would fall proportionately. That loss, Acheson felt, would violate the obligation of the government to its bondholders. He therefore resisted Roosevelt's importunities. As the President put it to Morgenthau, he had tried for six weeks to get the Treasury to find a way to buy gold, but it was "like punching your fist into a pillow."

At luncheon at the White House on October 19, 1933, Acheson still balked. Morgenthau, exasperated by this round in the endless debate, suggested locking all the lawyers who had ideas on the subject in a room together until they reached a decision. "That's fine," the President agreed. "Let them go to the Attorney General's office and do it." They did, and they returned with the decision Roosevelt wanted, for Attorney General Homer Cummings ruled categorically — though he did not put his opinion in writing for some weeks — that the Secretary of the Treasury, with the approval of the President, had the power to purchase gold in the open market.

Roosevelt intended the Reconstruction Finance Corporation to operate as the government's agent in executing his policy, and he planned to finance the purchases by selling short-term obligations of that corporation. At the meeting of the board of the RFC to vote on the sales, Acheson arrived looking "like a thundercloud." "I am opposed to our buying gold," he announced. "The President has ordered me to do it. I will carry out his orders." But he left it to Morgenthau, who attended the meeting as Roosevelt's "watchdog," to work out the details of the program with the Attorney General. "I have had the shackles on my hands for months now," Roosevelt told Morgenthau on October 23, "and I feel for the first time as though I had thrown them off."

4. Gold Buying

Every morning, beginning October 25, Morgenthau, Warren, and Jesse Jones met in the President's bedroom to set the price of gold for the day. Roosevelt "would lie comfortably on his old-fashioned three-quarter mahogany bed. A table stood on each side; on his left would be a batch of government reports, a detective novel or two, a couple of telephones. On his right would be pads, pencils, cigarettes, his watch and a plate of fruit. Hearty and refreshed after a night's rest, he would eat his soft-boiled eggs" while the others reported on the behavior of gold and commodity prices.

The price that the morning conference established on any given day made very little difference. The object was simply to keep the trend moving gradually upward, a little above the world price, in the expectation that commodity prices would follow. To prevent speculators from guessing what the price of gold would be, the conferees deliberately varied the daily increment, choosing figures that sometimes seemed arbitrary but always served their original purpose.

On October 21, the day before Roosevelt announced the new policy, the price of gold in London, the world's largest market, was $29.01 an ounce. On October 25, the first day the RFC bought American gold, the price in London opened at $31.02. At Morgenthau's suggestion, Roosevelt directed the RFC to buy at $31.36. He put the price up another 18 cents the next day. At tea on October 28 he discussed the long-range program. Morgenthau had had a dizzy day buying wheat; there were rumors that France and Great Britain might refuse to permit American purchases of gold in their markets; criticism of the policy at home was increasing. But Roosevelt, imperturbable, set his objectives for January 1, 1934, as 10-cent cotton, 50-cent corn, and 90-cent wheat. To start to reach these prices, he intended during the next week to raise gold to $33.02. His schedule called for putting the price Monday up to $31.98 and then adding daily for five days 28, 12, 28, 20, and 16 cents. He considered this schedule sufficiently erratic to confuse speculators, sufficiently high to affect world gold and commodity prices.

Roosevelt stuck close to this plan, but small deviations from his original estimates for daily increases left him on Friday, November 3, with a range of from 19 to 22 cents to add to the price of gold — the original estimate had been 20 cents. The President that day took one look at Morgenthau, who was feeling more than usually worried about the state of the world, and suggested a rise of 21 cents. "It's a lucky number," Roosevelt said with a laugh, "because it's three times seven." Morgenthau later noted in his Diary: "If anybody ever knew how we really set the gold price through a combination of lucky numbers, etc., I think they would be frightened." But as he later realized, Roosevelt had relieved a tense and gloomy moment by pulling his leg. He had also, his frivolity notwithstanding, hewed close to the plan that he had set almost a week earlier, and he continued daily to raise the price.

At first the RFC bought only gold offered within the domestic market. Soon the price within the United States rose above the world price. Consequently the dollar was worth more (or, in other words, had depreciated less) in London and Paris than at home. Morgenthau on October 27 therefore pointed out that it would be foolish to go much further unless the RFC began to buy gold abroad. Only in this way could the American purchases affect the world price of gold and other commodities. Only in this way could the United States offset any effort of the countries on the gold standard or in the sterling bloc to prevent the dollar from depreciating in terms of their currencies. The President had hoped to confine purchases to newly mined domestic gold, but the persistent gap between the domestic and foreign price compelled him to agree with Morgenthau.

That decision had large implications. They could buy gold abroad only by operating in foreign exchange, traditionally the province of private bankers who bought and sold foreign exchange themselves or worked indirectly through the Federal Reserve Banks, whose policies they governed. By taking over control of foreign exchange the federal government would reveal even more than it already had the President's intention to manage the currency. That was bound to frighten bankers who believed that they alone understood the techniques of their calling. Furthermore, the initiation of foreign exchange operations would surely be considered a declaration of monetary war. American gold purchases abroad would appreciate foreign currencies, alarm foreign nations about their potential loss of trade, perhaps set off a wave of competitive international currency depreciation like that which had followed England's departure from the gold standard in 1931.

To take charge of the foreign exchange operation Roosevelt called upon the Governor of the New York Federal Reserve Bank, George Harrison, an urbane, experienced, conservative financier who was conscious and jealous of the traditional powers of his office. Harrison insisted on having full authority over the technical aspects of his job, to which Roosevelt agreed, but the President hesitated to accept the banker's suggestion that the United States talk with the British and French before beginning to trade in gold abroad. "Every time we have taken the British into our confidence," he remarked, "they have given us a trimming."

After further thought persuaded him to let Harrison go ahead, the President thoroughly enjoyed the shocked surprise of the Europeans. The French, Harrison reported, had nearly jumped out of their skins. Governor Montague Norman of the Bank of England, a die-hard Tory whom Roosevelt called "old pink whiskers," heard Harrison's news about American plans with incredulity. "This is the most terrible thing that has happened," Norman wailed into the transatlantic telephone. "The whole world will be put into bankruptcy." Harrison's instinct was to reassure Norman, but Roosevelt and Morgenthau, picturing foreign bankers with every one of their hairs standing on end in horror, caught each other's eye and began to roar with laughter. Within twenty-four hours, Roosevelt told Morgenthau, he expected to "see the whites of the eyes of the enemies," and he expected Harrison to shoot.

By November 1, when operations in foreign exchange were bringing the Administration's gold policy into full play, the disciples of orthodoxy were vigorously attacking the President. As the month wore on and the price of gold moved up, the Chamber of Commerce, the American Legion, the American Federation of Labor, and the Economists' National Committee on Monetary Policy condemned gold buying and cheered Al Smith's bitter denunciation of the Roosevelt "baloney dollar." The President also had his defenders. Spokesmen of the Committee for the Nation and for the Farmers' Union urged him to advance the price of gold even more rapidly, and in reply to Al Smith, Father Coughlin, the Detroit radio-priest and inflationist who was then approaching the crest of his astonishing popularity, gave his national audience their choice of "Roosevelt or Ruin!"

Within the government the conflict of opinion was most serious in the Treasury Department, where Dean Acheson and others still opposed the President's policy. On several occasions Morgenthau openly expressed his annoyance with them. Once, after he had criticized Acheson for failing to prepare a formal statement on the price of gold, the Under Secretary snapped back: "Why don't you move into Mr. Woodin's office?" Morgenthau, hurt by this retort, replied: "Dean . . . I live each day for itself. . . . I am neither a schemer nor a plotter." Jesse Jones was unable to resist joining in the raillery. "What other orders have you for us?" he asked Morgenthau, who, again upset, said: "Don't do that to me, Jesse."

As long as Acheson dawdled, Roosevelt had to have someone outside of the Treasury on whom he could rely. On October 27 he had told Morgenthau that he could not decide whether to fire Acheson. Two days thereafter, addressing a meeting of his advisers on financial matters, Roosevelt said that if he had not begun buying gold and other commodities, there could have been "an agrarian revolution in this country." He explained what Jesse Jones was doing for cotton and how Morgenthau was buying wheat for Harry Hopkins. "Gentlemen," he continued, "I have called you together to inform you that the question of buying gold is an administration policy. We are all in the same boat. If any one does not like the boat, he can get out of it." Looking around, the President added that he meant no one in particular but everyone in general. Nevertheless, to Morgenthau Acheson looked "very miserable and very sick through the whole thing."

Acheson's disturbance persisted, partly because the Attorney General had yet to put in writing an opinion sustaining the President's authority to buy gold, partly because economists within the Treasury questioned the wisdom of the policy, largely because on principle the Under Secretary himself still disapproved of it. On November 1 Acheson had a row with Jesse Jones about RFC procedures. About that time he left with Roosevelt a handwritten, undated letter of resignation for the President to accept if and when he wished.

Acheson's hesitancy, Morgenthau observed, was making government especially difficult. The time for contemplation had passed. Like Roosevelt, Morgenthau was engrossed in deciding what policy to pursue and only then with finding a legal foundation for it. While the Under Secretary of the Treasury was searching his soul about the legality and the ethics of buying gold, Oliphant, with Morgenthau's consent, was searching his library for authority to have the RFC buy silver, too. Many inflationists in and out of Congress believed that such purchases would also help raise commodity prices. The plan was not adopted, but in explaining it to Roosevelt, Morgenthau suggested jokingly that instead of taking it up with Acheson, the President first get the Attorney General to rule and then tell Acheson about it. "You devil," Roosevelt replied, "you are just as bad as I am."

"Well," said Morgenthau, "who taught me?" Roosevelt roared.

At the breakfast conference of November 13, the President asked Morgenthau to stay after Jesse Jones left. He said he wanted to talk about Farm Credit, but he began on a different subject. "I had a very interesting and confidential conversation with Mr. Woodin," Roosevelt remarked. "I have suggested to him that he take a leave of absence without pay." "I am going to write him a letter," he continued, "in answer to one which he has written to me suggesting that we get somebody to become Acting Secretary who knows government and knows finance." He paused. Then he said: "I have decided that that person is Henry Morgenthau, Jr."

Morgenthau was "so dumbfounded" that he "broke out in perspiration" while Roosevelt went on: "You made good for me in Albany, and you are one of the two or three people who have made an outstanding success in Washington, so let's you and I go on to bigger things. . . . We will have lots of fun doing it together." Still staggered, Morgenthau, as he recalled, "managed to get something out about how much I appreciated the opportunity . . . walked over and shook his hand."

On November 16 Roosevelt accepted the undated resignation of Dean Acheson, who held the office for which Morgenthau was designated. Later, Roosevelt told Morgenthau that he had consulted no one about the appointment. Acheson first heard of the changes, according to his recollection, after the President announced them to the press, but Acheson could hardly have been surprised, for he had made no secret of his discomfort. In years to come he and Morgenthau were to work together effectively on different problems, and Morgenthau was to gain a large respect for Acheson's courage and integrity. In 1933, however, he felt Roosevelt had to let the Under Secretary go.

"The President," Morgenthau recalled years later, "wanted a Treasury Department which would play its proper role in his campaign on prices; he wanted a Secretary who would be loyal and would try to get things done; so he threw me in to plug the hole." Under his direction, the battle to keep prices up continued. The price of gold was raised to $34.01 an ounce on December 1, to $34.06 later that month, to $35.00 in January, a price that has remained unchanged for over three decades. It was not the President alone who was pleased. Walter Lippmann, publishing his column in the Republican New York *Herald Tribune,* derived "a sense of assurance" from the changes in the Treasury. "We are delighted in your appointment of . . . Morgenthau," the president of the American Farm Bureau wired Roosevelt. "We feel he is the friend of we folks and will help give us an honest dollar." "You are fortunate," wrote an officer of the Committee for the Nation, "in having a man like Mr. Morgenthau who will have the strength and courage to carry out the monetary policy."

Gold buying had less dramatic results than its advocates expected. By mid-November, the price of gold in London again lagged behind that set in Washington. The price of wheat did not quite touch 90, Roosevelt's objective, but after passing 89 in mid-November, slumped again to 85. While the government raised the price of gold 17 per cent, the price of cotton rose only 14 per cent, of corn 7 per cent. The general index of all farm products actually fell off a little during November and December in spite of the gold policy, the purchases of cotton, corn, and wheat, and the reduction in planting arranged by the AAA. But the average of thirty key industrial stocks increased in proportion to the price of gold, for the dollar value of these industrials reflected the inflation. Conversely, government bonds fell three points between the end of October and mid-January, for the real income their interest earned shrank as the dollar was devalued. These changes, however, did not restore the balance between agricultural and industrial prices that Warren had hoped to redress. Warren's theory was simply wrong.

Yet there were important gains. When prices were falling and threatening to fall further, the President and his advisers had reversed the trend. Devaluation ultimately facilitated a considerable rise in prices within the United States. That had been Roosevelt's objective. Devaluation also lightened substantially the burdens of farmers and other debtors. The depreciation of the dollar permitted them, as Roosevelt had intended, to pay their debts "more nearly at the price level at which they were incurred." And devaluation was ultimately followed, as Roosevelt had promised, by stabilization of the gold value of the dollar.

Compared to what Roosevelt might have done — to raising the price of gold to $40 as the Committee for the Nation urged, to printing three billion dollars of paper currency, to remonetizing silver at 16 to 1 — the gold-purchasing program was modest. European nations on the whole resented the policy, but no nation had for several years shown much regard for the economic convenience of others, and in 1933 the pressure on the President was such that he had to do something.

Roosevelt and Morgenthau seized the particular tool that seemed best to them at the time, and they used it boldly. They made the manipulation of the value of the currency an open and admitted instrument of public policy. This in itself signified the intention of the New Deal to free government from the decisions of bankers who, whatever their talents, had fallen into the habit of timorous inactivity.

The gold buying program, for all of its faults, represented the best spirit of the first ten months of the New Deal, which energized the federal government as it had never been energized before. That was the source of the exciting, satisfying, buoyant mood of the New Dealers. For a reporter from the *New York Times* Morgenthau phrased it very well: "There is a new sense of social responsibility and interdependence . . . implicit in the administration's policy. . . . It looks forward toward a more stable social order, but it is not doctrinaire, not a complete cut-and-dried program. It involves the courage to experiment. Behind it is the conviction that no prosperity can be permanent which is not shared with all elements of the population."

As much as his achievement in FCA, Morgenthau's dauntless-ness had won him promotion. Roosevelt could not afford, in a season of great crisis, to have around him obstruction or even reluctance. The President was not intolerant of dissent (he had permitted Morgenthau constantly to criticize the AAA), but he was impatient with the doubts that stifled action. The luxury of self-searching had to await a quieter time. In 1933 those with power had to use it fast and joyously.

III

THE DOLLAR AT HOME

AND ABROAD

1934–1936

1. The Department of the Treasury

As SECRETARY OF THE TREASURY, Morgenthau commanded the most extraordinary department in the federal government. It collected and disbursed billions of dollars a year, borrowed money, bought and sold gold and silver, supervised the national banks, and kept the government accounts. The Treasury did much more than manage the nation's finances. It also administered a multitude of services whose annual operating budget was exceeded only by those of the Army and Navy, and whose combined activities took the full time of the largest police force and one of the largest staffs of lawyers in the federal establishment.

Under the Treasury the Coast Guard patrolled the oceans for icebergs and the coastal waters for smugglers and amateur sailors in difficulties; the Bureau of Narcotics pursued peddlers of cocaine and marijuana from the Bronx to Nob Hill; the Secret Service guarded the President and combatted counterfeiting; the Bureau of Engraving and Printing manufactured dollars, stamps, and bonds; and the Public Health Service examined immigrants for contagious diseases, campaigned against syphilis, and studied American diets. In addition, the Procurement Division built post offices and courthouses, arranged competitions for paintings and sculptures, purchased thousands of tons of cement for public buildings and dozens of footballs and baseballs for the recreational use of public servants; the Bureau of Customs examined the baggage of hundreds of travelers, evaluating jewelry, tweeds, pipes, and toys, apprehending both smugglers and petty chiselers; and the Alcohol Tax Unit rooted out moonshiners and bootleggers. Above all, the Bureau of Internal Revenue, a constant companion to every citizen, collected his income and estate taxes and his pennies when he smoked or attended the theater or purchased gasoline.

Over all this and more Morgenthau presided, carrying the final responsibility for what went right or what went wrong, making the final decisions about organization, personnel, and policy — at all times, as he put it, running his own show. His hours were long and intense. As he had for years, he arose at about six in the morning. He began his day by glancing through a few leading newspapers, usually the *New York Times*, the *Wall Street Journal*, and the Washington *Post*, reviewing reports taken home the night before, and often telephoning one or two of his staff who learned not to expect to sleep beyond seven-thirty. After breakfast he ordinarily walked the two miles from his home to his office in company with a colleague, discussing some problem scheduled for further consideration later in the day.

Arriving at his desk by eight forty-five, the Secretary usually checked first on international exchange rates and on the trading that had already begun in London and Paris markets. At nine-thirty he held his morning staff meeting, attended by six to ten of his top advisers. There followed mid-morning conferences with officials of the Federal Reserve Board, or with representatives of the State Department or of foreign countries involved in an international monetary agreement, or with members of any one of the half-dozen committees of which Morgenthau was chairman or of the dozen other committees on which he served. When Congress was in session, he was often on the Hill, sometimes twice a day, testifying on legislation or appropriations. Except on Mondays, when he regularly took luncheon with the President, he ate at his desk, often with a colleague, a congressman, a newspaperman, a banker, an economist, a businessman, or a visitor from abroad. In the afternoon there were more meetings, more telephone calls, more conferences, correspondence to read and to answer. He was fortunate to be home by six, and he gave several evenings a week to homework. Now and then he could fly to his farm for a weekend, but ordinarily his was a six-day week and his Sunday was as much a time for study as for rest. No one in Washington, saving only the President, had more to do; no one worked harder.

2. The Gold Reserve Act

Simply by virtue of assuming office as Secretary of the Treasury — he became Secretary in his own right in January 1934, after the dying Woodin resigned — Morgenthau was forced to look upon familiar questions from a new angle. In the first months of his tenure, the demands of the devaluation program absorbed his energies, and he had now to resolve the monetary problems, national and international, related to gold buying. The exchange fluctuations which the rising price of gold produced could not long be permitted to disrupt international trade. As 1934 began, Roosevelt and Morgenthau therefore wanted to set a relatively permanent price for gold. They had to do so if the government was to realize the profits from devaluation. The increase in the price of gold gave a larger dollar value to the nationalized American gold stocks, but the Treasury could not enter the gain on its accounts until the price of gold was stabilized. The estimated budgetary deficit for 1934 gave that problem immediate importance.

Most significantly, the dollar was again appreciating relative to other currencies, particularly the pound. Morgenthau and Roosevelt ascribed that development to the deliberate policy of the British government. In 1932 the British had created the Exchange Equalization Account, equipped with a special fund for trading in foreign exchange. Its purpose was to prevent unwanted fluctuations of the pound sterling. Morgenthau, as he later recalled, became excited when he concluded that the British agency was "fighting" him. For his part, Roosevelt concluded that the British wanted to maintain their own favorable trading position and their own liquidity. With all this in mind, both men considered it imperative for the United States to have an instrument capable of checking British influence on international exchange.

On January 15, 1934, Roosevelt sent a special monetary message to Congress. "The time has come for a more certain determination of the gold value of the American dollar," he said. He already had authority to fix the lower limit of revaluation of the pre-1933 dollar at 50 per cent. He now asked Congress to set an upper limit of 60 per cent. To permit the Secretary of the Treasury "to bring some greater degree of stability to foreign exchange rates," Roosevelt also recommended "that, out of the profits of any devaluation, there should be set up a fund of $2,000,000,000 for such purchases and sales of gold, foreign exchange, and government securities as the regulation of the currency, the maintenance of the Government, and the general welfare of the United States may require."

Inflationists, still powerful in and out of Congress, objected to limiting revaluation, while officials of the Federal Reserve System questioned the propriety of authorizing the Treasury to buy and sell foreign exchange and government securities through a Stabilization Fund. The Treasury, they argued, lacked the necessary experience and leadership to exercise these functions, which were classically the prerogatives of private bankers and privately governed central banks. The friends of the Reserve System in the Senate therefore sponsored amendments to establish a board of directors to administer the Stabilization Fund, to restrict its transactions to foreign exchange, to require public reports of its operations, and to limit its life to two years. Only the last of those amendments survived, and it was modified to permit Congress to renew the Fund. On January 30, 1934, Congress passed the Gold Reserve Act by impressive majorities, the House voting 370 to 40, the Senate 66 to 23. The measure followed the Administration's prescriptions. The next day a presidential proclamation and Treasury regulations put the new law into effect, setting the price of gold at $35 an ounce, thus reducing the dollar to 59.06 per cent of its pre-1933 gold content.

Treasury policy put the United States on a limited gold standard. Acting as the agent of the Department, the Federal Reserve Bank of New York could sell gold to the central banks of foreign nations on the gold standard whenever the dollar reached the gold-export point, the price of $35 plus the cost of transportation. If gold rose above that price, it would profit the Treasury to sell. Such sales would in turn bring the price back to $35, the level the Administration wished to maintain. The law and Treasury regulations permitted American traders to buy gold abroad as they always had, but when they shipped it to the United States, they had to sell it at $35 an ounce to the Treasury. If gold was cheaper than that in foreign markets, private arbitragers were sure to buy it. Alternatively, the Treasury could make direct purchases of its own to hold the world price at the American figure.

The old gold standard no longer existed. Not since April 1933 had Americans been permitted to own gold or freely to convert paper currency into gold. Further, although the government now agreed to take all gold at $35 an ounce, the sale of gold was at the discretion of the Treasury. It could at any time stop sales or change their conditions. The President had the right at any time to devalue to 50 per cent of the old parity. The new standard, subject as it was to change, was a matter of convenience. Roosevelt called it the bullion system; Morgenthau described it as "the 1934 model gold bullion standard . . . streamlined . . . air flow . . . and knee action. . . . It's the one which suits our own need."

The Gold Reserve Act completed the alterations in the monetary system that had begun with the nationalization of gold. Before 1933 the United States had accepted gold as the standard of value to which the currency had to conform; the Federal Reserve System had maintained the currency in terms of gold. Now the government no longer considered that maintenance desirable. Under the traditional gold standard, flights of capital from the United States, depleting American monetary stocks, might have interfered with cheap money policies or with deficit spending. The new arrangements simplified the pursuit of those policies, which the President and his advisers deemed essential to the public good. The Administration acquired effective control over the exchange and gold value of the dollar, which permitted the protection of the internal credit structure from the influence of foreign monetary changes. Neither the deliberate or inadvertent devaluation of a foreign currency had any longer to affect the domestic value of the dollar or to touch the level of American prices. Perhaps most significantly, as Morgenthau repeatedly noted in retrospect, the Act turned over to the Treasury much of the authority for the management of credit and currency, and thus made monetary control an instrument of national policy.

3. The Supreme Court and the Gold Clause

As Morgenthau began to exercise the authority the Gold Reserve Act conferred upon the Treasury, he made heavy purchases which established the American price all over the world within about two months. For all of the incoming gold the Treasury issued equivalent, noncirculating, inconvertible certificates to the Federal Reserve System. These increased reserves provided a base for a vast expansion of credit and currency. The expansion made money more available, "easier," precisely as the New Deal intended, for easy money (or low interest rates) helped potential commercial borrowers, and industrial borrowing for the expansion of plant or inventory would put men to work and help move the economy out of depression. However, as Morgenthau realized, easy money, though one condition for revival, was not in itself sufficient. Unless businessmen took advantage of low interest rates, the level of investment would not rise.

The expansion of gold reserves made it possible to market government securities at lower interest rates. That permitted Morgenthau gradually to reduce the carrying charge on the debt and to handle effectively the existing and pending federal deficits, much of which the government spent on essential relief and recovery projects.

But by 1935 Morgenthau had become skeptical of the further devaluation of the dollar, which inflationists were urging. A higher gold price, he knew, would mean even larger American gold purchases, which by further depleting the reserves of countries still on the gold standard, would surely push them off and perhaps lead to unending competitive devaluation. The Secretary was reluctant to disturb the exchange and bond markets which the Treasury was bringing under control. He did not think devaluation had failed, but he and his advisers could see no domestic benefit in pushing it on. Aware of these views, Roosevelt in August 1935 suggested — partly in fun, partly as a test — that he might consider changing the price of gold. "Please do not tease me," Morgenthau replied, "it is too early in the morning."

Political rather than economic considerations had persuaded the President, to Morgenthau's dismay, seriously to propose tinkering with the price of gold in January 1935. At that time the Supreme Court was weighing the constitutionality of the Joint Resolution of June 3, 1933, one legal basis for the Administration's gold program. That resolution declared it to be against public policy for contracts to provide for payment in gold or in any particular type of currency. It forbade such provision in the future, and it made all contracts, past or future, payable in whatever coin or currency was legal tender at the time of payment. Many private contracts, especially bonds, had been written in earlier years to provide explicitly for payment in gold dollars of the pre-1933 weight and fineness. Much of the bonded debt of the United States was written in this manner, and many bond holders believed the Joint Resolution unconstitutional deprivation of their contractual rights. If the Supreme Court agreed, it would jeopardize the New Deal's gold policy.

The Administration hoped for a favorable decision. Its brief maintained that it had suspended gold payments and allowed the dollar to fall in order to save the economy by stopping deflation, but that the instability in foreign exchange and domestic prices which inevitably followed the cutting loose from gold was intolerable as a long-range condition. Therefore, the government argued, it had fixed the price of gold at $35 an ounce and established the Stabilization Fund to maintain that price. Throughout the formulation and execution of this twofold policy, the Administration had been determined that all Americans should suffer or benefit equally. Since the gold clause could not be inserted in private bonds not originally containing it, equality of treatment was possible only by striking the clause from previously existing private and public contracts. For the same reason the government had required all holders of gold and gold certificates to surrender them and accept payment in dollars of the new value.

If the Administration reversed its position on gold while the judges were discussing their decision in conference, Herman Oliphant told Morgenthau, it would weaken the government's case. Oliphant, who had moved to the Treasury as its General Counsel and Morgenthau's closest adviser, believed that the stability in the price of gold, which had remained at $35 for a year, gave the judges confidence in the Administration and might reconcile them to the abrogation of the gold clauses. "Even a hint of possible change," he wrote, "might destroy that confidence."

At luncheon with Morgenthau and Homer Cummings on January 14, Roosevelt seriously questioned that reasoning in what Morgenthau considered one of the most unpleasant hours he had had since coming to Washington. The President said he wanted to keep things in an unsettled state until the Supreme Court handed down its gold decision. The only way the man in the taxicab could become interested in the gold case, he contended,

was if the story were kept on the front page. Roosevelt therefore wanted bonds and foreign exchange to fluctuate in such a
way as to suggest crisis. If things were in constant turmoil and
the case went against the government, the man in the street
would say, "For God's sake, Mr. President, do something about
it." Then, if he did something about it, the country would
"heave a sigh of relief and say thank God." Cummings, who was
in charge of the presentation of the case, vigorously agreed.

In reply, Morgenthau, as he later noted, "argued harder and
more intensely than . . . ever before" in his life. He said that
he did not advise Cummings on legal matters and did not expect
Cummings to advise him on financial matters. Congress had
given him the Stabilization Fund as a trust, and his conscience
told him to use it as it was intended. He could not conceivably
encourage uncertainty. When he had entered the Treasury a
year earlier, Morgenthau reminded Roosevelt, things had been
chaotic. Step by step, he felt, he had stabilized foreign exchange
and the bond market. He had built up the confidence of the
country in himself and in his Department, and he expected to
keep that confidence. "Mr. President," Morgenthau said, "you
know how difficult it is to get this country out of a depression
and if we let the financial markets of this country become frightened for the next month it may take us eight months to recover
the lost ground."

Nevertheless, Roosevelt pressed Morgenthau "very very hard,
arguing all the time for the political effect." Finally Morgenthau
began to fear that the President might order him to obey, in
which case he would have to refuse and resign. To avoid that
possibility he pointed his finger at Roosevelt and said: "Mr. President, don't ask me to do this."

"Henry, you have simply given this thing snap-judgment,"
Roosevelt replied. "Think it over."

"Let's all three of us think it over," Morgenthau said, rising to
depart.

On the telephone the next morning, Morgenthau considered
the tone of the President's voice "particularly nice." He felt that
Roosevelt must have slept on the matter and that "my advice was

going to prevail." That evening they both attended a dinner at the Vice President's. Roosevelt was at Mrs. Garner's right, Morgenthau on her left. Leaning back in his seat, the President said across his hostess's back: "Well, Henry, I am glad to see that you are smiling again." Then he turned to Mrs. Garner: "You know, Henry was very serious for an hour yesterday. . . . I was arguing with him about the gold case and in arguing I often take the side of the opposition in order to bring out the various points but of course I didn't believe in these arguments." Looking over at Morgenthau, Roosevelt continued: "Henry feels much happier tonight and I see he is smiling." That, Morgenthau wrote in his Diary, was the method Roosevelt took to inform him that he had not meant what he had said the day before, or at least that he had changed his mind. In any case, Morgenthau knew he had won.

On February 18, 1935, the day the Court handed down its decisions, Morgenthau and some of his staff awaited word in the executive offices adjoining the White House. Shortly after noon a flash from the UP ticker reported that the Court was in session. Morgenthau rushed into Miss LeHand's office and told her to get the President. In what seemed like less than a minute, Roosevelt arrived smiling to take his regular place at the Cabinet table. His secretaries hovered around him during the tension preceding the final word.

Minutes later the Supreme Court's decision came over the telephone. By a margin of one vote the judges for all practical purposes favored the government. The majority upheld devaluation for essentially legal rather than economic reasons. In substance the Court concluded that repudiation of the gold clause was constitutional in private contracts but not in government bonds. However, the majority also ruled that the plaintiff in the government bond case had proved no loss and therefore had no remedy. The result, to which the minority entered a stormy dissent, protected the Administration, though Chief Justice Hughes in rendering the opinion scolded the President. The gold policy was safe.

The Court's reasoning was complicated and its temper unfriendly, but those around the Cabinet table were nonetheless grateful. They sat and talked for about an hour with the atmosphere "very jolly." Roosevelt was "very natural, laughing and smiling practically all the time." "It certainly was one of the big moments of my life," Morgenthau later reflected, "and it was an experience to be with him."

4. Toward Stabilization

The decisions in the gold clause cases, sustaining the Administration's monetary policy as they did, gave Morgenthau freedom to concentrate upon preserving the exchange ratios among the dollar, pound and franc. He had no doubt about the desirability of stabilization. Instability of exchange, his foremost advisers agreed, checked world recovery. Americans would not freely invest their funds at home if the dollar was sinking on the world market, and there would be no recovery in the United States until private investment was resumed on a larger scale.

Roosevelt, while not opposed to *de facto* stabilization, was not excited about it. He did not believe the United States could get other nations to agree upon stabilization until they had established their internal price levels to their own satisfaction, just as he felt he had now done. Like Morgenthau, he hoped to avoid still another round of devaluation, and he was willing to have the Secretary try.

The State Department, in contrast, was hostile to the new departure. Hull had concluded that the stagnation of British industry would force a further depreciation of the pound. He believed the United States should cooperate, let the dollar appreciate, and adopt conservative monetary policies in order to increase business confidence at home. He went so far as to suggest returning to the pre-1933 pound-dollar ratio, and to incorporate his views in a memorandum intended for circulation to American embassies in Europe.

Morgenthau denounced the memorandum to the President as one of the most anti–New Deal broadsides he had seen in a long time. The thought of sending it to the American embassies, the Secretary said, "made my blood boil." Roosevelt was equally angry. "J. P. Morgan has as much influence in the State Department as he ever did," he remarked. He also permitted Morgenthau to remind Cordell Hull of the agreement putting the Treasury in charge of stabilization.

Yet Morgenthau could move only slowly toward *de facto* stabilization. He began in the spring of 1935, when the French suffered a severe currency crisis. The political instability that had characterized French government for more than a decade contributed to uncertainty about monetary policy and was in turn complicated by the international tensions produced by Adolf Hitler's accession and gradual assumption of dictatorial power in Germany. The German threat and the possibility of European war that it raised, as well as persisting unemployment and gloom within France, persuaded French capitalists to convert their francs to gold, sell the gold for dollars, and invest them in the United States, where the government was stable, the economy improving, and the chance of war seemingly small. To a lesser degree, they also sold francs to buy pounds sterling. The Bank of France was therefore gradually losing its stock of gold, and continuing pressure would ultimately force it to suspend gold payments and devalue. That might provoke devaluation elsewhere, but the strong sentiment among French conservatives called for the retention of the gold standard, and in spite of pressure from inflationists, the government of Premier Pierre Flandin agreed.

Morgenthau attempted to force three-way cooperation to sustain the value of the franc, but in spite of his efforts, the Bank of France refused to ask the Bank of England for credit to help support the franc, while the British for their part were agreeable only to unofficial ventures to supply that support. Morgenthau fell back therefore on an informal, bilateral arrangement of his own with the French. As it worked out, the American Stabilization Fund bought enough francs to see France through her immediate crisis, and that development, while providing no permanent international mechanism, at least pointed the way toward cooperation among the three powers.

Almost a year later, in April 1936, Morgenthau again interceded. At that time both the British and American treasuries were anxious about a renewed flight from the franc that followed Hitler's march into the Rhineland. The French, Morgenthau predicted, would soon have either to devalue or to impose controls on the export of gold and the purchase of foreign exchange. "England," he told Roosevelt, "is holding up the franc." It was time, he argued, to define American policy toward the British.

In conference in April 29, 1936, the President stressed the importance in having the first move come from the English. Morgenthau reminded him that since 1934 the United States had not done so badly. "You and I, of course," Roosevelt replied, "started with no knowledge of this subject but the two of us have done well and have been able to more than hold up our end. The trouble is that when you sit around the table with a Britisher he usually gets 80% of the deal and you get what is left. Tell them that. Tell them if we got 45% we think that we would be doing well. As long as Neville Chamberlain is there [as Chancellor of the Exchequer] we must recognize that fundamentally he thoroughly dislikes Americans." As Morgenthau observed to his Diary, the President thoroughly distrusted the British.

But with Roosevelt's consent, Morgenthau reached Chamberlain through an intermediary. The Englishman replied that "in the difficult times through which we are passing and in the perhaps still more difficult days to come, the closest and most friendly contact between the two Treasuries is desirable." "I am scared," Morgenthau replied. He had been out for sea bass and caught a sailfish.

With strikes sweeping France and the European situation deteriorating, Morgenthau, on June 3, 1936, asked Roosevelt whether he might proceed to give the British formal assurances about Anglo-American currency transactions. As the Secretary had feared, Roosevelt objected. He "started on a long harangue that he thought we ought to have a secret commodity price index with which we could manage the dollar. . . . He felt that his message to the Conference, in July 1933, should be our text and Bible." Morgenthau replied that "if we could indicate to France that both England and ourselves would not try to devalue further if France would make a clean-cut devaluation at this time, that it might assist France to make up her mind . . . and we might be able to bring about world stabilization between England, France and ourselves." Roosevelt was "quite excited and enthusiastic about the idea," and with his support, Morgenthau communicated his suggestion about Anglo-American restraint in the face of French devaluation to the British Treasury's representative in Washington.

As it developed, neither the French nor the British were yet ready to act. The new French Premier, the Socialist Leon Blum, was pledged against devaluation, and his Ministry of Finance considered it impossible for his government directly to approach Great Britain. He refused even to be quoted as personally favoring devaluation. So, too, the British government was unwilling to take any initiative. Morgenthau was discouraged, but not wholly without hope, for the French decided to send a confidential emissary to Washington. With his arrival, the prospects for a monetary alliance might grow. Indeed, at the very time that Anglo-French conversations about gold seemed impossible, Morgenthau was applying significant economic pressure against Germany. That maneuver, important in itself, gave to the French and the British governments alike growing confidence in the Secretary and in the United States.

5. Countervailing Duties

When Adolf Hitler, defying France and England and violating the Versailles Treaty of 1919, ordered German troops to occupy the Rhineland in March 1936, he demonstrated that he meant to pursue the program of conquest which his speeches and writings had long advocated. He had already provided significant evidence for his intentions in the policy of economic aggression of his Minister of Finance, Dr. Hjalmar Schacht. Under Schacht's direction, Germany was weaving a web of bilateral agreements through which she could force her economic will on other nations. Schacht had also developed a system of export bounties. By the use of various devices, including "scrip" marks (marks purchasable from the government at a discount but convertible within Germany at face value), German exporters received large subsidies in their competition for world markets, including the market of the United States.

German currency practices had begun to worry Morgenthau in November 1935. Herman Oliphant, who was an implacable opponent of Hitler and all that he stood for, then told the Secretary that in his opinion the tariff laws of the United States made retaliation mandatory. The Tariff Act of 1930, he held, forced the Treasury's hand. Section 303 of that Act provided that whenever any nation bestowed a bounty on the export of any article which was dutiable upon admission to the United States, the Treasury had to levy an additional duty equivalent to the net amount of the bounty. The Act called upon the Secretary of the Treasury to make all the regulations necessary for the identification of such articles and the assessment and collection of additional duties. Under Section 303, Oliphant concluded, action was mandatory once the Secretary had established the fact that a bounty was being paid.

The crux of the problem in the case of Germany was whether or not currency manipulations constituted a bounty or "grant" within the meaning of the Tariff Act. It was Oliphant's view that the Supreme Court in two decisions had given to the word "grant" the widest possible definition, clearly inclusive of the devices which Germany had adopted. The Treasury, moreover, had received complaints from American manufacturers and their congressional representatives about German subsidies to various products including, among others, bicycles, plumbing accessories, cutlery, optical instruments, gloves, aluminum foil, microscopes, and steel tools.

The Executive Committee on Commercial Policy, an interdepartmental coordinating body, disagreed with Oliphant. Currency manipulation, it believed, had to be regarded as a special case of currency depreciation. The application of countervailing duties would tend further to disturb already abnormal international monetary relations. Furthermore, where interpretations of Section 303 were in doubt, the committee felt that general economic considerations should be given weight. The United States both had been a victim of monetary dislocations and had itself contributed to them. It would therefore, in the opinion of the committee, be unfortunate if the United States attempted to take special measures against currency procedures of other countries. The committee noted, too, that Germany was experiencing genuine difficulties in dollar exchange, that her purchases of agricultural products from the United States had already decreased, and that much existing German-American trade was possible only because of Germany's currency policies. Further, the Department of State was trying to persuade Germany to remove important discriminations against American trade, and the inauguration of countervailing duties would create an unfavorable atmosphere for the negotiations. For all those reasons Secretary of State Hull strongly endorsed the conclusions of the committee.

At luncheon with the President on April 14, 1936, Morgenthau reported that the Treasury Department was working on the issue of countervailing duties, but that the Department of State opposed action. "If it is a borderline case," Roosevelt said, "I feel so keenly about Germany that I would enforce the countervailing duties." Still, he wanted an opinion from the Department of Justice.

On April 30 Golden W. Bell, the Assistant Solicitor General, completed a memorandum on the issue. The concern of the Department of State about economic policy was so great, Bell observed, that it was difficult for the Department to dissociate policy and law. He found the State Department's fears about foreign trade entirely justified. But if German currency practices fell within the contemplation of the law, the Secretary of the Treasury was under a mandate to impose the duties, and only action by Congress could relieve him. And German practices, he maintained, constituted the bestowal of bounties and grants within the meaning of the Act. The law therefore required the imposition of countervailing duties, but Bell recommended that the Treasury, the State Department, and perhaps also the President, consider the question further, for it was so complex and so sensitive that possibly an effort should be made to change the law.

Morgenthau wanted to act. On the question of Germany, as he put it to Roosevelt on May 12, he had no choice. "Is that right, Mr. President?" "Yes, that is right," Roosevelt replied.

Ten days later the President directed Morgenthau to confer with the Secretary of State and the Attorney General to "try to find an immediate method of carrying out the law. I am convinced that we have to act."

"If this law is carried out it is difficult to see where it will end and I am afraid that it will break down our whole international trade program," Cordell Hull argued at an interdepartmental meeting on May 29. ". . . Whenever things go wrong, at the present time the tendency seems to be to hit the other fellow in the nose and we do not think this is the right way to proceed. We want to work things out in a spirit of fairness and good fellowship."

"I would like you to get my position very clear on this," Morgenthau replied. "I . . . have held up the decision for a great length of time simply to convince myself that I have looked at it from every possible angle but I cannot see any way out."

That afternoon the President agreed. "As long as the law is clear," Roosevelt said, "there is nothing for you to do but carry it out." He expressed entire satisfaction with Morgenthau's position and with his proposed procedures for giving publicity to the forthcoming order on countervailing duties. Morgenthau was relieved that the question was settled. As he put it to his Diary: "I thanked him for the backing he had given me and told him that the whole situation had been most difficult for me."

At his press conference on June 4, 1936, Morgenthau released the Treasury decision imposing countervailing duties on Germany, effective June 30. The press release explained that the decision had the approval of the Attorney General. The amount of duties to be imposed on any particular product was to be determined by an estimate of the subsidy granted that product by the currency practices of the German government. This was to result, for example, in an increase in the duty on cameras, toys, and dolls imported from Germany of 45 per cent, on cotton and rayon gloves of 39 per cent, on surgical instruments of 56 per cent.

German newspapers at once expressed their pained surprise. Adopting the argument which their government was also to use, German editorial writers argued that the devaluation of the dollar had made it necessary for their government to contrive its own methods for handling currency. The German government officially requested a postponement of the effective date of the order pending discussion of possible adjustments in German-American trade relationships. Indeed, German officials talked of applying new protective legislation against the United States unless some satisfactory arrangement could be made to delay the application of the Treasury ruling.

Neither this implied threat nor the objections to the decision from American cotton exporters had any effect, for Morgenthau could not and would not delay enforcing the law. When his ruling became effective, Germany submitted a formal protest to the Department of State. At the same time the German ambassador asked whether the Treasury would discuss ways in which Germany might finance her trade with the United States in a manner which would not violate the Tariff Act. The Department of State replied that any emissary coming to the United States should have clearly in mind that the law on countervailing duties was mandatory.

In spite of continuing protest from Germany, from American importers of cameras and other German products, and from the Department of State, the Treasury stood firm. Supported by Oliphant's repeated invocations of the law, Morgenthau permitted no exceptions or postponements in the application of the duties. His deliberate intransigency impressed Dr. Schacht's emissary to Washington, who advised his government to capitulate. On August 4 Germany abandoned the procedures which had provoked the United States Treasury to retaliate. On August 10, 1936, the Treasury announced withdrawal of the duties.

"Contrary to the fears of the State Department and the bluster of the German press," Morgenthau later pointed out, "the Treasury policy worked. . . . It was the first check to Germany's career of economic conquest." It also established a propitious atmosphere for Morgenthau's discussion of monetary cooperation with the confidential agent of Leon Blum.

6. The Monick Mission

On June 20, 1936, the special French emissary, Emmanuel Monick, reached Washington. Long a devaluationist, Monick had been at odds with Governor Tannery of the Bank of France, whose tenure had ended when Blum came to office. Monick had substantially persuaded Blum of the necessity for devaluation of the franc, but Blum believed that, in order to preserve his coalition, he had to get on with social reform before attempting monetary change. Yet at Monick's suggestion, the Premier had included in his speech in defense of the franc a caveat about possible realignment in the event of an international understanding. In sending Monick to the United States, the French Premier revealed an inclination toward devaluation.

When Monick arrived, Roosevelt was preoccupied by the proceedings of the Democratic National Convention which was meeting to renominate him. Morgenthau therefore began the conversations. Monick said at the outset that he was instructed to try to negotiate a currency agreement between France and the United States, if possible to include Great Britain. His mission was highly confidential. Were it to become known that he was in Washington to discuss devaluation, the Premier might have to repudiate him for political reasons.

The United States, Morgenthau replied, looked with favor upon a moderate devaluation of the franc. Great Britain agreed but insisted that France approach her directly. What would happen, Monick asked, if the three countries reached an agreement and then Germany devalued more than she already had and began to dump goods? If France, England and the United States could join hands, Morgenthau said, they would be so powerful that he doubted any nation could fight them singlehanded in a currency war.

England, Monick charged, was keeping the three democracies apart. On that account France wanted a network of currency agreements.

"I would no more sit in on a world monetary conference," Morgenthau replied, now quite excited, "than jump out of this window. I have seen what you can do with the Stabilization Fund and how you can move the thing around. If Germany started a monetary war, in the first place let's be practical. They can do that any time today. And you and England and ourselves would be alone and we would have no method to fight them. . . . In the Treasury, two weeks ago, we set up countervailing duties against Germany. . . . I would like to go into the German thing afterwards, but right now . . . Great Britain . . . will not do anything until your country speaks to them. . . . You can do it here."

Grateful for that statement, Monick talked freely with Roosevelt at the White House on June 23. His real reason for coming to Washington, he admitted, was the European political situation. The small countries surrounding Germany, especially Poland, were collapsing. Holland and Belgium were defenseless. Should Germany attack again as she had in 1914, Belgium would not and could not resist. He drew this dark picture, Monick explained, to emphasize the importance of lending immediate strength to the French government, which was in a precarious state. He sought what it needed, British and American support in a program of devaluation.

Roosevelt reminded Monick that the British government considered London the center of international banking. In dealing with the British, one had always to consider their "amour propre." He felt the British would be extremely reluctant to accede to any French request unless the French went directly to them. In his opinion, three-cornered conversations should be held simultaneously. Monick suggested beginning at once in Washington.

Roosevelt demurred. The British would consider discussions in Washington to be under American aegis. It would be better for the French to send similar and simultaneous communications to London and Washington. In that event, London would presumably inform Washington that it had received a message and request the views of the American government. A quick exchange would then take place, and in that way the French government would probably achieve its purpose. Monick gave the impression that he would act on the President's advice.

At the Treasury the next day, Monick said that he had begun to realize his mission would not be as empty as he had feared. But the form of the matter was important. Devaluation had to occur in such a way that the French people would accept it. The battle to keep on the gold standard had become for the French a battle of honor. If France moved, she would have to answer to the Dutch, the Swiss, and the Poles. Morgenthau said that someone had to take the lead. "But we are prepared to take the lead," Monick exclaimed. Things were so bad in France, he said, that there was as yet no agreement about how to inform the public. It would have to be done subtly, in a way that was not humiliating.

Morgenthau observed that "in American language" Monick was saying he wanted "to dress it up and make it look attractive to the French people as a French accomplishment."

"That's not exactly my point," Monick replied. "I want some dressing, but this dressing is not French dressing, I would say."

"As long as it is not Russian dressing," Morgenthau said, "I am satisfied."

"What we want is a dressing of something general," the

Frenchman said. "We want a peace dressing. . . . Some months when the political situation will have been cleared, then I hope I shall come here to talk declaration with you . . . but we want this feeling of peace and not only to France, but to the world that really this is monetary peace which is coming now. . . . We must give the feeling in France that the battle is over, and that it is the beginning of monetary peace and some form of collaboration between the stable currencies."

Monick then got down to figures. He suggested the pound sterling seek its point of equilibrium between $4.75 and $4.97 (the traditional rate of $4.86 was right in the middle of that spread). This was essential, he said, for France did not want to make any move that left the pound completely free to fluctuate. As for the franc, he suggested a range between $0.0475 and $0.0497. France would use the profit from devaluation to establish a fund to manage the franc.

Morgenthau was pleased. "If France has a stabilization fund," he said, "England has one and we have one . . . the three would . . . work together . . . as each one took care of its own currency."

On June 30, preparing to leave Washington, Monick brought Morgenthau a cable from Paris expressing the gratitude of the French. Europe, Monick said, was going to have to choose between democracy and totalitarianism. Uncertainties, monetary uncertainty not the least, bred fascism, provoked governments "to neglect the liberty and the heart of the people." Now, after his conversations with Roosevelt and Morgenthau, after hearing the President's stirring attack on fascism in his speech accepting renomination, Monick could for the first time see a way out for France.

"Your coming here," Morgenthau replied, "made things easier. . . . It is the exchange of views which gradually will bring about the stabilization we all hope for, but it takes time."

Indeed it did. Mid-August came and went without results. The French government was delaying because domestic politics were so tense. Nevertheless, Morgenthau continued to discuss his objective with the English.

Because those discussions were obviously also clearing the way
for an eventual Anglo-American understanding about gold, Oliphant and others in the Treasury feared they might be interpreted as a repudiation of the gold policy initiated in 1933–1934.
The Republicans might charge the Administration with abandoning an unsuccessful experiment. Morgenthau disagreed. "I
will tell you something, gentlemen," he said. "I have found that
the best kind of politics is to do your job well and not think
about the political effect on the election. I have done that ever
since I have been with Roosevelt and I think I have met with my
share of success and to stall this thing because an election is coming I think is just wrong, I just would hate to do it. I don't think
in the long run it's good politics — politics in the sense of good
Government."

7. *The Tripartite Pact*

During the last days of August 1936, France again suffered serious losses of gold. Blum took them as his cue to maneuver toward devaluation. The French draft agreement, which the
Treasury received on September 9, was unsatisfactory. It called
on England and the United States to maintain the prevailing
pound and dollar rates while the franc was lowered. It envi-
sioned cooperation among the three central banks with each assuming the task of holding its own national currency within
agreed limits. It cited, as the final objective of the contracting
parties, a general return to the international gold standard.

Working with representatives of the State Department on an
American reply, Morgenthau and his aides, on September 9,
1936, took exception first of all to setting precise rates which
were to remain firm. "We are not ready for that," he said, "because when the United States Government puts its name to it we
can live up to it, but the other fellows cannot." As to making a

return to the gold standard an ultimate objective, Morgenthau observed, "that is not the Roosevelt philosophy. I cannot say that." He then said what he was ready to do: "I think we ought to agree on very wide points at the beginning — plenty of fluctuation . . . as we gain some experience and find that it is working out successfully then these points can be gradually narrowed down. This will have to be a gentlemen's agreement. . . . England is going to come back and say, well, under these conditions, will you give up gold? And under these conditions the answer is, yes, as between these points. . . .

"This agreement would have to be a gentlemen's agreement; we would do everything possible to make it successful, but we would have to watch our internal price level just as they would. I would rather put it this way instead of saying that we will not agree to this and we will agree with that. I think we ought to make them talk as to how much they would devalue. We think this is a fine move and this is what we have been waiting for, for three years, and we will do everything possible to make it successful."

An American reply along those lines completely satisfied Cordell Hull. And Roosevelt, who had been motoring through the Great Smokies, considered the Treasury's draft "better than good." Particularly pleased that Morgenthau had deleted all references to the gold standard, the President had only one recommendation. The draft had preserved the language of the French proposal suggesting the three central banks cooperate to manage the currencies. Roosevelt wanted to eliminate the central banks. The three treasuries, he said, should manage their currencies. This was more than a matter of vocabulary. It emphasized Roosevelt's conviction, and Morgenthau's, that monetary policy was the obligation of government, not of private finance.

The British endorsed the American plan, but the French still held out for an ultimate return to the gold standard. "This thing is a lot of hooey," Morgenthau commented on September 17. "It may be very nice for the French people, but there is nothing in here that the President and I have said on monetary things. . . . If we knew how much they were going to devalue, I think

we could get a joint statement very quickly. But as long as we
don't know, I think all talks about the statement are useless. . . .
It goes without saying that we cannot enter into any agreement
which will definitely tie our hands or which looks forward to a
return to the gold standard." Roosevelt concurred. "It's terrible," he said of the French proposal. "It gives me a pain."

The Treasury staff had adjourned and reconvened when in
mid-afternoon Friday, September 18, Merle Cochran, the Department's representative, called from Paris. The French, he
reported happily, welcomed changes in phraseology. The Americans could write the agreement as they chose. He also had information on the extent of devaluation, but he was apparently
concerned lest a telephone operator overhear that secret.

"*Können Sie Deutsch sprechen?*" Cochran asked.

"What's that?" said Morgenthau, whose German was weak.

"*Können Sie Deutsch verstehen?*"

"*Ja.*" (Hopefully)

" *— von vier und zwanzig bis zwei und dreissig —*"

"Yes," Morgenthau said, relieved. "I got that." Then he
began to roar with laughter. "Excuse me, Cochran. I suppose
nobody else in the world speaks German either. Next time try
Turkish."

"Chinese," said Cochran.

Cochran's German meant a devaluation of the franc by from
24 to 32 per cent which in turn meant an exchange rate of from
100 to 110 francs to the pound. The British, Cochran said, could
probably stand at least 100, but Neville Chamberlain was not in
London, and there would be no decision until he returned.

"In other words," Morgenthau replied, "nothing could interfere with an English week end." But as the Secretary told Cordell Hull a few minutes later, he was "much more hopeful." The
French figures on devaluation were not impossible, and he expected the British to accept them.

The Treasury began immediately to draft a stabilization
agreement. Their plan was for each government to issue an independent statement. To protect against misunderstanding, they
intended to clear each statement with every participating government and then to have the statements released simultaneously.

The Treasury's draft was straightforward. The government of the United States, it read, after consulting with the British and French governments, joined with them to safeguard peace and restore order in international economic relations, to promote world prosperity and raise living standards. All the nations, of course, had to take full account of the requirements of internal prosperity, but the United States welcomed the opportunity to reaffirm its purpose of maintaining the greatest possible equilibrium in international exchange. France had informed the United States of her decision to devalue. The United States as well as Great Britain welcomed this decision and proposed through their own actions to minimize any exchange disturbances resulting from the French readjustment. The three governments would cooperate to that end, convinced that their policy was linked to the development of international trade. They invited the cooperation of other nations and they attached particular importance to an immediate attack on existing systems of trade quotas and exchange controls.

The draft delighted Morgenthau, who reviewed it with his advisers the evening of September 18. "I can't change it," he said. "I think it is swell." But he wondered about adding a warning to countries that might try to damage the agreement. Besides inviting "the collaboration of other nations," he thought they might say: "We feel that the three countries are strong enough to resist the interference of any other nation." As he put it to his staff: "In other words, we ask you to get on board, but look out — don't try to wreck this thing or we will be on your neck. This is a threat to Italy and Germany — don't try to undervalue because you are going to go under. . . . this is a notice to Japan, Germany and Italy that we don't stand any monkey business. . . . This is a notice to the boys — *Achtung!*"

"We have numerous potential causes of war now," a State Department spokesman complained. "I don't like to bring into the arena as another cause of war national action as regards the value of currency and I think if you bring it out in such terms you are directing public opinion to regard these words as so valuable."

Morgenthau interrupted: "Shall we be very frank with each

other? . . . There is a difference of approach on these things. I
am not saying I am going to do this thing. What I am trying to
forestall is particularly Germany and I am thinking also of Japan.
It's very easy for them to change their yen rate and the only
country that does not suffer through this is Japan. We definitely
suffer temporarily and so does England . . . I think we are at an
immediate disadvantage until the realignment takes place. Now,
why not at this time simply serve notice to any country, but
don't let's mention any country, that the three countries who are
trying to accomplish something in monetary peace won't brook
any interference. . . . And again using Germany, if Germany
should immediately devalue forty per cent this is notice to her
that we will all get together and take steps to protect ourselves."

The Secretary did agree to using temperate language which
the State Department accepted. The United States, the resulting
sentence read, "trusts that no country will attempt to obtain an
unreasonable competitive exchange advantage and thereby
hamper the effort to restore stable economic relations which it is
the aim of the three Governments to promote." This quiet
warning exactly suited the Secretary. "After three months," he
teased, "I have won against the career diplomats. Three cheers!"

On September 19 Roosevelt approved the completed draft,
which Morgenthau then transmitted to Paris and London. The
initial response from both capitals was favorable, but final word
was delayed while Chamberlain, back at his desk on September
21, pondered his own reply to France. Meanwhile, the French
continued to lose staggering quantities of gold and Morgenthau,
as he put it to Hull, was "just a little bit shaky in the knees about
the whole thing, because it is so important."

Roosevelt's political instincts influenced the Treasury's
thinking about cross rates for the dollar, pound, and franc.
The President wanted a five-dollar pound. Sterling was at
$5.07. He was willing to let it drop to $4.90, but not to the
traditional, pre-1931 level of $4.86. "We can't go out and talk
about a 4.86 pound," Morgenthau told his staff. "We didn't pick
this time. . . . Five weeks before election and a 4.86 pound are
impossible." To his relief, the British, responding to an Ameri-

can statement about cross rates, said they took for granted a five-dollar pound with a ten-cent leeway up or down. Morgenthau's advisers saw no reason why the United States could not maintain that rate. "You have given me the assurance I wanted," Morgenthau told them late in the evening of September 24. ". . . All right, I'm going to bed."

On the morning of the 25th, Merle Cochran called from Paris with a summary of the British comments on the proposed American text. The Chancellor of the Exchequer accepted it fully, but it was British policy to let the pound find its natural level. Possibly this level was $5; possibly it was lower. The French government, while also satisfied with the American text, would request authority to devalue from 25 to 34.35 per cent, with a mid-point of about 30 per cent — slightly more than Morgenthau had expected. The government would use ten billion francs for a stabilization fund and allocate the rest of the profit from depreciation for current expenses. A cable from London confirmed Cochran's report, and in a later message Chamberlain suggested issuing the simultaneous declarations at approximately 3 P.M. American time, on September 25.

Morgenthau then called Roosevelt. The President, "sick and tired" because Chamberlain constantly referred to himself as "the Chancellor of the Exchequer" and to Morgenthau by name, recommended the following reply: "The Secretary of the Treasury is glad to have Mr. Chamberlain's note. . . . It is a matter of opinion as to whether under the new circumstances a natural level of the pound would be at five dollars. . . . However, as long as Mr. Chamberlain understands that we believe the five-dollar level to be the appropriate one . . . without agreeing to Mr. Chamberlain's present thought of a lower rate between the dollar and the pound, the Secretary of the Treasury believes that this is not an obstacle that need prevent the issuance of the simultaneous statements in order to carry out their broad, useful and indeed essential objective."

"This is the way I feel," Morgenthau said. "I think the French are going to do it anyway. . . . I can explain that this is not ideal; that the peace of the world is at stake and that for that reason we are going along. Here is the interesting thing. The real big financiers are going to be tickled to death with this; they are going to consider this the real turning point for world peace and there is nobody among the big financial crowd who can criticize you and that is where your real opposition comes from. I am almost dazed. I have the British in the other room. I have tied up the telephone from two o'clock overseas. I hope you have had a good lunch. I have had none."

At 4:20 P.M. Morgenthau spoke with Cochran. The earliest hour at which everything could be straightened out, he noted, was midnight Paris time. "Well," Cochran said, "we'll try and keep the President up then, if we can."

"How does one keep the President of France up?" Morgenthau asked. "What's going on at the Montmartre tonight?"

The Secretary talked again with Roosevelt about 5 P.M. "The French," he said, "have accepted our . . . draft in toto without changing a word. I handed this thing to the British around four o'clock, and I told them that I wanted some kind of an acknowledgment from the Chancellor and that they should phone him, but that we would not release the various messages until we heard from the Chancellor, so the French and ourselves are sitting here waiting. . . . Hull is just tickled pink. He thinks it is the greatest thing that has happened."

Waiting for the British was hard for the French. Cochran later described the scene in Paris: "I was seated in the chair of the Minister of Finance. With him and his colleagues and assistants pacing the floor of the magnificent Empire salon, in the old Louvre palace which he occupies, glancing at their watches, grinding cigarette stubs into the marvelous carpets, and listening to the rumble of voices from the press representatives outside their door, made the situation extremely tense. Finally, you told me that the British had arrived at your office. We then waited until you had studied the reply. When you let us know that this was satisfactory and that we were in final agreement, there was great relief on the French side."

That occurred at 6:35 P.M., September 25, Washington time. Chamberlain, taking note of the American views, agreed that they constituted no obstacle to publication of the declaration. He proposed to use the American text and to release it at once. "The British are going to release this now at once," the Secretary told Cochran on the telephone, "so I say it might be all right to release it."

There was one small task left. To Roosevelt Morgenthau sent a jocular telegram: "A special messenger has just arrived from the French Embassy and wishes to inform me that the President of France wishes to go to bed. Please advise me what I should do in this great emergency."

Just before 8 P.M. he received a reply: "The President says . . . to tell Embassy to employ any American visitor now in Paris. Costs on the French Government — no commissions or liabilities."

The fun added to Morgenthau's ebullience. "I am thrilled —," he told Roosevelt on the telephone, "so thrilled I don't know what to say."

The Tripartite Agreement immediately won general applause. Belgium, Switzerland, and Holland, even Italy, quickly announced their adherence to its principles and soon thereafter officially joined the "currency club." The London *Times* expected that it might "prove to be a step, the first of several, towards the ultimate stabilization of the world currencies." The Manchester *Guardian* expressed the hope that now "the way to European economic cooperation will become easier." American newspapers and commentators were equally enthusiastic. Walter Lippmann, in a column similar to editorials written throughout the nation, called the agreement a "sure foundation" for escaping the "evil results" which had been building up since the collapse of the gold standard in 1931.

The French Minister of Finance, perhaps the most relieved of all the negotiators, thanked Morgenthau personally in a letter of October 5: "The French Parliament has enacted our proposal for the realignment of the franc. It is delighted with the agreement of the three great democracies. . . . In turn, I congratulate myself on the adherence of almost all the nations of the world to our common declaration which put the definite end to the monetary war and opened the road toward the 'economic peace' — so essential to peace among nations. . . . I do not know how to find words sufficiently expressive to convey to you the thanks of President Leon Blum and his Government, and of myself, for the energetic, enthusiastic and wholehearted cooperation which you have given us. I hope that this collaboration will continue in the work toward world economic peace which must be achieved if peace among peoples is to be attained."

8. A Bearish Interlude

On Saturday, September 26, the day after the announcement of the Tripartite Pact, Morgenthau had to use the Stabilization Fund to sustain the value of the pound. The markets in London and Paris were closed when sterling fell to $4.94 in New York. Morgenthau did not want sterling to close low, for that would make it seem as if the Treasury, in spite of the Tripartite Agreement, either could not or would not control fluctuations of exchange. He therefore immediately instructed the New York Federal Reserve Bank to buy $1,000,000 worth of sterling for the Stabilization Fund at the lowest price at which it could be had. Within fifteen minutes the Fund acquired £50,000 at $4.91.

Reporting the purchase, the New York Federal Reserve Bank explained that the Russian government had an order in to sell £1,000,000 at the best price. Morgenthau asked at once why he had not been told that before. Clearly the Russian selling order was pulling sterling down. The Secretary directed the Bank to pull out all buying orders and to tell the Chase National Bank, which was handling the sale for the Russians, that the Federal Reserve Bank would buy the entire £1,000,000. "They are trying to break down this agreement and I am calling the President and will ask him whether I can give this out publicly," the Secretary added.

"I want your permission," Morgenthau told Roosevelt, "to announce that the Russian Government tried to break this thing and that we bought the one million pounds sterling that they had ordered dumped on our market. Before I actually do it, I want to call you back once more. The negotiations are going on right now between the Federal Reserve Bank and the Chase. Those bastards want to break this thing so that Blum cannot get his support. In talking to Paris this morning they said that the only people who were fighting Blum on this is the Communist Party. We are the only market that is open and they are trying to break the market here."

At a press conference later in the day, Morgenthau described what had happened. "This is . . . the only instance today," he said, "of any government, any bank, or any individual trying to artificially influence the foreign exchange market in the United States and I point out that both London and Paris are closed and I sincerely hope that this incident will not be repeated."

On September 28 Winthrop Aldrich, the president of the Chase National Bank, telephoned Morgenthau. The Russian transaction, Aldrich insisted, was perfectly ordinary business, necessary because Russia had to pay $6,000,000 to Sweden and therefore had to sell pounds to get dollars. He agreed that the timing was bad and that the sale drove down the market; but he thought Russia, trying to cover as rapidly as possible, had had to act on a Saturday when only the American market was open. He saw nothing sinister in his customer's purpose. "Let's say there was nothing sinister," Morgenthau replied, "but I mean on the other hand they weren't willing to cooperate with every other country in the world and give this thing a chance."

Talking later with his friend Arthur Sulzberger, the publisher of the *New York Times*, Morgenthau mentioned his "particular satisfaction" in breaking "this idea that there was any relationship between us and Russia." He considered Aldrich's explanation of Russia's behavior stupid. Sulzberger, agreeing, pointed out that the Russians could perfectly well have used pounds to pay the Swedes.

The Russians were furious about Morgenthau's statement to the press. It was absurd, the Tass Agency maintained, to get excited about an ordinary banking transaction "effected by the State Bank through the Chase Bank in New York." The Russians also asserted that they had needed over $6,000,000 for payments in Stockholm. That was not true. They could have paid in pounds or, as Morgenthau contended, they could have waited to convert the pounds until all the money markets were open. The Secretary had had ample reason for acting and ample grounds for suspicion.

He also saw the amusing side of the episode. "I have had more fun," he told Roosevelt. "Aldrich had me on the phone explaining what a wonderful government Russia is; how we misunderstood them; that this was a legitimate transaction. I told him that I would take his word for it, but why did they have to do it on Saturday? That everybody else waited, but they could not. Today the Chase received a telegram from the Russians which practically says, we told you to sell the one million pounds sterling at the best. Why did you sell it at the worst? . . . Here is Aldrich, close to Landon,* and he comes out and makes a statement showing that he is befriending the Russians." Aldrich had learned, Morgenthau concluded, that he was no longer "running the Treasury of the United States."

Although in a campaign year Roosevelt preferred not to mention it, the United States had come a long way since the London Conference. As economists pointed out, the Tripartite Agreement of 1936 provided an essential means for international monetary exchange. It gave the French government the international endorsement it needed for devaluation, gave the British a broader base for managing the pound, and helped the American Treasury manage gold policy.

Those benefits were essentially technical, but technical operations had broad implications. The democracies had accepted the American price of gold as the basis for evaluating their currencies. They had utilized special instruments, stabilization funds or their equivalent, to act as the agencies for that operation. Stabilization funds had originally been considered emergency weapons; now they were recognized as the successors to central banks in

* Alfred M. Landon, the Republican presidential candidate in 1936.

international finance. The participating governments, furthermore, had entered into a monetary relationship which acknowledged that the international values of their respective currencies were a matter of mutual interest. They had demonstrated their concern for keeping order in international exchange. Although perhaps tentatively, their agreements established international comity where previously there had been hostility or suspicion.

The old gold standard was gone, as it happened not just for a season but for a long, long time, perhaps for ever. Under its operations money had been as much a measure of value as a medium of exchange. The gradual divorce of Europe from gold after 1931, the gradual divorce of the United States from gold during 1933 and 1934 left money primarily a medium of exchange. The advocates of the old gold standard had often asserted that it was not manipulable. It was presumed to respond mechanically to automatic operations of internal and external economies. But that was not necessarily an asset. Other standards could be manipulated, and in a time of internal stresses and international difficulties, management was in order. Initially the New Deal, like other governments, had conceived of monetary management primarily as a device for solving internal problems. Certainly that had been Morgenthau's purpose in the fall of 1933, when he advocated the gold purchase program. But gradually the United States government, in large part because of Morgenthau's changing ideas and capable direction, came to view the management of money as vital not only for domestic recovery but also for the support of democratic nations in a troubled world.

Morgenthau did not conceive of himself as abandoning the policies initiated in 1933, but rather as expanding and adapting them to the large needs of the Atlantic community. It was cooperation among gentlemen rather than exact stabilization that the Tripartite Agreement assured. None of the participating nations was to abandon its concentration on internal needs, but all of them, conscious of the political and economic dangers of fascism, were resolved thereafter to devise and protect mutually beneficial monetary arrangements.

Roosevelt and Morgenthau had consistently favored placing ultimate responsibility and authority for monetary policy in the Treasury rather than the Federal Reserve System, an agency of the private banks. The internationalizing of the management of money for mutually beneficial purposes reinforced their preference. Money was one factor in international health, and for consultations on international health, the appropriate doctors were the governments of the world. Where money was the issue, the Treasury spoke for the United States. That gave Morgenthau a clear mandate in one sphere of foreign policy. Hull resented this division of authority over foreign affairs, but it served Roosevelt's purposes, for he could rely on Morgenthau to face up to situations that Hull preferred to avoid, and he could in any crisis decide which of his two secretaries to support.

From the beginning there was no question in Morgenthau's mind but that the agreements he was negotiating had large political meaning. His conversations repaired constantly to political themes. He and his associates in the Treasury did not want to see France go the way of fascism. They were disturbed by the German threat to France and to Belgium. The Tripartite Agreement was scarcely an offensive against totalitarianism; Europe was not ready for that. But it was an early reaction to fascism, the first evidence that the Western democracies could profit collectively from mutually acceptable concessions.

"Japan," Morgenthau suggested, "thought . . . there would be . . . revolution in France. And while everybody was worried over there, this was the time to jump on China. . . . Japan . . . has backed down. . . . This has caught her unaware as it caught Germany, and this thing has steadied Germany and Japan." There was something in that analysis. The Tripartite Agreement and its supplements, the evidence of friendship among the United States, England, France and the small democracies, probably did temporarily give pause to Germany, Italy and Japan. Though he knew difficult days lay ahead, Morgenthau could for the moment feel "like the cat that swallowed the canary . . . very pleased."

IV

STATECRAFT FOR SILVER

1933 – 1936

1. "Something for Silver"

THE STRUCTURE of congressional politics prevented Franklin Roosevelt from ever forgetting his campaign promise to "do something for silver." He had to do much more than he intended, for the powerful friends of that metal effectively imposed their purpose upon the New Deal. To Morgenthau's dismay, it fell to the Treasury to execute the policy they devised. He never got rid of it, but he did learn to minimize its unfortunate domestic and international effects, even to use it, as he used gold policy, to encourage resistance to fascist aggression. This was political alchemy of a very high order.

Foremost among the agitators for increasing the price of silver were the owners and managers of silver mines and their employees. They had some natural allies. Silver was so often found with other metals that any subsidy it received enriched the producers of zinc, lead, and especially copper. Those mining interests, strong in the sparsely populated mountain states of the West, carried great weight in the Senate. There, during the 1930's, the silver bloc included at least twelve and, some congresses, up to sixteen men, many of them senior Democrats and skillful tacticians.

Their objective was to commit the government to buy all the

silver produced in the United States at $1.29 an ounce, the arbitrary value established by Congress for the silver which the Treasury owned and used as money. The market price of the metal during 1933 was about 45 cents. Obligatory federal purchases at $1.29 would provide a handsome subsidy and, according to the reasoning of the silver bloc, raise the price of silver on world as well as domestic markets. This in turn, the silverites argued fatuously, would increase the purchasing power of China and other countries on a silver standard and thus create a potentially vast market for American goods. In fact, of course, an artificially swollen price would drain those countries of their silver reserves.

Proponents of inflation, sympathetic allies of the silver bloc, wanted to have the government make greater use of silver for monetary purposes, either in coins or as a reserve for paper money. That objective was part of the historic cult that fed on resentment against Wall Street and international bankers who, according to the folklore, used the gold standard to further a sinister conspiracy against farmers. By no means guileless themselves, inflationists and silverites, contriving to enlist other interest groups, proposed using silver to pay pensions to veterans and subsidies to cotton growers.

The silverites and inflationists struck hard in January 1934, during the debate about the Gold Reserve bill. Senator Burton K. Wheeler of Montana, an agrarian Democrat, introduced an amendment making mandatory the purchase of 50,000,000 ounces of silver a month until a billion ounces had been added to the monetary reserve. Although Roosevelt expressed his own and the Treasury's opposition to the amendment, it failed by only two votes. Even that margin was possible only because the President accepted a substitute proposal giving him authority to issue paper money against all silver the Treasury might acquire. The authority was merely permissive, but it was clear that Congress intended to demand more.

On March 10, 1934, the House Coinage Committee reported out a bill designed by Representative Martin Dies of Texas. It provided for the sale of surplus farm products abroad in return for payments in silver at a premium of 10 to 25 per cent above the world price. It had the support of the Committee for the Nation and of the radio priest, Father Charles E. Coughlin, whose sermons on cheap money were commanding huge audiences every Sunday. In contrast, the Economists' National Committee and 85 per cent of the members of the American Economic Association opposed additional silver purchases at any price. The Dies bill horrified them, the financial community, the President, and the Secretary of the Treasury.

Because Roosevelt was politically vulnerable, Morgenthau led the Administration's resistance. His strategy throughout the spring of 1934 was to try to delay action by proposing further study of silver prices, and meanwhile to build up public antagonism against a mandatory program by revealing the influence of speculators in silver. Concurrently he tried to satisfy producers of silver by sustaining the price of the metal through timely Treasury purchases in the London market. On March 15 he told the press that he had "still . . . to be shown that silver . . . is a cure-all," and he hinted that the Treasury's investigations of speculation implicated some of the champions of silver in Congress.

Both statements backfired. "The Secretary of the Treasury and his expert advisers," said Key Pittman, Nevada Democratic senator and the most ardent and inelegant of silverites, ". . . know little about silver. . . . They are misadvised by . . . learned professors who know less about silver." Congressional friends of the metal, angered by Morgenthau's remark about speculation, complained so bitterly that the Secretary in another public statement exonerated them. In the House, Speaker Henry T. Rainey, a silverite for four decades, suspended the rules and called up the Dies bill, which passed by a vote of 258 to 112.

Morgenthau nevertheless kept trying. He had decided in February to send Professor James Harvey Rogers of Yale to investigate monetary conditions in the Orient. Rogers, he announced in March, would report back on whether or not an increase in the price of silver would foster Chinese imports of American goods. Again the silverites were unimpressed. It was "the height of asininity," they said, for a professor prejudiced against silver to attempt to learn anything by interviewing Chinese coolies. This kind of argument would not yield to reason. Puzzled, Morgenthau asked Senator Henry F. Ashurst, a mild-mannered Arizona Democrat, why he took silver so much to heart. "My boy," Ashurst replied, "I was brought up from my mother's knee on silver and I can't discuss that any more with you than you can discuss your religion with me."

Ashurst's spirit prevailed in the Senate Committee on Agriculture and Forestry, which on April 10 unanimously reported out a much amended version of the Dies bill. The measure owed its new form largely to Democratic Senator Elmer Thomas of Oklahoma, one of the most stubborn inflationists in Washington. It now provided for the nationalization of all domestic silver and for the mandatory purchase of 50 million ounces a month in the world market until the price reached $1.29 or until American prices generally reached their 1926 level. The silver chips were down.

At a conference with the silverites on April 21, the President made plain his unyielding opposition to mandatory legislation. Privately he endorsed two defensive maneuvers of Morgenthau. The Treasury sold some of the gold it held in London in order to buy silver there and push up its price. Morgenthau hoped this would gradually ease the pressure within Congress. He expected to get quick relief by "springing" the roster of silver speculators which the Treasury had been compiling for several months. At Roosevelt's recommendation, he stretched out publication of the twenty-six pages of names over three days, beginning April 24, 1934. There were no congressmen on the list, but it did include Frank Vanderlip and others of the Committee for the Nation, William Jennings Bryan, Jr., and Miss Amy Collins, the treasurer of Father Coughlin's Radio League, who had speculated in silver with funds the priest had solicited. Coughlin at once denounced Morgenthau and his investigation, but on the Hill the Treasury's list did little good. Congress ignored Morgenthau's recommendation for a complete investigation of silver speculation, and

Thomas's bill held the loyalty of what seemed to be a majority of senators.

On April 27 Roosevelt asked the Cabinet whether to compromise or to attempt to prevent all legislation. The consensus was for compromise, especially since a veto would be "most embarrassing for Congressmen at election time." To avoid a veto, the President had to negotiate. In the process, he and Morgenthau endeavored at all costs to prevent Congress from making silver purchases mandatory, for that would challenge the independence of the executive and run counter to national financial needs.

Negotiations reached fruition on May 8, when Roosevelt and the silverites agreed upon phraseology for legislation and for an executive message recommending it. With the President's support, Pittman introduced a bill authorizing the Secretary of the Treasury to buy silver until it constituted one-fourth of the nation's monetary reserve or until its price reached $1.29. He was to make his purchases "at such rates, at such times, and upon such terms and conditions as he may deem reasonable and most advantageous to the public interest."

The compromise won over enough of the silverites, especially those who were concerned primarily with subsidizing the industry, to be sure of enactment. For one of its features Morgenthau was the outstanding spokesman. This was a tax of 50 per cent on the profits from domestic silver trading. Its purpose was to limit the gains of those who had bought silver speculatively and then lobbied for a subsidy. As the Secretary told the press, "we are not going to let fifteen or twenty people clean up twenty-five or fifty million dollars through a monetary program of the Government." Eight or nine of the silver senators were quite enthusiastic about the bill, he added, and he was perfectly satisfied with it himself.

By large majorities both the House and the Senate passed the Pittman Silver Purchase Act, which Roosevelt signed on June 19, 1934. Its permissive features represented a considerable Administration victory, but Roosevelt had yielded under pressure, and as part of his bargain he conceded even more by committing himself orally to execute the Act "enthusiastically." Morgenthau made the same promise. The law, he said, was a direct mandate he was obligated to follow.

This, too, was subject to interpretation, for with the stock of gold rapidly increasing in response to the gold purchase program, the amount of silver needed to constitute one-quarter of the monetary base also rapidly increased. When the Act was passed, 1,200,000 ounces of silver would have met the requirement, but before the end of 1934, gold stocks had climbed to the point where 125,000,000 additional ounces of silver were necessary, and each year this figure rose. Alternatively, of course, the Treasury could have put the domestic price of silver at $1.29 an ounce. Morgenthau did not believe that even enthusiastic execution of the law involved granting so gross a subsidy. His mandate, he realized, forced him to serve silver more generously than he would have liked to; but as he viewed it, it did not permit the easy achievement of either of the alternative goals, and it did not commit the Treasury to inflation.

2. Executing the Mandate

Morgenthau immediately minimized the inflationary dangers of the silver program. Exercising the discretion the law allowed him, he issued silver certificates in one-, two-, five-, and ten-dollar denominations on the basis of the actual cost of the metal, not its statutory price of $1.29. As the Treasury released the certificates, furthermore, it retired Federal Reserve Bank notes and National Bank notes, which prevented any significant increase in the supply of paper currency. Indeed, to the dismay of men like Senator Thomas, between June 1934 and June 1935 the total monetary stock rose only 11 per cent, the per capita circulation of currency only 3 per cent.

To mollify the silverites, who would otherwise have sponsored mandatory, inflationary legislation, the Secretary, on June 28, 1934, put an embargo on shipments of silver from the United

States except under government license, and then, in August, began aggressively to buy the metal at home and abroad. The Treasury nationalized silver, in accordance with Roosevelt's instructions, when its price reached 49.5 cents an ounce. Also at the President's direction, Morgenthau kept buying until the world price climbed to 64.5 cents, the figure he was paying for domestic bullion. He continued his purchases until the domestic price reached 71.11 cents, with world prices following it, and then hoped to hold back to prevent a further increase, for at 72 cents Mexico, still on a silver standard, would have to abandon that standard. But the Secretary could not yet stop. Speculation on the world market carried the price above 72 cents in April 1935. To restrain the market, the Treasury began on occasion to sell silver, pushing its international price down to 65 cents, a departure that the Senate inflationists protested. They also created a special Senate Committee on Silver, a watchdog group to keep tabs on the Treasury's activities and to keep pressure on both Roosevelt and Morgenthau.

As the Secretary, conscious always of the demands of silver's guardians, continued to buy heavily, he could not avoid draining silver from the Orient and Latin America. In October and November 1935, the Treasury acquired more silver than ever before in a two-month period. The strain on countries attempting to maintain a silver standard was unbearable. In November China gave up and offered to sell the United States 200,000,000 ounces. The British in Hong Kong offered 100,000,000 ounces. Although Morgenthau declined both offers, he could not stop the flood of silver to market. Early in December, Hong Kong nationalized silver and began immediately to sell it in large quantities in London. If the Chinese were also to dump their stock, not even aggressive purchasing would sustain the price.

In his Diary on December 8, 1935, Morgenthau summarized the situation:

> During the past week our silver purchasing policy has seemed to me more and more stupid. It is now clear that exclusive of the newly mined silver we are simply siphoning the silver out of China through two channels — one, Japan and the other England. Going

back three or four years I find that the normal exports of silver
from Japan are between six and nine million ounces per year. For
the first nine months of 1935 they exported sixty million ounces.
This silver can only be gotten into Japan by smuggling it out of
China and somebody is making the difference between 40.5¢, approximately what you can buy silver for in China, and 65¢ the
world price. . . . All week . . . there has been an extra amount
of silver pushed on the London market. . . . It must be the Hong
Kong monetary reserve silver.

   For us to continue to take all . . . silver . . . at a fixed price
when we can unquestionably get it for much less than 65¢ so goes
against my better judgment that I decided it was time to act . . .
because at the rate we are going we will buy up all the floating
silver in the world, drive all the silver-using countries off silver,
and for the use of paper money — and then what have we. . . .
I telephoned the President . . . and told him what I had in mind
and that I wanted to drop silver and told him the reasons why. To
my surprise, he readily acquiesced. . . . I was dumbfounded that
he jumped at the idea so quickly because heretofore he definitely
wanted to keep up the price of silver. Perhaps he is getting a little
tired of it too.

To the Treasury's monetary experts, Morgenthau disclosed
that he hoped to see a drop to 40 cents, the price at which there
was no profit for anyone smuggling out of China. He foresaw
no resistance from Congress, for Senator Pittman had said he did
not care what happened to the world price so long as the price
for newly mined domestic bullion did not fall.

   Eager to put the speculators to rout, Roosevelt had the Treasury buy silver in all markets in order to take business away from
London. In dealing with London, the Treasury was to turn the
tables completely and permanently, to say nothing about a price
but instead to force the brokers to propose one. This was a mandate Morgenthau could execute with real enthusiasm. As he put
it to his Diary on December 12: "I am trying . . . to take the
artificial support away from the silver market . . . to get it
down . . . where the world will support the price for whatever
the intrinsic value of silver is. . . . Our silver program is the
only monetary . . . policy that I cannot . . . justify . . . but
if I could expose it . . . now it would save us much grief."

While preventing any sudden collapse in price, he gradually but relentlessly drove silver down until on January 20, 1936, it reached 45, where it leveled off.

The Administration thereafter abandoned even the pretense of seriously executing the Silver Purchase Act. In 1936, the President and Secretary even dropped the domestic price to 64.5 cents, half of the statutory price. But earlier, for over a year, Morgenthau, prodded by Roosevelt, had felt that congressional politics compelled him to buy silver aggressively, to push up its market price, twice to raise its domestic price. The results were so devastating that after December 1935 not even politics could persuade him to continue. Silver, he had learned, was a special form of madness.

3. Repercussions Abroad

American policy created special problems for nations using silver as a basis for their currency or producing the metal in large quantities. Mexico was affected both ways. Much of her circulating media consisted of silver pesos with a bullion value in 1934 of 71.9 cents an ounce in American money. Management of this coinage was to become difficult when the market reached 72. On the other hand, the boom stimulated by American purchases was to benefit the important Mexican silver industry, and rising silver prices to permit Mexico to acquire dollars to redress an unfavorable balance of trade. Indeed, the American program provided an incidental but significant subsidy to Mexico's depressed economy and sometimes shaky government.

As it worked out, American policy, under Morgenthau's guidance, during 1934 and 1935 subsidized Mexico by establishing an inflated price for one of her major exports. Even after the Treasury let the market drop, Mexico was able to sell her silver bullion at a better price than that which would have prevailed without the American Silver Purchase Act. Mexico's continuing difficulties were in large part occasioned by the failure of her officials to guard her currency system against rising silver prices and later by their speculative handling of her monetary reserves.

China had greater trouble. The Chinese had valued silver for centuries as a store of wealth and a medium of exchange. Producing none, they imported more than any other nation and consequently benefited from the low prices of 1930–33. Thereafter, China's insecure government, weak economy, continuously unfavorable balance of trade, and susceptibility to Japanese aggression made her especially vulnerable to the dislocations arising from American silver policy. As the price of the metal rose above its value as currency, Chinese nationals smuggled it out for quick sale in world markets. So also did the Japanese, who found smuggling not only a profitable trade but also a useful device for weakening China and the government of Chiang Kai-shek. Speculation by Chinese bankers and businessmen, some of them closely identified with the ruling Soong family, made matters worse.

In October 1934, alarmed by American purchases, the Chinese asked the United States to confine buying to American silver. Morgenthau, as he told the Department of State, could not grant the request while Roosevelt insisted on executing the Silver Purchase Act aggressively. After consulting the Treasury and the President, Hull had to tell the Chinese that the mandate from Congress governed American policy. He could only suggest that China sell her silver and use the proceeds to acquire gold.

This answer satisfied neither the Chinese nor Hull nor Morgenthau. Minister of Finance H. H. Kung, obviously harassed, in a cable of December 10, 1934, asked the United States either to lower the price of silver or to provide a credit for Chinese currency reform. Both Morgenthau and Hull wanted to help, but they disagreed about how to do it. The Department of State, taking the view that the Chinese government lacked sufficient administrative control to manage for itself, urged the Treasury to stop buying silver or at least to reduce the price to 45 cents.

As Morgenthau told Hull again and again, no modification of silver policy was politically possible. The United States could best help China, Morgenthau believed, by assisting in the reorganization of her currency. He ascribed Hull's opposition to that course to an undue sensitivity for Japan's opinion. The Department of State was taking pains not to violate the so-called Amau Doctrine, an official Japanese statement of policy that asserted Japan's interest in any developments involving China. Morgenthau was of the opposite mind. Japan's demands on China, unabating after her conquest of Manchuria in 1931, seemed to him to threaten the peace of the Orient and of the world. Impatient with what he considered Hull's appeasement of Japan, Morgenthau was prepared to use monetary aid to China as an instrument of political support. Otherwise, he feared, the United States would lose all influence in the Orient, leaving the area entirely to Japan and Great Britain.

Roosevelt, who seemed to Morgenthau sometimes to share his views about Asian politics, had distinct opinions of his own about Chinese finance. "Please remember," the President wrote Morgenthau in a private memorandum of December 4, 1934, "that I have a background of a little over a century in Chinese affairs. . . . China has been the Mecca of the people whom I have called the 'money changers in the Temple.' They are still in absolute control. It will take many years and possibly several revolutions to eliminate them. . . . I am inclined to believe that the 'money changers' are wrong and that it is better to hasten the crisis in China — to compel the Chinese people more and more to stand on their own feet without complete dependence on Japan and Europe — than it is to compromise with a situation which is economically unsound and which compromise will mean the continuation of an unsound position for a generation to come." Roosevelt, unwilling to alter American silver policy for the sake of the Chinese, was obviously not supporting the proposals of the State Department, but he was also clearly less enthusiastic than was the Treasury about helping China reform her currency. He apparently intended for the time being merely to observe.

The conflict over American policy reached a first resolution on December 17, 1934. The State Department then rejected several Treasury suggestions on the grounds that each tended toward bimetallism and would entail administrative commitments in China objectionable to the Japanese. Roosevelt, also opposed to encouraging bimetallism, tempered his usual stand on silver and instructed the Treasury to conclude a purchasing agreement with the Chinese. According to its terms, the Treasury was to buy silver only from the Chinese central bank, and to buy it in sufficient quantity to keep the world price from falling below 55 cents, the highest level to which Morgenthau's advisers thought the Chinese could adjust. The agreement was terminable on one week's notice. Pressure from the silver bloc forced its cancellation in two weeks. Morgenthau then again began to buy aggressively in London, the Chinese again complained, and the Secretary could only suggest that they appeal to the congressmen who had written the law.

Morgenthau also invited the Chinese to send a financial representative to Washington, but this too came to nothing. While the Chinese delayed, Hull proposed canceling or postponing the visit because he feared that if conversations failed, the effect on the whole world would be bad. In a "very gentle and polite manner," Morgenthau explained that he had told the Chinese to come with some proposal of their own. Hull was agreeable to proceeding on that basis; but Roosevelt, when he learned of objections from the silverites, called off the project.

During the next several months Roosevelt left his subordinates to their own resources. Morgenthau in that period gave considerable time to studying intelligence reports of the Department of State about Chinese affairs. He was shocked, as he was to be frequently during the next decade, by Chinese standards of personal and public morality. In order to combat the Communists in outlying provinces, Chiang Kai-shek's Nationalist government had to depend upon organized bands of brigands who systematically profited from trade in opium, gambling, and prostitution. Some of these guerrillas seemed more adamant in their resistance to Japanese expansion than did the Generalissimo himself. Those conditions were hard for Morgenthau to stomach, but he felt he had to, for Japan's intentions were alarming. American agents reported that the Japanese were making extraordinary economic demands. They wanted to have a Japanese appointed chief inspector of Chinese customs, to revise the Chinese tariff to favor the importation of Japanese products, to prevent China from negotiating any foreign loan without Japanese participation, and to standardize the currency of Japan, China, and Manchuria. Japan was reported to believe it would facilitate the last objective if she adopted the silver standard. That intelligence supported a hunch of the President that somehow American silver policy was hurting the Japanese. It obviously hurt China more. Morgenthau could not reverse it, but the spectrum of Japanese purpose increased his desire to assist the Chinese government. The question was still how to proceed.

An opportunity arose on October 28, 1935, when Chinese Ambassador Sze offered Morgenthau 200 million ounces of silver. China had given up. She was leaving the silver standard, Sze explained, and had to sell her bullion either directly to the United States or on the world market in order to acquire foreign exchange for the management of her new currency. Here at last, Morgenthau believed, was a strictly monetary problem that he could handle without reference to the Department of State.

The Secretary, as he told Roosevelt, had in mind purchasing 100 million ounces at once, and more if the deal proved successful, provided that China would deposit the proceeds in New York, use them exclusively for stabilization, appoint two Americans to a stabilization committee of three members, and tie the yuan to the dollar at the established rates for gold of $35 and silver of $1.29 an ounce.

Before negotiations could proceed, the Chinese on November 3 nationalized silver, ordered its exchange for legal tender notes, and tried to stabilize the yuan at the existing level of about 30 cents. The prospect of inflation and of possible Japanese interference caused near panic in Shanghai markets. Alfred Sze hurried to Morgenthau's farm to explain what had occurred. He carried a note from the Chinese treasury which did not specify how China would use the proceeds from the proposed silver sale, or whether her new currency was to be on a gold or silver basis, or whether it was to be linked with the pound, the yen or the dollar. The communication, Morgenthau told Sze, was vague and unsatisfactory. If the Treasury bought the silver, it would be acting in direct opposition to Congress's intention of enhancing the monetary use of the metal. He had, too, to treat the matter as a monetary question only, and consequently to be sure that the proceeds from the purchase would not be diverted to military supplies. With Roosevelt's approval, he insisted that China meet his terms.

The Chinese accepted all of Morgenthau's conditions except that tying the yuan to the dollar. As Sze explained, China could do no more than state the level at which she intended to maintain the yuan. She could not link it to any foreign currency.

"We have our politicians and our public and our future to think of," Morgenthau said. "We are not going to invest $65,000,000 and you tie your money to sterling. . . . You made this move and we want you to succeed. We feel that it is best for both countries to have the yuan quoted in terms of dollars instead of in terms of sterling. You people are playing poker and you are bluffing. . . . You have to pick the kind of money you are going to tie the yuan to."

On November 6 Morgenthau discussed the situation with the President, whose "snap judgment," as he put it, called for accompanying any purchases of Chinese bullion with "some sort of qualifying memorandum" linking the yuan and the dollar. Senator Pittman was of a similar view. The Chinese, however, were unyielding, and the State Department considered a link unnecessary. Morgenthau's own advisers gradually came to agree.

At the White House on November 9, 1935, Morgenthau, after a long review of the whole problem, suggested buying something on the order of 25 million ounces of silver to tide China over.

"My idea would be 20 million ounces which we may consider as a bet on what may develop in the future," Roosevelt commented. "Yes, I think that is the best thing we can do. That is, to go along without making any radical changes in the price of silver and see what happens."

This was at best a makeshift solution, but the President was not yet prepared to risk offending the silver bloc by dropping the world price, and both Morgenthau and Roosevelt were unwilling to purchase the entire amount China had offered without larger assurances than she would give.

The Chinese were desperate. "The Chinese ambassador is waiting in an outer office," Morgenthau told Roosevelt on November 13, "and he has now agreed . . . that they will keep the money over here; that they will keep us fully informed; that they will only use the money for stabilization purposes. Yesterday the Yokohama specie bank raided the Chinese currency and China only has about thirty-five or forty million dollars in gold and foreign exchange, and in order to fight it and hold it up, they want a commitment on the one hundred million ounces of silver." Morgenthau wanted to tell the "poor devils" that he would take up to 50 million ounces. Roosevelt said to go ahead.

"I am trying to make it as easy as possible for China," Morgenthau told Sze, "because we want to see you out of this trouble and I am willing to go through with this agreement on my word of honor and yours. . . . The only reason for doing it is that everybody seems to be against you and we will not ask for any trade preferences at this time. I take it that on all of the silver that the Chinese wish to sell, that they will give us the first chance and after we agree to buy these 50,000,000 ounces that you will not turn around and sell 50,000,000 ounces more to the English." Sze immediately agreed and the sale was consummated.

In mid-December Japan again raided Chinese exchange and China asked the Treasury to buy another 50 million ounces of silver. Sze also requested information about future American silver policy. Morgenthau hesitated. As he explained to the ambassador, there was such outright speculation in China (much of it by Chiang's official family) that the Treasury could not reveal its plans for changing prices. Informed that the Chinese treasury was thinking of selling 200 million ounces of silver in world markets, Morgenthau suspected Finance Minister Kung of contemplating some double-dealing. He was disturbed too because the Chinese, contrary to their promise, were not providing adequate data about their monetary policy. Though the Secretary remained sympathetic, he therefore declined China's requests for another silver purchase. He pressed instead to have a special envoy come to Washington for extended talks. The Chinese agreed, and dispatched K. P. Chen on the mission. Chen, a self-made man, struck Morgenthau as the most honest, sincere, and dependable of all Chinese financiers.

In the weeks preceding his arrival in Washington early in April 1936, and during the six weeks of conferences that then ensued, Morgenthau and his staff received voluminous reports about China. The material was as much political as economic. It had to be, for politics affected China's monetary problems and her interpretation of them. Politics also affected Morgenthau's response. Silver was his fulcrum, but his concern related always to the balance of forces in the Orient.

The "complete picture" as China painted it was discouraging. China had adopted a program to balance her budget within eighteen months in order to avoid inflation, but revenues were falling and expenditures were difficult to cut. The communist threat in the provinces and the need to maintain a posture of defense against possible Japanese aggression kept military costs high. Further, loan and indemnity payments were heavy and would remain so through 1940. Chinese currency was vulnerable even though its reform had been introduced under technically favorable conditions. China's exchange reserves were too small to insure stability in the event of a prolonged attack by Japanese banks. The reserve, moreover, was largely in silver, and when silver depreciated as it had in the previous weeks, it impaired public confidence. Now that China was off the silver standard, she would welcome higher prices for the metal.

China, as Morgenthau was told in confidence, also wanted a back door by rail to British Burma so as to be able to cope with Japanese aggression from the Pacific. And she wanted the United States to buy more silver at advantageous prices and thus to provide the foreign exchange for stabilizing the yuan. The need for financial support was imperative, as was the need for a public announcement that the United States was rendering that support.

Morgenthau considered it essential to cultivate the Chinese will to resist Japan. He could do so, he believed, by focusing upon the monetary problem. "Talking for the United States government," he said at his first meeting with K. P. Chen on April 8, "the only interest that we have in these financial discussions is to help China. . . . As far as the Treasury is concerned, it is purely monetary. We feel we can be instrumental in helping you and in the long run we will be helping ourselves. We feel it is very important to the world peace to help China strengthen her currency, because the way I see it, that is the center of the whole thing as far as China goes. . . . In discussing this thing, we have no axes to grind."

On April 12 Morgenthau, on the basis of his staff's advice, decided to offer China a contract for the purchase at the market price of five million ounces of silver each month during the remainder of 1936. This would be in line with agreements already concluded with Mexico and Canada. It was so hard to ascertain the real facts about China's situation that he preferred making gradual purchases to consuming immediately a large block of silver. Further, since the Silver Purchase law authorized the Treasury to buy silver until it equaled one fourth of the monetary reserves, continuing purchase of a reasonable amount from China could be construed as fulfilling the terms of the Act.

At luncheon the next day, Roosevelt asked a great many questions, especially about Chen's politics. After assuring him that Chen was anti-Japanese, Morgenthau said: "If Hitler can protect himself in Europe so that he will not have any conflict on his hands on either of his borders . . . he is very apt to join hands with Japan and attack Russia." Roosevelt agreed that was a possibility. China was in bad shape, Morgenthau continued, and unless the Japanese were diverted by a conflict with Russia, China's chances of pulling through were poor. That weakness, he suggested, had inspired his plan to buy five million ounces of silver a month. Roosevelt expressed no objections.

Treasury conversations with Chen set conditions for continued American silver purchases. Chen agreed to recommend the coinage of new silver yuan and half-yuan pieces and to suggest larger allotments of silver to industry and the arts. He was also willing to consider increasing the bullion and foreign exchange in the currency reserve. He admitted that the yuan seemed pegged to sterling because it had been quoted that way. By altering their system of quotation, the Chinese would make it obvious that the yuan was geared to no other national currency.

Completely satisfied, as were his advisers, Morgenthau on May 12 submitted a draft of a Chinese-American monetary agreement that Chen accepted. To avoid bringing in the Department of State, Morgenthau made the agreement between the Chinese Ministry of Finance and the United States Treasury, not between the governments. It made no reference to credits or loans but instead to the furnishing of dollar exchange. Only the Chinese and American governments were to know that the United States would provide $20 million against the deposit of 50 million ounces of silver. Morgenthau also proposed to buy 75 million ounces of silver, starting with 12 million ounces for the month ending June 15 and continuing with nine million ounces each month through January 15, 1937. The price was to be the current market price, and the Chinese could elect to have payment in gold. Proceeds from these sales were to be left in New York, where the Chinese could use them only for stabilizing the external value of the yuan. The details of this arrangement were also to remain confidential.

With his staff Morgenthau also prepared press releases designed to stimulate confidence in Chinese currency. In the text used in China on May 18, 1936, the Ministry of Finance announced that it had made "definite arrangements" to increase "the gold and foreign exchange of the note issue reserve." It promised "supplementary measures of monetary reform" to assure "the continued maintenance of an independent currency system not linked to any foreign monetary unit and the permanent stability of the Chinese currency which will inevitably lead to greater economic improvement and prosperity of the Chinese people."

With the help of the United States, China was able during the next year to manage her currency. The operation of the Silver Purchase Act had forced her off silver, occasioning large distress, but Morgenthau had gradually modified policy enough so that in the end the Treasury provided the assistance that permitted China to enjoy a period of unprecedented stability in both the internal and external value of her money. In that time, in spite of Japan's continuing hostility, Chiang Kai-shek extended the control of his government.

Like the Tripartite Pact with France and England, the silver agreement with China marked the end of an evolutionary phase in American monetary policy. Morgenthau had adjusted the gold and silver programs, instituted essentially for domestic purposes, to international monetary and political conditions. Within the limits of his authority, he had begun to develop technical devices to encourage resistance to fascist aggression. His achievement was timely, for the forces of oppression were on the verge of a great offensive. Monetary diplomacy could not prevent it, but when it came, the Treasury alone of American agencies had established foundations from which to meet it.

The President stood behind his friend. Like the good general in the analogy he so often drew, Roosevelt would not go out too far ahead of his army, but he was not averse to using an adventurous scout. He suffered Hull's hesitancy, but he also gave Morgenthau the opportunity to make stronger commitments across both oceans than did the Department of State, to go farther than most of the American people realized, farther than most of them — had they understood — would probably have condoned. And to his chief's satisfaction, Morgenthau did as much as he could.

V

ESSENTIAL SPENDING

1934—1937

1. A Difficult Job

THE NATIONAL BUDGET had never presented more troublesome or important problems than it did when Morgenthau assumed office. In 1933, as he later put it, "the economy of the country had literally come to a standstill." But Roosevelt's "vision and courage brought a scared and sullen country to life again. He gave people jobs . . . stopped mortgage foreclosures, dared to throw all the resources of the federal government into the battle to save bank deposits, homes, farms, and individual self-respect. It was worth every penny it cost. In those early days there was no time for careful planning or for detailed coordination. We were in a race against hunger and revolution, and we had to act fast."

The race permitted no feasible alternative to unprecedented peacetime spending. That spending and the deficits it produced involved Morgenthau in every aspect of federal policy. Charged by the Constitution with making "a regular statement and account of the receipts and expenditures of all public money," the Secretary of the Treasury had to know whether budgetary procedures achieved the objectives of economy and efficiency in the conduct of government. He had to ascertain how new spending proposals related to existing costs and to probable revenues, and whether those proposals served national policy.

Some of these responsibilities fell also to the Director of the Budget. In 1921 Congress had created the Bureau of the Budget, placing it in the Treasury Department, but making it responsible to the President, who appointed its Director. The Bureau was to assist the President in preparing a comprehensive budget and to strengthen his authority over the executive departments. Those changes lightened but did not remove the burdens of the Secretary of the Treasury, for his Constitutional obligations remained just what they had always been, as did his official and legitimate concern about public finance and national fiscal policy.

The actual working of government depended less upon blueprints than upon people. The Director of the Budget in 1933 was Lewis Douglas, a former congressman from Arizona who propounded rigidly orthodox ideas about fiscal policy with ability and insinuating charm. His orthodoxy troubled many New Dealers who thought it held back the battle against depression. As Morgenthau put it, he and Roosevelt "felt that Douglas' policy involved too great a gamble with human lives; that we could not stop the essential spending necessary to keep people alive, to keep the farms producing, to keep the government functioning without doing irreparable harm to the recuperative forces of the country. Yet we differed from Lew Douglas, not over whether a balanced budget was our ultimate goal, but over what sacrifices of relief and reform we were prepared to make in order to get it right away."

With some twelve to fifteen million Americans looking for work, the Administration had difficulty finding enough money for relief. Morgenthau helped the search for funds. In February 1934, at the risk of incurring an additional deficit, he assigned $150 million to the Federal Emergency Relief Administration. He was also reconciled to further deficits. At luncheon with the President on August 13, 1934, he submitted the draft of a speech which said that the Administration looked forward to a balanced budget. Then "a rather dramatic thing happened." The President tried to rewrite the statement, but finally said he did not see how Morgenthau could make it because the budget could not be balanced even in the fiscal year 1936, the period July 1, 1935–

June 30, 1936. There had been nothing provided for unemployment or for public work. "Well," Morgenthau replied, "cross it out."

The Secretary did not hesitate. For him, relief and recovery came first, a balanced budget second. Lewis Douglas was of a different view. He was willing to accept the dole, the cheapest form of relief, but he opposed public works. Already disturbed by the Administration's gold policy, Douglas found the prospect of a budget in continuing imbalance utterly alarming. On August 30, 1934, he resigned.

Morgenthau never forgot the episode. "I drove up the winding road to Roosevelt's house at Hyde Park," he later wrote, "and, at the door, was told the President would see me upstairs immediately. He was taking a bath." He sat up straight in the bathtub, looked Morgenthau directly in the eye, and said: "Henry (with great emphasis), in the words of John Paul Jones — we have just begun to fight." The previous evening, he explained, Lewis Douglas had quit. Roosevelt had tried to persuade him to wait until December 1, appealing to him as a patriot and, with the forthcoming Congressional elections in mind, as a Democrat. But Douglas declined. To Morgenthau, the President seemed "terribly upset and hurt. He said that he told Douglas that ten years from now he would be very sorry for what he had done." And he added: "Henry, I give you until midnight to get me a new Director of the Budget."

Morgenthau was worried about the spending program himself. In the first place, he recalled,

> I wanted all spending for relief and public works to be coordinated under a single head so as to avoid duplication and administrative confusion. In the second place, I wanted a scheduled tapering off of spending so that we could look forward to a balancing of the budget.
>
> It was with these two objectives in mind that I asked the President whom he was considering as Douglas' successor.
>
> He took my breath away by saying, "What do you think of Tom Corcoran as Director of the Budget?"
>
> This seemed to me absolutely out of the question. Tom Corcoran was a first-class lawyer, a first-class political operator, a first-

class accordion player. But I felt sure he knew very little about finance and could not be relied upon to keep a tight rein over the spending policies.

So I hastily suggested Daniel Bell, then my Commissioner of Accounts and Deposits in the Treasury Department for the job. Fortunately Roosevelt liked the idea, and Bell was made Acting Director.

That evening, at a clambake at the Morgenthaus', Roosevelt had a cocktail alone with his host. "You could tell," Morgenthau observed, "that he had a great weight off his shoulders. As the evening went on he began to sing songs and you could tell from the way he acted that a great load and worry was off his mind. As a matter of fact the people closely associated with him said that they had never seen him sing and be so jolly as he was that night since he became President."

Morgenthau was also pleased. Dan Bell, who was to remain Acting Director of the Budget for four years, was precisely the kind of dedicated civil servant whom the Secretary found indispensable. Bell had advanced from post to post within the Treasury Department since coming to work as a bookkeeper in 1911. If he had any political affiliation, he never revealed it. A talented and diligent man, unselfishly loyal, he held Morgenthau's confidence and returned it in full. They worked together with singular harmony of purpose and method.

They were determined "to ride herd over the spending program," for they believed, as the Secretary said, that "the various agencies who are doing the spending, their eyes are always bigger than their stomachs." Their appetite and lack of direction fostered extravagance which, as Morgenthau saw it, impeded recovery. "I wanted to see a free private enterprise economy as flourishing as the twenties but operating more soundly and more equitably," he explained years later. "It seemed vital to me that the government try sincerely to build a feeling of confidence in its financial operations so that businessmen would be encouraged to take over their proper role of invigorating the economy. I did not believe in the notion that a large, permanent deficit was necessary to 'compensate' for inadequacies of private investment, or for deficiencies of private purchasing power. Nor, I think, did the President or any of his close advisers in 1933–34."

In September 1934 the Secretary and his staff did believe that Roosevelt was getting "a lot of poor advice." In order to identify and eliminate waste, Morgenthau suggested establishing some control over the spending agencies. Douglas had been bitter because Roosevelt in January 1934 withdrew an Executive Order only three days old that put the independent agencies under supervision of the Bureau of the Budget. Morgenthau persuaded the President to let him refurbish the Order for possible use in the future. More immediately, he got Roosevelt to call the spenders together for a series of meetings beginning October 1. At these the Treasury hoped to obtain a coordinated estimate based upon national needs and assets. "We certainly have a difficult job ahead of us," Morgenthau wrote. "Just where it will all end, heaven only knows."

2. Search for a Program

In March 1933 the New Deal had had to improvise a relief program. About twenty-one million people were receiving some kind of public assistance, but the states and localities had practically exhausted their resources for rendering aid. The burden of sustaining life rested upon the federal government, which had neither precedents nor plans for the action that Roosevelt courageously promised. Under these conditions, the New Deal's achievements during the next eighteen months were magnificent but disorderly.

Harry Hopkins brought his indomitable energy to the direction of the Federal Emergency Relief Administration. It disbursed an initial $500 million, largely in the form of grants which the states distributed as dole; but Hopkins, who considered handouts degrading, in the fall of 1933 devised the short-lived

Civil Works Administration, which spent about $1 billion during the next half year putting men to work — some four million of them — on small federal projects. Many of these were hastily conceived, some were of little permanent value, but the experience of the Civil Works Administration and the gratitude of those it hired confirmed the belief of Hopkins and Roosevelt that only work relief, as opposed to direct relief, could preserve the spirit of the able unemployed during the distracting months of depression still to come. To provide a system within which work relief could proceed efficiently and constructively, Hopkins and his associates in September 1934 were preparing plans for the President and, with his approval, for Congress.

Morgenthau had no precise knowledge of Hopkins's plans, but he did know that the business community by and large opposed work relief, preferring the dole because it was cheaper and because employers feared that government competition for labor would force increases in wages. Morgenthau, in contrast, shared Hopkins's humane purpose and had no objection to incurring federal deficits in accomplishing it. He wanted, however, to keep expenditures to a minimum, and on that account to reexamine the nature and cost of proposed work relief projects, the capacity of those projects to provide jobs for the unemployed, and the pace at which projects would need financing. These considerations governed the Treasury's response to the competition for federal funds between light and heavy public works — between Hopkins's work relief program and Harold Ickes's Public Works Administration.

That competition had begun in the spring of 1933. The National Industrial Recovery Act then provided $3.3 billion for public works. The advocates of the appropriation expected PWA to stimulate heavy industry by spending the money for projects like dams that called for huge quantities of steel, cement, and other capital goods. But Ickes had criteria of his own. Determined to use his funds for durable projects of permanent social and esthetic value, he pursued his high purpose with maddening deliberation. As Morgenthau recalled, Ickes "was so anxious to keep graft and politics out of the public works program that he practically spent money through a medicine dropper. Ickes's slowness in making decisions was sometimes a real handicap. The important thing was to alleviate unemployment crises but because of insufficient advance planning the public works projects were frequently slow in getting started and therefore expenditures for them were sometimes being made after instead of before the crises had passed their peaks."

Hopkins, in contrast to Ickes, gave first priority to providing as much work as possible, as fast as possible, at as low a cost per man as possible. Morgenthau therefore favored channeling the bulk of federal relief expenditures through Hopkins. Ickes resented this preference, considered Hopkins wasteful and Morgenthau meddling, and fought both with pugnacious obstinacy.

On October 1, 1934, Morgenthau entered the White House for the first of several conferences with Ickes, Hopkins, and Roosevelt. Three days of discussion gave the Treasury nothing to go on. Even Roosevelt, when Hopkins and Ickes submitted their plans, pointed out that item after item was impractical. As Morgenthau saw it, Hopkins simply "yessed" everything the President said. Ickes at one point asserted that it made no difference whether the government spent $5 billion or private industry spent an equal amount. At this "classic remark" Morgenthau thought any conventional economist "would almost pass out." The President kept reverting to his own scheme for building four cross-country highways with four north-south intersectors fed by various branches. Construction could begin where unemployment was highest, he said, and the government could build and sell houses on large plots along the completed roads. After elaborating this dream, he asked Morgenthau whether the information which the conferences had developed satisfied him.

The discussion, the Secretary replied, left him "absolutely cold." Roosevelt said Morgenthau sounded like Russell Leffingwell, a Morgan partner who believed that large federal expenditures would retard recovery.

"I wish I had half his brains," Morgenthau answered.

In a sarcastic manner the President then asked if Morgenthau had any better suggestions. The Secretary requested reports from engineers qualified to state when projects might begin and how much they would cost. The government, he said, was contracting for public works without paying any attention to the problem of taking people off relief. He believed all public works had to be handled by one agency, directed by one man with the authority to make policy for the purpose of relieving unemployment and reducing relief rolls.

Morgenthau could tell that Roosevelt did not like this speech; and Hopkins called it unfair, arguing that Morgenthau could not reasonably expect him to come in with finished plans. After another half hour of talk, Roosevelt directed Ickes and Hopkins to have the Corps of Engineers submit estimates on all projects, covering costs, time schedules, and employment potentialities. He wanted a complete survey in time for a further conference to be held in Warm Springs in December. He would then, he said, take up the question of what kind of organization should run the program, and in January take his plans to Congress.

Roosevelt's concluding instructions pleased Morgenthau, who was even more encouraged by a "thrilling meeting with the President at his bedside" two days later. Roosevelt said he had tried to catch Morgenthau's eye so that he would stop suggesting that one organization manage public works. He agreed with Morgenthau but did not want at that time to start Ickes and Hopkins fighting. Morgenthau said that Hopkins ought to keep track of the entire operation. Again Roosevelt agreed, except that he thought Ickes should be left alone to finance municipal improvements. Morgenthau questioned even this, but he left the President with a "distinct feeling of encouragement . . . that he and I were seeing absolutely eye to eye on this program."

His optimism was premature. On December 2 he and Roosevelt, Ickes, and Hopkins began at Warm Springs to review what were purported to be final plans for public works. "You could have knocked me over with a feather," Morgenthau reported in his Diary, "when Ickes pulled out of his portfolio five copies of his program. It seemed unbelievable to me that we had all been sitting around there for a couple of days and Ickes had not given any of us a chance to see the program." It was only a lot of "lump sum figures," in Morgenthau's opinion, without relevance to the need for using public works to hire the unemployed. Hopkins spoke "rather loosely" about taking four million men off relief, but Morgenthau, pleased that Roosevelt was short with Ickes, made it clear to the President that the Treasury still had nothing definite with which to calculate the dole, the projects, or the necessary financing.

Sensing again the antagonism between Ickes and Hopkins, Morgenthau that evening urged the President to put one man in charge. "In a very emphatic and rather angry tone of voice, Roosevelt shouted: 'I will get a program within forty-eight hours. I am going to get my program first and I will not settle as to who is going to run it until I get my program.'" "I am sorry, Mr. President," Morgenthau said. "I think you are wrong."

Though the relief program remained as amorphous as it had been before the first conference about it, Roosevelt decided late in December to ask Congress for $4 billion of new money, which Ickes and Hopkins maintained they could spend. Morgenthau told the President categorically that they could not, but he knew he was making no impression, and he realized that the actual spending was not his job. He concentrated therefore on helping Bell find unexpended funds from earlier appropriations to stretch out relief in 1935 and, if Congress consented, to supplement the $4 billion of new money for 1936.

On December 26, 1934, Roosevelt for the first time carefully considered finances for fiscal 1936. With Bell and Morgenthau at his side, he took $937 million of unobligated monies away from emergency agencies that had been sitting on their appropriations. Seeing that Roosevelt "got a kick" out of making these subtractions, Morgenthau immediately persuaded the President to dictate letters instructing the agencies to cease obligating funds until further notice.

Pressing on, Morgenthau suggested that if the 1936 deficit were less than that for 1935, the Administration could argue that it had broken the back of the depression. If, on the other hand, each year's deficit increased, he did not see how to stop Congress from forcing the Treasury to print paper money.

Roosevelt, pencil and paper in hand, tried to figure out from every angle how the Administration could make it appear that the peak of expenditures would fall in 1935, the current fiscal year. After calculating for a long time, he decided to use the estimates submitted by the departments rather than the less dramatic figures of the Bureau of the Budget which Bell felt were closer to being accurate. Bell considered this procedure "just . . . faking," but Morgenthau was pleased because he thought that at last he was making real headway in getting the President to face basic issues.

At the White House the next afternoon, however, the Secretary realized to his dismay that Roosevelt was trying to placate Ickes. Morgenthau therefore made an emphatic "stump speech" about balancing the budget except for relief and about the dangers of "paper inflation." Roosevelt swung over to his side, and between them they swept Ickes off his feet and "just left him gurgling and murmuring to himself."

After Hopkins and Ickes left, Roosevelt, "grinning all over," implied that he had made it easy for Bell to take away Ickes's unexpended funds. Silently to himself, Morgenthau said: "Franklin, old boy, you had Bell and me here to help hold your hand while you performed the most difficult operation on Ickes and thank God that I was there to back you up."

Out loud, the Secretary reviewed the reallocations Roosevelt had approved. He also gave the President a draft of a budget message, including a page written entirely by Charles Merz of the *New York Times*, which Roosevelt accepted verbatim. That page seemed to Morgenthau, as to Merz, essential from the standpoint of business confidence and sound economics. Although a substantial measure of recovery had been achieved, it said, unemployment was still large, and increasingly the responsibility of the federal government. Therefore, the Administration could not completely balance the budget for 1936, but the President was submitting a budget which balanced except for expenditures for relief. That deficit, incurred as it was to meet the emergency, would decline as rapidly as private industry could reemploy.

At a final meeting about the budget message a few days later, Roosevelt again approved Morgenthau's formulations. "I will most likely never again have to face as serious a financial problem as the one I have just gone through with the President," the Secretary confided to his Diary, "and I now feel that I have nothing to worry about from Congress as I do not believe that any group would have the nerve or the backing to try to bust this budget which is balanced except for relief."

Again he was overoptimistic. Early in January Roosevelt secretly allotted Hopkins an extra $125 million. On January 21, 1935, Bell reported that Roosevelt had assigned $67 million to land reclamation. The pattern persisted. "The result," Morgenthau wrote in his Diary, "is that everybody is angry and frothing at the mouth." While Ickes, Hopkins, and other administrators struggled for funds for their agencies, while Roosevelt made his genial private arrangements with each of them, Morgenthau and Bell had no sure way of estimating, much less of controlling, the size or rate of federal expenditures. They had small reason to expect much improvement from the new relief bill then before Congress.

3. The Four Billion Eight

In April 1935 Congress passed the Emergency Relief Appropriation Act providing the funds for which Roosevelt had asked — $4 billion of new money and $880 million unused from previous appropriations. A few economists had advocated spending twice that amount, but the Administration received all it had asked for, the largest peacetime appropriation in American history up to that time. The law stipulated that a unified agency was to administer the work program; that the projects were to be permanent contributions to the nation; that the government was to pay a "security wage" larger than the dole but smaller than the wages paid by private industry; that preference was to be given to self-liquidating projects which directly employed labor and were located in distressed areas; and that local communities were to resume caring for unemployable paupers. Those stipulations met Roosevelt's prescriptions, but the Senate complicated the administration of the Act by insisting on confirming all appointments to jobs paying more than $5,000 a year and by specifying in the statute how some of the money was to be allotted. The former provision injected politics into the work program; the latter limited the Executive's flexibility.

Although the provisions of the Act did not compensate for what Morgenthau considered the inadequacies of planning for work relief, he hoped that Roosevelt would now give Hopkins unquestionable authority for the direction of expenditures. While the bill lay before Congress, the President had delayed decision about a program director; but in April, to Morgenthau's distress, he put Ickes in charge of an Allotment Division and Hopkins in charge of a Projects Division, which he was soon to reorganize as the Work Progress Administration. This separation of responsibility, Morgenthau believed, would hamstring the program. Worse still, as he put it in his Diary, the idea of Ickes as Chairman of the Allotment Division and Harry Hopkins in "some nondescript job just made me sick."

"Racking his brain" for some way to concentrate authority for the whole program and to free Hopkins from dependence upon Ickes, Morgenthau concluded that the best man in Washington for the "top job" would be Joseph P. Kennedy, a Boston Democrat then Chairman of the Securities and Exchange Commission. A successful stockbroker with frankly conservative views, Kennedy had the respect of the business community. Though he had opposed the work program at one time, he had come to support it enthusiastically.

On April 13 Morgenthau talked with Roosevelt "as one Dutchess County neighbor to another." "Please remember, Franklin," he began, "that I cannot get anything more out of politics in this life so what I am going to say to you is motivated by the desire to serve my country and you and nothing else." As it was then arranged, Morgenthau said, the "$4 billion 8" setup would surely fail, and if it did, Roosevelt would not be reelected. He suggested the President put Kennedy in charge. Kennedy, he argued, had made an outstanding record, could handle people, and was popular with congressmen and newspapermen. Roosevelt was dubious. "The trouble with Kennedy," he said, "is you always have to hold his hand." But after further consideration, he exuberantly proposed appointing an "Assistant to the President in Charge of Public Works," who would "really run the show"; and for that job Kennedy, he thought, would be "all right."

On April 22 Roosevelt had a new plan. He would make Ickes simply senior member of an allotment board and set up a small, intermediary committee to supervise all expenditures. There Kennedy would sit at the President's side as the secretary. "I can't yet tell either Hopkins or Ickes," Roosevelt confided to Morgenthau, "that Kennedy is going to be over them. They will have to learn that gradually." But Kennedy, he said, had already accepted the appointment. Later that day Kennedy told Morgenthau he was going to turn the job down, because he could not work with Ickes.

The next day, Roosevelt came up with other proposals. He would not tie up funds beyond July 1, 1936, and he would allocate them only after checking with Hopkins to see how many people in project areas were on relief rolls. Each million dollars allotted would have to provide employment for about a thousand people. The President also intended to spend at least half the money directly on wages, and he wanted to get back as much as he could in rentals and tolls, even if the length of time for repayment was longer than customary. Those criteria, however, did little more than elaborate the provisions of the statute; and Roosevelt, rejecting Morgenthau's recommendations, left Ickes as Chairman of the Allotment Board and Hopkins as Administrator of the WPA.

As Morgenthau saw it, the danger was that Ickes would divert funds to projects only remotely beneficial to the unemployed, while Hopkins, disbursing what he could of what remained, would spend generously but wastefully. "Some day," Morgenthau noted in his Diary in July 1935, "if we keep on spending money at the rate we are and in such helter-skelter, hit and miss method, we cannot help but be riding for a fall unless we continue to decrease our deficit each year and the budget is balanced. If we are not able to do this, I do not want to be the sole goat and . . . be under terrific pressure from all the money cranks and crackpots to pull out some more white rabbits out of the hat and do some unsound economic trick in order to correct other unsound measures which the administration had taken. . . . It seems to me that we are not making any headway and the number of unemployed is staying more or less static. The unfortunate thing in this administration is that nobody seems to be trying to fit our unemployment program in with the long distant viewpoint so that we will gradually cut down on unemployment and in that manner reduce the federal expenditures to maintain the unemployed. I think that ninety-five per cent of the thinking in the administration is how to spend money and that possibly five per cent of the thinking is going toward how we can work ourselves out of our present unemployment difficulties."

At luncheon with Roosevelt on July 23, Morgenthau reported that Georgia was the only state that had returned its unemployables to community aid. Elsewhere there were almost a million unemployables on federal relief rolls. Roosevelt at once went "into a long harangue . . . how for years there had been ten families in Hyde Park, that the town had always taken care of them but now the federal government is taking care of them and that there is no reason why these ten families should not be thrown back on the town and that there must be thousands of communities who have similar situations and who could take care of their chronic unemployables."

Suddenly switching direction, but still on the side of retrenchment, Roosevelt said he was going to tell Ickes to stop letting contracts for slum clearance after September 1 because heavy projects, slow to start, could not be shut off.

Taking advantage of the President's mood, Morgenthau

pointed out that some three and a half million people remained on work relief irrespective of improvements in private employment. He suggested that if recovery seemed likely, Roosevelt should make a speech after Congress adjourned referring to his promise to decrease expenditures if conditions permitted, and explaining that he had been spending slowly because (and from here on Morgenthau spoke with his tongue in his cheek) he had expected recovery in the fall and did not want to waste money. "If that is not the darnedest sophistry," Morgenthau wrote in his Diary, "I do not know what sophistry is," but Roosevelt, after listening, "made a perfectly magnificent address right then and there and by the time he was finished, knowing my F.D.R., I believed he was fully convinced that all the ideas he had expressed were his own — which encouraged me tremendously because I felt I had gotten my ideas across."

He had not, for Roosevelt's gestures toward retrenchment were few and small. The lingering depression with its accompanying unemployment kept the government from real economies. Indeed, on November 15, 1935, Harry Hopkins told Morgenthau that he would need at least an additional $300 million in the current fiscal year. At first "unsympathetic and cold," Morgenthau "asked him how he could go before Congress and ask for more money when so much was being wasted." But typically, after reflection, Morgenthau promised to find $3 to $5 million for direct relief.

Hopkins was grateful for this and other emergency contributions to the relief program. "No one did more than you to support that program," he wrote Morgenthau years later. "Many times when the days seemed pretty dark you were the one who helped influence a favorable decision on behalf of the millions who were out of work. . . . Never once in the long history of unemployment relief did you fail." Morgenthau was proud of that accolade, for Hopkins, he realized, had always at heart the interests of those at the bottom of the ladder. So did the Secretary. Their common humanitarian purpose transcended their disagreements about method.

Yet method, too, made a difference, for the efficient use of relief monies was as important for the unemployed as for the budget. As Morgenthau put it on November 11, 1935, it was perfectly asinine to talk about balancing the budget immediately. It could not be balanced if decent attention were to be given to human needs. But relief could be put on a businesslike basis. That was his objective while he and Bell worked on the 1937 budget with Roosevelt in Warm Springs on November 26 and 27. They halved the requests of the Civilian Conservation Corps, cut down the funds for road building, and arranged to discharge rapidly the personnel engaged in winding up the affairs of the National Recovery Administration, which the Supreme Court had declared unconstitutional. Looking for another $150 million, Morgenthau suggested taking it from Ickes's Public Works Administration. To his delight, Roosevelt concurred. Weighing these and other savings against the Treasury's revised estimates of revenue, Morgenthau in December 1935 hoped to balance the 1937 budget exclusive of relief with a couple of hundred million dollars to spare.

There remained three dangers. The Supreme Court had found the Agricultural Adjustment Act unconstitutional, and invalidated the processing tax which had defrayed the expenses of supporting agricultural prices. The Administration was determined to continue to support prices, but Congress had yet to provide new taxes. Congress, furthermore, seemed ready to pay the World War I veterans their bonus but unwilling to use taxes for that purpose. And Hopkins and Ickes, still warring with each other, had again only vague suggestions for spending the money they demanded. Morgenthau, as 1936 began, knew that the battle for efficiency in spending had yet to be won. Indeed, the Congress, bent upon paying a bonus to veterans, was about to complicate the Treasury's task.

4. The Bonus

With the coming of depression, World War I veterans had begun agitating to collect the bonus which Congress had authorized in 1924. The Adjusted Compensation Act of that year promised them payments based upon length of service plus interest compounded from 1925 to 1945 when the bonus was to become due. The interest would make it at maturity worth two and a half times the initial value of the grant. But the veterans, working through their powerful lobbies and supported by most inflationists, asked to receive the full amount at once in cash, more than $2 billion. Over Hoover's veto Congress authorized loans on half the face value of the adjusted compensation certificates, but pressure for full payment continued, and in every year after 1929 bonus bills were introduced.

Among the opponents of the bonus, none was more dogged than Morgenthau, who viewed premature payment as an unsound, unwarranted, even immoral subsidy to a special-interest group. The issue first caught his attention in April 1935 when the House of Representatives, after considering several proposals, passed the most radical, a bill sponsored by Congressman Wright Patman, Texas Democrat, professional veteran, and cheap-money advocate. This measure called for issuing greenbacks to pay the full face value of the bonus certificates. The prospect of printing the money bothered Morgenthau even more than did the alternative of further unbalancing the budget. Like Roosevelt, he preferred paying the bonus by issuing interest-bearing bonds, but he hoped the President would not limit Executive resistance to a compromise about methods of payment. Though Jack Garner warned him that "that damn thing's got a lot of strength down in the Senate," Morgenthau thought Roosevelt could make a veto stick.

The President also took a strong position initially. Meeting

with Morgenthau, Bell, and General Frank T. Hines, the head of
the Veterans' Administration, on April 22, 1935, Roosevelt opposed bonus legislation on any terms. In the past, he said, the
advocates of the bonus had always broken their promises. He
objected to any legislation conflicting with his budget estimates
or discriminating in favor of special groups. He agreed with
Morgenthau that the Treasury should insist on new revenues to
offset any bonus payment, and he endorsed the Treasury's idea
of using an inheritance tax for that purpose.

On April 23 the Secretary advocated that tax to the Senate
Committee on Finance, but the committee reported out the Patman bill without incorporating the tax, and the Senate passed the
bill with the provision for printing greenbacks by a vote of 55–
33. The next move was the President's.

Now Roosevelt wavered. At luncheon on May 6, he told
Morgenthau in strictest confidence that Garner had convinced
him it was wise to get the bonus out of the way in 1935 and not
have it as a political issue during the campaign the following
year. He intended to veto the bill, but if he acquiesced in letting
Congress override his veto, he calculated that everyone would
forget about it in three or four days.

Morgenthau was dismayed, for he was sure that only strong
Executive intercession would prevent Congress from overriding
a veto. For ten days he marked time, but he was ready for a fight
when, at Roosevelt's request, he went to the White House on the
evening of May 16. There he found the President "in a very bad
humor," complaining that "my sinus hurts me." Doubtless the
conflict between Congress and his advisers contributed to Roosevelt's headache. In a petulant mood, he read aloud a draft of a
bonus veto. It was not good. He then reviewed the notes which
General Hines and the Treasury staff had prepared. These
lacked spirit. As Morgenthau said, only the President himself
could write the veto.

Dropping his pout, Roosevelt turned to the job at hand at
about a quarter to ten and dictated steadily for an hour. Occasionally Morgenthau broke in to make a suggestion. Until one in
the morning the Secretary, alone with Roosevelt, urged him to

battle to the finish. As he put it in his Diary, he "kept pacing up
and down in front of him making one campaign speech after another." Finally, Roosevelt's face "lit up in a great smile. He
raised his two fists in the air and shook them and said, 'My god, if
I win I would be on the crest of the wave!' I saw that I had
convinced him and stopped arguing."

The next day Marvin McIntyre, one of Roosevelt's personal
staff, argued "very heatedly" that "he guessed that Jack Garner
knew more about politics" than Morgenthau did. "I do not give
a whoop what Jack Garner said," Morgenthau shot back. "I
think that this is the thing for the President to do."

Encouraged by the President's agreement, Morgenthau decided to concentrate all his energy on defeating the bonus. On
Saturday, May 20, he directed Steve Gibbons, the Treasury's
most gifted agent in handling Congress, who was ill, to get to
work on his telephone. "You know," he told Gibbons, "the
President's gone right out on the end of the limb on this bonus
and I'm going with him. . . . And so far as I can find, I'm the
only member of the Cabinet that gives a Goddam what he's doing."

The Secretary used his own telephone to recruit support.
Among others, he talked with Frank Gannett, the upstate New
York publisher, William S. Paley of the Columbia Broadcasting
System, Harper Sibley of the National Chamber of Commerce,
Charles Michelson, the talented publicist of the Democratic National Committee, and Joseph P. Kennedy. To Roy Howard of
Scripps-Howard he complained that the newspapers spent all
their time talking about what the veterans wanted and not what
the taxpayers needed. "America doesn't know what's happening
to it," Morgenthau said. "It's just another Wayne B. Wheeler
shoving prohibition down their throats."

"I have been living, breathing and half sleeping on the bonus
for the last three days with the President," Morgenthau said at
one point. ". . . The address that he's going to give to Congress
is the most striking and the most forcible since his inauguration."

It was going to be a terrific fight, the Secretary believed. The
enemy was "greenback printing press and greenback inflation."

Therefore, he was willing to enlist Jouett Shouse of the Liberty League, a turncoat Democrat bitterly opposing the New Deal, and willing also to arrange radio time for Owen D. Young, a conservative Democrat who had been a possible candidate for the Presidency. By noon of May 20 Morgenthau felt that he was making real progress in organizing the press and the radio in the President's behalf. He went to the White House exuberant, only to have his spirits dashed. Patman had called earlier with twenty-two colleagues. As Morgenthau put it in his Diary:

> Had lunch with the President and told him what I was doing about the Bonus. I was rather surprised to find a sort of coolness. . . . He said, "You know we may have to compromise. . . ." I said, "What do you mean?" He said, "Well we might have to pay the present bonus. . . ." I said, "Mr. President, there is nothing like that in your speech. You say definitely that you are against the bonus." He said, "Why yes, but how can I tell what kind of a bill they may pass." He said, "Patman asked me point-blank this morning if I was against all bonus legislation or whether I had an open mind and I told him that I had an open mind because how could I know what they might pass."
>
> I had a sort of sinking feeling and found myself sort of gradually crumpling up and I said, "If you want me to go on please do not talk that way to me because I am building a bonfire of support for you in your veto message." He said rather quickly with a smile, "Let's agree that I will not talk to you about any compromise if you will not talk to me about any bonfire." He said, "In other words, never let your left hand know what your right is doing." I said, "Which hand am I, Mr. President?" And he said, "My right hand." He said, "But I keep my left hand under the table."
>
> This is the most frank expression of the real F.D.R. that I ever listened to and that is the real way that he works — but thank God I understand him.

The real F.D.R., as Morgenthau knew, also loved a good fight, and on Sunday he trimmed again for battle. The Morgenthaus, Rosenmans, and Roosevelts went sailing on the President's yacht. It was a beautiful day and the President was in a grand humor. After luncheon Morgenthau asked him for permission to keep pressure on Congress. "Henry," Roosevelt said, "I give you carte blanche to anything that you want."

On Monday, May 22, the President broadcast his message, delivered before a joint meeting of the House and the Senate. The federal government, he observed, had already provided veterans with insurance, hospitalization, vocational training and rehabilitation, preferential employment, the promise of a bonus in 1945, and the privilege of borrowing up to 50 per cent on their certificates. Payment in 1936 of the debt due in 1945 would mean appreciating the certificates $1.6 billion, expending overall $2.2 billion. This would violate completely the principles of the 1924 settlement. The bill would also impede recovery. It would weaken the federal debt structure. Furthermore, the deceptively easy method of payment by printing greenbacks would simply give rise to similar demands by other interest groups. This could lead ultimately to uncontrollable inflation and the destruction of the value of savings. Authorizations and appropriations, the President continued, had been and should be predicated not on mere spending but on the sounder basis of preventing homes and farms from bankruptcy, of restoring industrial productivity, of safeguarding bank deposits, and most important of all, of giving relief and jobs through public works to individuals and families faced with starvation. There were before Congress bills providing old-age and unemployment security which would help not only veterans but all Americans. Only this kind of general legislation truly served the welfare of the country.

A generally favorable press heightened Roosevelt's joy in the contest. Congress was considering a substitute measure authorizing three means of financing a bonus — through greenbacks, bonds, or out of the $4.8 billion. "If they send me the so-called three-headed bonus bill," the President said, ". . . I am going to tell the country that I have been forced to make my choice and I am going to pay the bonus out of the four billion eight, which will leave about one billion eight for relief purposes, and every man who loses his job on relief projects can thank the veterans' lobby in Washington." With a smile of triumph, he concluded, "What do you think of that?"

Morgenthau thought it was tremendous. "Oh, you devil," he said. Roosevelt roared.

The Senate sustained the President's veto, and the question was closed for the year. Or so Morgenthau hoped. The Patmanites, however, filed a petition making another vote on the vetoed bill mandatory in January 1936; veterans' organizations continued to agitate; and in September the American Legion passed a resolution favoring a bonus unfettered by association with greenbacks. That proposal would be hard to beat.

It was in September also that Roosevelt wavered again. Out riding with Rex Tugwell and Morgenthau, he suddenly announced that he was going to act on the bonus before he departed on a trip through the West. Morgenthau said he was "just too tired" to discuss the issue. If Roosevelt had insisted on paying the bonus, the Secretary later wrote in his Diary, "I would have resigned on the spot."

The President did not press the matter, though he explained that if he paid the bonus after his trip, people would say he had done so because he had a poor reception out West. That argument, Morgenthau told him, was "just pure bunk." Roosevelt was really worried, he felt, that the bonus might prove embarrassing in 1936.

On September 4 Morgenthau wrote the President a personal and confidential letter. He had "almost literally passed out," he said, when Roosevelt took up the bonus during their drive. He had been thinking of almost nothing else since, and he had come "to the very definite and positive conclusion that from the standpoint of the welfare of the country and yourself that you should not make any announcement on the bonus prior to your message to Congress in January." The President's "magnificent and courageous veto" precluded retreat. Furthermore, the Treasury was financing $1.7 billion, and an announcement about the bonus either during or after the financing might have disastrous effects on the market. Every bondholder would consider it a breach of faith on the part of the government. "Certainly any private corporation which had filed its statement with the Security Exchange Commission and then came out with a financing and immediately after that incurred a large additional debt would be subject to the severest chastisement. . . . I fail to see any differ-

ence between this example and an announcement now that the
bonus will be paid. I most strongly urge you, first as your Secretary of the Treasury and second, as one of your true and tried
friends, to do nothing about the bonus for the balance of this
year. My own conviction is that the bonus should not be paid
until maturity, and the reasons are covered so admirably in your
veto message that it would be impossible for me to add anything
further. However, if you feel that politically it is necessary to
do something about the bonus, then it seems that the time and the
place for you to make a statement about the payment of the
bonus would be in your message to Congress when it meets in
January and subsequently explain how you propose to finance
the bonus payment in your budget message."

That counsel prevailed. Roosevelt, it developed, had been
needling his Secretary of the Treasury with the malice of fatigue. The legislative session of 1935 had been exhausting, involving as it did the $4.8 billion, the bonus, a new banking act, a
difficult revenue measure, social security laws, and other reform
legislation. At the end of October, after both men had had a
vacation, Morgenthau found the President restored. "He and I
together are almost two different men from what we were when
I last saw him in September," he wrote. "You again get the feeling that he has strength and reserve power and confidence in
himself and the power to inspire confidence which certainly
seemed to be lacking during July, August and September. I realize how tired I was and I suppose the President was just as tired."
Roosevelt admitted as much. He knew, he said, that their
September conversation about the bonus had almost brought
Morgenthau to tears. "After election we both must take regular
vacations, irrespective of what is going on and never permit ourselves to get so tired again," Roosevelt said. ". . . I was so tired
that I would have enjoyed seeing you cry or would have gotten
pleasure out of sticking pins into people and hurting them."

In mid-November 1935, however, Roosevelt's state of mind
counted less than did congressional sensitivity to the veterans'
vote. With the campaign of 1936 approaching, some bonus bill
was bound to pass. Morgenthau urged leaving the financing to
the Treasury, for he intended, if he had to, to raise the money in

an orthodox manner, by selling securities in the market. That would disturb the business and financial community less than would any alternative scheme.

Early in January 1936 the House of Representatives passed a bill authorizing full payment of the bonus without specifying the method of payment. The President, noncommittal about a veto, thought there was no chance of defeating the measure in the Senate, but he permitted Morgenthau to speak out. Testifying on January 14, the Secretary explained that the Treasury had to raise more than $9 billion before June 30, 1937. Bonus legislation would increase this to $11.3 billion. New taxes would in any case be necessary, but a bonus would make them heavier, and whatever their incidence, the Treasury would have to work hard to keep control of the money market. If there had to be a bonus, he recommended paying it in bonds bearing no coupon but accumulating interest progressively.

The Senate Committee on Finance pushed the bonus bill along, but modified it to adopt Morgenthau's suggestion for payment. On January 20 the Senate passed the bill, 76–16, and the House quickly concurred, 346–59.

After these votes, a veto could be only a gesture, but Morgenthau hoped Roosevelt would stand by his principles. At the White House on January 23, the Secretary noted in his Diary, "the President did not say a word but took a pencil and paper and began to write. After he had written a little while, I said to him, 'What is it, approval or veto?' and he smiled and said, 'You know perfectly well what it is. You never had any doubts what I would do,' and I said, 'Yes, I did, but I was afraid to let myself think about it!' "

The veto, which Roosevelt wrote in longhand and sent to the Hill the next morning, referred Congress to the message of the previous year. Morgenthau congratulated him on his courage. Four out of five congressmen had none. Filling the veteran's pocket before asking for his vote, both houses rapidly overrode the veto. It remained only for the Treasury to print and mail the bonds, prepare to convert most of them to cash, and plan the necessary financing.

Morgenthau had lost, but there were compensations. He took

great satisfaction in seeing Roosevelt, after some equivocation, join him in a positive fight against a deplorable but seductive measure. He had succeeded, largely by influencing the President and through him the Congress, in defeating the Patman bill with its paper money clause. He had persuaded the Senate to arrange the financing of the bonus according to the Treasury's preferences. Yet the bonus in any form threatened his budgetary objectives and therefore rekindled his zeal for economy. In so far as possible, he intended to make the lenders and spenders save much of the money the veterans were to receive.

5. Lenders and Spenders

The growing antagonism of the business community toward the New Deal disturbed Morgenthau as 1936 began and marked the prospect of another presidential campaign.

> For a number of days [he noted in his Diary on February 2] various articles which I have been reading plus what has been happening in Congress plus the information that naturally comes across my desk has convinced me that the President is extremely vulnerable to attack on his spending program. Furthermore, the whole fiscal policy of the government is at the cross-roads depending upon how we are going to pay for the new agricultural program, the bonus, etc. The final straw was Dr. Gallup's article in the Sunday paper showing that only 2 per cent of the people that he polled wanted new taxes. . . . Today I had a chance to do plenty of thinking and . . . I telephoned the White House for an appointment and got one for 5:15. . . .
>
> The President saw me immediately and I stayed with him a little over an hour — Miss LeHand being present serving us tea. He was fixing his stamps while I talked to him. I told him that I understood . . . that the Republicans were going to concentrate on attacking him on his spending program — just the way he had attacked Hoover. "But," I said, "the Republicans have ten times as much material as you had three years ago . . ." Furthermore, that

with the exception of the first six months that he was President all of the publicity that came out of the White House was "spending" and "more spending" and not a single word about economizing; that it was still time to talk and practice economy and that if he waited very much longer they would simply accuse him of doing it for the political effect. To my great surprise he sat there very quietly, nodded his head, smiled at me and said, "You are right." He never argued back at me once, except to say, "They have overlooked and misinterpreted what I said in my Message to Congress — that I pointed out that as business improved we would gradually curtail expenses." I said, "Yes, that was very nice but you have done nothing about it." Again he said, "You are right." I have never seen him so gentle or so receptive to suggestions.

The President then said, "What would you suggest doing?" I said, "Well I, as Chairman of your Lending Committee, could call them together and possibly do something but that would not help you any. You have got to do it and let the word go out that you called a meeting in order to begin to save." He said, "Whom should we call — Missy — take this down. I suggest that Jones, Fahey, Ickes, Myers and Stewart McDonald come." * I then said, "What about Tugwell" and he said ,"No, don't let's have Tugwell. He is in a sort of new business of lending to farm families in distress, and if we call him in it will start up a whole new line of thought and argument." I said, "Fine, that will make the meeting that much easier." And he let me get away with that. The President also did not want Chester Davis.†

Then, to my surprise, he said, "Let's have another meeting on Thursday and talk over the four billion eight." I said, "Frankly, I have been afraid to bring that up." He said, "Why not?" Then I told him that I did not think we would spend more than 250 million dollars in January and this seemed to surprise him greatly and he said, "At that rate Hopkins will have enough to go until July 1st, although he has been telling me that he could not last after 1st of May." (A month ago Hopkins said he could not go until the 1st of April.) The President said, "I would have gotten around to the 4 billion 8 long ago but I have been waiting for Bell to come back.‡ I made inquiries and found that Bell would not be back for a week." We both agreed that it was not necessary to

---

* The heads, respectively, of the Reconstruction Finance Corporation, Home Owners' Loan Corporation, Public Works Administration, Farm Credit Administration, and Federal Housing Administration.
† Then head of the Agricultural Adjustment Administration.
‡ From a brief vacation.

wait for Bell. The President then said, "Well whom should we have to that meeting" and I said, "Ickes and Hopkins" to which the President replied, "Hopkins is away but that does not make any difference we can have Williams* in his place . . . and," he added, "yourself." Again I was almost speechless, at the way he let me write the whole ticket.

I then said, "I have one more suggestion to make. I think you ought to get a national figure who is a good friend of yours in whom you have confidence and who believes in you and make him Director of the Budget so that the public will know that you are really interested in trying to economize." He agreed to that. We discussed various names but could not really arrive at any conclusion. I was very much amused at Miss LeHand seriously suggesting Bill Bullitt and the President said, quite curtly, "No, no, he is all wrapped up in international diplomacy and knows nothing about this" to which Miss LeHand answered, "But he would like to." . . .

If the President will really go through with this program and begin to talk and *practice* economy it may be the turning point in his whole hold on the people because there is no question that many many people are really worried about this spending program because they can see no end to it.

Roosevelt struck vigorously for economy at a February 4 meeting of the Interdepartmental Loan Committee. Jesse Jones, he said, could reduce his authorizations for borrowing and his administrative expenses, slow up grants of loans, and accelerate demands for payment. If he could tell Congress that the Reconstruction Finance Corporation no longer needed a $100 million authorization, Congress could repeal the authorization, and thus remove a potential obligation on the Treasury. Jones argued that reducing his administrative costs would not aid the Treasury, since these expenditures came out of RFC profits. Morgenthau said that fifteen agencies had economized under the supervision of the Bureau of the Budget, and he wanted the RFC to follow suit. Roosevelt added that a reduction in administrative expenses would also have a good psychological effect.

Still resisting, Jones said he was refusing applications for loans every day, and that he could not call in his loans to banks with-

* Aubrey Williams, Hopkins's Deputy Administrator.

out weakening their capital structures. Morgenthau replied that RFC estimates of receipts and expenditures were further out of line than those of any other agency. The RFC did not spend up to its estimates, Jones snapped, because of his efficiency in holding expenses down. He was not hurting the Treasury since the Treasury discounted his estimates anyhow. It hurt the Secretary of the Treasury's heart once a month — gave him high blood pressure, Roosevelt interjected.

As discussion proceeded, the group agreed that the Home Owners' Loan Corporation could not cut back its authorizations, and the Agricultural Adjustment Administration could not determine what it might save. Henry Wallace was unwilling to surrender funds for conservation and reclamation, and uncertain about how much he could recover from authorizations for cotton loans. Ickes, too, battled to keep his money.

The meeting had settled nothing, but Roosevelt, moving at his own pace, on February 18 slashed away. From the authorizations of RFC and its affiliates, he cut $660 million. The Farm Credit Administration lost $80 million of authorizations for crop loans. From the Federal Housing Administration and the Home Owners' Loan Corporation respectively, the President took $750 million and $805 million. Morgenthau was delighted.

Further, as he had promised Morgenthau he would, Roosevelt was reviewing the budgets of the spenders. Here the familiar difficulties remained — the rivalries of Hopkins and Ickes, the inadequate data on unemployment and on project costs, the unevenness, indeed the uncertainty, of economic recovery. Before the first session with the spenders on February 6, Roosevelt said to Morgenthau: "I must not talk too quickly or too much about saving, otherwise the impression will go out that I am afraid I am licked." Actually he was enormously confident. Morgenthau thought Hopkins would need $250 or $300 million more to carry through the end of June. "That is too big," Roosevelt said. "They will not need more than $200 million. The thing is working out just the way I thought it would and . . . on July 1 we will have left $1 billion out of the $4 billion 8."

That afternoon Roosevelt opened the conference with the

spending agencies by emphasizing the need for additional funds for the WPA. The problem, he said, was to keep the existing number of people on the work relief payroll until July 1, 1936, without asking Congress for additional funds. He had told Hopkins to reduce WPA rolls as fast as possible, transferring employees to public works projects under the supervision of other agencies or to private industry as re-employment progressed. He thought Hopkins could cut back as spring weather approached. He would permit the various agencies to continue their authorized programs until about April 1, when he could more accurately estimate WPA needs for the period through June 30. He would then transfer to WPA authorizations which the other agencies did not absolutely require for fiscal 1936. After the 1937 appropriation was available, he would return to each agency whatever he had taken away.

Roosevelt also talked economy to congressmen. It was essential to have a decreasing deficit, he said, for if the deficit rose in fiscal 1937, the Treasury would be unable to market government bonds. Morgenthau, who had been taking this line for many months, noted to his Diary: "I wanted to go over in the corner and hide my face and grin but instead of that I sat back as though it was an entirely new idea to me . . . and . . . said, you are perfectly right, Mr. President. . . . If he will only keep on talking and thinking along the same lines my troubles are over."

Hopkins was cooperative. "The record," he told Morgenthau in March, "is always that the money is going to relief, but in reality we got only about half of the $4 billion 8 for relief. . . . I have never told anybody that I can't do this or that because we do not have the money; we have always met the thing head on, but the other fellows just keep ducking. I am getting darned sick and tired of this. The people we are handling are the people who don't eat unless we give them relief. We want to see one bill for W.P.A. and not let anybody ride on the coat tails of this bill."

On March 6, Morgenthau and Hopkins, supporting each other, took their case to the President, who quickly accepted their view that the 1937 relief bill should ask for money exclusively for WPA. He was less willing to accept Morgenthau's estimate, which Hopkins confirmed, that they could get by for about $2 billion. "Oh Henry," Roosevelt said, "you are going to take bread away from starving people."

"Oh I am not," Morgenthau replied. "You can't say that to me when up to date Hopkins, for relief purposes, has gotten less than half the money out of $4 billion 8."

The President seemed to be persuaded, but just as Morgenthau was ready to say three cheers, Roosevelt returned to an idea he had proposed the previous week. He would ask Congress for only $1.5 billion. That would be enough, he would say, if industry put another million men to work, but if industry did not respond, he would need to ask for more later. The scheme distressed Morgenthau. "Mr. President," he said, "you will not fool anybody with this trick because you are not saying when you come back to Congress what the amount of money will be that you are going to ask for."

Quick as a flash, Roosevelt replied: "Oh no I am not going to tie my hands and that would be spoiling my whole plea."

"Mr. President," Morgenthau continued, "you know perfectly well that industry is not going to put any such amount of people back to work and you are not fooling anybody and the only people who are going to suffer are the unemployed who will not know where they are at. Why don't you tell Congress that you want $1 billion 960 million and that if industry puts people back to work that we will use that much less money."

"No no that will not do at all," Roosevelt said, "that spoils my whole plea."

"Why not ask for enough money to last you until February 1," the Secretary suggested.

"No," Roosevelt said, "that will not do."

Morgenthau persisted until the President gave in. In his message to Congress on March 18, 1936, he used the formula the Secretary had recommended. From previous appropriations he could carry over $1 billion; the regular budget allowed $600 million for the Civilian Conservation Corps; besides this money, Roosevelt said he would need $2 billion for relief. But he asked

Congress only for an initial $1.5 billion of the new money, all for
the WPA. This, he explained, would be adequate if private business absorbed an increasing number of workers.

Roosevelt knew Morgenthau was satisfied. "Wait until next
year, Henry," he said one day in April. "I'm going to be really
radical."

"What do you mean?"

"I am going to recommend a lot of radical legislation," the
President said, giving Morgenthau a sort of quizzical look.

"You are going to be very careful about money spending."

"Yes, I am," Roosevelt answered.

"Well then," Morgenthau said, "I do not care how radical you
are on other matters."

But soon Hopkins again alarmed the Secretary. Desperate for
money, Hopkins proposed paying workers after July 1 for what
they did in June. He could then draw upon the appropriations
for fiscal 1937. Morgenthau begged Roosevelt not to permit this
juggling. If Hopkins had his way, he predicted, everyone would
say "not only will the billion and a half not last, but they have
nicked it already. . . . It is all a fake." Morgenthau proposed
an alternative. "I have sent a lawyer over to Tugwell," he said,
"to check up and see if all of the $48 million which he has to
spend on the purchase of land has been obligated and, if not, they
should cancel the unobligated balance." The President approved. Early in May he also, at Morgenthau's urging, turned
over to WPA five per cent of all unobligated funds, about $30
million, enough to last through June. "I want you to give me
your word of honor," the Secretary said to Hopkins ,"if we do
this, you will not come back to me and say, you must give me
part of the $1 billion 500 million." Hopkins promised. But those
who mistrusted the Administration, even if they had known
about that promise, would have put little stock in it.

As the presidential campaign got under way, the Republicans
increased the tempo of their attack on New Deal spending. Unbalanced budgets, they maintained, forbode disaster which only
the return to power of the Grand Old Party could prevent. The
assault bothered Morgenthau, for he saw how persuasive was the
Republican case to bankers and other men of means whose busi-

nesses brought them regularly into contact with the Treasury. But he hoped completely to deflate the opposition by stealing its argument. On July 9 he took his morning text from an unlikely contributor to the *Saturday Evening Post*, Gertrude Stein: ". . . Who is to stop Congress from spending too much. . . . Who is to stop them?" The answer, of course, was Roosevelt, whom Morgenthau advised to make some decision that would dramatically "demonstrate to the country once and for all whether or not you really intend to curtail expenditures."

Roosevelt did not. The severe drought that had settled on the West imposed upon the federal government increasing costs for agricultural relief, seed loans, resettlement, and reclamation. These obligations made retrenchment impossible and delayed unification of relief spending, which the President in any case resisted. Furthermore, his sure political instinct told him that the Republican cult of economy was making no impact. Let the Republicans do the talking, he suggested to Morgenthau, instructing him to cancel a proposed speech on the budget.

Roosevelt of course intended to do some talking himself. As he had in 1932, so in 1936 he planned to deliver a speech in Pittsburgh on balancing the budget. It was an objective in which he still believed, and though he did not want to tie his hands, he hoped to contrive a formula for a persuasive address. Morgenthau first heard the speech on the evening of September 30 at the White House, where he found Corcoran and Rosenman at work with the President. On October 1 he registered his impressions in his Diary:

> The President began to read draft 3 of his Pittsburgh speech. When he got through I told him I thought it was a terrible speech and I wished he wouldn't give it. He said, "I have to give it." He had no other speech and had to finish this in an hour and a half. . . . I went up to see the President, while he was in his bedroom entirely alone, and told him that I couldn't release the speech, that the President of the United States just could not make any financial mistakes and if he would trust me I would promise to get it to him sometime this morning. . . . He smiled and said that was okay. . . .
>
> During the discussion earlier in the evening I pointed out to the President that he made the statement that "we will balance the

budget sooner than we expect" and that if he made that statement he simply would make himself the laughing stock of America. I told him that Bell and I feel that if he would be tough that he could balance the budget in '38 and still allow a billion dollars for relief. He said, "All right" and I said, "Now wait a minute" and I called on Miss LeHand to listen carefully to what I said. I said, "This decision has to be yours and nobody else's." He said, "Well I can say the Secretary of the Treasury says the budget can be balanced in '38" and I said, "*You* have to say it because nobody can balance it but *you* and both Bell and I feel it can be done."

In the draft that came to us as draft 4 the President said, "The Treasury advises me that the budget can be balanced" and we crossed that out and wrote a very powerful statement for him to speak. . . .

I made it clear to Tommy Corcoran that neither Bell nor I could plead with the President to make the statement "that the budget could be balanced in '38," that the President would have to make that statement himself.

The "very powerful statement" which Morgenthau proposed committed Roosevelt to leaving "no stone unturned to balance the federal budget for the fiscal year of 1938." Bell drafted a milder alternative. He also suggested that the President, if he wanted to provide himself with a hedge, might simply say that he expected to balance the budget within a year or two.

Roosevelt settled for the hedge in his public address of October 12. "The big fellows in New York will like this," Morgenthau predicted. "This is what they have been waiting for." The Secretary, however, aware of the President's measured selection of words, discounted their significance. Bemused rather than disappointed, he joked about the speech with his staff. At their instigation he dictated a message to a Republican friend. "Taking it for granted that your sense of humor is as good as it used to be, I am writing you the following personal letter. Now that Landon has come out for balancing the budget within four years and President Roosevelt has said . . . that he will balance the budget in a year or two . . . how do you feel?"

Temporarily Morgenthau relaxed. Politically "things" were "so lovely," and the last fortnight of a national campaign was an impossible time for serious discussion of fiscal matters.

6. Compassion in Practice, Prudence in Theory

"For all his ability and selflessness," Morgenthau recalled, "Hopkins did have an undeniable appetite for practical politics. He loved maneuvering, and he loved being in the know when great plans were under way. Moreover, he had supreme confidence in his own capacity for improvisation and would often embark cheerfully on huge programs without a full conception of the expense and of the difficulties involved. Harry and I got along well basically . . . though we had occasional sharp differences . . . when he confused need with politics."

That confusion, Morgenthau concluded, had moved Hopkins to hold relief expenditures above the level of his assets during the campaign of 1936. Immediately after the election Hopkins had therefore to devise means of stretching the balance of his depleted funds. He proposed to drop from his rolls in mid-December some 250,000 dirt farmers of whom about half would need direct relief, to drop also about 150,000 urban families and 25,000 administrators and supervisors. As of January 1, 1937, he intended to make localities pay for materials, thus cutting his average monthly costs per man from $65 to $50. Those policies, he calculated, would permit a saving of $25 million a month.

There was no need for Hopkins to explain the implications of his plans to Morgenthau, for the Secretary saw at once that he was caught again in a "squeeze play." As he put it, Hopkins and his staff "would wait until the last minute before letting Bell and me know they were overspending. Then they would appeal to our emotions by reminding us of the plight of the jobless." Trapped by Hopkins's preelection largess, Morgenthau had to find the money to sustain the unemployed through the winter of 1937.

"We might as well be realistic about this thing," the Secretary said. "In the first place, from the standpoint of human needs, this is not the time to make the dramatic reductions proposed; I would much rather start with a consideration for human beings. . . . I will say right now that if you try to go through with this program of rapidly reducing the number of people on your rolls, you are going to have cracked heads and state militias used. I do not think you should do it. . . . I will sweat blood for you to take care of the months of January, February and March; but you have got to help in reducing costs beginning the first of next July."

"There is something much more important to consider than you or me," Morgenthau argued at a meeting on relief on December 8, 1936. "The people will blame the President. What I am trying to think of is the President's interest and the country's interest. . . . I would rather see you refuse to replace the normal turnover . . . than to see drastic cuts made at this time of the year."

The only thing the President could not defend, Hopkins replied, would be the abandonment of people who needed relief, and WPA was not going to do that. But he admitted the problem was tough.

"If you can find 150,000 people now on relief rolls who you say now are not in need of relief," Morgenthau said, "how are you going to answer the charge that you must have known before November that these people were not in need of relief? How can you explain in the month of December, two weeks before Christmas, that you can find 150,000 on the relief rolls not in need of relief, when you could not discover this excess in your rolls a month earlier?"

Hopkins, visibly annoyed, argued that the President did not have "to take the heat" until he got back from a visit to South America. The time to cut the rolls was while he was away. "The place the budget is unbalanced is in my shop," Hopkins said. "There's going to be some headaches in the cutting, no matter when the cutting is done. If we cave in every move we make, we are never going to get anything done."

"It is rather unusual," Morgenthau broke in, "that I should be here as Secretary of the Treasury pleading with you to spend

money. What I do not want to see in this country is violence
and broken heads."

"You cannot assume that I am going to do that after three and
one-half years' experience," Hopkins snapped. After further argument he agreed to explain the situation to the press. "There
are two things I do not want to say," he concluded. "The first is
that there is no money; I have never said that; I do not want to
say it now. And second, that this is being done on the President's
orders; I never tell anybody that."

The Secretary had still to find the money. As always, Ickes
and Tugwell resisted any diversion of their funds — "fudging on
their figures," Hopkins and Bell believed. After revising Bureau
of the Budget estimates, however, Bell on December 29 reported
exuberantly that the pace of recovery had resulted in unexpectedly large tax yields, regular departmental expenses were below
previous predictions, and the deficit for fiscal 1937 would therefore be smaller than that for 1936, even if Congress made an additional appropriation for WPA.

The timing of the revised estimates was especially significant,
for on the previous day Morgenthau had discovered that the case
for a balanced budget was under serious attack. At the White
House on December 28 he found Roosevelt enervated by a bad
cold, "fuzzy," out of sorts. Bell's draft of a budget message was
terrible, the President said. He seemed to prefer a long memorandum he had received from Marriner Eccles, parts of which he
read aloud. "I feel too low and my mind is not functioning to
try to concentrate on the budget," Roosevelt complained. Toss-
ing the memo to Morgenthau, he told him to take it and Bell's
draft and "do something" with them.

Marriner Eccles, Chairman of the Federal Reserve Board, had
been one of the first and was then one of the most influential
Americans who advocated a deliberately unbalanced budget as
the key instrument for recovery. A Utah Mormon, banker, and
businessman, confident, self-assertive, ambitious, and energetic,
Eccles first came to Washington as a special assistant to Morgenthau on housing. Quickly conscious of Eccles's large talents,
Morgenthau was one of those who recommended him to Roose-

velt for the Federal Reserve appointment. He helped Eccles win
a long struggle for confirmation from the Senate, where Carter
Glass and other conservatives opposed him. Not without fric-
tion, he and Eccles worked together to see the Banking Act of
1935 through Congress. Endowed with enlarged powers by this
Act, resistant to the Treasury's increasing involvement in international and domestic monetary policy, Eccles clashed with
Morgenthau over questions pertaining to the management of the
national debt, interest rates on federal securities, and the disposition of inflowing gold. Most profoundly, Morgenthau and
Eccles differed about the budget.

Eccles's December memorandum on the budget advanced, in
his own words and in his own spirit, the ideas which had been
given their classic statement by John Maynard Keynes. An attempt to balance the budget, Eccles argued, would put the country into an economic tailspin. The popular analogy between the
debt of an individual and the debt of a nation was utterly false.
The crucial consideration was not the size of the deficit but the
level of national income. It would be unsafe to slash federal expenditures until the expansion of private enterprise took up the
whole slack of employment. Meanwhile deficit expenditures
were a necessary, compensatory form of investment which gave
life to an economy operating below capacity. Ultimately they
would lead to restored business activity and increased national
income. An attempt to balance the budget for the fiscal year
1938, Eccles maintained, would be dangerously premature,
would lead to a new wave of deflation and reverse the processes
of recovery thus far set in motion. This would spell doom for
the Democratic party, perhaps even pave the way for totalitarianism.

Morgenthau disagreed completely with the whole drift of
Eccles's thinking. Constant or increasing deficits, he believed,
would impair the government's credit, force Congress to start
the printing presses, precipitate runaway inflation and national
disaster. Progress toward a balanced budget, on the other hand,
would protect the value of government securities, win the confidence of private enterprise, and result in an upturn of private

investment that would sustain a new prosperity. So Morgenthau had thought on taking office; so he believed in 1936; so, indeed, he believed throughout his life. He would not stint in caring for the needy unemployed, but he would not relax his purpose of balancing the national budget precisely as he balanced the budget for his farm.

For Morgenthau, therefore, Eccles's memorandum was a tremendous challenge. If he failed to "dynamite" Eccles's point of view, he wrote, he would "find that Eccles will become the President's fiscal adviser." Bell was no less astounded and dismayed. The revised estimates of the Bureau of the Budget seemed to him and to the Secretary to constitute an overwhelming rejoinder to Eccles. The new figures, they agreed, demonstrated that recovery was well along, that the annual deficit was shrinking, that a balanced budget was in sight. "Golly," Morgenthau said on December 29, 1936, "I think we all got every reason to face the new year with the greatest of complacence and comfort."

On December 30 Morgenthau and Bell took their case to Roosevelt. Surprised by the improved figures, the President teased Bell, who, he said, had been holding out on him.

Without argument, he subscribed to the long-range fiscal program the Treasury advocated. Assuming a constant rate of recovery, it predicted a budget for fiscal 1938 in balance except for the cost of servicing the debt, a budget for fiscal 1939 in balance in all respects.

During the winter and early spring of 1937 Roosevelt, pleased and relieved by the prospect of decreasing deficits, stuck hard to economy, though retrenchment remained difficult. In March the governors of six industrial states protested against Hopkins's schedule for removing 600,000 people from relief rolls by the end of June. They accused the President, Morgenthau reported to his staff, "of saying for the last few years that he would take care of every hungry man. . . . He would have to live up to it. . . . Whereupon the President said, we will have another meeting and Hopkins and the Secretary of the Treasury will look it over and see what appropriations and what money we have and recommend what money we can transfer from other agencies to Hopkins. . . . Then the Governors had us for one hour afterwards and they were pretty ugly and tried to get Hopkins to say that . . . he would not lay off any more people. Hopkins said, the only person who can say that is the President."

Raiding "some of Mr. Roosevelt's pet projects," Morgenthau and Bell transferred $250 million to WPA, enough, Hopkins promised, to see him through May. Roosevelt did not object. As Hopkins remarked, he was "getting tough" about money. When the governors returned in April to fight against proposed reductions in WPA for fiscal 1938, the President was equivocal. He would stretch federal funds as far as possible, he said, but he would not make any promises about appropriations. Bad news from the Bureau of the Budget seemed only to stiffen him. For the period January 1 through March 30, 1937, revenues were off. Roosevelt responded with an Executive Order of April 7:

> It is my desire that the heads of the executive departments and independent establishments . . . will immediately . . . survey . . . expenditure requirements . . . for the remaining months of the fiscal year 1937. It is apparent at this time that the revenues of the Government . . . will be materially less than the amount estimated in my budget of last January; and, hence, the deficit will be far greater than was anticipated unless there is an immediate curtailment of expenditures.
>
> You will carefully examine the status of appropriations for your activities with a view to making a substantial saving by eliminating or deferring all expenditures which are not absolutely necessary. . . . You will report to me through the Acting Director of the Budget not later than May 1, 1937.

Morgenthau rejoiced. "I wish you'd hear the President talk about balancing the budget to Eccles," he told his morning group on April 5. "God, if he'd only say publicly what he told him, it would be marvelous." It was perhaps sufficiently marvelous that the next day Eccles, calling at the Treasury, completely reversed his earlier position. He intended to impress Roosevelt with the urgency of balancing the budget for 1938, he said, and he hoped Morgenthau would join him. With some amusement Morgenthau replied that beyond a certain point one could not press the President.

Beyond a certain point, as Morgenthau also knew, one could not hold Roosevelt too closely to any course. Time would show how frugality weighed against congressional politics, how a decline in public spending would affect the general level of economic activity, how fiscal conservatism weighed against social deprivation which the President and Secretary alike bemoaned.

Still, Morgenthau indulged himself in some sense of triumph. Without shortchanging the unemployed, without arresting reform, the Administration had excellent prospects for balancing the budget for fiscal 1938 except for the cost of servicing the debt. Prudence had won over spending, perhaps largely because recovery seemed so real, and best of all, from Morgenthau's point of view, Roosevelt appeared to be dedicated at last to unflinching economy. "The President," the Secretary said after the budget message for 1938 had been drafted, "gave me . . . everything that I asked for and I told him that I was entirely satisfied. It was a long hard trying fight but certainly at some time during the weeks that I argued with him he must have come to the conclusion that if he wants his Administration to go forward with his reform program he must have a sound financial foundation." The summer of 1937 was the sunniest season Morgenthau had known in many years.

VI

TAXATION

1934—1937

1. Revenue and the Redistribution of Wealth

THE PROBLEMS of depression, the cost of relief, and the inequities in American society gave taxation special importance as an instrument of public policy during the 1930's. Tax schedules affected more than the government's income. They had significance, too, for national recovery and for social reform. "The primary interest of the Treasury . . . relates to . . . revenue," Morgenthau said early in his term. As long as he was Secretary, that interest was to predominate. As he also observed, however, "taxation in any form has many collateral effects . . . and . . . there is a national duty to avoid tax laws which produce undesirable social consequences and a like duty to correct evils produced by existing tax legislation."

Every tax program had to compromise among its several aims, and as changing conditions warranted a changing emphasis, Morgenthau concentrated now upon one, now upon another aspect of the tax problem. During his first months in office, while other issues absorbed him, he nevertheless set forth the principles that guided his policies. The New Deal, he told the House Ways and Means Committee late in 1933, had an overwhelming mandate to improve the position of the underdog. Wealthy individuals were in far the best position to bear additional burdens, and increases in their income and estate taxes would have the desirable effect of reducing huge disparities in economic power. Before the Senate Judiciary Committee in 1934, he recommended closing the loopholes through which rich men and corporations avoided taxes, he emphasized the need for a constitutional amendment permitting taxation of the income from federal and local securities, which were tax exempt, and he appealed for additional funds for enforcement. He could say nothing more specific, for he was under instructions from Roosevelt to leave the choice of new taxes to the Congress, and to comment only on the estimates of receipts from alternative schedules. The Revenue Act of 1934 raised slightly income, estate and gift taxes in the higher brackets, but it was at best only a beginning.

Indeed, the Treasury did not fully develop its own policies until December 1934, when Morgenthau took his proposals to the White House. The first called for a graduated inheritance tax to supplement the existing estate tax.* Such a tax would bring the proportion of revenue the United States collected from estates closer to that collected by the British government. Because inheritance taxes could be in large part avoided through gifts made before death, the Treasury further suggested either raising gift taxes or taxing gifts as ordinary income.

These recommendations envisaged some redistribution of national wealth, a prospect that men of means naturally found radical. Their attitude in no way deterred Morgenthau, for, as he saw it, gross economic inequities were dangerous not only in themselves but also because they seemed to justify the demands of men like Huey Long for frankly confiscatory programs. Long promised to make every man a king on $2500 a year. The aged Dr. Francis E. Townsend won thousands of followers, especially in the Far West, by proposing $200 a month for all over sixty years old. Compared to such panaceas, the Treasury's recommendations were mild.

The second item in the Treasury's program was an intercorporate dividend tax designed to break up holding companies.

---

* An estate tax falls upon the total estate a man bequeaths; an inheritance tax upon the individual shares of his heirs.

Herman Oliphant had pressed this scheme upon the Secretary as a means of preventing a recurrence of the skulduggery which had so marked the 1920's. Adventurers owning only a minority of a corporation's stock had been able through holding company devices to control a corporation, waste its assets and manipulate its securities for their own gain. Morgenthau saw in taxation the leverage to make holding companies reorder their affairs. As things stood, only the corporation first earning income paid a tax on it. The Treasury now proposed that each corporation receiving dividends from that income should also pay taxes. This would make holding companies with several tiers of subsidiaries unduly expensive. The Treasury also recommended revising the corporate income tax so as to make business mergers unattractive. For the long run, Morgenthau suggested scaling the tax on corporations according to their size.

A third major item in the Secretary's report to Roosevelt was a tax on undistributed corporate earnings. He asked, too, for the taxation of future issues of federal and local government bonds, and for a reduction in tax exemptions for mineral depletions.

Not until June 1935 did Roosevelt, by then impatient with the "economic royalists," decide on his own tax program. He singled out as essential four items: the tax on corporations, graduated to check the growth of monopoly; the intercorporate dividend tax; higher surtaxes on individual incomes; and the inheritance tax. The message he sent to Congress on June 19, 1935, was part of a developing Administration attack on economic bigness, which the President now looked upon as a remediable evil. Wealth in the modern world, he said, resulted from a combination of individual efforts. In spite of the "great importance in our national life of the . . . ingenuity of unusual individuals, the people in the mass have inevitably helped to make large fortunes possible." The transmission of these fortunes from generation to generation, was not consistent with American ideals. Accumulations of wealth, moreover, perpetrated "great and undesirable concentration of control in a relatively few individuals over the employment and welfare of many, many others." He therefore recommended an inheritance tax, and in order to make "vast concentrations of capital . . . carry burdens commensurate with their . . . advantages," he also proposed a graduated tax on corporate income.

This unequivocal endorsement of tax reform pleased liberals in both parties, but it was not at all clear, as Morgenthau quickly discovered, whether Roosevelt wanted Congress to act at that session or whether he would fight for more than a nominal inheritance tax. The President's intentions were obscured in his puzzling relationship with the cautious Chairman of the Senate Finance Committee, Pat Harrison of Mississippi. Harrison, a masterful parliamentarian who used his considerable power gently but effectively in the cause of fiscal conservatism, opposed the inheritance tax. Roosevelt told him, Morgenthau learned, that that tax should exempt approximately $300,000, which the Secretary considered far too much. Worse still, Morgenthau found it hard to understand the President's shifting tactics.

They changed rapidly during the week after his message. At first Roosevelt stood against having the Senate attach major taxes to the House's resolution extending nuisance taxes — excises on a variety of consumer goods. Harrison, too, apparently with the consent of the White House, spoke out for leaving major reforms to the House, where revenue legislation was supposed to originate. He also advocated postponing the inheritance tax to the following session of Congress. But twenty-two progressive senators agreed to keep Congress in session until it adopted the President's program. Responding to that pressure, Roosevelt and the Democratic congressional leaders announced after a conference of June 25 that they would drive for immediate action. The next day Harrison said the Senate would take the initiative. Yet a day later, the Senate returned to the original schedule, leaving the initiative with the House; Roosevelt told the press he had never intimated that Congress should push through such an important measure; and Harrison, though he was obviously surprised, remained unruffled at this sudden reversal.

These developments gave Morgenthau no indication of just what Roosevelt expected from him. Perhaps the President was not sure himself. He was involved in so many things — among others, antitrust and banking bills, social security, and a bill to regulate the bituminous coal industry — that he had inadequate time for studying revenue legislation. Without pressing him, Morgenthau tried to get his signals straight. He did not know, he told Roosevelt at luncheon on June 26, 1935, how to reply to a request for the Treasury's working papers on the inheritance tax. Roosevelt told him to stall.

"Mr. President," Morgenthau asked, "just strictly between the two of us, do you or do you not want your Inheritance Tax program passed at this session?"

"Strictly between the two of us," Roosevelt said, "I do not know, I am on an hourly basis and the situation changes almost momentarily."

On July 8, Morgenthau testified before the House Ways and Means Committee. Roosevelt had told him he would not resist a movement for adjournment before a revenue act was passed, but he had also said he wanted the Treasury to stress taxing inheritances as if they were annual personal income, a method he had earlier asked Morgenthau to "soft-pedal." This change of heart encouraged the Secretary, who in his testimony emphasized the importance of the revenue that a high inheritance tax would yield. The Ways and Means Committee included the inheritance tax in its bill, but the Senate, increasingly resistant, shared the skepticism of the conservative press about Morgenthau's references to revenue. Roosevelt's hesitation made the Treasury's situation difficult, as did his rejection of one of Harrison's candidates for the Board of Tax Appeals. The senator now favored increasing the rates of the estate tax, which, he argued, would be easier to administer.

Harrison prevailed. The Revenue Act of 1935, which the Senate Finance Committee drafted, was nevertheless a landmark in the history of American taxation. Though the committee in the end rejected the inheritance tax, it increased estate taxes markedly and raised individual surtax rates on incomes from 59 per cent at the top to 75 per cent. As the Treasury and the President had recommended, it imposed both a graduated corporate income tax and a tax on intercorporate dividends. The Act assured the Treasury of new revenue, though less than Morgenthau had wanted. To his gratification, in spite of its limitations, the Act advanced the principles he and Roosevelt had advocated.

The Treasury could measure its success by the dismay of most wealthy Americans. Roy Howard, for one, originally a supporter of Roosevelt, now wrote that businessmen were "frightened," convinced that the new law "aimed at revenge rather than revenue." That interpretation characterized the hostile thinking of those in high income brackets, whose opposition to the New Deal grew as the Treasury pressed for the adoption of significant parts of its program which the Revenue Act of 1935 omitted.

Politicians have a natural reluctance to levy new taxes in an election year. Roosevelt was no exception. Generally satisfied with existing schedules, he was also anxious to avoid another fight with Democrats on the Hill. In September 1935 and again in his annual message of January 1936, the President announced that he would request no new taxes. Three days later, however, on January 6, the Supreme Court ruled the Agricultural Adjustment Act unconstitutional, invalidated the processing tax and thereby deprived the government of $500 million of annual revenue. When, in the weeks that followed, Congress overrode the President's veto of the bonus, obligating the government to the expenditure of an additional $2 billion, neither the White House nor the Treasury was willing to tolerate the impending deficit. Election or no election, Roosevelt, like Morgenthau, considered new revenues essential.

Between January and March, Morgenthau and his assistants, often cooperating with representatives of other federal agencies, worked continually on a tax message for the President. At first Roosevelt, who doubted whether Congress would increase income taxes, advocated a general processing tax. Morgenthau objected on several grounds. Manufacturers would pass on a processing tax by increasing prices, which would create hardships for those with low incomes. Indeed, federal and local consumption taxes already constituted too large a part of the total tax structure. Morgenthau was also worried because the Department of

Justice believed the Supreme Court would probably find any new processing tax unconstitutional. Especially on that account, he preferred to increase taxes on personal incomes, estates and inheritances, particularly in the higher brackets.

But the Treasury had to be political, to formulate a program that could win the enthusiasm of the President and the Congress. In this pass, Morgenthau, urged on by Oliphant, reverted to a proposal he had made in December 1934 for a tax on undistributed corporate earnings. Under the existing laws, directors of corporations who did not need larger personal incomes could leave their company's earnings in the corporation as surplus profits and thus save much of their personal income tax, especially surtaxes on high levels of income. In such cases small stockholders did not receive dividends on the full earnings of the securities they owned. A tax on a company's undistributed profits would increase the disposable income of small stockholders and penalize tax avoidance by the wealthy.

Morgenthau viewed the undistributed earnings tax primarily as a device to increase revenue by combating tax avoidance. The Treasury estimated that about $4.5 billion in corporate profits would not be distributed in 1936. If that sum were subject to an undistributed profits tax, or paid out in dividends to be taxed as personal income, the government might gain as much as $1.3 billion. Oliphant, who was for several years the foremost proponent of the tax, was more concerned with its possible bearing on recovery. Like Rex Tugwell and Marriner Eccles, he believed that the distribution of profits in dividends would increase consumer spending, which would stimulate the economy. He also thought he could write the tax so as to protect corporations which were reinvesting undistributed earnings in plant and equipment.

As they studied the tax, Oliphant and Morgenthau developed a special interest in its possibilities as an antitrust instrument — a device to force large corporations, no longer able to retain their earnings for capital expansion, to compete for new funds in the money market with their smaller competitors. Under the existing system, large corporations, by retaining their surpluses, could block innovation by their own subsidiaries and withhold profits from stockowners who might otherwise have invested in more venturesome enterprises. Thus the accumulation of surpluses perpetuated business oligarchy and tended to inhibit the whole investment process on which recovery depended.

On February 19, 1936, Roosevelt approved the concept of an undistributed earnings tax, for which the Treasury was to draft an appropriate message to Congress. Influenced largely by Oliphant, the Department made a major change in its proposal. It planned to substitute for all corporate taxes one undistributed earnings tax adjusted closely to ability to pay. This would eliminate the "double taxation" of business profits, first as corporation income and then, after it was paid out in dividends, as individual income. At the same time the undistributed earnings tax would provide increased revenue by practically forcing the distribution of profits to stockholders, thereby subjecting wealthy individuals who received those earnings to high surtaxes. Years later Morgenthau remarked: "I wonder what corporations today would give for such a system!"

The Treasury's completed draft provided the basis for the message Roosevelt delivered to Congress on March 3. Far more than Morgenthau had expected, the message excited an immediate opposition which mobilized powerful forces on the Hill. For weeks to come, the legislative struggle burdened the Secretary and his staff. As it began, Morgenthau was already under extraordinary strain. He was conducting important monetary negotiations with China, France, and England. The last stages of the bonus debate had depleted his emotional energy. In his fatigued state, he contracted a respiratory infection so severe that he had to take several weeks off. He and his wife were in Sea Island, Georgia, during much of the time in which the House of Representatives debated the tax bill, but in spite of his absence, which some journalists misinterpreted to mean a lack of sympathy with the President's proposals, the Secretary followed the course of the measure with a solicitous interest.

Oliphant carried the weight of the Treasury's case before the House Ways and Means Committee, played the pedagogue "rather brilliantly," according to reports Morgenthau received, and "did a splendid job, using just the right technique in almost every instance." The committee's bill incorporated the undistributed earnings tax, the Treasury's major objective, though it also retained in reduced form some other corporation taxes which the Department had suggested eliminating. Chairman Robert L. ("Muley") Doughton, who was convinced less by Oliphant's arguments than by his own deference to Administration policy, guided the bill through the House in just over a month.

In that period, opposition to the undistributed profits tax gained momentum. David Lawrence, one of many critical columnists, called it a tax on prudence; Arthur Krock considered it "reckless" and "bewildering"; Raymond Moley, now frankly aligned with the enemies of the New Deal, attacked the whole concept of "reform through taxation" which, he said, would strip industry of all surpluses, throw businessmen into "paroxysms of fright" and force the guiltless rich "into rags and tatters." The Republican minority of the House Ways and Means Committee agreed, asserted that the revenue bill had Communist approval, that it would lead to instability, regimentation, further waste of public money, and continuing depressions.

On May 7, 1936, only a few hours after the Senate Finance Committee concluded its hearings, Pat Harrison told Morgenthau categorically that approval of the House bill was out of the question. Harrison favored retaining the tax on corporate income and superimposing a small, flat tax on undistributed earnings. That solution, the senator maintained, would assure the collection of a substantial amount of revenue without violating the principles of Roosevelt's message. With only one exception, the committee and its staff were of the same view.

Morgenthau found other conservative Democrats wholly of Harrison's opinion. As he put it to his staff on May 11, he had done a lot of thinking over the weekend, and had practically concluded that the Treasury was "up against a stone wall" and needed some "alternative bill in our vest pocket." "I have come to the decision," he said, "that I cannot take the risk of giving up something that I have in hand, namely: $1,132,000,000 in revenue, for a possibility of getting roughly $1,700,000,000. It seems to me that there are too many dangers surrounding the possibilities. . . .

"I do not believe there is a living person who can guarantee that the Supreme Court will not tie up the tax bill immediately after it passes and we will be short all of our revenue. The thing is too great a risk for me to take. . . .

"You can ask me why I did not do all this two months ago. My answer is that I was sick away from the office for two months. I should have had this bright idea two months ago, but I did not. I have it now. I would rather be sorry now than be desperate a year from now."

That evening the Secretary met with Harrison, Doughton, and Roosevelt. The President, influenced by Marriner Eccles, seemed to favor amending the House bill. "As to what happened over at the White House," Morgenthau told his staff, "I had a swell glass of orange juice. . . . Doughton kept saying, 'You can't let us down. . . . We are sick and tired of giving in to the Senate.' The President said, 'We are not trying to let you down. I want a bill which will force distribution of surplus earnings and get me the revenue.' Pat was sort of vague and . . . so when he went out I said, 'What are you going to do . . . ?' and Pat answered, 'Evidently the President is not ironclad on what he wants, but we do know that he wants a bill which will carry out his principles . . . and we are getting that, but he has . . . not definitely told us just how to do so.' I don't think that is so bad."

Later that evening one Treasury expert, who thought the President's vagueness left the department "right out on a limb," threatened to resign rather than testify. When Morgenthau ordered him to join Oliphant before the Finance Committee, he consented, but almost wept. Oliphant was no happier. "When you were before the House Committee," the Secretary told him on May 12, "you assumed the responsibility. . . . You devoted yourself almost exclusively to this for two or three months. . . . It is up to you to go through with it."

Faced the next day with persisting hostility from the Senate, Morgenthau once and for all gave up "the idea that we will get the bill as it passed the House." As he put it on May 18, "We will have to reluctantly and gracefully recede." He would accept Harrison's general plan, but with important modifications. The senator, along with three other Democrats on the Finance Committee, now proposed raising the corporate income tax and adding a flat 7 per cent tax on undistributed profits. Roosevelt insisted on a graduated tax on undistributed profits, as did Morgenthau and Oliphant, who emphasized the importance of graduation for preventing tax dodging and for adjusting schedules to capacity to pay. All three, moreover, wanted, in so far as possible, to save the House's face.

On May 22 the President tentatively decided to take the issue to the people. He told Morgenthau to prepare a letter to Harrison "of not more than a page and a half or two pages" dwelling upon the importance of the principles which a graduated tax on undistributed earnings would advance. "Now, Henry," he said, "whatever you put in this letter it just can't be anything but right. . . . You just can't put anything in . . . unless you are sure."

The assignment was impossible. No short letter could be simple enough for the man on the street to understand, yet accurate enough to prevent experts from picking holes in it. Furthermore, Morgenthau feared that a public letter would infuriate Harrison and split the Democrats in the Senate, which would be embarrassing during an election year. He therefore on May 25 urged Roosevelt to forget the letter and talk with Harrison. The President instead gave Morgenthau that job, directing him to tell the senator that the Administration would conduct a fight on the floor unless the committee wrote a bill that forced the distribution of profits.

Morgenthau tried to see Harrison the next day, but the senator was ill. In any case Morgenthau thought the right man to consult was Majority Leader Joe Robinson, who was best qualified to "count noses" willing to support a minority report endorsing the Administration's program. Robinson, moreover, considered the Finance Committee's bill a mess and was anxious to work out an alternative that would satisfy the President and the House Ways and Means Committee.

Somewhat reluctantly, Roosevelt on May 26 conferred with Robinson and the Finance Committee Democrats. The next morning the President was pleased with himself. "I do not think you realize the significance of last night's meeting," he said to Morgenthau.

"I'm afraid that I do not because I was very tired last night," Morgenthau replied.

"Well I had my nerve with me," Roosevelt said. "I tackled the lion in his own den. I went up against the majority members of the Finance Committee knowing that the majority were against me. I told them a thing or two, didn't I?"

Morgenthau thought not. "I gave him no encouragement," he reported to his staff, "and did not sit there at his feet and say what a great guy he was because I did not feel that he had done a good job . . . and I will be very much surprised if the Senate Finance Committee gives in to his wishes. The fact that I did not sit there in glowing admiration . . . put him in a bad humor and . . . he let me have it."

The Secretary's assessment of the conference was accurate. Roosevelt had not sufficiently defined his position to give his friends in the Senate anything to go on. Alben Barkley was prepared to do what he could, and Robinson would like to have bound the Democrats to Marriner Eccles's tax plan, but in the absence of instructions, they lost command of the situation. The Administration faced the possibility of a major legislative defeat from the conservative wing of its own party.

Barkley, the Administration's unofficial negotiator during the meetings of the conference committee of the two houses on the revenue bill, needed all the help he could get. The Senate conferees would not condone the steeply progressive undistributed earnings rates which Oliphant still recommended. The House conferees, claiming that they had acted according to the President's specifications, refused to budge from their own bill. "Your damned old tax bill," Barkley told Morgenthau on June

16 after a week of futile negotiation, was in trouble. The Democratic Senate conferees were going to submit a proposal preserving existing revenues and adding a tax on undistributed profits graduated from 5 to 25 per cent. Their strategy was to keep the President out of it until the last minute, but Barkley felt that if they got nowhere that day, it would be important somehow to persuade the House to work something out.

After the committee meeting that morning, Doughton called Morgenthau. The House conferees were pretty obstinate, he said, and the Senate conferees would not accept the House bill or any bill that did not carry a straight corporation tax. Doughton then asked whether the Secretary believed in retaining the existing taxes. "I feel that at this stage that we can't just throw all that overboard," Morgenthau replied.

Clearly pleased, Doughton maintained that this had been his conviction all the time. As their conversation ended, Morgenthau turned to his staff and said confidently: "I have just settled the tax bill."

The dénouement was rapid. On June 17 the conference committee sent the Treasury four proposals for estimates. After examining the calculations, the committee reported out a bill that met the approval of both houses and struck Morgenthau as the best available solution. The Revenue Act of 1936 retained the corporate income tax, as the Senate conferees had demanded, thus insuring the revenue about which the Secretary would otherwise have worried. The measure added a modest graduated tax on undistributed profits, as the House conferees had insisted, thus in Morgenthau's opinion establishing the principle for which he and Oliphant had struggled so long. This and other new schedules, the Treasury estimated, would yield about $800 million of additional annual revenue.

The Act fell short of the ideal, but it included, Morgenthau believed, every concession the Treasury could wring from the Senate. It protected the budget. As he saw it, it took another step toward industrial democracy. It prevented one common form of tax dodging. The debate about the legislation, moreover, gave so much publicity to tax avoidance that the Treasury could confidently demand the closing of other loopholes. Particularly in an election year, these were large achievements.

Morgenthau remembered them as among the most difficult of his career. "The undistributed profits tax," he recalled twenty years later, "was sort of a revolution. The opposition from the conservative press and big business, and their influence in both parties on the Hill, made a terrific impact. Nobody in the Treasury wanted to testify. . . . I had to stand like a column of concrete but I had the backing of F.D.R. He wanted to wipe out special privilege. We both got real excitement and pleasure out of this thing, out of laying a cornerstone for a new America. It was the kind of thing that kept the United States from being another Rome."

2. *Closing the Loopholes*

Tax avoidance was an old problem that had assumed new dimensions. Probably no one ever enjoyed paying taxes, and very few deliberately paid more than they owed, but as Morgenthau put it in 1937, "tax ethics today are where business . . . ethics were in the 1890's." The Treasury could handle outright criminals, but it was more difficult to deal with rich men who hired clever counsel specifically for the purpose of working out techniques for remaining within the law while avoiding taxes, for exploiting loopholes in federal revenue statutes and inventing tax-saving devices which neither Congress nor the Treasury had foreseen. Even in the 1920's the tax structure had become so complex, tax questions so difficult, that adroit lawyers could often frustrate the intention of Congress. As taxes rose during the New Deal, wealthy taxpayers grew bolder in their maneuvering. One "economic royalist" bragged that he and his kind would continue to employ their art "as long as that bastard is in the White House." Their success decreased revenues and threatened to demoralize honest taxpayers who could not help but resent the ability of the wealthy to escape their obligations.

Andrew Mellon, who personally took advantage of the law's loopholes while he was Secretary of the Treasury, generously refunded or abated $3.5 billion to rich taxpayers and their corporations. Though rates during Mellon's time in office were low, he suggested that the prevalence of tax avoidance proved the need to reduce taxes. Morgenthau, in contrast, considered the higher rates of the 1930's eminently just, and the toleration of tax avoidance, a crime against society. "Do not come in here with a belligerent attitude as though you were righteous," he said to the attorney of one offender who had crossed the line of legality. "There isn't a day passes where they don't hire some political lawyer or some shyster who thinks he can get in the back door of the Treasury. And let me tell you, there is no back door! . . . Who do you think the United States Treasury is? The United States Treasury belongs to the people. . . . We are here to do our job fairly and honestly and see that the people are protected."

In that spirit Morgenthau spurred the prosecution of criminal charges of tax evasion which the government brought against Mellon in March 1934. The Treasury alleged that Mellon had submitted fraudulent returns and was deficient more than $3 million in taxes and penalties. Mellon denied the charges, asserting in return that he was the victim of political persecution.

To plead the government's case before a federal grand jury in Pittsburgh, Morgenthau recruited Robert Jackson, who reported that the Republican press was accusing him of ruthless tactics. "You can't be too tough in this trial to suit me," the Secretary said.

Jumping up, Jackson replied: "Thank God I have that kind of boss."

"Wait a minute," Morgenthau went on. "I consider that Mr. Mellon is not on trial but Democracy and the privileged rich and I want to see who will win."

In court Mellon won. The grand jury refused to indict him and the Board of Tax Appeals in 1937 ruled unanimously that he "did not file a false and fraudulent return with the purpose of evading taxes." The law, the Board observed, cloaked every man "with presumption of good faith in his business dealings." The Board also found errors in Mellon's return that made him deficient some $400,000 in taxes and interest. His attorneys and the Bureau of Internal Revenue, alike anxious to avoid further litigation, in 1938 settled out of court for slightly more than $480,000, a solution both sides interpreted as accepting the fairness of the Board's decision.

Mellon was exonerated, but as the Commissioner of Internal Revenue put it, "the facts elicited and precedents set in the Mellon case have been of great importance." Indeed, they constituted a kind of primer on the loopholes in the revenue laws. Mellon, while Secretary of the Treasury, had solicited from the Bureau of Internal Revenue "a memorandum setting forth the various ways by which an individual may legally avoid tax." Under oath he later admitted to using five of the ten devices the memorandum listed. Those and other schemes sharply reduced his tax payments.

In Morgenthau's view, Mellon's methods revealed a serious discrepancy between legality and morality. Things that the courts approved outraged the Secretary's personal sense of justice. He could hardly contain himself as he reviewed the record. Mellon in 1931 had created a charitable trust and reported gifts to it of five paintings valued together at more than $3 million. He took a deduction for those gifts after the Treasury had disallowed certain losses he claimed on the sale of securities. Though he had not yet begun to build or to endow a gallery for the works of art which remained in his personal control, the Board of Tax Appeals found the charitable trust valid, and permitted him an income tax deduction of over $80,000.

Mellon, like most other rich men of the time, reduced his inheritance, estate, and gift taxes by passing on to his children during his lifetime the greater part of his fortune, though he retained the income from that fortune for himself. He made more dramatic savings by transfers and sales among his various personal holding companies — "incorporated pocketbooks," the Treasury called them.

The Secretary was both angry and alarmed because Mellon's

techniques, multiplied many times by many men, slashed federal revenues. One of the most costly escapes was not even subtle. The rich alone could afford to invest in federal and local securities which carried low rates of interest but were entirely tax exempt. Even Mellon had called for repeal of the exemption, which Roosevelt specifically asked Congress to remove in 1936 and Morgenthau condemned annually. In 1937 tax leaks threw off the Treasury's estimates. Revenue, the President told Congress on April 20, was $600 million below predictions. Though the Republicans blamed New Deal bungling and inefficiency, Morgenthau and his associates were sure that the source of the trouble was wholesale tax avoidance. Roosevelt had planned to take the problem to Congress in November. On April 26, 1937, accelerating his schedule, he directed the Treasury to hurry its report.

The President, Morgenthau told his staff, "wants to say flatly that our estimates and our method of estimating were correct, but the citizens — that's the word he used — found a trick way of finding loopholes. And then he wants us to go into considerable detail as to what those loopholes are. . . . He wants to make a recommendation to Congress . . . that these loopholes be closed and that they be retroactive. And he said he does not want to wait until next fall and he wants particularly . . . to show the items which are held up by court action."

A quick audit of individual returns in New York on incomes of $100,000 or more, of some smaller incomes, and of the deductions claimed by various corporations and personal holding companies, persuaded the Treasury that taxpayers had not invented any new devices for avoidance but were employing old methods more widely. The resulting threat to revenue receipts strengthened Morgenthau's preference for seeking remedial legislation at once, as Roosevelt had suggested, rather than waiting until autumn for the full report of the Joint Committee.

"Henry," Roosevelt said on May 17, throwing himself back in his chair, "it has come time to attack, and you have got more material than anybody else in Washington to lead the attack. Did you notice how downcast Jack Garner was at Cabinet? Well, when I saw Jack before Cabinet, rather than give him a chance to attack me, I attacked him. People like Garner, Senator Bailey, Walsh of Massachusetts, and numerous other conservative Democrats, knowingly or not, are getting prepared for a Conservative Democratic party. They won't go along with any reform measures, and they are only interested in balancing the budget. . . . Now, it's up to you to fight."

Roosevelt was so excited that Morgenthau could not help laughing. "Why are you laughing?" the President asked.

"Because you are such a wonderful showman," Morgenthau replied. "I don't know what's going to happen. I can't guess what I have got that is so useful to you."

"You and I have kept quiet while they have talked so about the Federal revenue being short five or six hundred million dollars," Roosevelt continued. "They have been unfair and lumped it altogether, not distinguishing between the money we lost through court action and the rest of the decrease in taxes. The time has come when we have to fight back, and the only way to fight back is to begin to name names of these very wealthy individuals who have found means of avoiding their taxes both at home and abroad. What do you think of it?"

Morgenthau was exceedingly happy, as he put it, to be able at that moment to produce a memorandum which Roosevelt read with relish. It was just what he wanted, the President said, or it would be when he recast it with more "punch." "In the words of Theodore Roosevelt," he concluded, "my spear knows no brother. I want the Treasury to start working at once on the speech for me. I want to name names. I'm going on the air and tell this story."

Roosevelt's dudgeon did not abate. On the evening of May 17 Morgenthau returned to the White House to explain that his staff questioned the legality of making public the names of tax dodgers. The President, however, stood fast. Much impressed by his intensity, Morgenthau recaptured it the next day for his advisers: "The question is whether we are going to have a Fascist government in this country or a government of the people, whether rich men are going to be able to defy Government and refuse to bear their burdens. Are we going to make progress in liberal government or is it going to take a revolution finally to settle the question? The rich are getting richer in this country and the poor poorer. In France they met this problem by successive revolutions. If it had not been for the revolutions, a few men would own all France today.

"Such men as Garner, Robinson, Doughton and these men who are fighting the court plan* are against the President on the real issues. There has got to be a fight and there has got to be a purge. . . . Let us give the President what he wants, without quibbling as to whether this or that is legal. The President is intelligent enough to decide what he can use."

Leaving the question of tactics to Roosevelt, the Treasury prepared a letter on tax avoidance that named names and an alternative document omitting them. The President liked the material, which Morgenthau delivered on May 21, but he asked for at least twenty-five additional names for possible inclusion in a radio address which he was considering as a supplement to a message to Congress about loopholes. He agreed to delay decision about using names until he had reviewed the data more carefully. Morgenthau had concluded that the President should confine his remarks to methods of avoidance and use as his vehicle a letter to the Chairman of the Joint Committee on Taxation. Specifying names, the Secretary thought, "would stir up class hatred unnecessarily." Any mention of them was bound to be discriminatory. One famous automobile manufacturer who had incorporated his yacht might be the sole object of attack although at least twelve others followed the same practice. The depletion allowance, which saved millions of tax dollars, could not be associated with individual taxpayers. Even without names, Morgenthau believed, a letter to the Joint Committee would "have a terrific effect."

The Treasury's analysis of the ways around the revenue law was in itself commanding. One resident of Baltimore, for ex-

---

* Roosevelt's proposal to increase the size of the Supreme Court, a device through which he could have named enough sympathetic justices to bring the Court to support, instead of invalidating, New Deal measures. The Senate defeated the plan.

ample, had established sixty-four trusts in favor of his wife and three children which saved him over $485,000 in taxes in one year. Two partners in a brokerage house in New York had forty trust funds as well as twenty-three personal holding companies that made possible innumerable transactions for the reduction of tax liabilities. Other wealthy taxpayers took their wives and children into partnership or registered stock in the names of employees and relatives subject to lower surtax rates. One man saved $50,000 in 1936 by taking four minor children into his firm.

Many taxpayers abused the privileges of pension trust. Revenue acts for ten years had tried to encourage pension trusts for aged employees by allowing corporations special deductions for contributions to them. But clever lawyers had advised their clients to set up pension trusts and take deductions even though the only employees covered by the trusts were directors and other high officials. In one instance a corporation deducted $43,000 annually for a pension trust for the benefit of its two chief owners. One of them would retire at sixty-five with a pension of $1725 a month, the other with $1425 a month.

Another common method of avoidance was the incorporation of personal companies in foreign countries where taxes were low. One New Yorker, whose personal return showed no taxable income for 1936, owned with his two daughters a Canadian holding company which received dividends during the year in excess of $1,500,000 from American concerns. Even bolder was an American army officer who inherited the entire stock of a large business. Late in 1935 he became a Canadian citizen. Within six days he organized a corporation in the Bahamas, transferred his stock to it, and apparently planned to sell the stock through the new corporation in order to avoid the tax on capital gains. His gall unlimited, he then asked the Secretary of War whether he could continue to draw his pension from the United States Army.

Six Americans saved almost $550,000 between 1932 and 1936 by purportedly paying a large single premium for policies in a foreign insurance company in the Bahamas, immediately borrowing back most of that sum, and then claiming large tax deductions for interest on the loan, though in fact they paid no interest.

Domestic personal holding companies became especially popular after Congress reduced their taxes for 1936. In that year one family saved $791,000 in surtaxes by manipulating its incorporated pocketbook; another man saved $322,000; still another saved more than $140,000. A celebrated newspaper publisher, with ninety-six companies, managed to make it almost impossible, and certainly extraordinarily expensive, for the Bureau of Internal Revenue to follow his transactions.

Many rich people incorporated their luxuries and hobbies in order to cut tax payments. One millionaire established a personal holding company which owned his yacht and $3 million in securities. It rented the yacht to him and used part of the income from the securities to pay depreciation costs, operating charges, and the wages of captain and crew. Similarly, seven Americans saved in aggregate $244,000 by incorporating their country houses. One woman carried this farce so far that she paid her husband a salary for managing her home.

The largest boons derived from deductions for percentage depletion in oil and mining. Since 1928 mining companies had been allowed from 5 to 27½ per cent of gross income as an allowance for depletion, even though they might have recovered the whole cost of their property. In such cases, the deductions were a gift from the United States which cost the government several million dollars a year. Simplest of all methods of avoidance were the tax exempt bonds. Five wealthy men in 1937 each owned between $14 million and $32 million of those securities.

His data in hand, Roosevelt on June 1 sent a special message to Congress. He quoted a letter of May 29 from Morgenthau reporting that tax avoidance and evasion were "so widespread and so amazing both in their boldness and their ingenuity" that further action without delay seemed "imperative." The President was "indignant." The "clever little schemes" of men of wealth undermined the foundations of society and subverted the "decency of American morals." Congress, he was sure, would want to make the "present tax structure evasion-proof." As a first step, in accordance with the Administration's plan, Congress created the Joint Committee on Tax Evasion and Avoidance and empowered it to hold hearings, to subpoena witnesses, and to procure from the Treasury all the information it needed, including the names of offenders.

Roosevelt's message blew up a storm of self-righteousness. Disclosures of tax tricks, even though they were legal, were going to be unpleasant for the tricksters who attacked the President before the Joint Committee could embarrass them. Republican newspapers led the charge: Roosevelt had an "obsession against the rich"; his message was a "red herring" intended to hide the failures of the New Deal; the real evaders were not the rich but the poor, whose incomes were not subject to direct tax; the tax problem could be solved only by repeal of the unfair undistributed profits tax.

The wealthy themselves most fiercely denied the imputation of immorality. Returning from Europe, J. Pierpont Morgan said, according to several accounts: "I object strenuously to treating income tax evasion as a moral issue. . . . It is not up to us taxpayers to repair the mistakes of Congress. It is just as bad to pay too much as to pay too little." The public outcry at this candor impelled Morgan partially to retract. He had spoken, he explained, before reading Roosevelt's message or Morgenthau's letter. "I certainly have no sympathy with tax dodging . . ." he added, "and had no thought of defending such practices. What I strongly feel is that, when a taxpayer has complied with all the terms of the law, he should not be held up to obliquity for not having paid more than he owed."

This "exposition of Christianity" aroused the President's scorn. "Ask yourself," he wrote a New York lawyer, "what Christ would say about the American Bench and Bar were he to return today?" One of Roosevelt's cousins replied in a public letter condemning the New Deal and asserting the right of a taxpayer to claim every exemption the law allowed. The President's ire rose. His cousin, he said, was maintaining that because he did not agree with the laws passed by a properly elected Congress, he therefore had a right to evade taxes as long as he could get away with it. "That being your belief," Roosevelt concluded, "I do not hesitate to brand you as one of the worst anarchists in the U.S."

The rancor became more intense while the Joint Committee conducted hearings between June 17 and June 28. The committee did not employ special counsel, as Roosevelt had hoped it would, but the President assigned Thurman Arnold, a crack lawyer from the Department of Justice, to help the Treasury prepare evidence and testimony. "Everyone in tax trouble," Morgenthau told his staff, "is against Mr. Roosevelt."

As the hearings continued, an "almost unbelievable tale" unfolded. Never had the wealthy looked worse to the American people. The committee's interrogation led the Treasury to name names: June 24 it listed sixty-seven "large, wealthy taxpayers who, by taking assets out of their personal boxes and transferring them to incorporated pocketbooks, have avoided paying their full share of taxes." Among those using this device, "perfectly legal" as the Treasury admitted, were Andrew W. Mellon, Thomas W. Lamont, John J. Raskob, Pierre S. du Pont, Alfred P. Sloan, Jacob Ruppert, Roy W. Howard, and William Randolph Hearst. Lamont was quoted as frowning upon paying taxes that could be avoided. Sloan, who, it developed, had also incorporated his yacht, explained that he and his wife had paid taxes on 60 per cent of their income, given half of the balance to charity, and incorporated the yacht to avoid unlimited personal liability. "No conscientious citizen," Sloan said, "desires to avoid payment of his just share of the country's burden. I do not seek to avoid mine. . . . While no one should desire to avoid payment of his share . . . neither should any one be expected to pay more than is lawfully required."

This statement, like those of Lamont and J. P. Morgan, went right to the heart of the matter. No one, not Roosevelt, not Morgenthau, not the Joint Committee, was accusing the men whose names were made public of breaking the law. On the contrary, the Administration wanted to change the law precisely because, as it stood, it enabled those men to reduce their taxes. They felt that the Administration was persecuting them because they were rich and because they were, with few exceptions, Republican. Roosevelt and Morgenthau, on the other hand, attacked as they did in order to protect federal revenues and to eliminate what they considered unethical tax behavior.

Moved by the evidence the Treasury produced, the committee reported out the Revenue Act of 1937, which both houses of Congress passed unanimously and Roosevelt signed on August 28. The new legislation taxed domestic personal holding companies at rates equivalent to the highest surtaxes on personal income. The Act also limited deductions of expenses for incorporated yachts, country estates and the like. It made more difficult any artificial deductions for losses from sales or exchanges of property. It reduced the incentives for creating multiple trusts to avoid taxes. It also radically altered the treatment of foreign personal holding companies and removed a differentiation favoring nonresident taxpayers. The Department of Justice had found a way to stop the use of foreign insurance companies for tax avoidance, but various loopholes, as the Treasury explained, remained unclosed. Congress did nothing about pension trusts, about percentage depletion allowances, or about tax exempt securities, a matter which the Treasury had not chosen to raise at the hearings because no one had yet proposed a practicable and constitutional remedy. In spite of those deficiencies, the Act of 1937 saved the government between $50 and $100 million a year.

It was a significant victory for the majority of Americans who resented the habits of rich tax avoiders even though they were legal. Roosevelt and Morgenthau had consistently maintained that the wealthy should bear the increased costs of government. Those costs, as Morgenthau so often said, were designed to assist those at the bottom of the economic ladder. He and the President took pride in the frankly redistributive impact of New Deal taxation. Now the government had shown that it would not brook the frustration of its purpose. Particularly because it underscored what he believed to be a major moral issue, the Revenue Act of 1937 pleased Morgenthau more than had any of its predecessors.

VII

RECESSION

1937–1938

1. A Statement of Policy

HAWAII IN MIDSUMMER 1937 was a good place for relaxing. The problems of the Treasury seemed comfortably remote and in any case under control. Hopkins was following Morgenthau's prescriptions, Congress had made tax avoidance satisfyingly difficult, business conditions seemed promising. Morgenthau found it easy, therefore, to enjoy his family and his leisure. Twenty years later he remembered fondly the beauty of Molokai Island and the wonderful time he had with his children sailing in Pearl Harbor. There, he also recalled, Japanese fishing vessels had unrestricted views of American naval installations — a condition the military partially corrected after he called it to their attention. Most vividly Morgenthau remembered reviewing at Hickam Field the armed forces stationed in Hawaii. Roosevelt had assigned him that duty, largely in order to emphasize the presence in the islands of the Secretary of the Treasury. "Henry," the President had explained, "as you go East you have to be more and more formal."

Parades and sunshine, the green palms, the ivory sand, the bright blue water, for all their attractions could not entirely keep Morgenthau's mind away from Washington. The plan, which he had never approved, for the reorganization of the Supreme

Court, and the wave of sit-down strikes had, he thought, cost Roosevelt middle-class support during the first half of 1937. The President could regain the lost esteem, Morgenthau believed, only by balancing the budget. Committed to budget balancing on its own merits, the Secretary now had political reasons for making it his first order of business.

Warnings of a possible recession seemed to him to confirm his purpose. The satisfactory level of business activity, his advisers wrote him in August, had rested upon a backlog of unfilled orders. Unless increased buying replaced this backlog, production would fall off. Commodity prices were already tending downward and commodity futures had reached new lows. But the Research Division saw no need for collapse. Low interest rates, new residential construction, and increased purchasing power would sustain recovery unless these factors were offset by a decrease in federal spending. Here Morgenthau completely disagreed. Recovery, he believed, depended on the willingness of business to increase investments, and this in turn was a function of business confidence. In his view only a balanced budget could sustain that confidence.

Back at his desk in mid-September, Morgenthau was glad to find Roosevelt in a frugal mood, but a report from the Treasury Research Division in October disturbed him. It noted that fifteen different indexes revealed an ominous decline in national economic activity. And over the telephone, Earle Bailie, a New York financier whose judgment Morgenthau respected, expressed alarm about the relentless selling that plagued the stock market on October 11. Bailie felt that deflation had reached a point serious enough to affect federal revenues. There was, he said, a "lack of confidence bordering almost on disorder, or you could use the word panic, if you wanted to, but that would be putting it a little strongly." Further, the railroad situation had worsened. The roads were beset by rising costs and their financial problems were disturbing banks and insurance companies which held railroad bonds. The stock market was not absorbing new equities. Recent issues of Canada Dry and Bethlehem Steel had faltered. Perhaps most seriously, the utility industry was frozen pending the Supreme Court's decision on the constitutionality of the Act breaking up holding-company systems.

Morgenthau thought it was up to the President to clarify policy on public utilities, and at the urging of his staff, he promised to have a heart-to-heart talk with Roosevelt about that matter and perhaps also about capital markets. The Secretary's primary interest, however, remained the budget.

He had some strong allies. On October 12, 1937, Roosevelt told Congressmen Doughton and Vinson of the House Ways and Means Committee that he wanted to wipe out the $270 million deficit predicted for the fiscal year 1939. The Treasury, he said, had urged him to be rough, to insist on economy. At once Doughton and Vinson said they, too, wanted him to be rough. As Morgenthau put it in his Diary: "The President told them with a real 'burr' in his voice that he expected to balance the Budget; that he wanted enough money to balance the Budget; that he expected to keep expenditures down so that he could balance the Budget, and that if any Committee passes an appropriation over and above his estimates he would immediately serve notice on that Committee that they must find the additional revenue."

Henry Wallace seemed also to be veering toward Morgenthau's view. Immediately after the Cabinet meeting of October 12, Wallace said, according to Morgenthau's Diary: "Mr. President, as we are now approaching a balanced budget don't you think that you ought to call some of us together and see if we can't think up some suggestions to encourage private business enterprise so that they can go ahead and take up the slack which would be left due to the government's ceasing spending." This, in Morgenthau's words, was music to his ears, and he was equally pleased by a memorandum Roosevelt sent Wallace on October 14: "During the next two or three weeks I think it is very important for you and the farm organizations to keep in touch with the Treasury in order that we may avoid a program which would unbalance the budget. As I said in Cabinet, if we adopt a farm bill for 'balanced abundance' it must balance itself financially. . . . That is why I think you and the Treasury should keep in close touch."

With Roosevelt holding checkreins on Wallace, Morgenthau concentrated on Ickes and Jesse Jones. The best news the business community could receive, the Secretary asserted, was that the Reconstruction Finance Corporation and the Public Works Administration were through. "Now listen," the Secretary told his staff, ". . . do you mind if I go ahead, because I never, never felt that I was more right than I am now. Now, if I am wrong — I'm shooting the works, and if I'm wrong — I'm doing what I always have done since I've been Secretary; I'm willing to stick my neck out, and if I'm wrong — I'm always willing to risk my job if I think I'm right, because I think it's worth risking, and I'm perfectly willing to risk my job for this. . . . I'm willing to bet my job as Secretary of the Treasury that I'm right. . . . We're going to sweat this thing through because we think we're right."

He appeared, Morgenthau later recalled, at last to be within sight of his goal. Then on October 19, "Black Tuesday," the stock market disintegrated. Seventeen million shares changed hands while prices skidded, as Morgenthau put it, "amid an hysteria resembling a mob in a theater fire." Steve Early telephoned him from the White House to say that telegrams were pouring in asking for the closing of the exchange. The Secretary recommended keeping all exchanges open. At one-fifteen in the afternoon Roosevelt telephoned. The White House, he said, had the jitters, especially Early and Jimmy Roosevelt. "I was quite rude to them," the President added. Morgenthau said that retailing and the housing industry were as good or better than they had been. Though railroads and United States Steel were off, foreigners had bought American stocks, and there was as yet no indication of money leaving the country.

On October 20 the market recovered a little, but October 19 precipitated a policy crisis in Washington. While developments that day strengthened Morgenthau's convictions, they shook Roosevelt's faith in budget balancing and gained a hearing with him for the advocates of countercyclical spending. That policy had begun to gain currency in academic and governmental circles after the publication in 1936 of John Maynard Keynes's classic, *The General Theory of Employment, Interest and Money*. Within the Treasury itself, the Secretary's chief advisers had begun to think in Keynesian terms. Morgenthau, as always, permitted a free expression of opinions at variance with his own, but he was unpersuaded by his associates and they were too loyal to take their views over his head to the White House.

Outside the Treasury, however, there were influential proponents of compensatory spending. Marriner Eccles, for one, had been preaching that gospel on and off for five years. Now he had capable allies who proposed, as he did, to transform spending from a temporary expedient to a permanent instrumentality of government. The economist Leon Henderson had predicted a business slump in his "Boom or Bust" memorandum of the spring of 1937. His forecast gave Harry Hopkins, for whom Henderson was then working, arguments for resuming a spending policy. Tommy Corcoran, sensitive to the play of personalities at both ends of Pennsylvania Avenue, was the political brains of the spending group, Morgenthau believed. Ben Cohen, a highly literate and imaginative liberal lawyer, and Lauchlin Currie, an energetic New Deal economist, assisted in the formation of policy, and Jimmy Roosevelt, then acting as his father's assistant, was generally sympathetic to their ideas. The decline in economic activity and the catastrophe on the market gave their case enhanced prestige. Whenever private investment fell off, they warned, only an expansion of government economic activity could maintain a satisfactory level of production and employment.

Wedded to his own antithetical convictions, Morgenthau continued to resist proposals for expenditure. He also advanced plans, first formulated a month earlier, to speak out in public, with the full authority of the Administration, in behalf of a balanced budget. To that end he had accepted an invitation to address the Academy of Political Science at the Hotel Astor in New York City on November 10, 1937.

Morgenthau told his staff on October 20 that he wanted his speech to emphasize that balancing the budget would be the biggest fiscal job anyone had ever faced, particularly because of the slump in business conditions. He thought he would do Roosevelt a kindness by "putting" his "own neck out" and saying it could and would be done. Would he, he was asked, consent to unbalance the budget for fiscal 1939 if it were necessary to provide another $500 million for work relief? Morgenthau replied that he would not. If it came to that there would have to be another Secretary of the Treasury:

> I won't stay and knowingly and consciously have an unbalanced budget in order to correct the mistakes made by other people. . . . We have come to a crossroad. The crossroad is when private business needed the money which the Government has been taking up to this time, and we are at that crossroad now. I don't see why we can't use those words. . . . The time has come. And the only person around here who is not in line is Wallace and Wallace wants private industry to do it. . . . The President wants private industry to do it. . . . And it's not balancing the budget which is putting the stock market down. Then why the hell should we unbalance the budget to cover up the mistakes of other people? For four years we have carried the burden of mistakes made by other Departments.

A week later he had begun to hedge. He still felt, as he told his staff, that the best thing he could do for his country was to devote the first part of the speech to a discussion of why the Administration wanted a balanced budget. But then, of course, he would have to explain the realities of the situation. Funds were still needed for relief and for the Civilian Conservation Corps; the agricultural program would be expensive, and $700 million were already committed to public works. He wanted his address to make it clear that it was just as dangerous to economize too quickly as it was not to economize at all. He wanted it just as clear (the Keynesians in the Treasury had made their mark) that he was not yet willing to recommend a broader tax base, even in order to balance the budget. That would be deflationary. He intended to balance the budget by cutting costs, not by increasing revenue, though this might limit him to balancing his cash budget, leaving uncovered the expenses of debt retirement.

But as the days passed, all business indexes suggested that the slump was developing into a full-blown depression. To Morgenthau's dismay, Roosevelt was beginning to listen to the advocates of compensatory spending. While he listened, he gave no indication of the policies he intended to pursue.

That indecision, perhaps deliberate, worried Morgenthau, who believed quick action imperative. On the evening of November 2 he telephoned his chief. The country, the Secretary said, was headed into another depression, and Roosevelt should do something about it. Morgenthau proposed calling together a number of people over the weekend to discuss gold, intending by this remark to suggest that easier money would encourage investment. The President got "very excited, very dictatorial and very disagreeable." He quoted at great length a man he described as a "wise old bird" who had said that business was deliberately causing the depression in order to hold a pistol to his head and force a retreat from reform.

"A great deal depends on who this person is," Morgenthau said coldly.

"It is not necessary for you to know who that person is," Roosevelt replied.

After thinking it over, Morgenthau concluded that the "wise old bird" was the President himself. In any event, Roosevelt had been "extremely rude," as Morgenthau himself had been something less than tactful. Mrs. Morgenthau, who overheard the conversation, said to her husband that his "voice sounded like drippings of an icicle."

Roosevelt concluded their talk by objecting to the firm declaration for a balanced budget in the draft of the National Academy speech the Secretary had sent to the White House. Taking pen in hand, for him an unusual gesture, on November 3 Morgenthau wrote an anguished note: "As I told you over the telephone last night I have had to come to the conclusion that we are headed right into another depression. . . . You told the newspapers that your first interest was the one-third of the nation who are ill-nourished, ill-clad, ill-housed. This part of our population is also my deep concern and therefore, I am bringing this matter again to your attention in writing. I hardly need tell you that the first to feel another depression will be this same one-third. This cruel process has already begun. Mr. President what can we do to stop it?"

Roosevelt was unmoved. At Cabinet the next day, obviously in an acid mood, he said: "Of course, I am glad to hear from the various members of the Cabinet their sad story of how bad business conditions are. Last night when I went to bed, alongside of my bed was the darnedest letter you ever saw from Henry." He grimaced. "It was just terrible." Now angry, he continued: "I am sick and tired of being told by the Cabinet, by Henry and by everybody else for the last two weeks what's the matter with the country and nobody suggests what I should do."

There was complete silence. Morgenthau gathered his courage: "You can do something about public utilities. You can do something about the railroads. You could do something about housing. Above all, you must do something to reassure business."

"You want me to turn on the old record," Roosevelt said.

"You asked me," Morgenthau replied. "What business wants to know is: Are we headed toward state Socialism or are we going to continue on a capitalistic basis?"

"I have told them that again and again."

"All right, Mr. President, tell them for the fifteenth time. That's what they want to know."

"That's what they want to know," Jim Farley echoed, and Wallace also backed up Morgenthau.

Farley thought it was the best Cabinet meeting they had ever had, and Morgenthau in his Diary noted: "This is the first time in my experience that the Cabinet had ever talked on a man to man basis with the President and that we did not sit back and either talk trivialities or listen to him."

His spirits high, Morgenthau resumed work on his speech. "This thing has gotten so important," he told his staff, ". . . it's a question of the whole policy being at stake now." Almost as he spoke, Marriner Eccles arrived to explain, as Roosevelt had suggested he should, his interpretation of the developing recession. One trouble, Eccles said, was the high cost of labor which was forcing prices up, particularly in the building trades. As long as this situation continued, people would not build houses and railroads, would not lay track or construct new facilities. Small business, Eccles went on, needed tax relief, but the best way to stop the recession, he concluded, would be to speed up expenditures through Hopkins and Wallace.

When the Secretary showed him a draft of the speech, Eccles called it deflationary. Frugality would have been nice a month ago, he said, but not now.

After Eccles left, Morgenthau told his staff that he thought the President wanted to sit tight, as if he were in a poker game, to see who could last longer, the advocates of spending or the advocates of balancing the budget. Meanwhile, Morgenthau said, he felt the ground was slipping from under their feet. He was afraid Roosevelt would do nothing. And in spite of Eccles's objections or Roosevelt's doubts, he did not believe his ideas were deflationary.

A balanced budget was still Morgenthau's goal when he went, on November 8, for luncheon with the President. Most of their conversation took a different turn. Roosevelt was depressed. Fascism, he said, was making gains throughout the world, as the Rome-Berlin-Tokyo Pact suggested. Brazil was veering that way. Take the situation in the United States, he said. Four or five people might get together, talk it over, and decide they had to have their own man in Washington. Even though he said every so often that he wanted business to make a profit and that he believed in property rights, business did not believe him. The President thought there were about two thousand men who had reached the conclusion they had to block the New Deal, to go on strike against government. He had to decide whether to continue to go forward or do what Hoover had done and call in groups of people to try to cure particular situations one at a time in conference. He was going to see Harry Hopkins and his economists later that day, Roosevelt continued, and on the next day see another group, and then later talk with Gerard Swope, a business spokesman, and others about housing, going on from there to a discussion, again with business interests among others, about the utilities. But the President kept reverting to the possibility that American industrialists would gradually, as their thought crystallized, conclude that they had to get their own man in the White House.

Occasionally Morgenthau interrupted to ask if there was something that Roosevelt was trying to say that he did not understand, some special point he was trying to make, but the President said no, he was just thinking out loud. He had tried to define the New Deal to his oldest son, Morgenthau said. His conception of what Roosevelt had accomplished, he had told the young man, was that "the United States has come through this terrific turmoil and that the individual in this country still had the right to think, talk and worship as he wished." Roosevelt interrupted, "And add to that the right to work."

After luncheon, in his Diary Morgenthau wrote that he did not know exactly what the President was trying to get across. He supposed Roosevelt was attempting to frighten him by waving the fascist flag. But this was not necessary. Morgenthau knew without being told how bad conditions were. On the other hand, when Roosevelt finished, Morgenthau had felt that the President was fighting like a cornered lion, that he did not want to be tamed, and yet that he did not know where to put his strength to bring about recovery. Of course, Morgenthau conceded, fascism was spreading. It was therefore vital for the United States to avoid an industrial slump because it would give the enemies of liberalism an opportunity to take solace in the failure of the world's strongest democracy.

As Morgenthau judged, Roosevelt was troubled, as yet uncertain about policy, and consequently bent upon keeping discussion open while he made up his mind. Only a few hours after his luncheon with the Secretary, the President talked with Eccles, who was temporarily cheered when Roosevelt seemed impressed with a memorandum prepared by Leon Henderson and Lauchlin Currie, among others, "indicating how a reduction in government spending had helped precipitate the recession." Eccles hoped that the spenders had carried the field, but, as he was to learn, this was not entirely the case.

The President, working over the draft of Morgenthau's speech, questioned a section reading: "This Administration is going to do everything possible to promote a continuation of recovery and to balance the budget through cutting expenditures. But I wish to emphasize that in no event will this Administration allow anyone to starve." Dissatisfied, Roosevelt added: "Nor will it abandon its broad purpose to protect the weak, to give human security and to seek a wider distribution of our national wealth."

"If you want to sound like Huey Long, I don't," Morgenthau said. The emphasis of the speech, he thought, should not be on reform but on the budget. Yet he realized that Roosevelt thought business was conspiring against him, and he knew that when the President was in that humor, nothing could change it. The Secretary would have liked a stronger statement, but even the words the President approved depressed Eccles, "baffled" him, because he was sure that the views Morgenthau expressed in New York were the opposite of what Roosevelt had seemed to endorse in the memorandum of Henderson and Currie. He was right.

On November 10, 1937, Morgenthau arose before the meeting of the Academy of Political Science. Parker Gilbert of the House of Morgan introduced him politely to a serious and on the whole conservative audience that included some of the wealthiest businessmen of the city. The speech the Secretary was about to give had been "checked and double-checked — every word, every syllable, by the President." By and large it resembled its earliest drafts. For the four years ending June 30, 1937, Morgenthau began, the war against depression had necessitated federal expenditures $14 billion in excess of receipts.

We deliberately used an unbalanced Federal budget . . . to meet a great emergency. That policy has succeeded. The emergency . . . no longer exists. I am fully aware that many of our problems remain unsolved. I am aware that there still remains a considerable volume of unemployment; that the speculative markets have recently been under severe pressure; and that our business indices have recently shown a declining tendency. I am further aware that some persons contend that another great spending program is desirable to ward off the risk of another business depression.

I claim no prophetic insight into the future. But, after giving serious and careful consideration to all of these and other factors, I have reached the firm conviction that the domestic problems which face us today are essentially different from those which faced us four years ago. Many measures are required for their solution. One of these measures but only one, in the present juncture is a determined movement toward a balanced budget. . . . We want to see private business expand. We believe that much of the remaining unemployment will disappear as private capital funds are increasingly employed. . . . We believe that one of the most important ways of achieving these ends at this time is to continue progress toward a balance of the Federal Budget.

Someone laughed. It was probably, Morgenthau later decided, a drunk, but there were in the audience many men who wondered whether any Democrat could honestly say what they had just heard. The atmosphere as much as the interruption upset the Secretary, who was always a nervous speaker, but he braced and went on. In four fields he contemplated cutting costs: highway construction, public works, unemployment relief, and agriculture. But there was a point beyond which reductions were impossible without crippling essential activities. The government could not consider "such things as weakening our national defense, and slowing up or abandoning flood control, soil erosion prevention, and relief for the aged and the unemployed. Such a course, I believe, would not have the approval of . . . the American people."

This sounded much more like the voice of the New Deal which Wall Street thought it understood and knew it disliked. The mood of the audience, as Morgenthau sensed it, was unsympathetic, and he was increasingly tense as he came to his concluding points: "We are definitely in a transition period between unbalanced and balanced Federal budgets: but I firmly believe that there is just as much danger to our economy as a whole in moving too rapidly in this direction as there would be in not moving at all.

"Relatively few persons realize the striking fact that the net improvement this year in the budgetary position of the Federal Government as estimated will amount to more than $2 billion.

In other words, the net deficit this year is estimated at less than $700 million as compared with more than $2 billion 700 million last year." A pause here, an adjustment of the pince-nez, a triumphant tone: "This . . . provides the best answer to those who . . . have publicly despaired of our ability to balance the Federal budget. . . .

"This Administration is going to do everything possible to promote a continuation of recovery and to balance the budget through cutting expenditures." Another pause. Relish now for the words Roosevelt had inserted: "But I wish to emphasize that in no event will this Administration allow anyone to starve, nor will it abandon its broad purpose to protect the weak, to give human security and to seek a wider distribution of our national income."

Morgenthau had given everything he had. He had advocated precisely the policy the business community had been urging upon him, knowing as he did so that the President, by siding with Henderson and Eccles, might make him look foolish. There was, he said later to his staff, not one technical flaw in the speech, and he thanked them for their help in drafting it. The hard work, the high purpose, the great strain surrounding the occasion made the Secretary especially sensitive to the reception accorded his efforts, to the silent unbelief of the very men he was trying to help, to the disconcerting laugh that seemed to symbolize their temper. Herman Oliphant was furious. "We sit here and lose the feel of what the typical leadership of American finance is," he said, "and it's very illuminating to realize the hopelessness of trying to work with them." That seemed to Morgenthau to be the counsel of defeat. In spite of the poor reception given to his speech, he intended to push on.

2. "*A Different Set of Delusions*"

Roosevelt, during the first weeks of 1938, was both waiting and groping — waiting to see whether the economy might right itself, delaying definition of major policy while he discussed the recession with businessmen as well as public officials. The captains of industry and finance seemed to the President to have little to offer. They were not accustomed, he told the Cabinet, to thinking of the whole nation or even of businesses other than their own. Officers of corporations handling automobile installment loans had, for example, suggested that the Federal Reserve Board restrict the rediscount rate on installment notes. Amazed at their proposal "for strict government regulation," Roosevelt told them that "if such restrictions were generally applied we would not have state socialism but fascism." The President also reported that the automobile manufacturers admitted privately that they had oversold the market in 1937. He was therefore asking them, as he was asking other businesses, to work out for themselves ways to prevent extravagant production and extravagant selling.

As far as new investment went, Roosevelt felt that there were not enough opportunities for men of moderate means, nor did such men know where to get reliable advice. They had $15 billion in savings banks at nominal rates of interest although public utility bonds, he judged, were an excellent buy to yield 5 or 6 per cent. But the President saw no way to say so publicly.

He had told the businessmen that he needed confidence as much as they did. If they hit him on the chin, he said, he was going to hit them in the nose.

The advocates of countercyclical spending received timely support from their intellectual mentor, John Maynard Keynes, who on February 1, 1938, wrote Roosevelt an unsolicited letter about the recession. The key to recovery, Keynes maintained, was spending. Easy short-term money and the creation of an adequate system of relief, important though they were, could not and would not in themselves suffice. Recovery depended upon large-scale recourse to public works and other investments in capital goods guaranteed by the government. The Administration, he suggested, was especially subject to criticism for its "wicked" handling of the housing problem. Housing was by far the most important aid to recovery because of the large and continuing scale of potential demand, its wide geographical distribution, and the relative independence of housing finance from the stock exchanges. Keynes therefore advised putting "most of the eggs in the housing basket," and making absolutely sure that they were hatched without delay, if necessary through the use of direct subsidies.

He also criticized the deadlock on utilities. A good deal of what was alleged about the "wickedness" of the utility holding companies, he said, was surely "wide of the mark." "The real criminals" had cleared out long ago. Personally he thought there was a great deal to be said for the ownership of all of the utilities by the government, but if public opinion was not yet ripe for that he saw no object "in chasing utilities around the lot every other week." He considered it wise instead to "make peace on liberal terms," guaranteeing fair earnings on new investment and a fair basis of evaluation in the event of future government purchase. He spoke, too, of the railroads as potential sources of substantial demand for new capital expenditures. Nationalize them, he wrote, if the time was "ripe"; if not, "take pity" on the overwhelming problems of their management, and "let the dead bury their dead." "To an Englishman," Keynes said, "you Americans, like the Irish, are so terribly historically-minded!"

The recession, Keynes continued, was also in part psychological in origin. For this he blamed the President's attitude toward businessmen. "Businessmen," Keynes proposed, "have a different set of delusions from politicians; and need, therefore, different handling. They are, however, much milder than politicians, at the same time allured and terrified by the glare of publicity, easily persuaded to be 'patriots,' perplexed, bemused, indeed terrified, yet only too anxious to take a cheerful view, vain perhaps but very unsure of themselves, pathetically responsive to a kind word. You could do anything you liked with them, if you would treat them (even the big ones), not as wolves and tigers, but as domestic animals by nature, even though they have been badly brought up and not trained as you would wish. It is a mistake to think that they are more *immoral* than politicians. If you work them into the surly, obstinate, terrified mood, of which domestic animals, wrongly handled, are so capable, the nation's burdens will not get carried to market; and in the end public opinion will veer their way."

Morgenthau read Keynes's letter with special interest, for Roosevelt instructed him to answer it. The task was agreeable. It gave the Secretary the chance to speak for the Administration, and by a calculated silence to reject advice he disliked. He was deliberately noncommittal. "It was very pleasant and encouraging to know," he wrote, "that you are in agreement with so much of the Administration's economic program. This confirmation coming from so eminent an economist is indeed welcome. Your analysis . . . is very interesting. The emphasis you put upon . . . housing . . . is well placed."

Roosevelt, accepting Morgenthau's noncommittal reply for his own signature, could have had no doubt about what it implied. Morgenthau therefore felt that he still had an opportunity to conquer the recession without capitulating to the spenders. In February and March he recommended a number of remedies which were intended, in one way or another, to force or to induce a degree of private spending that would make a Keynesian policy unnecessary and undesirable. Keynes and his disciples, Morgenthau insisted, had a set of delusions all of their own.

3. Some Shots in the Arm

At the Treasury staff meeting of February 7, 1938, Morgenthau recalled the "bust-up" of the summer of 1933. Roosevelt had then turned to him, he said, to take the shackles off his hands, when everybody else in the Administration had failed. Either because he had been courageous or young or foolhardy, Morgenthau continued, he had taken a chance. He had "read up" on Warren and Pearson, and initiated the gold-buying program. That program might not have been "profoundly important," he said, but it had its own "small importance." It was all "very nice" for people to say they wanted no more monetary tricks, but if somebody did not try to provide a "shot in the arm" for the economy, they would get instead $8 billion of extraordinary expenses.

The Secretary and his advisers had in mind another venture in "easy money." The background for their proposals lay in previous developments during 1936-37. In those years, prematurely as it happened, the New York financial community, especially the officers of the Chase Bank, had come to fear inflation in the United States. Their anxieties much influenced the thinking of the Federal Reserve Board, Marriner Eccles not the least. Under pressure from Eccles, Morgenthau and the Treasury had agreed, though reluctantly, to two departures that were intended to constrain an expansion of bank credit. First, the Federal Reserve Board increased the reserve requirements of its member banks. That action gave banks less latitude than they had had for making loans against their assets. Second, the Treasury "sterilized" the gold then flowing to the United States in growing quantities from Europeans worried about the possibility of war. By sterilization, the Treasury simply confined gold received in America to vaults for safe storage and did not issue gold certificates against the metal. Those gold certificates would otherwise have moved on to the Federal Reserve and swollen the base against which banks could issue currency and generate credit for loans. Once the gold was sterilized, then, it was insulated from the American banking and monetary systems. Both sterilization and the increase in reserve requirements in considerable degree reversed the easy money policy of the early New Deal. Now, in 1938, Morgenthau wanted at the least to cease sterilization, at the most, actually to desterilize gold and decrease reserve requirements. Those moves would increase the lending capacity of the banks and thus lead to reductions in interest rates which in turn, as the Treasury saw it, would provide an inducement for renewed private investment.

With the acquiescence of the British, the skeptical consent of Marriner Eccles, and the agreement of the President, the Treasury in mid-February, 1938, announced that it would no longer sterilize gold imports or domestic gold production unless they together exceeded $100 million in any quarter. Drawing if necessary upon gold in the inactive account, the Treasury would add $400 million annually to bank reserves.

Among possible outlets for the easier money, Morgenthau gave high priority to investment in the utilities. Oliphant hoped to encourage such investment by having the government supervise the reorganization of a public utilities holding company (and perhaps later also of a railroad) in order to prove that a properly financed corporation could operate profitably. He proposed forcing into receivership one of the many public utilities companies in default of taxes. Acting as receiver, the Treasury could cooperate with the Securities and Exchange Commission to restructure the company, acquire new capital for it in private markets, and put it on a sound business basis.

"Bring the public utility to me," Roosevelt said when he learned of the plan late in January. "I have lived and worked with this all my life. In ten minutes I will show you how to reorganize it." It was his ambition when he left the White House to reorganize a railroad "either on constitutional or unconstitutional lines." Meanwhile he was "crazy" about the idea. The Secretary liked it too. "If I could prepare and develop, in all its details, the reorganizing and refinancing of public utilities and demonstrate that it could be done," he wrote in his Diary, "I don't know of anything that would be more helpful at this time and then if we could also do a railroad I think it would be a real help towards putting the country back on its feet because there are three things the public is talking about — Public Utilities, Railroads and Housing and, if we can get this started, it will go a long way toward putting the recovery machinery into gear." But as it worked out, various legal complications made the timely execution of Oliphant's project impossible.

Morgenthau had also turned his attention to housing which, as Keynes had said, was another vital area for investment. The Secretary believed that the government should rely primarily upon loans to encourage private building, whereas Senator Robert Wagner and Jimmy Roosevelt, among others, preferred direct grants and other forms of federal aid. With the President's support, Morgenthau persuaded Wagner to include in his 1938 housing bill provisions for loans to private cooperatives and limited dividend corporations. The Secretary also blocked programs Jimmy Roosevelt sponsored for using WPA labor and RFC funds to build small, low-cost, prefabricated homes, some of them on suburban land which the Farm Security Administration had acquired. Those plans, Morgenthau objected, would alienate private real estate interests and businessmen, duplicate or compete with the expanding operations of the Federal Housing Administration, and run up the federal deficit perhaps as much as $7 billion. His arguments convinced the President.

To Morgenthau, as to others in Washington, the ability of the cement, steel, and plumbing industries to sustain prices for their products while other prices were falling, seemed to impair the entire recovery effort. At Oliphant's instigation, the Secretary in mid-1937 had directed the Treasury Division of Procurement to consult the Department of Justice before accepting any bids that seemed noncompetitive. Oliphant wanted all federal agencies to adopt that procedure, and Solicitor General Robert Jackson, fully in agreement, was eager also to prosecute the men who were destroying competition and fixing prices. The recession intensified the antitrust sentiment that had been rising within the Administration for more than a year. In December 1937, Jackson publicly blamed monopoly and big business for the country's economic ills, as did Harold Ickes. As the year turned, Leon Henderson attributed the collapse of recovery to a shortage of purchasing power which derived, he said, from a too rapid rise in prices, especially monopoly prices. "Business has convicted itself of monopoly. . . ." Jackson had earlier written Roosevelt, in a vein which exactly suited Morgenthau. "The people can be made to understand this issue. I think you can seize this subject in a way that neither your economic nor political enemies can withstand."

The thought had long since occurred to the President, who in mid-February 1938, after consulting the congressional leaders, decided to make an issue of monopolistic prices. He immediately directed Morgenthau to consult the appropriate agencies and prepare a suitable statement about the problem. As discussion began, Henry Wallace, while agreeing that Roosevelt had a magnificent opportunity to speak out about prices, was afraid that the President might do some "moralizing," which would have an unfortunate effect on the psychology of the economy. Others hoped the President would set forth a broad policy for the government to follow during the next several months, while Morgenthau thought he intended to refer only to price trends, not to positive action.

To resolve these differences of opinion, Morgenthau appointed a working committee from the staffs of the Departments of Treasury, Labor, and Agriculture, which on February 16, 1937, submitted a tentative statement about prices. Recovery, it read, depended upon a steady increase in real income. In working for that increase, the Administration had been concerned necessarily with the relation of prices of groups of commodities to each other and with the movement of the general price level. Though the price level had fallen during the last six months, some prices remained high. Those for materials used in residential construction were still above the level for 1929. The artificial maintenance of these and other monopolistic prices was accentuating the deflationary pressure on competitive prices, especially those for food and raw materials. The government, therefore, should proceed against monopoly while it also tried to raise prices that were too low.

"Well," said Roosevelt when Morgenthau and his collaborators called at the White House, "this is a new kind of meeting to take place in my office. This seems to be a case where the pupils are going to tell Teacher."

"If you will pardon me, Mr. President," Morgenthau replied, "I don't think it is quite that. You will recall that you asked me to prepare some material for you on the price situation and the Administration's price policy. So, I called in all these people so that we could get together something on which we all would be united. I think they have done a first-class job. I think when you read this you will find that it is an excellent statement of your position and I think it would be very helpful indeed in the present business situation if it is used."

The President was cautious. "Well," he said after some discussion, "I don't know about a formal statement. . . . I don't often issue Presidential statements unless it is on a very unusual occasion."

As Morgenthau later put it, the President took "some time to warm up to having us give him this program. He seemed to resent it." Roosevelt complained that the language of the draft was rather technical, and said there had to be something definite for him to tell the housewife.

The drafting committee provided that addition quickly. "The average family," they wrote, "will benefit from the business recovery which a balanced price structure will foster. Increased employment and more continuous income should more than offset any increase in the cost of living. . . . Incomes of most families will increase while the costs of what the housewife buys should show little change."

So amended, the statement suited the President, who released it on February 18, attributing it to the heads of the three departments that had prepared it and to the Federal Reserve Board, which had endorsed it. Morgenthau "felt so good" he called

Wallace "to chin." "My gosh," Wallace told him, "I feel just as good as you do."

The statement on prices had a lasting effect in providing a mandate for an attack on monopoly. On February 22 Morgenthau suggested that the Federal Trade Commission, the Department of Justice, and the Department of State could cooperate in fighting monopolistic prices. One of their first studies focused on cement. The Bureau of Reclamation was a major purchaser of cement, and the Division of Procurement believed that if it could buy for that bureau and ultimately also for the Army Engineers, the Navy, and the Department of the Interior, the government could alter its purchasing policy so as to put pressure on cement manufacturers to reduce their prices. Morgenthau and his advisers also thought that the cement industry might be particularly sensitive to tariff changes. "I've been around this town five years now," the Secretary said, "and if you want to get something done, you've got to . . . pick one thing. . . . So we are taking on a big job."

As the Treasury developed its plans, Solicitor General Robert Jackson recommended some useful modifications, and Cordell Hull, while questioning the efficacy of renegotiating cement schedules in reciprocal trade agreements, gave the general program his enthusiastic support. Not so Henry Wallace, whose department included the Bureau of Public Roads. The government, Wallace objected, had known all along the cement people were violating the antitrust law. The thing to do now was to persuade them to listen to reason. If the country did not get recovery, he continued, it would not elect a Democrat in 1940. It would therefore be a mistake to irritate big business. "This is just the kind of stuff that the President loves," Wallace warned Morgenthau. "This is red meat for the President. We mustn't give anything like that to the President at this time."

But with Hull and Jackson behind him, Morgenthau on March 21, 1937, sent the President three recommendations, which Roosevelt at once approved. First, he concentrated cement purchases for all federal agencies under the Division of Procurement. Second, he required successful bidders on contracts for cement for the federal government to make their product available at the same price to all individuals doing work under government contracts. Third, he authorized grand jury investigations of collusion in the cement industry if anything developed in the negotiation of contracts that warranted such investigations. He also directed Morgenthau to get bids on cement f.o.b. mill in order to destroy the system in which producers set prices without regard to varying costs of delivery.

Roosevelt was in no mood to heed Wallace's warning, which Morgenthau relayed. The Administration, the President said, should not get together with big business. He was not going to let the flag down for anyone.

"The first time I let it down," Morgenthau replied, "you send me home. . . . The only thing that keeps me going is the moral uplift in this thing."

Signing the cement orders, Roosevelt beamed. "Now get plenty strong," he said. ". . . We're going into training for the heavy-weight championship."

Morgenthau was delighted. The best way to stimulate building, he was sure, was to knock down building costs. And the red meat of antitrust would, he hoped, dull the President's appetite for a menu of spending.

Marriner Eccles had restated the case for spending in an undated memorandum for Roosevelt, but the President was still not ready to move. "As I see it," Morgenthau said at luncheon on March 14, "what you are doing now is just treading water . . . to wait to see what happens this spring."

"Absolutely," Roosevelt replied.

4. Stampede

On March 25, while Roosevelt was on vacation at Warm Springs, the stock market had taken another sickening dip. This, as Morgenthau later observed, was the signal for new activity on the part of the spenders. Harry Hopkins, armed with memoranda from Leon Henderson and Aubrey Williams, camped on the President's doorstep. Before Roosevelt left Georgia, he decided he had to spend his way to recovery.

Morgenthau received his first intimation of the change on April 4 when Wallace telephoned him at Sea Island, where he was vacationing. The President, Wallace said, was "rarin' to go." He had instructed Wallace and Jones to work out a program for housing, flood control, rural rehabilitation, and loans to industry. He was also planning, Morgenthau learned two days later, additional appropriations for the Civilian Conservation Corps and the Works Progress Administration.

At the Cabinet meeting of April 5, as Morgenthau was later told, Roosevelt complained that congressional leaders were thinking of going home after passing bills on the Navy, taxes, and government reorganization. This would be fiddling while Rome burned, he said. He had done a lot of reading at Warm Springs, and he had reports from all branches of the government. The situation was bad not only for the country but also for the Democratic party, which might lose the fall election if conditions continued as they were.

The requests for funds he had already made, Roosevelt said, would at best maintain the existing state of affairs without making possible any improvement. Those requests included $1 billion 250 million for relief for the first seven months of the fiscal year 1939, $50 million to keep three hundred CCC camps going, and $300 or $400 million for the RFC. He was now thinking about what additional action to take.

Farley recommended expanding the post office building program, but the President said that money for post offices would go mainly to country towns, where unemployment was less severe than in the cities.

Garner thought the national debt was already enormous and wondered whether the country could stand any more. He also believed that the government had to move more people out of the cities into rural areas. As between the success of the Democratic party and the success of the country, the patriotic Vice President declared for the country.

Roosevelt said he was for the country, too, but that if the

Democrats were defeated in the fall, a third party might arise and
the Republicans win the election of 1940. That would mean the
ruin of many New Deal reforms. He wanted to spend money,
he explained, in such a way as to bring it back to the Treasury
ultimately; what he needed was suggestions for how to do so.

Knowing Roosevelt as he did, Morgenthau realized he had to
meet him part way. On the train from Sea Island to Washington
he wrote a carefully calculated "Memorandum for the President," which he intended to deliver as soon as he arrived on the
evening of Sunday, April 10. The time was propitious, Morgenthau began, for Roosevelt to present to the people a comprehensive statement of policy. He should state first his long-run objectives and describe the major legislation needed during the coming
two years to attain them. That legislation should include the
creation of some kind of transportation authority, appropriations
for the investigation and prosecution of monopolies, a wage and
hour law, and the taxation of tax-exempt bonds. Second, the
program should consist of an outline of specific steps, administrative as well as legislative, which Roosevelt proposed to take in
order to eliminate inefficiencies and failures in parts of the New
Deal already under way. Third, Morgenthau suggested the President prepare a comprehensive government spending and lending
program, coupled with measures to stimulate private re-
employment. It was most important, the Secretary wrote, to put
to work immediately the ten million or more unemployed. But
that did not excuse waste. In formulating a program, the Administration would have to correlate expenditures with the geographical distribution of unemployment.

The recession had destroyed Morgenthau's hopes for balancing the budget in 1939. But he still favored minimizing the total
deficit, relying insofar as possible on lending rather than spending, concentrating spending insofar as possible on relief and
work relief rather than on large-scale public works, and making
the lending and relief policies handmaidens of a central purpose
to spur private investment.

Roosevelt had come to quite different conclusions. On the
night of April 10, Morgenthau had a long and unhappy talk at

the White House with the President, Hopkins, and Jimmy Roosevelt.

"We have been traveling fast this last week and have covered a lot of ground," the President said, "and you will have to hurry to catch up."

"Mr. President," Morgenthau said, "maybe I never can catch up."

Roosevelt smiled. "Oh, yes, you can — in a couple of hours." With that he presented his ideas. Morgenthau's heart sank. It was clear that Hopkins had "sold" the President on spending. Ickes was to be put back into the business of lending money to states and municipalities. The United States Housing Authority was to have its loan authorizations doubled. The Federal Housing Administration was to build $500 million worth of houses. A transcontinental highway was to be started. And so on. Morgenthau listened and then read his own memorandum, with its emphasis on private reemployment.

When he finished, the President asked, "You are in agreement with this?"

"What you have outlined not only frightens me but will frighten the country," Morgenthau replied. "How much is it going to cost?"

"Oh," Roosevelt said, "we have all of that . . . we have all that."

Morgenthau asked to see a list of proposed expenditures, but none was forthcoming. "Please, Mr. President," he said on departing, "don't decide on this until you sleep on it."

The Secretary arrived at the Treasury the next morning depressed and angry. "I don't mind telling you gentlemen what I heard last night," he said to his staff. "The way it was put up to me last night just scared me to death — worse than I've been scared — and the thing hasn't been thought through. And fear begets fear — I mean . . . the President's attitude . . . in 1933 was, let's be calm and do things and overcome fear, but fear begets fear. . . . They had a conference — lasted an hour before I came — in advance of my coming — and I think the whole thing is finished, and there hasn't been a single person in the Treasury that knows a single thing about this. . . . I'm awfully afraid that the cards are all stacked against us."

The new program, Morgenthau went on, would wreck the RFC before Jones had a chance to get started. If Ickes and Hopkins as well as Jones were lending to municipalities, there would be an awful mess. The spenders had carried the day and the President, too. "They have just stampeded him during the week I was away. He was completely stampeded. They stampeded him like cattle."

Morgenthau left his staff to attend a late morning conference at the White House at which Roosevelt revealed his plans to the congressional leaders. It might not be necessary, he said, to increase existing WPA rolls beyond 2,600,000 but in all probability that many people would still be on work relief through the summer and the following winter. The $1 billion allowed for WPA for the fiscal year 1939 could not suffice. Unless the sum were increased, Hopkins would have to let 500,000 or more people go. WPA needed at least $1.25 billion more, the Farm Security Administration $150 million, the National Youth Administration at least $50 million, and the Civilian Conservation Corps $50 million simply to keep the boys in CCC camps who were already there. Roosevelt said he was also studying the loan situation, and he implied that besides whatever Jones could lend, the government would have to do a lot of spending of its own on public works.

Just before the meeting adjourned, Morgenthau broke in. The congressmen, he said, might be interested to know what the budget was going to look like for the coming fiscal year. He told them he thought revenue would fall below the January estimate by $900 million; that additional expenditures, including those Roosevelt had mentioned but excluding money for lending and pump-priming, would increase the deficit for 1939 to $3.5 billion at the inside. This, as he later recalled, gave everybody quite a shock.

After the meeting Roosevelt and Morgenthau had lunch. Usually this was a gay and friendly meal, but not that day. The President said coldly that Morgenthau had no right to bring up the question of the deficit in the morning conference, that the Secretary should have spoken to him first. He was going to take care of the unemployed, Roosevelt added, no matter how much it cost. "You can call Steve Early," he said vehemently, "and he will tell you that nothing is settled. You are just jumping at conclusions."

"No use getting angry," Morgenthau said. "No use in yelling at me. It does not do any good."

"Now at last I have heard the program," Morgenthau told Jimmy Roosevelt on April 12, "and I wish you would take the following message to your father. 'After giving the matter further consideration, I will let you know whether or not I can finance it.' "

"Well, of course you can finance it."

"I don't know, Jimmy."

As he put it later, the Secretary was deeply shaken. With a heavy heart he went home late and tossed in bed. Sometime in the early morning he made an anguished decision. For all his loyalty to the New Deal, for all his love of Franklin Roosevelt, he could see no choice but to resign. It was the blackest hour in his entire career.

Keeping his intentions to himself, Morgenthau telephoned Roosevelt to ask for his "day in court" — half an hour to go over the whole program. He next called Cordell Hull, who also opposed spending and wished Morgenthau the best of luck. At ten-thirty that morning of the unlucky 13th Morgenthau walked sadly to the White House.

"Mr. President," he said, "I am going to say something which is one of the most difficult things that I have ever had to do, but if you insist on going through with this spending program I am seriously thinking of resigning."

Roosevelt responded with a long dissertation on the solidarity of the British cabinet — how each member was bound by the decision of the majority and how they all stood or fell together. "You just can't do this," he said. "You have done a magnificent job, and you have kept your own counsel."

"After all," Morgenthau said, "nobody in the Treasury has

had time to study this program, and we have not been consulted
as to whether it can or cannot be financed; furthermore, whether
it will achieve the results you desire."

The President then, as Morgenthau recalled it, became excited.
If the Secretary resigned it would mean the destruction of the
Democratic party, the creation of a third party and the loss of
the Administration program in Congress. Morgenthau, moreover, would go down in history as having quit under fire.

"The trouble with you," Roosevelt said, "is that you are
piqued and sore because you have not been consulted."

"No, Mr. President," Morgenthau said, "neither of those statements is correct. You are asking your general, in charge of
finances, to carry out a program when he had nothing to do with
the planning."

Obviously uncomfortable, Roosevelt indicated he would like
to close the discussion. "I've got Baruch waiting," he said.

"Let him wait," Morgenthau said. "This is more important."

They parted without resolving their difficulties. Roosevelt
simply would not listen to the talk of resignation, and Morgenthau for the moment saw no alternative.

As he later recalled, he spent the next few hours in a gloomy
daze of indecision. But gradually the relative values of the situation began to sort themselves out, and his position began to clarify itself. He and the President had disagreed over an issue concerning which, it was fair to say, there were, at the very least,
two sides. It was also a technical rather than a moral issue; a
difference about means, not ends. And it was but one of the
many issues involved in the Roosevelt Administration.

Morgenthau might disagree with Franklin Roosevelt about
spending, but they were in agreement on most other broad questions. They shared the same deep conviction that the first concern of government should be for the masses of the people.
They shared the same deep conviction that the democracies of
the world had to prepare for an impending war with the forces
of aggression. Morgenthau asked himself whether he should
jeopardize those common objectives, whether he should withdraw from the common struggle, because of his opposition to

one phase of the President's program. He still had, he realized, a splendid opportunity to make relief efficient, to improve the banking system and tax structure, to mold a foreign economic policy helpful to the democracies. More important, was he to desert the man he admired and loved second only to his father, because of a single disagreement? At the bottom of his heart, he knew his greatest usefulness was in the service of Franklin Roosevelt, and he could not abandon him. So Morgenthau stayed on.

Roosevelt took his program to the people on April 14. For four and a half years, he said, recovery had proceeded apace, but in the previous seven months there had been a setback. The recession had not yet turned to disaster. National income, for example, was almost 50 per cent higher than in 1932. Banks were not in trouble and the federal government had accepted the responsibility for relief. Yet many people had lost their jobs. In his message to Congress during the previous session, he had said that if private enterprise did not provide jobs, government would have to take up the slack. During the last two months it had become apparent that the government had to take aggressive action.

First, he recommended appropriations to maintain the existing rate of government expenditures for work relief and similar purposes. These included additional monies for WPA, for Farm Security, for the National Youth Administration, and for the Civilian Conservation Corps, in all about $1 billion 250 million more than he had estimated the previous January. Second, to provide additional bank reserves, the Treasury would desterilize about $1 billion 400 million of gold and $1 billion of additional credit would be made available by reducing reserve requirements.

In Roosevelt's judgment these two steps were insufficient to start the economy upward. He therefore needed a third kind of government action. In order to add purchasing power by providing new work, he recommended that the United States Housing Authority undertake immediately about $300 million of slum clearance projects. He also planned to renew the public works program as soon as possible to provide $1 billion of permanent public improvements, $100 million more for federal highways, $37 million more for flood control, and $25 million more for federal buildings. This, he observed, would not only help the American people but would give democracy courage the world over.

In 1959, looking back on the budget crisis of 1938, Morgenthau was not sure who had been correct. Later, the huge outlays for defense and war and then for the cold war persuaded economists and thoughtful businessmen to revise "orthodox" conceptions. Certainly an unbalanced budget did not need to be an automatic disaster, as many people thought in 1938; certainly government spending could assure levels of production and employment undreamed of then. Still, as Morgenthau later put it, his position in 1938 was based on the hope that the country could get along without calling upon sustained government spending to make up for the deficiencies of private spending — on the hope that the system might run on its own power. Though twenty years later the whole weight of modern economics was against him, he still thought a balanced budget should have been given a chance.

5. Taxation in Recession

Under the guidance of Roswell Magill, a professor of tax law whom Morgenthau had recruited to government, the Treasury staff presented a study of tax revision that incorporated much of the thinking of the new economics. A year-to-year balance in federal revenues and expenditures, it asserted, would be a superficial and unrealistic aim for the tax structure. Taxes instead should be designed to yield sufficient revenues to balance expenditures over a number of years, perhaps a decade. "In periods of recession," the report explained, "such a tax structure will produce a marked decline in revenues at the very time when the financial requirements of the Government are likely to increase substantially. The result is a budgetary deficit, which is financed . . . by the sale of interest-bearing obligations. . . . The effects of the borrowing will be stimulating to the national economy.

"In the opinion of an important body of present-day economists, a business depression is characterized by a lack of balance between saving and investment. . . . The unpromising or threatening outlook causes individuals and institutions to withhold funds representing bona fide savings from current investment in concrete, durable goods; and this withholding creates a volume of unemployment of both labor and capital, corresponding to the excess of such savings over current investment. If such abortive savings are borrowed by the Federal Government and expended in the current employment of labor and capital, the effect is to increase the national income by virtually the whole of the sums so borrowed, or even more. . . .

"If, in contrast to borrowing, the Federal Government attempts to meet its current expenditures by the imposition of new taxes, such degree of success as is obtained tends to be achieved at the expense of the entire economy."

Morgenthau never accepted that reasoning, but with characteristic respect for the ideas of his chosen advisers, the Secretary sent the report to the Joint Committee on Taxation. Further, though he differed with its premises, he agreed with most of its recommendations. It proposed eliminating many excise taxes, reducing the allowance for mineral depletion, and increasing taxes on modest estates and on personal incomes in the medium brackets. It especially urged the repeal of some corporate taxes and the revision of others in order to make the total impact of corporate taxes proportionate to business size and business profits. Roswell Magill and his associates found the undistributed earnings tax a useful economic and social instrument, but they suggested establishing a steeper graduation, starting with a lower rate, and providing preferential treatment for small corporations.

Roosevelt had similar ideas. In conference with Democratic congressional leaders in November 1937, he spoke emphatically in favor of retaining the undistributed earnings tax. He was amenable to reductions for corporations with incomes of $15,000 or less in order to permit them to expand plant or build up reserves, but he warned against the possibility of corporations defeating the purpose of the tax by readjusting their capital structures. Too much wealth was controlled by two hundred big corporations, the President said, as he urged the congressmen to work out a system for lowering taxes on small businesses while raising them on large ones.

The Senate Finance Committee was already proceeding on its own. Pat Harrison had never liked the undistributed earnings tax and now Joe Kennedy had convinced him that it was forcing corporations into receivership. The senator wanted to act at once, during the special session of Congress sitting in the fall of 1937, and to press also for the repeal of the capital gains tax.

Harrison had powerful friends whose influence grew as the recession worsened. One of the heaviest lobbies ever to descend on Congress appeared during the last week of November to demand tax revision. Among those who testified, Kennedy, Hopkins, and Bernard Baruch advocated the immediate repeal of the undistributed profits tax. It was characteristic of Kennedy and Baruch to oppose any tax that business found distasteful, and Hopkins, according to the guesses of some columnists, itched for business support for the presidential nomination in 1940, but they all also believed that tax reduction would encourage private investment. Indeed Jesse Jones and Eccles, too, as well as a number of professional economists, called the undistributed profits tax a cause of the recession.

If Congress cut taxes hastily, the President held, he would keep it in session until it made up all the resulting deficiencies in federal revenue. But in the House as in the Senate, Congress defied the Administration, and the House Ways and Means Committee reported out a bill that eliminated all but a semblance of the undistributed earnings tax. In a nation-wide radio address, Harrison advocated tax reduction as an essential spur to business confidence. Roosevelt, urged on by Morgenthau, intended to answer the senator early in April, but the President was preoccupied by the spending bill, and while he delayed, the Senate accepted Harrison's schedules and the revenue bill went to conference, where representatives of the two houses began to reconcile their differences. Roosevelt then asked Morgenthau to prepare a letter for the conference committee which "the man in the street" could understand.

By April 13 Magill had drafted a letter attacking the deletion of the undistributed profits tax and the weakening of the capital gains tax as repudiations of New Deal principles. The low rate on capital gains would benefit primarily speculators like Baruch and Kennedy, while the amendments to the undistributed earnings tax would encourage the kind of tax avoidance the Revenue Act of 1936 had attacked.

Jimmy Roosevelt and Steve Early suggested that the letter was politically dangerous at a time when business conditions were so bad. It would also, they argued, antagonize the Senate without accomplishing anything. Morgenthau was furious. "What about the 130,000,000 people who were under the impression that the President wants certain principles in the tax bill," he said, "and he keeps quiet and lets the thing pass without saying anything?" Roosevelt signed the letter.

The President, however, aware of his opponents' strength, was prepared to make the best trade he could. If the Senate did not go along with the Administration, he said, he was thinking seriously of vetoing the bill. Magill feared the Treasury would lose everything but its underwear before the trading was over. Morgenthau thought they had already lost even that. When the bargaining ended, the conference committee had retained a low flat tax on capital gains and, while paying lip service to the undistributed earnings tax, made that tax so small that it was fruitless.

On May 18, 1938, Roosevelt reviewed the situation with Morgenthau and Magill. Magill reported their conference at length:

> The President . . . jokingly called attention to the fact that the Secretary of the Treasury had made no recommendation as to the President's action on the bill, but had merely asked for a conference to discuss the subject. . . . The Secretary asked whether he had not been pretty cagey in framing his letter that way. The President then asked whether we had considered that he had three

possible courses of action. He could sign the bill, he could veto it
or he could keep it for ten days and it would then become a law
without his signature. . . . The President said that . . . he inclined to the third course . . . The Secretary observed that he
liked that better than the President's previous suggestion of signing the bill but issuing a statement at the same time. . . .

The President said . . . under this bill the individual with a
small capital gain of $5000 would pay 15 per cent and the individual
with a $500,000 capital gain would also pay 15 per cent. This was
a clear violation of the principle of taxation according to capacity.

The Secretary said why not sign the bill promptly and issue no
statement. The President seemed impatient with this suggestion.
He said he wanted to take time and go over a memorandum on the
subject. The Secretary said that after he had gone over the memorandum he might ask the advice of the Cabinet. For instance, it
might well be to get Mr. Farley's view on the political side. The
President said the question was one he had to decide for himself,
that it would not be interesting to ask the Cabinet about it since he
already knew what their views were.

Though Roosevelt seemed set on letting the Act become law
without his signature and then explaining why he had done so,
Oliphant recommended a veto. The striking fact about the Act,
Oliphant maintained, was that it so obviously revealed Baruch's
influence on Harrison. New Deal opponents of the bill were
calling it outright the Baruch bill. Many Washington columnists
interpreted it as a victory of Baruch over Roosevelt.

Roosevelt appreciated Oliphant's spirit but hesitated to take
his advice. For several days he withheld his final decision. Then,
using material which the Treasury had supplied, he analyzed the
Revenue Act on May 27 in a speech which neither Morgenthau
nor Harrison had known he was going to deliver. It was a commencement address at the high school in Arthurdale, West Virginia, an impoverished industrial town which Mrs. Roosevelt had
made a special effort to reconstruct. Though the occasion was
an unlikely one, the President broadcast his speech, and Steve
Early drew the attention of the press to it. It was full of fight.

For a great many years, Roosevelt said, the United States had
accepted the principle that taxes ought to be levied on individuals
and families in accordance with their ability to pay. The new tax
bill, though it had some good features, threatened that principle.

The penalty it imposed "for withholding dividends to stockholders," Roosevelt explained, "is so small . . . that it is doubtful, very doubtful, whether it will wholly eliminate the old tax avoidance practices of the past." Worse still, he said, the bill taxed "small capital profits and large capital profits at *exactly the same tax rate*. And that, my friends, *isn't right!*"

Roosevelt was sure the audience could understand his problem: "If I sign the bill — and I have until midnight tonight to sign it — many people with some justification will think I approve the abandonment of an important principle of American taxation. If I veto the bill it will prevent many of the desirable features of it from going into effect.

"Therefore, for the first time since I have been President, I am going to take the third course which is open to me *under the Constitution*. At midnight tonight this new tax bill will automatically become law, but it will become law without my signature, without my approval."

The address infuriated Harrison. He blamed Morgenthau, and not without some cause, for Magill and Oliphant had contributed extensively to the documents on which the President based his address. So angry was Harrison that it was months before he was again willing to speak to the Secretary, but as Roosevelt observed, the senator had already strayed off the reservation. Whatever his mood, moreover, he had had his way on the Revenue Act.

For Morgenthau the defeat was galling. He had, in a sense, lost the battle of the budget twice, once to the President and once to the Senate, for the Revenue Act would reduce federal income. He had lost, too, a battle of principle, for the Act, as Roosevelt had said, encouraged tax avoidance and imposed inequitable schedules. All in all, the Secretary had a dismal spring in 1938.

Discouraged, but not for long depressed, Morgenthau decided to reconsider the arguments of those whose policies he had been opposing. Late in June, just before sailing for France, where he looked forward to resting after the most exhausting six months he had yet spent in Washington, he instructed his staff to review for him the whole problem of the public debt, of public spending, and of a compensatory budget. A number of professional economists had put a bug in his ear, he said, and he was particularly impressed by the writings of Gunnar Myrdal, a Swedish Keynesian. "We distinctly need a fresh viewpoint on this thing," the Secretary told his staff. "I mean we've taken this defeatist attitude right along, that it's something to be terribly ashamed of. Maybe it isn't. I don't know."

The analysis that awaited him on his return from Europe, however, failed to win him to countercyclical spending. Roosevelt, too, was still a doubter. As he and Morgenthau sat down together in the fall of 1938 to examine prospects for the fiscal year 1940, the President "seemed quite disturbed and shocked at the figures. He . . . indicated that what we might do from here on was to require a reduction in Hopkins's monthly expenditures as Ickes's monthly expenditures increased. He thought that possibly there was not the same ratio of employment but that we could work out some method to show a proportionate reduction." Back at the Treasury, Morgenthau presented the probable figures for the deficit in 1940 — figures swollen by the needs of national defense — and asked each of his associates if he had anything to say. "Not now," one of them replied. "I feel awfully sick."

"I had my stomach removed about two years ago," the Secretary said. ". . . I'm not going to take 1940 for granted. I may be a damn fool, but I'm not going to do it."

He would fight the battle of the budget again, and so would Roosevelt. Neither was really reconciled to an unbalanced budget. Both, however, believed the federal government had the responsibility to relieve the distress of unemployment, indeed the responsibility to provide full employment. Roosevelt went further than did Morgenthau in advocating large-scale public works, but the Secretary differed with his chief only in degree, not in purpose. Both, furthermore, believed that government had the responsibility for preserving free enterprise. Roosevelt by the fall of 1938 counted largely on antitrust activities to do so. Morgenthau had come to rely more upon removing deterrents to private investment; had come to side with Harrison in

favor of reducing taxes on business, including the shadow that
was left of the undistributed profits tax. "Either we're going to
fix the taxes . . . to encourage the people to risk their money
. . ." he said, "or the only other alternative is more deficit
finance. And while I am here I want to . . . encourage private
capital."

He had always wanted to. The recession did not alter his
creed, though experience persuaded him to change his tactics.
Yet free enterprise was for him, as for Roosevelt, only one part
of the image of a good society. As Morgenthau said in a commencement address of his own, it had been vital for the New
Deal to arrest the decline in the lives and fortunes of the American people, to serve American youth, to build homes, wipe out
slums, and discipline the buccaneers of the financial world. It
was tragic, he observed, that abundance alarmed some Americans. There had been a short circuit between production and
consumption, and this had yet fully to be repaired. But the Administration was at work on it, and he hoped the young men of
Temple University would join the national effort to produce a
life of plenty for everyone.

That, as he noted, had become of special importance because
of the encroaching challenge of totalitarianism. The United
States had to succeed, to prove that by democratic processes of
free enterprise and competition, of free votes, of freedom of conscience and expression and opportunity, the nation could reach a
condition of universal plenty. Not for its own sake alone, not
for the sake of its people alone, but also as an example to men
everywhere threatened by fascism and Communism, the United
States had a mission which the New Deal was furthering.

That mission, as the Secretary interpreted it, also involved the
fashioning of a foreign policy suitable to the time. In the fall of
1938, as during the previous year, the problems of the budget
and the direction of reform, urgent though they were, provoked
no greater anxiety than did portentous events abroad. Those developments increasingly engaged Morgenthau's attention, for
like the President, he sensed that his generation all over the world
had to keep its rendezvous with destiny.

VIII

THE TREASURY

AND FOREIGN AFFAIRS

1937 — 1938

1. The Stage

DURING 1937 and 1938 Morgenthau could not rid himself of a sense of impending disaster abroad. The entire creed he had learned as a youth — democracy, the rights of man, the rights of weak nations — now trembled before the advance of totalitarianism in Europe and Asia. Like Roosevelt and most other Americans, Morgenthau knew that war was an awful prospect, but he recognized the overwhelming necessity of resisting fascism, if need be at the risk of war, indeed, if need be, ultimately by war itself.

It was in that respect, he later observed, that he differed most from those of his countrymen who made peace their sole objective. He differed, too, with the State Department, for he found its approach, as he put it ten years later, "timorous" and "conventional," dominated by the "foreign-office mentality" — the notion that you got things done by being a generous host at diplomatic banquets. There were, of course, exceptions to that point of view, and Morgenthau respected the realistic contributions to foreign policy of Sumner Welles, the Under Secretary of State, and Herbert Feis, Hull's economic adviser. But Secretary Hull, in Morgenthau's opinion, was obsessed by his trade agreements program and misled by the Anglophilism and the hesitancies of career diplomats. Consequently the State Department as a whole failed to realize that Japanese militarism and European fascism had released new and ugly forces which, as Morgenthau saw it, could not be controlled politely.

As Secretary of the Treasury, Morgenthau was responsible for foreign monetary policy, and before 1937 he had revealed the directions he would take. His negotiations with China about silver, and those with England and France resulting in the Tripartite Pact, had provided instruments of limited effect for stiffening democratic resistance to Germany, Italy, and Japan. During 1937 and after, he acted in his own sphere more often and more vigorously than before, and he also urged constantly upon the President a more forceful general policy than any other member of the Administration, save Harold Ickes, was yet prepared to advocate. Morgenthau's perceptions about the totalitarian threat, however, were far larger than his means to combat it, and that imbalance tormented him constantly.

2. Arms and the Franc

As 1937 began, Vincent Auriol, the French Minister of Finance, urged the democratic nations to supplement the Tripartite Pact with further economic and political arrangements which would, among other things, open up the possibility for disarmament. In private Auriol told the Treasury's special emissary in France that he was worried about the continuing outflow of gold. That outflow reflected a lack of confidence in the franc arising from deepseated economic difficulties. Some of those grew out of the efforts of the Popular Front government of Leon Blum to pursue a program of reform opposed by conservative Frenchmen, including many investors. Holders of francs also feared the enormous additional strain which the need for military preparedness imposed upon the French economy. Although Auriol main-

tained that there was no immediate prospect of further devaluation, the arms race was severely complicating the management
of the franc.

On February 6 Neville Chamberlain in a confidential message
to Morgenthau described the increasing difficulties of the Blum
government. The Secretary, as he noted in his Diary, immediately telephoned Roosevelt:

> I said I thought the most significant thing about it was that Cham-
> berlain sent me a message more than what was in it. The President
> said every time the French have a crisis they seem a little worse
> off. I said we were only talking about what we would *do in case of
> war*, but were doing nothing to try and *stop war*. I said I . . .
> wanted to talk to him about the plan he had mentioned to me
> about . . . going possibly to Holland and try and call in various
> leaders from various countries and try and talk sense to them. (He
> mentioned this to me maybe a year ago.) What I *did not say* is
> that I feel the only way to stop war is to try and stop this mad race
> to arm that is going on in Europe. After all we would have noth-
> ing to lose and everything to gain. Everything points towards war
> in Europe and surely sooner or later we will be dragged into
> it. . . . The cost of arming is what is breaking down the Treas-
> uries of the World. I hope the President will let me help him work
> this out. I don't believe that Hull and Norman Davis* ever will.
> They just don't have guts enough. The President has the courage
> and I hope to be able to convince him that if the world is to be
> saved the next move is up to him.

On February 9 Morgenthau lunched with Roosevelt. "The
world is just drifting rapidly towards war," the Secretary said.
"We patch up the French situation every so often but with the
constant increased percentage of their budget going for war purposes we really cannot help them. The European countries are
gradually going bankrupt through preparing for war. You are
the only person who can stop it."

With a smile on his face, Roosevelt replied: "I feel like throwing either a cup and saucer at you or the coffeepot."

---

* Norman Davis was a veteran diplomat, internationalist, and advocate of disarmament, on whom Hull leaned. Morgenthau considered Davis an "unimpeachable gentleman" but an overcautious counselor.

"Or throw both, but why?"

"Well," Roosevelt continued, "I had Hull, Norman Davis to lunch and Davis said, the only person who can save the situation is Roosevelt and then I said to Davis how, and Davis said by sending a secret envoy to Europe." Roosevelt paused. "Another Colonel House."

"Hull's philosophy," the President went on, "is that through his trade treaties he would increase world trade and take up the slack of unemployment as the individual countries gradually disarm."

"I am not in disagreement with Hull," Morgenthau said, "but his policies will take five years to feel the full effect. He may only have five months before we have a world war and if we do and it lasts two or three years you can be sure we will be drawn into it. Would you have any objection to my sending a secret confidential message . . . to Neville Chamberlain asking him if he has any suggestions to make as to how we can keep the world from going financially broke due to constant increased cost of armaments?"

After thinking a moment, Roosevelt said: "No, that will be all right."

"Are you sure?" Morgenthau asked.

"Yes, I am sure."

"You know my idea," Morgenthau said, "is that if there are any negotiations to be conducted it is to do them here and not send anybody abroad."

"That is right," the President replied.

"I certainly had a most interesting and constructive lunch," Morgenthau recorded in his Diary, "and if I can be helpful in doing something to get the world to disarm I will die happy."

Two days later, on February 11, Morgenthau gave the representative of the British Treasury a communication "from one finance minister to another . . . the thing that is breaking down the credit of the big countries . . . is armaments. That affects your Treasury and . . . is the basis of the French troubles, the Japanese troubles, and looking at it as a financial matter and not as a diplomatic has he any suggestions to make to me whereby he and I might make some start to stop the arming that is going on all over the world."

While he awaited a reply from Chamberlain, Morgenthau on February 16 again suggested a disarmament conference of the major powers. Roosevelt, who seemed favorable to the idea, said that if he called a conference, he would invite just about half a dozen countries. He would tell their delegates that the problem was theirs, and send them to some other building to work out a solution and come back with it. He would offer no advice about political issues, the President added, but he would try to get disarmament started at an accelerating pace over a five year period. Any nation refusing to comply with the majority rule, he said, should then be hit by an economic boycott imposed by the others at the conference.

Dumfounded though he was by Roosevelt's rapid and elaborate response, Morgenthau did not expect any quick developments from his chief's musings. French ineptness in the management of the franc would not have disturbed the Secretary if he had felt that the possibilities for disarmament were real. Clearly, however, they were not. So persuaded, Roosevelt made no gesture toward summoning a conference. And whatever hopes Morgenthau had dared nourish were dashed when on March 26, 1937, he received Neville Chamberlain's reply to his query about disarmament.

Chamberlain had received the message, he wrote Morgenthau, with great interest, and discussed it with both Prime Minister Stanley Baldwin and Foreign Secretary Anthony Eden. He wanted to say "how warmly they all three appreciate this evidence of Mr. Morgenthau's and — as they understand — the President's earnest desire to find some way in which the United States — possibly in conjunction with the United Kingdom — could help in preventing the outbreak of another war. Beset as they are with the difficulties and risks inherent in the present political situation in Europe, the Chancellor and his colleagues had given their most anxious consideration to this message."

In order to gauge the possibilities of averting war, Chamber-

lain continued, it was necessary first to consider where the menace lay and what the causes were that kept it alive. "These
causes are both political and economic," he wrote, "and it is
sometimes difficult to disentangle them . . . but Mr. Morgenthau is undoubtedly right in saying that the needs of armament
programs are responsible for a good deal of the economic
troubles in Europe and these programs are in turn the result of
political considerations." Yet, Chamberlain observed, the main
source of fear of war was Germany. "No other country, not
Italy, since she has her hands full with the task of consolidating
her Abyssinian conquest, not Russia with all her military preparations, certainly not France, England or any of the smaller
Powers, is for a moment credited with any aggressive designs.
But the fierce propaganda against other nations continually carried on by the German Press and wireless . . . the intensity and
persistence of German military preparations, together with the
many acts of the German Government in violation of treaties,
cynically justified on the ground that unilateral action was the
quickest way of getting what they wanted, have inspired all her
neighbors with a profound uneasiness. Even these islands which
could be reached in less than an hour from German territory by
an airforce equipped with hundreds of tons of bombs cannot be
exempt from anxiety."

Germany's aggressiveness, Chamberlain believed, arose from
her desire to make herself so strong that no one would venture to
withstand whatever demands she might make for European or
colonial territories. "With this intention in her heart she is not
likely to agree to any disarmament which would defeat her purpose. The only consideration which would influence her to a
contrary decision would be the conviction that her efforts to
secure superiority of force were doomed to failure by reason of
the superior force which would meet her if she attempted aggression."

England was rearming, to the gratification of many nations,
but the British government had "no doubt whatever that the
greatest single contribution which the United States could make
at the present moment to the preservation of world peace would

be the amendment of the existing neutrality legislation. Under this legislation an embargo would be imposed on the export from the United States of arms and munitions, irrespective of whether a country is an aggressor or the victim of an aggression. It is obvious that the existing neutrality law and . . . any extension of it to include raw materials, suits the requirements of a country contemplating an aggression, which can and would lay up large stores of war materials with the knowledge that its intended victim will, when the time comes, be precluded from obtaining supplies from one of the greatest world markets. The legislation in its present form constitutes an indirect but potent encouragement to aggression, and it is earnestly hoped that some way may be found of leaving sufficient discretion with the Executive to deal with each case on its merits."

Chamberlain realized that the question, apart from its international aspects, was a matter of domestic controversy within the United States, and that it might well be impossible for the American government to take the step he recommended even if the Administration so desired, but in view of Morgenthau's request for his opinions, Chamberlain was expressing them "without reserve."

In this mood he turned to a related issue:

Japan . . . is another Power with far-reaching ambitions which affect the interests of this country . . . not with the same intensity as those which touch her very existence, but in highly important respects. The strain upon our resources is therefore seriously aggravated by the necessity of providing for the protection of our Far Eastern and Pacific interests, especially as the most favorable moment for any enterprise in that region injurious to our position there would be precisely when we were engaged in hostilities in Europe. The conclusion of the recent German-Japanese agreement is an indication, if one were needed, that if we were seriously involved in Europe we could not count even on the neutrality of Japan. Anything therefore which would tend to stabilize the position in the Far East would . . . ease our position there and safeguard us against added embarrassment in the event of trouble in Europe.

Even if the Japanese were to change their attitude, Chamberlain went on, the British would welcome an exchange of views with the United States "on the possibility of taking this opportunity to try to put relations between the United States of America, Japan and Great Britain on a footing that would ensure harmonious cooperation for the protection and development of their respective interests." Chamberlain concluded by expressing his earnest trust that "some form of collaboration" might be possible between the United States and Great Britain, since he was "profoundly convinced that almost any action common to them both would go far to restore confidence to the world and divert the menace which . . . threatens it."

There it was. The British government saw no chance for disarmament. Reading Hitler and his purposes more accurately than he was to read them later, Chamberlain in effect asserted the futility of attempting to negotiate. Morgenthau had hoped that the prestige and strength of the United States, personified in Roosevelt, might bring the Germans to see the impossibility of an arms race and of aggression. Chamberlain shared that hope, but what he urged was not a move for disarmament but a basic change in the structure of American neutrality legislation.

Morgenthau sympathized with the Chancellor's recommendation. The Neutrality Act embargoed the shipment of arms to all belligerents; before 1937 was over, it was amended to permit the President to embargo also other commodities he chose to list. In this manner the Congress expected to insulate the United States from hostilities overseas. The result, as Chamberlain said, and as Morgenthau and a minority of Americans recognized, was a backhanded invitation to aggressors. Given the posture of the Department of State, Morgenthau could not begin to follow the Chancellor's prescription in the Orient. It was not that Chamberlain was wrong, but rather that Morgenthau had no way to operate within the boundaries of action that Chamberlain defined.

3. War in China

In May 1937, H. H. Kung, the Chinese Minister of Finance, had
cabled Morgenthau to ask whether the Treasury would buy 50
million ounces of silver which China had in New York. Kung,
who was then attending the coronation of George VI, had failed
to negotiate a loan in London. He needed foreign exchange to
preserve his currency reforms, and he hoped to sell his silver during his forthcoming visit to the United States.

Morgenthau was at first reluctant to make the purchase. The
Treasury, he held, had already done everything possible for
China. But almost immediately the Secretary softened. With
Chiang Kai-shek again putting his affairs in order, Roosevelt
wanted to treat the Chinese "extra nice." Morgenthau, moreover, deemed it appropriate to save Kung's face, to give him
something to take home. He therefore decided to purchase 12
million ounces of silver, provided that Kung used the proceeds to
increase China's gold reserves.

On July 8 Morgenthau gave Kung the good news, explaining
that Roosevelt had instructed the Treasury to do everything it
could to keep China strong. Frankly pleased, Kung commended
the American point of view, since a "strong China" meant security and peace in the Far East. What Kung was trying to say,
one of his associates explained, was that Morgenthau was a great
statesman.

"Listen, Dr. Kung," Morgenthau replied, "I bought all your
silver; you don't have to give me anything more."

"Well," said Kung, "I sold the silver to you cheap. I bought
your surplus gold."

The meeting closed with laughter, but at an ironic time, for
Kung had remarked on peace and stability in the Far East in ig-
norance of the news which had yet to reach Washington: Japanese and Chinese troops had clashed at the Marco Polo Bridge

near Peking. The undeclared Sino-Japanese War began just before the conference reached its conclusion. Henceforth, keeping
China strong was to prove more difficult than ever. Henceforth,
indeed, the Treasury was to be unable to confine its negotiations
to the monetary aspects of diplomacy.

The undeclared war immediately raised questions about American policies. At Cabinet meetings of August 6 and 13, 1937,
Vice President Garner urged the withdrawal of American troops
in the Peking area, a policy also demanded by a resolution then
before the Congress. Roosevelt explained that the complete
transfer of the embassy and its protective troops to Nanking had
been delayed three years earlier at the recommendation of the
State Department. He had accepted that advice which, in retrospect, he judged unfortunate. Roosevelt also reminded Garner
that American troops, as well as those of other countries, were in
China in order to maintain a sufficient total complement of foreign components to protect all Westerners. This policy rested
on a gentlemen's agreement which in present circumstances the
United States could not very well violate. The Chinese situation,
Hull added, was extremely complicated. An orderly withdrawal
in agreement with other nations would be given one interpretation, whereas the Japanese would consider a scuttling departure
to signify a complete retreat of the United States from the Pacific. That would mean giving up American influence and damaging American trade in approximately half the world.

When Garner then objected to risking war for the sake of
business, Hull replied that he believed all the major powers
should gradually withdraw from China, and he planned if necessary to take the lead in doing so. The only purpose of the American troops, he repeated, was to protect American nationals from
irresponsible mobs. Roosevelt, who was also reassuring, told
Garner the Administration was basing its policies in the Far East
"on the hope of Japanese disaster, which could be produced by a
rise in the strength of Russia and China and a revolt on the part
of the Japanese population against militarism." The Cabinet
then decided to inform American residents in China that ships
would be held in readiness to take away all women and children

who wished to leave. Those who remained would stay at their own risk.

The President had to make an even more difficult decision about whether to recognize a state of war between China and Japan. On the advice of the State Department, he did not. A proclamation of a state of war, the Department argued, would lessen the possibility of composing the differences between the belligerents, and increase the chances of American involvement, which might follow hard on a Japanese invocation of belligerent rights to restrict neutral commerce.

So long as the war was undeclared and officially unrecognized, the Neutrality Act did not apply, and both China and Japan were free to make purchases in the American market insofar as they had available funds and reasonable expectations of delivery. In both respects, the Treasury believed, Japan had an advantage, for her finances were far stronger than the Chinese, and whereas there was no problem in shipping materials to Japanese ports, the Japanese fleet blocked access to China. Nevertheless, some material got through, and there would be more if the Chinese were able to work out overland transportation from Burma and other areas outside of Japanese control.

Morgenthau's predisposition to help China was confirmed by the political analyses he received from his Research Division in September. In the long run, the Division believed, a Japanese victory would greatly increase the chance of general world war, if only by encouraging other fascist nations to aggression. Germany was quite prepared to fish in troubled waters; and should Japan achieve success, the probability of a German move against Czechoslovakia would become great. Moreover, if Japan won a clear and decisive victory, the moment might be propitious for a joint German-Japanese attack on Russia. The peace of the world, as the Treasury saw it, was tied up to China's ability to prolong resistance.

During the fall of 1937, however, various diplomatic efforts failed to assist the Chinese. At their request, the League of Nations investigated the undeclared war. A League report of October 6, which the United States endorsed, blamed Japan for the hostilities. The previous day Roosevelt, speaking in Chicago, had compared world lawlessness to an epidemic. "When an epidemic . . . starts to spread," he said, "the community . . . joins in a quarantine of the patients . . . to protect the health of the community against the spread of the disease. . . . There must be positive endeavors to preserve peace." Just what the President implied has never been clear, and probably was not entirely clear to him, but he did not, he later explained, have sanctions in mind, and as isolationists attacked his message, he obscured his purpose behind a vague discussion of the importance of peace. He also did not, it developed, intend to pursue a policy of collective security against aggressors, at least not yet. At the Brussels Conference of November 1937, the United States and the European democracies reaffirmed their concern for the territorial integrity of China, but took no significant action against Japan. On their part the Japanese, defying both the conference and the League report of October, indicated that they would tolerate no outside interference with their China policy.

There was little in these developments to sustain Chinese resistance. Cordell Hull offered nothing more. Though he continually remarked the importance of international treaties and international law, he avoided the question of China's territorial integrity. China had reason to wonder whether she had any friend.

Morgenthau, resolved to be friendly, did not know how far the State Department would tolerate his monetary diplomacy, but he responded as generously as he could to China's overtures. On November 29 he began to consider a request for a bid on 10 million more ounces of silver. He wanted to tell the Chinese that he would buy 50 million ounces from them during the next ten weeks. He also wanted to extend for another year the agreement permitting China to borrow foreign exchange against gold on deposit within the United States. But before proceeding toward either of those goals, he asked Roosevelt for advice.

The President on December 2 instructed him to consult the Secretary of State. He would personally tell Hull, Roosevelt added, that he was inclined to go along with both of Morgenthau's proposals, but that both might be affected by any future proclamation of American neutrality. In the absence of such a proclamation (and Roosevelt said he would issue none unless the Japanese or Chinese declared war), the United States, the President believed, should continue its friendly policy just as if there were no hostilities.

The State Department had no official comment to make about Treasury purchases of Chinese silver. Informally, however, Hull advised Morgenthau to keep free of any commitments he would have to follow through should there be either a declaration of war or an application of the neutrality legislation. The customary rules of international law did not pertain to loans to belligerent governments, but Hull's legal adviser held that the purchase of silver from China would be against those customary rules if there were a formal declaration of war.

The State Department's indirect opposition to the proposed silver purchase led Morgenthau to restate his case entirely apart from its bearing on conditions in the Orient. The purchase of 50 million ounces of Chinese silver, he suggested, had as its real purpose the stabilization of the dollar, for China would be able to buy dollars by selling the gold she received for her silver. This kind of transaction was a tested device for improving the regulation of foreign exchange, specifically for maintaining the parity between the yuan and the dollar. The State Department, however, in a memorandum of December 6, 1937, expressed reservations about the Treasury plan. Since the Treasury said that the transactions in question could not be regarded as a loan or credit, and since the Treasury had made similar agreements with countries other than China, the State Department did not see how the arrangements could properly be considered as rendering the United States unneutral. But since the transaction was of a somewhat novel character, the State Department suggested retaining some freedom of action. It recommended that the Treasury include a provision making future extensions contingent on "any possible questions of neutrality that may arise." The Treasury might also tell the Chinese that, in the present judgment of the Department of State, such contingencies would not in fact arise.

After reading and rereading the memorandum, Morgenthau said he could not understand whether the State Department was telling the Treasury yes or no. He therefore turned to Roosevelt, who on December 8 called the memorandum "the most stupid . . . I have ever read. When they recommend that we add to the agreement to give China a foreign exchange loan a statement 'This may be cancelled in case of a Neutrality Proclamation,' this would be playing into the hands of somebody like Senator Nye." *

"Or the Japanese," Morgenthau added.

"Fix up an agreement with them right away in writing," the President directed.

Despite the hesitations of the Department of State, the Treasury bought the Chinese silver and extended to China for six months the privilege of procuring dollar credits against gold held in the United States. Those policies, conveniently redefined as ventures in monetary stabilization, were in fact efforts, however modest, to help the Chinese to purchase the materials of war which they desperately needed. They were soon to require much more help, but Morgenthau had given them at least a psychological lift. He had found a way around, and Roosevelt had stood behind him.

Franklin Roosevelt — the President — sensitive, perhaps to a fault, to the isolationist sentiment in the country and on Capitol Hill, buried the concept of quarantines beneath the caution of the State Department. Franklin Roosevelt — the man — indignant at Japan's brazen aggression, rejoiced in the uninhibited response of his like-minded friend, the Secretary of the Treasury. If Cordell Hull was Roosevelt's book of rules, Morgenthau, as Mrs. Roosevelt often said, was her husband's conscience.

* Gerald Nye, a leading Senate isolationist.

4. The Panay

On December 12, 1937, Japanese military airplanes bombed and
sank the United States gunboat *Panay* and destroyed three
Standard Oil Company tankers twenty miles up the Yangtze
River from Nanking. They machine-gunned the survivors of
the American ships, killing three and wounding others. Japanese
army motorboats also machine-gunned the *Panay*, and Japanese
personnel boarded that vessel although they could plainly see the
American markings on the ship, including the large ensign she
flew and two large flags painted on her upper deck.

Roosevelt, "deeply shocked," told the State Department to
render a protest to the Japanese Emperor, and Hull on his own
account also instructed the American ambassador in Tokyo to
impress upon the Japanese government "the gravity of the situation and the imperative need to take every precaution against
further attacks on American vessels and personnel." Yet neither
Hull nor his advisers believed that the United States was in a
position to send sufficient naval forces to the Orient to require
the Japanese to behave. Further, the Department of State was
conscious of persisting pressures from the American people for
the withdrawal of American troops from the Far East, and of
persistent opposition to the tone of the President's quarantine
speech. Hull therefore proposed to confine American policy to
demanding an apology, indemnities, and punishment of the officers who had directed the attack, as well as assurances that similar incidents would not again occur.

The Japanese ambassador on December 13 described those requests as "wholly reasonable," and the Japanese Foreign Minister
called on the American ambassador in Tokyo to deliver "a profound apology." There was no question but that the Japanese
government would repudiate the deliberate but unauthorized action of their army on the Yangtze. Consequently, Hull appar-

ently never even considered the possibility that the attack on the *Panay* might lead to a rupture in diplomatic relations or to war.

Roosevelt, who was more bellicose, told Morgenthau on December 14 that there were lots of ways of declaring war. In the old days, he said, sinking an American naval vessel would have in itself constituted a cause of war. Now it was not considered such, but Roosevelt wanted Morgenthau to find out what authority he needed as President to take possession of all the belongings of the Japanese government and its citizens in the United States, and hold them against payment for the damages the Japanese had caused. If he lacked authority to do this, he wanted to know how he could do it anyhow, and what anyone could do to him for having taken matters into his own hands.

A quick review of the available figures led the Treasury on December 15 to conclude that Japan and her citizens held about $72 million in short-term funds and something between $55 and $125 million in long-term securities, as well as merchandise, ships, and real estate valued between $25 and $50 million. The grand total ranged between $152 and $247 million, most of which the Japanese could convert into pounds sterling within a few hours. Yet Herman Oliphant, with his customary resourcefulness, proposed a plan for sequestering Japanese funds if Roosevelt found that necessary. As Oliphant explained in a detailed memorandum, under a 1933 amendment to the Trading with the Enemy Act, the President could proclaim a national emergency and issue regulations prohibiting or restricting exchange transactions. The proclamation could be drawn in general terms, reciting the necessity for forestalling events which might plunge the country into war, for quarantining the war situation, and consequently for providing a basis for indemnity as well as for protection against future acts. On that basis the President could expressly prohibit banking and foreign exchange transactions and monetary exports in which the Japanese government was directly or indirectly interested.

Surprised and delighted by Oliphant's memo, Roosevelt exclaimed: "My God, I completely forgot about it." He also directed Morgenthau to examine the scheme further.

As a first step, Morgenthau proposed sounding out Sir John Simon on the transatlantic telephone. Simon, now Chancellor of the Exchequer in the government of Prime Minister Neville Chamberlain, had been British Foreign Secretary in 1931, when Japan invaded Manchuria. At that time he had seemed pusillanimous to the American Secretary of State, Henry L. Stimson. Morgenthau thought a telephone call would stiffen the British. It would be "a bombshell to Simon," but Wayne Taylor, an Assistant Secretary of the Treasury, thought it would also be dangerous for the United States. Taylor asked whether the President was willing to go beyond regulations to war. If necessary, Morgenthau answered, the United States would fight. After all, he continued, "they've sunk a United States battleship and killed three people. . . . You going to sit here and wait until you wake up here in the morning and find them in the Philippines, then Hawaii, and then in Panama? Where would you call a halt?" Taylor said he would wait quite a while.

Morgenthau, disagreeing "1000 per cent," said that economically, psychologically and financially, the country was ready for a war basis. He could see no reason for waiting for the Japanese to strike again.

"Well," Taylor replied, "of all the cockeyed things in the world that we can do that would be more cockeyed than the last World War we got into, this would be it."

"Now listen, Wayne," the Secretary said, "I am under great strain; I can't always stand having you do this to me. . . . I have yet to find you come in and say, well, Henry, I'll help you on this thing. But when you say that . . . what the President wants is cockeyed, I object."

Taylor replied that he had said that to get into war would be cockeyed.

Morgenthau still objected: "Has anybody said we were going to get into war? I say to you this is what the President wants. I think it's all right. I'm going to do what he asked me to do. . . . Now, be reasonable. . . . I'm only a human being, Wayne."

"I think that this particular thing we have to think through, and I don't think we have," Taylor answered.

"Well, I'm very sorry," Morgenthau said, "but this is what the President wants. Personally, I think it's a marvelous idea. . . . For us to let them put their swords into our insides and sit there and take it and like it, and not do anything about it, I think is un-American and I think that we've got to begin to inch in on those boys, and that's what the President is doing. . . . How long are you going to sit there and let these fellows kill American soldiers and sailors and sink our battleships?"

"A helluva a while," Taylor said.

Even Hull didn't feel that way, Morgenthau said, and Oliphant assured Taylor that they had been over the legal side of the problem. The Constitution gave to Congress the power to declare war, but American legal precedent was reasonably clear that the Executive had the authority to resist violence. That was all very pretty, Taylor replied, but if in the circumstances the particular move under discussion led to war, he was absolutely opposed to it.

"We are," Oliphant protested, "in a situation where not acting is just as fraught with consequences as acting."

Taylor was not so sure. "There is no reflection on the President," he said to Morgenthau, "and there's no reflection on you. I'm talking about the possibilities . . . of going through with this thing, and where do you go?"

Morgenthau explained again that he was acting as Roosevelt's agent. He had been told to explore the matter. And he thought the time had come for the United States to tell the Japanese to behave, because otherwise "it's only a matter of five or ten years before we'll have them on our necks."

"Well," Taylor said, "that's where I disagree."

At that point, Morgenthau had to go off to a Cabinet meeting. When he returned he reported that Roosevelt had pulled out Oliphant's memorandum, without explaining what it was, and said, "We want these powers to be used to prevent war. . . . After all, if Italy and Japan have evolved a technique of fighting without declaring war, why can't we develop a similar one?"

Vice President Garner thought that only real force would have any effect on the Japanese. Roosevelt, however, believed

that economic sanctions could be made effective. "We don't call
them economic sanctions; we call them quarantines. We want to
develop a technique which will not lead to war. We want to be
as smart as Japan and as Italy. We want to do it in a modern
way."

After concluding his account of the Cabinet meeting, Morgenthau, frankly excited by Roosevelt's enthusiasm for sanctions for
peace, put in his telephone call to Sir John Simon. He was calling, the Secretary said, with the knowledge and the approval of
the President. He was operating through the Treasury rather
than through diplomatic channels, and his message was for Simon and Chamberlain alone. But Simon, who remembered that
Stimson in 1931 had misunderstood him on the telephone, interrupted to say that in England foreign affairs had to be conducted
through regular channels. He was nevertheless sure that Chamberlain would consider the call all right.

Morgenthau then explained that while the United States was
awaiting a Japanese reply to the American note about the *Panay*,
the Administration was exploring various methods for handling
an unsatisfactory answer. Under the Trading with the Enemy
Act, the President had the authority to declare a national emergency and "under such an act the idea would be to keep this
nation quarantined against a war." That would involve complete exchange control, including control both of bank credits
and gold movements. Unless the United States had cooperation
in such a policy, however, it would not be very useful, and Morgenthau wondered whether Simon might not like to think the
problem over.

"Yes," Simon said. "Now, look here, Dr. Henry Morgenthau,
thank you very much for even consulting me. I do appreciate
your speaking about a rather technical thing. . . . And, of
course, when you use a long-distance telephone, it's hardly possible to grasp details . . . and I am certain that if we are going
to do this we must really have the opportunity of looking at this
act you speak of and considering it in some detail." He suggested Morgenthau have the British ambassador cable the Foreign Office.

"Frankly," Morgenthau said, "we didn't want to put it in writing."

Simon replied that in the past he had not found that long-distance telephone calls were always understood. In England they tried to discuss business as far as possible through their offices. He was at dinner, his soup was getting cold, and he could not send a note to the Prime Minister until the following day. "I don't want it to be said hereafter," Simon continued, "that a suggestion was made to us and I didn't understand and the consequence is that if they had only acted differently something else would have happened. You know what happened in the case of Stimson. And I don't want there to be any misunderstanding."

"I didn't know how you felt about telephone calls," Morgenthau said.

"I don't think well of them," Simon said, "for this sort of purpose, to tell you the truth because I can't make a proper record. . . . I want to do everything that is helpful and frankly it is very difficult — our own methods in this country are rather the mode of our habits."

Morgenthau replied that it was an American habit to use the telephone freely; and Simon, laughing, said that he knew it, but England was a small country, and "we have a system that is completely confidential."

So did Roosevelt. Following new instructions from him, Morgenthau cabled Simon on December 18: "In pursuance my telephone conversation with you it is obvious that the subject is corollary to but an essential part of naval conversations and studies about to be made. The British Ambassador and your Foreign Office have been advised. With full concurrence of Secretary of State Hull we are asking the American officer who will shortly arrive in London to see you and obtain your views on the economic phase which I discussed with you by telephone Friday evening."

The President had decided to send Captain R. E. Ingersoll of the United States Navy to London to investigate "with the British Admiralty . . . what we could do if the United States and England would find themselves at war with Japan." Roosevelt was still interested in Oliphant's memorandum, and he wanted the Treasury to draft regulations governing foreign exchange, but he was not in as great a hurry as he had been. Though he was uncertain about Japan's assurances of friendship, he had, as Morgenthau put it, cooled off a bit.

By December 21, when the regulations were ready, the White House gave no indication of wanting them. That afternoon, furthermore, Morgenthau heard from Simon. He had given Morgenthau's complete message of December 17 to Prime Minister Chamberlain and Foreign Secretary Eden. He was pleased that Ingersoll was coming to England. But the British, lacking powers similar to those of the American Trading with the Enemy Act, could not cooperate in monetary action against Japan without requesting special legislation from Parliament, and without first consulting the dominions.

Most important, Simon said that study and experience had convinced the Chamberlain government that all aspects of such a problem as the Japanese crisis had to be considered together, and no separate decisions could be made about economic, political or strategic factors. Simon himself believed that long-range economic pressure would not produce immediate results, and was therefore hardly worth while. The application of immediate and drastic pressure was, in his view, indistinguishable from other forceful devices. Though he did not say so explicitly, Sir John implied that such forceful methods were not yet in order. The Treasury understood him to be saying "no," indirectly, politely, but emphatically.

There was, as it developed, no occasion for action. The Japanese government made a full apology, promised to pay the reparations the United States had requested, gave firm assurances that the episode would not be repeated, and agreed to punish the officers at fault. On December 23 the United States officially accepted the apology, and the matter was closed. Hull had never expected any other resolution, and though Roosevelt had contemplated retaliation, Japan's apology made it unnecessary as well as unwise.

As it later worked out, Ingersoll did not meet Simon. At Morgenthau's direction, he left it to the Chancellor to ask for an interview, which Simon did not do. Ingersoll talked with Eden and with the British Admiralty, but he did not discuss Oliphant's proposal, which remained where Roosevelt had put it, in the drawer of his desk, a memento, in a sense, of a difference of opinion within the Administration that had resulted in no conflict of policy. That difference of opinion was to persist, but the Japanese apology eased tensions, and Morgenthau's concerns in monetary diplomacy soon focused again on Europe.

5. Munich

During July and August 1938, while Morgenthau was in France, both for a holiday and for consultations about the persisting weakness of the franc, general war in Europe seemed more imminent than at any time since 1914. Hitler's frenzied demands for the Sudeten area of Czechoslovakia, supported as they were by German mobilization near the Czech border, provoked the Czechs to mobilize in turn. The Nazis, invoking their mad logic, made Czech mobilization the occasion for further protest and new demands. France was committed to go to war with Germany if Hitler invaded Czechoslovakia, and in that case Great Britain might be drawn in. But in Paris and London official opinion wanted to resolve the crisis short of war by devising a settlement acceptable to Hitler.

Morgenthau had no leverage for strengthening the will of the Western powers to resist the Nazis. Another round of French devaluation had already weakened the Tripartite Pact, and France now had more monetary problems. As the new French Minister of Finance, Paul Marchandeau, put it, the growing — and inevitable — military budget could only further strain the government's credit. He could not hold the franc at its existing level for long without new support from the United States. Rumors of an impending devaluation exacerbated his difficulties,

and he hoped that Morgenthau would make some public statement jointly with France and Great Britain indicating the steadfastness of three-power cooperation in monetary policy.

Morgenthau, who doubted the usefulness of words, preferred
the possibility of using the American Stabilization Fund to buy
francs for future delivery, which would provide the French
fund with dollars for sustaining the "spot" (or immediate) value
of its currency; but the British, whose cooperation was essential,
lacked authority to deal in futures. The Secretary therefore fell
back on words and on August 24, boarding the *Normandie* for
his voyage home, announced, as he had so often before, his desire
to be a friend to France.

As the Sudeten crisis mounted, France and England needed a
friend. The public statements of Roosevelt and Hull gave them
small comfort. Both the President and the Secretary of State had
reminded the American people in mid-August of the need for
international cooperation to check lawlessness and preserve
peace, but both had stopped far short of advocating foreign
commitments. Roosevelt's caution may have reflected a conviction that Chamberlain was bent on appeasing Hitler. In any case,
the declared American opposition to entanglements surely intensified the Prime Minister's trepidations.

Privately the President was beginning to look for devices short
of entanglements that would help the British and the French, and
perhaps also restrain the Germans. To this end he asked Morgenthau on August 30 to have his staff think about setting up a
special fund for French and English gold, "just for safekeeping."
Roosevelt thought it would help psychologically to indicate to
the world that the democracies had gold resources in a safe
haven. He also wanted the Treasury to consider plans for ex-
pending that gold for arms and ammunition.

On August 31, 1938, Morgenthau, calculating the odds on war
as no better than 50–50, gave his staff half a day to prepare the
plans Roosevelt had requested, and to complete arrangements for
the imposition of exchange controls on one hour's notice. That
afternoon they offered him three possibilities. Wayne Taylor
proposed that the Export-Import Bank open special accounts for

the governments of England and France, and operate in effect as their agent for converting their gold into dollars for the purpose of making purchases of war materials. Oliphant favored arrangements under the Tripartite Pact permitting Great Britain and France at any time freely to withdraw or to export any gold which they held under earmark in the United States. A third plan called upon the President once again to apply countervailing duties, and perhaps ultimately an embargo, against Germany.

At 4:15 P.M. on August 31, Taylor, Oliphant, and Morgenthau conferred with Roosevelt. "I gave you the germ of an idea," the President said, obviously pleased, "and you come back with three golden kernels." At first he particularly liked the Taylor proposal for the Export-Import Bank because he considered it more dramatic than the other plans. He wanted also to be told immediately how, if Germany went to war, he could impound every German ship in American ports. Because time was short, he said, Morgenthau should at once go over to the Department of State and show all the plans to Hull. In "a very meek voice," Morgenthau asked Roosevelt if he would mind telephoning Hull first. After the President put the call in, Morgenthau again "meekly suggested" that Roosevelt ask Hull to come to the White House. Roosevelt, nodding, said to the Secretary of State: "I have hatched a chicken. Do you want to come over and look at it?"

After Hull arrived, Roosevelt, reading aloud Oliphant's plan for utilizing the Tripartite Pact, stressed the advantage of action before war. Hull said he would have to sleep on it. He said also that he thought there was such a thing as doing too much at that time. Roosevelt's recent speech about the need for international cooperation, the pending trade treaty with the British, and then the proposed expansion of the Tripartite Agreement, Hull argued, were apt together to "get the American people up on their toes" over the European situation. As an alternative to the Treasury plans, Hull preferred one of his own — "to put the heat" on the Austrians for payment of their debt to the United States, and thus, perhaps, to embarrass the Germans.

The advantage of the Treasury approach, Morgenthau suggested, was that the decision about the Austrian debt rested exclusively with the Germans, whereas the decision about the Tripartite Pact rested with the United States.

Roosevelt emphasized the importance of taking steps at once in order to show the German government exactly where American sympathies lay. He then took a stronger line on the question of countervailing duties. He said he thought Hull should send for the German ambassador and tell him the United States might apply the duties if Germany went into Czechoslovakia. No, Roosevelt mused, he would send for the German himself. He might put it this way: "It's a hundred to one shot that I will do this if you go into Czechoslovakia." Or he might phrase it instead: "I hope you won't force my hand."

As Hull, still resistant, got up to leave, Roosevelt told him not to show the Treasury memoranda to anyone in the Department of State. This was a Treasury matter, the President said, and the State Department, except for the Secretary, was not supposed to know about it.

Back at his office, Morgenthau opened his mind to his staff: "My own feeling is that if we are going to do anything, the time to do it is in the next 48 hours, as I think that the offer we are making under the Tripartite would be most reassuring to the British and the French and I think if the President decided to do both, that it would give the German general staff and Dr. Schact something to think about, and if this is a 50–50 question everything that we can add on the score for peace is just that much to the good. But time is the essence! And it ought to be out in the papers . . . and the President ought to send for the German diplomatic representative."

The President did not. Either his own reflections or Hull's opposition persuaded him to put the Treasury plans aside. They were, of course, of limited value for resolving Europe's crisis. Hitler, for one, was probably not of a mind to be restrained by embargo, and Chamberlain, for another, had probably passed the point where an easy convertibility of gold to munitions was sufficient to bolster his spirit. But the Treasury proposals had at least one indisputable asset. Had the President chosen to adopt them, had he chosen to put himself publicly on record as prepared to do as much as the law permitted to aid the democracies, he might have given heart to the thousands of Englishmen and Frenchmen who needed every potion of courage the United States could provide.

There was, after all, a moral as well as a political reason for speaking out. It was this that Morgenthau so clearly understood. Unlike the President, the Secretary was not responsible for foreign policy; unlike the President, he was not the elected representative of the whole American people. Except for public opinion, Roosevelt might have gone along with his Secretary of the Treasury; except for the influence he supposed Hull to have with the Congress, he might not have been so moved by the reservations of his Secretary of State. As it was, he could not see his way clear to following the path which the Treasury had cut at his instigation. Because Morgenthau realized all this, he kept his faith in his chief, but he could not help but feel the pain of helplessness, the anguish of what Henry Stimson once called a "policy of amoral drift."

The Secretary, as he told Roosevelt, was particularly disturbed by reports from London. Chamberlain had told American Ambassador Joseph P. Kennedy that if the issue were one simply between the Czechs and the Sudeten Germans, an amicable settlement might be possible. The Prime Minister feared that England might be forced into a war, but he definitely would not go unless forced. Some of his colleagues, Chamberlain added, thought Hitler had to be stopped now or never, but he himself rejected that thesis. If Hitler struck, Chamberlain would influence the French to stay out, and even if France went in, some time would elapse before the British followed.

Though Ambassador William Bullitt in Paris believed the British would respond more courageously, Roosevelt was worried. The British press said that Lord Halifax, the Foreign Secretary, had asked Kennedy what the United States would do if Great Britain did fight. As Roosevelt put it: "It is a nice kettle of fish." The President, angry that Kennedy had not berated the British press for inaccurate reporting, also suspected that the Ambassador was deliberately leaking information. Roosevelt considered Chamberlain "slippery," giving one story to the French and another to the Germans; he thought Halifax's inquiry was designed to put Washington on the spot, and he concluded that the Prime Minister was trying to place the blame for fighting or not fighting on the United States. The President was especially perturbed over Kennedy's apparent preference for appeasement. The Ambassador had submitted for clearance a speech he planned to deliver in Scotland in which he intended to say: "I can't for the life of me understand why anybody would want to go to war to save the Czechs" — a sentence the State Department promptly struck out. "Who would have thought that the English could take into camp a red-headed Irishman?" Roosevelt said to Morgenthau. "The young man needs his wrists slapped rather hard." The Treasury's plans were in his middle drawer, the President concluded, and he could always get them out in a minute.

But as Hull again recommended, the United States did nothing. French Foreign Minister Bonnet, who rivaled Chamberlain as an advocate of avoiding war at any price, proposed on September 8 that, if the need arose, Roosevelt act as arbiter, and on September 12 that the United States urge Hitler not to use force. Still Washington stood pat. By September 13 war seemed so close that Morgenthau took steps to send American gold in London back to the United States on American naval vessels. He acted, he told the President, to avoid the possibility of the destruction of the gold in an air raid, but even this small gesture disturbed Hull, who objected when he discovered that the Navy was stationing a battleship at Gravesend until further notice. He withdrew his objections only after Morgenthau assured him that "that battleship is being held at my request" for the purpose of removing gold, not of showing the flag.

On September 15 Chamberlain flew to Berchtesgaden for the first of what were to be his three conferences with Hitler. Hopes for peace briefly rose in London and Paris, but Hitler's renewed denunciations of the Czechs, and Czechoslovakia's show of resistance, left matters still boiling.

On September 19 Morgenthau had a chance to talk frankly with the President, who thought the Czechs would fight. Morgenthau agreed. Roosevelt thought he ought to get word to the French that, if they became involved, they should stay behind the Maginot Line and with other countries surrounding Germany conduct a defensive war, shut off German supplies on land and sea, and thus bring the Germans to their senses. Again Morgenthau agreed. A defensive war, he believed, if properly executed, had a 60–40 chance of bringing Germany around. "If the various countries should attack Germany," Roosevelt added, "they only have a 40–60 chance of being successful."

The President gave Morgenthau the feeling that he was ready to go rather far in demonstrating American sympathy for a defensive war. As to the existing crisis, not yet a war, he said: "The time has passed for speeches on my part." Morgenthau asked him how he was going to get his messages to England and France. "That is my worry," Roosevelt said. ". . . I guess my best bet is the old boy up at the British Embassy." * If he acted at all, the President continued, it would be that afternoon.

Pressing his luck, Morgenthau criticized Hull more openly than he ever had before. "You know Mr. Hull," he said to Roosevelt, "as represented to the public, is about 100 per cent different from the real Mr. Hull." After the President "agreed readily," Morgenthau went on: "You know last June or July you put up to him the question of assisting the Chinese and he followed his usual policy by trying to wear all of us out and then do nothing."

"That is right."

"You know, Mr. President," Morgenthau added, "if we don't stop Hitler now he is going right on to the Black Sea — then what? The fate of Europe for the next 100 years is settled."

The following day, September 20, the prospects for the fate of Europe seemed grim indeed. According to analyses Morgenthau received, the British and French cabinets both accepted the Chamberlain plan for solving the Sudeten problem by permitting Germany to annex those areas in which a preponderantly Ger-

* British Ambassador to the United States, Sir Ronald Lindsay.

man population lived. The British and French people were deeply chagrined by this surrender to the diplomacy of intimidation, but at the same time relieved to escape the immediate consequences of war to which their own military weakness had rendered them vulnerable. The Czechs, however, were extremely bitter, and it would require great sagacity on the part of the Czech government to get the people to accept the concessions.

"War is probably avoided," Leon Blum, now the leader of the opposition to the incumbent French government, remarked, "but under such conditions that I, who have never ceased to fight for peace and for many years have dedicated my life to peace, cannot feel joy and that my emotions are divided between a cowardly relief and shame." Democrats everywhere felt the same way.

In further conferences with Chamberlain on September 22 and 23, Hitler made new and bolder demands on Czechoslovakia. This produced a spurt of resistance in France, where Chautemps deserted the peace party, and Bonnet almost alone stood for peace at any price. There seemed an increasing chance that the Czechs would reject the German terms. In that case France and Britain would have to confront the war they had tried so hard to avoid. Morgenthau, without influence on the direction of events, exercised his available authority and informed the French that if they decided to go ahead with exchange controls, he would be glad to cooperate with them.

On September 24 Bullitt recommended that if the British and French rejected the German demands, the President should urge England, France, Germany, Italy and Poland to confer about ways and means of preserving peace, and offer to send an American representative to such a conference. Roosevelt liked the suggestion, but Hull argued that the Germans were armed to the teeth, bent on aggression. Only a display of force, he thought, could deter them.

In any event, Roosevelt abandoned Bullitt's idea for fear that it might have "untoward domestic effects." Instead, early in the morning of September 26 the President sent messages to Hitler, to President Benes of Czechoslovakia, to Chamberlain and Premier Edouard Daladier, reminding them of the dangers of a rupture and urging them to continue negotiations toward a "peaceful, fair, constructive settlement."

At this point in the crisis, Morgenthau, in spite of his earlier support of a stronger policy, could see no alternative to Roosevelt's move. As he put it to his staff, the Secretary could not bring himself "in the middle of the Munich crisis" to advocate a boycott of Germany. Economic pressure would not keep Germany from going into Czechoslovakia. A boycott might give Hitler an excuse to tell the German people that a Jewish Secretary of the American Treasury was trying to strangle their nation economically and that they would have to fight. This was too big a risk, Morgenthau believed, for the limited good which a boycott might bring. But he still thought that a gesture of resistance was in order, and he was quite prepared not only to extend a credit to the Chinese but also to consider a boycott against Japan, for in the Pacific, he felt, such action was less likely to precipitate war.

Meanwhile, the State Department invited all governments to support Roosevelt's appeal for negotiations in Europe, and the President personally asked Mussolini to work to that end. In a second message to Hitler on September 27, Roosevelt asked again for a peaceful settlement of existing differences. The use of force, he said, might lead to a general war "as unnecessary as it is unjustifiable." Still sensitive to American opinion, the President added: "The Government of the United States has no political involvements in Europe, and will assume no obligations in the conduct of the present negotiations. Yet in our own right we recognize our responsibility as a part of a world of neighbors."

Neither Roosevelt's appeal, nor his careful self-exclusion from the conversations he urged, influenced Hitler's decision to call the Munich conference. Hitler was willing to talk only because he knew Chamberlain and Bonnet were prepared to give him what he wanted. By the time of Roosevelt's appeal, the question was whether the Nazis would take the Sudetenland by force or without it. The President apparently believed that postponing war might give France and England a chance to work out with

Germany "a new order based on justice and law." Though
Morgenthau had no such optimism, he still felt relieved that for
the moment war had been averted. When the tickertape at the
Treasury reported that Hitler had agreed to a conference, the
Secretary called Roosevelt and said, "I want to be the first to
congratulate you."

The settlement at Munich was as bad as Morgenthau had
feared it might be, almost as bad as war. The Czechs yielded the
Sudetenland and all their vital fortresses to Germany. In return
Czechoslovakia received French and British guarantees of her
new frontiers, guarantees which, considering the events of the
previous months, seemed peculiarly unreassuring. Some observers spoke hopefully of Chamberlain's broad vision and tireless
patience, and of the importance for the democracies to appreciate the need for correcting maladjustments growing out of the
Treaty of Versailles. This last was exactly Hitler's line. More
astute analysts recognized that the brutal debate in the British
Parliament about the Munich conference made it clear that
Chamberlain had had to make a virtue of necessity. Great Britain and France were physically and morally unprepared to face
the Germans and had therefore agreed to terms which Hitler
dictated. It was still too early to judge whether Chamberlain was
a sentimentalist expecting an era of peace which would depend
on Hitler's willingness to be moderate, or a realist who had
avoided an initial disaster in order to prepare a stronger resistance. The latter possibility provided the only solace Morgenthau could find in the Munich settlement.

6. Postlude to Munich

In the days after Munich, the Treasury had under consideration
three ways of strengthening democratic resistance to fascism — a
credit to China; a program of economic aid to nations of the
Western Hemisphere; and a plan for increasing duties on Ger-

man, and possibly also Japanese, imports. The last possibility appealed to the Secretary.

"It's a waste of my time to walk across the street to tell the President of the United States to do this in the case of Germany and Japan because we don't like their type of government," Morgenthau told his advisers. Roosevelt would agree that the Japanese method of warfare and conduct of government were outrageous, but Hull would argue in return that the imposition of duties was unneutral. "What I'm begging you to say," Morgenthau went on "is that it's illegal for the President not to act. See? Now if it's just a question of judgment . . . I can't get anywhere. But if you say to me that as Secretary of the Treasury the law directs me . . . to act . . . I've got something to work with."

The best way to speed things along, Morgenthau concluded, was to urge the President to approve a credit for China and loans to Latin America, a "financial Monroe Doctrine." He outlined his ideas and put his staff to work drafting an appropriate letter.

The letter was ready for the Secretary's signature on October 17, 1938. In sending it to the President, Morgenthau made the strongest statement on foreign policy he had yet ventured. "The events of the past weeks have brought home to all of us the increasing effectiveness of the forces of aggression," the letter began. "Since 1931 we have seen, succeeding each other with briefer and briefer intervals between, the fall of Manchuria and the invasion of China, the conquest of Ethiopia, fomented unrest in Latin America and in the Near East, armed intervention in Spain, the annexation of Austria, and the dismemberment of Czechoslovakia — all in seven short years."

There was no reason to expect the aggression to stop. Japan at first had wanted only Manchuria, then north China. "Now," the argument continued, "she will not be content with less than the whole of China. Italy wanted only Ethiopia; and now she wants control of North Africa. Germany wanted only equality in armaments, then the remilitarization of the Rhineland, then Austria, then Czechoslovakia, now Poland. The current claim of an aggressor power is always its last — until the next one."

With grim clarity the Secretary forecast the future: "So well have the aggressor nations mastered the tactics of aggression that a victory in one part of the world is followed by outbursts of aggression elsewhere." The history of the last seven years taught an obvious lesson. "Let us not repeat the short-sighted mistakes of Britain and France," Morgenthau wrote. "The impact of the aggressor nations upon American life and American interests has so far, to be sure, been more insidious than overt but it will be too late if we wait until the effects are obvious. Who in France as late as 1930 would have dreamt that in less than a decade that great democratic nation was to become a second-rate power, shorn of influence in central Europe, dependent upon a grudging and demanding ally for security? Who would have expected that Great Britain's might would be challenged in the Mediterranean, that her economic interests would be brushed aside in China, and that the Premier of England would hurry to Hitler to plead that he be not too demanding or impatient, and to plead, moreover, in humble tones lest the dictator take umbrage and demand more?"

What then was the United States to do? "Let us *while we can peacefully do so* try to check the aggressors. Let us not be placed in the position of having to compound with them. Let it not be necessary for the President of the United States to fly to Tokyo and in humble manner plead with the Mikado that he be content with half the Philippines rather than wage war for the whole. Such a possibility may seem ridiculous now, but no more ridiculous than Chamberlain's flight to Berlin would have seemed seven years ago."

Long before most Americans, Morgenthau had read the words of the great champion of the cause of freedom. As his letter to the President put it: "In March of this year Winston Churchill called upon England to act, saying 'if we do not stand up to the dictators now, we shall only prepare the day when we shall have to stand up to them under far more adverse conditions. Two years ago it was safe, three years ago it was easy, and four years ago a mere dispatch might have rectified the position. . . . Now the victors are the vanquished, and those who threw down their arms in the field and sued for an armistice are striving on to world mastery.' The basis for the present humiliation of England was laid in 1931, when England failed to join the United States in disapproval of Japanese aggression in Manchuria. The basis of either humiliation or war for the United States is being laid today by a foreign policy that shuts its eye to aggression and withholds economic support from those who resist."

Appealing to the Franklin Roosevelt he knew, his old friend, and not to "the President" taking counsel from the Department of State, Morgenthau went on: "I know you are firmly convinced, as I am firmly convinced that the forces of aggression must be stopped. By whom if not by us? I believe that we are the only country in the world now in a position to initiate effective steps to stop aggression by peaceful means. Once the United States takes the lead in developing an effective program, democratic forces in all countries — even those now submerged in the aggressor nations — will take heart. In England and in France groups within the government and without will be stimulated and encouraged to press for parallel action.

"To use our great financial strength to help safeguard future peace for the United States, and to make your 'Good Neighbor' policy really effective, we should introduce at once a program of peaceful action on two fronts — in the Far East and in Latin America. In these two areas we can move most effectively and with the least complications."

The Latin American nations needed capital to develop their resources free from foreign intervention: "Unless we assist them, they will become a helpless field for political and economic exploitation by the aggressor nations. Already some inroads have been made in that direction. Now, after the Munich agreement, we may expect that Germany, Italy, and Japan will become bolder and more effective in their attempts to establish areas of economic and political support to the south of us. We can stop that penetration by an intelligent use of a small proportion of our enormous gold and silver holdings."

More even than Latin America, China needed American assistance. "It is yet possible for such aid to be of decisive help," Morgenthau argued. "Sanguine as I desire to be, I am forced to the view that without substantial financial aid given promptly the Chinese resistance may soon disintegrate. By risking little more than the cost of one battleship we can give renewed vitality and effectiveness to the Chinese. We can do more than that. By our action we can further the struggle of democracy against aggression everywhere.

"I am pleading China's cause with special urgency because you have on numerous occasions told me to proceed with proposals for assistance to China. All my efforts to secure immediate substantial aid for China have proved of no avail against the adamant foreign policy of doing nothing which could possibly be objected to by an aggressor nation. I need not tell you that I respect the integrity and sincerity of those who hold the belief that a course of inaction is the right one, but the issues at stake go beyond any one of us and do not permit me to remain silent. What greater force for peace could there be than the emergence of a unified China?" Morgenthau's reasoning was persuasive. Largely because of his continuing agitation, China in December got $25 million from the Export-Import Bank to purchase American agricultural and industrial goods. That was less than Morgenthau asked for, but it was a start.

As Morgenthau's letter to Roosevelt had said, "the measures we may adopt can be developed as the specific occasions requiring assistance may arise." It was first necessary, he noted, for the United States to accept in principle "the need for *positive action*." To that principle the Secretary was fully committed.

BOOK TWO

YEARS OF URGENCY

1938-1941

IX

TOWARD A GOOD SOCIETY

1938–1939

1. President and Secretary

FOR SECRETARY OF THE TREASURY Henry Morgenthau, Jr., as for the President he served, the autumn of 1938 was a season of gloom. In spite of all of its accomplishments, the New Deal was at bay. The recession that had begun a year earlier had yet to lift. The course of domestic reform, still incomplete, stood impeded by the growing resistance of conservative Democrats in the Congress. Roosevelt's efforts in the fall elections to help dedicated New Dealers defeat his opponents within the party had for the most part failed, and the Republicans, for the first time in a decade, had made substantial gains in both the House and Senate. The slump in business, the surliness of the business community, the new confidence of the Democratic Right and of the Republicans called into question, as had no previous set of conditions, the effectiveness and the future of Roosevelt's leadership. Sensitive as always to his environment, Roosevelt seemed to lack the confidence and the energy that had marked his ebullient seasons.

Morgenthau understood Roosevelt's mood and the reasons for it, but like others around the President, he realized that positive leadership had never been more imperative. In the autumn of 1938, democracy in the United States could not afford to be cautious. The nation was becoming the last best hope for free men in a world that had begun to crumble before the encroachments of totalitarianism. England and France had just surrendered the Sudetenland to Hitler, whose appetite for conquest had thus been whetted rather than appeased. Italy was poised to share the spoils that Germany might seek, and in China, Japanese aggression was closing in on the capital of Chiang Kai-shek and his overpowered forces.

The collapse of spirit of the governments of France and Great Britain exemplified the weariness which for the time characterized Western man. It was a weariness that many Americans shared. Persisting depression and unemployment had persuaded the timid among American liberals that democratic efforts for recovery and reform had been futile. Persisting retreats in Asia and Europe before the forces of Nazism and Fascism seemed to suggest that democrats abroad were faltering in valor as well as faith. Many even of the brave at home remained opposed to any American involvement across the oceans.

Morgenthau, in contrast, believed that the United States had no choice but to enlist at once in the defense of decency and freedom. He wanted Roosevelt to take the lead in mobilizing American opinion and policy in support of England, France, and China, and in defense of the free governments of the Western Hemisphere. It was necessary, he was sure, to confront the Axis resolutely, to make it clear that democracy would fight before it would again appease. Only in that way, the Secretary thought, only through strength and determination, could the democracies persuade the aggressors that the alternative to decency was war. Even so, war might come, for there was little evidence that either Hitler or Mussolini or their friends preferred peace to battle. Consequently, Morgenthau believed that the United States should announce that it would assist the victims of aggression, and should begin to build its own defenses. To those ends, the President would have to convince the American people of the urgency of the danger and of the obligations of their democratic heritage.

The proof of the viability of that heritage depended on a continuing and successful effort to build a good society at home. The United States, in Morgenthau's view, had an exemplary as well as a militant function. It was incumbent upon the nation to demonstrate that democratic governments could wrest prosperity from depression and could distribute to all citizens plentiful shares of comfort and dignity. It was incumbent on the nation also to order its public affairs according to the prescriptions of its ideals — to discipline excesses of private power; to keep government responsible to the whole people; to use government, so responsible, to advance the conditions and opportunities of life for everyone. For recovery, then, and for reform, as much in 1938 as in 1933, presidential leadership was necessary.

Morgenthau retained a basic confidence that things could be set right. He had, to begin with, an unimpeachable faith in the strength and the purpose of the American people once they were aroused. He had, secondly, an equal faith in the capacity of Franklin Roosevelt to galvanize their purpose and their strength. Finally, he understood his President. Underlying the hurt of defeat, underlying the mood of caution, Roosevelt had reservoirs of energy and skill. He was, as Morgenthau had known for twenty years, the most ardent, the most daring democrat of his time. If the President's astute sense of political situation persuaded him of the temporary need for caution, his unfailing concern for a good society at home and a democratic world abroad held him to a permanent dedication to constructive action.

Roosevelt understood his friend and valued his qualities, confided in him, used him, and returned the affection he received. The President realized, moreover, that Morgenthau was not only a friend, but also a kind of conscience, a man who shared his hopes and ideals, and had the courage to speak up when those ideals were at stake. Like Morgenthau, Roosevelt in the fall of 1938 knew they were at stake. Yet the two men differed, as they sometimes had before, about means and emphases. They had grown together in their common purpose, but their separate obligations and temperaments had on some issues thrust them apart. The President, stouter and grayer, wearier in body though not in spirit, had to weigh the private counsel he received against his best perceptions of the public mood and of congressional responsiveness. The Secretary, still usually tense and remote with strangers and still usually relaxed, even playful, with his intimates, Roosevelt not the least, attended less to the demands of politics than to what he considered the obligations of the Treasury Department and the responsibilities of a loyal adviser to his chief. He therefore now and then proposed ventures that the President found too bold or too unpopular for the tolerances of politics.

Still, at bottom their relationship remained close and sure. The President could rely on the Secretary's unwavering loyalty; Morgenthau, in matters of principle, enjoyed Roosevelt's confidence and support. And principle defined for the Secretary the policies that could shape the good society at home.

2. *Treasury Blueprints*

Morgenthau was determined to use federal authority to ensure honest business behavior, to prevent the growth of clusters of private economic power so large that they overwhelmed potential competition, and to protect the funds of small stockholders and depositors. He had never shared the enthusiasm of the early New Deal for "rationalizing" the economy, for constructing great industrial and agricultural organizations, for suspending the antitrust laws. Rather, Morgenthau belonged to the antimonopoly tradition which had flowered in Washington since 1935. He was solicitous of small business, suspicious of big business, and especially wary of the motives of the giant institutions of American finance. Those attitudes, often upsetting to the business community, animated his attempt to alter the structure and the practices of the Bank of America, the key unit in the financial empire that stretched from the Rockies to the Pacific.

In particular, the Secretary objected to the bank's use of current earnings for the payment of dividends, rather than for the creation of adequate reserves, and to its involved dealings with the Transamerica Corporation, the holding company that controlled it. "The President," Morgenthau told the Comptroller of the currency, read the Treasury's report on the bank and "said it is the damndest thing he had ever read."

But there was nothing illegal about the bank's dividend policy, however undesirable it appeared to the Treasury, and for its part, the bank agreed to increase its capital funds $30 million. That increase, by improving the ratio between deposits and capital, gave more protection to depositors. The bank also agreed to establish a reserve against certain losses, while the Treasury endorsed a loan to the bank by the Reconstruction Finance Corporation of $25 million.

All in all, the agreement struck Treasury officials as a triumph for their policy. As Morgenthau put it to his staff on March 13, 1940: "I think this is the longest fight I have been in on the financial front and everybody . . . that has lasted . . . deserves a tremendous amount of credit." The lawyers from the Securities and Exchange Commission congratulated the Treasury on a "swell victory," and the head of the Federal Deposit Insurance Corporation told Morgenthau that for the first time the Gianninis had "recognized any authority in bank supervision."

While public supervision kept bigness from becoming badness, it was also necessary, Morgenthau believed, to revitalize business confidence as the key to recovery. He therefore dedicated his tax program of 1939 to the growth of private enterprise.

The President's budget message of January 1939 was a deliberately ambiguous document. Roosevelt instructed the Treasury to work out a budget no more than $2 billion out of balance and based on a predicted national income of $60 billion. The Treasury was also to propose taxes to raise an additional $1 billion. This meant that if national income rose the budget would actually be in balance. Cool toward any reduction in existing taxes, Roosevelt tended to favor only one new tax, a levy on income from interest on state and municipal bonds, which would both produce revenue and close another door to tax avoidance.

Among the economists whom Morgenthau consulted, Jacob

Viner, long an adviser to the Secretary, argued that a sales tax would reduce the deficit without intensifying the already deadening impact of taxation on enterprise. But the President would not accept that regressive recommendation. Harry White, the Treasury economist whose main duties pertained to monetary policy, preferred to raise revenues by increasing the federal estate and gift taxes. Alvin Hansen, a professor of economics at Harvard and perhaps the leading American Keynesian, argued against reducing the federal deficit and against any new tax that would, like the sales tax, diminish consumer spending. Instead, Hansen urged stimulating consumer spending by postponing the collection of social security taxes. By and large Marriner Eccles agreed. But Morgenthau stood against the Keynesian heresy. He simply would not, Morgenthau said, "sign a statement that I think we need deficits, and boast about deficits — I just couldn't do it. . . . The only way we can get this country out of the present mess is to get a national income up to around 80 or 90 billion dollars. And . . . I told the President . . . he ought to weigh every proposal that comes in to him — 'Will this add or subtract from national income?' "

As he left Washington to inspect the fleet for several weeks, the President on February 17, 1939, declared that, since the Administration planned no new taxes, business had every reason for confidence. "I am very glad that the President made that statement," Morgenthau cheerfully told his press conference on February 23. "Speaking only for myself the thing that bothers me is that businessmen I see have what I would call a 'what's the use' attitude about going ahead. . . . That attitude is . . . preventing businessmen from . . . taking normal business risks. I sincerely hope that Congress will take a careful look at the tax law and see whether there are any deterrents that are . . . holding back businessmen from making future commitments. Businessmen ought to feel that the Administration wants them to make money. . . . Of course we must have additional revenue, but in my opinion the way to make it is for businessmen to make more money."

At luncheon at the White House on March 6, 1939, the President, fresh from his cruise, told Morgenthau "that in 1936 and 1937 business fell off sharply due to curtailment of expenditure . . . that we would increase expenditures and in that way bring about recovery." Morgenthau hastened to turn the discussion to the tax program. "I gave him my little talk about wanting to make 1940 a prosperous year on account of the effect it would have all over the world. . . . The President seemed pleased that our suggestions did not include losing any revenue. He gave me a long lecture that business thought that they had us on the run and if they got adjustments in the taxes they would want adjustments in other fields.

"I told him that . . . I thought business conditions were such that we could, within a month, have a boom." Roosevelt asked whether such a boom would last through 1940. "I can't answer that," Morgenthau replied, "but I know it is there for the asking and the doing, and if you try to postpone it until next fall it may not be there and I would make the most of this opportunity." Later Morgenthau added: "I have a sign on my desk 'Does it contribute to recovery.' I would like to give you one." The President, Morgenthau felt, was in "a very attentive and . . . very friendly mood," but "of course how he will react . . . to our program is another matter."

Roosevelt's reaction two days later was skeptical. The Treasury's proposals called for repeal of the capital stock and excess profits taxes, reduction of the top surtax on individual income, and a major revision in corporate income taxes that reduced rates to 17 per cent on corporations with net incomes between $10,000 and $25,000 a year, 20 per cent on those with incomes up to $50,000, and 22 per cent on those with still larger profits. The President categorically opposed any reduction in personal or corporate income taxes. The Treasury, he said, was bringing him a "Mellon plan of taxation"; he hoped the Department had made no such suggestions off the record to Congress. "This is a matter of politics," the President said. ". . . The people on the Hill want to put us in the hole. . . . They will take your recommendations and say that does not go far enough and will go much farther and say 'Look what we did.' "

Looking right at Morgenthau, the President said, "I think that sign you have on your desk 'Does it contribute to recovery' is very stupid." He went on "to give . . . me a long lecture that while he would concede that this would be helpful for the rest of this year and possibly into 1940, as a result of what he called the complete turnabout position on the part of the Treasury as to where we were two years ago, this would put a man in as President who, as he called it, would be controlled by a man on horseback, the way Mussolini and Hitler are. This lecture went on and on, he saying that this was going backwards and that this simply would mean that we would have a fascist President."

"I disagree with you," Morgenthau said when the lecture ended. The Secretary felt "that if we had recovery in 1940 that that would enhance our chance greatly of having the next President a liberal President and that furthermore the situation was a very tight one in the world and that recovery in the United States was terrifically important at this time in deciding the fate of what kind of Government we would have in the rest of the world."

The domestic situation, Roosevelt replied, did not play an important part in world affairs. A prosperous year in 1940 would not elect a liberal President. "You come to me on my farm in Hyde Park in 1941 and say there has been a catastrophe and somebody . . . has called out the troops and you will call on me to come to the aid of the country and I will tell you that this thing has been brought about by this sort of thing you were talking to me about today."

Changing to a teasing tone, the President said that Bernard Baruch had constantly favored reducing surtaxes. For once, Morgenthau replied, he agreed with Baruch. "Well," Roosevelt said, "are you willing to pay usury to get recovery?" Morgenthau said, "Yes, sure." As he left Roosevelt called after him, "For God's sake, don't be innocent."

The President especially opposed repeal of the ineffective remnant of the 1936 undistributed earnings tax, which the business community was determined to get rid of. Pat Harrison was amenable to repeal, as he had always been. Morgenthau believed that what was left of the tax had become only an irritant. Roosevelt, in contrast, wrote the Secretary on March 25, 1939, that he did not see "how you and I can forget or bury the fact that two years ago one of the principal reasons for advocating the undistributed profits tax was to prevent very rich people from leaving their earned income in corporations controlled by them, with the effect of avoiding both personal and corporate income tax payments. That is a matter of fundamental principle."

Late in April 1939, Morgenthau at luncheon asked the President to read the statement he had prepared for Congress on taxation. Roosevelt replied that until mid-June he would be tied up with the visit to the United States of the King and Queen of England. Morgenthau, he added, was spoiling everything. Relations with Congress had been in good shape for months, but, if Morgenthau wanted to mess them up, the best way was to go up on the Hill and make the statement. The Secretary said that Roosevelt could not know what he wanted to say unless he read his draft. Though Roosevelt refused, Morgenthau persisted, until the President later studied the draft, making interlineations along the way. Those interlineations deleted every specific suggestion for change. Yet Roosevelt left untouched Morgenthau's general remarks about the need for private investment and about the importance of sound public finance.

In his most soothing manner Roosevelt on May 6 chatted about the prospects for recovery. He was willing, he said, to have Morgenthau speak optimistically on the Hill about enlarging national income, but not about the details of taxation. "As far as I am concerned," Morgenthau told his staff, "I could go up cheerfully and talk about balancing the budget . . . but I just never thought of it. . . . Don't ask me what it means or anything else. I had about two hours. I was dragged through the knothole ten times. All I can say is I am alive."

"You know," Morgenthau had told Miss LeHand, Roosevelt's secretary, "the President put the roller over me. And then he saw a little bit of Morgenthau sticking out, so he ran the roller over me again." Later the Secretary said: "They have pushed me so far they will find the real Morgenthau. . . . I am sick and

tired of straddling." Still, after his conversation at the White
House, Morgenthau realized that he was less committed to any
change in taxes than to his unshaken persuasion that the budget
had to be balanced. At a meeting with the Democrats on the
Ways and Means Committee, the Secretary delivered a revealing
soliloquy:

> I have got my responsibility to my country, which comes first.
> . . . We have tried spending money. We are spending more
> than we have ever spent before and it does not work. And I have
> just one interest, and if I am wrong . . . somebody else can have
> my job. I want to see this country prosperous. I want to see peo-
> ple get a job. I want to see people get enough to eat. We have
> never made good on our promises. . . . We have said we would
> give everybody a job that wanted it. We have never taken care
> of the people. . . . There are four million that don't have that
> much income. We have never done anything for them. . . .
> We have never begun to tax the people in this country the way
> they should be. . . . People who have it should pay. . . . It's
> never a good year to have a tax bill, but I think it's a darn good
> year to begin to balance the budget. . . . The biggest deterrent
> of all . . . is that the country does not know when the end is in
> sight and this unbalancing of the budget . . . that's what frightens
> people. . . . I say after eight years of this Administration we have
> just as much unemployment as when we started. . . . And an
> enormous debt to boot! We are just sitting here and fiddling and
> I am just wearing myself out and getting sick. . . . When I have
> got to become a deficit spender and believe in this compensatory
> theory, the President ought to get somebody else to sit in this
> chair. . . . I am loyal to him and have been with him longer than
> anybody else, but I can't appear before you people and stultify.
> That's why he made the suggestion that you begin hearings and
> don't invite me up. He knows me. . . . He knows I won't stultify
> myself.

But Morgenthau knew he was beaten. At luncheon on May
16, Harry Hopkins assured him that he had been doing everything possible to sell the Treasury's tax program to the President.
"I didn't let him know how badly we were licked," Morgenthau
noted immediately after their meeting. "Didn't see any sense in
letting him know how low I was or anything else . . . and what

my relationship with the President was. . . . He said the trouble is that he and I have been sold down the river by people close to the President on this tax program. . . . He said he agreed with Walter Lippmann that there are people in this town who don't want recovery. . . . There are a lot of the younger fellows sitting around who talk things over who don't want recovery, because they want Government to stay on the top deck.

"So then Harry said something about a crowd going over and putting over a spending program and selling Hopkins and me down the river. So I said, 'Harry, you used to do a pretty good job on me yourself.' (That was for dessert.) . . . To have him sit there and complain that he and I . . . poor things! We are having things put over on us through the back door, even with strawberries, I could not take it! I did it with a smile. He laughed. . . .

"He said the trouble with the President today is this! In the first place, he's bored with his job. He's tired and he's cranky. So I said, 'Well, he will get more tired and more cranky as business gets worse and that's why I want to see business get better.' He says today the President listens to Bob Jackson, Leon Henderson, Eccles, and he said the economists he has confidence in are Henderson, Currie and Lubin. . . .

"In other words, 'Life is just a bowl of cherries' but most of the cherries are rotten!"

Two days later, May 18, 1939, Morgenthau called on Eleanor Roosevelt, often his confidante in times of trouble. She understood his temperament, his hopes, his dedication to her husband. Morgenthau trusted Mrs. Roosevelt more than anyone outside of his own family. During his hour with her, he

started right in and told her all the trouble that I have been having. Told her how Franklin had been bullying me, browbeating me and being thoroughly unpleasant. She said that for some time now he has really not been feeling well and when he is like that he takes it out on people close to him whom he knows will take it. . . .

She kept asking me what I thought was motivating him. I told her that I pieced together a picture from listening to Franklin, Hopkins and Tommy Corcoran that the program was to rush Congress out of town, first getting another spending program through and next year doing things like taxation and other difficult matters because if we did them this year the people would forget about them next year, when Franklin ran again for President. I told her that I thought Corcoran and Cohen were wielding the greatest influence today.

I said that I was beginning to think that the President was trying to get rid of me and as far as I was concerned I would be tickled to death to go home. She said, "Of course you would. I understand perfectly. You have no reason to stay here. . . . I am quite sure that it is not correct that he wants to get rid of you because you can tell by little things that that was not so." . . .

I told her what I wanted was prosperity in 1940 for so many reasons and amongst others was the fact that if we had a prosperous year the President's whole attitude, his health, would be so different. I said, "If he would only reverse himself now and announce that he was going to keep Congress here until Christmas if necessary and get through a recovery program." Eleanor Roosevelt agreed with me entirely . . .

I told her how every time I would agree to a suggestion that the President made and I thought I had satisfied him, he would withdraw and I would find him asking for additional changes. After having gone through these experiences a number of times I had come to the conclusion that he really did not want a tax bill. Eleanor said, "Why don't you take in your statement and say to him firmly now this is your last chance to make some suggestions because I am going up on the Hill and make a statement." I said, "It would not work because when I tried to include his suggestions I found that it would just make me sound and look ridiculous." I told her what I was thinking of doing when I got a definite call to come on the Hill was to see him and say that I wanted to go on the Hill, as his Secretary of the Treasury, with this statement and if he did not approve he could get another Secretary of the Treasury.

She made no comment. I then read the statement to her and when I was about finished she said, "That is a wonderful statement. It is the clearest and best explanation on the tax situation that I have ever heard." . . .

I left the statement with her and I told her that if she would be willing to accept the responsibility I would like to place myself in her hands as I felt that Franklin and I were rapidly drawing further and further apart. She said she was going to talk to the President. . . . And she said two or three times, "I am sure, Henry, that the President is not trying to force you out."

While Morgenthau was turning to Mrs. Roosevelt for help, Senator Harrison was taking command of tax matters on the Hill. The senator felt that some tax relief was in order, and he wanted the Democrats to get credit for providing it. So long as there could be safeguards against tax avoidance, Roosevelt agreed in mid-May to the repeal of the undistributed profits tax. He told Cordell Hull privately that he was now in favor of a tax program during the current session of Congress, which Hull reported to Morgenthau at a Cabinet meeting on May 19. At that meeting, according to Morgenthau's Diary, the "President said he and his wife had a discussion on economics in this country. . . . When he got through he gave me a searching look."

He also let Morgenthau reach an accord on taxes with the committees of both houses. On May 25 Roosevelt endorsed their views. After leaving the White House that day, Morgenthau told Pat Harrison that he had come away "with complete agreement and he now says that I can say, when I appear publicly, that what I say has his approval. . . . I did not know until he read my statement how he would feel. . . . It looks awfully good. I congratulate you and myself." More progress, the Secretary felt, had "been made in the last couple of days than there has been in the last couple of months."

On May 27, 1939, Morgenthau testified, as he had hoped to for so long, before the House Ways and Means Committee. Referring at the start to the world situation, he emphasized the need for the "preservation of our democratic form of government." To that end, he recommended a four-part program: "Promotion of free enterprise and private investment . . . attainment of full business recovery . . . maintenance of our public finances in a sound and unassailable position, and . . . a just distribution of national income." Though the necessary expenses for national defense would prevent balancing the budget that year, the crisis abroad made it essential for the country to give "serious attention to our future fiscal position and redouble our efforts to attain full recovery."

Coming to specific recommendations, Morgenthau repeated two that Roosevelt had earlier made, one for extending the excise taxes, another for making all government salaries and interest on all government securities subject to federal and state income tax laws. He also repeated his own suggestion for postponing increases in Social Security taxes. Finally, Morgenthau turned to those taxes "which have been characterized as likely to hinder business expansion and development." Among them he listed the undistributed profits tax which, as he pointed out, now produced little revenue but had prominence "because of the widespread emotional criticism" long directed against it.

The spokesman of the National Association of Manufacturers expressed himself as "one hundred per cent" in accord with the Secretary. So, in large measure, was Congress. Late in June it passed the Revenue Act of 1939 substantially in the form that Harrison had earlier approved. Though the Act did not incorporate all of the Treasury's suggestions, it removed some of the major vexations of business, including the undistributed earnings tax, and it extended the excise taxes. To the President's satisfaction, Morgenthau in July published a Treasury decision which interpreted the Revenue Code in a manner designed to prevent the accumulation of undistributed corporate profits for the sake of tax avoidance.

Morgenthau was happy with the result. He hoped the general conservative approval of the act foreshadowed new private investments and with them a significant upturn in the business cycle. That would ensure the additional revenue needed to offset federal spending which he had been endeavoring to minimize during all the months of the controversy over the tax law.

3. To Lend Rather than to Spend

In May of 1939, in connection with his work on the tax bill, Morgenthau began to formulate an alternative to federal spending. Recovery, he believed, could be promoted by federal loans for the construction of self-liquidating projects. The Secretary had always favored such loans over spending for public works. The Treasury could not recover money it spent except indirectly through tax revenues, but it could receive steady income from tolls or fees to repay loans on roads, bridges, or public housing.

As Morgenthau put it to Tom Corcoran on May 22, 1939, if business got worse, the President would become more and more sour: "I compared the present situation to his last year as Governor of New York where he had begun to slip and part of the reason was that people criticized him for the mounting debt in New York State. I said his trying Jimmy Walker in the courageous manner which he did turned the tables in his favor." Roosevelt now hesitated to fire his hopelessly inadequate Secretary of War, Harry Woodring of Kansas, for fear of losing the Democratic delegation from that state at the convention of 1940. "If wheat next year is 50 cents," Morgenthau told Corcoran, "no Democrat will get the delegation. If it is one dollar, a Democrat can have it and Harry Woodring won't have a blankety-blank thing to say about it." If the President could get his mind off delegates and onto recovery, the delegates would come along too.

Roosevelt, Morgenthau suggested, should meet every night for a week or more with advisers he trusted to work out a recovery program. He should then announce the program to the public on the radio and keep Congress in session until it was enacted. Then, whenever the program met with success, the White House could put out a press release claiming credit for Roosevelt, whereas when something went wrong, one of the departments could take the blame for it.

Corcoran, though sympathetic, thought that little could be done. He went "on a long rampage on what complete disorganization there is in the office of the White House and why the President frittered his time away so much and . . . the way Steve Early sat on everything that everybody wanted to do . . . and how Pa Watson is good as a doorkeeper but that was all. That Sam Rosenman had said the President still runs the United

States as though it was the State of New York and he wants to do it on a personal contact basis and that the President has never really learned how to run his own office.

"Then Corcoran got really violent in his discussion of [Joseph] Kennedy and [Arthur] Krock. He said that Krock was running a campaign to put Joe Kennedy over for President; that if any prominent Catholic gets in the way he's to be rubbed out. . . . If anybody with financial training gets in the way, he's to be rubbed out. . . . Corcoran also said that they were sick and tired of having to do the political end of the dirty jobs that the White House gives them to do; that they would like to get on doing something constructive. . . . Again and again he said that everybody in Washington was licked; that they needed something like my idea."

"Of course the thing we must do is to get Roosevelt the re-nomination," Corcoran concluded. "What I think is," Morgenthau replied, "that we've got to get recovery in 1940 and that will take care of getting us another successful Democratic candidate." To his Diary the Secretary added: "I did not answer him as to how I felt or where I stood on Roosevelt's running for a third term. . . . I will stake my reputation that if the President will reverse himself and will go to town on a positive program, from that day on he gets well and if he doesn't . . . he will get . . . more like Herbert Hoover was the last year he was President." But Roosevelt, Corcoran reported a few days later, was so "tough and mad" that Morgenthau would have to let his plan "hang and cure a while."

When the end of the tax controversy softened the President's temper, Morgenthau assigned almost his entire staff to developing his recommendations for "a good recovery program." As he explained it on June 4, 1939, it would "take care of the people in the lower one-third and, second, would at no place compete with private capital and, third, would be self-liquidating. I had in mind . . . slum clearance . . . highways and bridges and tunnels. . . . [Harry] White suggested a corporation to buy land for farm tenants; loans to South America and China . . . and . . . a loan to Russia.

"I suggested an exchange of cotton for manganese from Russia . . . organizing a corporation which would sell bonds against the already existing utility projects . . . self-help cooperatives in all cities and country towns . . . expansion of food tickets for surplus food . . . and . . . an informal board which would be a social service and work planning board. . . . I said I did not want to get into a discussion . . . as to compensatory budget or pools of unused savings . . . but that this was my program."

Two days later Morgenthau discussed his plan with the Fiscal and Monetary Advisory Committee. "I don't pretend for a minute that it's going to solve the unemployment problem," he said, "but I think it's going to help. . . . If it did nothing else but make it possible that we'd put enough people to work so that they wouldn't have to ask for another appropriation from the Congress after the first of the year, that would be an accomplishment." Many of the Secretary's ideas appeared in a memorandum the committee then prepared for the President. With Marriner Eccles and Budget Director Harold Smith, Morgenthau took the memorandum to the White House. Roosevelt "liked it enormously. The only thing he questioned was where we said, 'the local authorities hadn't done their share of investing and spending.' He felt they had reached their debt limit. He kept saying, 'Where is the white rabbit and where is the cabbage to feed the white rabbit?' . . . The President told us to have a recovery program ready for him to send to Congress not later than the first of July and to surround it with all kinds of secrecy — no leaks.

"I showed him at length my program . . . and he said, 'Let's try and make it a self-liquidating program entirely.' I said to him, 'Now, Mr. President, I also want it, in no way, to compete with business.' And he said, 'In no way compete with business.' . . . So we are to go back a week from tomorrow with a program and the thing that pleases me so much is I have been saying now for months we had to do it . . . and I have been told consistently the President would not agree to it and he has."

Within a week the Fiscal Committee had prepared a list of specific self-liquidating projects for housing, for the relocation of indigent farmers, for rural electrification, and for toll roads, canals, and bridges. On the morning of June 14, several hours before the committee was to see the President, Morgenthau went alone to the White House. He suggested drawing a map showing the various structures the federal government had built in every county in the United States during the past seven years. Roosevelt, enthusiastic, thought that perhaps the Young Democrats could do that. Morgenthau then proposed picking out ten strategic states and appointing a small committee to steer public works as much as possible to them. "Of course," Roosevelt immediately replied, "that's the thing to do. . . . Have you got a list of the money ready for me?" Morgenthau had. "I haven't enjoyed any meeting that I have had with the President as much as this one in . . . a year and a half," the Secretary later noted in his Diary. ". . . I reminded him what I had done for him in New York in getting up the tax saving figures on a county basis. . . . I am very cheerful."

Roosevelt's response to the Fiscal Committee's recommendations was equally cheering. As each project was explained, the President endorsed it. At his instruction, the responsible agencies prepared a letter on the lending program for his signature. Dated June 21, 1939, and addressed from Roosevelt to Senator James Byrnes, the letter began by opposing further appropriations for state and municipal public works, for those appropriations would decrease the funds available for relief, which was more important. There was a better way, the letter continued, to accomplish the laudable purposes of the public works bill than through direct federal grants. "The great majority of people of this country have come to realize that there are certain types of public improvements . . . which should be undertaken at times when there is need for a stimulus for employment. At such times the Federal Government should furnish funds for projects . . . at a low rate of interest, it being clearly understood that the projects themselves shall be self-liquidating and of such a nature as to furnish a maximum of employment per dollar of investment." After asking for authorizations for loans for the kinds of projects the Fiscal Committee had earlier specified, the letter also, following Morgenthau's original blueprint, called for loans to foreign governments for the purpose of promoting American trade. The proceeds of those loans were to be spent only in the United States and to be used only for the economic development of the borrowing country.

Though Democratic leaders in both houses of Congress were initially receptive to the President's proposals, the party's rank and file and the Republican opposition balked. The lending bill needed the Administration's unequivocal support. That was not forthcoming, for Jesse Jones interpreted the bill as a backhanded criticism of his own Reconstruction Finance Corporation. At first he insisted that his agency should handle any lending. Conceding to this whim, Roosevelt arranged to make one of Jones's subordinates the head of the RFC and to promote Jones to the new office of Federal Loan Administrator with authority to supervise his old agency among others. But Roosevelt's tactic failed to enlist Jones behind the bill. Skeptical about the value of expanded lending, wounded that Roosevelt had evolved his program without consulting him, Jones quietly sabotaged the Administration.

Congress rejected the bill. "Jesse Jones is in the dog house, very much in the dog house," Roosevelt later told Morgenthau. "He's responsible for killing the Lending Bill." Jones, Morgenthau predicted in reply, would "wheedle himself back into your good graces." And so he soon did.

The President's mood about money remained fickle. "I am sick and tired of having a lot of long-haired people around here who want a billion dollars for schools, a billion dollars for public health," Roosevelt said to the Secretary in mid-July 1939. ". . . Just because a boy wants to go to college is no reason we should finance it." Interrupting, Morgenthau said, "Franklin, you don't expect me to swallow all this, do you?" Roosevelt said yes, he did. "The whole time the President was talking," Morgenthau recorded in his Diary, "I had a broad grin on my face, which he didn't seem to object to. But he wouldn't smile himself."

By the summer of 1939 neither man was any longer concentrating on domestic issues with the old intensity. Reform, recovery, the assistance of the "lower third," all these were important in themselves, and important also as evidence of the American style in a world where democracy was increasingly out of vogue. But even while he strove to assist business recovery or to balance the budget, Morgenthau had had to give more of his time and much more of his anguish to foreign and military policies. There, far more than in his ventures on the domestic scene, the Secretary had to sense the mood and depend on the support and constancy of the President.

X

IN THE GATHERING STORM

1938–1939

WAR CAME closer to Europe in the fall of 1938 than it had since the armistice twenty years earlier. Even after France and England yielded at Munich, few thoughtful men on either side of the Atlantic regarded the settlement as more than temporary, at best a humbling purchase of time for preparation against the day that fighting would begin. Americans remained reluctant to believe that war, if it came, would involve them. Indeed, most of Roosevelt's advisers still preferred to glue their attention to domestic issues. The President, less deluded, believed that few months of peace remained, that modern war touched every nation, and that the United States was sadly lacking in the minimum requirements for defending itself and the Western Hemisphere. He realized, too, that the true frontier of American defense lay not at the waterline but in the capacity of democracies to resist aggression in Europe and in the Far East.

Roosevelt was not yet ready to state his beliefs to a public unwilling to share them and downright antagonistic to acting upon them. Still, he spoke with increasing candor to those around him. He needed their advice and support in piecing together the defense and foreign policies for which congressional action was indispensable. He also needed their help, even their urging, to sustain his own convictions and to bolster the political courage necessary for awakening the country to its dangers and its obligations.

No one in Washington was more committed to assisting the democracies or more ardent in furthering national defense than Morgenthau. As Secretary of the Treasury, he had under his authority the Division of Procurement, the government's most versatile purchasing agency. Charged, too, with the direction of American monetary policy, Morgenthau had long conducted negotiations about economic and financial questions of international significance.

In autumn 1938, the degree to which Roosevelt leaned on Morgenthau was one measure of the degree to which the President intended to further his personal convictions in face of congressional and political opposition. Within the Cabinet, only Harold Ickes shared Morgenthau's sense of crisis. Secretary of War Harry Woodring, an isolationist, had little stomach for plans to expand the Army and the Air Corps, and Secretary of the Navy Charles Edison had no more spunk. Cordell Hull remained, as he had long been, uneasy about ventures that might provoke the Axis countries, for, though Hull detested fascism, he tended to believe that peace was conditional on the self-restraint of Germany, Italy, and Japan. The caution of the State Department and the sluggishness of the War Department forced Roosevelt often to turn to Morgenthau, who, for his part, constantly prodded the President to bring the country to a state of readiness.

1. Foundations for National Defense

Whatever the issue, domestic or international, the dominant intelligence on Morgenthau's staff was his General Counsel, Herman Oliphant, who had an unfailing gift for solving problems in the face of what seemed to be insuperable legal or administrative

obstacles. Most respected of Treasury officials in other government agencies, Oliphant, along with Herbert Gaston, was the
most dependable of Morgenthau's subordinates. It was to "Old
Reliable" that Morgenthau looked as he directed his staff to the
issues of national defense in the fall of 1938. The General Counsel was then ill — fatally ill — though no one was as yet aware of
it, but in the several months that remained he served his chief as
he always had with vigor and insight.

At Morgenthau's instruction, Oliphant in September began to
investigate ways to acquire strategic materials which were in
short supply. Neither the President nor the Congress had supported the requests of the Army and Navy for stockpiling appropriations. Oliphant's preliminary study confirmed an immediate
need, earlier identified by Herbert Feis of the State Department,
for chemicals and manganese. The insignificant funds available
to the armed services for buying those commodities could be expanded, Oliphant noted, by loans from the Reconstruction Finance Corporation to the Export-Import Bank and from it to the
Federal Surplus Commodities Corporation. In that manner the
Administration could begin at once to acquire critical materials.
But Roosevelt, though interested in the scheme, would not go
ahead without congressional endorsement, nor would he yet seek
that endorsement. The President, Morgenthau gathered, was
hoarding his diminished influence on the Hill against unpredict-
able contingencies arising out of European affairs.

Roosevelt was also guarded in his response to Oliphant's recommendations for controlling prices. In September 1938 the
Treasury's Division of Procurement wrote Morgenthau that a
European war would lead to increased demands for American
steel, tools, and machinery, and therefore to inflation in the
prices of the very items the government would need for its own
national defense. The Division recommended the immediate
planning for price controls to be based on the voluntary cooperation of industry, labor, and the public. That suggestion struck
Oliphant as wholly inadequate. He and his liveliest assistant,
Oscar Cox, joined representatives of the Departments of Justice,
Commerce, and Agriculture in urging Roosevelt to employ all

available federal authority to forestall price rises. The necessary power was at hand, Oliphant believed, if Roosevelt would appoint dedicated New Dealers, not businessmen, to use it. But the President, while relying upon Leon Henderson, Oliphant, and other liberals, approved only a further study of the problem.

Morgenthau took part personally in Roosevelt's early deliberations about an aircraft program. On October 20, 1938, the Secretary returned from the White House in great excitement to tell his staff of the President's intention to develop production of 15,000 airplanes a year. Roosevelt had in mind building eight new factories near cities where there were reservoirs of trained labor, and working those plants around the clock in three shifts. Harry Hopkins believed that plan would absorb many of the unemployed. He was ready to start building the plants if money could be found to buy the land. That posed a problem for Morgenthau, who determined at once to educate himself in the details of the program. "Next week," the Secretary said, "I'm going to school with General Arnold. . . . Practically every morning, beginning Monday morning." Roosevelt thought he could build the planes for $25,000 each, less than half of Morgenthau's private estimate, but expense did not worry the Secretary. He wanted only to provide whatever was needed "to defend this country against an aggressor . . . or any group of aggressors." He was "all bucked up over this thing. . . . Tickled to death the President is thinking of making this country so strong that nobody can attack us. . . . We want enough planes to take care of the whole South American continent, too."

As one step toward that goal, Roosevelt issued an Executive Order giving the Treasury's Division of Procurement authority to determine purchasing policies for aircraft as well as certain other military items. To enhance the Division's efficiency, Morgenthau in November 1938 decided to replace its aging chief, Admiral Christian J. Peoples, with a younger, more vigorous man. Captain Harry Collins, USN, an experienced and faithful subordinate, actually ran the Division as its assistant chief until, several months later, Morgenthau recruited as acting chief a senior and talented Sears, Roebuck executive, Donald Nelson, who was to play a major role in the administration of defense and war production. The Secretary also tried to strengthen the procurement arms of the services. "At my suggestion," he noted in his Diary, "the President is going to invite three of the leading manufacturers in America who are not interested in airplane activities to come down at a dollar a year and later take full charge of production after the Army has turned over to them the blueprints of the models that they want."

Those invitations were indefinitely delayed by indecision about aircraft models and numbers. Roosevelt on November 12, 1938, tried his most recent thoughts on Morgenthau, Harry Hopkins, and the Assistant Secretary of War, Louis Johnson. Johnson, though egotistical and tactless, was alone among top War Department officials in his energy. He had completed calculations on the production potential of the aircraft industry. The Army wanted to reserve that production for two new models it considered better than any in the world. Roosevelt emphasized the need for new capacity, for building eight or ten factories at once. Though he still expected the WPA to construct and operate one or two of them and to produce about 20 per cent of all military aircraft, he seemed to Morgenthau "to be leaning more and more towards giving the private manufacturers the first chance, and I guess he has become convinced that in England, particularly, the Government has been unable to manufacture planes in their own plants."

On the basis of discussions with Morgenthau and the War Department, Herman Oliphant worked out a definition of general objectives. His recommendations called for the full utilization of existing facilities of the aircraft industry, for the development of additional facilities, including some government-operated plants to set a yardstick for prices and production, for the adoption of the mass-production techniques that had been effective in the manufacture of ships and automobiles, for research subsidized by the government, and for government controls to prevent monopoly and to encourage invention. Oliphant also advocated centralized government purchasing to hold down prices and insure competition among suppliers. He recommended, too, the

suspension of the Buy America Act to permit the purchase overseas of materials in short supply, lower tariff schedules on all aircraft parts which seemed overpriced at home, and inexpensive
federal credit and technical assistance for new or financially
weak aircraft plants which promised to provide both capacity
and competition.

At a "momentous White House meeting" of November 14,
1938, Roosevelt reviewed his plans for American defense, particularly those for aircraft production, with a group from the
Treasury, Justice, and War Departments, including senior Army
and Navy officers. The President began by revealing his latest
information about the situation in Europe. He said that France
had less than 600 planes she could put in the air; England, from
1500 to 2200; Germany from 5500 to 6500 first-line planes and
about 2000 second-line; Italy about 2000 first-line planes and
1000 second-line. The discrepancy between the democracies
and the fascist nations was increased because production in
France was very low with little sign of improvement, and that
of England was not much better.

"The President then pointed out that the recrudescence of
German power at Munich had completely reoriented our own
international relations; that for the first time since the Holy Alliance in 1818 the United States now faced the possibility of an
attack on the Atlantic side in both the Northern and Southern
Hemispheres. He said that this demanded our providing immediately a huge air force so that we do not need to have a huge army
to follow that air force. He considered that sending a large army
abroad was undesirable and politically out of the question.

"The President's next point was that in 1917 it took the
United States thirteen months after its declaration of war to put
the first plane on the battle front in Europe. . . . Hereafter
there would be no such period of grace. We must have resources, plans and equipment for putting a large number of
planes into actual operation at any time on short notice.

"He said there was a second reason why we had to have a large
supply of planes and in this connection significantly said, so far
as I can remember his exact words, 'I am not sure now that I am

proud of what I wrote to Hitler in urging that he sit down around the table and make peace. That may have saved many, many lives now, but that may ultimately result in the loss of many times that number of lives later. When I write to foreign countries I must have something to back up my words. Had we had this summer 5000 planes and the capacity immediately to produce 10,000 per year, even though I might have had to ask Congress for authority to sell or lend them to the countries in Europe, Hitler would not have dared to take the stand he did.' In a similar vein he elaborated the proposition that our foreign policy needs implementation."

The President's almost exclusive emphasis on airplanes disturbed Army and Navy representatives who advocated a balanced expansion of the services, but they agreed with Roosevelt on the nation's need for 10,000 planes a year and for the capacity to produce twice that number. The lack of privately owned facilities persuaded Roosevelt, as he had earlier told Morgenthau, that the government would have to provide about a fifth of the necessary new capacity, and he was convinced, too, of the desirability of adopting the procurement policies Oliphant had recommended.

Between mid-November 1938 and early January 1939, when the President took his defense program to the Congress, Morgenthau had no occasion to review it. While the Army worked out the details of its requests for aircraft, while the Treasury staff continued to help draft economic plans, the Secretary concentrated upon defending America by strengthening her democratic friends. Yet he also had in mind the unsolved problems of procurement, and in January he urged the President, without effect, to put defense industries on a longer work week, to add extra shifts, and to recruit more skilled labor. If the aggressors knew that the entire American machinery and tool industry was going to be utilized, they would, Morgenthau argued, be less apt to attack. "I believe," he wrote, "we should do everything possible to prevent a European war until England and France are prepared to meet it. In the meantime I think the people in the United States should strive for peace, but I also believe that peace is so important to the future of the world that we should be prepared, and willing, to fight for it if necessary.

"In presenting this thought to Americans we must understand that the United States will stand to lose more in the case of a general war than any other country, because another world war will make it necessary for the United States to participate in a much bigger way than we did in the last in order to maintain our type of civilization."

2. Planes for France

In October 1938, Jean Monnet, the French financier, came to Washington to inquire confidentially about purchasing military aircraft from American manufacturers. Monnet's mission was sponsored by William Bullitt, United States Ambassador in France. Without an adequate air force or the facilities to produce one, France, Bullitt knew, would either have to yield again to Hilter's demands or crumble before his might. Bullitt was worried also about French finances, for the rising defense budget had weakened confidence in the franc, and investors, afraid war was imminent, were further debilitating the French currency by selling it for dollars.

In their Washington talks, Morgenthau offered Monnet American cooperation in the application of exchange controls and other devices to support the franc. Much interested, Monnet brought the word back to Paris. But Premier Daladier rejected the American proposals as politically impracticable. Monnet also reported that his American conversations persuaded him that France might obtain delivery of about 1000 airplanes before the end of July 1939. Daladier accordingly authorized him to buy the planes, provided that their specifications and delivery date met French requirements. In December 1938, Monnet, accompanied by three aviation experts, again arrived in the United

States with authority to negotiate contracts, arrange for financing, and, if necessary, establish a purchasing corporation.

Roosevelt, who had encouraged the French to send the mission, had done little to prepare to assist it. Apart from his willingness to permit the French to spend their money for American aircraft, the President by mid-December had decided only, as he told the Cabinet, that any foreigners coming to any department with letters of introduction or credentials should not be received until after the Department of State had certified them.

On December 16, 1938, Monnet, accompanied by Ambassador Bullitt, called on Morgenthau. "I told Mr. Bullitt," Morgenthau recorded in his Diary, "in front of Mr. Monnet, that until Sumner Welles should call me up and say this is cleared with the State Department, that nobody in the Treasury would talk to Mr. Monnet." When Bullitt protested, Morgenthau said: "I am sorry. I have to work with Sumner on a lot of things besides French planes, but I wanted you to know that all avenues . . . are closed until Mr. Welles gives me a green light."

The next day Welles sent word from Roosevelt that the Treasury could help Monnet. Morgenthau at once directed the Frenchman to talk with Captain Collins, the acting director of Procurement. "Triple confidentially" they began to investigate the possibilities for placing French orders with American firms.

While Monnet explored various channels of credit, his expert associates selected for purchase the P-40, a new pursuit ship which Morgenthau described as the "best plane in the world." The General Staff of the Army was reluctant to let the French buy the P-40, and Roosevelt, too, hesitated. "Think about it again," Morgenthau suggested. ". . . If your theory [is] that England and France are our first line of defense, then if you want them to be our first line, let's either give them good stuff or tell them to go home, but don't give them some stuff which the minute it goes up in the air it will be shot down. No sense in selling them that which is out of date." American factories, Morgenthau told his staff, were "all sitting waiting for the Army to make up its mind and they could get out, this winter, one thousand planes before the Army is ready."

Of a similar opinion, Roosevelt on December 21, 1938, signed an order which, as he put it, "for reasons of state should be kept as confidential as possible," permitting the French to inspect and purchase American planes, provided that their orders were filled "so as not to interfere with U.S. new orders this spring." When Morgenthau gave that order to Monnet the next day, he "made it entirely clear that the President is anxious that every opportunity be given this mission to purchase these planes in such volume as to meet their needs, providing their arrangements can be completed and orders given and deliveries made with sufficient promptness so as not to interfere with U.S. Army orders for the same types of planes." The Secretary also impressed the French with the necessity for "absolute secrecy as far as other Governments are concerned." Monnet promised to comply.

The War Department deplored the President's decision. Though Roosevelt had yet to take the Army's program for airplanes to the Congress, and though Congress was still months from acting upon it, senior Air Corps officers feared that French orders would delay American deliveries. They also opposed letting any foreign government acquire the latest types of American pursuit planes and bombers. Their objections impressed Secretary of War Woodring, who in any event believed that Europe's troubles were under no conditions America's concern. Assistant Secretary of War Johnson, while personally at odds with his chief, was nevertheless sensitive to the views of the Air Corps and, like Woodring, resentful that Roosevelt had turned the French mission over to Morgenthau.

It was the uncooperative attitude of the War Department that had forced the President to do so. Roosevelt also considered the Treasury's Procurement Division the only agency capable of coordinating French purchases with the requests of both the Army and the Navy. Unlike the Army, the Navy was happy to work with the French, but it was never comfortable in harness with its fellow service, and Morgenthau had to keep peace between them while he pushed the Army toward the President's objective.

From the start the War Department's policies distressed Morgenthau. On December 22, 1938, Louis Johnson told him that the Army had decided against ordering a four-engine Boeing bomber priced at $400,000. Boeing was therefore considering an offer from Japan of $800,000 for the plane and its plans. "This is just impossible," Morgenthau said. "You can't do that." Johnson argued that Boeing deserved compensation for the money it had spent in developing the plane. "That's just too bad," Morgenthau replied, "and you can't do it." When he reported the story to Roosevelt, the President concluded that Johnson must be crazy. He also endorsed Morgenthau's suggestion for letting the French have the Boeing plane. Johnson then called Boeing, which proved much less money-conscious than he had been. "Their attitude has been perfectly grand," he reported to Morgenthau.

That same day Secretary Woodring tried to block the entire French program. Besides the P-40 fighter, the French wanted a Douglas attack bomber. In a memorandum to Morgenthau, Woodring said that both were still valuable military secrets. The Army was now willing to release the pursuit plane for inspection, but it wanted to keep the bomber under wraps.

On December 29 Woodring wrote that he would reveal no secrets to the French until Morgenthau assured him their orders were bona fide and in no way impediments to the Army's program. "Since I cannot undertake to guarantee the French orders," Morgenthau wrote Roosevelt the next day, "I am unable to proceed further in this matter so long as Secretary Woodring maintains his present attitude." Morgenthau told Woodring that he was "very much disappointed" that the Secretary of War had tried to put him "on the spot by writing a letter placing such limitations . . . on the program of assistance to the French." Woodring replied that he was under pressure "from his own shop . . . with the claim that not only his Army officers, but members of Congress were critical of the proposed action with respect to the French." Congressmen, he added, were raising hell about "all the taxpayers' money that we have had for development and experiment being . . . given away. . . . All I wanted to do, Henry, was simply to protect you in the matter."

"But I don't . . . want to be protected," Morgenthau ob-

jected. ". . . The President said they can see these planes."
Though still querulous, Woodring then issued the necessary
orders.

Turning to Monnet, Morgenthau on December 31 said: "The
whole United States Army is opposed to what I am doing
and I am doing it secretly and I just can't continue, as Secretary
of the Treasury, forcing the United States Army to show planes
which they say they want for themselves." The French would
have to "come out in the open and say a mission is here." That
announcement would generate immediate support, particularly
from manufacturers and labor. Monnet promised to get a ruling
from Paris. Meanwhile, he reminded the Secretary, their efforts
created the best hope for peace. "This airplane thing is common
to the whole European situation," Monnet said. "Germany takes
this threatening position because she knows that the other countries are afraid of being bombed . . . and that they have not the
means of retaliating. The moment the Germans know that the
others have a force for retaliating, it may change the whole situation."

During the first two weeks of January 1939 the Navy agreed
to let the French have half the Dodd bombers being produced.
Indeed, Captain Collins believed the Navy's plans of releasing
every alternate plane exactly suited the requirements of national
defense. But the Army had yet to understand the importance of
French money for expanding airplane capacity. Convinced that
the President would never get what he wanted the way things
were going, Morgenthau had drafted an Executive Order for
Roosevelt's consideration that gave the Procurement Division of
the Treasury responsibility for all purchasing for both services.

As impatient as Morgenthau, Roosevelt on January 16, 1939,
summoned Treasury, War, and Navy officials to the White
House. The President demanded immediate assistance for the
French. Secretary Woodring complained that the Douglas
bomber contained many secret elements and had been built partially with government funds. Selling the plane to the French,
he argued, would put the President in an embarrassing position.
When Louis Johnson asked directly whether he wanted the

plane released, Roosevelt replied that he desired exactly that. Again and again he repeated his wish "that every effort be made to expedite the procurement of any types of plane desired by the French government."

The President's unequivocal statement cheered Monnet, to whom Morgenthau relayed it. Paris, the Frenchman said, would deal directly with the United States government, as Morgenthau had urged. An official announcement was presumably imminent. But even before an announcement, Roosevelt's command brought the Army into line, and General "Hap" Arnold, the head of the Air Corps, telegraphed to his subordinates in California, instructing them to demonstrate the Douglas attack bomber to the French mission. The French were to inspect the bomber stripped of its secret accessories, to be permitted to fly in it and to undertake negotiations for its purchase.

Woodring, Johnson, and General Arnold, although obeying Roosevelt's orders, remained discontented. On January 23, the day the French mission reached the West Coast, Captain Collins found Johnson "quite mad . . . very sarcastic." Late that day the controversial bomber, while making a bank, went into a spin at 400 feet and crashed, killing the test pilot, injuring the French observer and ten bystanders, and demolishing nine automobiles. On January 26, 1939, the Senate Committee on Military Affairs heard secret testimony from General Arnold about the crash. The next day the New York *Herald Tribune* and Washington *Post* published "information . . . elicited from a committee witness." The papers contended that Arnold had said that "permission to ride in a new, test plane which embodied military and technical secrets, had not been obtained from any officer of the Army or from the War Department, but from the Treasury." Arnold was in part misquoted. He had made it clear to the committee that all secret equipment had been removed from the airplane. He had said, too, that the War Department knew the French were going to inspect the plane. Yet he had also permitted the committee to get the impression that the Treasury issued the orders for the flight.

On the Hill on January 27, Morgenthau faced the antagonism

of isolationist Democrat Bennett Clark of Missouri, long a critic of the President. Clark asked just what the Treasury had had to do with putting a French air expert "in a plane supposed to embody the very latest development . . . for American national defense." Morgenthau responded with a detailed history of the French mission. The War Department, the Secretary said, had promised to cooperate in the President's wishes for the clearance of the Douglas plane that had crashed, and General Arnold had himself sent to the West Coast a telegram authorizing the test which resulted in tragedy.

Clark asked whether Morgenthau thought it was "going beyond the extreme limit, to render the courtesy of permitting them to learn American military secrets." The airplane was the property of the Douglas Company, the Secretary replied. The United States government had no proprietary interest in it. It had been brought down to the municipal airport at Los Angeles, where anyone in the world could see it. "It was secret enough," Clark interrupted.

The next to testify was Assistant Secretary of the Treasury Herbert Gaston, who had just come from the President's press conference. There, Roosevelt had said that the Cabinet, in the light of the idleness of most American airplane factories, had found it desirable to get French orders as soon as possible. The Cabinet had also decided there was no legal barrier to those orders since they would involve only cash, not loans. Neither the Treasury nor the War Department, the President said, had objected to French inspection of the Douglas plane, which had yet to be accepted by the United States government. Asked why the Treasury had been involved, Roosevelt replied, "For two very simple reasons: first, the Treasury Department was interested in building up American industry . . . and second . . . the Procurement Division worked in close cooperation with the Army and Navy in the procurement of many types of supplies."

Senator Clark doubted the President's veracity. The Douglas plane had yet to be entered into a competition for Army orders, he agreed, but General Arnold had testified that the manufacturer intended to enter it soon. The senator could still not understand why the Procurement Division was in the picture. Again, Morgenthau explained that "the President himself requested it."

Clark and his fellow isolationist Senator Gerald Nye pressed Secretary Woodring on the same issue. "We got our instructions to carry out this procurement by the French Mission," Woodring said, "under the direction of the Secretary of the Treasury." When Clark then asked if there had been any superior authority, Woodring replied: "The Secretary of the Treasury has already testified that he got a letter from the President."

Now Senator Nye, aware that the War Department had resisted the President's policy, asked Morgenthau whether the Army had originally discouraged cooperation with the French. Morgenthau turned the question to Woodring, who, dodging it, said that everyone had been in accord before the French went to the West Coast. Clark then referred to General Arnold's statement that the air force program would take "all of the airplane productivity of the United States for two years." Again Woodring ducked, replying that that depended upon how much money Congress made available.

The French, Morgenthau interrupted, wanted to place orders at once, whereas Congress had yet to authorize the American program. The French "would pay for the development cost and their orders would be out of the way and be delivered before Congress voted the money, and the Army would have a chance to have that competition later, and . . . we would get the plants into production that are idle now." Sixty-five million dollars to hire American working-men was "good stuff." Further, the French had pledged that none of the planes would leave France or be shown to any other power.

But Woodring told the committee that he had informed Morgenthau the airplanes could not be delivered to the French by July 1, 1939. By implication, he confirmed Clark's objection, and Arnold's, that the French order would interfere with the Army's purchasing.

The hostility of Clark and Nye had the predictable effect of getting Roosevelt's "Dutch up." At Cabinet meeting, Mor-

genthau reported, "the President said to proceed as before . . .
to go right ahead with the French . . . and let them buy what
they want."

The President also vented his annoyance on Morgenthau during a long conversation on January 31. "You had a terrible row
with Woodring," Roosevelt complained. He blamed the Secretary for bringing to the Cabinet the Treasury's draft of an Executive Order putting all military purchasing under the Procurement Division. "That was too much of a shock to Woodring,"
Roosevelt said. As Morgenthau put it in his Diary: "There was
no sense in explaining my action as I felt it needed no explanation."

Roosevelt next chided Morgenthau for telling the senators he
had a letter from the President. "I didn't," Morgenthau answered. "You told me that I could say that you had given me
instructions which I repeated to the Committee but I scrupu-
lously refrained from saying I had any letter from you and it was
Harry Woodring who let that cat out of the bag. . . . Woodring got very angry, particularly when I said that the French
wanted to get these planes by the first of July."

The Secretary, Roosevelt went on, had had no right to give
the committee a copy of the order Arnold sent to the West
Coast. "I was confronted with two alternatives," Morgenthau
said, ". . . I could . . . say that General Arnold was a liar or I
could produce the orders which he had issued, making it possible
for the French to see these planes, and inasmuch as I didn't want
to call General Arnold a liar, I had no choice in the matter. . . .
Woodring got all excited because he said we had broken faith
with him. . . . It turned out, upon investigation, that Louie
Johnson had known all about what we were doing . . . but had
withheld the information from Woodring. It seems to me that
most of the difficulty that I have met with is on account of the
constant clash between Woodring and Johnson."

Roosevelt, who did not like to hear about the mess in the War
Department, said: "You know I have plans to clean up that situation." Morgenthau revealed his doubts: "Mr. President, you can
take six months or a year to clean up some other situations in

other departments but in the case of the War Department it is a matter of days because, for your international speeches to be effective, you must be backed up with the best air fleet in the world and, if we are going to do that, it is a matter of days to get the thing in order. . . . After all, you gave me a mission to perform, namely, to get the French these planes and I have done it. I have been successful." Though still irritated, Roosevelt replied: "That is right."

Woodring, still surly, took his first opportunity to tell Roosevelt "how terribly" Morgenthau had acted on the Hill and "what terrible advice" Morgenthau had been giving. The President was by no means yet cordial to Morgenthau — their disagreements about taxation were to keep them apart for another five months — but Roosevelt was also oblivious to any remark of his Secretary of War. More important, though his mood toward his friend remained sour, he knew that Morgenthau had brought the French mission to a successful conclusion. In mid-February, assisted by the Procurement Division, the French signed contracts for air frames and engines with a number of manufacturers, including Martin, Douglas, Pratt and Whitney, North American, Wright, and United.

"I appreciate very much the confidence and support you gave me personally and gave us in this French plane affair," Monnet told Morgenthau in March 1939, "and I do think the result of it . . . has been of tremendous importance." If it had not been for Morgenthau's "firmness of attitude . . . this would not have gone through." The Secretary was still nursing his wounds. "For a month I went through hell," he replied, ". . . one of the most unpleasant experiences I ever had. Terrific! But now . . . it is fine."

Apart from the President's lingering resentment, Morgenthau had reason to rejoice, though the manufacturers delivered their orders more slowly than they had promised. Even so, before Labor Day 1939, the French had received all of their first order of Martin bombers, most of their basic trainers from North American, half of their dive bombers from United — in all just under half their total order of air frames but less than a third of

their engines. With Woodring and Johnson both still in office
and American aircraft production still chaotic, that was as good a
record as possible. It was not good enough. Morgenthau had
been entirely right in urging the President to reform procurement procedures. Both men had been wise in recognizing the
importance of the French orders which, Edward R. Stettinius,
Jr., later judged, "were almost revolutionary in their effect
upon our aviation industry, and laid the groundwork for the
great expansion that was to come."

At the height of his troubles with the Senate, Morgenthau expressed his own feelings to his staff: "On account of all the criticism of one kind and another . . . I just want to say this for the
benefit of this group: that . . . what I have done to assist the
French get planes — I am delighted I was able to do; if I had to
do it, I would do it all over again. . . .

"What I have done . . . I believe in; other people in the Administration may or may not change, but I . . . am proud of the
part that I was able to play."

3. Preparedness in the Treasury

The Nazi seizure of Czechoslovakia and Memel in the spring of
1939 provoked Roosevelt to instruct the Treasury to define the
action the federal government could take, without recourse to
new legislation, for the protection of American interests. Morgenthau assigned that task to his new General Counsel, Edward
H. Foley, Jr. Recruited from the Interior Department in 1937,
Foley had gained experience as Oliphant's assistant and insights
into the labyrinths of Washington as Tommy Corcoran's intimate. Gregarious, affable, widely acquainted in the Democratic
party, Foley was a steady and loyal performer. Before the end
of March he had completed a survey of the powers available to
the government, the Treasury in particular.

The Secretary of the Treasury could, with the President's approval, reinstate controls over foreign exchange by revoking the general license under which transactions had been authorized since 1933. He could stop sales and exports of gold and silver, and regulate, even nationalize, currencies and securities held or owned abroad by American citizens. He could use the Treasury's General Fund, the Stabilization Fund, and other resources to support the government bond market and the exchange value of the dollar. He could also sterilize all gold held under earmark for foreign governments. In those and other ways, he could prevent foreign nations from using their assets in the United States in a manner inconsistent with American interests.

Apart from its powers over money, the Treasury, with the assistance of other governmental agencies, could help to control commodity and security prices by establishing stand-by regulations over markets. The Department could also, if Roosevelt so directed, create a central office to represent the purchasing missions of foreign nations and the procurement agencies of the federal government. That office would have the size and prestige to hold down the prices of manufactured goods and to discipline the producers of scarce items.

Finally, the President, operating through the Treasury, could regulate ship movements. He had authority over traffic in arms. He could prevent the departure of vessels engaged in the conduct of hostilities. He could expand the list of materials essential for American security and stop the sailing of ships carrying them. If the President declared the existence of a national emergency, the Secretary of the Treasury could issue orders governing the anchorage and movement of vessels to and from territorial waters of the United States.

After studying Foley's report, Morgenthau decided to bring to Washington four men of administrative experience to assume responsibility for the sensitive areas over which the Treasury had authority. He wanted Tom Smith, a banker whom he had often consulted, "to look after banking"; Basil Harris, a New York businessman, "to look after shipping and Customs"; Earle Bailie, another banker who had advised the Department on earlier occasions, to take care of "foreign exchange and the stock exchange"; and, to oversee all purchasing, Edward R. Stettinius, Jr., the United States Steel president who had prepared for Roosevelt recommendations on the organization of national defense. "My thought," Morgenthau said on April 10, 1939, "is each one will . . . have his desk and have his whole organization set up, so if there should be a war the organization is there and all he has to do is come down here. I am going to get the President's okay so I can begin to function."

Roosevelt approved three of the Secretary's choices, each of whom went to work at once, but the President argued that Stettinius would not have the guts to keep the price of copper from rising too high. Morgenthau "disagreed warmly with him on this" and rejected Roosevelt's counterproposal for appointing instead President Robert Hutchins of the University of Chicago or James M. Landis, Dean of the Harvard Law School. "The President is wrong," Morgenthau noted, leaving the post vacant. ". . . I think we need a practical fellow like Stettinius."

With Roosevelt's consent, the Secretary discussed with the interested federal agencies "what we would do in the case of a world war, as far as stocks are concerned." Though the State Department objected, Morgenthau on April 16, 1939, submitted to Roosevelt drafts of Executive Orders, all cleared by the Attorney General, for regulating transactions in foreign exchange, transfers of credit, the export of gold and currency, and the registering of foreign-owned assets in the United States. The orders gave the President exactly what he had asked for, the means to shield American interests from the shock of war. He was pleased, Roosevelt said, with the progress Morgenthau had made.

The Secretary was less successful in trying to win the President to a program for purchasing strategic materials. On April 11, 1939, he suggested to Roosevelt a billion-dollar venture for the preclusive buying of oil, tin, and manganese. The price would be cheap, the Secretary said, as a "quarantine" against aggression. "The President seemed intensely interested," Morgenthau noted in his Diary, "and said one of the difficulties to overcome would be the cry that Germany would let out that this was a plan to encircle her and how would we answer such a statement. The President told me that he had an idea which he would like to do if the State Department would only let him, namely, he'd like to write a letter to Hitler and Mussolini suggesting that they give sacred guarantees that they would not absorb any other countries in Europe and that if they were willing to give such guarantees that he in turn would be willing to meet them at the Azores and sit around a table and discuss disarmament and world trade. I said I thought that that would be a splendid first move because if they turned him down then he would have a good excuse to go ahead with my plan and he said, 'That's exactly what I had in mind.' "

After reflection, Roosevelt did not adopt Morgenthau's proposal or comparable recommendations of the War, Navy, and State Departments. He appointed a committee to investigate stock piling, but asked Congress for only $10 million for that purpose, far less than a useful minimum.

Still, as Commander-in-Chief, Roosevelt speculated about American policy in case of war. "He . . . says," Morgenthau told his staff on April 20, 1939, "that he is going to have a patrol from Newfoundland down to South America and if some submarines are laying there and try to interrupt an American flag and our Navy sinks them, it's just too bad. . . . In other words, he is going to play the game the way they are doing it now. If we fire and sink an Italian or German . . . we will say it the way the Japs do, 'So sorry.' 'Never happen again.' Tomorrow we sink two. We simply say, 'So sorry,' and next day we go ahead and do it over again. . . . It is what he has in mind. . . . He is going to be not too strict on lending money [to the democracies] to buy our goods, merchandise, which isn't talking in terms of munitions. He's going to follow the new method of when someone gets in your way you sink them and apologize and do it again next day."

Though American planning continued through the late spring and early summer of 1939 — Roosevelt then completed the arrangements for his patrol — the sense of crisis on both sides of the Atlantic eased briefly while European statesmen pursued negotiations to postpone, hopefully to avert, the outbreak of war. In August Morgenthau left for Scandinavia for conversation with the treasuries of Norway and Denmark, and for a month's vacation. While he was there the negotiations for an accommodation collapsed. When Baron von Ribbentrop reached Moscow to complete a nonaggression pact with the Soviet Union, war seemed inevitable. Germany pressed her demands against Poland, which left France and England the choice between another groveling defeat or an honorable resistance.

On August 22 the Treasury representative in London reported that the City expected war momentarily. That day Roosevelt authorized an interdepartmental conference which reaffirmed the decisions about the exchanges that had been made the previous April. On August 25 the President instructed the Treasury to put into effect Morgenthau's stand-by orders for regulating the movement of ships. On August 28 the Coast Guard cutter *Campbell*, which had been cruising near Scandinavian waters, picked up Morgenthau at Bergen, Norway, and set out for Newfoundland, where he could meet a plane for Washington. The voyage, memorable for its unfailing dirty weather, got the Secretary to his desk just after fighting began in Poland.

Back in his office on September 4, Morgenthau was satisfied with the efficacy of the Treasury's advance planning and the responsible performance of his subordinates. He found, too, a kind of relief in confronting an open and declared war instead of another bloodless Nazi gain, another timorous democratic retreat. He had hoped, as had all decent men, that war might be avoided. He believed in 1939, as he still did two decades later, that the democracies could have prevented the war if they had stood up to Hitler sooner. He realized, moreover, that the United States had been as remiss as England or France. American isolationism, the Senate's refusal to modify the Neutrality Act, the hesitancies of the State Department, all these had disheartened Great Britain and France, and encouraged Hitler and Mussolini to believe that the world could be theirs at small cost. Now the cost for everyone was to be enormous and tragic.

XI

THE "PHONY WAR"

1939–1940

WHEN NAZI TROOPS broke the uneasy peace of Europe, most Americans sympathized with the Poles, the immediate victims of aggression, and with Poland's allies, France and England. Nearly all Americans realized that Adolf Hitler had brought war to Europe, nearly all hoped for Germany's defeat. Most of them knew that England and France would need American materials; over 40 per cent believed that if the democracies were in danger of defeat, American troops would have to fight across the ocean. But, short of Allied defeat, the American people and even more, the Congress, were resolved to keep out of the European catastrophe. The Senate especially was subject to the assumption, which had gained credence during the 1930's, that Wall Street, American munitions makers, and Allied propagandists had brought the United States into World War I. This belief underlay the Senate's refusal, only weeks before the German invasion of Poland, to amend the Neutrality Act of 1937 prohibiting the export of any arms or munitions to any warring power.

Sensitive to opinion on the Hill and yet determined that England and France should be able in time to procure munitions in the United States, the President proceeded with calculated caution. The political setbacks of 1938 left him unsure of his influence. Further, while he considered an Allied victory imperative, he did not entirely trust the stamina of the French, and he had some reservations about the British, particularly Prime Minister Neville Chamberlain, whom he found disdainful and irresolute. Roosevelt was always uneasy about British colonialism, always afraid of losing a round in negotiation to London, always conscious that British and American interests were not identical. He had no doubts about the impelling common cause, the eradication of Nazism, but he had continuing doubts about specific policies for cooperation to that end. Especially, the President remained suspicious of the New York financial community, so long in opposition to the New Deal, and of Wall Street's ties to London. These attitudes increased his caution.

During the first half year of war, developments in Europe tended to confirm rather than to challenge the presidential mood. After his rapid conquest of Poland, Hitler awaited spring weather before striking again, and the French, at least many of them, let themselves believe that their defenses were impregnable. In this time of "phony war," while Allied strategists thought in terms appropriate only for the previous war, appeasers still had an audience in England and France, and some Americans, especially isolationists, predicted a negotiated peace. Those who understood the Nazis, men like Leon Blum in France, Winston Churchill in Great Britain, Henry Stimson and Henry Morgenthau, Jr., in the United States, did not lose their sense of dread and urgency, but they had only moderate success in making themselves heard.

1. Cash and Carry

The President would like to have persuaded Congress to substitute for neutrality legislation an immediate return to the traditional practices of international law. The strength of isolationist sentiment, however, forced him to ask only for a lesser change, one that would eliminate the embargo on the export of arms and munitions. The rapidity with which the German troops conquered Poland indicated the need for amending the law in order to allow the British and French to purchase war materials. The failure to achieve even that in the summer of 1939, Roosevelt was sure, played into the hands of Hitler.

On September 21, 1939, Roosevelt addressed the Congress, which had just reconvened. Congressional leaders of both parties had indicated that they would repeal the embargo only if sales of munitions were limited to "cash and carry" and American credits were forbidden to belligerents. Accepting those conditions, the President also emphasized the inconsistency of the arms embargo. It permitted the sale of unfinished weapons and war materials while prohibiting the export of finished implements of war. Consequently, it did not protect neutrality, whereas by its repeal, which would assist the opponents of Nazism, "the United States will more probably remain at peace than if the law remains as it stands."

The drafting of the new legislation fell to Senator Key Pittman, Democratic Chairman of the Foreign Relations Committee. Pittman, chary of any pressure from the State Department or the White House, proposed to eliminate the embargo at a price which staggered Cordell Hull. The senator intended severely to restrict both American shipping and private credits to belligerents. Even so, his bill met opposition from isolationist organizations throughout the country and from most Republicans in Congress.

The Treasury became involved in the Neutrality bill over the question of credits. The Foreign Relations Committee wanted to limit the discretion of the President by providing that short-term commercial credits to belligerents might not exceed ninety days; that if any belligerent defaulted, no new credit might be extended; and that the President was to inform Congress every six months about credits outstanding. Like Hull, Morgenthau felt that Roosevelt should avoid endorsing a proposal which so restricted the presidential power. Yet Morgenthau also saw that even short-term credits would help to finance the transactions of the French and British governments, which were denied federal assistance by the provisions of the Johnson Act of 1934.* Indeed, as Morgenthau reported to Roosevelt, Senator Johnson had told Treasury representatives that his bill was not designed to eliminate short-term credits. "That's wonderful," the President said. "That's fine!"

Debate in the Senate clearly established the intention of Congress to forbid federal agencies to advance any credit or loan to belligerents. Though the Senate voted down a proposal of Robert Taft incorporating that prohibition, Pittman construed his committee's bill to cover "precisely one of the amendments offered by the distinguished Senator from Ohio." Further, on October 19, 1939, Senator Robert Wagner wrote Morgenthau that Taft and others were afraid the Stabilization Fund might supply currency to the democracies. To head off an amendment preventing that possibility, Morgenthau immediately replied that the Fund had been "used solely for the express purpose set out in the statute . . . namely, to stabilize the exchange value of the dollar."

In the end, the Neutrality Act of 1939, while permitting belligerents to buy munitions for cash and to carry them home in their own ships, attempted to prohibit all other transactions that might draw the United States into the war. The policy of the Congress, Pittman told representatives of the Executive departments on November 30, was to forestall any situation in which the United States would have to make strong representations to any belligerent, or as a result of which public opinion in the United States might be aroused.

Anticipating the repeal of the embargo, the democracies began early in September 1939 to prepare to purchase American munitions. Roosevelt at first leaned toward having them create a corporation to do their buying. "I have not told them either to form a corporation or not to," the President said to Morgenthau on September 19. "In other words, they can do it either . . . way but it . . . should not be an American bank or an American banking house." As the President later added, Winthrop Al-

---

* The Johnson Act prohibited government loans to nations in default of their World War I debts to the United States.

drich had consulted him about having the Chase National Bank represent the English. "I thought you were a bank," Roosevelt had said; "I didn't know you were a merchant." After Treasury experts pointed out technical objections to the use of a corporation, involving taxation, publicity, and other matters, Roosevelt, still circumventing Wall Street, advised the British to appoint a government purchasing mission.

The British and French also explored with the Treasury the question of how to handle their accounts. The President wanted the accounts open to him so that he would know exactly what orders the Allies had given to vital American industries. When Morgenthau suggested amending the Neutrality Act to require all nations to keep open accounts, Roosevelt said: "No. If I want them to do it, I will just tell them to. I don't need any law." It would be enough, he added, for the Treasury to lead the French and the British to the New York Federal Reserve Bank.

The chief opposition to the proposal came from Ambassador Joseph P. Kennedy in London, who thought it was a mistake for the United States to advise the British against the use of a commercial bank. "This appears dangerous ground to me," he cabled. His objection, as Roosevelt and Morgenthau interpreted it, stemmed largely from his desire to keep matters as much as possible in his own hands, rather than under the control of officials in Washington. The ambassador may also have desired to avoid the association of any partially public institution, like the Federal Reserve Bank of New York, with the French and the British. He had grave doubts about the war and he questioned the ability of the Allies to defeat the Germans. As Roosevelt put it to Morgenthau: "Joe Kennedy . . . has been an appeaser and always will be an appeaser. . . . If Germany or Italy made a good peace offer tomorrow, Joe would start working on the King and his friend, the Queen, and from there on down to get everybody to accept it. . . . He's just a pain in the neck to me."

Morgenthau, who agreed, was pleased that Sir John Simon, the Chancellor of the Exchequer, followed the Treasury's advice. On October 30, 1939, Simon cabled that the English would open a special account in the New York Federal Reserve

Bank, make access to it available to the Secretary of the Treasury, and keep in close touch with the American government about all financial arrangements in the United States. Early in December the French announced that they would take similar action.

Meanwhile, the British and French governments concluded an agreement for coordinating most of their economic activities, including shipping, airplane production, raw materials, munitions, food, and oil. This pooling of resources made it desirable to establish a single Anglo-French purchasing mission which would prevent the Allies from bidding against each other. It would also ease Morgenthau's responsibility for keeping French and English orders from interfering with the procurement programs of the American armed services. Jean Monnet was made chairman of the Anglo-French Co-ordinating Committee in London and the American mission was assigned to a Canadian, Arthur Purvis, who had no personal ties to the New York financial community. With the announcement of his appointment and the opening in December 1939 of a British account with the New York Federal Reserve Bank, the Allies completed their basic arrangements for buying American war materials. Morgenthau, fully satisfied with their plans, had already begun to investigate their cash resources for carrying them out.

According to Treasury estimates, British and French nationals together held some $15 billion of gold, American securities, and American properties which they could realize within two years after the start of the war. Half of these assets were owned in the United Kingdom, about a quarter in the British dominions, the balance in France. The British could liquidate about a third of their total holdings relatively easily, but they could give up a second third only with permanent injury to their economy and the last third "only if England were desperate." Yet solely by realizing their assets could France and England obtain American goods, for both nations had long had an unfavorable balance of trade with the United States and now had no products or services available for sale across the Atlantic. Both were doubly barred from American credits, by the Johnson Act because they were defaulters, by the Neutrality Act because they were belligerents.

Both the United States Treasury and the Securities and Exchange Commission had a lively concern about British policy. In order to prevent disturbances in the stock markets, they were eager to have the British make continual, controlled sales rather than dump securities at irregular intervals. Morgenthau also wanted to protect the value of the huge American gold holdings, of gold itself as the keystone of international exchange, and of the long-standing New Deal policy to buy all gold offered the United States at the rate of $35 an ounce. He hoped, therefore, that the British would retain as much of their gold as they could, and liquidate their securities continually in order to reduce their reliance on gold sales. He also hoped to obtain from the British accurate data about their assets, for his estimates were admittedly inexact.

The first reports he received from Ambassador Kennedy were disquieting. "England is busted now," Kennedy cabled. Montague Norman, Governor of the Bank of England, considered the financial situation "worse than tragic." Fearing inflation and even defeat, Norman predicted that whether or not the English won the war, Europe would have to return to medieval trading practices. All the world's gold and currency, all European assets, as Norman saw it, would end up in the United States, and "there will be no hope for the world . . . at least none for Europe."

While Norman's characteristic gloom reinforced Sir John Simon's ordinary indecisiveness, Kennedy complicated American negotiations with the government. His status at the Court of St. James's, he argued in October, would suffer if he were not permitted to counsel the British about their securities program. "That is what the President definitely doesn't want," Morgenthau told his staff. He also informed the British embassy that Roosevelt preferred discussions about English securities to take place in Washington, but Kennedy continued to interfere in London.

In spite of Kennedy's advice, and in deference to Morgenthau's wishes, the British government announced the first requisitioning of American stocks owned by British citizens on February 8, 1940. Two weeks later, Morgenthau advised them to sell. "It went off beautifully," the Secretary commented. The British made "no bones about it." Admitting that they had also consulted J. P. Morgan and Company, they said they would have been "extremely foolish" if they had not had advisers of that kind. Morgenthau agreed. The House of Morgan, as a broker for the British, would collect a commission which the Secretary considered properly earned. But Morgenthau was also "very frank" in return. "It has nothing to do with J. P. Morgan's ability," he said, "but there is in the minds of the public in the United States a certain phobia against them, because they feel that they more or less symbolize . . . the one institution that got us into the last war. . . . The children in the schools are taught that. . . . And . . . by using them exclusively as your advisers . . . you are going to stir up that feeling and it will undoubtedly . . . react unfavorably on your government. . . . I am not in any way saying that they are not . . . perfectly honorable people . . . [but] I think that sooner or later you may regret it."

In April a second British requisitioning and sale left the exchanges unruffled, but the mounting need for dollars forced England also to accelerate its sales of gold. Some Americans, expecting a German victory in the war, feared it would render gold worthless. Their anxieties gave rise to rumors that the Treasury would abandon its gold-buying policy, rumors Morgenthau tried to still in a public address that Roosevelt endorsed. Kennedy was urging the President to ask the Congress for legislation prohibiting the further purchase of gold. Perhaps the ambassador, pessimistic about England's ability to resist the Nazis, was trying to protect American interests, but his recommendation could have had the effect only of impairing England's capacity to obtain dollars with which to buy the means for continuing the war. Roosevelt, at Morgenthau's suggestion, wrote Kennedy that the United States Treasury was pursuing "the only policy with respect to its gold purchases that is compatible with the public interests." Kennedy, by implication, was to keep his hands off.

From September 1939 to April 1940, as Roosevelt's designated agent for dealing with the Anglo-French Purchasing Mission, Morgenthau had been increasingly involved in British procurement, and increasingly concerned that the British sell the assets to cover their expenses. He was not ungenerous. On the contrary, it was his intention to help the democracies as much as possible. But the Neutrality Act put all purchases on a cash and carry basis, and the Secretary wanted to make sure that British and French procedures were coordinated with the condition of American stock markets and the direction of American gold policy. He felt he deserved their help, particularly since he was giving to them the largest fraction of his time. Indeed, while he was appropriately jealous of American interests, he was making an unparalleled effort to supply the Allies.

2. *The Liaison Committee*

Shortly after Thanksgiving 1939, Morgenthau had his first long conference with Arthur Purvis, the head of the Anglo-French Purchasing Mission in Washington. The Secretary was immediately impressed with his guest, a man of medium height, well built, with strong features, gray hair, and piercing blue eyes under heavy black eyebrows. Purvis's manner combined force with charm and distinction. His slight Scottish accent lent piquancy to his speech. He was at once energetic and versatile. He held a degree in music from the University of Edinburgh; he was widely read and traveled; he had long experience in industry and had also, with great success, dealt with unemployment problems in Canada. Now he had assumed responsibility for a spending program that would run into billions of dollars. His boldness, his frankness, his straightforward way of doing business, his honesty and courtesy, his extraordinary energy, and his dedication to his crucial job made him one of the most valuable of all those serving the British Empire. These characteristics also won

Morgenthau's trust and affection. Indeed, save for Franklin Roosevelt, Morgenthau felt closer to Purvis, as their relationship developed, than he did to anyone else with whom he ever worked.

"Profoundly and passionately interested in the issues of the war," as the British later put it, the Secretary was dedicated to assisting the democracies, but he was also obliged by temperament and by office to prevent Allied buying from disrupting the American economy or rearmament program. He insisted, therefore, that the Allies coordinate their purchasing so as to avoid competition with the United States government. By the end of the first week of December 1939, he was reaching a position from which he could provide significant help. Though the Secretary had expected to have only temporary responsibility for the Allied purchasing program, Roosevelt decided to extend that duty. At Morgenthau's suggestion, the President appointed a Liaison Committee to work with the Anglo-French Purchasing Mission, and named as its chairman Captain Harry E. Collins, the acting director of the Treasury's Division of Procurement. "Let me explain what I have been doing, during the last month or two, without anybody knowing it . . ." Morgenthau told the new committee. "In addition to Collins getting information, the French and English have been giving it to me directly. . . . I get this and walk it over to the President. Did you know what I did on the search lights for them? . . . I got them every other one. It was that kind of thing I was able to do, with the President's backing. I have carried this thing. . . . It's getting to be too big. . . . So I recommended to the President, yesterday, that he set up an informal board composed of the . . . Paymaster General of the Navy . . . the Quartermaster General of the Army . . . and the Director of Procurement. And have you three meet, informally . . . with one representative of the French Embassy and one representative of the British Embassy . . . at least once a week. . . . You three people are to communicate with the President. . . .

"For example, the English . . . want a thousand motors and . . . the Army has turned them down. Wouldn't do it. . . .

Then the question comes up here of priority and this whole question of priority, prices, availability, you three men would . . . keep . . . fed to the President."

Roosevelt had deliberately kept off the committee both Secretary Woodring and Assistant Secretary Johnson, whose feud was crippling the War Department and embarrassing the Administration. When Roosevelt on December 6, 1939, officially appointed the Liaison Committee, Woodring objected. The Army and Navy Munitions Board, he argued, was handling the military program capably, and the War Department saw no reason for bringing in the Treasury. Woodring, who disapproved of foreign buying that in the least conflicted with the Army's plans, thought that his department, rather than Collins's committee, should pass on foreign orders. In a memorandum of his own, Assistant Secretary of War Johnson took a similar position. Roosevelt replied in a sharp letter of December 13: "I think you fail to realize that the greater part of such purchases is not, in the strict sense of the word, munitions — probably well over 50 per cent of the purchases will consist of articles and raw or semi-raw materials which are primarily of civil use. . . . With all due deference to the Army and Navy Munitions Board, it is not as experienced in making purchases as is the Procurement Division. . . . In any event, the coordinating committee . . . will have representatives of the Army and Navy on it, and I am perfectly willing to have the Quartermaster General and the Paymaster General represented by officers who are also members of the Army and Navy Munitions Board — expecially when it comes to purely military . . . materials. Finally it must be remembered that we are not at war, that we are trying to keep prices in this country down, that the work of the committee deals with civilians, and that the general fiscal and purchasing policies of the Treasury are very definitely involved. That is why I think I should let the present arrangement stand."

The War Department continued, however, to criticize the Liaison Committee and its decisions. Late in January 1940, Morgenthau, his patience gone, asked Steve Early, the President's press secretary, to release a White House endorsement of the committee. Louis Johnson, Morgenthau said, "was dishing out . . . dirt about me, namely, that I was more interested in the Allies than I was in my own country. . . . The whole War Department . . . have fought us to a standstill on this thing and the President . . . wants to do it this way. Woodring and Johnson argue with him so he has to use me. All right! I think I am serving my country. . . . I may have to take the rap. . . . But get this thing together tonight." On January 23, Early released a statement that the Treasury had drafted and the President had authorized. "Keep those two boys, Woodring and Johnson, straight," Roosevelt told Morgenthau privately, "or try to keep them straight."

That instruction in effect pertained also to Purvis and René Pleven, his French associate. Morgenthau had continually to bring them to accommodate their requests to American conditions while he attempted to show the War Department the legitimacy and the utility of the Allied program. In handling that doubly delicate assignment, the Secretary followed three broad policies. First, he encouraged the British and French to make purchases as large as possible, for he believed they were not arming fast enough and he knew that deliveries on their orders would often be delayed. Second, he tried to direct their buying in a way that would enhance American productivity, an objective they were glad to cultivate. Last, he sought to protect both the Allies and the American armed services from profiteering.

The most important and controversial of Allied orders were those for airplane frames and engines. The American Air Corps officers, short of planes and worried by the slowness of American manufacture, were reluctant to release the latest types of aircraft to any nation. They were stubbornly slow in recognizing that Allied orders would enlarge American capacity and that Allied use of new American types would test those planes under battle conditions. This opposition rarely flagged.

During the half year in which the French and British developed detailed plans for major orders, their purchasing officers made a series of small requests for aircraft. In January 1940 they were especially eager to obtain modern pursuit planes. The Allies, Morgenthau believed, "should place orders so that they take every other one of the Army and Navy planes now in production that they can use. I am afraid they are getting planes now which will be one cycle behind their enemy's." On January 8 he recommended to Roosevelt allotting to the French 25 of the first 81 P-40's for which the Army had contracted. The President agreed. "I did a magician's trick for you," Morgenthau told Pleven, "pulled 25 planes out of the hat!" Better still, Roosevelt had said that "he would like to see our industry on such a basis that on short notice we could produce 30,000 planes a year. I said that if he had that in mind, we certainly ought to avail ourselves of the opportunity of building up our industry through the purchases of the Allies. He agreed it was most important."

Specifications for the major Allied airplane order began to reach Washington in March 1940. The British and French wanted to buy at least 5000 air frames and 10,000 engines, preferably twice the number of each. If the aircraft were to be satisfactory for use in 1941, the Allies had to have access to various types of superchargers which the United States armed forces had developed but not yet released, and access also to certain engines and designs still classified as secret. Typically, Woodring, Johnson, and particularly General "Hap" Arnold refused the necessary permissions. Morgenthau had therefore once again to take the Allies' case to the President.

"Oh boy," Morgenthau reported to his staff after a White House conference of March 12, 1940, "did General Arnold get it!" Roosevelt had said there was to be no more resistance from the War Department, no more leaks from Johnson and Arnold to the Republican and isolationist press. Uncooperative officers would find themselves assigned to duty in Guam. In every respect the meeting had gone exactly as Morgenthau hoped it would:

> I told the President . . . that if he wanted me to do this job, that my effectiveness was just being ruined by Johnson and Arnold and I can't function that way. . . . I told him . . . that both from a strategic standpoint and business recovery, this was the most important thing in Washington. And if he wanted me to do this thing, he would just have to do something.

Well, he was tremendously impressed with these airplane production figures and employment figures and he immediately tried
to get hold of Steve Early and Pa Watson. . . . He said . . . if
we had had a war . . . we would have had all this machinery set
up, but lacking a war I had to coordinate . . . this thing. . . .
Early reminded the President that he was in the War Department
at the time Arnold was there and Arnold was running a mimeo-
graph machine on government time and government stationery
sending out propaganda against the coordinated air force, and was
working against, at that time, Secretary Weeks. And the President said, "Well, if Arnold won't conform, maybe we will have to
move him out of town." . . .

And the upshot of the meeting was Early and Pa Watson have
sent for Louie Johnson. . . . The President, in very forceful language, said that Johnson has to announce that he likes this Board;
he likes to have Secretary Morgenthau in charge of it; he likes to
have Captain Collins in charge of it, and that it is functioning well
and that he and Arnold are going to conform. Furthermore, Early
is going to tell him that from now on, no publicity from the War
Department except from the central bureau, and Arnold has to
keep his mouth shut. He can't see the press anymore. And they
are going to announce that there were 25 P-40s released over there
and Early is going to announce the airplane production figures. . . .

I was amazed! . . . I went at 1:30 and left there at ten minutes
of four, and . . . the President talked nothing but this and he
said . . . to Early and Watson, "These foreign orders mean prosperity in this country and we can't elect a Democratic Party unless
we get prosperity and these foreign orders are of the greatest importance. . . . Let's be perfectly frank." And he's right! . . .

Watson says, you can't at this time let either Woodring or Johnson go, politically. . . . Well, the President was swell. It was . . .
just the question of either backing me up or not and it shows when
the President wants to he can take two hours to get a thing
straightened out.

Roosevelt instructed Woodring either to go along with the
program or resign. Woodring yielded, and, on April 10, 1940, at
the Treasury, Purvis and his associates signed a stack of contracts
for 2440 fighters and 2160 bombers. The new and pending contracts brought total Allied commitments in the United States to a
round billion dollars.

The American models and designs had been released only on the condition that the Allies would pay a part of the cost of research and development, but Purvis and Pleven felt strongly "that the amounts of money being charged them" were entirely too high. With their American purchases rising and their dollar assets diminishing accordingly, they tried desperately to have their previous expenditures for the development of American models and the expansion of American industry offset the charges against them for the new orders. As Pleven complained to Morgenthau on April 12, 1940, the Allies were being asked to pay a share of costs even where a model had already been fully developed. Every time the French spent a million dollars for something "which is not actually our expense," Pleven said, "it reduced by twenty-five the number of pursuit planes" they could buy, which had an adverse "morale effect."

Recent history, Morgenthau replied, compelled the United States to make the charges to which the Frenchmen objected. "As you know," the Secretary said,

> the fight we went through on our neutrality legislation and lifting the embargo was a very, very difficult fight and there are a great many people in this country who think we shouldn't . . . sell you armaments. . . . There are other people who think that if you are going to spend your own money here, you are entitled to get the best instruments of war that money will buy. Between those two poles there is a big ocean. Now — there are people in our Army who are not pro-Ally. . . .
>
> So a plan had to be worked out which would be acceptable to the Army and which they could . . . sell to . . . our Congress. . . .
>
> The Army . . . have told the people on the Hill . . . that . . . the Army has had difficulty in getting these companies to develop more advanced models where they have to do it out of their own pocket.
>
> Therefore, the Army has worked out a formula. . . . And I want to say, after listening to the thing and knowing that the President, myself, Mr. Woodring, Mr. Johnson, and Mr. Edison have to defend this before Congress, that the Congress of the United States at the moment is satisfied, I don't see any other way of giving this to you people. . . .

This is the Administration policy and I have gone into it very, very carefully. . . . We have an election coming along. We have to be on firm ground and on this program the Administration could from the house tops shout it and explain it and we have nothing to apologize for. We don't have to do anything secret on this. It is something that I am perfectly willing to go anywhere and defend because I feel on this we are not being injured as far as our national defense is concerned through your program being superimposed on our industry. . . . You will simply have to take my word for it. . . . It's the only way I see that we can go along with you.

"That is good enough," Purvis immediately replied. ". . . We are very glad to have it all in the open so we could understand." As his visitors left, Morgenthau told Collins he thought Purvis understood but "Pleven was going to cry." "He was crying," Collins said.

With the settlement of the question of development funds, negotiations over the Allied airplane program were complete. "I've turned myself inside out on these purchases, and so has the President," Morgenthau reflected. But it had been worthwhile. General George Marshall told the Secretary in May that the Anglo-French orders had given the country four times the airplane manufacturing capacity it would otherwise have had. Taken together, Allied and American orders in the year ending May 14, 1940, had accomplished "an enormous expansion" of the airplane industry. The number of employees had multiplied by two and a half. Plant facilities had grown, and subcontracting with them. An average rate of production of about $12 million a month in 1938 had risen to $50 million a month, and prospective foreign orders would push that figure much further in the ensuing years.

"Harry Hopkins," Roosevelt told Morgenthau on April 29, ". . . paid you a great compliment in that he said anything you give Henry to do he does it and if something goes wrong and he's attacked on the floor of the Senate or House he takes it right on the chin." In his Diary, the Secretary then noted: "It has taken the President one year to admit that he was wrong and that he did not treat me nicely . . . when I took it on the chin and not only without any help from the President but, I suspect, some encouragement from him to the War Department to give it to me on the chin. But instead of his saying it to me directly, he puts it into the mouth of Harry Hopkins. As a matter of fact, this is the first time he has ever told me he was pleased with what I was doing."

But in other matters the Secretary's involvement yielded less happy results.

3. What Aid for Finland?

Imbued with the spirit of independence, the Finns during the late fall and winter of 1939–1940 resisted Russian invaders with a bravery that heartened all free men. Beyond any previous victim of aggression, Finland merited the financial support she needed to buy essential munitions in the United States. Minister Hjalmar J. Procopé asked for a minimum loan of $50 million, a request Roosevelt referred to Morgenthau. The Treasury, the Secretary promised, would examine Procopé's "list of merchandise" to see "whether we can work out some method to help you. . . . I admire the courage of your people."

As a first, small gesture, Morgenthau persuaded Roosevelt on December 4, 1939, to order Finland's current payment against her debt from World War I set aside until Congress had a chance to pass legislation turning the money over to the Finnish Red Cross. Though only about $180,000 was involved, Morgenthau looked "awfully pleased walking back from the White House." He also spurred Jesse Jones to arrange a credit of $10 million, all the Export-Import Bank had uncommitted. Yet as Procopé said on December 15, the ten million "does not help us very much. . . . We need much more money. . . . We need . . . guns and airplanes and shells." He wanted Morgenthau, when Congress reconvened, to plead for an adequate sum, but the Secre-

tary told him that "there is only one man who can settle that and
that is the President." Roosevelt, Procopé replied, had been
"wonderful and he really understands better than any head of
state in the world."

Roosevelt had publicly condemned Russia's "resort to military
force," calling it the "dreadful rape of Finland." As an earnest
of his indignation he had declared a moral embargo against the
Soviet Union. But anxious to avoid new difficulties on the Hill,
he withheld Administration endorsement from the various bills
for aid to Finland introduced in January. The President was influenced by the counsel of Hull, who argued that support for a
loan to Finland would convince isolationists in the Congress that
the Administration intended to take a similar position in behalf of
France and England.

Hull's continuing trepidations led Roosevelt to send a message
to Congress so weak that even the State Department was surprised. While acknowledging the sentiment for assistance to Finland, Roosevelt also referred to the "undoubted opposition to the
creation of precedents which might lead to large credits to nations in Europe, either belligerents or neutrals." The facts about
Finland, he said, were just as fully "in the possession of every
member of Congress as they are in the Executive Branch . . .
and the matter of credits . . . is wholly within the jurisdiction
of the Congress." The President suggested helping Finland to
finance the purchase of American agricultural surpluses and
manufactured products, but he stopped short of recommending a
loan for buying arms. He simply left the Congress, obviously
indisposed to act, with full responsibility for the Finnish problem.

Opposition to a loan even for nonmilitary expenditures prevented the Senate until mid-February from adopting a bill
which, without mentioning Finland, increased the capital of the
Export-Import Bank. The bill also provided that the bank
should not make loans for arms, munitions or implements of war,
or for more than $30 million to any one country. This bland
measure languished in the House until the end of February,
when a Soviet victory was already in sight.

"The Finns certainly seemed to be up against an impossible situation," Morgenthau wrote his father while Congress debated. "Once the Russians break through . . . we will curse ourselves for not having given the Finns some real help. The cost of one new battleship given *now* to the Finns would be the best investment we could make." Communist lies and distortions, the Secretary believed, had fed the isolationist mood in the country and on the Hill. "It is amazing," he said, "the propaganda which is going around." To combat it, Morgenthau ordered a memorandum prepared for Mrs. Roosevelt. "All of these young youth people are doing everything they can to stop giving aid to Finland," he said, "and I would like to give her factual information to prove that Finland is a democracy." He would not "do business," he remarked on another occasion, with any group that was "Soviet minded."

He had also found it impossible to do business for the Finns. They had tried to use their meager resources to purchase some modern aircraft, but Morgenthau had had to agree with the Air Corps that no planes were available and none could be diverted from forthcoming deliveries without crippling the English and French who were still capable of carrying on the war against totalitarianism. In March 1940 Finland had to surrender.

The defeat reminded men with views like Morgenthau's, though they did not need reminding, of the ironies and unrealities of the position of the United States in world affairs. To be sure, in the six months of the "phony war" the Neutrality Act had been amended, the Anglo-French Purchasing Mission had set to work, the friends of democracy had received some mild balms and the enemies of freedom some superficial stings from American policy. But no democratic nation could, on the evidence, expect to get from the United States — the richest country in the world — any help beyond what it could barter for or buy. Those with the dollars could not, on the evidence, be sure that the United States — the most industrialized of nations — was capable of producing enough of the sinews of modern warfare even for its own defense. The American people — by their own lights the most democratic in the world — had yet to recognize, much less to assume, the responsibilities inherent in the implications of their splendid creed. A reminder, little heeded, of the deficiencies of American attitudes and policies, Finland's surrender was also, though none yet knew it, the first portent of a terrible but instructive spring.

XII

DISASTER IN EUROPE

APRIL – JUNE 1940

Expecting a long war, lulled by the first slow months of hostilities, underestimating then the scope of Hitler's madness, the free men of Europe in the spring of 1940 learned suddenly and too late of their nakedness before the Nazi fury. On April 9 the Germans struck, overran Denmark, smashed the Norwegians and the British defending Norway, opened the awful blitzkrieg — the screaming, unhampered, diving bombers, the thundering tanks, the high-haughty-stepping troops — that within three-quarters of a hundred days would thrust the borders of oppression across almost all that remained of democracy on the continent. The edges of the racing night of fear, blacking Europe out, cast ghostly shadows westward across the ocean and beyond, and in the dust of encroaching disaster America at last awakened to its vulnerability.

1. Protection for Foreign Funds

Sleepless in the early hours of April 9, 1940, Morgenthau heard on his bedside radio the first war bulletins. At dawn he summoned his staff to a nine o'clock meeting at the Treasury. Before leaving the house, he telephoned the New York Federal Reserve Bank and asked Vice-President Allan Sproul to request the large commercial banks in the city to agree temporarily to hold all Danish and Norwegian assets. Then, on the telephone to Hyde Park, where Roosevelt was just arising, hastening to Washington, the Secretary got the President's approval for the steps he had just taken.

Morgenthau's immediate concern was to keep American funds and securities owned by Danes and Norwegians out of the reach of the conquering Germans. The cooperation of the directors of the New York Federal Reserve Bank gave the Secretary a start toward his objective, but the bankers were uneasy. They feared that if they held the Scandinavian funds indefinitely without legal warrant they would become liable for damage suits. The President, at the Treasury's recommendation, agreed to issue an Executive Order freezing the funds, provided the State Department approved, but Hull, though desiring to protect the funds, worried about acting without prior congressional approval. While he hesitated, Morgenthau fretted.

The freezing of Danish and Norwegian assets, in all some $267 million, would cover the small fraction untouched by the informal moratorium of the New York bankers. More important, it would prevent the Nazis from transferring those assets to Germany. It would also, as Morgenthau later emphasized to the newspapers, furnish some security against American loans to the two invaded countries. Most important, a freezing order would warn Germany that if she invaded other, richer nations, she would not be able to appropriate the larger bank deposits and security holdings of their citizens in the United States. Finally, Morgenthau believed, it would notify the Germans that Roosevelt "doesn't like what they are doing." For all those reasons, the Danish minister in Washington was "very much pleased" by the Secretary's initial action, and the President was "very insistent that all balances be frozen."

"I've just talked to the President," Morgenthau told Hull on April 10, "and if we're going to carry out the President's wishes . . . we should get out an executive order . . . which gives us complete control rather than on a volunteer basis." Later that day Roosevelt prohibited, except by license of the Treasury, all exchange transactions in which the Danish and the Norwegian governments or their nationals had any interest. The Department, Morgenthau told the press, would permit no withdrawals except upon proof that Germany would not be the beneficiary. "The purpose of this," he said privately at his morning staff meeting of April 11, "was that after all, we have become the safe deposit vault of the whole world for safe keeping of this money . . . and we want to make a hundred per cent sure that . . . we continue to keep it for the original owners." As Assistant Secretary of State Adolf Berle put it to Morgenthau later that day: "You and the Danish minister and the President and I are building a Denmark in our heads for the time being. . . . Obviously there isn't any Danish government. There's a German government there. . . . And we're just arranging there's going to be a Denmark existing somewhere . . . and just keep on going until the Germans get out of there."

On April 19 Morgenthau recommended that Roosevelt issue a supplemental order covering securities. "We went ahead and got out the second order," he told the press on April 29, "and, having gotten that out . . . not to be dragged through the courts and give the lawyers a chance to get some fat fees . . . we . . . let the Congress tell us whether they approved it or not. . . . It is a terrific responsibility taking over these monies, and we have tried to handle it very fairly. There hasn't been a single complaint from any bank or importer or exporter that I know of."

The need for controls broadened in May, when the Germans, their victory in Norway complete, turned on the Netherlands, Belgium, and France. In the first hours of May 10 the President was constantly in touch with his again sleepless Secretary of the Treasury. At 12:15 A.M. Roosevelt called Morgenthau at home. "Be ready to shoot in exchange control on Holland, Belgium, Luxembourg first thing in the morning . . ." Morgenthau scribbled on his bedside pad. "He cannot get anyone in Europe on telephone. Thinks there is a big raid on in England. Afraid they will attack Sweden." Ten minutes later Morgenthau had talked with Cordell Hull: "I said I thought I ought not to get out executive orders as President suggested until I knew more. I could freeze all exchanges in the morning on volunteer basis first. Cordell agreed . . . I ought to check first thing in the morning." But the matter could not wait: "President called at 2 A.M. Definitely get out executive order as of 8:30 Eastern Standard Time for Holland, Belgium, and . . . Luxembourg. I should come to the White House at 10:30." Advancing the schedule, Roosevelt signed the order at 7:55, and five minutes later Morgenthau sent telegraphic instructions to the presidents of all Federal Reserve Banks.

The Treasury established effective control over the funds of the countries that had fallen to Hitler. Yet, as Morgenthau told the press, German funds themselves were not controlled. If a Danish, Norwegian, Dutch, or Belgian national owned shares in an American corporation that declared a dividend, the Treasury would not permit remittance to the individual. Instead, the money would be held for him in the offices of the corporation. But a German national would get his dividend. "I know it doesn't make sense," the Secretary said. The Treasury was doing its best, but the United States was still at peace with Germany, and the Treasury could do no more without coming closer to a state of war. Though he did not say so, Morgenthau was himself eager to control all foreign funds, including Germany's, but Hull for months to come held Roosevelt back.

Even so, the orders already issued revealed the intention of the Administration to minimize, however slightly, Nazi gains from conquest. They revealed also the Administration's belief that someday the frozen assets could be returned to their rightful owners, that someday the Germans would be driven out. They represented, too, one part of Washington's hectic response to the alarming events abroad.

2. Protective Mobilization

The German invasion of Scandinavia brought the President to support the Army's program for expansion which he had sidetracked the previous September. When the war in Europe began, Chief of Staff George Marshall asked for authorization to bring the regular army up to strength, but Roosevelt by Executive Order permitted only a partial increment. Further, the President pared the Army's requests for appropriations to train and equip its recruits. While Army planners set their needs at close to one billion dollars, Roosevelt asked Congress for only $853 million. Though Marshall told the Congress that that figure was "modest" (a soft synonym for inadequate), the House cut it almost 10 per cent. This parsimony, along with Roosevelt's restraint, prevented the buildup of a balanced force, an Army in which all units — not just the Air Corps — were growing.

Marshall, the foremost advocate of a balanced force, warned the Secretary of War when the Nazis moved in April that "the increasing gravity of the international situation makes it appear necessary for me to urge a further increase in our state of military preparation." Air force and ground force alike needed development. The Nazi victories in May convinced Congress, as argument had not, that defense took precedence over economy, and Roosevelt, at once cultivating and responding to the new mood on the Hill, called for estimates to provide the necessaries for the Protective Mobilization Plan. So did the Congress, now in a hurry. But the need for haste, the pace of German gains, and the conflict between the air and ground forces, imposed an unavoidable confusion on Army estimates.

Disturbed because the War Department was "feeding to the President little pieces here and little pieces there," none of them encouraging, Morgenthau invited General Marshall to give him an integrated and complete plan for expansion. Marshall had al-

ready impressed those who knew him with his judgment, his gen-
tlemanliness, and his composure, qualities which were to make
him the most distinguished American soldier of his time. Morgenthau had had few dealings with him, but at their long meeting
of May 11, 1940, the Secretary's forty-ninth birthday, he realized at once that he was working at last with a wise and temperate spokesman for the Army. His respect for Marshall and his
confidence in him were complete then and thereafter.

"Just remember," the Secretary began, "it is all new to me."

"We should be allowed immediately to increase the strength of
the regular Army," the General replied. ". . . I want to get
. . . started just as fast as we can." The Army needed funds
for mechanization, for paying the troops, for their travel, subsistence, shelter, clothing, medical facilities, and signal equipment.
It needed modern machinery, indeed even shovels, to build barracks. It needed rifles, field guns, anti-aircraft guns, ammunition,
training planes, fighting planes and bombers. These initial, indispensable supplies would cost some $640 million.

"I don't scare easily. I am not scared yet," the Secretary said.
Marshall nodded: "It makes me dizzy." "It makes me dizzy,"
Morgenthau said, "if we don't get it."

It would be essential, the General went on, to avoid confusion
on the Hill by differentiating carefully between total mobilization, still in the remote and uncertain future, and immediate expansion. Morgenthau urged Marshall to make that clear to the
President. Even for the smaller goal, certainly for the larger, expenditures for new capacity to produce critical items would become tremendous. "Please emphasize that," Morgenthau advised, for if Roosevelt understood the financial requirements of
the Protective Mobilization Plan, it would make him more amenable to the costs of the lesser program. "Another recommendation I am going to make to the President," Morgenthau said,
". . . I think there should be only one person go on the Hill and
that is General Marshall. . . . In view of what has happened, I
don't think you are going to have any trouble. . . ."

If Marshall alone testified, Morgenthau thought, the Senate
would see the virtue of a balanced military buildup. "We can't

have the Air Corps," the Secretary said, "asking for 400 heavy bombers, as though that were going to solve the whole picture." That was exactly Marshall's opinion.

After Marshall left, Morgenthau called the White House. "We've been getting along great guns," he told Pa Watson, Roosevelt's military aide and poker companion. ". . . He's been asked to come up on the Hill and give some confidential figures. . . . It seems to me that before he goes up it would be a great advantage for him if we could see the President." Watson, an admirer of Marshall, agreed.

Two days later, on May 13, Roosevelt met with Morgenthau, Marshall, Woodring, Johnson, and Budget Director Harold Smith. "When we got in to see the President," Morgenthau later recorded in his Diary, "Johnson had not seen Marshall's memorandum and I don't think Woodring had . . . as there was constant disagreement and bickering before the President.

"At first, the President was entirely opposed to Marshall's program and when I put up a strong argument for it, he said, with a sort of smile and sneer, 'I am not asking you. I am telling you.' And my reply was, 'Well, I still think you are wrong.' He said, 'Well, you filed your protest.'

"The trouble was this memorandum of Marshall's took him entirely unawares and it was quite evident that he was really not familiar with the problem, but as time wore on he did really accept everything in Marshall's program with the exception that he said he was willing to ask for the money for the plants, to get them started, but not for the money with which to manufacture the article in the plant. He said that could be done next January or March. . . . He said we should get together and come back tomorrow.

"When I left the room, first Woodring and then Johnson said would I please call them together. So did Harold Smith. Johnson then saddled up to me and said, 'You had better do this, because after all you are really the assistant President,' and I vehemently told him if he wanted to ruin my usefulness all he had to do was to say it out loud. He said, 'Oh, I won't say it to anybody, but that's what you are.' "

Actually the reins remained in Roosevelt's hands. Before the meeting had ended, Morgenthau suggested that only Marshall appear before Congress. "Quick as a flash the President said, 'Why do you want to go up on the Hill? . . . Tell them to wait. I am going to have a message. Don't go up and tell them anything.'"

Above all, Morgenthau was "tremendously impressed with General Marshall. He stood right up to the President . . . and Woodring sat there in a corner and never opened his mouth. And in the outer room, Johnson and Woodring sat there and never talked to each other."

Over aviation Johnson and Marshall clashed again that afternoon. The General had a revised schedule of materials "which could neither be overlooked nor reduced if a national defense program were inaugurated. To disregard this list would be to walk right into the middle of a national scandal." Both air and ground forces, he argued, should, like the Navy, be at least 75 per cent mobilized at all times, and for that purpose the ground forces needed a larger share of the defense budget than Johnson allowed. Further, even though the Allies were receiving four-fifths of the planes being produced, the Air Corps "did not have sufficient pilots trained to handle" existing plane capacity, much less the increased capacity for which Johnson was pressing. Supporting that analysis, Morgenthau suggested that Marshall "write the ticket for the Air Corps."

Those estimates, Marshall's list of requirements for the ground forces, and Morgenthau's various suggestions provided much of the raw material for Roosevelt, whose message to Congress nevertheless emphasized his own goals. He called for an immediate appropriation of $896 million and for authorizations for $286 million more.

"For the permanent record," Roosevelt also said, "I ask the Congress not to take any action which would in any way hamper or delay the delivery of American-made planes to foreign nations which have ordered them, or seek to purchase more planes. That, from the point of view of our national defense, would be extremely shortsighted." The immediate problem was to expand production: "I should like to see this nation geared up to the ability to turn out at least 50,000 planes a year."

Roosevelt had supported the modernization of a balanced army and, as Morgenthau had expected, uninterrupted cooperation with the democracies. No longer niggardly, Congress appropriated the needed billions for American defense. Mobilization was under way.

3. Darkness in Europe

As the Nazi storm swept across Holland and Belgium and sent French and British troops reeling in defeat, the Allies pleaded for the opportunity to spend their dollars, previously held in reserve, for American weapons, old or new. French Premier Paul Reynaud begged for planes and destroyers. From London came an impassioned call for arms. The Chamberlain government had resigned, leaving to Winston Churchill a perilous command. On May 15, 1940, Churchill told Ambassador Kennedy that he expected Germany to attack the British Isles within a month. Like Reynaud, the Prime Minister asked for all the planes and destroyers the United States could spare. So long as he held office, he promised, England would never surrender, even if she had to carry on the fight from Canada. Kennedy was stirred, but he feared the United States, if it met Churchill's request, would hold the bag for a lost war. "It seems to me," he cabled Roosevelt, "that if we had to fight to protect our lives, we would do better fighting in our own backyard." That was the counsel of miscalculating prudence.

Fortunately, Churchill also appealed directly to the President. In a message of May 15 he warned of the probability of Italian intervention and of a Nazi invasion of the United Kingdom. Prepared to resist alone if necessary, he hoped for all possible American aid short of an alliance in the war. Besides ships and planes, the British needed anti-aircraft guns, rifles, ammunition, steel, and tools. On the day that Churchill cabled, Arthur Purvis told Morgenthau of the substance of his message. On May 17, two days later, Purvis delivered a further petition from Jean Monnet repeating Churchill's requests and adding iron, ferroalloys, aluminum, plywood, and precision instruments. The previous evening Roosevelt had reviewed an identical list with Morgenthau, whom he commissioned to see what he could get the Army to release. Churchill had enlisted two stalwart friends.

"If I was the President," Morgenthau told General Marshall on May 17, ". . . I would make you make the decision." It was bound to be difficult. Only the previous day Roosevelt had asked Congress to endorse his program for producing 50,000 planes a year. Secretary Woodring doubted that the Army could legally sell any military property. Most of his senior officers doubted they could spare any. At the Treasury Marshall asked General Arnold just how badly it would set back the pilot training program if he sold 100 airplanes to the Allies — only three days' supply at the rate they were being shot down. It would cost six months, Arnold judged. "We have got to consider the psychological effect on both sides of the water," Marshall then said. "Of course, on this side, that is a political consideration and not a military consideration. On the other side it is a military consideration. . . . It is a military consideration to us that the Allies succeed in stopping this flood. . . . This whole thing has a tragic similarity to the pressure for American men in 1917. . . . We have got to weigh the hazards in this hemisphere of one thing and another. I have taken the risk of not concentrating our talent in the immediately operating squadrons, except in the more desirable, the symmetrical development of the whole program. . . . If I do this, that accentuates the ineffectiveness of the Air Force. It is a drop in the bucket on the other side and it is a very vital necessity on this side and that is that. Tragic as it is, that is that."

"There will be no pressure from me," Morgenthau assured him, and Marshall, reflecting overnight, did not change his mind. "Considering the uncertainties of the situation in . . . the Western Hemisphere and . . . the defense of the Panama

Canal," he wrote the Secretary on May 18, "I regret to tell you that I do not think we can afford to submit ourselves to the delay and consequences involved in accommodating the British Government in this particular manner." England could have no extra pursuit planes; "the damage to training would be too great."

On May 22 Marshall reviewed with Morgenthau the whole range of the emergency British and French requests. "Our situation in bombers is very serious," the General said, ". . . because we have this antiquated force in Panama and Puerto Rico and Hawaii as well as . . . in the United States." As to other matériel, he continued: "We have ignored the legal requirements, both of the Neutrality Act and of the law which states exactly how we will declare things surplus and we have ignored the political implications of any action. We have addressed ourselves simply to the proposition, duly safeguarding our situation of national defense . . . of . . . what . . . might we spare if means were found of getting it over to the Allies. . . .

"The shortage is terrible and we have no ammunition for anti-aircraft and will not for six months. So if we gave them the guns they could not do anything with them. . . . Anti-tank guns, the situation is similar, a shortage. .50 caliber, our situation is the same.

"Now we come to some things we can do. Browning .30 light machine gun. I feel we can release 10,000 as they stand, unmodified, because we have a great many. Automatic rifle, unmodified, I feel we can release 25,000 without jeopardizing ourselves. Enfield rifles, I feel we can release 500,000. Those we can declare surplus and manage that under the law. . . . 75 mm. field guns, of the British design that fires either American or French ammunition, I feel we might release 500. . . . Mortars, we can release 500 of those and 50,000 rounds of ammunition." Over and beyond that list, there were other items which the Army had declared surplus, but which the State Department had decided could not be sold to belligerents. If the State Department could be brought to reverse its opinion, the Army, while short of explosives, could let the British and French buy some powder-making machinery.

During the last week of May British requests came in faster than Marshall could find surplus material for sale. On May 29 — the day the British began to evacuate their troops from Dunkirk on the coast of France, a day of surpassing gallantry in grave defeat — Purvis brought Morgenthau a proposal for assigning the Allies weapons of modern design on order for the American Army. The United States would ultimately benefit, Purvis argued, from the experience of manufacturers with what were still new designs. The British had yet to present all their requests, but Purvis knew that within the next few months they would want at least 1000 to 1500 medium-sized tanks, at least 1000 37 mm. anti-aircraft guns, probably 1000 anti-tank guns of the same caliber, between three and five hundred 90 mm. aircraft guns and 1000 3-inch anti-aircraft guns. For all these weapons they would also need ammunition, and they hoped, too, to get at least 1000 heavy tanks equipped with large cannon. Motor torpedo boats and nitrocellulose powder were top priority items right away.

Morgenthau could make no promises. The torpedo boats, for example, brand-new naval weapons, could not possibly be defined as surplus equipment; the "destroyer thing" was "out." Yet there was cause for hope. "There has been all the pressure possible," the Secretary said, "and all the sympathy but we have to find a way frankly to get around the law. . . . I am going to tell you a story about General Marshall. When he was in charge of American soldiers at Tientsin. To show you, he wanted to get instructors to teach his soldiers Chinese and he had no money . . . . The most valuable thing he had in the compound to sell was manure from the stables. So he advertised it for sale, but said you have to supply services, contractors, to get this manure and 'services' were teachers to teach soldiers Chinese, and on that basis he got the teachers."

"You are very reassuring," Purvis said.

Congress, Morgenthau continued, would not authorize the release of the kinds of new equipment England needed, but some progress had been made toward finding a way to transfer surplus gear to a belligerent. Though Woodring held that surplus equipment could be sold only to neutrals and then only by negotiation of the State Department, Sumner Welles had a rather different interpretation. To be sure, Welles acknowledged, a direct sale of arms and munitions to a belligerent would violate American neutrality under international law, and would also breach the Neutrality Act, but Welles, Marshall, and the attorneys in the Treasury and Justice Departments believed that the Army could sell surplus items to private manufacturers who could in turn sell them to the British or French without violating any law. As an added convenience, an act of July 11, 1919, made it possible for the government to sell surplus without public advertisement.

Purvis during the first week of June asked for everything on Marshall's list of surplus — "the whole damned lot." "The Attorney General and ourselves worked out an opinion which he signed," the Treasury's General Counsel reported to Morgenthau on June 4, "together with a memorandum explaining how the Secretary of War could operate under the opinion. . . . We went over this morning and talked to Marshall and Marshall had made up his mind when we got over there that he was going along and it was simply a question then of talking to the Secretary and . . . that problem was relatively easy."

The full British order evolved at conferences on June 5, 1940, the day after the completion of the evacuation of Dunkirk. "We had lost," Churchill later wrote, "the whole equipment of the Army to which all the first fruits of our factories had hitherto been given. . . . Never has a great nation been so naked before her foes." American surplus afforded at best a meager wardrobe, but Purvis eagerly contracted for an extensive inventory of guns and ammunition — all prices "as is" and "where is." "I am delighted to have that list of surplus matériel which is 'ready to roll,' " Roosevelt wrote Morgenthau on June 6. "Give it an extra push every morning and every night until it is on board ship!"

The American "miracle of deliverance," as Churchill called it, was to consume over a month, during which British ships carried their precious cargoes to England only, for in that time the dwindling French resistance on the fields of battle evaporated entirely. "You can't tell what this means abroad," Purvis said.

"It just means everything to them. Just means everything."

To a well-organized minority of Americans it seemed to mean too much. The isolationist America First Committee, its adherents and sympathizers, either denied that there was any German threat to the United States or argued that, if there was a danger, Great Britain played no significant role in meeting it. So it was that Colonel Charles A. Lindbergh, the most prestigious of the American Firsters (and one of very few Americans to accept a decoration from Hitler), publicly warned against supporting England on the grounds that national defense depended on keeping arms and munitions at home.

Lindbergh was a Cassandra, but for all his prophecies, American opinion was gathering swiftly in sympathy for the British and in perception of the significance as well as the courage of their cause. Both the President and Morgenthau were especially heartened by the attitude of Wendell Willkie, a candidate of growing appeal for the Republican presidential nomination. "An overwhelming number of people in this country," Willkie said, "believe that we should give all possible aid, short of war, to the Allies." William Allen White, the celebrated Republican editor of the Emporia, Kansas, *Gazette*, speaking for himself and for the Committee to Defend America by Aiding the Allies, telegraphed the President that "as an old friend, let me warn you that maybe you will not be able to lead the American people unless you catch up with them. They are going fast."

Yet neither White nor Willkie, nor the mass of Americans whose opinions they represented, fully realized how little there was to sell to the British. The War Department, even Morgenthau had to admit, was "scraping bottom," and though he and Marshall were doing all they could to advance the President's policy of maximum latitude in defining military surplus, though they had long been moving faster than public opinion, the Axis was proceeding at much greater speed.

On June 10 Italy declared war on Britain and France; the Reynaud cabinet, about to fall, fled Paris; France stood twelve days from formal surrender; and England, almost defenseless, lay exposed to Nazi invasion. That evening Roosevelt spoke to the graduating class at the University of Virginia at Charlottesville. "The Government of Italy," he said, ". . . has manifested disregard for the rights and securities of other nations. . . . The hand that held the dagger has struck it into the back of its neighbor." The United States could not safely become a "lone island in a world dominated by the philosophy of force. . . . Overwhelmingly we, as a nation . . . are convinced that military and naval victory for the gods of force and hate would endanger the institutions of democracy in the Western World, and that equally, therefore, the whole of our sympathies lies with those nations that are giving their life blood in combat against these forces."

Roosevelt came then to a declaration of American policy, a policy to which he had been moving gradually since the war began, a policy which Morgenthau and others had uninterruptedly urged upon him. "We will pursue two obvious and simultaneous courses," the President said. "We will extend to the opponents of force the material resources of this nation, and at the same time we will harness and speed up the use of these resources in order that we ourselves . . . may have equipment and training equal to the task of any emergency and every defense. All roads leading to the accomplishment of those objectives must be kept clear of obstructions. We will not slow down or detour. Signs and signals call for speed — full speed ahead."

Within that formidable commitment, dictated by the tragedies of a ghastly spring, Morgenthau remained responsible for organizing the transfer of American "material resources" to the United Kingdom, the sole active "opponent of force." He had already accomplished all his chief had asked and more than the laws of his nation had at first seemed to permit.

XIII

A BALANCE OF NEEDS
JUNE–NOVEMBER 1940

THE GERMAN CONQUEST of France forced the leaders of state in London and Washington to reassess their national situations under the pressure of extraordinary anxiety and confusion. As Churchill warned the British cabinet, "However indomitable the spirit of the country, the task of maintaining a resistance . . . will be well-nigh insupportable unless we are able to draw assistance on a large scale from the New World." Lord Lothian, the British ambassador in Washington, told the State Department that the "immediate sale" — the questions of costs and resources were now temporarily irrelevant — of all kinds of munitions was "of the utmost importance if the impending attack on Great Britain is to be beaten off before winter sets in." Roosevelt's address at Charlottesville, sustained as it was by the movement of public opinion, brought American policy into theoretical accord with those English objectives, but neither the President nor his advisers had yet decided how to surmount the political and logistical obstacles that stood between hope and fulfillment of the common transatlantic goals. The demands of national defense and the vagaries of American politics had yet to be adjusted to the necessities for British survival.

1. The Problem

Shaken by the fall of France, Congress provided unprecedented appropriations for rearmament and began to consider national conscription. But American military commanders, pending delivery of the weapons and supplies they could now order, strove to protect their inadequate stocks from diversion to Great Britain. The demands of hemispheric defense in themselves overtaxed the growing industrial capacity, which was patently insufficient to meet the needs of England as well as the United States. In practice, therefore, Roosevelt's Charlottesville commitment guaranteed the British only what they could convince the President they absolutely had to have. In his turn, Roosevelt had to persuade the American people and their representatives in Congress that his decisions were in the national interest. In this process neither he nor his advisers could ever forget the campaign of 1940. On no occasion did Roosevelt proceed without consulting those extraordinary sensitivities, at once daring and cautious, that had made him the champion campaigner of his generation.

Morgenthau, as ever, served both as conscience and agent for his chief. Characteristically, the Secretary deferred little to politics. He believed that strong policy would yield large votes, but he was alert to the limitations on policy that grew out of the mood of the Congress, and to the further limitations imposed by the sensibilities of the President. These led Morgenthau to temper his own readiness to sacrifice requirements of the Army and Navy in order to meet the minimum British requests. Churchill and his cabinet calculated their needs; Arthur Purvis managed the negotiations to satisfy them; Morgenthau in June and for weeks thereafter was their guide and influential advocate. His friendship with Purvis, the mutual trust and affection that enveloped their cooperation with warmth and grace, had become a major integral in the calculus of Anglo-American relations.

During the weeks that France was collapsing, as Purvis continually observed, England's strategic problems multiplied. Besides
the weapons to repel invasion, small arms and tanks, small craft
to harass landing barges, cannon, and the like, besides intercep-
tors and retaliatory bombers, she lacked destroyers, now more
important than ever, in the absence of the French fleet, both to
protect the home waters and to combat Nazi submarines in the
Atlantic and Mediterranean. Purvis on June 5 "asked the Secretary whether they could have any of our destroyers. The Secretary told him that he would ask for an appointment immediately
to see the President. . . . Upon his return . . . Morgenthau
sent for Mr. Purvis and said, 'I saw the President and spent
twenty minutes with him, although I had only asked for forty-
five seconds. He stopped everything. He said I could tell you
this, and you only, although I see no reason why you cannot
repeat this to Lord Lothian. There is a slight ray of hope. The
trouble is with Admiral Stark. On the Hill, he was asked the
question about selling destroyers. "Did they [the United States
Navy] need them all?" and he answered yes.

" 'The President ordered Stark over at 1:45 and he will try to
find out a way to work out getting ten for you. This is the first
time he has ever given me any . . . hope. If there is any way
possible he is going to do it. He is using the opinion of the Attorney General as a basis for it.' "

But that opinion permitted the sale only of surplus equipment,
and the Navy was unwilling to consider even old destroyers,
built for duty in World War I, as surplus. The Congress, too,
was not yet of a mind to condone the release of any ships. Those
obstacles encouraged the President to underestimate England's
shortage. Again with Purvis on June 11, 1940, Morgenthau said:
"Well, now, to call a spade a spade . . . the figures that we have
on the losses of . . . destroyers, do not seem to impress . . .
the President. . . . The thing he has [a report from Churchill]
doesn't show that the English . . . losses in destroyers have
been very great."

"I think that this is very much up to us," Purvis replied, "to
show our hand." On June 16, pending the receipt of more data

about the destroyers, the Englishman submitted a list of other most pressing needs, including pursuit planes, heavy bombers and dive bombers, mosquito boats and at least one hundred flying boats — "of extreme importance for anti-invasion purposes."

But Washington counted in ones and tens instead of hundreds. On June 17, Morgenthau saw Roosevelt: "Told him that Arthur Purvis was coming for supper and wanted to know whether I should continue to give the English the same assistance that I have given the English and French up to now. He said absolutely! I said, for example, that they need four-engine bombers. He said, 'Haven't we got eight or nine obsolete ones that we could spare?' I said, 'Well, I think we ought to be able to spare ten.' He said, 'That's fine. . . . You have been doing grand work and continue to give the English the same help.' "

Ten planes were only a gesture, as Morgenthau knew. More important were his successful efforts to help turn over to the British outstanding French contracts for procurement of munitions and planes. Still more significant were the destroyers for which Churchill pleaded in a message that Purvis delivered on June 18. Since the beginning of the war, France and England between them had lost 32 destroyers, Churchill said; 25 since February 1. Many more were inactivated because of damage. Of 133 destroyers in commission, only 68 were fit for service; in 1918 some 433 had been in use. And now, in 1940, at least 30 per cent of the destroyers capable of going to sea had to be kept near the British Isles to protect against invasion. Yet the German U-boat fleet, estimated conservatively at 55, was destroying vital British shipping. Worse still, the British could expect within the next four months to commission only 10 new ships, and they foresaw the necessity of increasing their forces in the Mediterranean to guard against German advances there. "We must ask, therefore," Churchill concluded, "as a matter of life or death, to be reinforced with these destroyers. We will carry on the struggle whatever the odds but it may well be beyond our resources unless we receive every reinforcement and particularly do we need this reinforcement on the sea."

"I just spoke to Grace Tully and told her I was sending over a most secret document in regard to the British destroyer situation," Morgenthau recorded in his Diary immediately after reading Churchill's message, "and I wish she would inform the President that it is my belief that unless we help out the British with some destroyers it is hopeless to expect them to keep going."

That night Roosevelt again said that he wanted "to give the English all the cooperation that we can," but "can" remained an uncertain word. Morgenthau implored Pa Watson to help him persuade the President to let the English have 12 B-17's, the new four-engine flying Fortresses. But just as Admiral Stark clung to the destroyers, so General Marshall, with much more reason, hesitated to release any Flying Forts. And Attorney General Robert Jackson ruled a proposed transfer of twenty motor torpedo boats "absolutely illegal."

The question, as Marshall said, was whether "we pour our slender means into a situation . . . over which we have no control and reduce ourselves to the point where we can't protect our own interests. . . . When it comes to the training of pilots, we are in a difficult situation. When it comes to ammunition, we are in extremely critical ammunition times." If England were invaded and her fleet came to American shores, the determination of policy would have to follow conferences with leaders of Congress as well as with the President, "yet Admiral Stark and myself were in agreement that it was unthinkable that we wouldn't do everything in our power to salvage the British fleet, but we would have to have a very definite basis on which to operate."

To establish that basis, Marshall and Stark and their associates soon undertook conversations with the senior officers of the British and Canadian services. At the same time the President at last appointed strong men as the heads of the Navy and the War Department. The coming to Washington of the new Secretary of the Navy, Frank Knox, and of the new Secretary of War, Henry L. Stimson, dramatically enhanced Morgenthau's opportunities for bringing Purvis's program to fruition.

2. Partial Solution

The changed mood of the War and Navy Departments reflected the character of their new heads. Yet eager though they
were to help the British, Knox and Stimson were troubled, as was
Morgenthau, by the impact of the new and very large appropriations for expanded purchasing for the American Army and
Navy. They did not want these additional orders to gum up
what had been ordered before. And they had to know exactly
what the British needed.

"If I were to cable to London today," Purvis told them on
July 23, 1940, "the feeling of discouragement that I had for a
moment last week, I think the effect would be very vital on the
course of the war, so if you will let me speak . . . I would appreciate it tremendously." One fact dominated: "That is, that
the extent of the orders, whether for air frames or engines,
placed in this country by England or France was not governed
by their needs as they saw them at that time at all. They were
governed by the productive output, capacity, of the industry, as
added to by the Allied money that was poured into the industry
and which has given that industry today a place which is valuable in the United States national defense. It would have been of
but little value but for that."

Purvis had never been able to buy nearly as many airplanes as
the British wanted, and "today we are unable to buy nearly as
many planes or engines as we want, as we need, in the face of the
fact the enemy has more." There were no surplus engines or
planes; there were only shortages. "I believe that a great deal of
misunderstanding . . . has come through a distinctive feeling
that there is some plus sign in the picture which came as a result
of the debacle in France. There is no plus sign; they are all
minus signs." In spite of the engines the British had been able to
acquire as a result of taking over French orders, they still had

many more planes than they had engines, and they were impatiently waiting for permission to order 12,000 more air frames with engines to match. "Airpower," Purvis concluded emphatically, "is vital."

After the Navy agreed to divert to the British at least 18,000 airplanes within the coming two years, Morgenthau wondered whether "the Army will come as clean." "The Army," Stimson replied, "is to be prepared or trying to be prepared to meet an emergency which might come very quickly. . . . Whereas Admiral Towers tells me that the Navy today is ready with its full quota of planes for action, General Arnold tells me that the Army is about 3000 planes short. . . . I have to consider an immediate emergency when these requirements for 1941 or 1942 seem like iridescent dreams."

Morgenthau calculated that the proper goal for American production had to be 3000 airplane engines a month for the British and 3000 more for our own Army and Navy. Government figures did not come close to that, and when he learned that there were still no plans for building capacity to the requisite magnitude, Roosevelt said: "My God! Haven't they done that yet?"

During a sleepless night Morgenthau decided to force the issue. The next morning, July 24, 1940, the Secretary gave Purvis bold advice. "The aircraft program of the United States can't be frozen," he said. "It can't have a ceiling. You've talked about how the British would like 3000 planes a month; say . . . you're ready to order them. . . . Don't worry about the authorization . . . you'll get it all right. . . . You've got to bluff . . . part or all of your British production facilities will be bombed — this country has got to take care of it. . . . I'll back you up."

The tactic worked. Later that morning, besieged by Morgenthau and Purvis, Roosevelt's production chief agreed to superimpose on production schedules an additional 3000 planes a month for British account, with the British undertaking some financing of plant expansion. The question of allocations of engines within existing productive capacity was left unsettled, but as Stimson wrote in his Diary, everybody on July 24, in contrast to the previous day, seemed cheerful and encouraged. That was certainly the temper of the President, who — as Morgenthau noted — "seems to want my advice and . . . follows the recommendations that I make," and also of the British ambassador. "Mr. Purvis came up to see me," Lord Lothian told Morgenthau on July 25, "and . . . he said the most marvelous performance he'd ever seen done by anybody was done by you yesterday. . . . It'll make a terrific difference to the whole future for the whole thing is lifted at last onto the right basis."

Yet no one could feel cheerful about England's immediate prospects.

In mid-August there was no assurance that the British could long hold out. While the battle for England continued in skies infested with German bombers, the threat of Nazi invasion also persisted, and Hitler's forces were poised for further conquests in the Mediterranean, further assaults against the Atlantic lines of supply. Immediately and at a minimum, the British had to have the destroyers for which they had been pleading since May.

3. The Destroyer Deal

On August 2, 1940, while Morgenthau was away on a few days' vacation, Dan Bell attended a Cabinet meeting in his place. "Mr. Knox," Bell reported upon returning to the Treasury,

> . . . gave an account of a conference he had last evening with the British Ambassador. He said that the British Ambassador called him while he was at dinner and told him he had a very important matter that he wished to discuss with him that evening. Mr. Knox stated that he went over to the Embassy and talked with the Ambassador for some time, and the Ambassador gave him quite a pitiful story. Mr. Knox seemed very much worried about the whole situation. The Ambassador made a great plea for fifty American destroyers and he wanted Knox to exhaust every means that he could think of before giving him a negative reply. He said the shipping situation in Great Britain is quite serious and unless they

get these fifty destroyers, he did not know what would happen to the British Isles. Mr. Knox said he then asked the Ambassador if his country had ever considered selling a part of the islands in this Hemisphere for these destroyers and other supplies. He thought that the British should understand that the United States would anyway have to defend these islands if we were called upon to defend this Hemisphere. The Ambassador said that he had not discussed this with his Government, but that he would be glad to take it up if Mr. Knox wanted him to. Mr. Knox asked the Ambassador if it would hurt the British Government if this desperate situation were made public in the United States in our discussion with the legislative branch regarding ways and means of transferring these destroyers to his Government. He said they would have to take that chance but the situation demanded action.

Mr. Hull was asked if acquiring any part of the British territory in this Hemisphere would violate the agreement just reached in Havana.* The President and Mr. Hull both thought that it might, and the President then suggested that probably we could lease a part of this territory along the same general lines as we are now leasing a naval base in Trinidad. There was then a general discussion of this whole question as to the ways and means which might be found to furnish the British the additional destroyers. Everyone thought it was quite important that if we did furnish the British these ships, that the British in turn would promise that no part of its fleet would under any condition fall into the hands of the German Government if the British lost the war, but that the British fleet would at least be sent to this Hemisphere. There was some question as to whether this should be part of a formal agreement or whether it might not be better to have it as an informal understanding.

Mr. Hull thought that about the only way to accomplish the transfer of the destroyers to the British Government would be to repeal that old law which prohibits such sale, and this repeal could not be accomplished without some very definite understanding between the President and Mr. Willkie. It was, therefore, suggested that the President have William Allen White, who not only has the confidence of the President, but also has the confidence of Mr. Willkie, come to Washington to thoroughly acquaint himself with this question by discussing it with the British Ambassador and Secretaries Hull and Knox. The latter two were instructed to pre-

---

* At the Pan American Conference, which supported the longstanding policy of the United States to object to transfers of territory in the Western Hemisphere.

pare a statement which Mr. White would take to the President at
Hyde Park . . . and after getting the President's approval, White
would discuss it with Mr. Willkie. If agreement is reached, an attempt will then be made to get legislation on the subject after
publication of the joint statement. Messrs. Wallace and Jackson
thought it poor politics to consult Willkie. Jim Farley thought it
an excellent thing to consult him, it was for the good of the country, and to him what was for the good of the country, was good
politics.

Morgenthau, again at his desk on August 7, received through
Arthur Purvis an imploring memorandum from Churchill: "The
need of American destroyers is more urgent than ever in view of
the losses and the need of coping with the invasion threat as
well as keeping the Atlantic approaches open and dealing with
Italy. There is nothing that America can do at this moment that
would be of greater help than to send fifty destroyers, except
sending one hundred. . . .

"I append a note prepared in the Admiralty and I propose also
to send a personal message to the President."

The Admiralty note indicated that Great Britain had started
the war with far too few destroyers, had since then lost the support of the French flotillas, and had now to fight alone against
the German and Italian fleets in order to guard the ocean lanes
from submarines, in order to blockade Europe, and in order to
protect the British Isles against counterblockade and invasion.
To those ends, the Admiralty needed between fifty and a hundred American destroyers — the more the better. They hoped
American crews might man those ships or at least get them to
England; but if necessary, the Admiralty was prepared to send
British crews to fetch them. "This number of American destroyers added quickly to our forces," the Admiralty said,
"might make a decisive difference to the future of the war."

Almost as badly they needed American flying boats, which
were, as it happened, ideally suited to England's situation. Here
again they hoped to get one hundred, if possible with American
crews. Finally, it would make a vital difference during the autumn if they could get large supplies of anti-aircraft guns and
ammunition.

Moved by England's plight, Roosevelt and his Cabinet learned on August 13 that Wendell Willkie was favorable to the possibility of transferring destroyers to England. On the next day Morgenthau stayed behind after luncheon at the White House to talk with the President, Stimson, Knox, and Sumner Welles. "As the meeting progressed," Morgenthau later noted in his Diary, "they drafted a cable on the destroyers which was to go directly to Churchill, and he, the President, would give a copy of it to Lothian. . . . The plan on the destroyers is that England is to give us land in Newfoundland, Bermuda, Trinidad, and some other places in exchange for the fifty destroyers. The President also mentioned giving them these twenty speedboats which we once had contracted and revoked, also five long distance four-engine bombers and five long distance Navy bombers. I mentioned letting the bombsight go with them, but they didn't seem to think well of that.

"The President asked whether he should conclude the deal with the English first and tell Congress afterward or tell Congress first. I said I thought he ought to tell Congress first, but the undercurrent of those present seemed to be he should do it first and tell Congress afterward.

"For the first time that I discussed the destroyers with the President, he seemed to have made up his mind. He read us a telegram from William Allen White . . . which was noncommittal, the implication being Willkie wouldn't give much trouble on this matter but would in no way guarantee that he wouldn't.

"Someone mentioned 250,000 Enfield rifles for the English, and Stimson spoke up and said he thought they ought to go to the Philippines."

On Friday, August 16, Morgenthau again "called on FDR at White House by appointment. Found R. Jackson and H. Hopkins already there. President had just started reading cable from Churchill which he said was entirely satisfactory. Discussion was then on how Roosevelt should handle it. Everyone agreed it should be done that day. It was finally Roosevelt's idea to do it at his press conference and only handle what we were to receive (namely airbases, etc.). He also got the idea on the spot that he would see Mackenzie King. Jackson and I persuaded him not to include the twenty speedboats . . . at this time as Congress had turned it down once.

"I found the President much more decisive again but not unpleasantly so. Hopkins contributed next to nothing but seemed very excited and eager to get idea over and Jackson not sure of himself."

After that meeting, Morgenthau was not again involved intimately in discussions about the destroyers. They lasted another fortnight. Roosevelt at his press conference of August 16 announced that negotiations were under way for the acquisition of bases in British territories, but under questioning he denied that those negotiations were connected with the issue of transferring destroyers to England. That statement may have seemed unavoidable to the President until Amdiral Stark privately certified that the exchange was essential to national defense. This he did by August 21, when Roosevelt called for a review of documents prepared by Sumner Welles turning over to Great Britain 50 destroyers, 5 Flying Fortresses, 250,000 Enfield rifles, and 5,000,000 rounds of ammunition. Stimson had then to beat off suggestions for sending the material to Canada instead of Great Britain. Attorney General Jackson had meanwhile advised the President that he could act without the prior consent of Congress. It remained to be settled exactly which bases the United States would lease and exactly what equipment England would receive. Further, Roosevelt insisted upon avoiding the appearance of an exchange, and at his instigation, Churchill on August 22 cabled that he had in view no contract or bargain or sale but rather two independent gestures of support between friendly nations, both in danger. With this message came a memorandum from Lothian to Morgenthau of British requirements. Besides the destroyers, the English still hoped to obtain torpedo boats, heavy bombers, flying boats, tanks, rifles, and ammunition, and enlarged commitments for deliveries from current production of pursuit planes. Morgenthau sent Lothian to the President, though he realized that Roosevelt was not carrying all the details of the problem in his mind, and he urged Stimson to try to keep the President alert and informed.

After further negotiations, Hull and Lothian on September 2,

1940, signed the final papers. Unfortunately, in the last days of discussions State Department officials lost sight of the full range of British needs, and the text of the completed agreements referred only to the destroyers. For the defense of England the airplanes and rifles were also vital, and Morgenthau, like Lothian, felt that the United States had at least implied the intention to deliver the other equipment. As Morgenthau put it to Hull, Roosevelt alone could judge the extent of the American commitment, and though he had rejected the request for torpedo boats, he had also said, "Get what you can, Henry."

It proved difficult to get much. On September 14, the Bureau of Aeronautics of the Navy Department reported that it had revised the schedule of deliveries of PBY-5 flying boats so that the British during 1941 would receive almost every other plane produced, but the Navy did not want immediately to release even five. On September 19 Morgenthau told Roosevelt "the English have got to have more planes. . . . I am working it out and I will go to it, but you are going to hear plenty about this."

The services were holding back largely because production was running behind schedule. In order to speed it up, the British and the Army agreed to concentrate on building only one type of pursuit plane, the P-40. They hoped thereby to increase production from 6 to 8 planes a day, from 132 to 176 a month. This development, along with a Gallup Poll prediction that Roosevelt would carry thirty-eight states in November, in Morgenthau's view accounted for the President's private assurance that the English could have what they needed, but that assurance guaranteed little without the approval of the committee on aircraft allocations.

To that committee on September 20 Morgenthau proposed an agreement in principle to assign the British half of the production of P-40's and flying boats. "All present," he noted, "were enthusiastic about the idea and said they would do what they could to push it along." Characteristically, however, the enthusiasm had in part evaporated five days later when General Marshall needed more basic equipment, including P-40's, for the Army's training program.

Morgenthau at this juncture admitted privately some loss of confidence in his ability to influence the President. He worried most of all about the tangle of communications that prevented him from getting all the data on the problem. "I just can't work that way," the Secretary told Purvis on September 26. "I don't care how many people get crossed up in England and I don't care how many people are all falling all over each other trying to do the same thing, that is their business. . . . But I can't give what I have given to this thing and not be informed and have you informed so that you can in turn inform me what is going on now. . . . There is some cable that went over the weekend on these rifles . . . that went from Churchill to the President. . . . There is something that went between them . . . Strong* is convinced that they can use some additional planes, but not anything like the quantity that I am talking about because they haven't got the pilots and won't have them. . . . If their training program is such that they are not going to have enough pilots next July . . . why have me upset everybody in Washington . . . because I am just going to be licked before I start."

Morgenthau told Purvis that he had had a bad time with Roosevelt the previous evening: "He threw figures at me as to what Churchill and Beaverbrook† had asked for and they just don't jive with what you told me at all. . . . I was up the stump last night for three hours. . . . The one person that they ought to take in their confidence is you and me, and I can't function like this. . . . Now, you had better get Churchill or Beaverbrook on the telephone. . . . You have never heard me talk like this before, but here we are in this whole thing, you know, and we have worked this thing up and everything, and then for them to treat you and me like this isn't right."

On September 27 Purvis reported that England and Canada were training pilots at a rate consonant with their requests for planes, and that those requests took fully into account current British production, which was being increased as rapidly as pos-

* Chief of Army Intelligence.
† Lord Beaverbrook, the powerful British newspaper publisher whom Churchill had made head of aircraft production.

sible. Morgenthau used that information later in the day to support the British case at the White House, where Stimson and Marshall raised disturbing objections. Speaking for the War Department, Marshall pointed out that the United States had only 49 large bombers fit for duty outside of those in garrisons at Panama and Hawaii. When he heard this, Roosevelt's head went back as if someone had hit him in the chest. "I think the President and Morgenthau," Stimson noted in his Diary, "at last got it into their heads in what a difficult position we were and I hope that will end the situation."

Yet there was no end to British needs. Knowing this, Stimson and Marshall themselves supported a compromise. By its terms, in return for 120 engines relinquished by the British to the United States to equip American B-17's, the Army released six B-24's to England and promised 20 more of those heavy bombers in the next six months. The British, moreover, received the rifles and bombsights they had asked for, and, pursuant to the Navy's earlier agreement, half of the flying boats coming off the production lines. "You haven't been turned down," Morgenthau told Purvis, who called the allocations "pretty good for one morning." Best of all, as Morgenthau saw it, "as a rule of thumb, from now on, the English will get half of everything."

London shared Purvis's satisfaction with the arrangements that completed the destroyer deal. Lord Beaverbrook cabled Morgenthau his gratitude "for your understanding of our problems." The "Beaver" had been able to pledge British pilots a flow of airplanes sufficient to carry them through battle to victory. "This pledge is only possible owing to help we derive from you. We cannot publicly acknowledge your assistance but we hope the day will come when you will visit us and receive from our lads the thanks we owe you."

The cable gratified Morgenthau as much as did Stimson's expression of confidence. At luncheon on October 1, 1940, when both men had begun to relax a little and to look ahead to pending problems of supply, Morgenthau said: "Now look. I have lots to do but the President has asked me to do this thing, and if you feel I can't be helpful I would be delighted to drop out of it."

"No, quite the contrary," Stimson said. "You have been very helpful."

"Stimson then said," Morgenthau noted in his Diary, "it wasn't me who bothered him so much but he felt the President went off half-cocked, and that he didn't give General Marshall and some of the other Generals a chance to be heard."

Like Roosevelt, Stimson valued Morgenthau's energy and ardor in England's behalf. The three men had together been the prime movers on the American side of the destroyer deal and its supplements. They had met or exceeded their own expectations of the political and military possibilities of sustaining England. Further, in November Roosevelt again carried the country. "This election," Morgenthau told his staff, "wasn't just electing Mr. Roosevelt. I think this election was to decide whether Democracy is to live. It has been decided . . . and I think the most important thing that I can do is to really see now that England gets some real aid. No more arguing about it. . . . Our only chance to keep out of the war is to let these fellows win. . . . It is a great day for Democracy."

But as November turned into December, it became more and more apparent that England also needed, and at once, American money. The exploration of that want and of the means to satisfy it, more even than the tasks already undertaken, was to test the skill in politics and the creative imagination in policy of the whole Administration, most of all, in some respects, of Morgenthau and the Treasury.

XIV

LEND-LEASE

DECEMBER 1940–OCTOBER 1941

Until the German offensive began in April, 1940, the British, in order to conserve their dollar resources, had held down their American orders and relied as much as possible on the production of the home economy and the Dominions. Thereafter, with German victories in Europe, with the increasing violence of the war on the sea and in the air, with the extension of the conflict to Greece (invaded by the Italians in October, 1940 and by the Germans the following spring) and to North Africa, British purchases in the United States approached astronomical proportions. At the same time, in spite of the construction of new plants, British production declined because of the Nazi bombings and the attendant blackouts and destruction. Future British requirements appeared almost limitless.

Toward the end of August 1940, the Chancellor of the Exchequer had warned Churchill that new expenditures in the United States during the coming ten months would run the British deficit up to £3 billion 200 million, a sum far beyond the holdings of the British Treasury. There were still ways of "scraping the pot" by requisitioning gold ornaments and works of art, pushing exports, and selling South American investments in the United States, though the last measure would bring only "rubbish" prices. All those tactics together could not raise more than a few million pounds. "The red light had gone up about finance," but even with their American orders riding through the autumn, the British chose not to signal across the ocean until after Roosevelt's re-election. Assured then of a sympathetic audience, they described their predicament, which the stunned Administration could fail to resolve only at the cost of inviting a total Nazi triumph.

1. Pounds, Shillings, and Pence

Returning to the United States from a quick journey home, Lord Lothian told the reporters on November 25, 1940, that Great Britain was "beginning to come to the end of her financial resources." The mode as well as the content of this "calculated indiscretion" astonished Roosevelt and his advisers.

Cordell Hull was skeptical. Morgenthau, like the President, feared that Lothian's remarks would antagonize Congress. Roosevelt told Lothian that the Administration considered a request for financial help premature; first the British must liquidate their estimated nine billion dollars of investments in the Western Hemisphere. American public opinion, Lothian reported to London, remained "saturated with illusions . . . that we have vast resources available that we have not yet disclosed . . . and that we ought to empty this vast hypothetical barrel before we ask for assistance."

Morgenthau was less deluded than the British surmised. The Treasury's own estimates of United Kingdom resources came to just over two billion dollars, which, as the Secretary realized, even if liquidated would still leave a staggering deficit. The issue, he knew, was not whether but how and when to provide some kind of help. On December 2, he discussed the whole question with the ambassador: "I told him that I was very sorry that he had made the remark which he did on landing about the British finances as that would date the matter in the minds of the public. I explained further what I meant by saying that if Senator Nye or any other senator called me on the Hill they would say, 'Well, on such and such a date Ambassador Lothian said the English were running short of money. By what authority did you let them place additional orders in this country?' This seemed to be a new idea to him. He said that he had made the remark on his own authority.

"I found Lothian very pessimistic. . . . He said that England had to import 43 million tons of goods a year and at the present rate they were importing only about 36 million tons."

Morgenthau had already started to investigate two specific British needs, one for merchant ships, the other for ordinance. The catastrophic pace of German sinkings of merchantmen had brought a flood of British orders for new ships in the United States. Congress had already appropriated some four billion dollars for the construction of more than a hundred warships, and the Maritime Commission was counting on building fifty merchant ships a year. This left no room in existing shipyards for the British orders. To Roosevelt and Morgenthau, Purvis early in November stressed the need for bottoms to carry the food which kept the United Kingdom alive. The United States, the President suggested, might "build the ships and then lease them to the British."

On November 28 Morgenthau raised that possibility directly with Admiral Emory S. Land, the head of the Maritime Commission. Land rejected the idea on the grounds that the United States would never support a large fleet of tramp steamers and would therefore be stuck after the war with nothing to do with ships it had built and leased. A month later the problem was partially solved when the British let contracts for new yards to construct sixty cargo vessels. There then began, as the result of British initiative and money, the enterprise identified with Henry J. Kaiser and his ultimate prodigies of production. But the idea of leasing ships to England, while temporarily abandoned, suggested a useful direction of thought.

On November 28, the day of Morgenthau's conference with

Land, Stimson sent the Treasury for approval a draft agreement allowing the British to order American types of ordnance. Stimson could not promise to relieve them of financing much of the plant expansion for their weapons, and Morgenthau doubted their ability to find the necessary dollars.

Over the weekend an answer emerged. On Monday, December 3, 1940, Roosevelt left aboard the USS *Tuscaloosa* on his first holiday since the campaign. That morning Stimson and Hull discussed England's problems, and after luncheon, they joined Knox, Jesse Jones, and Marshall at the Treasury. "Gentlemen," Morgenthau said as they gathered,

> the reason I asked for this meeting was the fact, frankly, I need a little company. Those of you in Cabinet know that on Friday Mr. Stimson announced that he had come to an understanding . . . as to the ordnance. In his memorandum . . . he pointed out that the other departments were affected as far as the financing was concerned.
>
> I asked the President for a chance to see him and he saw me . . . Sunday afternoon, and I needn't say that what I am saying now . . . is in the utmost confidence. I explained to him that . . . the English were wanting to buy . . . a little over two billion dollars worth of materials and . . . Ambassador Lothian had put us on notice that they didn't have enough money. I showed the President the memorandum . . . which explains our estimate of their assets. . . . His reaction to it was that he wanted us . . . to go ahead and build the additional facilities necessary to manufacture for the English what they needed. He wanted the Government to place the orders and then sell this material to them as it was manufactured. I asked him to write out something for me and I point out that it is written . . . "Secretary of War, Navy, Treasury. . . . Planes, munitions, use US R. F. C. funds for plant capital on US orders. . . ." I said, "Well, that isn't very definite," and his answer was, "All of you use your imaginations."
>
> Now, he has gone on his two-weeks trip. I have this request. I needn't explain to all of you what it would mean if we could tell the English they can't place any more orders. . . . But frankly I can't take this alone. I am willing to carry my share, whatever the responsibility is.

By June 1, 1941, Morgenthau continued, the British deficit would be at least $2 billion. Did the Secretary think, Jesse Jones asked, that the RFC could order the planes and guns and tanks and build the necessary plants? Morgenthau said yes. "Well," Jones replied, "I will have to get a little lower down in the chair." Knox, less hesitant, saw "no choice" but "to pay for the war from now on."

"This is the first time I have heard this," Stimson interjected, "and it strikes me as a very serious thing for the Executive to go on and permit without the consent of Congress. Now, in the first place, we mustn't deceive the British. I don't think you can split this in two. You can't let them commit for purchases . . . on the face of our building the facilities for them. We can't begin building the facilities unless you are going to let them — with an implied commitment on their part — unless you are going to let them put the orders in. Now, I think you have got to face the whole thing at once before you do that. . . . Can we do anything except on a basis with them? Certainly not, can we? I mean, it is going to war. Can we take measures that are going to put us in the position where eventually we will be committed to going to war just to save our investment or to save the purpose for which we made the investment, unless you have the consent of Congress?"

"You can't get an argument out of me," Morgenthau said, "about not going to Congress. . . . I mean, I can't argue against it."

"We have got to go to Congress," Jones agreed, "even though we were going to bundle it up and say, o.k. we will do it. We have got to go up there and get the borrowing authority."

Before taking the British case to the Hill, Morgenthau said, they would have to review the military situation. "It is a financial dilemma rather than a military," General Marshall replied. The English orders were "useful to us because they carry us beyond the two million man point in production of critical material. . . . They would carry us . . . to around three million men." Marshall was therefore eager to prepare for doubting congressmen a full study of the significance for the American Army of the British program.

It was the attitude of Congress that worried Morgenthau

when he met on December 6 with Sir Frederick Phillips, representing the British Treasury. Phillips had clear instructions from London. He was to request "a free gift of munitions and aircraft," if possible; otherwise, some kind of loan. But he was also to indicate that "repayment of a quasi-commercial loan can only, in our judgment, be effected after the war to the extent to which our exports to the USA exceed imports." Morgenthau believed the Congress would reject both alternatives unless it were fully persuaded the British had no other recourse. Further, the Secretary's sense of his own responsibility to the American people compelled him to take a hard line. "We haven't lost track of the magnificent fight that you are putting up," he told Phillips. ". . . We are conscious of it every day . . . but the fact that no move has been made that I know of, even to try to sell, some of the English companies in the United States . . . raises a doubt in some of the minds of the people here. . . . The President is perfectly conscious of this, and the path that you and I have to go down while you are here is extremely difficult and I want all the help that you can give me to remove these doubts. . . . It is a matter of convincing the general public of the determination, of just how far the English businessman is ready to go. It is a psychological matter as much as anything else."

Morgenthau wanted a complete list of all British holdings, securities, gold, and direct investments, differentiated according to estimates of their liquidity. Of necessity tough, he was also of equal necessity more alive to England's wants than ever before, for he had received from Lord Lothian a copy of the compelling letter Churchill sent Roosevelt on December 7, 1940. There the Prime Minister laid before the President Anglo-American prospects for 1941.

"Even if the United States was our ally," Churchill wrote after spelling out his strategic plans, "instead of our friend and indispensable partner we should not ask for a large American expeditionary army. Shipping, not men, is the limiting factor." Churchill needed help in maintaining the Atlantic route, and, even more, he needed the industrial energy of the United States. Yet the more rapid the flow of munitions, the sooner would

British dollars be exhausted. "They are already as you know," Churchill wrote, "very heavily drawn upon by payments we have made to date. . . . The moment approaches when we shall no longer be able to pay cash for shipping and other supplies. While we will do our utmost and shrink from no proper sacrifice to make payments across the exchange, I believe that you will agree that it would be wrong in principle and mutually disadvantageous in effect if, at the height of this struggle, Great Britain were to be divested of all saleable assets so that after victory was won with our blood, civilization saved and time gained for the United States to be fully armed against all eventualities, we should stand stripped to the bone. Such a course would not be in the moral or economic interests of either of our countries. . . .

"Moreover I do not believe the government and people of the United States would find it in accordance with the principles which guide them, to confine the help which they have so generously promised only to such munitions of war and commodities as could be immediately paid for. You may be assured that we shall prove ourselves ready to suffer and sacrifice to the utmost for the cause, and that we glory in being its champion. The rest we leave with confidence to you and your people."

Churchill had done exactly what Morgenthau had hoped he would do, and put himself in Roosevelt's hands. He had expressed with a force that none of his subordinates could match the determination of the English to carry the major burden of the common fight. In order to ensure the American contribution, Morgenthau had to hold the position he had taken with Phillips, to hold it, as things worked out, for years to come; but for the Secretary this was at worst a painful means to reach the goal he had most fervently at heart.

2. That "Foolish Dollar Sign"

The *Tuscaloosa* docked at Charleston on December 14, 1940, and Roosevelt returned refreshed, inspired, poised for one of the greatest efforts of all his years in office. "At lunch with the President," Morgenthau recorded in his Diary on December 17, "I found him in a very good humor, very quiet and self-possessed, and very proud of the fact that he didn't look at a single report that he had taken with him from Washington.

"The President said, after some story telling, that the first thing he wanted to ask me was whether the English had asked me for a loan. . . . I told him the whole story about Sir Frederick. . . .

"The President then said, 'I have been thinking very hard on this trip about what we should do for England, and it seems to me that the thing to do is to get away from the dollar sign. . . . I don't want to put the thing in terms of dollars or loans, and I think the thing to do is to say that we will manufacture what we need, and the first thing we will do is to increase our productivity, and then we will say to England, we will give you the guns and ships that you need, provided that when the war is over you will return to us in kind the guns and the ships that we have loaned to you, or you will return to us the ships repaired and pay us, always in kind, to make up the depreciation. . . . What do you think of it?' I said, 'I think it is the best idea yet. . . . If I followed my own heart, I would say, let's give it to them; but I think it would be much better for you to be in the position that you are insisting before Congress and the people of the United States to get ship for ship when the war is over, and have Congress say that you are tough, and say, well let's give it to them, than to have the reverse true and have Congress say you are too easy.' "

To the press that afternoon Roosevelt said there was no doubt

in the minds of "a very overwhelming number of Americans that
the best immediate defense of the United States is the success of
Great Britain in defending itself; and that, therefore, quite aside
from our historic and current interest in the survival of democracy in the world as a whole, it is equally important from a selfish
point of view of American defense, that we should do everything to help the British Empire to defend itself." The Axis was
waging war without money, he went on. The democracies had
to find non-traditional methods of their own. There was no
need to repeal the Neutrality Act or Johnson Act; nor was there
need for an outright gift to the British. Rather, the United States
could "lease or sell" to Great Britain that portion of its production of munitions that events demanded. He was trying, Roosevelt said, to get rid of the "silly, foolish, old dollar sign." His
analogy was to a man whose neighbor's house was on fire; in
such a case that man would not say: "Neighbor, my garden hose
cost me fifteen dollars; you have to pay me fifteen dollars for it."
No, he would connect the hose, help put out the fire and get the
hose back later. So it had to be with munitions. The President
could not yet explain the details, for the procedure was still
under study, but he would substitute for the dollar sign a "gentleman's obligation to repay in kind."

The President had scarcely finished talking when, with his
consent, Morgenthau told Sir Frederick Phillips that it was "all
right for him to place the order" — Roosevelt on December 19
defined that permission to cover "orders for anything they
wanted if they said they had the money to pay for it." That
cleared the way for England to satisfy some of her most vital
needs but left her with large problems of finance until Congress
reconvened and could act on Roosevelt's recommendation.

On December 30, Roosevelt assigned the Treasury the drafting of the Lend-Lease bill. "One of the most important things
that the President said," Morgenthau recorded in his Diary,
". . . was that . . . what he really wanted was authority from
Congress to go ahead and build the necessary arms for this country plus England, and that we should have a blank authority to
allocate as many of these combined orders as he might see neces-

sary at the particular time. In other words, he doesn't want ten million, let's say, for the United States, five million for England, and have the amount to England earmarked; and I got the impression that what he would like to have is to have Congress say, 'Go ahead and build fifteen million dollars worth of munitions,' and that he would say at the particular time what kind of munitions should go to a particular country.

"Of course, if he could get this authority it would be excellent, but I doubt very much if he will. But he is definitely counting on the Treasury to do the drafting . . . and he definitely wants it in a blank check form."

3. The Lend-Lease Bill

The preparation of the Lend-Lease bill involved Morgenthau in a familiar administrative pattern. Having received his orders from the President, the Secretary assigned to his staff the legal and financial preparations. As proposals emerged, he submitted them to conferences of Cabinet officers and agency heads. Then, under Roosevelt's sporadic supervision, the recommendations were cleared with the Democratic leadership on the Hill. This was less a struggle for domination than an exchange of ideas, sometimes easy, sometimes wearing.

The drafting of the bill fell largely to Edward H. Foley, the Treasury's General Counsel, and his associate, Oscar Cox. Their acumen and industry, and their tact in dealing with other departments facilitated the formulation of a complex and controversial measure. The British, the Secretary told them on January 2, 1941, had already prepared an inventory of requirements, but the American services had yet to complete one of their own. If, for example, the Army ascertained that it had to order perhaps ten thousand tanks, knowing as it did that the English needed some 5000, the Administration would go ahead and create facilities for the production of 15,000. The President believed that only a blanket authority in defense production would permit him to proceed with speed and efficiency without constantly going back to Congress for additional authorizations. Roosevelt had been "very clear in his discussions . . . that he wanted the extra facilities built." Both in constructing new plants and in transferring finished equipment, the President preferred to act directly, "no RFC, no monkey business . . . no corporations . . . he said, 'We don't want to fool the public, we want to do this thing right out and out.' "

Further, Roosevelt wanted control over allocations; "he doesn't want to tie it down that the English get so much . . . China gets so much." And he wanted authority to determine the method and terms for recompensing the United States for materials lent or leased. The American people, as Morgenthau saw it, "would just have to trust Mr. Roosevelt."

Before midnight on January 2 Foley and Cox had a tentative draft of a joint resolution providing for Lend-Lease. The next day they reviewed it with Ben Cohen, long a presidential brainstruster, now in the Department of State. On his recommendation they eliminated a provision that "no . . . transaction should be entered into in violation of international law as interpreted by the Department of State." Also at his suggestion, they broadened the powers of the President by making it clear that British ships could be repaired and outfitted in American Navy yards. It was not yet dinner time when they called on Supreme Court Justice Felix Frankfurter, whom Morgenthau had telephoned the previous evening to ask "whether he would be ready to look over our proposed legislation on how to lend war materials to England." Frankfurter recommended altering the wording of the draft so that the President's various powers for acting on behalf of any foreign government would be less particularized. He also suggested writing a preamble emphasizing, in quotable language, the importance of the legislation for national defense. This, he believed, would strengthen the bill's constitutionality. That evening, while Foley and Cox revised their handiwork, Roosevelt told Morgenthau to have them consult the Parliamentarian of the House of Representatives, for the President intended that the "aid to Britain Bill have the look of originating in the House."

On January 5, a Sunday, Morgenthau asked Foley to get the advice of Dean Acheson, at that time a private citizen devoting his crisp mind and large energies to supporting all aid to England short of war. Morgenthau's instructions in this instance represented a kind of landmark in the circulation of the New Deal's elite, for Acheson, under pressure from Roosevelt, had resigned as Under Secretary of the Treasury in 1933 because of his opposition to the gold-buying policies Morgenthau was prepared to carry out. The Secretary, who had always admired the gentlemanly manner in which Acheson had left his post, was delighted at last to enlist him again in a common purpose. He was pleased even more when in February 1941 Acheson returned to office as Assistant Secretary of State.

After seeing Acheson that evening, Foley discussed the latest draft with Secretary of the Navy Knox, who approved it, and with Secretary of State Hull, who asked him to go over the language with various of his subordinates. Foley and Cox then began a first summary memorandum for the President, which consumed their whole day Monday.

By January 9, Roosevelt, Morgenthau and Stimson had worked out legislative strategy for the bill with the Democratic leaders in Congress. On January 10 the bill was introduced in both houses with the symbolic number of H.R. 1776.

The Administration had then to organize support for the bill. Hull, with his usual distaste for controversy with the Congress, stubbornly declined to take charge of the measure and seemed reluctant even to prepare major testimony in its support. On January 13 at Hyde Park, Morgenthau asked Roosevelt to keep Hull from shirking his duty. "The President did not take my suggestion too well," the Secretary noted in his Diary. "He said, 'Hull is going to testify,' and I said, 'I know that but up to now in the Treasury we have done everything, even to preparing the statements for Barkley and Rayburn.' He said, 'I know that.' I said, 'We are perfectly willing to continue but I think, seeing that it goes before Foreign Affairs, that Hull ought to do it.'

The President said he would take it up the first thing . . .
when he got back. The important thing is that I have planted
the seed in his mind." But the seed produced no flower, and
Morgenthau found himself, as Roosevelt had intended he should,
the principal agent for the Administration throughout the many
weeks ahead.

During the ensuing debate, some members of the Administration and many of Congress seemed unwilling or unable to understand the severity of the British financial crisis. A fixed notion
about the "richness of the British Empire" fostered the delusion
that there were billions of dollars of assets hidden somewhere.
"The situation," Purvis cabled London, ". . . is difficult and
complex. . . . It is quite evident that even the most friendly
Cabinet elements do not find it easy to believe that our immediate
position is as grave as we know it to be."

At a Cabinet meeting of January 9, 1941, the "President said,"
wrote Morgenthau, "English must put couple of billion as window dressing as collateral." Though Roosevelt intended this as a
gesture to dispel congressional opposition, his suggestion implied
an expectation which England simply could not meet. He was
encouraged in his miscalculation by Cordell Hull, who maintained that the British could provide $2 or $3 billion. Morgenthau advised Sir Frederick Phillips to go right down the line to
Hull, Knox, and Stimson and tell the full story. "I have done it
until I am hoarse," the Secretary said. Hull, he felt, was not only
misinformed but also misdirected.

But Hull in the end gave unexpectedly strong and positive testimony. His statement, a part of which Roosevelt had written,
focused on the dangers confronting the Western Hemisphere
and the circumstances "which render imperative all possible
speed in preparation for meeting these dangers." When Congressman Tinkham, who made a career of hating the English,
suggested that Lend-Lease might increase the possibility of war,
Hull answered: "I want you to know that in my view there is
danger in either direction." On the whole, the bill, growing out
of the right of any nation to self-defense, set "the safest course."

Morgenthau, the next witness, began by presenting tables of

the estimated dollar expenditures and receipts for the British Empire, excluding Canada, for the calendar year 1941. Those tables, the data for which the British had provided, revealed an expected deficit of $1464 million. The tables indicated further that British gold resources, holdings of American securities, and investments in the United States and elsewhere in the world, even if entirely liquidated, could not meet that deficit. They showed, too, the United Kingdom's high tax rates and the rising costs which had now reached 60 per cent of national income for war purposes alone. As Morgenthau put it, "the British people are not only dodging the bombs and fighting for their existence, but . . . they are also making a stupendous effort to pay for this war by themselves."

Under questioning, the Secretary elaborated. England could sell her £3868 million of foreign investments outside the United States only with difficulty and at a huge loss. Her $33 million of gold was "scattered in various parts of the world . . . from which it cannot be shipped quickly or safely to the United States." British banks, citizens, and corporations had balances of $305 million within the United States which, in the view of their government, were "at the minimum level necessary for the continued conduct of business and are therefore not available for use." The British had already paid out and taken delivery on $1337 million of weapons and other materials; "when it comes to finding the dollars to pay for anything like they may need, they just haven't got it."

Turning away from finances, Hamilton Fish asked Morgenthau whether the Lend-Lease bill gave the President the power to seize foreign ships in American ports and turn them over to another country. The Secretary said it did not. Would the bill give the President the power to convoy shipments to foreign ports? Again Morgenthau said no. Did the bill authorize the President to give away part of the American Navy? Reading aloud the language of the bill authorizing transfers of defense articles and the section describing the terms for a return of direct or indirect benefits to the United States, Morgenthau replied: "I would not say he could give them away."

Would the Secretary, Fish then asked, object to establishing a ceiling on Lend-Lease expenditures at perhaps $2 billion? "I think that is a matter for the committee to decide," Morgenthau replied. "I think the situation changes so rapidly that nobody I've come in contact with can say what the ceiling should be, not only as to our defense but as to other countries." Fish was dissatisfied. "Don't you realize," he said, "that it does not put any limit on putting into the hands of one man power to spend unlimited funds?" On the contrary, Morgenthau pointed out, the bill carried no appropriation. Congress would have to come to that matter at a later date.

John M. Vorys of Ohio, another doubting Republican, declared himself "frankly amazed" at the smallness of British resources, and made Morgenthau admit that appropriations for the bill would surely force a raising of the American debt limit. Therefore, Vorys said, the measure should be entitled "Lend-Lose." In a similar vein, Tinkham asked why the English should not sell more of their listed securities. Morgenthau, tiring under the strain of the questioning, replied sharply that he had no authority to say "what Britain should or should not do."

"I am very sorry to say," Tinkham countered, irrelevantly, "I haven't the same confidence in the President you have."

"If you will pardon my saying so," the Secretary answered, "you are probably in the minority."

The opposition hammered at every aspect of Lend-Lease. Even Stimson's masterful testimony on the importance of the bill to American defense failed to impress men like Fish and Tinkham. They harassed Stimson, as they had Morgenthau, by raising issues, like the escort of convoys, that lay beyond the content, though perhaps not the long-run implications, of the bill. Outside the hearings such issues dominated the national debate. Attacking the arguments of the measure's supporters, Joseph P. Kennedy, resigned at last as Ambassador to the Court of St. James's, urged Congress to avoid involvement in a fight that was "not our war." Charles A. Lindbergh, the isolationists' champion, advocated a negotiated peace with Nazism and condemned Lend-Lease as a diversion of hemispheric strength. Norman Thomas, the Socialist leader, in invincible innocence implored Americans to forget the war and concentrate on domestic problems. Others impugned the integrity of British estimates and stressed the cost of Lend-Lease for the American taxpayer.

The House leadership found it necessary to propose an amendment calling for reports to the Congress every ninety days about everything to do with Lend-Lease which the President could divulge without injury to the public interest. They agreed, too, that nothing in the Act should be construed to give the President the power to use the Navy to convoy belligerent ships. By telephone Roosevelt endorsed those changes. Debate on the floor of the House, lasting only from February 3 to February 8, 1941, produced two more amendments. One provided that Congress might terminate the President's powers before the expiration of the Act. The other placed a ceiling of $1300 million on the value of military supplies already in hand or on order for the American services which might be transferred to foreign governments. But no limit was placed on future aid, and the bill passed by a persuasive majority of 260 (including 24 Republicans) to 165. The adverse votes of 135 Republicans suggested that sailing might be stormy in the Senate.

So it was, for three senators in mid-February moved to revise the Administration's original concept of Lend-Lease. Two influential Democrats, Senators James Byrnes of South Carolina and Harry Byrd of Virginia, aided constantly by Republican Robert A. Taft, proposed an amendment designed to give Congress the final voice about the production and transfer of military supplies. Taft argued that, as the bill stood, the President could lend or lease to foreign nations munitions procured under appropriations for the United States Army and Navy. Congress would then have no alternative but to grant new monies to the services. As Taft saw it, this challenged Congress's legitimate authority over money. Of much the same mind, Byrnes drafted an amendment requiring the President to obtain congressional authorization before disposing of equipment manufactured for the Army or Navy. Senator Byrd, going still further, had that amendment altered to specify that all aid to foreign governments had to be supplied out of funds voted exclusively for that purpose.

Those changes, Morgenthau believed, prevented the flexibility needed in procurement. He spelled out his case in a memorandum to the President of February 28, 1941, which was also signed by Stimson and by Under Secretary of the Navy Forrestal, in the temporary absence of Knox. The Byrnes-Byrd-Taft amendment, the signers maintained, crippled the original bill and the whole defense program by separating American military development from foreign aid.

Roosevelt, in bed with grippe, was disinclined to fight. Further, Hull found the memorandum "a little bit hard . . . to get my teeth in." Hull did not want to step in front of the President on the issue, he said, particularly since he felt that Roosevelt, Stimson, and Morgenthau had been handling the financial aspects of the legislation. Stimson told Morgenthau that he had warned the President that the amendment would "take the guts right out of the bill." Roosevelt had then given the impression he was handling the matter himself, but the President's voice sounded very husky, his cold was clearly worse again, and Stimson had therefore not talked for long. "I've done all that I dared do," he added, "towards stirring him up but you as his close personal friend perhaps now can carry the ball a little bit further and pull the string that will start Cordell going." Morgenthau, "with the man sick," did not want to call him up, but he sent the memorandum on the bill to the White House by special messenger, dispatched a copy to Harry Hopkins, who had recently returned from England, and by telephone urged Hopkins to lend a hand.

The resulting pressure persuaded Hull on March 2, 1941, to call a meeting of Morgenthau, Stimson, and Senators Barkley, George, and Byrnes. Their talk accomplished nothing. That night Morgenthau gave Hopkins "a very discouraging and gloomy report because that is the way I felt about it. I said the trouble was the President had not taken my original suggestion and asked Cordell to carry this bill. I suggested that Harry get the President to call up Hull and ask him how things went this morning. I said that is the natural thing for the President to do. Harry said that maybe Cordell had called the President, and I said, 'I'm sure that he hasn't because they weren't on that kind of a basis.' "

Unable to rouse Roosevelt or to budge Senator Byrnes, Ed Foley worked out a compromise in an effort to make the amendment less damaging. Foley's revision provided that the President could dispose of defense articles abroad under Lend-Lease unless Congress imposed specific restrictions. The revision satisfied the Senate which on March 8 passed the bill by a vote of sixty to thirty-one. Like the changes made by the House, those added by the Senate made the technical administration of Lend-Lease more difficult than Morgenthau or Stimson had hoped it would be, but did not vitiate the main purpose of the Act. Congress, as Roosevelt had proposed, had removed the dollar sign from foreign aid.

Roosevelt turned the administration of Lend-Lease over to Harry Hopkins, whose recent trip to England, as the President had intended it to, enlisted him in the cause which Morgenthau and Stimson had so long advocated. Harry Hopkins was to have command of a new agency that would report to a Cabinet committee. "I propose to administer the bill," the President wrote Morgenthau, "through . . . an Advisory Committee composed of the Secretary of State, the Secretary of War, the Secretary of the Navy and you. I am going to ask Harry Hopkins to act as Secretary of this Committee. . . . I do this because of his intimate acquaintance with the needs of Britain and his understanding of governmental relationships here."

Only to his own staff did Morgenthau express doubts. The current plan, he said, sounded "very nice . . . but I am just worried sick over it because . . . Hopkins isn't well enough. . . . My position has been . . that I am not going to do anything . . . in connection with the war stuff that the President doesn't ask me to do. . . . I think just at this time — I think it is very, very unfortunate that there is going to be a swapping of forces. . . . Here is this list of eighteen things the British want. Hopkins has been carrying that around with him since Sunday a week ago. The thing could have been mimeographed and everybody could have a copy and [be] working on it. That is what would have happened in my shop."

Yet Morgenthau was aware that his "own shop" could not perform the functions of both the Treasury and Lend-Lease.

The Secretary had already done his part. Dean Acheson remarked that Morgenthau "was entirely responsible for the fact
that . . . between Dunkirk and the first of the year . . . the
English kept on fighting." The words of Arthur Purvis in a
handwritten letter of March 13, 1941, pleased the Secretary
most: "Your note with its — to me — sad confirmation of the
break with your arduous work in the field of war supplies for
Britain, has reached me today. I can only hope, for my country's
sake as well as for mine, that that break will not extend to the
policy field. It would be a disaster if it did. . . . You have from
the start been a consistent and persistent friend 'in shade or shine'
and this also at a time when such friends were few and far between. The fact that your guiding skill was available to us in the
time of trial is far from the least of the debts we owe to the
President."

Beyond words lay the palpable results of Morgenthau's striving. A year after the German offensive in Europe had begun, a
year after Western civilization had seemed about to succumb, the
British were still fighting, stronger each day, secure most of all in
their indomitable spirit, but dependent also, as they long had
been, on American assistance. For that, as Purvis said, they had
Morgenthau, more than anyone but the President, to thank.

4. *Arsenal for Russia*

For the lack of a Purvis, for the lack of the energy and perception and personal warmth he brought to his task, for the lack,
too, of the understanding that characterized the relationship between responsible officials of the two English-speaking nations,
other countries met with far more difficulties than did England
in their experience with Lend-Lease.

Throughout the summer of 1941, the United Kingdom was
the primary recipient of Lend-Lease aid, though China also received some American weapons. Earlier, Nazi aggression in the

Balkans had spurred Greece to try to purchase American air-craft, but the scarcity already troubling the United States and England had permitted only a token sale. German victories in Greece, Yugoslavia, and Rumania prefaced the Nazi invasion of the Soviet Union on June 22, 1941. The President and his colleagues had then to decide whether and in what dimension to supply Russia with American munitions.

Morgenthau's reaction was exactly that of the British. On the evening of the invasion Churchill, reminding his audience of his lifelong opposition to communism, welcomed the Soviet Union enthusiastically as a partner in the struggle against Nazism. "Resolved to destroy Hitler," Churchill said, the English would give "whatever help we can to Russia and the Russian people. We shall appeal to our friends and allies in every part of the world to take the same course and pursue it, faithfully and steadfastly to the end." London immediately sent military and economic missions to Moscow. In the United States Sumner Welles endorsed Churchill's position. Regardless of the national abhorrence for communism, Welles said, "Hitler's armies are today the chief dangers of the Americas." To that statement public opinion was by and large favorable, though some rabid isolationists and anti-Communists hoped that the latest turn in the war would let the Russians and Germans destroy each other while the United States watched. Morgenthau harbored no such illusions.

While eager to assist the Russians, Morgenthau refused to serve as their American advocate for a general license for the purchase and export of munitions. That role, he believed, had to be played by the State Department. "Six months ago," he said to those urging him to act, "the President told me he wanted to stay on the fence as long as possible. He said he didn't care what the cost. Mr. Hull raised one of his worst rumpuses. . . . Since then they have done everything possible to drive them into the arms of the Japanese and the Germans, and I put it up to the President that we should bribe them, do business with them in any way to keep them neutral, and I believed it then and I thought it was a good policy, but . . . it was one of the worst rows that ever took place in Washington. I was right then. I am

right now But I am not going to rush into this thing. . . . Let
Mr. Hull come out and kiss the Russians on both cheeks. . . . I
can't be a weather vane. It is one thing to bribe them and try to
keep them neutral . . . but when it comes to this thing, let's just
sit tight and see."

Taking the initiative, Welles on June 24, 1941, drafted a general license for the Russians and a press release announcing it.
"The State Department requested," the release read, "and the
Treasury Department and the Department of Justice approved,
the issuance of the license." Morgenthau, who had insisted that
the language indicate where the policy originated, continued to
do no more than follow the State Department's lead. "Dean
Acheson came over here very, very hush hush," the Secretary
told his staff on July 3, "and . . . brought me a list of what the
Russians said they wanted. . . . The main thing was that they
want to let the Russians now have thirty or forty or fifty million
dollars worth of material, and the Russians want to buy it on a
five-year credit. Would I please tell Mr. Welles how the Russians could borrow the money, and unless you people . . .
argue awfully hard — I am going to call up Mr. Acheson and
tell him that the United States Treasury is not in the lending
business, I am not interested. . . .

"It is a question of policy. . . . Mr. Jones has all the authority for lending and I think if Mr. Welles wants to find out how
the Russians can borrow some money he should go to Mr. Jones.
. . . The State Department suddenly coming over and asking
my advice, it is just too much."

"It seems to me that the thing to do is take it up with the Loan
Administrator direct as you have in the past," Morgenthau told
Welles by telephone.

"What I wanted was your own judgment as to the desirability
of proceeding along this line," Welles said.

"Well," Morgenthau said, "I think that this is so much foreign
affairs that . . . it better be handled by the State Department."
Turning back to his staff, the Secretary continued: "I burnt my
heart out and Hull and Welles have gone there consistently, and
told the President, 'Morgenthau wants to run the State Depart-

ment and wants to run foreign affairs.' Hull told me that himself. And now they want my help. . . . But after what they put me through for eight years — they have got to get down on their knees to ask me. I mean I will never forget the tongue lashings that I have had from Mr. Hull about how I want to run his department and the sarcasm and everything else."

The sensitivities of the State Department had not entirely changed. All through July 1941, Welles delayed approving an agreement Morgenthau had proposed for buying Russian gold. Welles had no objection to the terms of the agreement; rather, he felt that the State Department should handle the American end, whereas Morgenthau and his assistants pointed to the Stabilization Pact of 1936 and to other similar precedents for Treasury negotiations with foreign authorities on monetary matters. By August 7, 1941, Morgenthau was "sick and tired of waiting" for State Department consent. So informed, Acheson studied the file on the matter, took it up with Welles that afternoon, and at once authorized the Treasury to proceed. The Secretary did so by writing the Russians that the gold policy of the United States would continue to apply for at least a year as it had since 1934. The government of the United States (the use of the word "government" instead of the word "Treasury" was deliberate) would purchase any gold Russia offered for sale on the same terms available to other nations.

The assurance was timely. A strong congressional minority was delaying legislation to permit Lend-Lease to the Soviet Union. Roosevelt stood back, partly in order to let public opinion develop in support of the Russians, partly in order to familiarize himself with the details of Russian requirements. To that end, he sent Harry Hopkins to Moscow. Meanwhile the Russians could obtain American equipment only for cash, and their dollar resources within the United States were slim. They could finance their purchases in the United States, as they told the Treasury on August 15, 1941, only by selling gold. They had $3 million of gold on the high seas and within the next six weeks would ship another $10 million, all of which they hoped the Treasury would buy before it actually arrived at American

ports. Before the day was over, with the approval of Hull and
Welles, Morgenthau decided to allow $10 million against future
delivery, with 5 per cent withheld until the gold reached an
American assay office. There was to be no interest.

Morgenthau also helped to expedite a Russian request for a list
of supplies, which the Treasury received on August 1, 1941. As
the Russians put it to Morgenthau, the war was moving very
quickly, but plans for concrete aid were moving very slowly.
Just three days ago they had given Welles an expanded list of
Russian requirements which he had promised to get to the President within the hour. Yet the Russians had seen Roosevelt two
days later and he had never seen the list. So also, the President
had promised to deliver a number of fighter planes, but the Army
had protested that it had none available. And in Moscow Hopkins had received an inventory of definite Russian needs but had
been unable to provide assurances that they could be met. The
Russians particularly wanted fighters and bombers, they had
been told there were no P-40 fighters available, but they had discovered the British had 150 of those planes still in crates and
awaiting shipment, and that there were 50 more undelivered
within the United States.

The distribution of military supplies, Morgenthau explained,
was the responsibility of the Lend-Lease administration, where
Oscar Cox, with whom he arranged an appointment, would give
the Russians a sympathetic hearing. Like the Secretary, Cox felt
that the delay on the P-40's was a "damned shame." The difficulties, it developed, arose partly because Stimson did not want
to reduce the number of fighters assigned the British, nor indeed
were the British happy with the thought of releasing any. But as
was so often the case with Soviet requests, the fault lay also
partly with the Russians, from whom Stimson had been unable
to get precise specifications about much of the equipment they
wanted, and who also stubbornly insisted, for reasons no American could understand, on having planes in crates in Great Britain
shipped back to the United States, carried across the continent,
and then transshipped by way of the Pacific to Vladivostok.

Yet this absurdity, which the Russians ultimately abandoned, in no way altered Morgenthau's conviction that American authorities, those in the War Department particularly, were responding ungenerously to Soviet pleas. At luncheon with Roosevelt on August 4, Morgenthau complained that Soviet Ambassador Oumansky was getting "absolutely the runaround." Though the President questioned that statement, he promised to bring up the matter at the Cabinet meeting that afternoon. He opened that session with a forty-five-minute lecture demanding priority for the movement of materials to the Soviet Union. As Morgenthau recalled his words, Roosevelt said: "I am sick and tired of hearing that they are going to get this and they are going to get that. . . . Whatever we are going to give them, it has to be over there by the first of October, and the only answer I want to hear is that it is under way." The President, whom Morgenthau had never seen more emphatic, directed most of his fire at Stimson, who looked "thoroughly miserable." "Get the planes right off," Roosevelt ordered, "with a bang next week." Besides the fighters, there was to be a token shipment of some rifles and four-engine bombers, five from American and five from British stocks. "I want to do all of this at once," Roosevelt said, "in order to help their morale."

When he had "sort of run out of steam," Roosevelt turned to Morgenthau, who said: "The trouble, Mr. President, is that with Harry Hopkins away Oscar Cox tells me that he just hasn't got enough authority to get anywhere . . . and that he does get the run around all the time." The President then said he would put one of the best administrators in Washington in charge of the Russian order "and his job will be to see that the Russians get what they need." For that assignment, he selected Wayne Coy, his liaison assistant to the Office of Emergency Management, within which there operated the agencies responsible both for production and for priorities.

Six weeks had elapsed since the invasion of Russia, Roosevelt wrote Coy after the Cabinet meeting, and "we have done practically nothing to get any of the materials they have asked for. . . . Please get out the list and please with my full authority use a heavy hand and act as a burr under the saddle and get things moving. . . . I have told the Russians that I am dividing things into two categories, first materials to be delivered on the Russian Western front in time to take part in the battle between September 1 and October 1 and secondly, those materials which physically could not get there before October 1. I have chosen that date because after October 1 we all doubt if there will be very active operations, due to rain, snow, etc. Step on it."

Within twenty-four hours Coy reported to Morgenthau that much of the trouble arose from a failure of communications. Stimson was now at last getting the specifications he required, and the Russians, as Roosevelt had stipulated, had been told that it was ridiculous to move the P-40's through the submarine zone, but that the United States would arrange to have 140 fighters sent from England by way of Archangel. Another 49 would come directly from the United States by way of the Pacific, while 5 British and 5 American bombers were proceeding by other routes. "I think what has happened since Cabinet," Morgenthau said, "is very encouraging, but 210 airplanes isn't going to last them very long. What about all the rest of the stuff?" Coy said that he and Cox were working on it. England, currently getting about 60 per cent of American production, would have to take less, for the major front of the war had shifted to the Soviet Union. Oumansky had told Morgenthau that since the Russians were doing 90 per cent of the fighting, they should get 90 per cent "of the stuff." That proportion was manifestly higher than suited either England or the United States, but Coy had already talked with Oumansky about the need for tripartite discussions of the matter.

"Well," Morgenthau commented, "they have just got to get this stuff and get it fast. . . . You can't treat them the way we treated the Greeks. . . . We just can't treat these fellows this way, because this is the time to get Hitler. We will never have a better chance. . . . And if we muff the ball — I mean, somebody has been looking over this country and the good Lord has been with us, but we can't count on the good Lord and just plain dumb luck forever. We have got the chance to do it now or never."

Grateful "for the Secretary's interest and help," Oumansky had yet to obtain sufficient funds to pay for the purchases Coy was arranging. On September 11 he asked for a Stabilization loan, which Morgenthau explained he could not make without consulting Congress. Opposition there, Morgenthau and Hopkins agreed, would prevent a loan, especially in the face of Russian reticence. No one, Morgenthau said, had ever been allowed to learn how much gold the Russians had, though it would not be surprising if they had as much as $1 billion. Hopkins felt the Russians should draw on their gold to pay for their orders, just as "England did for a long time." Oumansky, as the Secretary put it to his staff on September 12, 1941, "seemed a little bit annoyed last night. He came up to me all excited — he hasn't any money . . . he's down to $400,000. He was with the President for two hours yesterday, and I said, 'Look here, Ambassador, you always come to me at the last minute.' He is leaving tomorrow. He kind of resented that a little bit. This is the first time I ever criticized him. . . . I said, 'One o'clock my time today is the deadline,' but the President will have to call me up. . . .

"In the room here, an amusing episode. They had a little dinner last night of eighty-six people, and down at the other end Oumansky got up and made a speech giving the health of President Roosevelt, and I sat up at Madame Oumansky's right and Harriman* on the left, and he addressed himself to Harriman and wished him good luck. The dinner was a send-off to this mission. After he did that, Harriman leaned over and said, 'Are you going to give the toast?' I said, 'Oh, no, it is your mission.' . . . Finally he jumped up and said, 'I give the toast to Stalin.' . . . I would much rather have Averell Harriman give the toast to Stalin. He didn't recover all the rest of the evening. With eighty-six people, I think it wouldn't have been more than an hour before, 'Morgenthau proposes a toast to Stalin.' That is news. But if Averell Harriman does it, it is not."

Confusion about Russian finances alarmed Harry Hopkins, whose trip to the Soviet Union had convinced him of the vigor

---

* Averell Harriman was about to leave for Moscow to follow-up Hopkins's earlier discussions about Lend-Lease to the Soviet Union.

of Russian resistance and of the urgency of American aid. On September 23 Hopkins asked Morgenthau if there were any way in which the Russians could sell the United States more gold. They could if they wanted to, the Secretary replied, but he had no way of knowing their plans. "The thing's in a hell of a mess," Hopkins said, ". . . and I'll have to get the President . . . to see if he can make an appointment with you. . . . We're just getting licked right and left here on this god damned thing. I don't blame you. . . . It's up to the President. I can't control his time and his appointments. . . . It's very important that no-body offers to loan them any money and they can't use Lend-Lease, and we made this large size commitment and now, by god, we can't deliver on it. . . . It's just god damned discouraging."

"Just remember this," Morgenthau said, "that no matter what happens, I've got only one object in life and that is to see that Hitler gets licked. . . . So no matter what anybody does to me in town, I don't give a damn."

To Roosevelt that day Morgenthau wrote: "I was consider-ably disturbed by my telephone call from Harry Hopkins this morning in regard to the Russian financial situation. Quite frankly, I do not know anything about Russia's current financial needs. I am in almost daily contact with Treasury representa-tives in England, Canada and China. If you wish me to do some-thing in regard to the Russian situation, I would be glad to take it on, provided that you will explain to me personally just what it is you would like me to do."

The next evening Roosevelt telephoned, "very affable; voice dripping with honey." The President asked whether the United States could buy $10 or $15 million of gold, and when Morgen-thau reported that the Treasury could, indeed that it had already paid more than $5 million of the $10 million that had been ad-vanced against future gold deliveries, Roosevelt was surprised. He said that Harriman, when he had a chance to talk with Stalin alone, would ask how much gold the Russians had. Meanwhile, Morgenthau was to deal directly with the chargé at the Russian embassy, Andrei Gromyko. "It has been a long time since the President called me," Morgenthau noted, "and evidently he must want something done for Russia very badly, and I am glad I wrote my letter because it got the desired results."

The Russians, Hopkins informed Morgenthau on September 26, were asking for tremendous sums of money, but they did not have to have all of it immediately because they could not use it very fast. The United States could sell them only a small proportion of the planes and tanks under production, and there would be no opportunity for them to place large orders in advance the way the British had. "Here's the thing, Harry," Morgenthau said, "the President and you are going to have to make up your mind about. Does the President want me simply to chip out some gold or does he want me to look after their dollar requirements the way I do for the British Empire and China?"

"The President's position about the permanent thing is pretty much this," Hopkins replied, "that he's trying to get them cash now so they can work here from week to week on the things that are available. . . . That he's stalling a little to make up his mind and watching public opinion about how he's going to handle the major problem of when we get into four or five hundred tanks a month and airplanes a month, with each one you have to multiply by fifty or one hundred thousand dollars apiece — whether to use the RFC to loan them the money or to use the Lend-Lease machinery. Now, I wish that could be decided now. . . . The President thinks . . . apparently that he can't handle it now on the Hill. There's going to be an amendment to our bill* put in prohibiting the use of any of this money for Russia. . . . And the President's going to work awfully hard to get that defeated, and the more publicity he can get about that, the better. And that would, in the President's mind, indicate congressional intent . . . not to exclude Russia. . . . Which would give him a handle. . . . Now Jones . . . has got his RFC bill . . . in such shape that a similar resolution is going to be introduced, prohibiting him from loaning; and Jones is sure he can defeat that. So in either case, we'd have congressional intent and presumably at that point the President would decide how to handle it.

* The second Lend-Lease appropriations bill then pending.

"Now, in the meantime, the Army have agreed to give up some things immediately — some things that are important. . . . To do that now, legally, it requires cash. . . . My judgment is that it's about $25 million a month for the next three months. Jones has promised them $100 million . . . legally, he can advance that money whenever he wants to. . . . I've told Jones that this thing is going to cost at least 25 million a month, and it doesn't do any good to dole this out to the tune of 10 million a month. . . . Now, at the moment, our interest is . . . to have it in their hands, $25 or $30 million cash every thirty days until such time as the President decides how he is really going to handle this in a big way."

At the Cabinet meeting that day, Morgenthau and Hopkins reminded the President that the Treasury would buy all the gold the Soviet Union offered for sale. With Roosevelt's approval, Morgenthau during the first week of October volunteered to advance the Russians $50 million against gold deliveries during the coming six months. "The trouble," he then reported to the President, "seemed to be that the Russians had been told there was only $11 million worth of goods around, and my guess was that they were wondering why they should hurry about furnishing a lot of cash if they could get it all for nothing in a couple of weeks through Lend-Lease. If we had $50 million worth of goods laying around, the way Hopkins said we had, why didn't we tell them? The President said, 'You're right.' Then he asked me whether I had told this to Hopkins and I told him that I hadn't. Then he said, '. . . Be sure to tell him about it in the morning.' "

Moscow declined to comment on the offer to buy $50 million of gold, but on October 9 reported that another $5 million of gold was arriving in the United States, and Morgenthau then announced that the Russians had delivered gold several weeks earlier than their contract required. This announcement, the Secretary thought, would create a good impression on the Hill and with the public. He was ready, he stated, to give the Russians credit against any future deliveries they would guarantee. They quickly asked for $30 million, which, as Hopkins put it, was a "life saver for us . . . because we're getting . . . a hundred more planes . . . and about fifty more tanks, and . . . several thousand trucks. . . . They want them on ships right now."

By mid-October 1941 credit was ceasing to be a problem. In the House of Representatives there were only twenty-four votes in favor of the amendment forbidding Lend-Lease to Russia. That Administration victory cleared the way for the massive aid which Roosevelt had promised Stalin. Hopkins then sent Morgenthau a memorandum of terms for Lend-Lease to the Soviet Union. The draft demanded from the Russians a monthly payment in gold, a further payment of 1⅞ per cent interest on all materials delivered in any month beyond the worth of the gold payment, and ultimately full return of raw materials to offset the value of Lend-Lease shipments.

"This is not the way to do the thing," Morgenthau objected. "I think it is a mistake at this time to bother Stalin with any financial arrangements and to take his mind off the war. It would make him think we are nothing but a bunch of Yankee traders trying to squeeze the last drop out of him. . . . Do you feel or does the President feel that because the English paid down so much cash that we have to get so much gold from the Russians?" As with Great Britain, so with the Soviet Union, Morgenthau preferred to supply whatever the President considered appropriate, and to let arrangements for a quid pro quo evolve in the fullness of time. "I absolutely agree with you," Hopkins said. "I am going to put on my hat and go over to see Hull and try to sell him the idea. Then Hull, you and I should see the President."

But Hull, suspicious as always of the Russians and sensitive as always to opinion on the Hill, insisted on setting firm terms, and on October 29 Hopkins completed a new draft, more generous than the original, but still more demanding than what he and Morgenthau favored. The revised draft, which the Russians accepted, promised large-scale American aid of war materials and raw materials to Russia. Russian indebtedness for Lend-Lease was not to carry any interest until five years after the end of the war, and payments of interest were then to run over ten years.*

---

* The Soviet Union has never, in the years since the war ended, seen fit to meet the terms on which they received American Lend-Lease aid.

Under this agreement, the United States extended an initial Lend-Lease credit of $1 billion.

There remained unresolved the problem of allocating American production among the American services and the various nations eligible for Lend-Lease. Before the end of November Gromyko was again at the Treasury asking Morgenthau's help in obtaining planes and munitions, trucks, cars, chemicals, shoes, and various other materials. On November 26 the Secretary gave Roosevelt a memorandum on the Russian request. He did not like to take the matter to the White House, the Secretary said, but Hopkins was ill, and the movement of goods to Russia was much slower than it should have been. "The President shied away from the Russian matter," Morgenthau later noted in his Diary. "The President said, 'The trouble is they can't unload the ships fast enough in Archangel,' so I said, 'They can unload one a day, and we have only given Russia half a dozen ships.' It was finally left that the President would take the matter up with Hopkins. I don't want to convey the impression that the President was annoyed about the Russian matter. He was in a good humor but he just didn't want to go into the thing, which makes me believe he knows the situation is bad."

So it was, as it was also in the faltering deliveries of goods on order for the American services. The difficulty, as 1941 drew toward its end, lay not so much in the disinclination of responsible Americans to help the Soviets as it did in the paucity of American production. That condition was to improve only gradually during the year ahead. Yet the sum of accomplishments for 1941 was considerable; the enactment of Lend-Lease, the rising flow of supply to the United Kingdom, the beginning of a similar movement to the Soviet Union. In all this, Morgenthau had had a hand. So, of course, had many others; in the Secretary's judgment Roosevelt first of all, then Stimson, then Hopkins, and also their aides. As he worked with them, sometimes leading, sometimes assisting, Morgenthau had always the same motivation.

"It is for us to decide," he said in his commencement address at his son's graduation from Amherst College, ". . . whether we would rather die on our feet than live on our knees." His own answer to that question was unequivocal. American society, in order to survive, had not only to organize its own strength and share it with the enemies of Nazism; it had also at home and abroad to mobilize its economy and to stock its arsenal of economic weapons.

XV

DEFENSE ECONOMICS

1939 – 1941

WAR IN EUROPE had significant consequences for the international and American economies and for federal fiscal policy. On the international front, the United States had to make decisions about whether or not to engage in virtual economic warfare. At home, federal expenditures for preparedness, the purchases of the Allied governments, and later procurement for them under Lend-Lease, stimulated American industry and employment more than anything had since the great depression had begun. But the costs to the government, even before the inception of Lend-Lease, severely strained the Treasury. The Department had both to borrow more money than ever before and to work out changes in the tax laws that would produce much of the increased revenues the government needed. Further, from Morgenthau's point of view, the financing of American defense could not be permitted to impair either the social goals of the New Deal or the incipient recovery of the economy. The difficulties in the achievement of those varied purposes made the problems of taxation during the period of American preparedness as complicated as anything the Secretary faced. And as in previous years, Roosevelt's reluctance to confront the unpleasantnesses of revenue legislation and Congress's propensity to play politics with every tax bill obstructed Morgenthau's worrisome task.

1. Principles and Applications

Morgenthau based his financial program on conservative techniques. At his urging the Federal Reserve System in the fall of 1939 withdrew its support from the government bond market. In spite of the European crisis, as the Secretary predicted, the market remained steady without artificial props. Yet its steadiness, he believed, depended upon the confidence of investors, which would fade were Roosevelt to embark upon unorthodox policies. In response to a proposal to use silver certificates to increase the circulating currency, Morgenthau said he was "sick and tired of all this monkey business."

The Secretary was more impatient with the proponents of business-as-usual. During all the years of the New Deal, businessmen had argued that the government's social welfare policies damaged confidence and thereby impaired recovery. But in the absence of such policies, if any recovery had taken place, it would have benefited primarily the rich. Predictably, the business community held that new taxes on the profits from defense contracts would prevent "the revival of private enterprise . . . and thereby . . . the balancing of our federal budget." Morgenthau replied in a memorandum for his own staff. The United States, he wrote, stood as a bastion against both fascism and communism. The government had, therefore, to maintain the unity of all Americans by curbing extremes of suffering and avarice. A tax program, by tapping all special gains arising out of defense expenditures, would raise revenues for defraying the cost of preparedness and for assisting impoverished Americans. Further, Morgenthau intended taxes to prevent any group from finding economic profit in war, and thus from driving the nation needlessly toward it. He wanted also to use taxes to guard against inflation. In the coming period of increasing business activity, he believed it would be just and feasible to increase taxes on middle and lower income groups. But first of all he favored new taxes, including an excess profits tax, to keep any firm from deriving undue benefits from national defense.

In principle Roosevelt agreed. "If you take a plebiscite today as to whether the people would rather have price fixing by fiat or excess profits tax," he said at luncheon on September 25, 1939, "it would be an overwhelming vote for excess profits taxes. The people don't want to see individuals and groups profit here." When Morgenthau then asked him "about excess profits, increase the middle group and . . . the lower income group," the President replied "perfect tax program; simple; perfect!" At a luncheon on October 3, Roosevelt reported a conversation he had just had with seven congressmen. It was not enough, he had argued, simply to tax munitions; it was not enough simply to tax the man who made shells; it would be necessary also to tax those manufacturing the brass pipe and producing the copper that went into the shells. "The best tax is the excess profits tax . . . I told them," and for help in drafting one, he referred them to the Treasury.

For supplementary advice, the President turned to a skilled, liberal New York tax lawyer, Randolph Paul, who prepared a study which reached Morgenthau on November 11, 1939. Emphasizing the importance of a graduated tax on excessive business earnings, Paul defined them as the net rate of income greater than the average for a corporation during the period 1935–1938. The net increase, he held, represented profits accruing from the impact of the war upon the American economy. Yet in order to protect corporations which had had low earnings during the base period, Paul recommended exempting 8 to 12 per cent of total invested capital from any excess profits tax.

Paul had provided additional support for Morgenthau's principles. Public opinion also backed the Secretary. The isolationism of the 1930's rested on the conviction that bankers, munitions makers, and other war profiteers had primary responsibility for American involvement in World War I. Though this contention was vastly exaggerated, and though isolationist sentiment began to diminish even before the German spring offensive of

1940, there remained then and later strong popular demand to curb defense profits.

That demand had found expression in the Vinson-Trammell Act of 1934, which limited profits on naval aircraft and vessels to 10 per cent. As amended in 1939, the Act included army aircraft for which the permissible profit was raised to 12 per cent. Administration of the law fell to the Treasury, which, on Morgenthau's instructions, construed its meaning narrowly and vigorously. Therein lay a source of controversy, for the Treasury's policy struck the manufacturers of ships and planes as onerous, and their complaints won important support from procurement officials in the War and Navy Departments. The Treasury and the armed services also disagreed about the question of depreciation allowances in defense work, with the Army and Navy again advocating latitude. That view by November of 1939 impressed the President.

"You are hereby directed," Roosevelt wrote Morgenthau on November 9, "to work out a policy of depreciation allowance by which the abnormal investment in plant expansion that will be required of the airplane motors manufacturers will be absorbed over the life of the contracts or during the emergency period.

"You are further directed to consult with the appropriate committees of the Congress for the purpose of devising a permanent program whereby the facilities thus created will become a permanent part of the national defense."

Morgenthau resisted the implications of this directive. While eager to accelerate the production of airplanes, he believed that the Army and Navy should go directly to Congress for appropriations to build new plants rather than rely on the Treasury to circumvent Congress's clear intention by permitting quick tax write-offs. As the Secretary put it to his staff on November 29, he did not want to "do it through a devious way which would put . . . me . . . and the rest of us with our backs to the wall, defending why we permit munitions makers to make excess profits. To hell with them!"

To the Cabinet on December 4, 1939, Morgenthau explained

that the Treasury could permit a defense contractor to deduct from his income the cost of specialized machinery that was consumed or rendered obsolete in any tax year. But the tax laws, and the tone of ongoing committee hearings in Congress, prevented the Department from giving similar treatment to standard factory equipment or buildings which would have a useful life beyond the termination of defense work. Morgenthau was prepared, however, to support the Army and Navy in recommendations to Congress for appropriations or for changes in the tax laws which they deemed essential for national defense.

There followed a hot argument between Morgenthau and Secretary of the Navy Edison over a recent Treasury ruling that denied a rapid tax write-off to Consolidated Aircraft for certain buildings in which Navy planes were to be manufactured. Always uncomfortable with contention at Cabinet meetings, Roosevelt closed the debate by saying to Edison: "Charlie, what do you want to do, just give Consolidated a handout?"

When Edison later raised questions about contracts pending with Midvale Steel and Bethlehem Steel, Morgenthau held tight. "The President and I," he said, "are together on this thing, see, and I am sure that we are together with the Congress and the public on this, see, so if you don't mind my saying it, there is no use pleading on this question of excessive depreciation on buildings for a munitions maker. . . . I am willing to go across the street and recommend X millions of dollars for the government to put in the plant where you need certain things and the Army needs certain things. . . . I am willing to put the influence of the Treasury behind it." There, unbudging, Morgenthau remained, and Roosevelt pushed him no further.

2. New Taxes

The First Revenue Act of 1940, little more than a gesture toward what was needed that year, increased individual income surtaxes in most brackets, slightly increased corporate rates, and set a "defense" supertax of about 10 per cent on most of the other existing internal revenue taxes. It also broadened the individual income tax base by reducing personal exemptions, and it raised many excises. Morgenthau believed "a hundred per cent" that the Treasury and the Congress had quickly "to get to work . . . on real excess profits stuff." As he told his staff on June 28, 1940, "The President wants an excess profits tax . . . message. . . . Not a bill, just a message. It is the opening gun of the campaign." Opposed to war profits, Roosevelt was in a hurry to ban them so that the Republicans could not call the Democratic party a war party. But with the war in Europe and the Orient commanding his attention, Roosevelt had no time to study a tax bill. He had simply told Morgenthau to "make it tough."

But Senator Harrison wanted to postpone excess profits until after the election. So informed by Morgenthau, the President nevertheless persisted. "Mr. Roosevelt called me up and told me he just concluded a meeting with . . . the Big Four* and they were all in complete agreement with him," Morgenthau reported to Harrison on July 1, "that he should immediately send up a message on excess profits. . . . I pleaded with him; I did everything that I could to stop it; he wouldn't listen to me."

By July 10, the Treasury had completed a memorandum of principles for the President. It recommended rapid amortization for privately financed plants necessary for national defense, and it proposed repeal of the Vinson-Trammell Act, which affected only the shipbuilding and aircraft industries. These would be

---

* The Vice-President, the Speaker of the House, and the Democratic majority leaders in both chambers.

covered by enactment of a third recommendation for a steeply graduated, non-discriminatory excess profits tax. An appropriate schedule of rates, the Secretary believed, had to prevent defense profiteering and also yield significant new revenue. "I don't care how steep it is," he told his staff on July 16. The Administration would be damned for what it did no matter what the rates, and consequently "might as well do a bang up job. . . . You fellows can't make this thing too tough to suit me."

As it worked out, congressional conservatives in both parties kept the revenue bill buried in committee throughout July. Eager for action, Roosevelt early in August conceded to Harrison and Doughton full authority over the construction of the excess profits schedules in the bill.

Morgenthau was away on a brief vacation on August 2 when the President, during a Cabinet meeting, explained his decision to Dan Bell. As Bell reported to the Secretary, Roosevelt

> told me that he had made it plain . . . that we must have an excess profits tax bill this session; that he did not want to be bothered with the details of the bill but would leave that entirely to the legislative branch . . . but he did want to impress upon them that he had to have a bill of some kind this session and if there were any mistakes in it, they could be corrected at the next session. . . . The President then said he did not want this bill to get bogged down because of differences between the Treasury experts and the congressional experts. The main thing now is to get a bill through and then straighten it out next January. He said even the amount of revenue is not so important at this time. . . .
>
> Mr. Stimson . . . wanted to stress the fact that delay in enacting legislation covering the amortization question was holding up many contracts. . . . Mr. Knox also said it was holding up many . . . that industry was just not signing the contracts as long as this question remained open.

"I can boil down what happened yesterday," Morgenthau told his staff on August 5 after a session with Roosevelt at Hyde Park, "inside of the room and under the robes. I sat on the President's back porch. He was in a rocker and he says, 'I can tell you very simply how I feel. . . . I want a tax bill; I want one damned quick; I don't care what is in it; I don't want to know.

. . . The contracts are being held up and I want a tax bill.'
. . . I disagree with him a hundred per cent. I think he is en-
tirely wrong, but I am not President and I am not running for
President, and he is."

"The President asked me how we were getting along on the
tax bill," Morgenthau noted on August 14, "and I told him it was
a lousy bill." The draft completed by the House Ways and
Means Committee was "a terrible mess," filled with loopholes
permitting evasion of the excess profits tax, inadequate in raising
revenue, harsh on small business. Yet Stimson and Knox, as well
as the businesses they were favoring, stood behind the measure,
and Roosevelt, while sympathetic to the Treasury's argument,
stood aside. The Ways and Means Committee, overriding a liberal minority protest, late in August reported out its controversial draft.

The Senate Finance Committee further weakened the bill. Its
revised draft substituted a flat for a graduated corporate income
tax schedule. The Senate version of excess profits taxation gave
to each business a crucial option. It could calculate a credit
against its excess profits tax either on the basis of the return on
invested capital or on the basis of previous average earnings.
That option permitted almost a total escape from the excess
profits tax for corporations with high earnings in recent years
(including several large airplane companies), and for corporations with huge capital structures (including several major steel
companies).

But Roosevelt dodged a futile fight, and Pat Harrison, strug-
gling for his own bill — "the best bill we could have gotten" —
succeeded with little difficulty in having it reported out of the
Senate Finance Committee without amendment. That marked
the defeat of the Treasury's plan for the Second Revenue Act of
1940. The new legislation, Morgenthau wrote Roosevelt on
October 21, 1940, sponsored the very kinds of discrimination that
the President and the Treasury had for so many years opposed.
First, under improving business conditions, the excess profits
tax, violating the principle of ability to pay, would bear most
heavily on those corporations which in the past had had the poor-

est earning records. Second, the excess profits tax as the Congress had imposed it, by placing a grave handicap on growing businesses, would give to many established corporations a near monopoly in their industries. Third, the excess profits tax encouraged enterprises with high earnings to complicate their corporate structures in order to secure unfair tax advantages. Later experience bore out that analysis. Some corporations in defense industries made 30 or 50 per cent on their invested capital without paying any excess profits tax. The conservative mood of Congress, the sense of crisis in the defense emergency, the callousness of the War Department toward anything but production, all these helped to account for the result. In the fall of 1940, however, the Second Revenue Act served, as Roosevelt had intended, to quiet demand for some excess profits legislation. The President, in a campaign year, had decided to accept an imperfect law that would encourage the defense program, and he had obtained only that. Further, even after Roosevelt's reelection the powerful conservatives on the Hill yielded nothing to the Treasury's progressive views.

3. Foreign Funds

In the arena of international economic policy, the State Department was no more yielding. In June 1940 the Treasury began to reconsider the purposes of its controls over the funds of nations Hitler had overrun. The Executive Orders freezing those bank deposits, securities, and other properties had made their transfer subject to license by the Department. The controls had been imposed in order to prevent the dollar assets of the invaded countries from falling into the possession of the invaders, and also to protect American institutions from possible adverse claims arising out of the invasions. As the international crisis deepened, Morgenthau wondered about shifting the emphasis of the controls from benevolent protection to active economic warfare.

When Italy attacked France, Morgenthau wanted to freeze Italian funds, but to that time all controls had applied only to the victims of aggression rather than to the aggressors themselves. The Secretary, unable to alter that policy without the approval of the State Department, explored all possible courses both with his own staff and with Hull's.

There was, to begin with, the imminent need to extend controls to France, and the related advantage of extending them also to Switzerland so as to prevent the Germans there from working to acquire securities or other properties of Europeans who were citizens of the conquered nations. A broader venture contemplated the inclusion of Germany, Poland, Czechoslovakia, Italy, and Albania, on the ground, among others, that the United States could not completely prevent an aggressor from realizing looted assets without controlling the aggressor's own accounts. Further, by extending controls to Germany and Italy, the United States would be able more effectively to combat subversive activities of the Axis and also to regulate exchange operations involving Axis exports in the Far East. Still broader solutions contemplated covering the whole world, or all Europe except for Great Britain and Ireland, perhaps by issuing a general license for those two nations.

Those large formulas would multiply administrative costs and problems both for the government and for American business firms, would impair the status of New York as a free international financial market, and would probably lead to German and Italian retaliation against American balances abroad. Yet in Morgenthau's view, the benefits of a general freezing outweighed the liabilities. A broad policy would permit the Treasury to supervise the use of some $100 to $200 million of German and Italian funds, to reduce American remittances to the Axis countries, and, in the event of a weakening of the British blockade of Europe, to minimize exports to the Axis, even to the point of embargo. Such controls would also help to protect American security markets against large-scale selling by residents of Switzerland or in the name of Swiss firms. "My own feeling," Morgenthau concluded by mid-June 1940, "is that I would do it one-hundred per cent or do it exclusively of the British Empire."

Yet there were counterbalancing political disadvantages. The policy Morgenthau advocated would constitute an overt unneutral step, for which the American public, in Hull's opinion, was not ready, particularly if Germany countered with measures drawing the United States closer to war. Though Berle and James Dunn, among Hull's advisers, supported the Treasury's conclusions, the Secretary of State overruled them, and on June 17, 1940, won Roosevelt's endorsement.

German gains during the next six months brought Morgenthau to try again to make his case. As he told Felix Frankfurter, there was no one at the State Department with whom he could talk candidly except for Dean Acheson. Frankfurter recommended taking Hull to the White House to talk the question out in front of the President. Only Roosevelt, Frankfurter said, "can settle it, and decide and dispose of it." Morgenthau, skeptical, asked, "Have you ever known the President to work like that?" Frankfurter, laughing, urged the Secretary to humor Hull: "Listen, Henry, just remember one thing that . . . you can afford to do anything in the cause, number two, you're thirty years younger than he is."

"I am really terribly worried," Morgenthau wrote Hull on January 27, 1941, "that we have not frozen German, Italian, and Swiss funds. At your convenience, I would like very much to have a heart-to-heart talk with you on this subject, and see if we cannot arrive at a meeting of the minds as to what course to pursue in these difficult times." The talk took place in Hull's office on January 30, where the two secretaries were accompanied by various of their subordinates; but once again there was no meeting of the minds.

There matters stood until February 10, 1941, when Morgenthau returned from a short holiday in Arizona. At the White House he then "brought up the question of frozen funds and told the President about my conversation with the State Department the day I left, and he seemed very much interested. . . . As I said, I felt confident that while it would take us two years to get ready to get an army of a million four hundred thousand men fully equipped, that within two weeks we could have an effective economic warfare starting."

Since the previous June, Morgenthau added in a memorandum for the President of February 14, he had been urging the extension of controls to cover at least the property of the Axis powers in the United States. In the last few days there had been further evidence of the wisdom of that policy and of the danger of delay. The Axis nations were systematically converting their dollar assets to cash or removing them to places or agencies beyond the reach of potential American control. Since January 1, 1941, Italian agents had withdrawn from a single bank in New York over $6 million, always specifying that they wanted old currency. The Italian government in that time had built up a $10 million account with the Bank of Brazil. Within the previous month the Yokohama Specie Bank in New York had transferred to Brazil over $6 million, and the Treasury had just received word that that Japanese bank was negotiating with the National Bank of Haiti to take over all of its New York accounts and to handle all of its business in the Western Hemisphere. Further, companies ostensibly of Swiss and Swedish ownership had been creating dummy corporations in Haiti and Panama to hold American securities.

In a memorandum of the same day Hull again objected to a general freezing order. Exchange controls might curb espionage and subversion, but Ameican assets in Germany and Japan were worth four times the assets of those countries in the United States; Russia, if offended, might rush to the side of Japan; and Switzerland and Sweden toward Germany. The national interest, Hull argued, required only the registration of assets until a tougher policy became essential for the defense of the United States.

Undeterred, Morgenthau at a dinner party on February 20 worked hard on Norman Davis, the American diplomat for whom Hull had perhaps the greatest respect. "At first," Morgenthau noted, "Norman Davis took the same attitude that Hull has . . . but then when we got along in the discussion he said what he really believed in was that we should freeze all countries and then exempt our friends. In other words, he claimed to agree with the exact position which I have taken from the beginning."

By the end of February, Roosevelt had also drawn closer to that view. Adopting various of the Treasury's earlier suggestions, the President on February 26 sent a memorandum to Hull, Attorney General Jackson, and Morgenthau. He began by remarking the urgency of controlling the assets and properties of foreigners in the United States. "I am sure," he wrote, "that this is a matter that needs to be prosecuted at once, and, after considering the various proposals, it seems to me the most satisfactory one is to have a Committee composed of the Secretary of State, the Secretary of the Treasury, and the Attorney General to approve of any actions that are to be taken by the Treasury. It is clear to me that all three Departments are vitally involved, and I should like, therefore, to have the approval of all the Departments prior to any recommendation for action whenever a specific proposal is submitted to me for approval. Inasmuch as the Treasury is responsible for the actual issuance of the orders, I believe that it would be advisable to have the Secretary of the Committee chosen from the Treasury staff."

The solution was typically Rooseveltian. The structure of the committee gave special weight to Treasury influence, but the State Department retained a full veto. And within the committee, which began meetings the next day, the Treasury representatives and their counterparts from the Department of State failed at first in the least to alter the old impasse.

During the first week of March the issue reached crisis proportions. Germany had then invaded Bulgaria, and Morgenthau and Hull confronted each other over the question of whether to apply freezing controls to Bulgaria only, as Hull desired, or more widely, to the entire European continent, as the Treasury, with the support of Dean Acheson, advised. Again the President supported Hull, whose immobility contributed to Morgenthau's growing dismay. "As far as I am concerned, I am licked in the State Department. I can't do anything with Mr. Hull," Morgenthau told his staff. ". . . . On the oil to Japan, the question of doing something to keep Russia happy, or the question of freezing funds, all of those things which the President wants and I have just worked myself to a frazzle and Mr. Hull gets madder and madder at me and is a worse enemy and so forth and so on. Well, the President has him as a spokesman. He is his Secretary of State. I am through being the President's whipping boy on the foreign affairs stuff. . . . Let the President of the United States do it. . . . He tells me that is what he wants and I go ahead and try to bull it through and Mr. Hull gets mad at me. . . . Let the President of the United States tell Mr. Hull what kind of a document he wants."

Yet at the end of April Morgenthau took encouragement from Roosevelt's signing of an order freezing all Greek credits and assets, some $40 to $50 million. Greece was the fourteenth country to fall under exchange controls, which then affected over $4 billion. As the piecemeal extension of freezing spread gradually over Europe in pace with German conquest of the continent, the argument for holding back from a general order became weaker. On April 30, Acheson urged Morgenthau to try once more to enlist the Secretary of State. Understandably, Morgenthau hesitated, reluctant to "be all the time put in the position that we here are trying to push ourselves." The situation had changed, Acheson said, for "you are not pushing for something. It is we who are." In that case, Morgenthau replied, "let Mr. Hull say so. Let him say so formally, but I don't want to read in the papers that this is another plan of the Treasury bright boys."

Hull assented in part on May 5, 1941. He and Morgenthau and Jackson that day requested the President to enlarge the authority and increase the staff and budget of their committee so that it could make recommendations for the control not only of foreign funds but also of foreign trade and related matters. This proposal, which Roosevelt approved while keeping the committee informal, came close to creating the kind of board of economic warfare Morgenthau had suggested months earlier. On June 12, 1941, Hull went still further and signed a recommendation for freezing the funds of all European nations, provided

general licenses exempt, under stipulated conditions, Switzerland, Sweden, Spain, Portugal, and Russia. Explaining Hull's
new attitude, Acheson said that the Secretary of State now felt
that Hitler was working toward a united states of Europe, and
that controlling the assets of all the European neutrals might
play into the dictator's hands. But Hull at last recognized the
advantages of freezing German and Italian funds, especially to
prevent their use in propaganda. Since the State Department
formula represented a great advance, Morgenthau, as he told
Acheson, was "very excited and pleased. . . . I think we really
are going to make some headway this time." So they did, for
Hull's acquiescence provided the unanimity on policy which
Roosevelt had been seeking.

A month later, on July 17, 1941, Morgenthau, Hull, and Jackson commended a further step which the President also took. He
issued a proclamation authorizing the promulgation of a "proclaimed list of certain blocked nationals." The list was to consist
of individuals deemed to be acting for the benefit of Germany or
Italy or of nationals of those countries, and persons to whom the
exportation of various articles was held to be detrimental to the
interests of national defense. On those bases, freezing orders,
where necessary, could cover Swiss or Swedish or other neutral
citizens or firms. The first proclaimed list included more than
800 persons and businesses in the American republics. It gave the
Treasury substantially the authority which Morgenthau had
been seeking for more than a year. Meanwhile, he had begun to
demand not just the freezing of foreign funds but a whole system
of economic warfare, including embargoes on the shipment of
strategic materials to the Axis nations. It was his demand for an
embargo against Japan that brought Morgenthau, from June of
1940 onward, into his stormiest conflicts with the Department of
State.

XVI

IN THE GLARE
OF THE RISING SUN
JUNE 1940–DECEMBER 1941

HITLER'S CONQUEST of Western Europe had grave consequences in the Orient. The fall of the Netherlands and France shattered the power of those nations in Asia, while England's peril tied her fleet to the Atlantic and her home waters. French Indochina and the Dutch East Indies cowered before the threat of Japanese aggression. During June 1940, while the Nazis infested British skies, Japanese diplomats brought England temporarily to close access to the Burma Road, China's only useful avenue of supplies from the West.

The United States, hampered by deficiencies in military preparedness and by the burden of supplying Britain's most immediate needs, could not redress the balance of power in Asia. Yet limited means were available for deterring Japan. An embargo could reduce her access to critical stocks of oil and steel. So too, the provisioning of China could sustain the continuing resistance to Japan on the mainland and thus, in some degree, restrain her advance elsewhere. As ever, deterrence entailed risks. The senior officers of the Army and Navy persistently opposed any threat to Japan which might bring on a war for which the United States was unready. That was the position, too, of Cordell Hull and Sumner Welles. Ranged against them were Stanley Hornbeck, the State Department's expert on the Far East, Harold Ickes, Henry Stimson, and, often and vehemently, Morgenthau, all of whom hoped that Japan was bluffing, and believed that American determination might call her bluff and forestall aggression without provoking war. As the two groups argued, and as the strategy of Japanese encroachments unfolded, Roosevelt shifted his support now one way, now the other, enlisting fully with neither side. For Morgenthau, therefore, the process of making policy for Asia fell into the worrisome pattern of all policy in 1940, a pattern of continual competition for the President's influence, of continual conflict with the State Department and cooperation with the War Department, of continuous tension and sporadic success.

1. China: "Pretty Hopeless?"

On the morning of June 28, 1940, Morgenthau received two Chinese visitors whom he had known for years. One was Ambassador Hu Shih, the other, T. V. Soong, now in Washington as the personal emissary of his brother-in-law, the Generalissimo. "General Chiang Kai-shek wanted me to come over and see the President and members of the administration because of the changed situation in the world," Soong began. "We all had expected, hoped, that it would be victory for the democracies and now France has . . . collapsed and England is fighting for its very existence. This means a change in our world outlook as well as yours and . . . we would like to be able to consult . . . and . . . let the President know what is our internal situation, our military strength, our relations with various countries including Russia."

Soong explained that, even though the overland route was difficult, the Chinese were still getting supplies regularly from the Soviet Union, including all their airplanes as well as many pilots. The planes were "on a par with the Japanese as far as quality goes," but there were not enough of them. The Japanese were raiding Chungking daily with about 150 planes, against which the Chinese could send up only 20 or 25.

"Pretty hopeless, isn't it?" Morgenthau asked.

"Very difficult," Soong said, "but we still manage to shoot two or three down because we have pursuits and the Japanese still have to use bombers, which . . . are slower."

The Russians had made "no political demands," Soong reported. "Of course they must be interested in the Chinese communists, but so far . . . they have been very correct. Never even mentioned them." As for those Chinese Communists, they had a special army "which is not very large in numbers and not very efficient, because poorly armed and more fitted for guerrilla warfare than stiff pitched battles."

Chiang Kai-shek had guerrillas of his own, whose harassing operations provided the core of Chinese resistance to Japan. In order to pay these forces and to prevent the continuing depreciation of the currency, the Generalissimo needed an American loan. Both Soong and Arthur Young, Chiang's American financial adviser, had sought a Stabilization loan for more than a year. The decline in the value of the yuan, which had dropped from 16 cents in mid-1939 to 4 cents in May of 1940, portended a total collapse of Nationalist currency unless the United States furnished dollars or gold to support it. Further, Soong argued that China needed and could repay another American credit against shipments of tung oil and tungsten, which could be delivered, he contended, in spite of difficulties in transportation.

Friendly but dubious, Morgenthau concluded after studying the situation that the proposed loan was "beyond the legitimate scope of our Stabilization Fund operations." The Secretary's advisers persuaded him that Soong had exaggerated both the benefits of a loan and the dangers of a collapse of the Chinese currency. The Nationalist government, unable to control exchange operations, could not prevent either illegitimate flights of capital or Japanese raids on the yuan. Only if the United States was prepared to lose up to $100 million within the next year or two was there much hope of stabilizing the yuan at its existing level, and such a sum might be better spent on material aid to the Chinese. Furthermore, under existing law the Export-Import Bank could not offer China a new credit. In the Treasury's judgment, moreover, notwithstanding Soong's optimism, the debilitation of Chinese transportation made almost impossible the delivery of significant quantities of goods. Indeed, the Chinese had placed less than $4 million of orders against the last $20 million credit they had received. Cargoes were piling up at Haiphong, and the Japanese were cutting off traffic out of Indochina. A new credit would serve only to bring prestige to Soong for arranging it and to Chiang Kai-shek for receiving it.

Persuaded by Morgenthau's analysis, Roosevelt rejected the repeated pleas of Soong and Young for a Stabilization loan and an Export-Import Bank credit. But like Morgenthau, the President wanted to assist the Chinese. According to Soong's report to Morgenthau on July 9, 1940, Roosevelt had suggested an American loan against Chinese tungsten provided the Chinese "would use that money to buy from Russia." Morgenthau, who suspected that that suggestion was "too simple to suit the President," first added an ingredient to the scheme by proposing to buy manganese from the Soviet Union "on condition that Russia help China," and then "tried to find out what he [Soong] had in mind in the way of a three-way loan and he had nothing." Soong still preferred an outright American loan and a credit for the purchase of weapons and construction equipment.

Morgenthau, in contrast, warmed to the possibility of a tripartite arrangement, but as Sumner Welles reminded him on July 28, 1940, the Russians were "very angry because we have frozen the Latvian, Estonian, and Lithuanian money. . . . He had talked to the President and the President agreed the matter ought to be postponed." Morgenthau agreed, too. He had explored the question of a tripartite exchange, he noted several months later, "because I wanted some place, somewhere in the whole government, some person who would carry out the President's mandate, do something to keep Russia on the fence so we can keep peace in the Pacific. . . . I wasn't carrying out my own personal wishes. It was what the President wanted."

Since neither he nor the President as yet saw any merit in a Stabilization loan or any point in a credit for procuring weapons that could not reach China, the Secretary had begun to urge instead an alternative policy for containing Japan, an embargo on shipments of oil and steel.

2. Partial Embargo

On two accounts, Morgenthau was distressed by the absence of government controls over shipments of oil and scrap to Japan. An embargo, he believed, would preserve those important resources for American defense and impair Japanese military strength. Further, at a time when aggression was sweeping across Europe, an embargo would signify the determination of the United States to resist it in the Orient. Hull, on the other hand, remained hesitant about using any of the weapons of economic warfare. The Secretary of State feared that withholding oil from Japan would drive the Japanese into the oil-rich Netherlands Indies. The disagreement between the two Cabinet officers contributed to Roosevelt's indecisiveness. Tired of evasion at the White House, Morgenthau urged the President to delegate responsibility over the export of strategic materials to one Cabinet department, though not necessarily to the Treasury. But Roosevelt, as the Secretary noted in his Diary of June 26, wanted "to do it his own way and wants to keep the authority under himself."

The President retained that authority by scattering it. He directed the materials and production divisions of the National Defense Advisory Commission to cooperate with the Administrator of Export Control in determining the extent and character of the restrictions to be applied to the export of ammunition, raw materials, and machinery essential for national defense. The Department of State was to issue the necessary licenses, but the Administrator, Lieutenant Colonel Russell L. Maxwell, was to serve

directly under the supervision of the President. It was "a wonderful and weird system" that exactly suited Hull. The appointment of Maxwell, in his view, "ended a long struggle initiated by
Secretary . . . Morgenthau to wrest from the State Department control over exports and imports of arms . . . and implements of war."

The struggle had not ended, for the new arrangements in no
way diminished Morgenthau's enthusiasm for an embargo. On
July 18, 1940, the Secretary dined at the British embassy with
Lord Lothian, Ambassador Casey of Australia, Secretary of War
Stimson, and Secretary of the Navy Knox. During conversation
after dinner, according to Morgenthau's memory the next morning, Stimson asked Lothian "how you can expose Australia . . .
to Japan by giving in to Japan on the Burma Road? . . . The
only way to treat Japan is not to give in to her on anything."

"Mr. Casey and I went to see Mr. Hull," Lothian replied, obviously upset, "and told him that we would say no to Japan if the
United States would join us. . . . As a matter of fact, we did
say no in the first instance, but the United States would give us
no assurance, so we had to say yes. . . . After all, you are continuing to ship aviation gasoline to Japan."

"Nobody," Morgenthau broke in, "has asked me or even suggested to me that we stop shipping aviation gasoline." Stimson
said that in speeches during the last year he had been making
precisely that point.

"If you will stop shipping aviation gasoline to Japan," Lothian
suggested, "we will blow up the oil wells in the Dutch East Indies so that the Japanese can't come down and get that . . . we
have felt that if we put too much pressure on Japan they would
go down and take those oil wells." At the same time the Royal
Air Force could concentrate its bombing attacks on German
plants producing synthetic gasoline.

His "breath . . . taken away," Morgenthau said he would
propose the idea "at once." Stimson encouraged him, remarking
incidentally that so long as Japan was tied down in China she was
unlikely to make excursions farther south.

On his way home from the dinner Morgenthau decided to proceed through Harold Ickes, who, during the last Cabinet meeting, had advocated a total embargo on oil in order to conserve declining American fuel reserves. If Ickes could now carry that case with the President, Morgenthau felt that it "would keep the State Department from opposing the idea . . . and then it would be up to us to find out and make certain that there is enough oil flowing from Venezuela and Colombia which the British could get to take care of themselves." If then the British "would blow up the wells, it would simply electrify the world and really put some belief in England." Destruction of the wells, Morgenthau surmised, would eliminate Japanese ambitions for the Dutch East Indies and thus encourage the Australians, who were "shaking like aspen leaves." Lothian's plan would entirely alter the situation in the Pacific, whereas "if we don't do something and do it fast, Japan is just going to gobble up one thing after another."

Morgenthau elaborated his thoughts in a memorandum of July 19, 1940, for Roosevelt and Ickes. That day at the White House the Secretary "told the President that this thing might give us peace in three to six months and he read the thing very carefully. . . . The President was tremendously interested. He said this is very much along the idea he had a couple of months ago whereby he was talking about blockading all of Europe and just leaving a small channel open directly to England through which all ships would have to pass. . . . He then went on down and talked about the wells in Iraq, and so on. After he had been going on about half an hour, they came in and said Stimson and Knox were outside and he said, 'What do you think of having them in?' I said, 'By all means,' they were great guys."

Sumner Welles — Hull was away at the Havana Conference of American Republics — also joined them, and there followed what Stimson described as a "very important conference on the general situation in the world." At an opportune moment, Roosevelt presented the proposal which he had just received, without attributing it to Morgenthau, but Welles maintained that it would cause the Japanese to make war on Great Britain. Morgenthau and Stimson "argued very hard . . . and Stimson gave his usual argument, that the only way to treat Japan is not to retreat. And then Welles talked about . . . making peace for China and Japan, that is what we want."

The meeting ended without a decision. Riled, Morgenthau told his staff about the "beautiful Chamberlain talk that I listened to Sumner Welles give. . . . Everything is going to be lovely. And after that then Japan is going to come over and kiss our big toe. . . . Thank heavens we have a Stimson with us." Thankful also for Ickes, Morgenthau still hoped for a favorable decision, as he soon explained: "Now, if we begin scrap iron, then the State Department will say Japan will fight, but they can't say Japan is going to fight if we are doing this as a matter of conservation and national defense. We will say no oil can leave the United States and that was the trick in this thing that pulled the main argument away from the State Department. . . . The State Department just drives me crazy."

To Roosevelt, in Hyde Park on July 22, Morgenthau telegraphed that "valuable strategic materials" were "slipping through our fingers every day." At the same time the Secretary suggested to Ickes that "if you could see your way clear, if necessary and the President wanted to use it, to say that no oil should leave this country for national defense and conservation . . . it would be terribly helpful." Ickes was glad to help, impatient with the way the State Department had "piddled around," and convinced that "if we'd stopped sending scrap iron to Japan a couple of years ago . . . the world would be different today." With his own opinion reinforced, Morgenthau called the National Defense Commission and asked Ed Stettinius whether he could "on an hour's notice . . . give us a justification for clamping on an embargo on scrap iron or scrap steel products." Within a few days, Stettinius concluded that supplies of scrap steel were already below the margin of safety, that exports should therefore be restricted, and that Japanese purchases might well be curtailed.

Anticipating that conclusion, Morgenthau on July 22, 1940, wrote the President to advocate the addition of petroleum, petroleum products, and scrap metals to the list of strategic materials subject to embargo. "I'm very glad you've done that," Stimson commented.

On July 24, 1940, the Secretary of War learned from the Fourth Corps Commander at San Francisco of immense Japanese purchases of aviation oil. Japan, the Army officer reported, while apparently trying to corner the market on deliveries for 1940, seemed uninterested in deliveries thereafter. Stimson at once telephoned Morgenthau, who urged him to send the *"most important"* report to Roosevelt. Morgenthau also wrote Roosevelt himself.

Persuaded at last, the President on July 25, 1940, issued orders, based upon Treasury memoranda, placing scrap metals and oil and oil products on the list of vital materials which were not to leave the country. The State Department, "terribly upset" according to White House reports, redrafted the orders to bring them into accord with its own emerging plans, which confined the embargo to high-octane gasoline, airplane motor oil, and tetraethyl lead, as well as number one heavy melting-grade iron and steel scrap. A total embargo on oil, the Department argued, would be "administratively tremendously difficult," whereas the revised rules would still seriously hamper the Japanese air force. Unimpressed, Morgenthau suggested that if the State Department could not handle the larger plan, it should "give it to somebody else to do." He also asked Stimson and Ickes to help him in the "big row." Both, in Stimson's words, promised "to go the limit on it."

That afternoon Morgenthau took to Cabinet meeting a letter of protest against the proposed change in the President's orders. That change, the letter read, "would be a most serious mistake, since crude oil and various other petroleum products can be converted into aviation gasoline and this restriction would not apply to diesel oil, used by submarines and tanks. . . . I understand that the State Department's objection is that the sweeping petroleum and scrap embargo could not be administered effectively. May I most respectfully suggest that if the Division of Controls of the State Department and the Administrator of Export Controls cannot administer this proclamation effectively the Treasury Department can. As a practical matter the enforcement of the embargo . . . is a comparatively easy problem. In the case of Foreign Exchange Control, which is a much more complex problem . . . the Treasury has not found the task impossible of achievement, nor has the effort expended been unjustified by the results achieved. The objections raised to the oil and scrap metal control reinforce a growing impression on my part that there is something very seriously wrong with the personnel or system in effect for administering the export controls."

The Cabinet meeting, as Stimson reported it, was frantic. Welles and Morgenthau struck out at each other as soon as it began, and "the President raised his hands in the air, refused to participate in it and said that those two men must go off in a corner and settle their issue. Accordingly, after the Cabinet meeting . . . Morgenthau and Welles got together and thrashed it out. I myself was very glad to find that my own views as to aviation oil had been apparently now accepted by the State Department, and also scrap iron. Morgenthau had apparently won his victory in substance."

Morgenthau considered the victory significant but incomplete. It was, as Stimson said, "a comparatively minor matter" that the State Department still controlled export licenses, but it was a major matter that Japan could still obtain most categories of scrap iron and steel, and crude oil which was convertible for aviation and other uses.

3. Parries and Counters

Simultaneously with the American decision to impose a limited embargo against Japan, the Japanese reached important decisions of their own. The new Konoye cabinet, after ten days in power, on July 26 and 27, 1940, agreed upon an "Outline of Basic National Policy," domestic and international. This called for "mobilizing the total strength of the nation" in order to settle the

"China affair," an objective that entailed the complete closing of China's access through the south to the rest of the world. For that purpose, and to establish a New Order in Asia, the government determined to tighten its ties to Germany and Italy, "to strengthen policies toward French Indo-China, Hongkong and the Settlements, to check assistance to the Chiang regime," and to press "the diplomatic policy" for obtaining oil and other raw materials from the Netherlands East Indies. These goals, which portended increased totalitarianism at home, were announced in guarded language to the Japanese people on August 1. At that time Japanese diplomats also protested against the American embargo, which had neither brought the Konoye government to its definition of policy nor decreased that government's resolve.

The Japanese also pressed their demands upon the French in Indochina. They wanted the right of transit for their troops, the right to construct airfields, and an agreement which would in effect bring Indochina within their economic sphere. Gradually the French gave in. Advised by the State Department that the United States could offer no armed assistance, the government in Vichy had little choice but to yield to Tokyo. In a political pact of August 29 the Japanese recognized the "permanent French interest in Indo-China," while the French in turn recognized the "preponderance of Japanese interest in that area."

Japanese gains moved the State Department toward a harder policy. On September 22 the French decided to permit Japan to station some 6000 troops in Indochina. Permission for those forces to march through the country to the Chinese border was imminent. The Japanese were continuing, too, to insult British nationals and other Westerners in China, while also increasing the pressure for guarantees of oil shipments from the Netherlands Indies. American Ambassador Joseph C. Grew in Tokyo, long an advocate of restraint, now concluded that Japan was "one of the predatory powers; having submerged all ethical and moral sense, she has become unashamedly and frankly opportunist. . . . American interests in the Pacific are definitely threatened by her policy of southward expansion. . . . If the support of the British Empire . . . is conceived to be in our interest . . .

we must strive by every means to preserve the status quo in the Pacific, at least until the war in Europe has been won or lost. This cannot be done . . . merely by the expression of disapproval. . . . Japan has been deterred . . . only because she respects our potential power."

That analysis impressed Roosevelt, who at a Cabinet meeting of late September opened discussion of American policy in Asia and the Pacific. As Stimson recalled that meeting, "Morgenthau and I pretty strongly supported" a complete embargo on oil which "fitted in with the President's own ideas of strategy. . . . The State Department has been getting a little weak on that point. . . ."

While supporting Stimson, Morgenthau also, as he told his staff, "got across today the most important thing I've done this year. . . . After Mr. Hull said he wanted to do something, then he went on to say that there is no use in doing anything on oil. So I said, 'Well, if they really want to do something to set Japan back on her heels, take the President's suggestion of a couple of months ago of the three-corner deal with Russia, China, and ourselves. That would really mean something to Japan. . . .' Of course, Stimson is always very helpful. . . . I drove it pretty hard. This went on for about twenty minutes to a half hour. . . . During the thing I said that if the President would direct me to do this, . . . with the help of Jesse Jones I would like to do it. . . . The conversation stopped and the President said, 'Henry, I guess you had better get hold of the Russians and start your talk.' So . . . Hull spoke up and said, 'Well, before you have the final arrangement and give it to the press, I would like to be consulted,' and I said, 'Well, absolutely. . . .' So . . . we are on our way.

"Hull is out on the end of the limb. He has twice scolded Japan if she goes into Indo-China. According to Hull, she is going into Indo-China and he is going to say, 'Boys, I am going to lend some money to Indo-China,' which they know they can't buy arms with. I'd pointed that out at the meeting. He is going to do something about scrap iron, but he won't touch oil, and I made a big talk on oil."

The Secretary was most excited about the opportunity to approach the Russians, but as Hull put it, "this Russian outfit — I don't think you could depend on them a split second to do anything for China more than what they are doing or would be disposed to do anyhow. . . . They are utterly as unreliable as Jesse James. . . . Now, we want to go as far as possible on a loan and on an iron scrap embargo as quickly as Japan settles in Indo-China, and it's a question of how far we can go without running too much a risk of a military clash. Now this sort of a loan to China would obviate that. They couldn't make serious complaints about a purchasing loan like we made before if the Chinamen are disposed. So I thought . . . of . . . avoiding possibly two brash acts with Japan all at once."

"Well, Cordell," Morgenthau replied, "unless you tell me definitely you object — this fellow will be here in twenty minutes — and I thought I'd very diplomatically just throw out a hint along the lines that the President asked me to. . . . I realize that it's a very, very ticklish thing and if the President hadn't specifically said to go ahead, I wouldn't have dreamed of doing it."

Minutes later Jesse Jones and Russian Ambassador Oumansky arrived at the Treasury, and on September 25 the Russian reported that the Soviet Union, while unwilling to link any exchange with the United States to China, was "prepared to deliver . . . raw materials. . . . There is a feasible route." "It seems to me," Morgenthau told Roosevelt on September 26, ". . . that it would be distinctly useful within the next day or two to conclude an arrangement by which we bought some manganese." He had told Oumansky, Morgenthau added, that "he would have to make the next move. He left me with the impression that he would, but I have my doubts."

At the Cabinet meeting of September 27, 1940, Hull, who had larger doubts, again objected to negotiations with the Russians, "saying in the strongest language," as Stimson reported him, "that they couldn't be trusted for a minute." Backing Morgenthau, Stimson said that "while I felt that Russia was just as bad . . . as Hull did, nevertheless she had very different interests in the Pacific than she did in Europe and . . . in the Pacific her interests ran parallel with ours and . . . probably she could be trusted to go along as far as her interests went and that was all we need ask."

That day the future of both Europe and the Pacific looked grim, for Japan, Germany, and Italy signed a new treaty in Berlin. They promised to cooperate with each other in their efforts "in Greater East Asia and the regions of Europe" to establish and maintain "a new order of things, calculated to promote the mutual prosperity and welfare of peoples concerned." They further agreed to assist one another "with all political, economic and military means" if any one of them was attacked "by a power at present not involved in the European war or in the Chinese-Japanese conflict." Manifestly, the alliance was intended to warn the United States against joining Great Britain in her war with Germany and against embarking on hostilities with Japan. Disturbed by the latter possibility, the Japanese on their own recognizances were resolved to avoid inciting the United States or England, and to improve their relations with the Soviet Union while they pushed onward against French and Dutch territories and on the Chinese mainland.

Morgenthau and Stimson, outraged by the new pact and yet instinctively aware of Japan's preferred diplomatic strategy, were more eager than ever before to tie Russia to American policy in the Far East. Yet a new approach through Chiang Kai-shek failed to win the Soviet Union to a triangular exchange agreement, and though negotiations went on in Moscow, Roosevelt on October 3 told Morgenthau that he expected the Russians to "continue their Mugwump policy of sitting on the fence."

Looking again to an alternative deterrent, Morgenthau and Stimson at the Cabinet meeting of October 4, 1940, urged "straight out" action that would "show the Japs we meant business and were not afraid of them." Both men advocated tightening the embargo on oil, but Hull still objected, partly because he had promised the Dutch government to do nothing about oil so long as Dutch talks with the Japanese were continuing. Roosevelt, though he had made the Treasury a kind of statistical clearinghouse for data about oil, remained unwilling to overrule his

Secretary of State, particularly with the election just a month away and the problem of aid for England never more severe. Scolding Morgenthau privately, the President had said pointedly that he and Hull were "handling foreign affairs."

4. China: New Commitments

Late in October the British reopened the Burma Road, which provided a rough route for moving weapons into China, but in the fall of 1940 the United States had no weapons to spare. Roosevelt therefore looked to other expedients. "The President," Morgenthau told his staff on November 28, 1940, "just called me up and told me in strictest confidence . . . that he is sending part of the fleet to the southern part of the Philippines. He is worried about China . . . and he wants me to make a Stabilization loan of fifty million dollars to the Chinese in the next twenty-four hours . . . and he is telling Jones to make another fifty. It would be a one hundred million dollar loan, and he says Cordell Hull insists that we put somebody in there to manage it. We lend them the money, but it would be under our direction, so he said I should get a hold of the committee chairmen and notify them that I am going to do this."

The committee chairmen were those congressmen whom Morgenthau had promised to consult "before we would use the Stabilization Fund . . . to assist a country in prosecuting . . . war." That promise now annoyed Roosevelt. "I am going to make this announcement," he told Morgenthau at the Cabinet meeting of November 29, "but I want your word, Henry, that if I make the announcement, even though Congress turns you down . . . you will go through with it. . . . It is a matter of life and death. . . . If I don't do it . . . it may mean war in the Far East." At a large dinner party that night where many of the guests were not members of the administration, Roosevelt put

Morgenthau right on the rack. "Let me tell you what happened in Cabinet," the President said. "I said I want some money, and I thought I would have a lot of trouble with Jesse Jones and it would be easy to get it from Henry." Then, according to Morgenthau's report, Roosevelt "went on and told the story about how nice Jones was and how he gave him fifty million dollars and what a mean cuss I was."

The next day T. V. Soong urged Morgenthau to hurry, even if he had to break his promise to Congress, for the Japanese had formally recognized the puppet Chinese government at Nanking, and Soong thought the world was waiting to see what the United States would do. "The Germans have made secret proposals to Chiang for peace terms," Welles explained, "and there is a danger of real psychological moral lapse as a result of this recognition of the one regime, and our hope is, of course, that this will act as an immediate counteractive. If you wait for two or three days, the effect might be too long delayed." Convinced, Morgenthau agreed immediately to make a public statement about the loan. Welles cleared it with the White House, and that afternoon a Treasury news release announced that the United States was contemplating a $100 million credit to China, half of it for "purposes of monetary . . . management as between American and Chinese currencies."

The Chinese were quietly unhappy about any surveillance over their parlous finances, and they were discontented with the actual deliveries during 1940 of American supplies — at best some $9 million worth, a meager amount even allowing for the months the Burma Road was closed. Tensions about the currency loan came to a head first, partly because factionalism within the Kuomintang led the Generalissimo to delay the appointment of a Chinese member of the committee to supervise the use of the money. Further, the G'imo declared the British nominee to that committee *persona non grata*. Morgenthau refused to advance any money until a proper committee had been selected, a position taken also by the British, who were contributing to the Stabilization Fund.

While arguing Chungking's case, Soong also suggested that

China would gain if her assets and Japan's were frozen in the United States. American control of Chinese assets would help the Chinese government to prevent leaks of dollars and bullion. Unless the United States also blocked Japanese assets, the Japanese would be able to move goods out of China into Japan and thence to the United States as Japanese products. Soong's suggestions reached the Treasury at the time that the State Department was bitterly opposed to any extension of freezing controls. The application of those controls to Japan, which in the view of the State Department would provoke retaliation, would also give the Treasury licensing power over all Japanese transactions, including oil imports, a prospect that was anathema to Hull.

Morgenthau was content temporarily to accede to Hull's wishes, partly because of the absence of reliable information about Chinese currency, partly because of depressing reports about other conditions in China — the swirl of inflation, the demand for a negotiated peace with Japan put forward by fascist factions within the Kuomintang, the persisting problem of the Communists, whom Chiang Kai-shek had yet either to mobilize as partners against Japan or to defeat as enemies for the control of the Government, and the indecisiveness and corruption of the G'imo's entourage.

Indeed, by April 1941 relations with the Chinese had, for Morgenthau, assumed the quality of mad inextricability that they were never to lose. Japan's diplomacy in Asia made China's fate both more important and less predictable than ever before, while the tragicomedy of Chiang's government, already beyond credulity or melioration, had at least yielded one good appointment, that of the expert and trustworthy K. P. Chen as Chinese representative on the Stabilization committee. By April Chiang Kai-shek had requested from the United States immediate Lend-Lease assistance, theretofore discussed but delayed; immediate payment of the full $50 million Stabilization loan, $30 million of which Morgenthau wanted to disburse at the rate of $5 million a month on evidence of sanity in Chinese finance; and the immediate imposition of freezing controls on Chinese and Japanese assets. Of these, the second was easiest for Roosevelt to grant. British and American requirements left little for China from Lend-Lease, and Hull still opposed freezing controls; but the loan had been promised, and the President wanted Morgenthau to turn over the money without regard for protecting it. At the White House on April 21, 1941, the Secretary received gentle but unequivocal orders: "The President said to me, 'We have to do something for the Chinese in order to save their face. . . . I want you to make that $50 million loan right away.' I did not say anything for a few minutes because I wanted a chance to get control of myself. Then I said, 'Well, Mr. President, that is just like throwing it away.' He said, 'I know but it is a question of face saving.' . . .

"The President then said, 'I'll tell you what to do, Henry. . . . Let them have the $50 million but get them to give you their word of honor that they will not use more than $5 million a month over the $20 million.' I told him that I would go along with that. The President really tried to be fair, and I wanted to help him with that."

In this improved mood, Morgenthau at the Cabinet meeting of April 25, 1941, supported all three of Chiang Kai-shek's proposals. He was willing, he told the President, to recommend advancing the entire $50 million without restrictions "particularly in view of the fact that K. P. Chen had been made chairman of the committee to handle it." To this Roosevelt of course agreed. Harry Hopkins, he added, would take care of the Lend-Lease matter, but on the question of freezing the Chinese and Japanese funds, Morgenthau would have to negotiate with the State Department.

5. *Japan: Firmer Lines*

The Treasury's responsibilities for monetary matters, and Morgenthau's personal involvement in the allocation of American materials of war provided natural bases for the Secretary's influence on China policy during the early months of 1941, but he had no comparable reasons for being involved in decisions about Japan. Though removed from discussions of Japanese questions, Morgenthau had some occasion for gratification with the decisions of the President and the Department of State, for they followed the broad outlines of the Treasury's earlier recommendations. On December 30, 1940, the embargo on exports of iron and steel scrap became effective, except for licensed shipments to the United Kingdom. During January and February 1941, a series of Executive Orders extended the licensing system and thereby cut off from Japan American supplies of various chemicals, abrasives, measuring and testing instruments; certain grades of copper, brass, zinc, nickel and potash; aluminum foil, oil-refining machinery, radium, uranium, calf and goat skins. Those orders were designed to keep Japan from obtaining materials essential to her war-making capacity, and the piecemeal application of economic pressure was intended to avoid serious provocation. In both purposes American policy was partially successful. Japanese imports from the United States declined steadily, and even though oil shipments continued in large quantity (to Morgenthau's distress), the pinch of other shortages helped gradually to persuade Japanese officials to consider seeking an accommodation with the United States.

That possibility was diminished by the incompatibility of Japanese and American global strategies. While the President gave first priority to the demands of American defense and the war in Europe, he welcomed conversations between British and American naval officers in Washington and in Singapore. Those talks prepared a foundation — still informal — for American, British, Commonwealth, and Dutch military cooperation in the Pacific as well as in the Atlantic, and confirmed Roosevelt's abiding purpose to try to avoid war in the East while at the same time checking Japanese ambitions in China, Indochina, and the Netherlands Indies, ambitions which carried the threat of Japanese attack against Singapore and even Australia. For their part the Japanese persisted in their aim to dominate Southeast Asia politically and economically, and to conclude the "China incident" satisfactorily, but always if possible while avoiding hostilities with the

United States, Great Britain, or the Soviet Union. The tensions in the Orient, then, while increasing, spent their force along the lines of familiar vectors.

While the desirability of accommodation beguiled both Japan and the United States, the resulting negotiations exposed the near irreconcilability of their fixed and conflicting objectives. In April 1941 both sides took positions from which neither was disposed to retreat. For the United States, Hull laid down the principles that constituted a "paramount preliminary" for serious discussions. These called upon the Japanese to respect the territorial integrity and sovereignty of all nations, to refrain from interference in the internal affairs of other countries, to support equality of commercial opportunity, to abide by the status quo in the Pacific area except insofar as that status might be altered by peaceful means, and, by implication at least, to withdraw from the Rome-Berlin alliance. While talking abstractly, Hull was clearly requiring Japan to renounce designs on Indochina, the Netherlands Indies, and Malaya, and to withdraw from China. Only on that basis would the United States for its part remove restrictions on trade, cease support of Chiang Kai-shek, and take steps toward closer political and economic ties with Japan.

Those demands, rooted in traditional American policy toward Asia, were too much for the Japanese army and government, and probably, too, for Japanese public opinion. The "China incident" had already consumed too much of money, life, and grandeur to be abandoned now by diplomatic fiat, and even the moderates in Tokyo saw a primacy of Japanese interests in neighboring areas of the mainland. Those more extreme were resolved to exploit the opportunities for imperial expansion presented by the war in Europe. That determination gained timely reenforcement from Japan's successful completion on April 13, 1941, of a neutrality pact with the Soviet Union. Still Roosevelt gave Morgenthau no encouragement to offer counsel about Japan.

But Morgenthau could not keep out of it entirely, as was indicated by his Diary entry about the Cabinet meeting of July 18, 1941: "They brought up the question about Japan and Sumner

Welles* said he thought in two or three days, most likely by the twentieth, the Japanese were going to move on Indo-China. When it came to my turn, I said to the President, 'I would like to ask you a question which you may or may not want to answer. What are you going to do on the economic front against Japan if she makes this move?'

"Well, to my surprise the President gave us quite a lecture why we should not make any move because if we did, if we stopped all oil, it would simply drive the Japanese down to the Dutch East Indies, and it would mean war in the Pacific.

"As I remember it, Welles then spoke up and said that they were prepared, though, to freeze Japanese assets, so I said, 'If you are willing to freeze Japanese assets, why not Chinese assets because it was of very little significance to freeze the Japanese, but by freezing the Chinese we get the money in Shanghai.' And the President said that's all right with him; Welles said that's all right with him, and the President said, 'As long as we point out we are doing the Chinese end at the request of General Chiang Kaishek.'

"Ickes then said it was very embarrassing to him that beginning this Sunday we would have to begin to put in rationing of gasoline in the East — embarrassing that all this oil was going to Japan and we really needed the gasoline here, so couldn't he, Ickes, say that in as much as they were getting considerably more gasoline now than they were a year ago that they prorate it and only give them an amount equal to what they had been getting over a given period? And the President agreed to that.

"So I said, 'Well, in the name of conservation, couldn't you drop gasoline from 87 octane to 67?' and the President said, 'Why don't you do it?' And I said, 'because the State Department won't let me.' So Welles said, that was all right with him. . . . The part that pleases me is if I had not raised the question, none of this would have happened because nobody else raised it."

The next day Welles instructed his subordinates to prepare the papers necessary for the steps Morgenthau had described. On

* Sitting in place of Hull, who was then ill.

July 23 the British reported that they had discussed the question of freezing Japanese funds with the Dominions, the Netherlands, and the Free French, and all had agreed to the policy. Dean Acheson feared that it might hasten new Japanese aggression, and the Navy thought that an enlarged oil embargo might produce an early Japanese attack against Malaya and the Netherlands Indies, but Roosevelt overruled their reservations when he learned on July 24 that the French had given in to the Japanese demands for suzerainty in Indochina. Confident that Germany had forced the French to do so, the President ordered the freezing of Japanese funds, along with the other contemplated restrictions.

The administration of the licensing system soon added substantially to the number and variety of products which the Japanese could no longer import from the United States. There then lay beyond their reach, in addition to the items previously embargoed, metals, machinery and vehicles, rubber, chemicals and pharmaceuticals. The cumulative lists covered everything in which there had been any substantial trade except for cottons. The Treasury, moreover, with the approval of the State Department, planned to issue few licenses for imports of Japanese silk or silk products, and to discontinue purchases of gold from Japan. Further, the Dutch government in the Netherland Indies on July 28 cut back sharply exports to Japan of oil, bauxite, and other commodities. While nominally Japan could buy low-grade oil in the United States in a quantity equivalent to her annual purchases of 1935–1936, actually the Treasury issued no licenses permitting payment for any oil exports either in the United States or elsewhere in the Western Hemisphere. Thus by August 1, 1941, the economic sanctions which Morgenthau and Stimson had been advocating for more than a year were at last complete and operable.

These sanctions, according to public opinion polls, won the overwhelming approval of the American people, who expressed increasing sentiment for taking a chance on war, if necessary, to hold back Japanese aggression. That had become the view also of Hull, who was angered by the duplicity of Japanese diplomacy as it was revealed by the MAGIC intercepts, the American breakthrough of the secret Japanese codes. "Nothing will stop them except force," Hull told Welles on August 4. ". . . . There is naturally going to continue to be an element of risk and danger in our course, if it is sufficiently firm and extensive to checkmate them. I just don't want us to take for granted a single word they say, but to appear to do so to what ever extent it may satisfy our purpose to delay further action by them." As Stimson understood Hull, he had "made up his mind that we have reached the end of any possible appeasement with Japan and there is nothing further that can be done with that country except by a firm policy." That, of course, had long been Morgenthau's opinion.

6. *To the Clasp of War*

By the summer of 1941, the hour seemed late to all men of Morgenthau's beliefs. Again and again totalitarianism had successfully challenged the humane and pacific society in which such men believed. In less than two years, the depredations of Germany, Italy, Russia, and Japan had ravaged the world, leaving a sturdy Britain, her Dominions, and an awakened United States the only powerful islands of democracy. To protect those havens and, in time, to extend freedom again, Roosevelt and those around him had embraced a logic composed in part of principle, in part of necessity. On principle, they would contest any further encroachments by the Axis and would aid its resistant victims where they could, even when such aid took the nation to the edge of war. Of necessity the United States would help not only the democracies but also any enemy of the Axis that had the will to fight. So it was that the Soviet Union qualified for Lend-Lease assistance. To the President and his advisers, Germany appeared the most powerful, implacable, and dangerous of the despoilers; Europe, the crucial sector in the battle. But the logic of the Administration, like the developments of the spreading war, encompassed the globe, and so it was that on principle the United States confronted Japan and, of necessity, championed China.

About China, Morgenthau, like his colleagues, had few illusions. The government of Chiang Kai-shek was weak, corrupt, and cynical, threatened by the apathy of most of its subjects, the arms of the Japanese puppet regime in Nanking, and the hostility of the communist camp. In midsummer 1941, according to the American ambassador at Chungking, operations on the Burma Road were "bad beyond belief." Ernest Hemingway, his theater of observation now China instead of Spain, wrote Morgenthau an alarming letter about the growing totalitarianism of the Generalissimo and his regime, the oppressive atmosphere of fear and betrayal at the capital and in the universities, the pro-Japanese sentiments of wealthy Chinese landlords and bankers, and the unreliability of the communist leaders, experts in the tactic of plausible slander. But all of these informants realized, as did Morgenthau, Roosevelt, and their associates, that the sorry government of Chiang Kai-shek was the only government in China with which the United States could work, the only government that represented Chinese sovereignty and independence.

That independence was still Japan's prime target and, in itself and as a symbol, a fundamental objective for American protection against Axis aggression. The Japanese, feeling the bite of American sanctions, worried too by the potential strength of Russia in Asia, were, as before, determined to have China but eager for a *rapprochement* with the United States. Aware of the dangers inherent in these contradictory goals, aware also of the impact on Japan of the embargo, the War Department hastened the rearming of the Philippines, the State Department tried to prolong negotiations, if possible to reach a successful terminus, if not, at least to gain time for the military buildup; and Stimson, talking with Morgenthau on September 18, 1941, promised "to stand shoulder-to-shoulder with me where we have stood before, and that is no let up on the economic pressure on Japan."

Morgenthau understood the implications of that resolution. On October 22, he moved to improve the efficiency of the internal management of the Treasury because "we are on the verge of a war." Yet the Secretary, along with the President and his military and diplomatic representatives, still hoped instead to keep peace in the Pacific on American terms, for peace would leave the country free to concentrate on the Nazi menace in Europe, and the nation's terms, if Japan accepted them, would break her link to the Axis, maintain the status quo in Southeast Asia, and guarantee the independence and self-government of all of China.

The unchanging conflict in purpose between the United States and Japan made the negotiations between the two nations during November 1941, as Cordell Hull later said, seem constantly "to come to a certain point and then start going around and around the same circle." During that month the Japanese were secretly readying an offensive from the island of Hainan to the Netherlands Indies and Malaya, as intercepts of their cables continually disclosed. Early in November the Japanese cabinet had decided to present two plans to Washington. Plan A proposed an overall adjustment in the Pacific; if it were rejected, Plan B suggested a *modus vivendi* that would perpetuate the uneasy truce. In Plan A the Japanese government expressed its willingness to accept the principle of nondiscrimination in trade in the entire Pacific region, including China, provided that the same principle were applied to the rest of the world. Japan would not renounce the Axis Pact, but she did agree to extend no further her "sphere of self-defense," and she voiced her wish to keep the European war from spreading to Asia. Japan insisted on maintaining her forces in China for "a suitable interval," at least twenty-five years, though she was prepared to withdraw from Indochina if China would accept her occupation.

The United States rejected these terms. As Hull explained, he could not guarantee that all nations would practice nondiscrimination in trade, though the United States was willing to do so. As for Japan's adherence to the Axis, it had to "disappear." And the United States would not alter its stand on the territorial and political integrity of China. Hull's response was abrupt, for his mood and the President's had been conditioned by their knowledge from MAGIC of Japanese preparations for attack during the period of negotiation.

Plan B, which the Japanese now brought forward, would have accomplished most of their program without hostilities. It called for an agreement by Japan and the United States to refrain from invasion of any part of Southeast Asia or the South Pacific "with the exception of French Indo-China." It also included mutual guarantees assuring both countries the raw materials they needed from the Netherlands Indies. It obligated the United States to unfreeze Japanese assets, to lift the embargo on oil, and to engage "in no activity which might put an obstacle in the way of Japan in her efforts to make peace with China," a euphemism for conquest. In return Japan would withdraw her army from French Indochina "wherever peace shall have been established between Japan and China or a just peace firmly established in the Pacific area." However, in the event of American participation in the European war, Japan would "automatically carry out what she understands to be the obligations" of the Axis Pact. Those conditions postulated a total reversal of American policy, an eventuality so unlikely that the Japanese army and navy pushed ahead with their war plans. MAGIC's window on that development confirmed the distaste of Roosevelt and Hull for any consideration of Plan B.

Yet before breaking off negotiations, Roosevelt on November 17 penciled out a note to Hull defining the minimum terms he would tolerate for a temporary easement in the Pacific. The United States would resume economic relations — "some oil and rice now — more later," if Japan would send no more troops to Indochina, or to the Manchurian border, or to any place in the South Seas, and if Japan would agree not to invoke the Axis Pact should the United States become involved in the European war. The United States would also "introduce" the Japanese to the Chinese but take no part in ensuing conversations.

At this juncture Morgenthau for the first time became involved in the ongoing discussions, the details of which he had not known. No perceptive observer needed the particulars of diplomatic exchanges or the revelations of the intercepts to sense the drift toward war. So it was with Harry White, who was carrying responsibility for the execution of the Treasury's stabilization policies. White believed that a creative economic policy could establish a basis for decent and prosperous peace in Asia. Like Morgenthau, White operated largely on surmise, but the Secretary found his memorandum about Japanese policy interesting, and on November 17, 1941, sent copies of it to Roosevelt and Hull on the chance that it might prove helpful.

If White's hopes were naïve, perhaps even fanciful, he nevertheless wanted to find a way to transform a threatening and powerful enemy into a good neighbor; a way to prevent a devastating war that would surely leave behind it a legacy of bitterness and disruption. Japan, he argued, could not possibly win a war against the United States. It would cost the Japanese their empire and their status as a first-rate power, and leave Asia in chaos. The United States had an equal stake in peace and stability in the East, especially in the face of the German threat in Europe. White suggested, therefore, that the United States withdraw the bulk of her naval forces from the Pacific, sign a twenty-year nonaggression pact with Japan, promote a settlement of the Manchurian question, advocate the placing of Indochina under the government of a multinational commission, give up all extraterritorial rights in China and persuade England to do likewise, repeal the immigration laws discriminating against Asians, negotiate with Japan a trade agreement giving her most-favored-nation treatment, extend to her a credit of $2 billion for twenty years at 2 per cent, set up a fund of $500 million — half to be supplied by Japan — to stabilize the cross rate between the dollar and the yen, and try to assure Japan access to raw materials.

For her part, Japan, in White's formula, would withdraw her military forces from China, restoring there the boundaries of 1931, and withdraw also from Indochina and Siam, recognize the government of Chiang Kai-shek, cease attacks on Chinese currency, give up all extraterritorial rights in China, extend to China a loan of a billion yen at 2 per cent interest, remove troops occupying Manchuria if Russia would pull back her forces on her eastern front, sell the United States up to three-quarters of her current output of war materials on a cost-plus basis, expel all

German technicians, officers, and propagandists, accord the United States and China most-favored-nation treatment, and negotiate a nonaggression pact with China, Great Britain, the Netherlands Indies, and the Philippines.

As Morgenthau saw it, White, while "shooting in the dark," had composed a "very amazing memorandum of suggestions." It appealed to the Secretary in part, surely, because he was ignorant of the hardness of Japan's position as expressed in negotiations with Hull, and ignorant, too, of the Japanese staging for a southwestward offensive, as revealed by MAGIC. But White's memorandum impressed the Secretary also because of its positive tone, and because its constituent recommendations not only pointed to an end of aggression in the Orient but also to the preservation of China's integrity and the development of her feeble economy. At the least, White had suggested a fresh approach to a stale impasse. Maxwell Hamilton, the veteran chief of the State Department's Far Eastern Division, called the memorandum a "most constructive one," while Admiral Stark and the office of General Marshall described the document as "satisfactory from a military standpoint."

Hull made the Treasury memorandum one basis among several for fashioning his answer to Japan's Plan B, which reached him on November 19, 1941, though White's proposals lost their distinctive character as the State Department proceeded to draft and revise the American reply. To the deliberations in that delicate and laborious process, neither Morgenthau nor his aides were privy. The Secretary of State forwarded his completed draft to the President on November 26. It reflected the established positions of both men. Hull began again with a statement of general principles which were to bind both the United States and Japan. He then enumerated various steps which the United States and Japan were to take at once. They were to attempt to conclude a multilateral nonaggression pact with Great Britain, China, the Netherlands, the Soviet Union, and Thailand. The agreement was to pledge the signatories to respect the territorial integrity of Indochina and to combine against any threat to it, as well as to abjure from seeking preferential treatment in the area.

Japan would withdraw all military, naval and police forces from both China and Indochina. The United States and Japan would in no way support any government or regime in China other than that of Chiang Kai-shek. Both would give up all their extraterritorial rights in China and try to get the British to do likewise. Further, the United States and Japan would negotiate a trade agreement on a most-favored-nation basis, remove restrictions on each other's funds, and work out a plan to stabilize the dollar-yen rate. Finally, no previous agreement with any third power was to conflict with these proposals or with the preservation of peace in the Pacific.

Had Morgenthau known about the contents of Hull's draft he would have approved of it, for like White's memorandum, it contained Japan and protected China. As it happened, however, the Chinese, themselves in the dark, misled the Treasury. On November 25 Morgenthau received a cable from Chiang Kai-shek, of which copies also went to Knox and Stimson, imploring the United States to make no concessions to Japan. The easing of sanctions, the Generalissimo said, even the consideration of that move, already the constant subject of rumor, would persuade the Chinese people that the United States had sacrificed them to appeasement. Their morale would collapse, as would the Chinese army's resistance to conquest. The United States, the G'imo urged, should "announce that if the withdrawal of the Japanese armies from China is not settled, the question of relaxing of the embargo or freezing could not be considered." This, of course, was already the position which Hull and Roosevelt had decided to assume, and emphatically the policy Morgenthau commended to the President.

On the morning of November 26 the Secretary called at the White House. "To show how things go," he noted in his Diary, "when I came in to see the President, his breakfast had already been brought in. He had not touched his coffee. He had some kippered herring which he had just begun to eat when Cordell Hull called up. He was talking to Hull and trying to eat his food at the same time, but by the time he finished the conversation his food was cold and he didn't touch it. I don't think the President ought to see me or anybody else until he has finished his break-fast." On the telephone to Hull, as in talking to Morgenthau, Roosevelt agreed to see Ambassador Hu Shih and T. V. Soong, and, he said, "I will quiet them down."

Soong's agitated state had alarmed Morgenthau. As he ob-served in his Diary after leaving the President: "I read the memo from Chiang Kai-shek and I think he has every reason to be dis-turbed. Soong told me that the agreement* with the Japanese provides for the withdrawal of all Japanese troops from French Indo-China with the exception of twenty-five thousand. We, in turn, are to unfreeze the Japanese assets and allow them to buy as much oil as they need, based on their monthly quota for their industrial uses (which, of course, they can fake). The Japanese are to be allowed to sell unlimited quantities of goods to us, pro-vided two-thirds of it is silk. The Japanese are to agree not to attack Russia and Siberia. This is lovely for us, but it leaves the poor Chinese holding the bag with twenty-five thousand troops right at their back door. T. V. Soong told me that the only thing which has helped so far is the freezing of the Japanese funds. This is having a terrific economic effect internally on Japan.

"He said something very interesting to the effect that Hull called in the English, Australians, Chinese and the Dutch, and Halifax † evidently was upset by a suggestion which was made and he said he would have to consult his government. Hull be-came very annoyed and said that it was up to the English to ac-cept the proposal without any comments, which seems to me rather highhanded. . . .

"I think the President will have more of a situation on his hands than he realizes when he receives Hu Shih and T. V. Soong, but I think they have every reason to be outraged."

Soong erred in his report about Hull's draft and about the English, and he erred further in his account to Morgenthau of his meeting with Roosevelt. Indeed, as the Secretary put it in his Diary of November 27, Soong was "not very clear," or at least "I didn't get too good a picture from what he told me. How-

---

* The agreement Soong thought the United States was negotiating with Japan.
† British Ambassador to the United States after the death of Lothian.

ever, it seems the President presented the facts to him in the following manner.

The reason that they were giving to the Japanese a memorandum which they called modus vivendi was because of the United States' concern about the Burma Road, and they were so anxious to keep that open. Furthermore, the President said he thought Chiang Kai-shek was much too excited. Furthermore, Hull said the Chief of Staff of the Army and the Chief of Naval Operations said they desperately needed three to six months to get ready in the Philippines. Soong says he knows from a very reliable source that this is not true.*

Soong told the President that if it was left to them as to whether the Japanese should get oil, embargo lifted on other goods, and Japanese given the right to export silk to the United States on the one hand as against protecting the Burma Road on the other that they would be in favor of not changing the economic status between the United States and Japan, and they would take their chances on the Burma Road.

The President at the meeting yesterday with Hu Shih and Soong told them that he had information the Japanese were moving thirty or forty thousand troops somewhere just north of Shanghai. He said he didn't have the details but the men are on the boats. The President said that to do such a thing in the midst of the conference is a definite breach.

Soong said he pressed the President pretty hard, and the President may have become annoyed at him. I told him not to worry, and that I was sure in his heart the President knows Soong was right, and he wouldn't hold anything against him. . . .

I understand that they heard from Churchill either yesterday or today, and that Churchill was opposed to the so-called modus vivendi, was absolutely opposed to giving the Japanese any oil, and objected to other parts of the arrangements. Most important of all, Churchill said that he couldn't agree to this modus vivendi on account of what it would do to the morale of the Chinese troops.

As near as I can make out three things happened yesterday: (1) the President saw Chiang Kai-shek's memo for the first time; (2) information was received that the Japanese were moving troops; (3) Churchill objected to the modus vivendi. Anyway last night Soong had a call from Stanley Hornbeck, who told him they had not heard from the ABCD powers, but they had presented a memo to the Japanese. It was not the modus vivendi memo but one

* Soong was wrong.

which had been prepared some time ago in case the United States was ready to break off with Japan, and they hadn't showed it to them because they felt confident that the ABCD powers would agree to it. This memo contained no economic factors but was more a question of sixteen or eighteen points.*

The President also told the Chinese yesterday that for the first time yesterday the Japanese learned about the large number of four-engine bombers in the Philippines. (I can't believe this because they had been there for a long time and you can't bring in four-engine bombers and not have the Japanese in the Philippines know about it.)

Soong feels that the matter is taking a definite turn for the better as far as their country is concerned, and maybe I was foolish but I told him I had prepared a letter to send to the President on this question but now that the thing seemed better I wouldn't send it. I told Soong that if things got worse, he should please let me know.

Morgenthau never sent the letter to which he referred, for the President needed no prodding to stand for precisely the policy which the Secretary then and later considered essential. He had, in a sense, deemed it essential ever since the fall of 1938, as the draft of his letter revealed. "The gravity of the situation," the Secretary wrote,

is my only excuse for writing to you on the subject uppermost in your mind and mine. We are both of us keenly aware — as indeed the country and the world are — that the negotiations with the Japanese are of the most profound import and that the decisions reached, whatever their nature, will have world shaking consequences. I am convinced that your many times expressed stand against appeasement is as firm as ever and that it is far from your intent that there shall be an Eastern Munich; yet I cannot but be deeply alarmed by the hints that have come to me of the direction of the negotiations.

These hints, for all the evasive language, give what seems to me a dangerous picture — a picture the full significance of which the American people are only beginning to grasp. I may be wholly wrong in my deductions as to what is being contemplated, but the situation is so crucial that I dare not refrain from speaking my mind.

It is because of your forthright and unyielding stand, it is be-

* Soong obviously had only a garbled understanding of Hull's memorandum.

cause you are the one statesman whose record has never been be-
smirched by even a trace of appeasement that the United States
holds its unique and supreme position in world affairs today. Not
the potential power of our great country, but your record, Mr.
President, has placed the United States and you, its titular head and
spokesman, in a position to exercise the leading force which will
bring ultimate victory over aggression and fascism.

Mr. President, I want to explain in language as strong as I can
command, my feeling that the need is for iron firmness. No settlement with Japan that in any way seems to the American people, or
to the rest of the world, to be a retreat, no matter how temporary,
from our increasingly clear policy of opposition to aggressors, will
be viewed as consistent with the position of our Government or
with the leadership that you have established. Certainly the independence of the millions of brave people in China who have been
carrying on their fight for four long, hard years against Japanese
aggression is of no less concern to us and to the world than the
independence of Thailand or French Indo-China. No matter what
explanation is offered to the public of a truce with Japan the
American people, the Chinese people, and the oppressed peoples of
Europe, as well as those forces in Britain and in Russia who are
with us in this fight, will regard it as a confession of American
weakness, and vacillation. How else can the world possibly interpret a relaxation of the economic pressure which you have so
painstakingly built up in order to force Japan to abandon her policy of aggression when that relaxation is undertaken not because
Japan has actually abandoned it, but only because she promises
not to extend her aggressive acts to other countries? The parallel
with Munich is inescapable.

The continuation and further intensification of our economic
pressure against Japan seems, in the light of all the opinions I have
sounded out, to be the touchstone of our pledge to China and the
world that the United States will oppose Japanese aggression in
the Pacific.

The eyes of nations and their peoples are centered on you as a
promise of a better life. There can be no diplomacy no matter how
attractive a promise of temporary peace may seem to some that is
worth the price of shaking the confidence of those who turn to
you for leadership, who turn to you as the answer of the false and
disastrous diplomacy followed abroad for so many years.

After our long association, I need not tell you that this is not
written in any doubt of your objectives, but I feel and fear that if
the people, our people, and all the oppressed people of the earth,

interpret your move as appeasement of repressive forces, as a move
that savors strongly of "selling China out" for a temporary respite,
a terrible blow will have been struck against those very objectives.
You have a supreme part to play in world affairs and you can play,
Mr. President, with complete effectiveness only if you retain the
people's confidence in your courage and steadfastness in the face of
aggression, and in the face of the blandishments of temporary advantages.

As Morgenthau knew, the President did not need to be reminded of the purport of that letter. On December 1, 1941,
Soong told Morgenthau, again in error, that the Japanese had
"backed down." Roosevelt reported otherwise. Morgenthau
asked for advice about the Treasury's forthcoming financing.
Roosevelt told him to go ahead, adding, "I cannot guarantee anything. It is all in the laps of the gods." But, the President said, it
was apt to be worse in the following week than in the week just
beginning. Still he did not tell the Secretary that MAGIC had
disclosed Japanese troop and naval movements, thrusts that
Roosevelt, Stimson, Hull, and Marshall thought to be aimed at
Southeast Asia.

On December 1 Morgenthau also consulted Welles. "I am
having a financing of a billion and a half," he said. ". . . I just
wanted to ask the State Department if something would be happening Wednesday, Thursday, or Friday of real importance — I
mean that might upset the people of this country — I would appreciate knowing it. . . . I'd like to know as soon as possible."

"I can tell you now," Welles replied. "I don't anticipate anything within that brief period; but if there's any change in that
belief on my part . . . I'll let you know at once."

Two days later Roosevelt supplied fuller information. "On
the Japanese question," Morgenthau recorded in his Diary of
December 3, 1941, "the President said he had the Japanese running around like a lot of wet hens. After he asked them the
question as to why they were sending so many military, naval
and air forces into Indo-China. He said that Kurusu asked to see
Barnie Baruch and a number of other people today to try to
bring influence to bear on the President. The President said, 'I

think the Japanese are doing everything they can to stall until they are ready.' The most important thing is that the President said he is talking with the English about war plans as to when and where the USA and Great Britain should strike, and that is what he is waiting for. I think the Japanese here in Washington have the instructions to do everything possible to keep the United States from getting in at this time or at least until such time as the Japanese can get their troops into whatever position they want."

Later that day Morgenthau heard that the Japanese were closing the New York branch of the Bank of Japan on December 4 or 5. The Japanese manager of that bank was planning to leave New York December 10, and to sail from the West Coast on December 16. Worried by this news, so laden with a sense of major crisis, the Secretary left a message at the White House, since Roosevelt "could not speak on phone until after supper."

Yet with a "clearance from the President," "an all clear signal," Morgenthau on December 4 announced the Treasury offering $1 billion of 2½ per cent bonds maturing 1967–1972, and $500 million of 2 per cents with a shorter maturity, 1951–1955. Those were strong terms, conceding little to the market, sustaining low interest rates — terms that had been established, as usual, after conversations between the Treasury and the Federal Reserve Board, the Federal Reserve banks in various districts, and bond brokers throughout the country. Had Morgenthau or his advisers felt that the market was apprehensive or feeble, the Treasury could not have set such thin coupons. And within twenty-four hours of the announcement the offering was oversubscribed, though it was to fall off badly for a few hours on the following Monday.

That possibility was far from Morgenthau's thoughts when he closed the books on the loan Friday night, December 5, 1941. He was looking forward to a short vacation in Arizona. Though war seemed nearer than ever before, on the basis of what he knew he saw no occasion to change his vacation plans.

On Sunday Morgenthau had luncheon with his family in a New York restaurant. As he left, his chauffeur gave him his first news of Pearl Harbor, and the Secret Service told him that the President had been trying for two hours to reach him. At once the Secretary boarded the plane that had been standing by to take him to Tucson and took off instead for an emergency meeting at the White House.

BOOK THREE

YEARS OF WAR,
1941-1945

XVII

STRAINS OF WAR

1941–1945

SICK FROM WORRY, the senior officers of the Treasury Department greeted the Secretary at eleven in the evening on December 7, 1941, when he returned from the Cabinet meeting at the White House. "It is just unexplainable," he said. "And they caught us just as unprepared as the others — just the same. . . . Much worse than anybody realized. . . . I was with Frank Knox when he got the report from Pearl Harbor, and that telephone conversation was taken down, and I read it, so I know the President read the same one in Cabinet. . . . Knox feels something terrible. . . . Stimson . . . kept mumbling that all the planes were in one place. . . . They have the whole fleet in one place — the whole fleet was in this little Pearl Harbor base. They will never be able to explain it."

Inexplicability contributed to the shock of the Japanese attack that forced the entire nation to face the unlimited emergency of war. For almost four years war dominated the lives of all Americans. The problems of waging war placed an ultimate strain on the federal government, especially on the President and his close advisers. War heightened their sensibilities, stretched their nerves, called forth their last reserves of energy.

1. Emergency Unlimited

Financing the costliest war in history imposed severe strains on the Treasury. One involved an exhausting effort to persuade the balky Congress to raise taxes high enough to cover one half the expenses. Another related to the "tremendous program," as Morgenthau put it, to defray the balance of expenses by borrowing. A third grew out of continual controversy with various federal agencies about the Treasury's effort to keep the purchase of bonds on a voluntary basis.

Except for Morgenthau himself, only Franklin and Eleanor Roosevelt cherished the Treasury's War Bond program. One day early in 1942 the Secretary walked over, as he had so often, from the fine old Treasury building to the White House for luncheon with the President in his office. Almost weekly for nine years the two had sat there together. "Henry," Roosevelt said, "you and I are the only people who understand it. Everybody else is against it, but we are going to do it." What they wanted to do was to persuade the American people voluntarily to buy bonds to finance the war.

A voluntary program, they believed, could raise sufficient funds to meet expenses not covered by tax revenues, and could absorb enough private income to relieve inflationary demands for goods and services in limited supply. A compulsory lending program, they thought, would produce little, if any, more money, while Congress, given the chance, would tend to hold back on income taxes if it enacted a forced lending bill. For 1942, Roosevelt and Morgenthau at first expected the bond drives to produce $8 billion, one billion more than a 10 per cent forced savings tax would have yielded. Equally important, voluntarism would work only if the Treasury mounted a vast sales campaign. Through that campaign, as Morgenthau put it and Roosevelt agreed, the Treasury could "make the country war-minded — there just isn't any other vehicle to do it."

Opponents of the Treasury's policy, men like Marriner Eccles and Budget Director Harold Smith, who considered voluntarism wholly inadequate for combating inflation, continuously underestimated the value placed by Roosevelt and Morgenthau on the psychological aspects of the successive sales drives. Again and again Eccles or Smith or others won the President or the Secretary to temporary or partial support for some kind of compulsory lending, but always Morgenthau was determined to preserve his machinery for selling the war, which included an Advertising War Council of volunteer copywriters. Fred Smith, an advertising executive whom the Secretary recruited as an assistant, called Morgenthau "the number two advertising man in Washington. His only peer is his boss." Morgenthau, Smith went on, "couldn't lay out an advertisement if his entire apple crop depended upon it. . . . But . . . he has a genius for knowing . . . sweat from bluff. . . . Perhaps the most important advertising decision he ever made was the decision to use *bonds* to sell the *war*, rather than vice versa. . . . He simply points out that people have been trying to sell thrift since the time of Benjamin Franklin, and not with very great success; while under his plan of selling the war first and bonds second, people are laying away more money in a couple of weeks than they had ever before saved."

In April 1942 the Treasury was emphasizing the importance for its bond sales of voluntary monthly payroll deductions, through which employees of large corporations contracted to purchase bonds regularly. Those systematic deductions also, as Morgenthau often observed, had a healthy, anti-inflationary impact. Roosevelt agreed. After inspecting the General Motors payroll deduction plan, one of the most complicated and expensive in the country, the President said: "I want a sign in everybody's window, not just saying, 'I bought a war bond,' but that 'I buy a war bond every month.'"

The ongoing sales campaign, directed to that goal, constantly received Morgenthau's personal attention. He ordered his special bond staff to prepare radio programs not only in English but in foreign languages for use in cities with large foreign-born

populations. He wrote dubious congressmen about the importance to the Treasury of the advertising sponsored by "public
spirited companies or individuals" who bought hundreds of millions of dollars a year of bond advertisements. "This is very
different from free advertising," Morgenthau noted, "in that it
provides a substantial amount of revenue to newspapers and
magazines. . . . The . . . Bond program has already given the
newspapers many millions of dollars in advertising from banks,
department stores, and other institutions. In the case of radio,
our most popular program . . . was sponsored and paid for by
two corporations, and was not in any sense free advertising." Indeed, the generosity of the contributing sponsors had made it
possible for the Treasury to avoid spending "one penny on paid
advertising in newspapers and magazines or on the radio since the
start of our . . . program."

The Department's budget covered other activities, including
the salaries of the professional staff in the bond office and the
costs of promotional films, of which one series featured Walt
Disney's Donald Duck. Ordinarily the Treasury also paid for
the use of billboards. At least once the layout displeased Morgenthau. "Is it necessary," he complained, "for us to get a Hol-
lywood actress swathed in mink over a blue-and-white print
dress to launch our new bill board campaign? Personally, I think
it is awfully cheap. Secondly, I would much rather have a girl
from Amalgamated Clothiers Union swathed in a pair of over-
alls."

In the spring campaign of 1942, Morgenthau for the first time
had his staff establish quotas for sales. He wanted quotas for
every state and county and an increase in the payroll savings plan
to carry it to at least 10 per cent of the gross payroll of every
important business firm. As things stood, about 45 per cent of all
employees were participating, with an average monthly allotment of about 4.8 per cent of their wages. Morgenthau intended
to double that record.

"We have got to step up the sale of War Bonds," he said in a
speech for the newsreels on April 20, 1942, "to a billion dollars
every month. Every community in this country will have to do
its share to reach this quota. All of us who earn regular pay

should set aside an average of at least 10 per cent of it every week for buying War Bonds. . . . It's not only smart to be thrifty, but our future depends upon it." To newspapermen, off the record, the Secretary stressed the significance of the campaign for national morale. "There are millions of people," he said, ". . . who say, 'What can we do to help?' . . . Right now, other than going in the Army and Navy or working in a munitions plant, there isn't anything to do. . . . Sixty per cent of the reason that I want to do this thing is . . . to give the people an opportunity to do something."

Morgenthau had to get results. If he slipped, voluntarism would fall with him. "Henry has promised to raise $1 billion a month and he's got his neck out," Roosevelt told the Cabinet on July 10, 1942, "and let him hang himself if he wants to or else . . . his head goes caput!"

"This is either the second or third time he has said this at Cabinet," Morgenthau reported to his staff. "And if sometimes I seem a little unreasonable in my pressure on you, it's remarks like this that are difficult to take. . . . I know each and every person is doing his damndest . . . but at times if I get a little overexcited, it's remarks like that which I think were most unfortunate before the Cabinet. . . .

"There are a lot of things which are going badly for him and I suppose he thought he would take a crack. . . . And sometimes it's awfully hard to take it." Alone with Roosevelt on July 16, Morgenthau "told the President that he had been pretty rough on me at the last Cabinet on War Bonds. . . . 'Well,' he said, 'There isn't a day passes that either Wallace or Miss Perkins doesn't go after me on compulsory savings. . . . What did I say?' I said, 'Forget it, but I thought you were pretty rough.' "

That December the Victory Loan Drive, as the Secretary reported at its conclusion, far exceeded his expectations. Aiming for $9 billion, the Treasury had raised $12.906 billion, "the biggest amount of money ever raised by any government in such a short time." This "grand response by the people" impressed the President, as did the success of later bond drives, and protected voluntarism, Treasury style, from the mounting criticisms of its opponents.

2. *Weeks of Particular Hell*

In the months before Pearl Harbor, Morgenthau had been devoting most of his time to the problems of taxation and the control of inflation, which were to continue to harass the Treasury for another two years. With conversion to war production, fewer goods and services became available for civilian consumption, while the accompanying spurt in employment raised personal incomes. Increased taxes, like increased savings, could effectively reduce the spending power of the American people, and thereby help to ease the rise in prices, while the resulting revenue from such taxes might meet — if the Treasury's purpose prevailed — about half the booming costs of war. Morgenthau wanted revenue legislation also to preserve the social goals of the New Deal, to distribute the burden of taxation on the principle of ability to pay, and to prevent any individual or corporation from exploiting the war for personal gain. Those objectives, along with his commitment to voluntarism in the bond program, governed the Secretary's thinking throughout the war, but he subjected his views deliberately to the criticisms of his expert advisers.

On matters of taxation, those advisers included Under Secretary of the Treasury Daniel Bell, whose responsibilities for debt management naturally involved him also in questions relating to revenue. As conservative as Morgenthau in his views about fiscal policy, Bell, like his chief, was prepared to embrace innovations that promised to reduce the need for federal borrowing. Accordingly both men, while hostile to Keynesian economics, accepted suggestions from Keynes's American disciples. One such disciple was Assistant Secretary of the Treasury Harry Dexter White. Though White's responsibilities lay in the area of monetary research and policy, he occasionally spoke out about taxation, and he continually supported the fiscal proposals of Alvin Hansen, the Harvard economist, of Ben Cohen, the President's counselor, and of other proponents of the new economics.

Assistant Secretary of the Treasury Herbert E. Gaston, who had been with Morgenthau in various capacities since 1929, gave the Secretary unequaled devotion and understanding. A veteran of agrarian reform movements and a dedicated New Dealer, Gaston, with the Secretary, stressed the importance of taxation as a vehicle for social progress. So, too, did the most influential new member of the Treasury staff, Randolph Paul, who came to the Department just before Pearl Harbor to take charge of the Tax Division and soon thereafter, in July 1942, became General Counsel. An experienced tax lawyer and economist, Paul operated, as one of Morgenthau's friends observed, in the tradition of one of his predecessors, Herman Oliphant — with "brains, imagination, integrity and the willingness to spend himself on a cause." Paul persuaded the Secretary to incorporate Keynesian devices in his recommendations to the President and to the Congress, while he also valued and sustained the general objectives of Morgenthau's wartime revenue programs.

In mid-March 1942, many of Roosevelt's advisers — among others Vice President Wallace, Secretary of Agriculture Wickard, Budget Director Harold Smith, Marriner Eccles, and Leon Henderson, the head of the Office of Price Administration — persuaded the President "to order basic staff and command work on the problem of inflation." Morgenthau, a member of the committee appointed to explore that question, disagreed with his colleagues and would not sign the report they sent the White House early in April. The report recommended a sales tax, a lowering of income tax exemptions, and the freezing of wages. The Secretary, no less worried than were the others about inflation, endorsed a six-point program devised by Randolph Paul. It proposed the freezing of prices at current levels; the rapid enactment of a tax bill; further necessary fiscal measures; wage adjustments to compensate for the rising cost of living; and direct controls over credit, inventory, and residential building. Further, Morgenthau commended the Treasury's voluntary savings program for which Eccles and Smith wanted to substitute compulsory lending. The Secretary summarized his views in a memorandum to Roosevelt of April 3, 1942:

"We should not leave a stone unturned to keep the cost of living as nearly as possible at the present level. You will notice . . . we have not limited ourselves to fiscal measures for we do not believe that fiscal measures alone are adequate to meet the situation. If we adopt a program of strict rationing . . . the amount of money available for federal borrowing will be greatly increased and it will come from sources which will not be inflationary. . . . There are radical points of difference between our conclusions and those of Harold Smith's group. . . . We feel strongly that it would be a mistake to yield to the clamor for a sales tax. . . . A sales tax . . . would get no more revenue but simply have shifted the source of revenue to the lower income groups.

"We object on the same grounds to lowering the personal exemptions. . . . We also . . . are in strong disagreement on the proposal to freeze wages, which we think unnecessary, impractical, and exceedingly dangerous."

Determined "to force a decision," the Secretary was especially angry with the Keynesian economists in Washington. "First they want inflation," he complained, "and they don't want any rationing or anything sensible about finances. They think that the Government can do the thing one day by pumping money in, and the next day they think the Government can do the thing by putting the brakes on the lower income groups, but I have yet to see a single one of them make a success of anything that they have undertaken. . . . I am sick and tired of the whole thing."

Smith, Eccles, and Leon Henderson were equally adamant. Following a futile meeting with Treasury experts on April 7, 1942, they went straight to the White House to press for their own plan. "Well," Morgenthau said when he heard about their foray, "I always say when you are doing a tax bill you have got to sleep on the floor so a fellow can't put a knife in your back." The Smith plan, the Secretary felt, would kill voluntary savings and wreck any chance for the recommendations the Treasury had made to the Ways and Means Committee. Taking his own case to the President on April 9, Morgenthau found Roosevelt "in sympathy with everything that we wanted," an impression which Eccles — to his distress — also gleaned. At the Cabinet meeting the next day Henry Wallace "got a little ugly" when the President supported the Treasury. The Department had, too, Morgenthau learned, the backing of organized labor, but Smith was attempting to woo it away. "These stupid asses around Harold Smith," Morgenthau told his staff, "in order to satisfy Labor . . . want to go after the rich people." Smith was therefore urging a 100 per cent tax on war profits, and Eccles a 95 per cent tax, though the Treasury was certain that anything above 80 per cent would hurt war production, a conclusion in which the War and Navy Departments agreed.

Alone with Roosevelt on April 15, Morgenthau said that Smith was "like a termite undermining the foundation of the Treasury. . . . I have heard him before a committee publicly say that he wanted to have the taxing authority of the budget as well as the expenditure. . . . He is constantly undermining us . . . and I wish that you would tell him to stop it." Roosevelt made no promises, though he did comment that Harold Smith was a very stick-to-it person. Still, Morgenthau was satisfied. "The President was very nice to me about it," he reflected after their meeting. "The last time I brought up the subject he resented it."

The President was also receptive to most of the Treasury's suggestions for his national address about inflation on April 27, 1942. "I really am terribly pleased on the President's message," Morgenthau announced to his morning meeting the next day, "because there is really everything in there that I fought for; . . . no ceiling on wages, we fought for rationing, and he has come out for rationing; we insisted on a ceiling on prices, and he has got that; he was very fine on the War Bonds; there is nothing about the tax thing that I couldn't endorse, so I would say that the Treasury got about 95 per cent compliance from the President, which I think is pretty good." So it was, especially after what Morgenthau had called "three weeks of particular hell . . . fighting the boys who wanted compulsory savings." The Secretary felt "a little weak," but "at least . . . in the clear."

Further, on April 28 the Office of Price Administration followed up the President's message with a major change in policy. Before that date OPA had experimented with selective price controls. Now it issued a General Maximum Price Regulation — "General Max" in the phrase of wartime Washington. Effective as far as it went, that order set the stage for the Price Control Act passed at Roosevelt's request in October. The new law broadened the field of price controls and provided for the first time for the control of wages. "General Max" and the directives supplementary to it proved themselves beyond the expectations of their sponsors. The price control program for the duration of the war held the line against inflation more successfully than did any other facet of government policy. But its success depended in considerable degree from the first on reducing inflationary pressures, a major objective of the Treasury's tax recommendations. In April 1942, those recommendations were faring badly on the Hill.

3. Two Hostile Committees

The House Ways and Means Committee, antagonistic toward almost every Treasury proposal, was proceeding to write a tax bill of its own. Indeed, the committee never seriously considered closing tax loopholes or adopting the Department's suggestions for steep increases on surtaxes on individual income and on estate and gift schedules. So, too, the committee shrugged off the President's unexpected proposal, one part of his message of April 27, for limiting individual income after taxes to $25,000 a year for the duration of the war. As the Treasury saw it, the larger problem was the limitation of excess corporate profits, but on that issue, too, the committee went its own way. By the end of April, Paul conceded that the issue was lost.

The congressmen who were fighting against taxes on individual and corporate wealth had contrived an effective tactic. By beating back the Treasury's recommendations and thereby reducing the revenue the new bill could raise, they could maintain that only a sales tax would provide the funds necessary for the prosecution of the war, only the sales tax would remove from consumer pockets money which would otherwise contribute to inflation. By the end of April, furthermore, as the President's message indicated, the need to control inflation had come to surpass even the need to raise revenue. At that juncture Morgenthau adjusted his own position. As he explained to the White House, the Treasury in March had asked Congress for $7 billion of additional revenue. Now the movement of prices and the cost of war indicated the need for more than $8 billion. Without surrendering any of his previous objectives, Morgenthau therefore recommended one change he had previously opposed. He suggested, as preferable to a sales tax, the lowering of personal exemptions so that the income tax would penetrate further down the scale of earnings and reach the lowest income groups.

Cool to the Treasury's revised view on exemptions, the Ways and Means Committee also resisted the Department's longstanding proposal for collecting income taxes at the source by regular withholding from payrolls. That scheme, some congressmen believed, would prove "a box of monkeys," impossible of administration. As the Committee finally drafted the Revenue Bill, it contained none of the Treasury's controversial recommendations and it promised to yield, according to departmental estimates, only $6.25 billion additional revenue, far less than the $8.7 billion which Morgenthau considered necessary. "Those fellows," he said, "just don't know there's a war on."

When the bill passed on to the Senate, Morgenthau told the Finance Committee of that body that "the people of this country want a courageous tax bill, and want it with the least possible delay." That kind of bill would have to include the reforms and the progressive schedules that the Treasury had earlier commended unsuccessfully to the House. Yet those provisions evoked little enthusiasm in the Senate. And, while Congress dallied, the continuing advance in prices was provoking demands for higher wages, was disturbing the economy, and impeding the industrial prosecution of the war. New, rapid, and powerful policies were past due "to prevent a calamitous rise in the cost of living."

On July 27, 1942, Judge Samuel Rosenman told Morgenthau that the President wanted an executive order freezing both prices and wages, and rolling agricultural prices back from 110 to 100 per cent of parity. Morgenthau feared that Roosevelt and Rosenman were developing a patchwork quilt of controls, with little regard for the needs of union labor. Their "Alice in Wonderland" scheme, the Secretary predicted, would fail. He preferred a more comprehensive and novel approach.

On July 29 the Secretary and his aides took their own proposal to Rosenman. It called for "expenditure rationing" to limit aggregate spending. Each individual or family would be able to spend for consumer goods only that amount of money for which the government had issued coupons. As the supply of consumer goods diminished, the government could reduce the volume of coupons issued. The system could also make allowances for variations in family size and income. "There is one thing about the Treasury," Rosenman remarked, "it certainly is resourceful." But as he soon reported to Morgenthau, the President was not "prepared to go that far" without the explicit consent of Congress.

Roosevelt held back partly because he preferred direct controls over prices and wages, partly in the hope that the Senate would make the tax bill an effective anti-inflationary instrument. As July became August and August September, Morgenthau begged the President to "take the bit in your teeth." Now the President held that the steps he contemplated necessitated a reorganization of the executive branch, which he could announce but not put into effect until Congress had had sixty days, under its statutory power, to disapprove his stated plans. "You are daring Congress to tell you that you cannot do it," Morgenthau complained. "I am just laying it before them," Roosevelt said, "and if they do not do something about it the plan goes into effect."

The plan, which Rosenman drafted with some help from Treasury experts, established an Economic Stabilization Administrator, charged with ultimate control over policy connected with profits, prices, wages, rationing, the cost of living, the movements of labor, private credit, subsidies, and related matters. The order establishing the new office provided too that, until the administrator ruled otherwise, all wages were frozen at current levels saving for adjustments necessary to meet the costs of living, to eliminate substandard conditions of living, to correct serious inequalities, or to reward increased productivity. Raises in salaries above $7500 a year were restricted even more tightly. A message to Congress in the first week of September explained the President's order, which, in the absence of congressional objections, took force early in October. Roosevelt then put Jimmy Byrnes in charge.

The success of the new venture, the Treasury believed, depended upon limiting pressure on established or intended ceilings. For that purpose, Randolph Paul and his talented associate, Roy Blough, originated a venturesome scheme that they first showed Morgenthau during the hot third weekend of August 1942. If the revenue bill, they said, in its final form, could produce $5 billion more than anyone had yet asked for, it would serve better than any set of regulations to hold down the cost of living. The device for raising that additional revenue, they suggested, was a spendings tax, a superior substitute for expenditure rationing. As Blough explained the spendings tax to the Secretary's morning group on August 24, it would be a graduated tax, supplementary to the income tax, on the whole sum which an individual or family spent, less stipulated allowances for necessities. A steeply graduated rate would in itself retard spending except for those necessities. Further, income saved rather than spent would be exempted from the tax. Progressive and efficient, the spendings tax would also yield substantial revenue and obviate the alleged need for a sales tax. If the tax reached too far into the pockets of lower income groups, some fraction of the resulting revenue could be defined as a compulsory loan, refundable after the war.

Enthusiastic about the proposal, Morgenthau had Blough explain it to representatives of the Federal Reserve Board, the

Office of Price Administration, the War Production Board, the
Department of Commerce, and the Bureau of the Budget. "The
principle of the plan was sound," they all agreed, as the Secretary then reported to Roosevelt, "and . . . it was a healthy step
in the right direction." He believed, Morgenthau continued,
that "the tax might well be suggested to Congress even at this
late stage in the progress of the tax bill. I am planning, with your
approval, to discuss it with Senator George."

Roosevelt permitted the discussion, and George had no objection to the Treasury's presenting its plan, but political prospects
for a spendings tax were poor. After little deliberation, the Finance Committee rejected it flatly. "The plan is dead," Senator
Guffey of Pennsylvania commented on September 4, 1942, the
day after Morgenthau had testified. "Not a man on the committee is for it." In the opinion of Senators Robert Taft and Harry
Byrd, the tax was "the most complicated and unworkable that
has been submitted . . . in nine years." The *Wall Street Journal* considered the spendings tax "an income tax walking about
on its hands," and a columnist in the *Washington Post* called it
"Morgenthau's morning glory. It opened Tuesday morning and
it folded before noon." That was enough for Roosevelt.
Though he had permitted Morgenthau to advance the plan, he
had himself never mentioned it, and now he refused to give it
any support. "I never make any recommendations to Congress
while a bill is pending before them," he told Morgenthau. The
Secretary was aghast. "It completely took my breath away," he
later told Herbert Gaston, "and I couldn't think quickly enough
to give him a few examples, because there are plenty of them.
. . . But I said something, and then he kind of broke down and
laughed, showing that he was trying to put something over on
me. Then he immediately made the statement, 'Well, you know,
Henry, I always have to have a couple of whipping boys,' to
which I replied, 'Yes, I realize that I am one of them and right
now I am getting plenty of whippings.' "

Nevertheless, as he told his staff, Morgenthau was "delighted
that we had the courage and the foresight to make this recommendation. . . . I don't want anybody around to take the atti-

tude that we have been licked. . . . It is the public who will get the licking."

So did the Treasury, at least in the eyes of the Congress. On September 8, 1942, the Senate Finance Committee officially voted down the spendings tax and adopted instead Senator George's plan for a 5 per cent gross income tax — a tax on all incomes in excess of $624, to be collected at the source, with certain provisions for a partial postwar credit. That measure would produce an additional $3.6 billion before refunds, a net after refunds of $2.5 billion. It would be hard to administer, it would bear unjustly on families with low incomes, it would produce less revenue and less of a check against inflation than the Treasury's scheme.

4. New Revenue "By Various Methods"

In November 1942, while the Treasury was starting a major bond drive and reviewing suggestions about taxation for the President's Budget Message of the following January, the Bureau of the Budget and the Office of Economic Stabilization moved together to take over the direction of revenue policy, particularly to persuade Roosevelt to support compulsory lending. As ever, Morgenthau bridled at a challenge to what he deemed his department's Constitutional prerogatives for making fiscal policy. "I just got to straighten out," he told Randolph Paul, " . . . who's going to . . . prepare the Tax Bill for the President."

The President's order establishing the Office of Economic Stabilization, Morgenthau reminded Jimmy Byrnes, the chief of that office, had said nothing about fiscal or monetary policy. Instead, as the Secretary accurately added, an early draft of the order had explicitly exempted those policy areas, and in announcing the creation of the new office, the President had orally

confirmed the exemption. "I had a pretty good talk . . . "
Morgenthau reported to his staff. "I went back through the
whole business right from the beginning. . . . He tried to sell
me that . . . anybody who holds this position and has to pre-
sent the whole thing on the cost of living has to include taxes.
And he said he knew nothing about the verbal statement the
President made the night it was announced. He never heard it.
. . . He says, 'You don't claim that you are over me, do you?'
I said, 'No, and you don't claim you are over me?' He says,
'No.' I say, 'Now, we are both here to lick inflation. We are
both here to save the President a headache. Can't we work together?' He says, 'Of course we can.' I said, 'That is what I want
to do.'

"Then he went on to say . . . he was relying on the Treasury to prepare the programs. . . . He will have to be watched,
that is all."

Before turning to the content of the tax program itself, Morgenthau asked Roosevelt for guidance about procedure. "What
I want to know," the Secretary said, " . . . is whether or not
you expect us to continue to prepare the tax bill as we have in
the past and present it as we have in the past."

"Absolutely," Roosevelt said.

"I didn't know whether Byrnes was thinking of something,"
Morgenthau said, "and I wanted to find out whether you said
anything to him or to the leaders on the Hill." Roosevelt had
not.

"This proves to me," Morgenthau later reflected in his Diary,
"that Byrnes is groping for power and hasn't gotten any directive from the President. It also proves I am right in thinking that
one should not be scared by anyone like Byrnes. The only thing
to do is go directly to the President and find out where you
stand."

Proposals for new taxes, Morgenthau told his chief aides on
December 2, 1942, should not be "too complicated," should
minimize difficulties in collection, and should avoid harassment
of business. He wondered whether "we can't take a brand new
look at the Social Security thing. Now, what they are proposing

in England is not only good for today, but it is good for the postwar, and it has many advantages over straight compulsory savings. . . . Every single person in England is going to be insured. They are going to get unemployment insurance; they are going to get sickness insurance, and the whole business.

"Now, the beauty of the study of the social insurance over something else is . . . you have got your mechanics. . . . It wouldn't be an additional burden from the standpoint of machinery. . . . We will just extend it." An extension of Social Security, with higher taxes at once but increased benefits only after the war, "would hit the volunteer war bonds" much less than would compulsory lending, while "last and most important," it would be "a damper on inflationary tendencies."

Yet social reform, Morgenthau learned, had few sponsors in wartime Washington, even within the Democratic party, and the Republicans had gained seats in both houses of Congress in the November elections. To the Treasury's dismay, Congress confined revenue legislation in 1943 to a measure that permitted taxpayers to cancel their obligations from 1942 while they also began to make current payments, either by payroll deductions or installments, on their 1943 liabilities.

Simply by making Americans current in their tax payments, Congress added $4 billion to federal revenues for 1943, but $12 billion of the President's stated goal remained to be raised. The problem of reaching that target provoked as much debate within the executive branch as it did between the Treasury and the Hill. Indeed, even Roosevelt seemed at first to have lowered his sights. "What we want," he told Morgenthau on May 27, ". . . is to get on the basis where we are paying for one-third of the war through taxes."

"Mr. President," Morgenthau replied, "you are wrong on that. We're on that basis. We are trying to get to a 50 per cent basis."

"You shoot at 50 per cent," Roosevelt said. "Get all you can . . . . You can tell them this for me. If I don't get more revenue before the end of this calendar year, I am going to put the entire blame on Congress."

Yet as Randolph Paul reminded Morgenthau, it would be September or October before any revenue bill passed, and if the new schedules were steep enough to provide additional revenue of $12 billion, they would be too steep for retroactive application to January 1, 1943. The difficulty confronting the Treasury was to persuade Congress to adopt schedules that would add enough new revenue in any calendar year. The cumulative effect of revenue legislation enacted since 1939 magnified public and congressional resistance to taxation, as did the conservative temper increasingly dominant in both parties. Roosevelt, Morgenthau knew, would do little to assist in overcoming those obstacles. "This sort of thing bores the President," the Secretary pointed out to his staff. ". . . It always has been like that. . . . You are going to get very little help out of the President. You never have on this thing."

The negative mood of Congress suggested to proponents of forced lending that only their policy could now serve to check inflation. Perhaps under their influence, Roosevelt in a press conference of June 8, 1943, indicated that both higher taxes and compulsory savings were needed to close the inflationary gap. "I didn't say," he added, "that a compulsory savings plan was an immediate necessity. . . . At the present time the public is supporting bond drives with a great deal of enthusiasm. As long as they continue to do this, I feel . . . the compulsory savings will not be necessary." But newspapers generally predicted, on the basis of the President's remarks, that Justice Byrnes was to take a "leading hand in tax policy."

Morgenthau was aghast. He considered both his bond drive and his authority over revenue policy endangered, and he opposed any compulsory lending or savings program other than a major revision of Social Security taxes and postwar benefits. "If I am to continue to be responsible to you for the development of tax policies," he wrote Roosevelt, "and to represent you before Congress on tax matters, it seems to me that this is the time to clear up the confusion. . . . Until this matter is cleared up, it seems unlikely that congressional leaders will pay serious attention to any suggestions that I or representatives of the Treasury may make." Roosevelt replied that Harold Smith, Jimmy Byrnes, and Byrnes's chief deputy, former congressman Fred Vinson, were cooperating on a draft of a tax message which would deal also with inflation and subsidies. "Each of the departments named," the President wrote, "have responsibilities in connection with the subjects. If I approve a tax program I would, of course, expect you to present it to the Congress as my program. Thereafter there would be no excuse for conflicting views. . . . You and the Director should get together and arrange to cooperate in this matter. Do not let the newspapers disturb you." When Morgenthau pressed him further, Roosevelt said: "This whole question of money is broader than it has been before and I . . . have to consult other people and instead of my coming directly — instead of Morgenthau going directly to Roosevelt and Roosevelt dealing directly with Byrnes, I want you and Byrnes to deal with each other."

But during June and July 1943, continuing attacks on his position worried the Secretary, who believed that they were inspired by Byrnes and other advocates of forced lending. Morgenthau also resented Vinson's direct negotiations with the House Ways and Means Committee, though Vinson explained that he was merely trying to establish a unified point of view with his former colleagues in Congress. "What the President has done," Morgenthau told his staff on July 22, "without having the courtesy to tell us, is that he has brought between himself and his Cabinet another group that he looks to to run it.

"He is not going to do it to me, and I am not going to take it. . . . I am willing to take this unjust criticism in the papers, but if the President is stupid enough to let me be undermined. . . . I want him to say so. . . .

"The pattern is perfectly obvious. Those people sit over there in the left wing of the White House and they are going to run the show. If they are going to, let them get the credit publicly, and the blame publicly — I am not going to be a shirt front for Vinson. . . .

"The point of my story is, here are four or five people, very ambitious . . . every one of them . . . a politician. . . .

They are maneuverers; they are finaglers. . . . They are much smarter than I am. They are interested in their personal ambition. . . . And that is what we are up against. . . .

"I want it straight from the shoulder. . . . I have been here ten years and your moral fibers begin to weaken after a while. . . . You can take a rubber band and keep pulling it, and after a while the thing just snaps. The things I could take five years ago . . . I can't take now."

He asked his staff to consider overnight the possibility of drafting a strong letter to the White House. Paul and Gaston, agreeing that the situation was intolerable, prepared that letter, which Morgenthau edited and then signed on July 27, 1943. "I am in doubt," he wrote Roosevelt, "whether you want me to go on doing for you what I've done in the past. . . . The whole atmosphere is one of doubt and uncertainty which I think will very greatly prejudice your ability to make recommendations on taxes to which Congress will give serious heed." Morgenthau therefore urged the President to give him "a clear and definite answer to two questions." First, was the Treasury to continue to coordinate the views of others in the Administration, and to present a tax program to the White House for the President's approval? Second, "Do you wish me to be in charge of presenting such a program?" to the Congress.

Roosevelt returned a classic answer, settling nothing, revealing no irritation, teasing but friendly. "AW HEN," he wrote on July 30. "The weather is hot and I am goin' off fishing. I decline to be serious even when you see 'gremlins' which ain't there!"

Back in Washington on August 10, the President had luncheon with Morgenthau. "I sent you a letter just before you left," the Secretary said, "in regard to this tax thing."

"Did you get my very snooty note," Roosevelt asked.

"Yes," Morgenthau replied, "I did and I didn't think it was snooty. I thought it was darling and I enjoyed it. I loved it."

"Now let me do the talking first," Roosevelt said. "In the first place, Jimmy Byrnes feels in his new position that taxes are a part of his over-all responsibility as well as other matters." Morgenthau interrupted. He had not referred to Byrnes but to Vinson.

"No, no," Roosevelt said. "Vinson has nothing to do with this. It is Jimmy Byrnes."

"Well," Morgenthau said, "look Mr. President, all I want you to say is that you want me to go ahead."

"You go ahead," Roosevelt replied, "as you always have. Get your tax bill ready — I take it you have a tax bill — and about the 24th I will be ready to see you and Paul and anybody you want to bring over to go over the tax bill with you and give you the okay. After that I would like to see George and Doughton."

"Do you really want a tax bill?" Morgenthau asked.

"You need 12 billion in taxes," Roosevelt answered. "So I think you should put up to Congress various plans which total 18 billion, so that they can pick a number of schemes which will raise 12 billion. . . . Now we used to give Congress a plan which would raise a definite amount and they didn't like it, so we have been giving them suggestions with the result that the newspapers said we had no plan. . . . Now, of course, we have a plan, but we have changed our method of presenting it to Congress. This year let's give them alternative plans to raise 18 billion dollars and then let them select what they want."

"The President," Morgenthau later noted in his Diary "was very firm in that he wanted me to go ahead as I always have done. . . . He also was very definite that he doesn't want to sign any memorandum to Byrnes or Vinson. He said, 'This is all one big family and you don't do things that way in a family.' He was very definite that he wants a strong tax bill."

He was very definite, too, that Byrnes and Vinson had a role to play. "Jimmy Byrnes talked to me," Roosevelt told Morgenthau on August 11, "about what you and I were talking about yesterday morning. . . . Jimmy Byrnes said that Bob Doughton said that he needs Vinson to help him, and that Vinson is the only man that can help him with the bill."

"That would be fine," Morgenthau replied. ". . . If he can give Bob Doughton any help, as far as I am concerned, that would be fine."

Morgenthau's own program also needed help on the Hill. In August 1943, as in January, he was "not willing to lower the

exemptions on the working people more than they are now."
He preferred to raise taxes on advancing corporate profits. He
also endorsed forced corporate (rather than individual) lending
according to a scheme that after the war would return funds to
the corporations for reconverting their plants to peacetime uses.
The heart of his policy still, he told his staff on August 17, was
an immediate, substantial increase in Social Security rates, calculated to yield $5.5 billion in new revenue. That increase, to be
followed only after the war with a broad expansion of Social
Security benefits, would accomplish the purpose of compulsory
lending while at the same time strengthening the fabric of American society. In this manner "at the end of twelve years Mr.
Roosevelt will have something to point to for the lower third of
this country," Morgenthau said. "To me that is much more important than all the rest of this stuff."

Walter George and Bob Doughton, Harold Smith and Jimmy
Byrnes disagreed. On the radio that night, Byrnes urged a large
compulsory lending program. "I was shocked," Morgenthau
wrote him. ". . . This statement is going to cause our State
War Finance Committees a great deal of trouble." There was no
reason for Morgenthau to be shocked, Byrnes replied, for the
Secretary had long known his view. Unless Roosevelt issued
specific orders forbidding him to advocate forced savings,
Byrnes would continue to do so — fair warning to the Treasury.

Other warnings followed apace. With the exception of the
Federal Reserve Board and the Social Security Board, all the interested executive agencies told the Treasury that the $12 billion
goal was too high. Late in August Roosevelt informed Morgenthau that he would accept $10 billion; early in September the
Ways and Means Committee suggested eight. After consultation
with the President, Morgenthau then grimly redefined the
Treasury objective as $10.5 billion, with increases in Social Secu-
rity to provide about half of that sum. The President would not
"put into writing" any definition of Byrnes's responsibilities, but
he did promise Morgenthau that he would "see that Byrnes
makes no more statements on compulsory savings." As for Morgenthau's "plan to consolidate social insurance with the tax bill,"

Roosevelt said, "I have been groping for something. . . . This sounds good and I like it."

The only people who really counted would support that kind of bill, Morgenthau replied, the people who were earning $3000 a year or less; "this will be good for those people, and it is good for America, because they are America."

Wholly dissatisfied, Jimmy Byrnes lost his temper at a White House meeting on September 9, 1943. Taxes, he said, as part of the problem of stabilization, had to be under his jurisdiction. Byrnes, according to the account of Randolph Paul, was "pretty bitter and hot. . . . The President tried to stop him a couple of times, but he slugged right on. . . . The Secretary didn't talk very much, but . . . he called the President's attention to that meeting . . . in which the President had said . . . that this Executive Order* did not contain any authority to issue directives to the Secretary." The Treasury, Roosevelt ruled, was to present and manage the tax bill on the Hill, but the President alone was the "responsible person," and the others "were serving as his agents in presenting the bill." On all questions of basic policy, decision was to lie with the White House. "I am the boss," Roosevelt said. "I realize that taxes fit into the inflation picture. . . . It is all in one picture. We must agree. . . . Then when we agree, I expect you fellows to go in and do the work just like soldiers."

Byrnes said he would not work for the bill unless he had a voice in it. He would take no orders from the Secretary of the Treasury. When he had left the Supreme Court to take over his job, he had done so in spite of a warning from Bernard Baruch that he could never handle it unless he had control over taxes. "I told Barnie," Byrnes said, ". . . 'I will take a chance.' . . . I have never had any trouble getting along with people previously. . . . I get along with Knox; I get along with Stimson; but I can't get along with the Secretary. He is the only man I can't get along with."

Angry as always when his subordinates fought in his presence, Roosevelt pounded the table. "I am the boss," he said again. "I

* Creating the Office of Economic Stabilization.

am the one who gets the rap if we get licked in Congress, and I
am the one who is in control. You people have to get together
on a tax bill and then we can work it the way I want which is for
the Treasury to present it . . . and the other people to work
behind scenes."

"I think you and I agree on this," Morgenthau said to Byrnes.

"I wouldn't agree with you," Byrnes snapped, "on anything."
And in spite of the President's remarks, Byrnes added: "I am
going to send for George and Doughton and see if we can't get a
bill."

"Livid," as Morgenthau later recalled, Roosevelt again
pounded his desk and repeated: "I am the boss, I am giving the
orders."

Four days later, on September 13, 1943, the President summoned the principals in the dispute to the White House, where
Paul and Morgenthau explained the Treasury's tax program with
its emphasis on Social Security. Quietly, Byrnes and Vinson,
after recalling their active interest in the Social Security legislation of 1935, analyzed the political obstacles to expanding Social
Security in 1943. The Treasury's intention to include medical
insurance in the Social Security plan, they predicted, would stir
up "more than a hornet's nest." Roosevelt, after reflecting overnight, told the group the next day that he thought the country
would favor an extension of Social Security if the matter were
properly presented. For a moment Morgenthau thought he had
won his case, but Byrnes interrupted to explain his scheme for
enforced savings, and Roosevelt swung over to that idea. In pencil the President wrote out a memorandum of his decision. It
called for raising an additional $5 billion through increments in
the graduated income tax. After the war taxpayers would have
an option of accepting a partial cash refund or a paid-up life insurance policy equivalent to the entire increase in taxes. Those
earning less than $3000 a year, who were to be exempt from the
new rates, would instead make additional contributions to their
unemployment and old age accounts under Social Security.
When Morgenthau said that the refundable tax proposal would
impede the pending bond drive, Byrnes suggested deferring dis-

cussion of the entire tax question until after that drive was completed. There matters were left until the group could meet with the congressional leaders the following day.

At that conference Roosevelt again presided. Working from a Treasury memorandum that reflected the discussions of the two previous days, the President suggested increases in excise taxes to raise an additional $2.5 billion, increases in estate and gift taxes to raise an additional $400 million, and increases in corporate taxes to raise an additional $1.1 billion. He went on to describe the refundable tax scheme he had devised, which would yield, according to Treasury calculations, between $3.5 and $4.5 billion.

That program, Doughton and George immediately said, could not survive in their committees. Their colleagues would vote down any higher payroll taxes. Personally opposed to any scheme involving a postwar rebate, Doughton preferred outright taxation even if it yielded less revenue.

The meeting left Morgenthau dissatisfied. "People like Byrnes and Vinson are going to get Congress in such a frame of mind that I can't work with them," he complained to the President privately. ". . . If they keep this thing up you and nobody but you can stop them." But Roosevelt assured him that "Byrnes was all right." And in his Diary, the Secretary shrugged the matter off: "The President's attitude toward me is always very friendly and I gather he thinks the whole thing is rather funny. So I don't see any sense in my becoming tragic about it, but I will just have to continue to look after my own interests."

To that end, the Secretary enlisted Harry Hopkins, Sam Rosenman, William Green, and Philip Murray behind the Treasury's Social Security plan, but Roosevelt received equally vigorous protests against the plan from Congress. "The only person," the President told Morgenthau on September 27, "who can explain this medical thing is myself. The people are unprepared." And so was the White House. "You don't want, I am sure," Roosevelt said to Walter George at a meeting the next day, "to have anybody come up and present a Social Security program at this time. . . . I know you don't want it. . . . We can't go up against the State Medical Societies; we just can't do it." As Morgenthau interpreted the meeting to his staff: "They're only interested in what they can get through Congress."

As the tax bill emerged in January 1944, it contained so many inequities and produced so little revenue that Randolph Paul, Herbert Gaston, and Dan Bell urged Morgenthau to recommend a veto to the President. Undecided, the Secretary consulted Byrnes on February 1, 1944. "If you ask your mother for a dollar," Byrnes said, "and she gives you . . . a dime, you're not going to turn the dime down. You go back for ninety cents this afternoon." But the arguments of Vinson, Paul, Bell, and Ben Cohen, now his general counsel, moved Byrnes, who sent Morgenthau a message on February 10 that "he had changed his mind about the bill" and now favored a veto. Morgenthau, in contrast, had come to believe the President should let the revenue bill become law without his signature, as he had in 1938. Roosevelt disagreed. With the Secretary on February 13, he said: "I am going to do what everybody is urging me to do. . . . I am going to veto it."

Randolph Paul contributed to the draft of the veto message, which Byrnes, Vinson, and Ben Cohen prepared. As Roosevelt sent it to Congress on February 22, that message condemned the revenue bill as "wholly ineffective" for meeting the budgetary and economic needs of the nation, and as "dangerous" in its provisions for "indefensible privileges for special groups." "In this respect," the President said, "it is not a tax bill but a tax relief bill providing relief not for the needy but for the greedy."

In a quick, hot retort, nineteen of the twenty-five members of the Ways and Means Committee declared that Roosevelt's $10.5 billion goal would have been "oppressive to tax payers and dangerous for the national economy," as well as a threat to "the solvency of all business." Alben Barkley, the Democratic Majority Leader in the Senate, long an effective lieutenant of the White House, went further. Resigning his post on February 23, he called the veto message a "calculated and deliberate assault upon the legislative integrity of every member of Congress. . . . If the Congress . . . has any self-respect yet left, it will override the veto." It did — the House on February 24, 299 to 98; the

Senate the next day, 72 to 14. Roosevelt patched things up with "Dear Alben," to whom he wrote a soothing letter and whose reelection as Majority Leader he urged upon the willing Senate Democrats. But the damage was done. Congress had passed a revenue act over a veto for the first time in American history, and Congress had so thoroughly routed the Administration that debate about taxation ceased for the duration of the war.

The newspapermen covering the Treasury warned Morgenthau that congressmen of both parties, bitterly resentful of the veto message, blamed it largely on Randolph Paul. Paul's prestige on the Hill, the reports added, had vanished, and the Secretary's was fading rapidly. Hoping to temper that hostility, some of Morgenthau's advisers suggested he explain to Doughton that the Treasury had opposed a veto. But Morgenthau preferred to take his beating. As he put it to his staff on March 1, 1944:

> The President did it his way; that is his privilege. I will never forget, after all, I am here as an appointed officer. . . .
> As far as the press is concerned, my statement, if they ask me, is this: "The President of the United States made up his mind. We gave him certain advice. What we gave him is his business and his business only, and I have no comment to make." . . .
> I told my wife — I made the rather trite remark that somebody would have to be the ham in the sandwich, as between the President and the Congress, and I was expecting to be it. . . .
> Now . . . somebody has to take it. I am perfectly willing to take it, but it does give you a gripe when a man like Byrnes will run to cover just as soon as it gets hot. . . . Anybody who is loyal to the President is going to get it.

Congress, not the Treasury, was the proper object of criticism and attack. Various economists believed the Treasury erred in not sponsoring a program for compulsory lending, but the kind of program that Jimmy Byrnes preferred would have met no better fate on the Hill in 1942 and 1943. Most important, both Morgenthau and Paul remained persuaded that their recommendations, potentially effective against inflation, also advanced the cause of social reform and preserved the voluntary bond program with the income for the federal government which it produced. There were also economists who contended that the Treasury was unwise in resisting a sales tax. Morgenthau disagreed, for his staff had calculated again and again that the yield from a sales tax would have been relatively insignificant, while its social impact would have been regressive.

Those issues aside, the Treasury's general policies stood on their merits. The taxes the department recommended were enforceable; they were designed to produce the funds needed to defray on a current basis at least half the cost of the war; they had the capacity to close the inflationary gap; and, unlike the recommendations of any other group in Washington, they reflected the spirit of the New Deal. In rejecting the Treasury's programs, the Congress damaged the economy, weakened the government's finances, rewarded those already overprivileged, and penalized the vast majority of Americans. Taxation for war ran counter to the purposes Morgenthau held highest — the mobilization of maximum resources to defeat the Axis; the construction of a good society in the nation and in the world.

XVIII

FINANCING THE GRAND ALLIANCE
1941–1944

DURING THE YEAR after Pearl Harbor, the United States and her allies suffered a succession of grave defeats. Japanese forces overran the Philippines, Malaya and the islands of the Central and Southwest Pacific, and were poised for an attack on Australia. In North Africa German troops, advancing past the western border of Egypt, threatened Cairo and British control of the entire Middle East. In Europe the Nazis marched to the outskirts of Leningrad and Stalingrad. While the Grand Alliance was on the defensive, the products of the American arsenal had to be distributed to sustain resistance to Axis gains across the globe, and to prepare for the counterattacks already planned. Launched in late 1942 and 1943, those thrusts turned the Germans back in Russia, cleared them out of North Africa, and drove them north in Italy — all preparatory to the cross-channel invasion of 1944 on which victory depended. So, too, in the Pacific, the Allies began at Guadalcanal the long march north toward Japan.

Morgenthau had no voice in the strategy of the Grand Alliance and very little in the logistics supporting it, but it did fall to him and the Treasury to find ways to finance the alliance in whatever volume the President and his military advisers prescribed. Now and then the Secretary assessed policy from the point of view of his ordinary departmental responsibilities, but when his conclusions diverged from those based upon the political and military considerations of the war, he invariably yielded. His was basically a staff position, and in that role, while candid in his advice to the President, he also, like a good soldier, executed unhesitatingly the orders he received. Those orders, moreover, because of Roosevelt's continuing personal trust in him, involved Morgenthau now and then in missions extending beyond the ordinary borders of the Treasury to questions relating to the prosecution of the war and the development of policy for the postwar world.

1. Russia: "This Is Critical"

Three days after Pearl Harbor, Maxim Litvinov, the new ambassador from Russia, called at the Treasury. He and Morgenthau had known each other since the negotiations that led to American recognition of the Soviet Union in 1933. Now Litvinov, of all eminent Russians the most popular in the United States, had returned to Washington. His predecessor, he said, had told him to go to Morgenthau when he needed help. He would be glad, Morgenthau replied, to assist the Russians in any way "that would aid in defeating Hitler."

An early opportunity arose on January 1, 1942. In order to purchase American materials unavailable through Lend-Lease, the Soviet Union arranged through the Treasury to borrow $20 million against delivery of gold within six months. The transaction resembled several completed during the previous half-year, and as Morgenthau and his assistants remarked, regular Russian gold payments had confirmed the integrity of the Soviets in meeting their contracts.

The United States was doing less well in fulfilling its Lend-

Lease commitments to the Soviet Union. Indeed, in the early months of 1942, deliveries to all allies flagged because of the growing crisis in shipping. The sea lanes to Russia, exposed both to Nazi submarines in the Atlantic and to Nazi air attacks from Norway, were especially vulnerable. Still, Morgenthau suspected that American inefficiency was contributing to the problem.

At his direction, Gerard Swope, the able president of General Electric who was on temporary duty with the Treasury, talked with Admiral Emory S. Land, the chief of the Maritime Commission, who was taking the brunt of the criticism for American shipping failures. Land, Swope reported on January 22, 1942, said "that he's been kicked all around by the President and also by Harry Hopkins . . . and that if anybody can run the thing better than he does, why they're welcome to it; but that they have already . . . sent thirteen ships to Russia, and they will send fourteen more this month." Land needed 639 ships and had only 400; under the circumstances, he was "just doing the best he knows how."

In the following weeks the procurement of supplies for the Soviet Union and the movement of those supplies to port, while erratic, proceeded more rapidly than did shipments. Goods piled up in New York and elsewhere on the East Coast while Russian complaints accumulated at the Treasury. Many of those complaints related to materials the Russians had ordered through the Department's Division of Procurement. Because the War Production Board had not given those orders a high enough priority, deficiencies had developed, largely in various kinds of steel and steel plate.

Morgenthau took the problem to Roosevelt on March 11. "I do not want to be in the same position as the English," the President said. "The English promised the Russians two divisions. They failed. They promised them help in the Caucasus. They failed. Every promise the English have made to the Russians, they have fallen down on. . . . The only reason we stand so well with the Russians is that up to date we have kept our promises. I suppose the reason we are behind in our deliveries to Rus-

sia is because we got into the war ourselves. . . . I would go out
and take the stuff off the shelves of the stores, and pay them any
price necessary, and put it in a truck and rush it to the boat. . . .
Nothing would be worse than to have the Russians collapse.
. . . I would rather lose New Zealand, Australia or anything
else than have the Russians collapse."

Morgenthau, the President said, was to see to it personally that
"the stuff" moved to Russia. Initialing a chit in his own handwriting, Roosevelt wrote: "This is *critical* because (a) we *must*
keep our word (b) because Russian resistance counts *most* today."

As the Secretary explained it to his staff: "The President said
he wanted me to get everybody together and say that as far as he
was concerned they had made a perfect monkey out of him, that
he couldn't stand for it. He would rather lose fifty ships off the
Atlantic Coast than have Russia fold up and make peace. It
would just have to be done. . . . I am quite excited."

At the conference the next day, March 12, 1942, Morgenthau read the President's order to officials from Lend-Lease, the
War Production Board, the Maritime Commission, and other
agencies. The President, he added, "just wasn't going to accept
any excuses." There were plenty of those. Edward Stettinius,
Jr., the head of the Lend-Lease Administration, blamed the Russians for their "failure to bring in their specifications on time."
They had submitted "Tiffany requirements. . . . They had
been told constantly for months, that they could have the steel
if they would take a standard type." In that case, Morgenthau
said, the President ought to have had a memorandum of explanation. "If it was mine to settle," he added later, "and you had a
certain kind of steel rolling out and it was 2 per cent nickel and
they wanted 4, I would give them the 2 per cent."

For the tie-up of freight cars at Norfolk and Philadelphia, the
Russians also bore some responsibility, for they had insisted on
using their own methods of designating railroad cars for loading
aboard ship. "It seems to me," Morgenthau said, "that before
they put in sixteen ships into Philadelphia that somebody might
have had the foresight to work out the rail traffic thing so that

the thing would flow smoothly to these ships and not have this jam which they have got there now." Representatives of the Railroad Administration admitted that was true, though they also felt that shippers had given them too little advance information to permit proper planning.

Admiral Land foresaw no quick solutions: "You were just singing a song for me here that is going to be sung right along, and that is going to get progressively worse. We haven't got enough ships. . . . The sinkings are going faster than the buildings, and there are a thousand other excuses that are not worthwhile even to go into. . . . A lot of this trouble . . . is the Russians themselves. It took me months to find out who was the shipping man that I could contact. I was passed around the ring like the ball in a football field."

As the discussion ended, Morgenthau asked for assistance in preparing a memorandum for Roosevelt describing the efforts being made to meet the commitments of the protocol. "These confessional meetings," he said, "are good for the soul. . . . From the way the President spoke yesterday, if you are short on something, take it and he will back you to the limit. . . . Filling his promises to Stalin . . . that came first over and above everything else."

The consequences of the meeting were considerable. Within a day, the War Department arranged for a change in authority over inland transportation that promised to accelerate loadings and thereby to relieve the shipping shortage by speeding turnabouts. "That's at least a little something done," Morgenthau reported to the President's secretary. ". . . Tell him I'm keeping after it." Roosevelt kept after it too. To the Cabinet on March 26, he stressed the importance of living up to American commitments; his word and the national honor were at stake. "He thought it was very important," Dan Bell, who attended the meeting, reported to Morgenthau, "that everybody understand his position in this connection and make every effort to deliver all of the items required under the protocol by July 1, when it terminates. He said he wanted Mr. Welles to begin discussing immediately with the Russians the question of renewing that protocol. . . . He also wanted to increase the amount under the new protocol."

"The whole question of whether we win or lose the war depends upon the Russians," Roosevelt told Morgenthau on June 16. "If the Russians can hold out this summer and keep three-and-a-half million Germans engaged in war we can definitely win." Losses on convoy runs to Murmansk were staggering, but Roosevelt remained sanguine through the summer. "I don't see any dark spots," he said in early September. ". . . I have said right along that if the Russians can hold on . . . we are all right, and I think they are going to."

"The amusing thing about the President," Morgenthau noted in his Diary, "is that he can state these facts coolly and calmly whether we win or lose the war, and to me it is most encouraging that he really seems to face these issues, and that he is not kidding himself one minute about the war. That, to me, seems to be the correct attitude for a commander-in-chief to take."

Heartening, too, was the improvement in the American delivery of materials to Russia. The first Lend-Lease protocol committed the United States to make available by June 30, 1942, goods estimated at a value of $750 million. By that date, the United States had delivered close to 80 per cent of the quota, and had also provided outside of the protocol other items that brought the value of the total to more than 100 per cent of the original obligation. That record partly reflected improved communications between the Soviet supply mission and American agencies, partly, the pressure on those agencies exerted by the President and Morgenthau.

In diminishing degree, similar pressure had on occasion to correct lags in shipments to Russia during the rest of the war. As Roosevelt put it in a memorandum of early January 1943, "the Army and Navy are definitely of the opinion that Russian continuance as a major factor in the war is of cardinal importance, and therefore it must be a basic factor in our strategy to provide her with the maximum amount of supplies that can be delivered in her ports. . . . In executing the Second Protocol and in planning the over-all program, . . . the necessity of meeting Soviet needs . . . must be regarded as a matter of paramount importance." By the summer of 1943 American performance, now under the Third Protocol, continuously met the standards the President had set. Morgenthau therefore had no further occasion to intercede.

American and British preparations in 1944 for the cross-channel attack contributed to the serenity of the relationship between the United States and the Soviet Union in the first six months of that year. Though Russia's political purposes, according to State Department analysts in Moscow, remained at variance with American expectations, political issues seemed remote with military victory still so distant, and Roosevelt valued Stalin's support for the Anglo-American invasion of Europe that American military planners so warmly advocated.

2. China: The Price of Friendship

China and Japan, enemies in the field for years, had yet to declare war on each other on December 7, 1941. Partly to show sympathy with the United States, China indicated her readiness to declare war, though she was delaying, her government said, in the hope — patently futile — that the Soviet Union might join her. So informed by T. V. Soong, Morgenthau also learned that in the view of the President and the State Department, China should declare war not on Japan only but also on Germany and Italy. China did so, but her usefulness as an ally depended on various uncertainties. Without substantial shipments of American materials, Generalissimo Chiang Kai-shek remained, as he had long been, incapable of significant military action. Further, the successful Japanese offensives of December 1941 and January 1942 cut off avenues of supply to China except by air across the Himalayas from India, a cumbersome and dangerous route. Those victories also accentuated the vulnerability of the whole

South Pacific area, including Australia and New Zealand. The United States and Great Britain were therefore eager to ensure China's resistance and to tie up a substantial Japanese force otherwise available for aggression elsewhere. In Roosevelt's interpretation, China's declaration of war gave her a status equal to that of the English-speaking belligerents, but that declaration also strengthened the Generalissimo's demands for extensive Anglo-American assistance, which the corruption within the Nationalist government threatened to waste.

Long an effective advocate of aid to China, Morgenthau had developed serious doubts about the honesty and efficiency of the circle around Chiang Kai-shek. Information he received early in December 1941 confirmed his suspicions that Chiang was financially irresponsible, uneducated, and brazenly unapologetic for the failure of his regime to advance the people's rights or welfare.

There was no serious dissent from that analysis by the American ambassador in Chungking, Clarence E. Gauss, or by most members of his staff, or most western newspaper correspondents, or by the Treasury officials who advised Morgenthau about policy for China. Foremost of those advisers was Harry Dexter White, whose counsel was later subject to particular attack because of postwar accusations, which he denied under oath, that he had been at one time a Communist or Communist agent. Whatever the merit of those charges, the attitudes toward China that White expressed during the war were close to the consensus of informed American observers. Even on questions of monetary policy, his major responsibility, he neither always influenced Morgenthau nor always agreed with him, but he did have a large and continuing voice in Treasury deliberations about many matters, China not the least.

About that there was no secret, then or later. First hired by the Treasury as a specialist in monetary questions, recommended by Jacob Viner, a distinguished economist, White in 1940 became Director of Monetary Research, a promotion he earned by his capacity for hard work, his success in the management of the Stabilization Fund, and his initiative in assisting the Secretary in related matters. "To make life easier for me," Morgenthau announced to his morning group the day after Pearl Harbor, "and . . . better for the Treasury, I want to give Harry White the status of an Assistant Secretary. He will be in charge of all foreign affairs for me. . . . I want it in one brain and I want it in Harry White's brain. He will tell Bell as much as Bell wants to know. . . . When it is some question of foreign matters, Harry will come in and see me and I will give him a decision and when the decision is made he will tell you about it. If it in any way crosses anything that you have got, he will come in first and see you and ask your views."

Cordell Hull, when Morgenthau informed him of White's new role, remarked that "he's a mighty suitable man . . . a very high class fellow." Increasingly of that opinion, Morgenthau in 1943 asked White "to take supervision over and assume full responsibility for Treasury's participation in all economic and financial matters . . . in connection with the operations of the Army and Navy and the civilian affairs in the foreign areas in which our armed forces are operating." And in 1944 Morgenthau made White an Assistant Secretary of the Treasury. "Harry," he then said to Roosevelt, "has done a swell job."

He had done so, the Secretary knew, against large personal odds. "He could be disagreeable," Morgenthau said years later, "quick-tempered, overly ambitious, and power went to his head." He was rude, abrupt, and impatient with opposition, which he often tried to circumvent by going outside of ordinary bureaucratic channels — a habit that could be identified with furtiveness or even confused with subversion. He appointed some assistants who were almost certainly members of the Communist Party, though Morgenthau did not know they were, and those assistants, in White's view, were as free to pass along information about Treasury policy to the Russians as was Averell Harriman, for example, free to talk to the British. But White did not himself hew to the line of the Communist Party. Further, he was also energetic, unsparing of himself, a bulldog in defense of his chief and the Treasury, and something of a hero to his subordinates who found him considerate, creative, attentive, and helpful. Morgenthau in all his years in office had no reason to question their impression, no reason to doubt White's competence or loyalty or value to the department.

White and his assistants, in the weeks just after Pearl Harbor, agreed with Roosevelt on the overriding need to keep China in the war; with Morgenthau on the desirability of combating corruption in Chungking; and with the Chinese themselves on the gravity of the problem of inflation. Money, early in 1942, provided one obvious means for executing American policy in China. The Chinese treasury and banking system desperately needed dollars to help arrest the accelerating depreciation of the fapi, the Chinese unit of currency. Inflation in China, in the opinion of the American Treasury and Ambassador, arose primarily from the pressure of demand on diminishing supplies of food, textiles, and hard goods, but the financial irresponsibility of the government made things worse.

Politics rather than economics provided the major justification for considering the $500 million loan that Chiang Kai-shek requested on December 30, 1941. It was intended, he admitted, to buttress the morale of the Chinese people after Pearl Harbor. As Ambassador Gauss pointed out, a loan of about $10 million would probably suffice to retard inflation. The primary benefits of a larger loan would be psychological. At the Treasury on January 9, 1942, Assistant Secretary of State Adolf Berle argued that $500 million was necesssary to strengthen the position of the Generalissimo who, except for the Communists, represented the only important resistance to the Japanese. That was the President's conclusion, too. "In regard to the Chinese loan," Roosevelt wrote Morgenthau that day, "I realize there is little security which China can give at the present time, yet I am anxious to help Chiang Kai-shek and his currency. I hope you can invent some way of doing this. Possibly we could buy a certain amount of this currency, even if it means a partial loss later on."

Following the President's lead, Cordell Hull defined official State Department policy. "The Generalissimo's proposal," he wrote Morgenthau on January 10, 1942, "has been given very careful consideration. I feel that, as an act of wartime policy and to prevent the impairment of China's military effort which would result from loss of confidence in Chinese currency . . . it is highly advisable that the United States extend financial assistance to the government of China."

Nevertheless Morgenthau hesitated. "The President and the State Department want me to make a loan to China," he told his staff on January 12, ". . . but . . . I would like to do this thing in the way that we could sort of kind of feed it out to them if they keep fighting, but I would hate to put $300 million on the line and say, 'Here, boys, that is yours.' "

With Morgenthau that afternoon, T. V. Soong "went through a long rigmarole, trying . . . to justify this loan." Quoting Chiang Kai-shek, Soong used a military analogy: "I can't tell you where I am going to put my troops, I've got to have my troops, and then I will tell you where I will put them." Responding to that metaphor, Morgenthau said that he would commend the use of American dollars to pay Chinese forces to attack the Japanese. "How about if we could pay these troops with silver dollars," he asked Soong. ". . . How would they like it?" Soong's face lit up. "What I am thinking of, " the Secretary continued, ". . . once a month to make you an advance for a month." As the Secretary explained it to his staff: "I was trying to think of some way so that while the boys fight they get their money, and if they don't fight, no money." He was also thinking, he said, of making the American dollar the basic unit of exchange for the whole world after the war. Direct support of the Chinese armies would be a step in that direction. Such support, moreover, was preferable to buying up fapi, for once a loan had been used for that purpose, the Chinese, Morgenthau was sure, would simply print more currency "just as fast as you get it."

Though Harry White and his assistants emphasized the disadvantages of his proposal, they did not sway Morgenthau. As he told his staff on January 13, 1942: "I was wholly indiscreet last night and enjoyed it. I first tried it out on Halifax, and it was all right. Then for one hour I got Mr. Churchill thinking about China. . . . I got him quite excited and I got Lord Beaverbrook quite excited." In the absence of significant assistance, the Secretary had told Churchill, Chiang Kai-shek might move closer to the Japanese and others of the "yellow-races." Churchill, as Morgenthau recalled, "conceded they might figure . . . you couldn't count on the white races." "If there is anything the United States Treasury wants to do," the Prime Minister said, "you take the leadership and we will go along with you. We will back you up 100 per cent." At least, Morgenthau concluded, "I got Churchill's mind on it. He was very much interested. They all seemed to like the idea of this business of the soldiers."

The State Department did not, but Morgenthau took the matter to the White House. Roosevelt, "very enthusiastic" about the payment of Chinese troops, as Morgenthau recalled his words, said: "The State Department doesn't know what they are talking about. Supposing I want to make an arrangement with Chiang Kai-shek, who is Chairman of that Board . . . and I want a million attack troops, and . . . I may want to take Shanghai. I may want to support the Philippines. I may want to do anything, but I need a million troops. . . . Now, I expect to pay for them. I will pay for them out of my own funds . . . as Commander in Chief . . . five dollars for maintenance, to the Government . . . per month, and five dollars to the troops themselves. . . . We will call it the D-E-M-O, democracy, the new currency."

That afternoon Morgenthau repeated the substance of Roosevelt's statement to T. V. Soong, and on January 21, 1942, Soong delivered Chiang Kai-shek's adverse reply. The Generalissimo "urgently requests that careful consideration be given to his original proposal. . . . This loan should be regarded in the light of an advance to an ally fighting against the common enemy thus requiring no security or other pre-arranged terms as to its use and as regards means of repayment." The State Department, in a similar vein, recommended a prompt and generous loan in order to secure maximum political effect, as did White, who advised, however, setting definite conditions so as to guarantee the greatest possible anti-inflationary impact of the loan.

Still uncomfortable, the Secretary telephoned Henry Stimson on January 28, 1942. Negotiations with the Chinese were difficult, Morgenthau said: "The attitude that they're taking . . . is — really . . . a hold-up. . . . This is what I'd like to get from you and General Marshall. . . . I'd like to come over and call on you . . . and go to school as to just how much are we or should we be worried that Chiang Kai-shek might stop fighting if certain things happen." At the War Department the next morning, Morgenthau learned for the first time that General Stilwell was going to Chungking to serve as Chief of Staff under Chiang, a development that Marshall considered encouraging. As for China, according to Morgenthau's notation in his Diary, "Marshall regarded the situation seriously" and Stimson had concluded "that at any price we should keep them going." Morgenthau, Stimson also said, had erred in offering to pay Chinese troops. He had done so, Morgenthau replied, only after discussions with Churchill, Roosevelt, and Soong. "Well," Stimson said, "you can't trust T. V. Soong. . . . In my experience of Orientals, if you say something to them as a proposal, they will always say yes . . . but they will get word to you in some round about way which often makes you think that they have double-crossed you, but they just can't say no to you."

Though his "heart wasn't in it," Morgenthau felt he had to handle the Chinese loan. "The President asked me to do it," he said, "and I would have to go and tell the President I didn't think I could do it, something which I have never done before." In that case, Stimson urged him not to permit any differences between the Treasury and the State Department to interfere. "I am pushing the matter," Morgenthau said. "Please do," Stimson replied, " . . . whatever the cost is."

Though not without personal reservations, push the loan Morgenthau did. "This is nothing but blackmail," Litvinov told him. The Secretary agreed: "Yes, and at a time when we have our back to the wall in the Pacific, I don't like it." But there seemed to be no alternative, and on January 29 he wrote Hull that the Treasury was ready "to go ahead at once. . . . You may wish to consider the desirability of the President and ourselves meeting promptly with the congressional leaders to advise them of the problem and to discuss the . . . methods of financial assistance. With their clearance, it would be possible for the President to make an immediate announcement that he and the congressional leaders are prepared . . . to grant China . . . the financial assistance requested by Chiang Kai-shek. The details could be worked out later."

After the Cabinet meeting the next day, Roosevelt chose to discuss the question of procedures in the Cabinet room, as Morgenthau later told his staff, "with everybody buzzing around and talking at the top of their voices." While they were talking, Hull kept looking around for Jesse Jones, who "was waiting just about three feet away from Hull and he dived right between Hull and the President. It really was funny. I mean, whenever there is anything like that up there, Jesse just sort of crowds himself, sort of leans over on them so he gets in on it. . . . It was going all right, but Hull . . . the last minute he brings him in and Jesse, smelling some new business,* he was only two feet behind . . . So he barges his chair right between Hull and the President, and I tried to explain the thing. . . . The President listened, and of course there was all this talking going on around. It was the most unfavorable circumstances that I ever presented anything in. Jesse . . . tried to get in and the President said 'Well, why can't you, Jesse, buy some goods?' and . . . Jesse said, 'I could lend them some money against some goods,' and the President said, 'No, no, that won't be any good.' I said, 'Mr. President, you might just as well do it right out in the open. So then . . . there will be congressional action, and that is what Chiang Kai-shek wants. . . . He wants the prestige of a loan backed by Congress to give him face opposite the Japanese.' So then Jesse said, 'Well, wouldn't it be just as good if it was from the President?' Well, of course, there was only one answer I could say. That was 'Yes.' So the President said, 'Well, explore it, Jesse, and if you don't find there is any way that you can do it, then Hull, Jones, and Morgenthau should go up on the Hill to-

---

* For his Reconstruction Finance Corporation or another of the several lending agencies he ran.

gether Monday and see the leaders.' . . . I am used to it. It is Washington, and it is the way they do business here. Now, if I didn't want the Chinese to get anything I would just sit tight and do nothing, but I do want the Chinese to get something, so I am going to call up Berle and tell him that."

Jones, to Morgenthau's surprise, proved to be wholly amenable to the Treasury's suggestions for procedure, which Hull also endorsed on January 31. Hull's hands, Morgenthau observed after they had talked, were "the color of pale yellow parchment, and shaking . . . it's terribly depressing." But the Secretary of State agreed to brief the President on the State Department's reasons for recommending the loan, while Morgenthau prepared letters of support to be signed by Roosevelt, Stimson, and Knox. Jones assisted in drafting the text for a Joint Resolution of Congress, which the President immediately approved. It authorized him "to loan or extend credit or give other financial aid to China in an amount not to exceed in the aggregate $500 million at such . . . times and upon such terms and conditions as the Secretary of the Treasury with the approval of the President shall deem in the interest of the United States." It was Jones, not Morgenthau, who altered the original draft of that resolution to include the direct reference to the Secretary of the Treasury. Later, another alteration in phraseology asserted, in the manner of the Lend-Lease Act, that China and her independent future were "vital to the defense of the United States."

"I read to him the joint resolution," Morgenthau noted in his Diary after seeing T. V. Soong that same day, " . . . and told him what we'd done and how we were going up . . . on the Hill, and he should let the Generalissimo know. . . . Soong said this would be very pleasing to the Generalissimo. . . . I told him we appreciated how much the Chinese had done during the last four years, and they of all people should receive help at this time."

"This proposal is a war measure," Morgenthau said in testifying for the loan on February 3, 1942. "The effective continuance of the Chinese military effort — so invaluable in our fight against the Axis Powers — depends largely upon the strength of the economic structure of Free China. . . . The Chinese financial and monetary system should be made as strong as possible."

Under questioning in executive session by members of the House Foreign Affairs Committee, Morgenthau admitted that he was recommending the loan at the urging of the Secretary of State and the Secretary of War, as well as General Marshall, and "as a political and military loan." Asked how the loan was to be administered, he replied that the Treasury would open a credit on its books in the amount of $500 million, and then discuss uses with the Chinese. He did not expect the Chinese to draw on the money immediately, but he did believe that it had to be granted in a lump sum and at once in order to buttress Chinese morale. He wanted to make it "taste as good as possible" to the Chinese; he did not want to drive a hard bargain. The loan might be used to curb inflation, but its real purpose was to keep the Chinese interested in the Allied cause.

Congress had no illusions about the joint resolution, which it quickly passed. Yet in his message to Chiang Kai-shek of February 7, 1942, Roosevelt had to maintain the pretense which he and his subordinates had cultivated. "The unusual speed and unanimity with which this measure was acted upon by the Congress," the President wrote, "and the enthusiastic support which it received throughout the United States testified to the wholehearted respect and admiration which the Government and people of this country have for China. They testify also to our earnest desire and determination to be concretely helpful to our partners in the great battle for freedom. . . . It is my hope and belief that use which will be made of the funds . . . will contribute substantially toward facilitating the efforts of the Chinese Government and people to meet the economic and financial burdens which have been thrust upon them by an armed invasion." Those words, as all American principals to the transactions realized, of necessity put into idealistic cadence the high price of Chinese friendship.

3. China: "A Peculiar and Interesting Situation"

During 1942 and 1943, American military strategy in the Orient looked to the relief of China through the reconquest of Burma and the reopening of the Burma Road, and to the build-up of China as the main base for an attack against Japan. Those purposes, always remote in these years, informed the increasingly irascible negotiations of General Stilwell with Chiang Kai-shek, guided the allocation of the slim resources that the United States could transport across the Himalayas, and established the bases for Morgenthau's responses to problems arising in the disbursement of the Chinese loan. The Treasury during 1942 and 1943 denied the Chinese nothing that the loan agreement permitted them to request, though the temptations to refuse were inherent in the persistent inefficacy of Chinese financial policy, which failed to pursue the most practicable courses to stem inflation.

In spite of his resulting impatience, Morgenthau bent the Treasury's efforts to the prevailing exigencies, which commanded agreement with China's preferences in the management of the money promised her. He began in April 1942, when H. H. Kung asked for the deposit of $200 million to the Chinese account at the New York Federal Reserve Bank. Kung also requested investment of the money in United States bonds and notes until the Chinese were ready to draw upon it. In time, they intended to use it to back the sale of securities to the Chinese public so as to absorb some of the fapi outstanding. Dan Bell thought it unfortunate that the Treasury would have to pay interest indefinitely on the securities that the Chinese bought with American funds loaned to them. But Morgenthau concluded that "it would be a mistake to show any hesitation in handing over the $200 million." He therefore "held his nose" and transferred the money. The Chinese Ministry of Finance made a fiasco of its sales of the dollar-backed securities, which were traded, the Treasury concluded, to the considerable personal advantage of members of the Soong and Kung families.

Nevertheless, Morgenthau followed Roosevelt's instructions to assist Madame Chiang Kai-shek, who arrived in the United States for a long visit early in 1943. At her urging and the President's, he conferred with various Chinese representatives about ways in which the Treasury could help the Chinese government control inflation. Kung particularly wanted to use $200 million of the 1942 loan to purchase gold in the United States for shipment to China and for sale there to absorb much of the currency which had been printed in such vast supply. The Monetary Division was dubious about the scheme. If the gold fell into the hands of the Central Bank, it would provide a further basis for extension of credit, a further invitation to inflation. But the sale of gold in small bars to Chinese merchants and businessmen might help, if the government refrained from printing new currency to replace whatever fapi were retired. In any case, Madame Chiang solicited approval for the plan, which Morgenthau granted in principle.

In July 1943, Kung asked for the $200 million with which to buy the gold. Morgenthau then reminded him of the large costs of shipping and the difficulties in executing the program, which might sacrifice important Chinese assets for postwar reconstruction. But on July 27, 1943, the Secretary agreed to a formal request from the Chinese Ambassador. "In order to avoid unnecessary raising of funds by the United States Treasury," he added, "it is suggested that transfers from the credit of the Chinese Government for the purchase of gold be made at such time and in such amounts as are allowed by existing facilities for transportation. . . . On receipt of requests from . . . China that a specific amount should be transferred . . . and be used for the purchase of gold, the necessary action will be taken." To that suggestion Kung agreed.

Three months later China asked for $50 million in accordance with the Treasury's promise. In a memorandum of a conversation with Morgenthau of September 29, 1943, Harry White wrote: "I said that I thought we ought to be tough with the Chinese on the question of earmarking $200 million of gold for gold sales. . . . The Secretary agreed. He said he thought that we should be tough in this matter and he told me to go ahead and let them have the gold only as rapidly as it could be shipped and sold in China." Though Kung did not call for much gold, the psychological effects of the announcement of the new arrangements seemed to help retard the rate of inflation during the last two months of 1943.

On that account, Morgenthau on December 18, 1943, suggested to Roosevelt a doubling of gold shipments as a further palliative, though not a cure, for Chinese inflation, for which "the basic reason," he noted, was the continuing "shortage of goods." The Secretary thought that shipments were already at $6 million a month. In fact, as White told him in January, they were far less than that, and farther still from the $12 million a month Morgenthau had suggested or the $25 million a month that Roosevelt then contemplated. Indeed, through the first half of 1944 total shipments came to only $2 million of gold, but they were adequate for meeting Morgenthau's justifiable order to let China have gold "as rapidly as it could be shipped and sold." Had sales moved faster, shipments would have, too.

Discussions about the gold program during the latter half of 1943 proceeded concurrently with negotiations relating to other aspects of China's inflation. The United States was spending on various military and civilian projects close to $20 million a month in China, would soon spend more, and could not conceivably afford to operate at the official rate. Morgenthau therefore explored the possibility of buying fapi directly from the Chinese government at a reasonable rate. There was little reasonable about Kung, who held that it was impossible to keep secret any special price he gave the United States, and that a departure from the official rate would undermine confidence in the fapi. Instead he suggested a de facto 40 to 1 ratio between the fapi and the dollar. Yet by November 1943, the real rate had dropped from about 100 to 1 to about 120 to 1 and was getting worse almost daily.

It was in November 1943, that Roosevelt and Churchill conferred with Chiang Kai-shek at Cairo, where "the talks," the

Prime Minister later wrote, " . . . were sadly distracted by the Chinese story, which was lengthy, complicated and minor." Complicated it certainly was. The Communists were harassing the Nationalist government, the Japanese were tempting that government to quit the war, the Burma campaign was beginning on a minor scale, and the success of the United States Navy in the Pacific — along with the impressive potentialities of the new B-29 long-range bombers — suggested the possibility of attacking Japan from the air, from China and from oceanic islands alike, without recourse to significant ground warfare on the continent of Asia. But the American Chiefs of Staff, counting on Chinese resistance to Japan to ease the path across the Pacific, temporarily won Churchill to endorse a major operation to recover Burma during 1944, and the Prime Minister also joined Roosevelt and Chiang in the Cairo Declaration that promised that "Manchuria, Formosa, and the Pescadores, shall be restored to the Republic of China."

Churchill and Roosevelt then moved on to meet Stalin at Teheran, where, the Prime Minister later recalled, "I at length prevailed upon the President to retract his promise" for the Burma campaign, though the strictly political agreement of Cairo, unaltered, received Stalin's approval. Stalin's interest was almost exclusively in the Anglo-American cross-channel invasion, which Churchill had resisted. At Teheran it was scheduled definitely for the spring of 1944, and landing craft and other gear needed for the invasion of Europe — the essential step in the defeat of Germany and in victory in the entire war — could not be spared for Asia.

Chiang Kai-shek had to settle for the status as one of the four great powers accorded him, but he was not content. He objected to the postponement of the Burma operation, "so disheartening" for the Chinese people, and he resented, too, Roosevelt's calculated indecision at Cairo about his request for "a billion gold dollar loan." As soon as he heard about the Teheran decision on Burma, Chiang reminded the President of China's economic condition, "more critical than the military," and asked again for the loan.

Back from Teheran on December 17, 1943, Roosevelt told Morgenthau about his resistance to that request. The trouble, the President believed, was that China had too much paper money; he had said as much to Chiang. Roosevelt was thinking about using dollars to buy up fapi in the black market. Then, when the war was over, the United States could redeem the Chinese currency after its value had gone up. The President was vague, as of necessity was Morgenthau when he asked his staff to prepare a memorandum on the plan.

That memorandum, dated December 18, 1943, presented what Morgenthau considered "the unvarnished truth." The Nationalist government had been issuing fapi at the rate of 3.5 billion each month, twice the rate of the previous year. The United States might meet its own expenses in China by purchasing fapi with gold or dollars in the Chinese open market, or it might double shipments of gold for sale by the Chinese government. Together those programs might retard inflation, but never to the degree that would result from increased shipments of food and other goods, which would depend upon future military operations. Certainly there was no need for a further loan, particularly since China had $460 million in unpledged funds in the United States.

The Secretary reported in his Diary that, on December 20, 1943, "the President very carefully in my presence read my memorandum on China for the first time. . . . He said, 'This looks good. . . . What would you think if I send your memo in toto to General Chiang Kai-shek?' I said, 'Nothing the matter with that.' So he said, 'That's what I am going to do.' "

That prospect appalled Cordell Hull. Circumstances in China were already bad, Hull told Morgenthau on January 1, 1944, and it might discourage the Generalissimo and those around him if the President simply dispatched a cable based wholly on Morgenthau's analysis. The Secretary of State wanted to send some kind of mission to assure the Chinese that the United States had "every disposition" to get at the merits of the situation. Further, another loan, Hull thought, might provide the cheapest way for steadying China.

Initially sympathetic to that analysis, Morgenthau on reflection concluded that the Nationalist Party could not long tolerate the "grafting family at the head of the Government." In that environment, an American mission could accomplish very little. He therefore urged Hull to follow the President's directive and send Chiang Kai-shek the Treasury's memorandum. But Hull, still reluctant, on January 4 suggested at least softening the text. Further, since Roosevelt had taken kindly to the idea of a mission, Hull felt it might be well to avoid any decision about a further loan until after the mission had reported back. Morgenthau, he suggested, might edit the memorandum with that in mind.

He had no further comment to make, Morgenthau replied. If Hull wanted the message changed, he would have to talk to the President. "To me it is one of the most striking things I have ever heard of," Morgenthau commented in his Diary on January 5, 1944. "Here the President . . . requests the Secretary of State to forward a message to the Generalissimo and . . . Hull tries to block the President and have it changed. I asked Miss Tully* if this had ever happened before and she said, 'No! . . . We didn't ask Hull for any comments. We just asked him to send it. . . . I'd like to know when this message goes forward.'

"If this happens to the President, it is no wonder that sometimes my messages don't go forward for weeks and also that I don't receive answers from them for weeks.

"To me the whole performance is just outrageous."

When the cable went out later that day, Hull had achieved some part of his purpose. He had persuaded Roosevelt to have Ambassador Gauss deliver the message by hand, and to temper the Treasury's tone by assuring the Generalissimo of the President's confidence and good will. "Sounds all right to me," Morgenthau commented about Hull's new procedure, " . . . and everybody's a good fellow except the Secretary of the Treasury."

In any case, Morgenthau was worrying less about the loan, which he considered a closed issue, than about the growing prob-

---

* Grace Tully, one of Roosevelt's secretaries.

lems of the United States Army in China. The Army, behind schedule in the construction of major airfields in the Chengtu area, needed fapi to pay Chinese labor and to purchase food and other supplies. General Brehon Somervell, the head of the Army Service Forces, in a memorandum to Morgenthau of January 3, 1944, said the "principal concern" was the "exchange situation," for the official rate remained twenty fapi to the dollar, a rate which would make American costs gargantuan. "Progress is being made," the Treasury learned from Chungking on January 13, " . . . on only four of the seven bases which China promised to construct and for which payment is to be made by the United States. . . . The war effort in this theater will seriously be impeded by the delay. . . . The United States Government has not committed itself to pay for these . . . bases at the official exchange rate and China is, therefore, holding up the work on them." All the Treasury wanted, Morgenthau told Somervell, was for the Chinese to build those bases; the question of the exchange rate could wait. Somervell agreed. "Nothing could be more conducive to lowering the prestige of China in the United States," Morgenthau then cabled to Chungking on January 15, " . . . than the knowledge that China was not cooperating fully . . . in the building of these airbases. I firmly believe that I speak in the best interests of China when I recommend that immediate action be taken for the construction of the remaining bases . . . leaving for future determination the final question of the U.S. currency equivalent."

Chiang Kai-shek replied in what Morgenthau considered "a very drastic cable . . . a very tough cable" to Roosevelt. In it, the Generalissimo argued that China needed the billion dollar loan to finance reciprocal aid to American military forces. If the Treasury opposed the loan, then the United States should bear its own expenses in China at the official exchange rate. If the Treasury rejected both alternatives, China "would have . . . no means as its disposal to meet the requirements of United States forces in China and consequently the American Army in China would have to depend upon itself to execute any and all of its projects, for to our great regret we would be placed inevitably in a position in which we could not make any further material or financial contribution, including the construction of works for military use."

The cable infuriated Morgenthau. "The billion dollar loan is out," he told White on January 18, 1944. The alternative, White warned, might cost Americans more. "Take it from me, I am not going up on the Hill," Morgenthau replied. " . . . They [the Chinese] are just a bunch of crooks, and I won't go up and ask for one nickle. . . . Supposing we tell them to go jump in the Yangtze River . . . The first thing to do is to find out from a military standpoint whether we can do this thing in some other way. . . . Is this something that I have got to stomach . . . or have you got some way to wiggle out and do something else? . . . If the Army tells me that we have just got to, well, that is something else."

The Army had also decided to be tough with Chiang. "China," Henry Stimson noted in his diary on January 19, 1944, "has been riding us pretty hard with the aid of Madame Chiang Kai-shek's influence over the President. . . . I do not fear that the Chinese are going to drop out of the war now that we are so close and I think that their present demands show a good deal of the Chinese bargaining." The Secretary of War had discussed Chiang Kai-shek's message with Generals Marshall and Somervell, as Somervell told Morgenthau that day. All of them were dissatisfied with China's attitude, with the small amount of actual fighting by the Chinese army, and with the breakdown of the airfield program. Indeed, the Army was prepared to stop building airports in China and instead to approach Japan from the sea. "Does that mean that the Army has made up its mind," Morgenthau asked, "that it could use other avenues of approach to Japan?" Somervell said it did.

With Marshall and Stimson, Somervell had drafted a cable answering Chiang Kai-shek's message to Roosevelt. The United States, it said, was fully prepared to bear all costs of its own war effort in China, but not at a fixed rate of exchange in the spiraling Chinese money market. The Congress would never be able to understand the need for such "unreasonable expenditures."

American faith and confidence in China had already been badly shaken. Now Chiang Kai-shek's demands, if they were met, would be disastrous to the war effort and "to both of our futures." But the United States would welcome any arrangement for paying for its military program in China in American dollars at a fair rate of exchange.

Pleased with the draft, Morgenthau telephoned Roosevelt for his approval. Although he was on the whole satisfied, the President censored a few phrases; "large expenditures," he said, would be better than "unreasonable expenditures." He was still opposed to a loan, but he thought a special mission to Chungking might ease the general situation.

The State Department was even more solicitous of Chiang's sensitivities. At meetings of January 19 and 20, 1944, with Treasury and War Department representatives, Alger Hiss, speaking for Cordell Hull, condemned the proposed message to the Generalissimo as "much too strong." Reluctantly the Treasury and War Department representatives cooperated in moderating the reply, and Roosevelt approved the amended version for dispatch to Chiang on January 26, 1944. It proposed, as an interim measure, American purchase of one billion fapi at a rate of 100 to the dollar.

In conversation with Ambassador Gauss on February 3, 1944, Kung held, as he had before, that China could not alter the official rate without breaking her "economic backbone." Even discussions of an alteration weakened confidence in the fapi, which would rally if China received a billion dollar loan for her reserves. He blamed the course of inflation entirely on the growing expenditures of the United States Army, and he claimed that China had actually repaid its previous $500 million loan in the form of various kinds of assistance to the American war effort. Referring to the possibility of Chinese collapse, Kung remarked that the Japanese had been making "some very good offers." Several days later the Ambassador delivered the official American answer: China's proposed exchange rate was unsatisfactory and unreasonable; there was no need for comment on the fatuity of Kung's arguments.

The rejection of the Chinese position forced reconsideration of American plans for China. In February 1944, General Clay reported the Army's decision. Recent events in the Pacific had again altered the strategic picture. American victories in the Marshall Islands made it possible to advance the timetable for a possible attack on the Japanese-occupied Chinese coast. For such an attack, large airfields within Chiang Kai-shek's domain were essential. Clay preferred therefore not to threaten retrenchment in China or to accept the Chinese proposals for a rate of exchange. He suggested instead that the United States, without formal commitment to any rate of exchange, immediately place $25 million to the account of the Chinese government, since the Chinese had already put up one billion fapi against which the Army had drawn. Both the State and Treasury Departments consented at once to that procedure.

According to the plan which the Army then worked out, at the beginning of each three-month period, the United States would pay a stipulated sum of dollars to China's account, for which the Chinese would advance fapi to the Americans. For any period of three months the United States would set the rate of exchange for these transactions at a figure between 100 and 200 fapi to the dollar. But while the amount of fapi obtained by the United States would be kept secret, China might publicize the American dollar "contribution" if it seemed desirable to do so in order to enhance the value of fapi. The settlement of accounts would be left for postwar negotiations. The American Embassy in Chungking on March 28 supported the proposal as the most realistic basis for discussions with Chiang Kai-shek, for it would save his face and avoid a showdown. For his part, the G'imo decided to send Kung to Washington to discuss cross-rates, while Roosevelt planned to send Vice President Wallace to Chungking for general conversations.

"I should like to take this opportunity to congratulate you," Morgenthau wrote Roosevelt on June 8, 1944, " . . . upon having faced and passed an important military crisis. General Somervell informs me that the United States installations in China are now practically completed. Thus the problem which you faced in January has been overcome and your major objective has been achieved." To be sure, inflation went on at its devastating pace. But Morgenthau felt "that despite the financial problems which arose to disturb the cordial relations of this government with the Chinese government, the course of the present financial negotiations is satisfactory and moving in the proper direction."

Though those negotiations were to prove less easy than he hoped, Morgenthau's pleasure in the apparent achievements of the previous six months had noticeably softened his mood. The quarterly exchanges of dollars for fapi, however much they created unsolved problems for the future, did permit the Army to sustain its program in China. Since the discussion of exchange rates had been deferred, Chiang Kai-shek had kept his prestige without receiving the controversial loan. Most important, the airfields, so far from completion in January 1944, were in June almost ready for use. American victories in the Pacific were soon to render those airfields unnecessary, but for the while they seemed vital for the war — almost as important as were the bases in Great Britain from which the invasion of Normandy was about to be launched. For two years and more, the Treasury had also been concerned continually with the financial aspects of relations between the United States and the United Kingdom, the very heart of the Grand Alliance.

4. Great Britain: "Nothing Decadent"

Morgenthau's many services to England, as well as his intimacy with the President, earned him a place at the Christmas party at the White House in 1941, when Winston Churchill made his first wartime visit to the United States just three weeks after the attack on Pearl Harbor. "I had the pleasure of sitting opposite Mr. Churchill last night," the Secretary told his associates the next day, "and watching him for two hours. . . . You know, he has a distinct speech impediment. . . . He would say practically nothing because he just wasn't having a good time. . . . You see him on one side of Mrs. Roosevelt and Beaverbrook on the other, and Beaverbrook's face is a map of his life, but on Churchill's face there is absolutely nothing. . . . He looked in good condition. He wasn't flabby, literally in the pink of health. . . . He asked three times to be excused after dinner so, he says 'I can prepare these impromptu remarks for tomorrow' * . . . After supper I sat next to him all through the movie. . . . When they showed pictures of Libya, he said, 'Oh, that is good. We have got to show the people that we can win.' . . . Beaverbrook, on the other hand, is very cocky. . . . He said that the President and I were the only friends they had right along."

Still a good friend to the British, Morgenthau in his negotiations with them was also a dogged protagonist of American interests. He was admittedly distrustful of what he considered to be the continuing influence of London financiers and of the Bank of England on the British Treasury, and he was unhappy about the appointment of Robert Brand, whom he identified with Lombard Street, as a British negotiator in Washington, first on matters of Lend-Lease, later as a representative of the Chancellor of the Exchequer. More important, Morgenthau considered Lend-Lease essentially a wartime measure, designed to guarantee to Great Britain and other allies of the United States the materials, military and civilian, without which they could not continue to fight. That was the view also, he felt, of the Congress. Consequently, he resisted British pressure for associating American Lend-Lease assistance with their needs for dollar and other assets in the postwar period. He did not want to compound British economic problems, or to push England to bankruptcy, which threatened her continually. But he saw no license for using Lend-Lease to build British dollar balances beyond a necessary minimum, which the British thought he underestimated.

His estimations reflected the calculations of Harry White, who sought openly, with the Secretary's approval, to make the dollar the dominant currency in the postwar world. An ardent nationalist in his monetary thinking, White also championed

* For a speech before the Congress.

postwar international monetary cooperation, the objective of his tireless efforts to establish the International Monetary Fund. In that cooperation, White expected the United States and the United Kingdom to provide the lead, but with the United States as the senior partner. Accordingly he, too, resisted, more vigorously than Morgenthau, any deliberate expansion of England's gold and dollar holdings.

In that stance, the Secretary and his assistant were opposed not by the British only but also by Secretary of State Cordell Hull, who considered large British assets indispensable for that free, international trade on which he pinned his hopes for a lasting peace. So, too, did Hull's chief representative on monetary issues, Assistant Secretary of State Dean Acheson. Further, Acheson, like the British, believed that the Treasury did not understand how poor England had become as a result of her wartime expenditures. He also, unlike Morgenthau, tended to defer to British rather than congressional sensitivities.

In London as Roosevelt's personal representative on October 16, 1942, Morgenthau began a series of conversations at the British Treasury. Those talks confirmed what had long worried him about the problems of British finance. But his fortnight in the United Kingdom increased his already large admiration for the courage of the English people. "I think the trip was very, very much worthwhile from every standpoint," the Secretary told his staff upon his return on November 2. He had seen a number of British factories, including the plant where they manufactured engines for the Spitfire airplane: "It is perfectly amazing how smoothly they run." He had spent one night with an English bomber squadron, one with an American bomber squadron, one day with the celebrated Polish fighter squadron. When the Poles saw a German, he said, "they fly square at him and if he does not give way they just crash him. We saw the very latest Spitfire which is better than anything the Germans have." The British, he went on, had complete aerial control of the English Channel and some fifty or a hundred miles beyond into France. That control enabled them to send convoys through the channel in daytime as well as at night, and thereby to avoid mines.

Morgenthau, much impressed by the British laboring force,

was pleased to find nourishing food available at low prices, and cheered by the great amount of activity on the streets, in buses, and in taxicabs — "the place humming with life."

"I think the thing which would interest you the most," he said, "is my own feeling that Hitler has seen his high water mark; that the worst is behind us, and it is not going to be as long a war as I thought it was. I am very, very much encouraged. . . . I think we ought to be able to lick those fellows in 1943 or 1944, because the English are so much further advanced than I dreamt. I mean their production is simply amazing. . . . I have come back definitely feeling that it is going to be very much shorter than I thought. . . . The English have made their mistakes, recognized the mistakes, and profited by them, and that is the important thing. This thing of calling the English a decadent race is just the bunk. There is nothing decadent about their leaders, the ones they have now."

What the women in England were doing, Morgenthau went on, was "just unbelievable." This was true alike for women in the armed services and in the civilian occupations, true of their housekeeping, their cooking and work in the barracks, their managing of buses and motorcycles. In the services, "as one person put it . . . they treat them like men, and they want to be treated like men. There is no nonsense about it. . . . If it were not for the women England would cave in today." The Secretary compared the contribution of the British women favorably to what the American WACs and WAVEs* were doing, with all of their saluting and pretty uniforms. In contrast, the war for women in England was "a hard, tough job; and do those people hate Hitler. You don't have to have any posters or propaganda — they just hate his guts, and they want to get at him."

The Secretary went on:

I was with Churchill three times, once on a trip to Dover, once at lunch, and once for dinner. He was in good form every time except the night his wife gave him a supper he did not like and so he did not talk all through supper. She said, "I am sorry, dear, I

* The WACs were Army, the WAVEs Navy personnel.

could not buy any fish. You'll have to eat macaroni." Mrs. Roosevelt was sitting right there. Then they gave us little left-over bits made into meatloaf. . . .*

Here is one little human interest story. When I had lunch with the King and the Queen alone, to make conversation, being an apple grower, when they brought in apples I asked if they had Cox's Pippins, which happens to be their best apple. The Queen was very much upset because she could not produce it, and the next day† this note arrived and some apples. The package was marked in her own handwriting, too. I think she is an amazing woman — an amazing person.

When we got through the King walked me down about a mile of hall to the front door to see me out. There was one servant present, that is all.

Poor Mrs. Roosevelt, I visited her at the palace. She had four bedrooms and she could not find any light switches. . . . When we went there at night to call on her — there is this big courtyard and you go in, there is complete darkness and nobody in the whole courtyard. I went from door to door trying to get in. . . . Finally I knocked at a door, it opened, and it happened to be the right place, so Mrs. Roosevelt said, "I have not a torchlight. I can't find the switches." . . . So I gave her my torch.

I had another experience. Not having this torch, the night I called for her to take her over to Churchill's I borrowed an Army torch. I came out with Mrs. Roosevelt on my arm and this torch, which had no cover on it — it was just loaned to me by the Army — and this British policeman says, "Don't you know you are supposed to" — I didn't say a word — "what are you doing with a torchlight that — oh, Mrs. Roosevelt!" . . .

The thing that pleased me as much as anything was a little speech Churchill made at Dover, in which he told the crowd I was the man that gave them the 100,000 rifles. . . . Bracken, to go one better, calls it a million rifles.

As for Brendan Bracken, the British Minister of Information, Morgenthau said he was "perfectly swell. I was really worried about that one and only press conference. They sit you up on a dais. . . . The Army arranged it. . . . There were about

---

* Twenty years later Morgenthau recalled the episode differently. As he then remembered either this or another occasion, Churchill "called his wife down for serving fish in aspic, and then sank down in his chair for the rest of the evening and came to life again only with the champagne."
† Or that very evening, according to Morgenthau's recollection in 1964.

ninety or a hundred press people. . . . Brendan Bracken introduced me with a little speech, and like in a radio hall to tell them
to applaud he goes like this before I start speaking . . . just like
on the radio. . . . In the middle of it I turned to Brendan
Bracken and in a very low voice said, 'Am I doing all right?'
Bracken could not have been nicer, and he and I hit it off right
from the beginning."

The hospitality and courage of the British did not alter the
Secretary's position about their dollar balances. On January 3,
1942, along with Vice President Wallace, Secretary of State
Hull, Secretary of War Stimson, and Edward Stettinius, he reported to the President. The United Kingdom now had accumulated about one billion dollars' worth of gold and dollars, an adequate figure. Any further growth in British holdings depended
primarily on factors within the control of the United States, such
as the volume of Lend-Lease aid, the volume of American purchases in England, and dollar expenditures for American troops
there. Morgenthau and the others recommended that the United
States hold British balances between $600 million and one billion,
discontinue shipments of civilian goods under Lend-Lease to
South Africa, and continue military shipments only on the basis
of equivalent reciprocal aid. A final recommendation called for
the appointment of a new committee to oversee Lend-Lease policy. To Morgenthau's satisfaction, Roosevelt on January 11,
1943, approved those suggestions and made the Secretary chairman of the committee.

It was not until July 1943, when British balances began rising,
that Morgenthau became seriously concerned again with the
financial implications of Lend-Lease.

In a memorandum for Roosevelt of November 1, 1943, he
called for reducing British balances to the one billion dollar level
that the President had approved in January. Besides cutting
down balances, the Secretary wanted to avoid adverse criticism
on the Hill and, wherever possible, to stop the practice of em-
ploying Lend-Lease for transactions which might better flow
through ordinary commercial channels.

Those criticisms received a sympathetic hearing from Leo

Crowley, who in September 1943 had become the head of the Foreign Economic Administration, a new agency created to direct Lend-Lease and other activities.* Crowley, as he told Morgenthau, was meeting continual difficulties in working with the State Department. So was Morgenthau, who knew from Harry Hopkins "that Hull had written a letter to the President . . . objecting strenuously to my heading up this committee on Lend-Lease with the British." The trouble was not just personal. Whereas Crowley and the War Department agreed with the Treasury's position on British balances and Lend-Lease, the State Department held an almost opposite view. That department, according to Dean Acheson, was prepared to support suggestions for eliminating "freakish transactions" from Lend-Lease, but not if the Treasury had the unexpressed but governing purpose of forcing British balances to any particular level.

That purpose, as Morgenthau had often argued, governed the policy of Congress. On November 5, 1943, the Senate Committee to Investigate the National Defense Program, through a statement of its chairman, Harry S Truman, asserted that Lend-Lease was never intended as a device to shift a portion of the United Kingdom's war cost to the United States, but only as a realistic recognition that the British did not have the means to pay for essential weapons and other materials. Further, Congress had been assured that Lend-Lease would be extended only where recipients were already fully utilizing their own resources. The next day Roosevelt discussed the question of British balances with Crowley. "I told Crowley," the President then informed Morgenthau, " . . . to keep them as they were, not to let them get any higher."

On November 14, 1943, Morgenthau explained to Lord Halifax the opinion now common to the Treasury, the Foreign Economic Administration, the Truman Committee, and the White House. British balances were nevertheless rising, the Secretary said, because the British had been lobbying successfully with the

* An Executive Order of September 25, 1943, establishing the Foreign Economic Administration, placed within its jurisdiction the Office of Economic Warfare, the Office of Foreign Relief and Rehabilitation Operations, the Lend-Lease Administration, and the Office of Foreign Economic Coordination.

State Department. In the long run, that practice might lead Congress wholly to abandon Lend-Lease. As Morgenthau later reported to his staff, he said to Halifax that "just because we were innocent in the international field, it was no reason why they should take advantage of us. I said that there were at least two committees — McKellar and Truman that were hot after us, and something should be done."

But the British blocked every effort to eliminate specific Lend-Lease transfers, as Crowley told Morgenthau on December 15, 1943, and the State Department continued to support the British case. At an interdepartmental conference on December 31, Cordell Hull explained that, in his view, an American policy for controlling the resources of the British government, even if it were based on reasons of domestic political necessity, would provoke a "very serious international situation." If Congress and the American people found out what British balances actually were, Crowley replied, Congress would criticize the responsible executive agencies, which would have great difficulty in explaining away what they had done. Neither he nor Morgenthau wanted to embarrass the President, but they did feel they had to call the issue to Roosevelt's attention.

They did so in a joint memorandum that described the growth of British assets, reviewed the mood of the Congress and asked the President to permit the Treasury and the Lend-Lease Administration to discontinue some parts of the non-military assistance rendered to the United Kingdom. There was no need, they said, for decision about the size of British balances. "Listen, you know, it is very interesting," Morgenthau said as he finished reading one draft of the memorandum, " . . . the French are sore at us in Algiers because we stopped Lend-Lease. We are trying to cut down Lend-Lease to the British; they get sore. I get a snooty, snooty telegram; Chiang Kai-shek sends for our Ambassadors and gives them hell, and this, and that, and the other thing. Just as soon as we quit being Santa Claus we become unpopular."

In a separate memorandum that incorporated Dean Acheson's advice, Hull wrote Roosevelt that he would go along with recommendations about specific Lend-Lease practices, but he also urged forthright conversations with the British about their gold and dollar balances. "I don't know any better way," Morgenthau commented, "to irritate the situation than to bring it to their attention. . . . I should think he . . . wouldn't insist that we continue to keep discussing this whole question with the English and get nowhere . . . as we have during the last twelve months."

"I agree," the President wrote Hull, Morgenthau and Crowley on January 5, 1944, "with the report of the Secretary of the Treasury and Mr. Crowley, and I understand that the Secretary of State approves the report but wished to take the matter up first with the British. Also, I understand that the Secretary of the Treasury and Mr. Crowley feel that they have been doing this for a year and have got nowhere.

"Therefore, I suggest that the matter be taken up once more with the British, but on the distinct understanding that I will be given a final report within thirty days, i.e. February 7, 1944, and will act finally thereon."

After several weeks of continual, futile debate, the Chancellor of the Exchequer on January 27, 1944, urged Morgenthau to put considerations of international finance above those of domestic politics. "We shall have many difficult problems to consider together in the coming months," he wrote. "My financial anxieties arising out of prospective external payments are increasing as the war advances . . . and it may be advisable that we should have an early exchange of views about what the position will be in the early postwar period. I am confident that in the future, as in the past, we can rely on your friendly cooperation."

That confidence was not misplaced, for Morgenthau by the end of January had come almost wholly to accept Acheson's attitude toward the negotiations. With so many issues troubling Anglo-American relations,* the Secretary did not want to strain transatlantic friendship. Still, he believed as he had for some

---

* Especially questions of politics and strategy in Europe, the Mediterranean and the Orient; but also ongoing negotiations of special interest to both Treasuries about military and occupation currencies, postwar international financial institutions, Argentine relations, and the problem of Jewish refugees.

weeks that a debate about British balances would draw blood, while modest and justifiable cuts in Lend-Lease aid would not. Accordingly, on February 2, 1944, he approved a program acceptable alike to Crowley and the British. It eliminated from Lend-Lease American purchases for British consumption of Caribbean molasses and sugar, of Icelandic fish, and of Canadian alcohol and petroleum products. Subject to further discussion about details, it also cut out some other nonmilitary items. The Lend-Lease Administration, retreating from an earlier proposal, contracted to continue to provide tobacco, certain paper products, agricultural machinery, and various shipping services. That retreat preserved $245 million of annual Lend-Lease assistance. The mutually agreeable cuts aggregated $288 million — less than Morgenthau had originally hoped for, as much as he thought he could now demand, and about half of what had been in controversy — a reasonable compromise. Content with the outcome, Morgenthau in the spring of 1944 was preoccupied with the course of the war, with issues relating to Allied advances in Europe and in the Pacific. Those and other international problems had been commanding his attention for more than a year. In dealing with them, as in the development of financial policy in China and the United Kingdom, he had found himself often in disagreement with the British or the State Department or both. Indeed, the matter of British balances, temporarily put to one side, was the least contentious of the international controversies in which the Treasury was engaged.

XIX

PRINCIPLES AND EXPEDIENTS

1942–1944

OUT OF THE Second World War Morgenthau hoped there would emerge a principled and lasting peace. To that peace he expected the United States to contribute the authority of its power and the inspiration of the spirit of the New Deal — of social justice, humanitarian striving, and popular and responsible government. Yet he realized that the precondition for that kind of peace was the defeat of Germany, Italy, and Japan. The stupendous task of victory again and again demanded expedients that threatened the very purposes of the struggle. In such cases, Morgenthau, like Roosevelt, deferred to military requirements. His style in the financing of the Grand Alliance revealed his general recognition of priorities. Irritated though he often was by the inflexibility of Soviet negotiators, he labored to speed the flow of arms to Russia. Recognizing the corrupt ineffectuality of the Nationalist government, he strove to make the dollar an instrument of the war effort in China. Similarly, he subordinated controversy over Anglo-American finance to the preservation of the most vital partnership the United States had.

Yet British policy in other matters disturbed him, as did the policies of various of his colleagues in Washington when they seemed to subvert his definitions of American interests or of appropriate principles for the governing of affairs among men and states. Morgenthau pursued those interests and principles with a calculated toughness and with an intermittent success that depended always on two variables: the degree of support he could elicit from Franklin Roosevelt, and the degree to which principle had to be accommodated to military necessity.

1. Invasion and Occupation Currency: North Africa

In July 1942, the United States began making detailed plans for taking the offensive in the European Theater. At that time the President still hoped for a cross-channel attack in 1943. Although that was to be postponed another year, American forces were within six months of landing in North Africa, and within a year of invading Sicily and Italy. Civilian authorities therefore prepared to meet their obligations in areas occupied by the army, and the Treasury bore special responsibility for the administration of finances.

In mid-July General Dwight D. Eisenhower, in command in the European Theater, asked whether American troops invading North Africa would use British currency, as he supposed, or whether the Treasury had an alternative plan. His own concern was to have available for American soldiers an adequate supply of negotiable currency in invaded and occupied countries. Morgenthau unhesitatingly rejected the thought of paying Americans in pounds sterling. Europeans and Africans, he believed, preferred dollars to pounds. He particularly objected to any system of paying American troops that would in any way appear to make them hired mercenaries; therefore, insofar as money and finance were involved, he wanted to distinguish between British and American military operations.

He was especially eager to prevent the British from assuming unilateral authority over European currency and finance. Eisenhower, the Secretary told his staff in August, had reported that the British were printing several million pounds with an overmark for use by all occupation armies in Europe, including American forces. Yet the Europeans Morgenthau saw in Washington had convinced him that their countrymen "like American money." Accordingly the Treasury arranged for the printing of dollars with a special yellow overmark for use in paying American troops and occupation expenses. "My suggestion," the Secretary said:

> . . . is that we use for both armies US dollars and that this would be the first foot in the door that the United States, when this war is over, is going to settle . . . what kind of Europe it is going to be. . . . Who is going to pay for it? We are going to pay for it. The English are going to be busted; . . . We might just as well say it, because we are going to do it anyway. . . . We are now going to say, "We recognize the fact that the United States is going to have to take the relief over in Europe, and in return for that . . . we will set up once and for all the kind of Europe that we expect."
>
> And the first question that is going to come up is this whole question of reparations. If we are going to go through this whole thing all over again of reparations and grinding the German people down again through malnutrition, through inflation, and through another Versailles Treaty . . . in another twenty-five years we will have another war. . . .
>
> The only way that this thing can be changed so that Europe might live at peace for one hundred years is if the United States will say, "All right, . . . we are going to set up the United Nations peace, tariff walls, and so forth . . . try to set up an ideal state that might be good for a hundred years." If we do, we are going to have to pay for it.

Roosevelt had said only a few days before: "Winston and I will write the Peace Treaty." There was no mention at all of Stalin. "I think," Morgenthau told his staff, "it had better be Franklin Roosevelt without Winston, and also I think it had better be the United States that does the international policing without Winston. I think it had better be the United States that decides that all of these munitions factories will be leveled to the ground and destroyed, and the munitions machinery, airplanes that can't fly more than two or three hundred miles, all the rest of that stuff.*

"Now . . . if we start going into these countries and the English are going to take the attitude right from the beginning, 'We are going to dictate the peace of Europe,' the whole thing is going to be repeated.

"That is a long speech for me . . . maybe . . . very Wilsonian, maybe . . . purely daydreaming, but lacking something like that, . . . my sons' children will be doing the same thing that my sons are doing." †

The United States would certainly have some of the influence Morgenthau described, Harry White suggested, but it was a mistake to assume the United States could dominate the world. If the Soviet Union and Great Britain were out of the picture, the United States would never get into Europe. There would be a negotiated peace. Even Woodrow Wilson had not tried to impose an American peace on Europe. Morgenthau disagreed. The United States had to play a major part in the settlement of Europe, he believed, on the basis of ideals Roosevelt had yet to define. "I sit around," he said, "and I hear these college students and these young people, soldiers and sailors, and there is nothing inspirational being raised for them." He had come, he admitted, a long way from the question of currency; he had, seriously and self-consciously, "been doing a little daydreaming."

Late in September 1942, as the date approached for the invasion of North Africa, the British Embassy opened conversations with the War Department about cross rates between the occupation pound and the occupation dollar. The English proposed a depreciated rate for the pound, in Morgenthau's opinion an undesirable step that might cause trouble for the dollar in postwar international exchange. The Secretary therefore directed Dan

---

* A prescription for Germany to which Morgenthau returned in 1944, see Chapter XXI.
† Henry Morgenthau III served as an Army officer under General George Patton in Europe; Robert Morgenthau, an officer in the Navy, served on ships that were sunk in the Mediterranean and in the Pacific.

Bell to intercede with Judge Patterson. "I don't care how forceful you are," Morgenthau said, "in telling Patterson that it is perfectly ridiculous to have a British Treasury official dealing with the War Department; he should be dealing with us."

The core of the problem lay in setting rates of exchange between the dollar and the French franc circulating in North Africa, and between the pound and that franc. The British cared primarily about preserving the pound-franc rate that already prevailed in those parts of French Africa in the control of Gaullist rather than Vichy forces.* Accordingly, London proposed for North Africa a rate of 43 francs for a dollar and 172 francs for a pound. The American Treasury, in contrast, wanted to set the rate realistically at 75 francs to the dollar, which was close to the existing black market rate of 100 francs to the dollar. The Treasury believed that a rate of 43 would rapidly slide off. In rebuttal, the British argued that that rate would have a beneficial political effect on the inhabitants of North Africa. After several days of discussion, Stimson and Hull, supporting Morgenthau, decided, in Hull's phrase, to "let it go at 75." So did the British.

For Morgenthau, that decision paled in comparison with larger issues that developed with the invasion of Algeria. To facilitate that operation, the President authorized his personal representative, Robert Murphy, to arrange for the assistance of the French Admiral Jean Darlan, who had remained strictly under the orders of the Vichy government. Murphy succeeded a few days after the fighting had begun; the French troops in Algeria ceased their resistance to American forces; and Darlan enjoyed American support until his assassination on December 24, 1942. As Morgenthau began to understand the degree of American involvement with Darlan, and as he reflected upon the exclusion from the North African operation of General Charles de Gaulle and his Free French forces, the Secretary feared that the United States had surrendered too much to military convenience. The State Department held that the reliance on Darlan had been "de-

* The Vichy French controlled North Africa; de Gaulle controlled parts of French Africa south of the Sahara. The British, who had on occasion fought against the Vichy French, were both cooperating intermittently and trading regularly with the Free French.

cided by the military commanders on the ground of military necessity . . . the chief purpose . . . being to assure . . . that
in time of great crisis there would not be any hostilities behind
their backs. . . . The President himself was not aware of the
details until they had already been arrived at. . . . General
Marshall has had the entire thing in his own hands from the beginning."

For the War Department, Judge Patterson offered a rather
different explanation. "It was a kind of desperate play," he told
Morgenthau on November 16, 1942, " . . . to get the French
fleet. . . . The White House knows about the thing, and . . .
it did not pass much through the War Department. We only
got some very superficial notice about it, and it was handled
through the State Department by this man Murphy." Still upset,
Morgenthau replied that Darlan's record "speaks for itself. It's
terrible." Further, the Secretary put full credence in a CBS news
report from London that American sponsorship of Darlan had
provoked alarm in Great Britain. Patterson sympathized with
those worries. Darlan, he said, was cold-blooded, loyal to no one
but himself. But Murphy was representing the White House,
even though he was more or less on General Eisenhower's staff,
and Patterson interpreted the situation as "one of those things
where maybe they thought you have to do the job with the tools
you have." Morgenthau shuddered at the "awful implications"
of the policy, which would disgust de Gaulle as well as "a lot of
people in this country."

Hoping to soothe Morgenthau, Henry Stimson asked him to
tea, where they were joined by Archibald MacLeish, representing the Office of War Information, and Associate Justice Felix
Frankfurter, who were also disturbed by the affiliations with
Darlan. Stimson and John J. McCloy, his assistant, who accompanied him, considered their perturbation "starry-eyed." In
Stimson's view, Eisenhower's deal with Darlan had produced
enormous benefits, particularly the laying down of the arms of
the French forces in the area. The Secretary of War therefore
gave his guests "a little talk, pointing out first the hazardous nature of our operation in North Africa and the perilous condition
in which our troops would have been in case there had been any

delay caused by the obstruction of the French." The Army, he assured his guests, was not making foreign policy, simply a temporary military arrangement. Responding to Morgenthau's suggestion that the United States take steps to control the character of French government after the war, Stimson argued that such an effort, impossible of execution, would violate the principles for which Americans were fighting. The Secretary of War felt that Morgenthau "after grunts and groans" had gone home "reconciled."

In that conclusion Stimson erred. He had been less persuasive than he thought, and Morgenthau less reconciled than he perhaps seemed. In his own Diary on November 17, 1942, Morgenthau recorded his impression of the previous afternoon:

> Stimson . . . read a three-page telegram from Eisenhower. . . . Eisenhower said he felt it was a military necessity to use Admiral Darlan, and he asked for authority to go ahead, but that if they didn't want him to do that, they should send a commission out at once to advise him. Stimson then told us that both Churchill and Roosevelt had approved what Eisenhower had done.
>
> When Stimson got through giving us all this background, none of which was very new, showing how necessary it was to use Darlan, and using him meant the saving of many American lives, somebody mentioned Edward Murrow's broadcast.* I had a copy of it in my pocket and I asked Stimson whether he didn't want to read it. He lost his temper and said he wasn't interested. . . . I just let it pass. . . .
>
> Then I went on and made a very passionate address on what I thought about Darlan. I said he was a most ruthless person who had sold many thousands of people into slavery, and that to use a man like that in these times, no matter what the price is, the price is too great. I went on to say that there is something else besides temporary military victories, and I said, "You can't tell me the whole campaign was set up with the expectation of using Darlan because the President told me that that wasn't so. . . . There is a considerable group of rich people in this country who would make peace with Hitler tomorrow, and the only people who really want to fight are the working men and women, and if they once get the idea that we are going to sit back and favor these Fascists, not only in France but in Spain, which is what we are doing every

---

* The CBS newscast from London reporting British criticism of the collaboration with Darlan.

day . . . , these people are going to have sit-down strikes; they're going to slow up production, and they're going to say, what's the use of fighting just to put that kind of people back into power? . . . If something isn't done about it and that idea once gets into the minds of the people, you will never be able to get it out. . . . Now for the English — Darlan is known as one of the most violent British-haters. How do you suppose the men and women of England feel about this. General Giraud also hates the English."

When I finished I could tell from MacLeish's face that he agreed with me. . . . Then Frankfurter said, "Yes, we agree with what Henry said." Then he began to try to fix a middle course, and I was never so disgusted in my life. Then he said, "What would you do if you had the decision to make?" I said, "That isn't the question. . . . The question is how to explain to the American people what this means, and we are going to let the State Department put in this kind of people. . . . If we do that, nothing will be settled and in another ten years we will have another war on our hands."

Stimson was quite flabbergasted at my vehemence. McCloy said nothing, but then one of them spoke up and said, "Well, you know that last Friday Eisenhower issued orders to Robert Murphy to take up with Admiral Darlan a matter of rescinding the Nuremberg Decree* and freeing all political prisoners." I asked them when that would be made public and they said they would have to wait until it was carried out. Then I said, "Well, somebody said that Murphy is living in the pocket of Darlan, and supposing Darlan refuses to carry out these orders." They had no answer for that.

Shortly before I left, Stimson said, "Give me that copy of Murrow's address. I want to read it." McCloy said, "Isn't that typical of the man? He gets mad and then he cools off, and he does what you ask him."

Frankfurter called me up as soon as I got home, and I was very disagreeable with him. . . . He wanted me to write the President a letter telling him that he should say . . . that all brutality and cruelty in North Africa should be stopped. It was typical of Frankfurter. He didn't say anything while we were all together; yet as soon as he got home he wanted to become "Mr. Fixer."

In his agitated state of mind, Morgenthau called on the President on November 17. As he entered, he said he wanted to talk

---

* The Nazi Decree calling for various kinds of deprivation for all Jews.

about North Africa, "something that affects my soul." Roosevelt listened for twenty minutes. The arrangement with Darlan, he then said, would permit the United States to achieve in two weeks what otherwise might have taken ten. "Darlan," the President continued, "says he hates Giraud* and the head of Dakar — the governor — hates Darlan, but Darlan drops in our laps because he is the only man who can represent the part of France which is still left. Darlan wants to save lives and in some way keep a semblance of power for Pétain†. . . . It is purely a military matter. . . . There is an old Bulgarian proverb which goes like this: 'You can walk with the Devil as far as the bridge but then you must leave him behind.' "

He was satisfied with that statement, Morgenthau said, but he thought it "terribly important" for Roosevelt to tell the American people that he had rescinded the Nuremberg Decree and urged freedom for all political prisoners in North Africa. He also wanted the President to say he was giving the North Africans the right to vote. "Well," Roosevelt said, "some believe that should be done and some don't." He had, he assured Morgenthau, told Eisenhower to have local people run all public facilities like electric power and water, and also given the General other explicit instructions. Since the President was "running the show," since he had made no promises of any kind to Darlan about the future, Morgenthau "under these circumstances, and knowing that it has saved thousands of lives," concluded that there was nothing more he could say. As he went on in his Diary: "I believe the President when he says he won't tie up with the Darlans and the Flandins‡ and I suppose that Eisenhower is looking at it purely from a military standpoint. McCloy says that both Eisenhower and Clark are soldiers and have no political ideas, that Eisenhower is a farm boy, and that it is merely a

---

* General Henri Giraud, chief of the French Army in North Africa, who succeeded Darlan as High Commissioner in North Africa after Darlan was assassinated. Giraud later signed his authority over to de Gaulle.
† Marshal Henri P. Pétain, head of the Vichy Government.
‡ Pierre-Etienne Flandin, sometime Premier and Foreign Minister in prewar France, at that time a member of the Pétain government in Vichy and a friend of Robert Murphy.

matter of military strategy. I hope they are all right, but I do believe the President, and I am confident that Stimson wouldn't be a party to a tie-up with any Fascist because his whole life has been against that kind of thing."

Roosevelt's clarifying public statement about Darlan and his public request for the liberation of all Nazi political prisoners in North Africa lifted Morgenthau's spirits. When he called the President the next day, November 18, to congratulate him on those statements, Roosevelt said he had decided about voting rights. In Algiers and Morocco the Arabs felt they had been discriminated against, for the Jews there were allowed to vote and the Arabs were not. Roosevelt considered that their domestic problem, and as he put it, removed "all the persecution status of the Jews and I am saying to the Jews and the Arabs, 'Forget about the voting for neither of you is going to vote. There will be no election until we are good and ready.'" All that, Morgenthau replied, was most heartening.

But Morgenthau was soon again disturbed, this time by renewed controversy over exchange rates. The North African French had agreed to the rates of 75 francs to the dollar and 300 to the pound only conditionally. Late in December 1942, General Giraud demanded a higher value for the franc. British authorities had continued to abide by the official rate of 43 francs to the dollar in their trade with Madagascar, where General de Gaulle held authority. Consequently the Gaullists enjoyed a more favorable and more prestigious rate than did Giraud, who resented his situation, and considered the issue political as well as economic.

Roosevelt settled the matter by his own lights. The British, the President told the Cabinet on January 8, 1943, considered De Gaulle's Fighting French the true representatives of the French people. Roosevelt did not agree. He intended to recognize no one as the head of the French government until France was liberated and the French people could act politically. In the interim, he deemed it essential to make it clear to the people of North Africa that they were under military occupation, with General Eisenhower in complete command.

At a Cabinet meeting on February 5, Roosevelt was full of entertaining anecdotes about his recent conference with Churchill at Casablanca. On this, as on many other occasions, he obscured, doubtless by design, the seriousness of his purpose, and precluded argument from his subordinates. He said that in North Africa he discovered that the Treasury and State Departments had fixed the rate at 75 francs to the dollar. He did not consider that a very good rate, because in converting francs to dollars, the arithmetic came out unevenly. He also found that the British had fixed a rate with De Gaulle at 43.90 francs to the dollar, again a poor figure for computation. So, as he put it to the Cabinet, Roosevelt decided to make it simple by establishing a franc rate of two cents, 50 to the dollar, which by happy coincidence worked out to 200 francs to the pound. "You have made an excellent story of it," Dan Bell complained, "but that isn't all there is to the picture."

Indeed it was not. The new rate overvalued the franc, precisely as Morgenthau had said it would. Further, the British still objected to applying it in Madagascar and Somaliland, where the Free French held out for the prewar rate. Any change, they argued, would shake confidence in the franc, the unit of currency they associated with the glory of France. For months to come, the softer rate in North Africa rankled Giraud and others who disliked De Gaulle. Still, Roosevelt's solution sufficiently placated Giraud to relieve the pressure on Eisenhower's military campaign. However casually, the President had served the interests of military efficiency and the politics of his North African allies, British and French alike.

Then and later, Morgenthau felt that Roosevelt had conceded too much. So also, the Secretary feared that American military government in North Africa moved too slowly toward democratizing the area and ridding it of the influence of those who had collaborated with the Nazis. As he saw it, the true interests of American finance and politics called for a more forceful, independent, and reformist policy not only in North Africa but also even more in Europe, the target for the next Allied attacks.

2. The Franc: Mirror of French Prestige

For American policy makers, the problems of France resembled those of no other nation, for, as usual, all France was divided into three parts during the months preceding the Allied attack on Europe. There was occupied France, the area in the north from which the Germans had to be driven. There was the government of France at Vichy, the creature of the Germans, established subject to their change of mind in the south. Roosevelt had dealt with that government in the expectation, only partially fulfilled, that such negotiations would ease the way to victory, as they had in some degree in North Africa. There was also the France of Charles de Gaulle, Free France, Fighting France — the union of brave and patriotic Frenchmen combating the Nazis in the *maquis* of occupied France and of Vichy France, under arms in French colonial areas, in spirit in exile in London, everywhere straining to erase the humiliation of 1940 and to restore France to her station as a great power.

De Gaulle, who personified that France, was head of the French Committee of National Liberation, the shadow-government that a host of loyal Frenchmen served. But the French Committee was not a government-in-exile in the view of the United States and Great Britain. De Gaulle's France, while an ally, had a legal status in Washington and London rather less than that of Belgium or Holland. Still, the assistance of De Gaulle's France, of the various resistance groups within geographical France, had special importance for the invasion, in which De Gaulle envisaged a major role for himself and his army. Indeed, for his part, De Gaulle considered the invasion an operation within his sovereignty, within the area under his legal authority. Churchill distrusted and Roosevelt disliked De Gaulle, who in turn resented the treatment he received. Roosevelt and Churchill, though not without disagreement within their own administrations, thought of France as a nation that could have no legal government until after liberation and free elections. Those conflicting assumptions complicated invasion planning, including the planning for a currency for France. And the conflict racked Morgenthau, whose loyalties, as always, were to Roosevelt, but whose sentiments, insofar as those loyalties permitted, lay strongly with the Free French.

A familiar issue confronted the Secretary in the late summer of 1943. Experience in North Africa had demonstrated by that time that the dollar-sterling-franc ratio set by the President at Casablanca overvalued the franc, just as Morgenthau had said it did. British and American financial representatives now advised that the rate made it impossible for French Africa to sell its exportable commodities on the world market. The Allied governments therefore had difficulty purchasing strategic materials in French Africa at prices based upon the official rate. A much lower rate was needed, one close to the Treasury's long-standing preference of 75 or 100 francs to the dollar. But the French Committee for National Liberation, interpreting the rate as a symbol of political prestige and a factor in national morale, wanted the 50 franc rate to apply in France after the liberation. After months of doubt, in May 1944, Morgenthau agreed with the understanding that an "equitable adjustment" for American expenditures in France might reflect a lower rate.

The French Committee had meanwhile made concessions to the United States on the question of currency. Initially, Morgenthau had endorsed the Committee's proposal, which the State Department supported, for franc currency for use by American troops during their operations in France. The Committee was to issue that currency, though the notes would carry only the legend: "La République Française." Secretary of War Stimson immediately objected. The United States, he argued, did not wish to recognize the Committee as sovereign in France, particularly during the interim between the invasion and a French election. For that period he demanded some kind of military money to be issued on the authority of the Allied commanders. The Free French replied that in Norway, Holland, and Belgium, Great Britain and the United States were planning to use the national

currencies, but Stimson pointed out that those nations had gov-
ernments-in-exile which the United States and Great Britain had
recognized; France did not.

Deferring to the War Department, Morgenthau on December
23, 1943, recommended a franc currency for military use in-
scribed on one side with the words "La République Française,"
and further "Émis en France." The currency would not indicate that the issuing authority was the Allied Military Commander. The reverse side of the notes would display a French
flag in full color and the words "Liberté, Egalité, Fraternité."
Morgenthau also recommended permitting the French Committee of National Liberation to place an order for currency of their
own design, which the Treasury would hold for release whenever the heads of government in Great Britain and the United
States so ordered.

Those suggestions won the approval of the War, Navy, and
State Departments, but not of the President. In a memorandum
to Morgenthau of January 6, 1944, Roosevelt objected to the
words "République Française." He preferred instead to say only
"La France." "In view of the fact that this will be issued by the
Allied Military Commander," he wrote, "I would put in the
middle, in color, the French flag, supported by the American flag
and the British flag on either side. I have no objection to having
the French Committee of National Liberation buy finished
French currency over here, but it cannot have on it the words
'République Française.' How do you know what the next permanent Government of France is going to be? My guess is that it
will be headed by a mandarin."

The omission of the phrase "République Française," John J.
McCloy said to Morgenthau on January 8, 1944, would be
"fraught with great danger. . . . The more we rap General de
Gaulle with republicanism, the better off we are." Morgenthau
wholly agreed. Later that day he and McCloy tried to convince
Roosevelt, who was adamant. "How do you know what kind of
a government you will have when the war is over?" the President asked again. "Maybe it will be an empire."

"That is just what we don't want to imply," Morgenthau

pointed out. ". . . It seems to me if you put on the words La République Française, it isn't going to tie your hands at all."

"Henry," Roosevelt said, "you talk just like the British Foreign Office."

"Mr. President," Morgenthau replied, "I have never been so insulted in ten years!"

But as the discussion continued, according to Morgenthau's Diary: "The answer always came back that he didn't want anything on the money which would indicate what kind of a government it was going to be. I argued and McCloy argued and while the President was in a grand humor, he had all his 'Dutch up,' and you couldn't budge him at all. He said, 'I have heard all these arguments. De Gaulle is on the wane.' . . . We got off the 'Liberté, Egalité, Fraternité'; he said we couldn't have that. He also asked for 'La France' . . . off. So it gets back to the flag and nothing else."

Harry White, upon hearing the Secretary's report, asked who Roosevelt thought would supplant De Gaulle. "He wouldn't say," Morgenthau replied. "But besides his own prejudice against De Gaulle, he now says that Stalin has no use for any Frenchman. . . . In the first place, the new government cannot include anybody — this is Stalin speaking — who has ever been a member of the French government before."

"Oh, oh," White interrupted, "Stalin is beginning to issue orders, is he?"

Replying indirectly, Morgenthau said Hull had come around to his position, though the Secretary of State still called "De Gaulle a polecat." Churchill, Morgenthau felt, was the main influence behind Roosevelt, but White noted that most of Churchill's subordinates supported De Gaulle, so that if Morgenthau were correct, the Prime Minister spoke only for himself. Whatever the influence, Roosevelt's views prevailed, and the French Committee, like the American Cabinet, had no choice but to go along.

American troops were not yet secure on the Cherbourg peninsula when De Gaulle provoked a new crisis in Franco-American relations that was embarrassing alike to commanders in the field

and to statesmen in Washington. From the Treasury's representative in London, Morgenthau heard early in June that De Gaulle
"had been acting up terribly. . . . He was . . . not only arro-
gant, but . . . actually vicious." He was especially angry that
the design for the franc on which his subordinates had agreed did
not name the Republic of France or the Committee of Liberation
as issuing authority. The omission, he held, undermined his dignity as the leader of the resistance to the Nazis, and challenged
the grandeur of the French republic and the French nation.

De Gaulle, so Churchill informed Roosevelt on June 9, 1944,
was demanding that General Eisenhower, in a pending proclamation about currency, refer specifically either to the "Provisional
Government of France" or the "Provisional Government of the
French Republic." If Eisenhower would do so, then De Gaulle
would issue a supporting proclamation of his own, putting his
endorsement and that of the Committee of Liberation on the
new francs. Churchill was worried. If General de Gaulle did
not endorse the issue, the notes would not have any backing, and
Great Britain and the United States would separately or jointly
be responsible to redeem them. Eager to avoid liability for the
currency, Churchill was even more intent on preventing De
Gaulle from causing difficulties for Eisenhower, perhaps by de-
nouncing the currency as false money. Further, the Prime Minister had examined specimens of the notes and found them very
easy to forge. He urged Roosevelt to look at the notes and to
decide whether England and the United States should allow De
Gaulle to obtain new status as his fee for backing them, or should
assume the burden for the time being, improve the issue later on,
and make the settlement at the peace table.

Disturbed by Churchill's cable, Morgenthau was embarrassed
by a radio broadcast from London that asserted that the French
National Committee had never been consulted about the cur-
rency. "I am not going to take this," the Secretary told Dan Bell
on June 10, "and I want a statement before sunset today that
Jean Monnet was in my office and agreed to the whole thing.
. . . I don't give a goddamn what the State Department, or the
War Department says, I want the public to know that I did this

working it out with Monnet . . . and with Mendès-France, the recognized . . . Minister of Finance."

The situation, Bell advised that evening, was too complex to be handled by pointing to that agreement. The Minister of Foreign Affairs for the Committee of Liberation, speaking from Africa, had condemned the Allies for printing any francs. The provisional government, he had said, could not "accord any legal value to the . . . paper." Of course the United States did not recognize the Committee as the provisional government, but there were those in Great Britain who believed that both English-speaking powers should do so at their first opportunity, and the question of the currency as it related to De Gaulle's status had become a matter of large political importance within Parliament and for Churchill. Those hoping to embarrass the Prime Minister, according to reports received in Washington, were using the currency issue as an excuse for demanding recognition of De Gaulle and his group as the government of France. Anything that Monnet or Mendès-France might say about previous arrangements with the United States Treasury would highlight a matter that the United States would do better, for the time being, to obscure.

Nevertheless, Morgenthau wanted to proceed. "I would get Jean Monnet in a room," he said. "I'd hold a gun to his head and make him sign a statement that he had approved this thing." But Monnet, Bell remarked, while approving the notes, had never approved of the United States' issuing them. So reminded, Morgenthau concluded that "as Secretary of the Treasury, . . . I should answer the President. . . . Should we assume responsibility for this currency, even if De Gaulle denounces it? . . . And my answer is: We've gone so far that we've got to assume responsibility." As to whether De Gaulle was to sign a proclamation supporting the currency, Morgenthau said that he would not advise the President; that question fell to the Department of State.

De Gaulle's conduct, Morgenthau felt, had been utterly outrageous. "With our men on the beaches of France," he said, "this fellow comes along and holds . . . a gun to our backs." In that

mood, the Secretary approved the draft of a reply for Roosevelt
to send Churchill which Bell, Harry White, and John McCloy
had prepared:

I share your view that this currency issue is being exploited to
stampede us into according full recognition to the Comité. Personally I do not think the currency situation . . . is as critical as it
might first appear. Nor do I feel that it is essential from the point
of view of the acceptability of the supplemental currency that De
Gaulle make any statement of support. . . . I propose that De
Gaulle should be informed as follows:

1. We intend to continue to use the supplementary franc currency in exactly the same manner as we have planned and as . . .
has been fully understood by Messieurs Monnet and Mendès-
France of the French Comité.

2. If for any reason the supplemental currency is not acceptable
to the French public, General Eisenhower has full authority to use
yellow seal dollars and British Military Authority notes. Accordingly, if De Gaulle incites the French people into refusing to accept supplementary francs . . . one of the certain consequences
will be the depreciation of the French franc in terms of dollars
and sterling in a black market which will accentuate and reveal the
weaknesses of the French monetary system. This is one of the
important reasons why we accepted the request of the French
Comité that we not use yellow seal dollars and BMA notes as a
spearhead currency. . . .

I would certainly not importune De Gaulle to make any supporting statement. . . . Provided it is clear that he acts entirely on
his own responsibility and without our concurrence he can sign
any statement . . . in whatever capacity he likes, even that of the
King of Siam.

As far as the appearance of the notes is concerned, . . . I have
looked at them again and think them adequate. I am informed by
the Bureau of Engraving and Printing counterfeiting experts that
they will be extremely difficult to counterfeit by virtue of the
intricate color combination. . . . The French representatives here
not only approved the note but were satisfied with the design and
the color.

After consulting Hull and Stimson, Roosevelt on June 12 sent
that message to Churchill.* Hull, Stimson observed in his diary,

* The President added only one sentence: "It seems clear that a prima donna
does not change his spots."

hated De Gaulle so fiercely that he was almost incoherent on the subject, and Stimson himself distrusted the General greatly. Roosevelt's position, Stimson believed, was correct theoretically and logically, but regrettably unrealistic, for circumstances required an immediate reconciliation between the British and American governments even if that entailed provisional recognition of De Gaulle.

Developments in England forced others to move toward Stimson's view. To Morgenthau on June 16, 1944, McCloy described the heated debate under way in London where Anthony Eden had thrown down a gauntlet to Churchill on the question of recognizing the provisional government of De Gaulle. Eden was making it a personal issue on which the future of the Churchill government might depend. Further, the British were making it seem as if the currency were just another American scheme. General Marshall, McCloy also reported, was in a white fury with De Gaulle. If the American people could know, Marshall had said, what De Gaulle had been doing to hamper the invasion — the actual military operations, if that ever leaked out, it would sweep "the whole damn thing aside," but the story was so outrageous Marshall feared that, if he released it, it would provoke too strong a reaction and play into the hands of American isolationists. More important, Marshall, like Stimson, felt that the need for Anglo-American cooperation during the fighting made it necessary to find some way to resolve disagreements about De Gaulle.

Stimson had contrived a formula for that reconciliation. The United States, he suggested to Roosevelt, should authorize Eisenhower to deal with the French Committee as the authority responsible for civil administration outside of the combat zone. That formula involved less than provisional recognition but more than Roosevelt would yield. The President, according to McCloy, told Stimson he did not want to compromise on a "moral principle." That principle, as Roosevelt saw it, guaranteed the French people a free election to determine their government. Accordingly, the President would not now permit that "jackenape" to seize the government. Indeed, he was unmoved

even by Stimson's suggestion that he pledge De Gaulle to holding an election.

Yet Roosevelt's reply to Churchill was reducing the tempera-
ture of the currency problem. The American threat to use yellow seal dollars like those employed in North Africa quieted the
Free French and their English supporters. Monnet and Mendès-
France, moreover, were taking steps to remind De Gaulle that
they had earlier consented to the American design for the supplementary francs. The matter of currency, Churchill believed
by June 21, 1944, was no longer critical. Still, the Prime Minister felt that the United States would be morally responsible for
redeeming the supplementary francs unless there were some further agreement with the French Committee.

Morgenthau intended to define the terms for any agreement in
Washington. With the help of McCloy, on June 23, 1944, he
prepared a draft reply for Roosevelt to send Churchill about the
redemption of the supplemental francs. There was no need, that
draft held, to assume that the United States and Great Britain
were responsible for the currency "merely because no understanding has been reached with the French Committee." The
Supreme Allied Commander alone had authority to issue currency for France. Ultimately, that currency would be redeemed
"like any other good currency by the government of the country in which it is issued," just as in the case of Belgium or Norway.

At first the Treasury's draft displeased the President. "I don't
like issuing money which isn't money," he said at a White House
meeting of June 26. After Dan Bell described the proposed
scheme in detail, Roosevelt relented. "These financial matters,"
he said, "are very difficult to explain to a layman." With one
small alteration, he then approved the draft. It put to rest
Churchill's worries about redemption.

There remained the fierce French sensitivities about sovereignty. The French Committee, Mendès-France admitted in a
letter to Morgenthau, had known of the American intention to
use the supplemental notes. The Committee, however, had never
agreed "on the matter of the issuing authority." Mendès-France

had never wanted a military currency issued on French territory, and had never meant to suggest that he believed a major political problem could be solved on the technical level.

Neither, of course, had Morgenthau, who had, rather, hoped that the technical solution implied a political understanding. On July 5, 1944, the Secretary suggested to John McCloy that Eisenhower issue a directive recognizing the French Committee and De Gaulle as a "de facto authority." That phrase, he felt, might suit Roosevelt better than had Stimson's earlier suggestion of "provisional" recognition of De Gaulle. McCloy, though he feared that Roosevelt would recognize the new phrase as an old horse, agreed to join Morgenthau in commending it to the White House. So did Hull. "We should like to suggest to you a fresh approach to the French situation," they wrote the President. The United States should deal with the French Committee either as the "civil authority" or the "administrative authority" or the "de facto authority" in France "to reach agreements on civil affairs administration along the lines of those reached with Belgium, the Netherlands and Norway." The agreements would be temporary, pending selection of a French government by the free choice of the French people, but the French Committee would become the issuing authority for the supplemental francs.

With De Gaulle then in Washington to be entertained and appeased, Roosevelt was unusually malleable. After designating his preference for the use of the phrase "de facto authority," he wrote across the memorandum Morgenthau had submitted: "OK in principle. Let me see the agreement first." On July 7, 1944, he approved the agreement, which followed the lines of the memorandum. "I am very pleased," Morgenthau told his staff, ". . . that I had a little part in it."

The settlement of the currency question relieved Eisenhower of one major irritation but left untouched another matter of concern to the Treasury. Prices in France rose dramatically in spite of the success of the Department and the Army in persuading American troops to save their pay and otherwise to refrain from stimulating demand. But the obligations of war prevented the United States Army from diverting transportation and supplies to a degree sufficient to relieve inflation. And in the meantime, American troops, during both the fighting and the occupation, like all soldiers in all times and places, looked for relaxation from combat or fatigue and for mementos of their service. In that search they spent some fraction of their pay on luxuries, whether perfume or wine or entertainment, all of which were beyond the reach of the impoverished civilian population. Consequently, the presence of the troops occasioned some resentment and contributed some dimension to inflation. The solution to those problems had to await the formulation of civilian policy and the application of necessary controls after normal channels of trade and supply could begin again to function.

Yet the experience in France, like the previous experience in other areas which the Allies reconquered from the Nazis, pointed to the kinds of difficulties which would harass the Allies when in time they gained power over Germany and Japan. There they would again confront the problem of inflation. And before they triumphed, they would have to settle questions of currency that involved the military efficiency and the political cohesion of the Grand Alliance. By June 1944, those questions, as they arose in planning for Germany, were already engaging Morgenthau.

3. Allied Military Marks

Significant planning for occupation currency in Germany commenced early in 1944, some six months before the invasion of Europe and more than a year before Allied troops reached the German border. Germany presented something of a new problem. In Belgium or the Netherlands or Norway, British and American forces were moving into territory held by the enemy but represented by a properly constituted and recognized government-in-exile. In North Africa and France, the French

Committee stood ready to assume authority. In Italy a hostile government reigned, but very rapidly that government was supplanted by a cooperative regime. In Germany, however, victory would initiate a long period of Allied military government in which the German people would have no voice. But the United States could not make unilateral decisions about currency or any other aspect of military government, for all plans for Germany began in 1944 with the assumption that the United Kingdom and the Soviet Union would cooperate in the occupation and would pursue unified political and economic policies.

The Treasury and the War Departments feared that if yellow seal dollars were used in Germany, local vendors would refuse to deliver goods for Reichsmarks and demand dollars instead. That would destroy the value of the Reichsmark, shake the economy, and impede supplies of food and other essentials for military operations. The two Departments therefore preferred printing Allied Military Marks designed to circulate alongside of Reichsmarks and serve as currency for payment of troops. The British agreed that the United States and the United Kingdom should provide occupation marks for the payment of troops and as a supplementary currency. As Averell Harriman reported from Moscow: "Great importance is attached by the British Government to the Russian Government's participation in this arrangement."

The first Soviet opinion reached the Treasury on February 1, 1944. The Russians felt "that the question of the kind of currency that would be used . . . in Germany was too important . . . for them to rush into a decision. . . . They were giving the matter further consideration." That delay, though characteristic, was crippling, for the Treasury and the War Departments considered it essential to begin printing currency not later than February 14, 1944, if production were to take care of Soviet requirements. The Treasury had at least to know whether the Russians expected to use the mark designed for the United States and the United Kingdom, and if not, what alternative they proposed to adopt.

Pressed for a decision, Soviet Foreign Minister Vyacheslav

Molotov responded on February 11 in a long letter to Harriman. The Soviet Union, Molotov wrote, shared the wish of the British and American governments to collaborate in the issuance of military currency for Germany during the period of invasion and occupation. The Soviet Union also agreed to American proposals for the design of that currency, and for printing on it the phrase "Allied Military Authorities." Further, the Soviet Commissariat for Finance considered it expedient to print serial numbers on all notes, and important to prepare a part of the printing within the Soviet Union "in order that a constant supply of currency may be guaranteed to the Red Army." In order to make the marks printed in Russia identical with those manufactured in the United States, the Commissariat for Finance needed a list of serial numbers, models of paper and colors, and plates for printing the various denominations of the currency.

The Russian request for the plates, received at the Treasury on February 28, elicited an alarmed negative from Alvin W. Hall, Director of the Bureau of Engraving and Printing. "To acquiesce to such an unprecedented request," he wrote Daniel Bell, "would create serious complications." It would make accountability impossible. Worse, by inviolable custom, bank note manufacturers retained possession of all plates they used for the printing of any currency or bonds for any country or bank. Hall urged the perpetuation of that rule. The contractor printing the Allied Military Authorities marks was under strong safeguards and heavy bond to insure against misappropriation, loss, or improper use of the plates, paper, or currency. A scandal might follow removal of those precautions, yet the Treasury could hardly force the Soviet Union to preserve them. Further, the process of manufacture of invasion currency, extremely complex in itself, had to proceed under ideal and controlled conditions which would be hard, if not impossible, to duplicate. Opposed to furnishing duplicate plates to anyone for any reason, Hall was "ready and willing to assist the Russian Government in the development of new designs of invasion currency for Germany" and to supply inks and paper for that purpose.

Indirectly, of course, Hall was proposing that the Russians

adopt an invasion and occupation currency of their own. That suggestion disturbed Harry White, who at a meeting on March 7, 1944, was "loath to turn the Russian request down without further review. . . . He called attention to the fact that in this instance we were not printing American currency, but Allied currency and that Russia was one of the allies who must be trusted to the same degree and to the same extent as the other allies. He wondered if it wouldn't be possible to talk to the Russian Ambassador here . . . without settling the question concerning the plates at this time."

At Morgenthau's home on the evening of March 18, Ambassador Andrei Gromyko said that the Russians, in spite of all the technical problems that the Treasury had reported, still wanted the plates. In a memorandum about the ensuing discussion, Harry White wrote:

> The Secretary replied that he was sorry that the Soviet government still wanted the plates after his explanation of the difficulties and that he had not expected that they would. . . . He said that since he had last spoken to the Ambassador that the Treasury had again contacted the Forbes Company about the request. The Forbes Company repeated its insistence that it could not go on with the contract if a duplicate set of plates were given out. The Secretary stressed the fact that we were prepared to make available to the Soviet Government the currency that they needed whereas if we were to give them a duplicate set of plates the matter would be delayed long beyond what he thought was the time schedule provided to us by the Army.
>
> He urged the Ambassador to send some of his representatives to the Forbes Company plant . . . to see the magnitude of the task. . . . The Ambassador responded that he would be glad to send these men up but he doubted very much if it would make any difference at all in the request of his Government. The Secretary then said he would get the exact information of the time that would be required to provide the necessary currency if the Treasury had to take the job over from the Forbes people, and also the time that it would require for the Soviet Government to begin production on a large scale if plates were sent to them now. He . . . would inform the Ambassador within forty-eight hours of the information he obtained.

Eager for a common currency, Morgenthau made another effort to win over the Soviet Union. At his instruction White called on Gromyko on the night of March 21, 1944. In a report to Morgenthau the next day, White wrote:

> I tried to expand on the reasons why it would require six to eight months to produce marks in the Bureau of Engraving and why it might be unwise to have the Army take over the Forbes plant under the War Powers Act and attempt to operate it. He kept coming back with a question which he asked a number of times, namely, why the Forbes Company should object to giving a duplicate set of plates to his Government. He said that after all the Soviet Government was not a private corporation or an irresponsible Government. . . .
>
> As instructed, I explained to him that Secretary Morgenthau was sending a letter to the Combined Chiefs of Staff containing an explanation of the situation together with a memorandum, asking them for a prompt reply. The Ambassador hoped to be able to get the reply soon, and I told him I thought he would.

Morgenthau's letter of March 22, 1944, to Admiral Leahy, the senior American representative on the Combined Chiefs of Staff, reviewed the whole problem, the difficulties in acceding to the Russian request for duplicate plates, the insistence of the Soviet Union on those plates, the question of the timetable. The Secretary sent a copy of the letter to Hull, who the next day cabled Harriman about the impasse. Gromyko, Hull noted, had received the Treasury's analysis of the technical problems and understood the Treasury's conclusion that meeting the Russian request would delay production. Morgenthau, Hull also said, had referred the question to the Combined Chiefs of Staff. "It is not expected," Hull continued, "that the Combined Chiefs . . . will favor the delivery of plates to the Russians, in view of this very considerable delay."

Replying to Hull on April 8, 1944, Harriman reported that the Russians would not budge. If the United States could not provide the plates, Molotov had said, "the Soviet Government will then be forced to proceed with the independent preparation of military marks for Germany in its own pattern."

As the matter then stood, pending further decision either by Hull or Morgenthau or the Combined Chiefs of Staff, Hall's wholly understandable technical reservations had to be weighed against Molotov's firm, contrary position. While Hall was incontestably correct in his interpretation of ordinary practice in the printing of currency in the United States, Molotov was by no means unreasonable considering the spirit and the exigencies of the time. In April 1944, Soviet-American relations were on the whole excellent. Neither the United States nor the United Kingdom had any palpable evidence to indicate that the Russians would fail to proceed with the developing plan for a cooperative, joint occupation of Germany. Further, just as Eisenhower wanted assurances that he would have in hand the currency he needed for his troops, so did the Russian military commanders want similar assurances, and naturally they and their civilian superiors felt that the supply of currency to Soviet troops would work out most efficiently if facilities for producing the currency were operating within the Soviet Union. In this as in other instances, Soviet representatives had grave difficulty understanding the posture of the American government toward private enterprise, especially toward a contractor attempting to influence an issue under negotiation with an allied foreign power. Most important, in the United States, as in Great Britain, the dominating concern for unified policy in Germany overbalanced the technical factors that motivated Hall. All those considerations lay behind the cable Hull sent Harriman on April 11, 1944: "We are trying to facilitate a favorable decision in connection with the Soviet request and in a few days we hope to telegraph you the scheme which we think will meet the wishes of the Soviet Government."

At the War Department on April 12, 1944, General John Hilldring, the Army head of civil affairs, told an interdepartmental conference that the issue of the duplicate plates was almost "too hot" for the Combined Chiefs of Staff. After working over five drafts of a reply to Morgenthau's query to Leahy, the Combined Chiefs had concluded that the question should not be settled on military grounds. On that basis, in a letter to Morgen-

thau on the following day, the Combined Chiefs suggested
that the Treasury should make the plates available to the Soviet
Union unless that step interfered with Eisenhower's requirements for AMA currency. There would be no interference,
Morgenthau ascertained, for Eisenhower's full order was almost
ready.

Equally important, the State Department supported the decision of the Combined Chiefs, as Morgenthau learned in a telephone conversation with James Dunn on April 14. Morgenthau
called Dunn to report that he was planning to tell Gromyko that
afternoon that the Treasury would provide the duplicate plates.
The Secretary wanted first to be sure the State Department approved. Aside from any military or technical considerations,
Dunn replied, it was the opinion of the State Department from a
political point of view "that if possible it was highly advisable to
have the duplicate plates furnished to the Soviet Government in
order that the three Governments and the three Armies entering
Germany would be using the same identical currency. The Soviet Government had informed us that if the plates were not furnished to it, that Government would proceed to produce a separate currency for use in Germany. It was our opinion that it
would be a pity to lose the great advantage of having one currency . . . which itself would indicate a degree of solidarity
which was much to be desired not only for the situation in Germany but for its effect on the relations in many other aspects
between the Soviet, British and United States Governments."

The British were of the same mind. It was technically improb-
able, they noted, that identical notes could be produced in two
different places, and they were therefore concerned about the
possibility of forgery or of low confidence in the AMA marks.
But that was a subsidiary question. "We fully realize," they
wrote, ". . . how desirable it is politically . . . to comply with
Russia's present request which seems to indicate a welcome readiness to cooperate. Provided US Authorities are satisfied . . .
we therefore agree that Russians should be given the plates."

Though Alvin Hall remained passionately unhappy, Morgenthau on the afternoon of April 14, 1944, told Gromyko that the

United States Government, eager to cooperate with the Soviet Union, would furnish duplicate plates, inks, paper, and, if the Russians wished, supplies of printed currency. As Hall later recalled, the Secretary instructed him to "do everything you can to give the Russians what they want," and on April 21 the Treasury delivered the plates and other materials to the Soviet Embassy.*

Years after the events, when Russian-American relations had deteriorated, critics of the Roosevelt Administration maintained that the decision about the duplicate plates derived from Communist influence within the Treasury and accounted for the inflation in postwar Germany. The latter assertions were silly. Postwar inflation visited every nation in the world, including the United States, but especially those that had suffered severe war damage, like Germany, France, and Japan.

The decision about the duplicate plates subordinated technical to military and political judgments. It was the joint decision of the Treasury, State, and War Departments, the Combined Chiefs of Staff and the British Government, with General John Hilldring, Assistant Secretary of State James Dunn, and Morgenthau as the major contributors to the final policy. No one of those men was in any sense a Communist or Communist sympathizer. All of them in 1944 were dedicated to the advancement of their common hope for successful cooperation among the Russians, the British, and the Americans throughout the postwar world, not least in Germany. And in that spring and during the preceding months, Morgenthau was also pursuing his own vision of decency and justice in international politics. On that account, he was at odds with the State Department and with the British

---

* The foregoing account of intra- and inter-governmental negotiations leading to the delivery of the plates to the Soviets may be compared to the recollection of Elizabeth Bentley, a self-confessed Communist spy who accused Harry White, among others, of complicity in her work. A War Department employee, she wrote, "brought me samples of the marks the United States was preparing for use in the German occupation. The Russians were delighted, as they were planning to counterfeit them. However, due to a complicated ink process this proved impossible — until I was able through Harry Dexter White to arrange that the United States Treasury Department turn the actual printing plates over to the Russians!"

Foreign Office over policies remote from the European battle-
ground, policies affecting American assistance for persecuted and
displaced Jews.

4. *"Those Terrible Eighteen Months"*

Years after he had left office, Morgenthau looked back on what
he called "those terrible eighteen months. . . . We knew in
Washington . . . that the Nazis were planning to exterminate
all the Jews of Europe. Yet . . . officials dodged their grim responsibility, procrastinated when concrete rescue schemes were
placed before them, and even suppressed information about
atrocities."

Long before the war and the worst of the pogroms, Morgenthau had worried about the European Jews whom politics put at
Hitler's mercy. He was, for example, a regular and generous
contributor to the American Jewish Joint Distribution Committee, whose agents were working for the removal of Jews from
Germany to the United States and other havens. But, as Secretary of the Treasury, he had little opportunity to deal with the
problem. Not a Zionist, always aware of British reluctance to
antagonize the Arabs by increasing Jewish migration into Palestine, Morgenthau also knew that American immigration laws,
about which Congress took an unyielding position, severely restricted the number of refugees who could enter the United
States. With Roosevelt, he therefore seized on other possibilities.

In November 1938, after Hitler had promulgated the Nuremberg decrees to the President's outspoken shock, Morgenthau
went to the White House with what he called "the first concrete
suggestion to make for the Jewish refugees." He had received a
letter, he said, proposing that the United States acquire British
and French Guiana in return for canceling the debts of the first
World War due from the United Kingdom and France. Roose-

velt was unimpressed. "It's no good," the President said. "It would take the Jews five to fifty years to overcome the fever." Roosevelt had instead the idea of a Jewish community in the Cameroons where there lay, he said, "some very wonderful high land, table land, wonderful grass and . . . all of that country has been explored and it's ready." But the geographers whom Morgenthau commissioned to explore the possibility of settlement in the Cameroons considered the probable cost of the project prohibitive and the potentialities for economic development poor.

The Intergovernmental Committee on Refugees, established in 1938, also found no place to which to evacuate European Jews. "The whole trouble is in England," Roosevelt admitted to Morgenthau in mid-1939. Since British politics in the Near East prevented the utilization of Palestine as a haven for European Jews, Roosevelt had "talked to the President-elect of Paraguay" and believed that if he could "get two or three people together . . . we could work out a plan." He was even willing to have it called the Roosevelt Plan, and if Morgenthau would give him a list of the thousand richest Jews in the United States, he was prepared to tell each how much money he should contribute. But Morgenthau brought Roosevelt down from his cloud. "Mr. President," he pointed out, "before you talk about money you have to have a plan."

It was no time to bring up the question of Palestine, Roosevelt told Morgenthau in July 1942, for "the English were terrifically worried" about an Arab uprising. By the end of the year, the President had a new dream. "What I think I will do," he said on December 3, 1942, "is this. First, I would call Palestine a religious country. Then I would leave Jerusalem the way it is and have it run by the Orthodox Greek Catholic Church, the Protestants, and the Jews — have a joint committee run it. . . . I actually would put a barbed wire around Palestine, and I would begin to move the Arabs out of Palestine. . . . I would provide land for the Arabs in some other part of the Middle East. . . . Each time we move out an Arab we would bring in another Jewish family. . . . But I don't want to bring in more than they

can economically support. . . . It would be an independent nation just like any other nation. . . . Naturally, if there are 90
per cent Jews, the Jews would dominate the government. . . .
There are lots of places to which you could move the Arabs.
All you have to do is drill a well because there is this large
underground water supply, and we can move the Arabs to places
where they can really live." But that fantasy was a long way
from fulfillment, and by June 1943, Roosevelt had moved only
to urge Churchill to bring the Jews and Arabs together for discussion. The President thought the Arabs could be bribed, but
the Prime Minister — though himself a long-time Zionist — disagreed. He was straining to avoid the Jewish question and to
keep the Middle East quiet at least until the war ended.

Meanwhile "those terrible eighteen months" had witnessed
new and frightful stages in Hitler's plan to exterminate the Jews
of Europe. Though Morgenthau did not become aware of the
full implications of that plan for American policy until 1943, and
then, as he later put it, in a "scramble of bits and pieces," a detailed report of the Nazi program reached the State Department
in 1942.* It came from a German Jew, Gerhart Riegner, who
had fled to Geneva, where he represented the World Jewish
Congress. Through private channels, Riegner got his ghastly
story to Rabbi Stephen S. Wise, the president of the American
Jewish Congress. Wise then asked the State Department to confirm the information, and at the Department's request, kept the
story to himself while Washington cabled an inquiry to the
American Minister at Bern, Leland Harrison. In November
1942, Harrison sent back full documentation for Riegner's report, which the State Department then told Wise he could make
public. The United States officially denounced the Nazi policy
of extermination on December 17, 1942, and Roosevelt declared
that it would be American policy to punish racial and political
murder.

A second report from Riegner on January 21, 1943, said that
Germans were killing Polish Jews at the rate of 6,000 a day and

---

* In order to avoid confusion, the account in this chapter proceeds chrono-
logically, but the Treasury did not obtain the full story until the winter of
1943–1944, and then only in scrambled installments.

in Rumania were systematically starving Jews and others to death. Those disclosures provoked requests from Americans of all faiths for governmental efforts to rescue the victims of Nazi brutality. The State Department, however, deferred action. In reply to pleas for assistance, it merely referred to the Intergovernmental Committee on Refugees, which had as yet accomplished nothing significant. The British were still cultivating the Arabs, and within the Department of State itself, those responsible for visas had admitted even fewer Jews than the small quotas for European immigration permitted.

As Morgenthau discovered months later, State Department officials also cut off the communications from Riegner. The Department's reply to Minister Harrison's cable of January 21, 1943, suggested that in the future he should not accept reports submitted to him for transmission to private individuals in the United States except under extraordinary circumstances. Those private messages, the reply said, circumvented the censorship of neutral countries, and in sending them Harrison risked the possibility that neutrals would curtail or forbid communication about important official matters. That directive was signed by Sumner Welles, then still Under Secretary of State, but Welles, who was personally entirely sympathetic with efforts to rescue the Jews, did not understand the implications of the order and may not even have seen it. Indeed, in April 1943, obviously unaware of the restrictions he had inadvertently approved, Welles asked Harrison for further reports from Riegner about the Jews. But in the interim, three months of silence had stayed the hands of those who would otherwise have pressed for American action.

In spite of the interruption in communications from Bern, enough information reached the Treasury to alert Morgenthau. On February 13, 1943, the *New York Times* reported from London that the Rumanian government had told United Nations officials that it was prepared to transfer 70,000 Jews to Palestine on Rumanian ships using Vatican insignia. As the *Times* noted, some spies might mingle with so large a number of refugees; further, tension between the Arabs and Jews in Palestine was already high; and there were logistical difficulties in arranging mass transportation for so many people. "The President," Morgenthau told Welles on February 15, "didn't know anything about it, and he said . . . to talk to you about it, and . . . would you discuss it with him." Welles, too, had learned all he knew from the *Times*, but the State Department ascertained through the American Embassy in London on February 18 that in essence the story was correct. "Officials who were in charge in Rumania of Jewish interests" had offered to transfer between 60,000 and 70,-000 Jews in return for a per capita ransom of £250. The American Embassy in Ankara, in a cable of February 23, added that the United States and British governments were also to provide assurances of safe conduct and the necessary visas. But the British did not want the refugees in Palestine, and Roosevelt, after months of uncertainty, in a letter to Hull of May 14, 1943, called for strict compliance with American immigration laws and suggested the possibility of North Africa as a temporary depot for some refugees if local authorities approved.

There matters stood until July, when representatives of the American Jewish Congress called at the Treasury to say that certain Nazi officials in Rumania could be bribed at an overall cost of $170,000 to permit the evacuation of 70,000 Jews. The money would have to be paid in local currency. Jewish merchants in Rumania, who had been able to conceal their resources, could make that payment if they were reimbursed either in dollars or Swiss francs, to be held for them in trust until the war ended. The World Jewish Congress would direct the entire operation from Switzerland, and the American Jewish Congress had already discussed the plan in general terms with the Department of State. For the Treasury, the proposal raised the question of whether to release dollars for the purchase of Rumanian currency. On July 19, 1943, Randolph Paul wrote Morgenthau that the matter had "been thoroughly discussed here in the Treasury and we have advised State informally that the Treasury is prepared to approve the necessary transactions on the basis of the facts now before us." Morgenthau then informed Wise that the department was "fully sympathetic to the proposal."

To Roosevelt on July 22, 1943, Wise explained that Morgenthau understood that the alternative to the exchange transaction was the death of the 70,000 Jews. The Treasury, he reported, would retain the dollars it released in Switzerland in escrow so that no funds could reach any representatives of the Axis until after the war. Roosevelt approved the plan orally, but Wise, in a letter to the President written right after their meeting, continued his plea by pointing out that the contemplated arrangements would "create such conditions within the Hitler territories as shall enable many Jews in those countries to survive, to escape deportation and ultimately to come out of those countries. . . . The whole arrangement is to provide especially for the saving of many little children. We feel that these funds may make possible the salvation of thousands of otherwise doomed beings, especially in Rumania, Slovakia and France, without . . . one penny falling into the hands of enemy representatives for the duration."

Morgenthau wrote Wise on July 23, 1943, that the matter was "now awaiting the further exchange of cables between the State Department and our mission in Bern regarding some of the details." In fact it was more complicated than that, for within the State Department, as the Treasury discovered on August 5, there was a division of opinion about the issue, with Assistant Secretary Breckinridge Long, to whom Hull had assigned responsibility, either opposed or dubious to the point of indifference. Foreign Service officers to whom Long listened, argued that the Germans would never consent to the necessary transportation arrangements, and that neither the British, the Turks, nor local North African authorities would agree to admit the evacuees. So informed, Morgenthau wrote Hull that Foreign Funds Control had been ready since July 16 to "take the necessary action to implement this proposal." Replying on August 7, Hull wrote that "the Treasury itself is entirely free to act on this matter and to grant the necessary licenses if it should so decide. In the latter event the State Department would be pleased to send the appropriate notification . . . to our Legation in Bern. . . . Any view that this would make funds available to the enemy is not correct; the funds would remain blocked in Switzerland until the end of the war."

Hull's quick cooperation reassured Morgenthau. The Secretary of State, unlike some of his subordinates, was clearly eager to assist in rescuing European Jews. Further, he seemed at last to have cleared the way for the dispatch to Bern of a cable communicating instructions to the legation there for the transactions that would permit the execution of the plan for Rumania.

But through no fault of Hull, the appearance remained at variance with reality. Not until September 28, 1943, did that cable go out to Bern. Replying on October 6, Harrison asked for specific orders from the State Department before acting on the authority granted by the Treasury. He then also said that in accordance with standing instructions concerning problems having to do with trading with the enemy, he had discussed the matter with British authorities at Bern who opposed the issuance of the license. It was another ten days before the Treasury learned of the reply, and October 24 before Randolph Paul, acting for Morgenthau while the Secretary was away, succeeded in obtaining a copy of the cable. On October 26 John Pehle, the head of Foreign Funds Control, furious that the State Department had still not directed Harrison to act, told Breckinridge Long that there was no need for British clearance before proceeding. But the British Treasury and the British Ministry of Economic Warfare held that the contemplated license would result in aid to the enemy.

Back in Washington, Morgenthau on November 23, 1943, reviewed the situation with Paul, Pehle, and others on his staff. The Secretary scolded Pehle for neglecting to consult the British himself, since there were, as the State Department had noted, standard instructions for consultation on all activities relating to trading with the enemy. But Morgenthau also realized, as Pehle pointed out, that the root of the difficulty lay in the reluctance of the British and of Hull's subordinates to support the Treasury's policy. The Secretary therefore suggested having "a very careful cable drawn up giving Winant all the facts and asking him whether he would please facilitate this on behalf of the Treasury. . . . That cable has to be signed by Hull, and in that way it does bring it out in the open. A cable going from me to Winant has to be signed by Hull and cleared."

The files, Pehle objected, were filled with cables which Treasury had originated and the State Department had sent. Those cables in turn were full of little remarks "like the Treasury wants this, the Treasury desires you to do this, and the Treasury this, and the Treasury that. And Harrison, unless he is a dumbbell, can see through that, that State is in effect saying this is what the Treasury wants you to do."

Morgenthau disagreed. He believed that Ambassador Winant could bring the British to heel, and he trusted Hull's good will. "So far," he said, "whenever I have gone to him direct he has been very good. . . . No one would like to see this come out in the open more than I. Unfortunately you are up against a . . . generation of people like those in the State Department who don't like to do this kind of thing, and it is only by my happening to be Secretary of the Treasury and being vitally interested in these things, with the help of you people . . . that I can do it. I am all for you. . . . I will do everything I can, and we will get it done. But don't think you are going to be able to nail anybody in the State Department . . . to the cross. . . .

"You men are very forthright . . . very courageous, and I back you up. . . . I will go just as far as you men will let me go. . . . All I can do is to bring this thing and put this thing in Cordell's hands. . . . Then it is up to him to get angry at his own people."

Randolph Paul drafted the letter to Hull, which Morgenthau softened considerably and signed on November 24. The letter reviewed developments in the Rumanian question since the previous June, lamented the delays that frustrated the program, and solicited Hull's assistance. Morgenthau also asked Hull to send Winant a cable requesting him to obtain from the British Ministry of Economic Warfare "the withdrawal of its objections to the issuance of the license."

Morgenthau's letter referred, too, to a related issue which had first arisen toward the end of the summer, when two cables from Bern reported the circumstances of Jewish children in France. The Nazis had deported some 4,000 children, ranging in age between two and fourteen, to undisclosed destinations — gas chambers, probably — in windowless box cars without food or water. Under German orders, the French police were attempting to take a census of another 6,000 Jewish children abandoned in France. Many of them had been hidden in private homes, about half in the Italian-occupied area of southern France. Local finances were inadequate for taking care of children who had been evacuated or for providing transportation and subsequent support for the Jewish children hidden near Paris. Relief organizations could not help unless they had permission to convert dollars to francs. Randolph Paul, after examining the problem, concluded that the Treasury should permit responsible philanthropic groups to arrange relief for refugees in enemy territory under stipulated safeguards: the relief organizations were to demonstrate that they had the necessary facilities and contacts, were to ensure that no foreign exchange would reach the enemy, and were to subject their operations to the scrutiny of American officials in neighboring neutral countries. Morgenthau approved that scheme, while also expressing a preference for working through the Quakers or the Y.M.C.A. rather than through Jewish relief organizations. But as in the case of Rumania, the Treasury needed State Department cooperation in order to proceed.

Replying to Morgenthau on December 6, 1943, Hull wrote that he understood the proposals for Rumania and France had never been developed in detail. Consequently, Harrison in Bern had been in a difficult position, authorized to issue a license to cover arrangements not yet adequately worked out. Further, Harrison felt the Treasury's conditions for the use of the license could not be met. The State Department, Hull concluded, had "the deepest sympathy for the desperate plight of the persecuted Jews in Europe. I have always been horrified at the unspeakable treatment which these poor people have received, and it has always been the policy of the Department to deal expeditiously and sympathetically with proposals offering hope of their relief."

Convinced that those arguments were meretricious, Randolph Paul especially resented Hull's tendentious conclusion. In a draft for Morgenthau, Paul argued that Harrison had known how to proceed under the license issued to the World Jewish Congress.

There had been no failure to establish safe mechanisms for exchange. Rather, officers of the State Department and representatives of Great Britain had held up the program. By and large, Morgenthau relied on Paul's analysis in the answer which he sent to Hull on December 17, but he also said that existing disagreements were insignificant in comparison with Hull's willingness to review the whole matter and with Hull's assurances that it was State Department policy to deal expeditiously with the proposal. Like Paul, Morgenthau believed that the Treasury's plans had provided proper safeguards for refugee operations in Rumania and France; unlike Paul, the Secretary was willing to subordinate controversy about what had occurred in order to invite cooperation about what had still to be accomplished.

British policy made that task difficult. On December 13, 1943, the Treasury received through Winant a statement of London's position. The Ministry of Economic Warfare, after "very full and careful consideration," agreed to licensing the transfer of funds for the evacuation of Jews from Rumania and France, but only to $25,000, and only under conditions preventing the movement of dollars to Nazi agents or other objectionable persons. The Ministry noted that the Foreign Office saw "grave disadvantages in general," which would be the subject of a longer dispatch. That arrived two days later. The Foreign Office was concerned "with the difficulties of disposing of any considerable number of Jews should they be rescued from enemy occupied territory;" the schemes under consideration were "greatly hampered by difficulties of transportation, particularly shipping, and of finding accommodation in the countries of the Near East for any but a very small number of Jewish refugees." It seemed to the Foreign Office almost impossible to deal with anything like 70,000 refugees, and therefore the British were "reluctant to agree to any approval being expressed even of the preliminary financial arrangements." Those objections perhaps accounted for the decision of the Ministry of Economic Warfare to confine its approval to only $25,000 of transactions, a small percentage of the funds needed to finance the combined Rumanian and French programs.

At last, Randolph Paul said at a Treasury staff meeting on December 18, 1943, they were "down to the real issue." The Ministry of Economic Warfare had accepted the scheme which Harrison had implied was unworkable. The question was not one of safeguards, as Pehle put it, but of foreign policy. The problem lay in removing that question from the State Department to some agency more sympathetic to the Jews. For that purpose, Morgenthau's subordinates urged him to recommend to the President the appointment of a commission on the refugee problem. The Secretary hesitated. He agreed that there was no doubt about the integrity of the proposed licenses, but he was not sure he could go to the President about a special commission without first enlisting Hull. In spite of his staff's continuing pleading, Morgenthau decided that he would return to the Department of State, armed this time with the stiffest possible memorandum.

Morgenthau's confidence in Hull's good will was well placed. On December 18, 1943, two days before he received the Treasury memorandum about the obstructionism of the British Foreign Office, Hull had dispatched a severe message of his own. "Your telegram," he cabled the Foreign Office, ". . . has been read with astonishment by the Department and it is unable to agree with the point of view set forth. . . . It is desired by the Department to inform you immediately of the fact that the philosophy set forth . . . is incompatible with the policy of the United States Government and of previously expressed British policy as it has been understood by us." That, of course, was precisely the view of Morgenthau, whose memorandum to Hull called for American policy "to facilitate the escape of Jews from Hitler and *then* discuss what can be done in the way of finding them a more permanent refuge."

On December 20, Morgenthau congratulated the Secretary of State on his cable. Back at the Treasury, he told his staff: "This is one of the greatest victories. . . . You fellows don't know old man Hull. He has his teeth in this thing. I have told you fellows consistently not to say a fellow won't come through until the facts are in." Hull had said, Morgenthau went on, that the trouble lay with "the fellows down the line," whose activities the

Secretary of State had been unable to review constantly and in detail. Now Hull was himself ripping through the red tape.

The State Department had already taken some important steps. Breckinridge Long, who had accompanied Hull at the meeting with Morgenthau, had personally drafted a license for exchange transactions in Bern and cabled it to Harrison. Long reported confidentially, moreover, that Rumania had attempted to sue for a separate peace. The United States had been unwilling to enter into negotiations at that time but had assured Rumania that if she conducted herself appropriately she would be given favorable terms when a peace could be made. In particular, the United States had urged improved treatment of the Jews, and within two weeks Rumania had replied that Jews in Transnistria were being repatriated in order to protect them from the Germans then retreating through that area. Still, Long was pessimistic about managing by any device, diplomatic or underground, to bring the Germans to assist the rescue.

Later, alone with Morgenthau, Long had complained that there were various people "down the line" who were making trouble in the State Department. "Well," Morgenthau replied, "Breck . . . we might be a little frank. The impression is all around [that] you, particularly, are anti-semitic." Long said he knew that to be the case and hoped Morgenthau would use his "good offices to correct that impression, because I am not."

"After all," Morgenthau said, "Breck, the United States of America was created as a refuge for people who were persecuted the world over, starting with Plymouth . . . and as Secretary of the Treasury for 135 million people — I am carrying this out as Secretary of the Treasury and not as a Jew."

"Well," Long replied, "my concept of America as a place of refuge for persecuted people is just the same."

Since Hull was now taking charge, Morgenthau had not even raised the question of establishing a committee. Hull's intervention produced prompt action. A cable from Bern on December 23, 1943, reported that Harrison had personally delivered to Riegner the license that Long had sent on December 18. Riegner had then selected the Geneva branch of the Union Bank of Swit-

zerland to keep in escrow funds to finance the evacuation of
Rumanian refugees, and he now proposed depositing in that
bank Swiss francs equivalent to $25,000, the sum which the Brit-
ish had approved. That money was to be in the name of the
World Jewish Congress, with authority for drawing on the account confined to Riegner, and to him only with the Treasury's
permission in each case that arose. Riegner was ready also to
explore the possibility, on the receipt of further funds, of evacu-
ating Jews from France to Spain and Switzerland. On December
24 Treasury and State approved those arrangements.

Building on that good start, John W. Pehle in Foreign Funds
Control began that week to help representatives of the Joint Distribution Committee secure the Swiss francs they needed, estimated at about $150,000 a month for 1944, to finance the evacu-
ation of Jewish children from France and to support the 3000
refugees already arriving in Switzerland. By January 3, 1944,
the Treasury had prepared the appropriate licenses and authorized the Joint Distribution Committee to make an initial remittance of $200,000 to Switzerland. The Treasury had also asked
the legation at Bern to take reasonable steps to facilitate operations under the new licenses and to report promptly on any difficulties encountered. Morgenthau, "surprised and pleased," as he
told his associates, at their initiative, considered them "impolitic"
for proceeding without explicit approval from the State Department. Further, he issued instructions on January 5 that all organizations in the field should be obliged to help all children threatened by the Nazis, not just Jewish children.

But the Secretary and his staff quickly realized that their energy exceeded their accomplishments. They were disturbed by
their discovery at the turn of the year of the way in which State
Department subordinates in the previous May had cut off the
flow of information from Bern. Worse, State Department officers, perhaps out of sheer bureaucratic inertia, had again inter-
posed a delay by neglecting to transmit the new licenses that the
Treasury had prepared for Bern. Most important, Morgenthau
learned on January 8, 1944, that the British government felt that
the movement of evacuees resulting from the proposed Ameri-

can financial measures would create problems in transportation and accommodation "which might be embarrassing not only to this government but to your own."

In a long conference on January 11, 1944, Hull was shocked by what Morgenthau reported, but he also seemed "harassed and weary . . . not . . . well informed as to what was going on . . . simply bewildered." Depressed, Morgenthau returned to the Treasury convinced that "Roosevelt wouldn't move on Hull, he never has; and Hull wouldn't move on Long." But the Secretary was ready now to ask Roosevelt to appoint the special committee earlier suggested by John Pehle.

The memorandum stating the case was prepared by Randolph Paul. It carried an unequivocal title: "Report to the Secretary on the Acquiescence of this Government in the Murder of the Jews." The first sentence moved that theme forward: "One of the greatest crimes in history, the slaughter of the Jewish people in Europe, is continuing unabated." Officials in the Department of State, Paul maintained, had willfully failed to act to rescue the Jews. Their procrastination, dating back to August 1942, had facilitated mass murder in Nazi Europe. Paul particularly condemned State Department restrictions on visas. Under the pretext of concern for national security, he said, Breckinridge Long and his associates had held immigration below available quotas. The memorandum, Morgenthau suggested, should also describe the role of the British Foreign Office. Otherwise its content and tone provided exactly what he needed for Roosevelt. So did the increasing possibility of congressional action to aid the refugees.

On January 16, 1944, Morgenthau told the President that he was deeply disturbed by conditions in the State Department. The Treasury, he said, had uncovered evidence indicating that subordinates there, defying Hull, were not only inefficient in dealing with the refugee problem, but were actually taking steps to prevent the rescue of the Jews. Pehle then explained the details to Roosevelt, who listened attentively. He also glanced at a draft of an executive order creating a War Refugee Board to consist of the Secretary of the Treasury, the Secretary of War, and the Secretary of State. Roosevelt, as Morgenthau later reported to his staff, "seemed disinclined to believe that Long wanted to stop effective action from being taken, but said that Long had been somewhat soured on the problem when Rabbi Wise got Long to approve a long list of people being brought into this country, many of whom turned out to be bad people. . . . In any event he felt that Long was inclined to be soured on the situation." But the President agreed that it was possible to facilitate the escape of Jews from Rumania and France to safety in Turkey, Switzerland, and Spain.

That evening, under Roosevelt's instructions, Morgenthau talked with Edward Stettinius. He told the new Under Secretary of State "in plain words," that "he was convinced that people in the State Department, particularly Breckinridge Long, were deliberately obstructing the execution of any plan to save the Jews and that forthright immediate action was necessary if this Government was not going to be placed in the same position as Hitler and share the responsibility for exterminating all the Jews of Europe." Upset by the facts which Morgenthau and Pehle then presented, Stettinius said that he was "not surprised about Breckinridge Long since Long had fallen just as badly and in an equally shocking way in the handling of the exchange of prisoners. Stettinius was very frank in his views on Long's failures and pointed out that in the reorganization of the State Department which he had worked out the only remaining function assigned to Breckinridge Long is Congressional relations." Like Roosevelt, Stettinius doubted that Long had meant to hurt the Jews; rather, he found Long, no longer a young and perhaps never a vigorous executive, inefficient in everything he handled. And like Roosevelt, Stettinius agreed with Morgenthau that the time for action had come. Examining the draft executive order, Stettinius said emphatically: "I think it's wonderful."

His endorsement satisfied the President who on January 22, 1944, established the War Refugee Board to assist the immediate rescue and relief of the Jews of Europe "and other victims of enemy persecution." That board was to cooperate with interested American and international agencies, to utilize the facilities of the Treasury, War, and State Departments in furnishing aid to Axis victims, and to attempt to forestall the plot of the Nazis to exterminate Jews and other minorities. An accompanying order to the Bureau of the Budget set aside one million dollars for initial administrative expenses, and Roosevelt announced that he expected all members of the United Nations and other foreign governments to cooperate with the board in its important task.

The terrible eighteen months had ended, though too late to help most of the Rumanian Jews. Morgenthau then and later grieved over the lost opportunities. As he put it, the fight had been "long and heartbreaking. The stake was the Jewish population of Nazi-controlled Europe. The threat was their total obliteration. The hope was to get a few of them out." With the War Refugee Board established, the hope lay, "in the few meagre months remaining," as it had never before, with "crusaders, passionately persuaded of the need for speed and action."

By mid-June 1944, the War Refugee Board had begun to fulfill that hope. Morgenthau's experience in getting the board established and in helping to oversee its early operations constituted his signal wartime success to that date in nurturing humanitarian purpose in American foreign policy. That success compensated, in part at least, for frustrations the Secretary had met. But success and failure alike contributed to his growing determination to spend his influence for the construction of a decent postwar world.

XX

IN THE NATIONAL INTEREST

1944–1945

MORGANTHAU SPONSORED American participation in international economic and financial affairs, and American assistance to other nations because he believed that no other course would permit the United States in the future to avoid a repetition of the depression and war of the previous decade and a half. Only a guarded altruism, as he saw it, would strengthen the national interest and assure the safety and prosperity of the country in a peaceful postwar world. It was his duty, he felt, to minimize the costs of internationalism, both during and after the war, to the American people. That objective demanded the rebuilding of a prosperous Great Britain, the cultivation of Soviet relations "not tainted with mutual suspicion," the incapacitating of Germany for future aggression, and the support of decent government and economic growth in China. Those goals, as Morgenthau interpreted them, in large degree depended on each other, and all, he was convinced, advanced the national interest.

So, too, as he saw it, did the two agreements signed in July 1944 at Bretton Woods, New Hampshire, agreements establishing the International Monetary Fund and the International Bank for Reconstruction and Development. As early as 1941 Morgenthau had directed Harry White to begin planning for those agencies. With Roosevelt's support, the Secretary had also encouraged White during the long preliminary negotiations with the British. Out of those negotiations there emerged, as a consequence of the superior bargaining position of the United States, formulations much closer to American than to British prescriptions. The Bretton Woods conference accepted those formulations with no major alterations. The Bank, in Morgenthau's expectations, would function as an important source of inexpensive capital for rebuilding the economies of nations devastated by the war and, in lesser degree, for assisting underdeveloped countries. The Fund, to which he gave more attention, would operate to prevent the kind of competitive devaluation that had harassed international economic relations during the 1930's. In both agencies the United States would have a dominant voice, and from both the American economy would benefit directly, as would also the economies of the other United Nations. As the developments of the spring of 1944 revealed, both Great Britain and China would need all the help they could get.

1. Balance Sheet for Chengtu

The meeting at Bretton Woods presented a new opportunity for settling the corrosive financial problems relating to American participation in the war in China. In June 1944 there remained at issue the question of an exchange rate between the dollar and the fapi and the calculation of the Chinese contribution to the war effort in the Asian theater. For some months, the War Department had been attempting to reach the necessary agreements with the Chinese, but Stimson turned the problem back to the Treasury, as he put it in his diary, because he did not want to have any catastrophe occur while he was dealing with the Chinese.

The Chinese rate of exchange, Stimson observed, was still declining, and yet no one had been able to show the Chinese how to stabilize it. Further, the United States had been incurring debts for the construction of airfields in China which, in terms of the official, inflated value of Chinese currency, amounted to billions of dollars. To press the Chinese case, Finance Minister H. H. Kung was on his way to the United States, along with his wife, a sister of Madame Chiang Kai-shek. As Stimson reported it, when Roosevelt learned she was arriving, "the President at Cabinet . . . threw up his hands in horror and said he thought he'd take to the woods!" So, in effect, did Stimson, by handing the Treasury responsibility for the financial negotiations.

Aware of the difficulties ahead of him, Morgenthau welcomed the promised assistance of the Army, but at the same time took pains to prevent the Chinese from playing one American agency off against another, as they so often had. "I just talked to Admiral Leahy," the Secretary noted in his Diary on June 27, 1944, "and I told him I understood the President was going to see H. H. Kung and that State and War and Treasury hoped that the President would not discuss exchange rates with Kung and that if he brought it up would the President tell Kung to take it up with the Treasury." At the White House the next morning, Roosevelt "immediately started off by saying that he had seen Kung, and from the way he talked I gather he got my message . . . because he said that he had told Kung to take this matter up with me. The President said . . . 'Why not give the Chinese a new currency similar to what we have done for France? . . . . I am not recommending it. I just want you to think about it.' Then he said that he had also talked to Kung about getting more goods over the Hump . . . because he said the only way to handle the inflation problem was by getting more goods. . . .

"The President said . . . 'What I am trying to find out, where is the Chinese Army and why aren't they fighting because the Japanese seem to be able to push them in any direction they want to.' "

The Americans had never been able to influence the Chinese when questions of money were at stake. As the Secretary knew, the Chinese, guarding their sovereignty with as much vigor as the French, would resist any American proposal for a new currency or for any other device that threatened to cost them either face or cash. For his part, Morgenthau wanted to give the Chinese everything they deserved, and everything beyond that which seemed to the Army necessary to strengthen Chinese participation in the war, but he was determined to resist the demands which the Chinese would certainly make for an exchange rate that would milk American taxpayers of hundreds of millions of dollars. Those were the views also of the able group whom Morgenthau recruited to work with him in the forthcoming negotiations. Senior among them was General Lucius Clay, at that time second in command in the Army Service of Supply, a toughminded soldier with a broad knowledge of finance and supply, and a ranging and acute intelligence in personal relations. Besides Clay, Morgenthau's associates included John Carter Vincent, a veteran Foreign Service Officer with long experience in Chungking and an extensive knowledge of Chinese affairs, and Solomon Adler, for several years the Treasury's special representative in Chungking.

The Chinese had recently offered to settle past and future obligations on the basis of an exchange rate of 60 to 1, whereas the actual rate was many times that figure. They also proposed that for each 60 fapi for which the United States paid them in dollars, they would credit 40 to reverse Lend-Lease. The Americans intended only to fulfill the precise commitment of Roosevelt's January 28, 1944 message to Chiang Kai-shek. "Since you say," Roosevelt had then cabled, "that your government is not in a position to continue any direct maintenance of American troops in China, this government, in order to cover all of its military expenditures, including such maintenance as well as construction, is prepared to place to your account the United States dollar equivalent of any Chinese funds made available under general arrangements that will be suggested by General Stilwell and the Ambassador." In keeping that promise, the Americans did not want to overvalue fapi or to place the Chinese in a position to claim that they had made a large, uncompensated contribution to the American war effort. A reasonable figure would reflect an actual exchange rate of about 120 fapi to the dollar.

With that figure tacitly his benchmark, General Clay explained the American position to the Chinese. To date, he said, the Army had paid $25 million toward financing airports and other installations. Now the Army proposed a final settlement, exclusive of food and lodging, as of June 30, 1944, of another $75 million. In the future, the Army would settle accounts every few months.

In a passionate reply Kung stressed his concern for Chinese-American friendship, his pride in Chinese sacrifices, and the difficulties of Chinese inflation. After acrid debate, Clay volunteered, in the interests of a "quick and prompt settlement," to raise the American offer to $100 million. Still dissatisfied, Kung focused his case on one item, the air base at Chengtu, which had been constructed for the use of B-29 bombers in attacking Japan. At the Cairo Conference, he said, Roosevelt had promised to pay for the Chengtu base. The Americans, Morgenthau replied, had no record of that promise.

That afternoon, Clay made another concession. The United States, he told Kung, would proceed "with the understanding that the 4 billion for the Chengtu airfield . . . would be presented by you as a claim under reverse Lend-Lease. . . . We would pay you the lump sum of 100 million dollars immediately, and in any reverse Lend-Lease agreement . . . you could, in addition to the food and lodging which you would put forward as a claim, include also this 4 billion." But still Kung balked. The private conversation between Roosevelt and the Generalissimo at Cairo, he said, made it impossible for him to accept Clay's formula; he could not yield without explicit instructions from Chiang Kai-shek. "Then we'll just have to wait," Morgenthau said. " . . . That is the best we can do."

Overnight the Americans drafted a telegram to Roosevelt reviewing the discussions. As Morgenthau saw it, the record proved that they had caught Kung "red-handed." But whether Kung was sly or merely sloppy, the American negotiators stood behind Clay's final offer. "We feel that the terms offered are more than fair," the telegram to Roosevelt said, "and we recommend a firm stand. We do not feel that there will be political repercussions in China which would warrant material deviation from the stand we have taken."

There matters stood for the rest of the summer of 1944. The exchange rate remained for Kung the crux of the matter. Even if conversations were confined to a lump sum payment, Kung constantly calculated the ratio between the dollars he was to receive and the fapi he claimed. In that pass, there lay open a new approach for the Americans. A recalculation of estimates that resulted in a reduction of the amount of fapi expended would yield, if payment remained at the figure offered in July, an exchange rate better than the 120 to 1 ratio which had then been tacitly proposed. Whether for that purpose or because of complications in its bookkeeping, the Army in the first week of October did submit revised figures, and those figures did establish an actual but unstated exchange rate of about 100 to 1.

On October 6, 1944, Morgenthau apologized to Kung for the changes in American calculations but also pointed out that the revision produced in effect a more favorable rate of exchange. Urging quick agreement, now partly to facilitate Kung's plans for necessary hospitalization, he repeated Clay's July offer. As the Secretary put it privately to his staff: "I have the rate in mind . . . but I still pay . . . in US dollars. I am not going to pay . . . in yuan."

On the telephone to Clay that afternoon Morgenthau tried to work out a figure that would appease Kung. "I'm going to make one final offer," the Secretary said. "I am going to offer him a gross of $150 million, of which we've paid 25. . . . In other words, I'm going to take advantage of that extra $25 million that you . . . said I could use if I wanted to." Wholly agreeable, Clay proposed going up, if necessary, to $185 million by adding $35 million to make the settlement cover the period through September 30. If that later period were to be included, the United States, Morgenthau suggested, should offer Kung about $200 million and let him interpret it at any "goddamn rate he wanted to."

Later that afternoon Morgenthau made Kung the last offer he had described to Clay. As the Secretary put it, he was taking $125 million for the period through June 30, adding another $60 million ($20 million a month for July, August, and September), and then adding still another $25 million, for a grand total of $210 million, which the Chinese could view as indicating any rate they liked. But Kung, increasingly prickly, suggested the United States pay the Chinese in fapi rather than dollars; the Americans could go into the Chinese open market and buy the currency they needed. Morgenthau declined to take that possibility seriously.

Kung, Morgenthau told his staff, had been "very nasty," and a month later Stimson described the Chinese Finance Minister as "the same oleaginous . . . gentleman as of yore," but Kung's case gained from the President's growing anxieties about the deterioration of the Chinese government and economy. Back from the White House on November 20, 1944, Morgenthau wrote: "Kung convinced the President that there's something in writing that said we would pay separately for these airfields. I told the President I'd never seen any such thing in writing. The President said he would send over to me the memorandum that Kung had left with him."

What was in writing, it developed, was the cable from Roosevelt to Chiang Kai-shek of January 28, 1944, that the Treasury had long since seen. "Our interpretation of this cable," Morgenthau wrote Roosevelt, "gives Dr. Kung no ground for any additional demand except for payment for board and lodging of American troops. . . . My offer of October to Dr. Kung works out at a rate of around 100 yuan to one US dollar on the basis of our Army's gross figures, around 90 on the basis of the Army's net figures, and around 110 on the basis of Dr. Kung's figures. This is most reasonable to the Chinese, in view of the exceedingly low purchasing power of the yuan and of the fact that it compares favorably with the black market rate which has risen . . . to 400 recently. . . . In order to facilitate settlement we have informed Dr. Kung that we have no objection to his putting in a claim for the cost of the Chengtu airfields on reverse Lend-Lease, making it clear, however, that we regarded the lump sum payment that we were offering as a final settlement of our outstanding obligations."

That analysis must have persuaded Roosevelt, for with his

support, Morgenthau remained firm. "I am operating here as the agent for Mr. Stimson," the Secretary told Kung on November 25, 1944. "I can't do any more than I have done." Kung also held fast. "I think maybe it would be much better," Morgenthau then said, "if I would simply write Mr. Stimson . . . that I have tried my best to get together with you with the information which he has given me. I have been unsuccessful." Now Kung complained. He had not been dealing with Stimson, he said, but with Morgenthau and the President, and Roosevelt, he asserted again, had promised to pay for Chengtu. "I feel very badly about this," Morgenthau replied. "I have tried my best to stretch every possible point. I feel that we have done everything within the spirit of the message from the President."

With the President, the War Department, and the State Department backing the Treasury, Kung could turn for aid to no important official or agency. On November 28, 1944, he yielded at last to the American terms.

There remained almost a month of dickering over details before the settlement was completed, but the major issues had been resolved to the satisfaction of both principals. As Morgenthau wrote on November 30, 1944: "We have settled with China. In paying them in dollars instead of yuan . . . I have saved the taxpayer millions of dollars." Other millions remained at stake.

In October 1944, when Kung had reopened discussions about Chengtu, he also asked the Treasury to expedite shipment of $20 million of gold which China had earlier requested. Sales of that gold, which was to be supplied as a part of the $500 million American loan of 1942, were to absorb some of the huge quantity of fapi outstanding in China, and thereby in small degree to combat inflation, unless the government of Chiang Kai-shek issued more fapi, as it probably would. In the opinion of Morgenthau and his staff, gold sales did provide some palliative for Chinese inflation, whose cure could result only from military victories that would permit American delivery of vast amounts of commodities to China, that would remove the Japanese occupation, and that would also, perhaps, prepare Chiang Kai-shek to adopt and enforce positive economic policies. At the least, gold shipments constituted a token of support and prestige for the Generalissimo.

During the summer of 1944 Harry White, as he told Morgenthau on October 5, had "stalled" because of the discrepancy in China between the official price of gold and the price at which banks actually sold the metal. Someone, White suspected, was making a profit from the gold sales, probably T. L. Soong — a brother of T. V. Soong — whose bank handled much of the gold the United States supplied. In spite of his suspicions, White now recommended that Morgenthau tell Kung that evening that he was going to get his $20 million. "Is that," the Secretary asked, "what I am going to pay for my dinner tonight?" Later in the month the Army transported the bullion, though it had to move it by ship because of the shortage of air space.

Morgenthau had little interest in the transaction. He had delegated responsibility for assessing the Chinese request to White because the matter seemed relatively trivial. Yet the Secretary had a large interest in the condition of Chiang Kai-shek's government, to which the gold shipment of October gave a public American blessing. In assessing the state of affairs in China, Morgenthau turned neither to his subordinates, who were aggressively bearish about Chiang Kai-shek's future, nor to his own judgment. Rather, he looked to General Patrick Hurley, Roosevelt's chosen agent.

Roosevelt had assigned Hurley a threefold mission: to maintain the existing government and work through the Generalissimo, to keep China in the war, and to unify the Chinese Army for a more effective military effort. But Hurley, as he informed the Treasury on November 15, 1944, considered the situation in Chungking distressing. Most of the officials at Chunking were interested only in preserving their own position. They regarded the American taxpayer as "a sucker" whom they could exploit indefinitely. Though they claimed to be democratic, they were really fascists opposed to the concessions necessary for the achievement of national unity. The Communists, in Hurley's opinion, genuinely wanted multiparty government and on the whole "offered a fine, liberal program." He was certain they were not receiving Soviet support. The achievement of unity in China would be a difficult task, but Hurley rejoiced in believing that he had brought the Communists to the American side. He also took heart from Roosevelt's recall of General Stilwell and Ambassador Gauss. Both men, he thought, out of sheer disgust had favored "pulling the plug and allowing the show to go down the drain." Now Hurley planned a more constructive approach. To abet that purpose, Roosevelt in December made him Ambassador to China, and Morgenthau on December 13 sent his "heartiest congratulations" for a "difficult and important assignment" in which the Secretary promised "every assistance" from the Treasury's representative, Solomon Adler, then about to return to Chungking.

On the following day White reported that the Chinese were requesting an acceleration of gold shipments. "We think it is unwise," White said, "in this very uncertain state of political development for them to get out as much gold as they want to get. . . . What we would like to do is raise a lot of objections. . . . We can continue to stall indefinitely. Is that all right with you?" Morgenthau said it was "as long as we let Ambassador Hurley know what we are doing." Because Hurley was attempting to bring the Chinese Communists into closer cooperation with Chiang Kai-shek, Morgenthau also approved a letter White drafted introducing Adler to Chou En-lai. At White's suggestion, the Treasury instructed Adler to ask Hurley "whether or not he feels it would help him to have this letter sent to . . . Chou En-lai." The Secretary, too, told Adler to offer his services to General Albert C. Wedemeyer, who had been appointed to succeed Stilwell as Commanding General in the China Theater. And in a letter of December 16 which expanded on his earlier telegram, Morgenthau wrote Hurley: "I need not say what a feather it would be in your cap if you were instrumental in bringing about political unity in China which would be the basis for the more effective participation of China in our common war effort. I do hope that you succeed."

In mid-December 1944, then, Morgenthau had taken Roosevelt's instructions to Hurley as the guideline for Treasury pol-

icy, had put the Treasury's Chungking staff at the disposal of
Hurley and Wedemeyer, and had made the Treasury's policy on
gold shipments conditional on Hurley's judgment.

In that spirit, Morgenthau on January 8, 1945, sent Adler a
cable about gold. White had recommended denying Kung's request for speeding shipments on the ground that deliveries were
justifiable only when they helped to fight inflation, whereas
under the current conditions they were benefiting only hoarders
and speculators. Rejecting that advice, Morgenthau explained to
Adler that the Chinese had asked for $80 million of gold bars and
$100 million of gold tokens, with another $100 million or more
in the very near future. Thus far, the Secretary cabled, he had
not given his assent because of the uncertainty in China and because of her postwar needs for foreign exchange. Now he instructed Adler to discuss the matter thoroughly with General
Hurley and "inform me as quickly as possible of his view."

Hurley in the next months failed to arrange the political rapprochement which he had thought close to hand. At the end of
February 1945, while still hoping for improvements, he recommended holding down gold shipments to about the same magnitude as in the past years. On that account, after further, adverse
reports from Chungking, Morgenthau gave Kung only a token
of gold.

"You'll be pleased to learn," he wrote Kung on April 12, 1945,
"that of the $7 million of gold to be exported to China during
the next few months, the first shipment of more than $1 million
has already left this country." Seven million, of course, was far
less than Kung had expected. In the same letter, the Secretary
rejected Kung's complaint, recently repeated, about American
dealings in the Chinese black market. "As for the question of
United States civilian and military personnel in China exchang-
ing U.S. dollar currency in the open market," he wrote, "both of
our governments have acquiesced in this practice because of the
general recognition that the official rate of exchange has not reflected real conditions. . . . I would be glad to consider any
proposal which would give fair Chinese national dollar equivalent for the expenditure of United States civilian and military

personnel in China as a substitute for the present practice."

In politics as in finance, in the spring of 1945 as in the spring of 1944, the problems of China defied American efforts to find solutions. Had it not been for the enormous stakes at issue — the winning of the great war in the Orient, the future of China in the world — it would have been hard not to laugh at the opéra bouffe in Chungking. Even those like Hurley and Wedemeyer, who later conveniently forgot it, blanched at the unabashed nepotism and corruption in the Kuomintang. Even they, moreover, misconceived the purpose of the Chinese Communists. And both of them, like the more veteran observers of the Army, the State Department, and the Treasury, believed that Chiang Kai-shek had contributed far less than lay within his grasp to the war against Japan; that the Generalissimo and his associates had failed, even within their limited capacities, to combat inflation; that conditions of life and of morale in China were at a distressing remove from the minimum requirements of decency and democracy.

Relying on Hurley's judgment, Morgenthau established a policy toward gold shipments that delayed substantial aid while offering token support. In the situation, there was no other logical choice. The policy he followed protected American gold which the Chinese would otherwise have squandered. Even had gold been sent in the quantities Kung requested, it could not have saved China from the economic and political disasters bred of prolonged enemy occupation, inept government, and internal revolution.

Yet Morgenthau's policy of friendship tempered by caution was in later years attributed to the influence of pernicious advisers. Critics of the Secretary's decisions maintained that Communists or Communist sympathizers within the Treasury had fashioned their counsel to the demands of a world-wide Communist conspiracy. The Secretary had leaned primarily on Secretary of War Stimson, Generals Somervell, Clay, and Wedemeyer, and Ambassador Hurley, no one of whom had ever had any attachment to Communism or its masters. When in time Hurley and Wedemeyer condemned the Treasury, they chose to overlook the unanimity of American assessments — including their own — of Chinese conditions and of appropriate American policy in the early months of 1945. Without exception, all responsible counselors had then concurred in the decisions Morgenthau made. And they had then all recognized, as Henry Stimson once said at a dinner party, and as Ambassador Hu Shih agreed: "There are in this room two real friends of China — Mr. Morgenthau and myself."

2. British Finances Again

The course of the war introduced questions of wartime relief and postwar reconstruction into Anglo-American financial negotiations. At the time of the attack on Europe, the British, in an aide mémoire to the State Department, proposed that the procurement of relief supplies for liberated areas should fall half to England, half to the United States. But "any . . . final settlement," they suggested. ". . . must be on an equitable basis and must be based upon a recognition of the relative financial strengths of the countries concerned. In this connection, His Majesty's Government desires to place on record their view that in the light of the difference in financial strengths between the United States and the United Kingdom, they would not be able to regard an equal sharing of the burden of relief in the military period between the two countries as an equitable settlement."

Though Dean Acheson approved of that proposal, the Treasury objected. Since England's contribution of relief supplies came largely from Lend-Lease goods shipped to the United Kingdom by the United States, Morgenthau would not interpret the division of responsibility as actually fifty-fifty. He was even more unhappy about predicating a final settlement on relative financial strengths. Acheson, he complained, "always takes the British view."

It was Morgenthau's opinion that it would cost less politically and financially to furnish 90 per cent of the relief supplies than to defer to the British. In Italy, he said, the United States had provided 80 per cent of relief but Churchill had used his 20 per cent as a lever for obtaining recognition of King Victor Emmanuel III and Marshal Badoglio, whom Morgenthau considered reactionary. Now the Secretary wanted the United States to assert itself, and if necessary to pay all relief costs. He also insisted on negotiating the final settlement on the basis of all relevant factors, of which relative financial strength was only one. Acheson satisfied Morgenthau by replying to the British that "the final settlement should be on a fair and equitable basis, in the determination of which no relevant factor should be excluded," but Morgenthau nevertheless wrote Roosevelt on June 16, 1944: "I cannot agree with the position of the United Kingdom . . . that any final settlement as regards supplies to the liberated areas . . . must be equitable but be based upon a recognition of 'relative financial strengths' of the two countries. I believe that the adoption of such a principle would be contrary to the best interests of the United States and would be so regarded by Congress and the people."

The issue was still unresolved when the Secretary flew to England in August 1944, to talk directly with Churchill and the Chancellor of the Exchequer about Lend-Lease and British balances during the coming period of the war. Both governments, expecting the defeat of Germany by the end of the year, had begun to examine their financial problems for the continuing operation against Japan. During Stage II — the British phrase for the period between the surrender of Germany and the surrender of Japan, which the Americans called Phase II — by joint agreement the United States would make the larger military contribution, with Great Britain and the Dominions bearing a fair share of the fighting. The Churchill government also hoped that with victory in Europe they could at last ease their severe controls on civilian life. Morgenthau sympathized with that hope but felt himself responsible for confining Lend-Lease aid to England during Phase II to reasonable proportions.

The Secretary found the British much worse off than he had supposed. Back in Washington on August 19, 1944, he reported his observations to Roosevelt and their conversation in his Diary:

> I told the President I had seen Churchill, who started the conversation by saying that England was broke. The President said, "What does he mean by that?" I said, "Yes, England really is broke." That seemed to surprise the President, and he kept coming back to it. I said that Churchill's attitude was that he was broke but not depressed about England's future. The President said that that was well put. . . . I said, "Well, he is going to tell Parliament about their financial condition at the right time after the armistice, and that when he does that he is through." So the President said, "Oh, he is taking those tactics now. More recently his attitude was that he wanted to see England through peace."
>
> I then told the President I had been very frank with Churchill, particularly after he told me that he had heard that I was unfriendly toward them. I said that I wasn't unfriendly but I didn't like their playing one person against the other, and that they had the temporary advantage over us. I said that I had merely been trying to carry out the President's decision given to me in January 1943, to keep the British balances down to a billion dollars. I then told him I thought the British should put all their cards on the table and approach this thing in a completely frank manner. I said that I thought Mr. Churchill should appoint a committee which would consider all these financial questions . . . and then he . . . should approach the President. I said the President should appoint a similar committee and he might ask me to do it. I said that we did make a study of suggestions for the President before I went to England . . . that there should be a committee here having to do with all financial matters. . . . I also told Churchill . . . that I made a similar suggestion to Halifax and nothing had happened.
>
> During the course of the conversation, the President kept coming back to England's being broke. He said, "This is very interesting. I had no idea that England was broke. I will go over there and make a couple of talks and take over the British Empire." I told him how popular he was with the soldiers and how unpopular Churchill was. I told him about the difficulty of finding someone to take me through the shelters because Churchill . . . had been jeered . . . recently, and that finally they decided on Mrs. Churchill and Lady Mountbatten.

Morgenthau also called on Harry Hopkins on August 19. The British, the Secretary said, wanted to reduce their production of munitions so as to increase their production of civilian goods. They realized that the United States had similar expectations, but the two nations were far from agreement about how much each might cut back. Any arrangements, Hopkins said, would have to await a complete review of conditions in both countries.

That review began in Morgenthau's office on August 24, 1944, with a report from Robert Brand, representing Chancellor of the Exchequer Sir John Anderson. During Stage II, Brand said, the British people would not tolerate 100 per cent mobilization. They needed fewer hours of work, more holidays, more consumer goods, and the economy needed to begin to reconvert for export trade. Though he had no exact figures, Brand was sure that the United Kingdom would continue to require food, oil, and shipping under Lend-Lease. The figures would become available only when Churchill had decided about the extent of Great Britain's participation in the Japanese war. At that point, settlement of the outstanding problems would be urgent, as would the beginning of discussions of Lend-Lease during Stage III, the period following the Japanese surrender.

He was eager to help, Morgenthau replied, but if he was to have anything to do with the matter, "it would have to be centralized in the Treasury; . . . he could not have the British Government representative going around back doors to various agencies. . . . The British would have to cooperate fully and make available . . . all of the information . . . wanted, and the British Treasury would have to deal only with and through the Treasury on the matter."

The suggestion, as Brand understood it, called for Churchill to appoint Anderson to work directly with Morgenthau on Lend-Lease questions. That was rather "too definite," Morgenthau replied. There would have to be a committee representing several agencies on both sides of the ocean. The President had yet to appoint one in Washington, and Morgenthau could not be sure that it would fall to him to head the American group. "I don't want to get over the idea that it's an accomplished fact," he said, " . . . because it isn't." But he and Brand agreed on the desirability of asking Churchill to stand by to appoint a responsible group to carry the British case. The next morning, August 25, 1944, as the Secretary wrote in his Diary:

"I asked the President what was happening in regard to the suggestion for an over-all committee on finance in this country and in England, and I said that Grace [Tully] had told me that he had sent a memorandum to Hull. He said, 'That's right,' and he seemed very much pleased with himself . . . but he said he had not yet heard from Hull.

"I then told the President that Sir John Anderson had asked me to let him know whether the President would consider the suggestion in a favorable light, and I had sent for Bob Brand and told him the President had received the suggestion favorably, and that he could send word back to that effect."

Far more than he told Roosevelt, Morgenthau as a result of his trip had persuaded himself of the need to sustain the British economy. As he said in private on August 25, "this has to be approached from the standpoint that Great Britain made this fight for democracy. Now we have got to help her. She is a good credit risk, a good moral risk, and we have to put her back on her feet. . . . Somebody smart enough has to think up a new name, other than Lend-Lease, because that will have been worn out. But we have got to do the thing to put her back . . . for a permanent world peace, and I look at this peace thing — a lasting peace, to me is becoming a religion."

In his official communications, Roosevelt was more restrained. "There has been a good deal of discussion within the several Government Departments relative to our Lend-Lease policy after the collapse of Germany," the President wrote several interested offices on September 9, 1944, "It is my wish that no Department . . . take unilateral action in regard to any matters that concern Lend-Lease, because the implications of any such action are bound to affect other Departments . . . and, indeed, our whole national policy. I am particularly anxious that any instructions which may have issued, or are about to be issued regarding Lend-Lease . . . to our allies after the collapse of Germany, be immediately canceled and withdrawn."

That directive cleared the slate for Roosevelt's scheduled meeting with Churchill in mid-September in Quebec, where the two would arrange military and financial cooperation for the prosecution of the war against Japan. Summoned, to his surprise, to that conference, Morgenthau received when he arrived a memorandum for Roosevelt from the British Treasury. The objective of Lend-Lease, it read, had been to satisfy England's justifiable military and civilian requirements beyond the reach of the fully-mobilized British economy. Of the munitions which British forces had used during the war against Germany, still under way, Great Britain herself had furnished a little less than 60 per cent, the United States about 27 per cent, Canada 10 per cent, and the rest of the British Empire, the balance. If the British Empire had to provide total British munitions requirements during Stage II, there could be insignificant reduction from conditions of full mobilization. Yet after five years of war, a considerable reduction was necessary for civilian morale, for rebuilding damaged cities, and for taking the first steps towards restoring the British economy. The British therefore suggested, as a yardstick for Stage II, that the proportion of their total munitions supplies received from Lend-Lease should be the same as in 1944. Besides munitions, they asked for Lend-Lease foodstuffs and raw materials sufficient to meet the reasonable needs of the United Kingdom, though not primarily for purposes of reconversion. The aggregate requirements would be about $3 billion during the first year of Stage II, as compared to about $3.9 billion for 1944.

It fell to Morgenthau to discuss the British memorandum with Lord Cherwell, Churchill's controversial and intimate adviser. A personal friend of the Prime Minister for many years, Cherwell — "the Prof." — had been a professor of physics at Oxford, a courageous experimenter in British aviation, and a steady and strong Conservative. Morgenthau found him "very keen . . . wonderful to work with — very frank, very direct . . . a breath of fresh air from the sea." Together they brought negotiations to the point where Roosevelt and Churchill were quickly able to reach agreement. They did so on September 14, 1944, in a conversation which Cherwell reported from memory the next day in a memorandum that Churchill and Roosevelt initialed:

The Prime Minister said that when Germany was overcome there would be a measure of redistribution of effort in both countries. He hoped that the President would agree that during the war with Japan we should continue to get food, shipping, etc. from the United States to cover our reasonable needs. The President indicated assent.

He hoped also that the President would agree that it would be proper for Lend-Lease munitions to continue on a proportional basis even though this would enable the United Kingdom to set free labor for rebuilding, exports, etc. E.g., if British munitions productions were cut three-fifths, U.S. assistance should also fall to three-fifths. The President indicated assent. Mr. Morgenthau, however, suggested that it would be better to have definite figures. He understood that munitions assistance required had been calculated by the British at about 3.5 billion dollars in the first year on a basis of the strategy envisaged before the . . . Conference. The exact needs would have to be recalculated in the light of decisions on military matters reached at the Conference. The non-munitions requirements had been put at three billion dollars gross against which a considerable amount would be set off for reverse Lend-Lease. The President agreed that it would be better to work on figures like these than on a proportional basis.

The Prime Minister emphasized that all these supplies should be on Lend-Lease. The President said this would naturally be so.

The Prime Minister pointed out that if the United Kingdom was once more to pay its way it was essential that the export trade, which had shrunk to a very small fraction, should be reestablished. Naturally no articles obtained on Lend-Lease or identical thereto would be exported or sold for profit; but it was essential that the United States should not attach any conditions to supplies delivered to Britain on Lend-Lease which would jeopardize the recovery of her export trade. The President thought this would be proper.

To implement these decisions the Prime Minister suggested there should be a joint committee. It was held that it would be better to appoint an ad hoc committee for this purpose on an informal basis in the first instance which could be formalized in due course.

Pending its report the United States departments should be instructed not to take action which would prejudge the committee's conclusions, e.g. production should not be closed down without reference to Lend-Lease supplies which it might be held should be supplied to Britain. The President thought that the committee should be set up but suggested that Mr. Morgenthau should head it representing him, and that Mr. Stettinius, who had taken such a large part in Lend-Lease, should also be a member.

Another memorandum of September 14, 1944, also initialed by Roosevelt and Churchill, confirmed and elaborated Cherwell's report. The two documents were the subject of further discussion on September 15, 1944. "I met at twelve today," Morgenthau noted in his Diary, "with Roosevelt, Churchill, Eden, and the Under Secretary for Foreign Affairs. We took up the question of Lend-Lease agreement for Phase II. . . .

"Churchill was quite emotional about this agreement, and at one time he had tears in his eyes. When the thing was finally signed, he told the President how grateful he was, thanked him most effusively, and said that this was something they were doing for both countries."

At the State Department on September 20, 1944, Morgenthau told Hull, Stimson, and Forrestal that Roosevelt had been casual about Lend-Lease while at Quebec. Hull complained about the President's failure to consult the State Department and to demand British concessions for postwar commercial policy in return for American aid. Roosevelt, he said, had given away the bait. Harry White, who had accompanied Morgenthau to Quebec, defended the Lend-Lease memorandum, but Stimson, siding with Hull, said: "There may be some flexibility, but not much." Cherwell and Halifax, Morgenthau said later that day, were ready to open negotiations about the exact figures for Stage II. "The way I would like to proceed," Morgenthau went on, "would be to sort of put them on the witness stand and ask them how much they wanted and why they wanted it, and then start in with whatever was agreed on at Quebec as to what . . . they would contribute in the Pacific. Then we would expect the Military to testify. . . . Churchill knows that the President is will-

ing to give them the works. . . . This committee is appointed
. . . with the attitude that . . . this agreement will be carried
out cheerfully. . . . Cherwell knows that the British have to
justify these figures." Were they to be justified, McCloy asked,
"in terms of the Japanese war?" Morgenthau said yes.

J. M. Keynes was to handle the British negotiations about
Lend-Lease for Stage II, while the British, as Morgenthau ex-
plained, were to "look to Mr. White." White was disturbed by
the appointment of Keynes, always a tough negotiator.
"Shouldn't monkey with the buzz saw," he said to Morgenthau.
But the Secretary, confident of the American position, replied:
"Not as long as the saw can keep turning. Sometimes its teeth
get kind of dull."

Essentially, Morgenthau and White approached negotiations
for Phase II of Lend-Lease from opposite points of view. The
spirit of the Quebec Conference, the Secretary said on October
6, 1944, was to prevail during the discussions with Keynes. British dollar balances had not entered the agreement between Roosevelt and Churchill. "Here is a client or customer or friend who
is broke," the Secretary continued, "but who is a good moral
risk, and we should ask this friend to state his entire program so
that we can analyze it. Then . . . we should . . . do a job for
England to make it possible for her to stage a comeback and
gradually meet her obligations. . . . I don't consider that the
dollar balances are yardsticks anymore. I think we might just as
well have this thing straight from the beginning." White objected to incurring any responsibility for putting England back
on her feet. The United Kingdom, he argued, could absorb endless billions of dollars, and any vague commitment to England's
future prosperity would threaten both the financial and political
position of the United States in the postwar world.

The British, Morgenthau replied, had made a magnificent
fight. England had been the bulwark against German aggression, the jumping-off place for the American Air Force. The
United States could not now permit her to "go under financially." He did not believe the British would ask for ten billion
in order to get five; Cherwell and Keynes would be honest with

the Americans. In return they deserved the most "careful attention" to the "domestic problems" that Great Britain faced.

Morgenthau also hoped that American generosity would induce the British to support his own political views. But the Secretary did not bargain hard, nor did he let his disappointment affect his judgment about Lend-Lease needs. He did not even take offense at Keynes's continual irritability. The ultimate agreement, he felt, was consistent with Roosevelt's instructions at Quebec.

The Secretary's letter to the President of November 25, 1944, began with that judgment. It then reviewed the points of agreement between the two English-speaking countries. The British, Morgenthau wrote, had asked initially for themselves and for the Empire for $3.2 billion of munitions, $3 billion of non-munitions, and $800 million of other special items — in all $7 billion of goods and services. After screening all the requests, the Americans had recommended $2.7 billion of munitions and $2.8 of non-munitions, a total of $5.5 billion — a substantial reduction from the first British estimates and some 50 per cent less than the level of Lend-Lease for 1944. "All schedules," Morgenthau continued, "both munitions and non-munitions, are subject to the changing demands of strategy as well as to supply considerations and the usual considerations of procurement and allocation."

The program, the Secretary explained, consisted of articles and services which the United Kingdom could not produce in time to meet the demands of war, or which the United States could produce much more effectively. Coupled with decreases in overall munition and manpower requirements for Phase II, the Lend-Lease agreement would make it possible for both the United States and the United Kingdom to release some resources for reconversion, for raising living standards, and for reviving exports.

Privately Morgenthau felt that he had obtained for the British everything possible, less than Cherwell had expected at the time of the Quebec Conference, more than Roosevelt would have yielded on his own. Winston Churchill would have been surprised had he known how much more generous Morgenthau had been than were such presumed friends as Bernard Baruch, a critic of the Phase II agreement. "American production and standards have held the world up for many years," Baruch had written Morgenthau. ". . . I am sure that those standards can win the peace. . . . But we ought not to do all of it. . . . Nothing can hold up many of these countries unless they modernize their business structure. For instance, does anyone know what England or France or any other country will permit an American to do in those countries?" Baruch, though he spoke only for himself, would have insisted, like Cordell Hull, on commercial privileges for American businessmen and investors. After the Phase II agreement was made public, Baruch on December 1, 1944, again wrote Morgenthau:

> Today I saw that certain agreements had been entered into between us and England, in which they get 5 billion and one-half dollars of Lend-Lease a year. . . . No one need think that by giving too much and weakening ourselves that we can help the rest of the world. We can weaken ourselves so much by giving away so many things before peace is here that no one will pay any more attention to us when we talk of world peace than they did at the Paris Conference. We must also measure the cost, not only in dollars, but in the derangement of our economy which inflation is bringing. . . . Winston Churchill said that he did not accept a portfolio to liquidate the British Empire. I should like to see either a full explanation of why all this is done . . . or simple Americans like myself will wonder if this action is of such a nature as to tend to liquidate the American standards of living.

For Baruch, and for thousands of like-minded Americans, Morgenthau had a ready answer. "The recent agreement on Phase Two of the Lend-Lease program," the Secretary wrote Baruch on December 23, 1944, "has no other purpose but to bring all of Britain's resources to bear on the earliest possible defeat of the enemy. By mobilizing the full strength of our allies in this struggle . . . we can shorten the war and in this way diminish the ultimate burden on our own economy. Defeating the enemy has been the sole purpose of the Lend-Lease program from the beginning and that is all that Phase Two of the . . . program is intended to do while the war with Japan continues." Great Britain, Morgenthau noted, had yet to ask for financial aid in the postwar period. Her problem would be to expand her exports enough to enable her to purchase food and other necessary raw materials. With the deterioration in her economic position that had already taken place, she would have to increase her prewar exports, as she had often pointed out, by at least 50 per cent in order to pay for her prewar level of imports. She could do so only in a world in which international trade and investment maintained a high level, and in which nations cooperated in stable and orderly exchange arrangements, such as those designed at Bretton Woods.

"What worries me most about your comments," Morgenthau continued, ". . . is not that you feel as you do, but that these arguments play right into the hands of the isolationists who are only too eager to capitalize on issues of this character to further their own objectives. Recent events in Greece and Italy* are already being exploited and it is not difficult to anticipate a recurrence of a wave of cynicism that will destroy the hopes for international cooperation until we are in the throes of another war. It is going to tax our capacity for self-restraint if we are going to give international cooperation a trial — let alone make a success of it."

Since his trip to Great Britain in August 1944, Morgenthau had moved to the van of those Americans who believed, as he put it in another context, that the future peace of the world depended first of all on "an economically strong and prosperous Britain." Yet as he had written Baruch, the Secretary, under Roosevelt's orders, had confined the agreement on Phase II to the period ending with victory over Japan. He had only hopes, not instruments, for rendering to England the assistance she would incontestably need thereafter. And as he implied in his letter to Baruch, for all of his differences with the British about political questions, he had made England's economic stability the crite-

---

* Demonstrations of democratic discontent, in some degree exploited by local communists, under the conservative regimes restored after liberation.

rion second only to military necessity for establishing the terms of aid. For its part, the United States, he believed, would have to follow a program for reconversion geared to the needs of its wartime allies and the control of their wartime enemies. The latter goal had brought him deeply into the debate over postwar policy for Germany.

XXI

THE MORGENTHAU PLAN
AUGUST–SEPTEMBER 1944

THE MOST controversial and agonizing episode in Morgenthau's public career grew out of his involvement in American postwar planning for Germany. When in 1944 he first approached that issue, the Secretary proceeded on the assumptions that guided his general thinking about the making of peace. His views on Germany both conditioned and were conditioned by his other major objectives: a prosperous Great Britain, a cooperative and friendly Russia, a liberal community of democratic nations in a world free from war. His views on Germany reflected, too, his personal interpretations of the particular conditions of the time and his personal assessments of the possibilities for changing them.

1. Background to Involvement

By the summer of 1944, the peoples and the leaders of the nations of the Grand Alliance had ample reason for their almost universal animosity toward Hitler's Third Reich. The Nazis had brutalized Germany, annihilated millions of human beings, stormed across Europe, and mistreated those whose lands they conquered. The British people, the sturdiest of Hitler's intended victims, believed almost to a man that, with victory, the Allies should punish the German war criminals, eradicate Nazism, disarm Germany, and impose upon her a period of military occupation. About the details of a victorious settlement there was less British unanimity, but public opinion polls estimated that two-thirds of all Englishmen favored the permanent separation of the Ruhr, the area containing some 40 per cent of Germany's industry, from the rest of the Reich, and an even larger percentage believed the Germans should help rebuild the nations they had damaged or destroyed. At least a majority wanted Germany broken up into several smaller states, while an articulate minority deemed the German people "incurably bellicose," and on that account proposed occupying Germany for at least a generation, controlling German industry, and eliminating its capacity to produce arms. The Russians, who had felt the full bestiality of the Wehrmacht, at the very least expected victory to bring with it a time of judgment for Germany, long the most active threat to Soviet security.

Though geography had put them beyond the reach of Hitler's forces, the American people were close to unanimity — 81 per cent according to the polls — in support of the policy of "unconditional surrender" that Roosevelt and Churchill had announced at Casablanca. Most Americans believed Germany would begin planning a new war as soon as she met defeat, and most therefore favored a reduction of Germany to a "third rate" nation.

Roosevelt, Churchill, and Stalin both reflected and shared the sentiments of their countrymen. The insistence of the President and Prime Minister upon unconditional surrender marked their refusal under any conditions to negotiate with Hitler. Beyond that, the foreign ministers of the three powers in Moscow in October 1943, had agreed on the occupation of Germany by forces of all three countries, on the creation of an inter-allied control commission, on the complete disarmament of Germany, and on the dissolution of the Nazi party. For the Russians, those were minimum terms. Foreign Minister Molotov also called for the partition of Germany. He demanded extensive reparations, but Cordell Hull proposed limiting them to a dimension consistent with a healthful "postwar world economic and political order." Yet Hull, unlike Anthony Eden, had no concern for legal formalities in the ultimate treatment of Nazi leaders and war criminals. The foreign ministers, with the later approval of Roosevelt, Churchill, and Stalin, agreed that after the war the Germans responsible for atrocities would be "sent back to the countries in which their abominable deeds were done in order that they may be judged and punished according to the laws of the liberated countries," and major criminals, those "whose offenses have no particular geographical localization," would be punished "by joint decision of the Governments of the Allies." Finally, in order to draft terms for surrender and to suggest machinery to oversee the fulfillment of those terms, the foreign ministers created the European Advisory Commission, a three-power organization which was to begin its work in London.

A month later, in November 1943, the Big Three met for the first time at Teheran. There, as in Moscow, there were differences about significant questions but also agreements about important principles. So, to begin with, Germany was to be divided into three zones for occupation purposes, with a fourth, combined inter-Allied zone to be located in Berlin from which common policies would be administered during the period of occupation. But Stalin had ambitions for German territory which Churchill would not yet concede, and Roosevelt put off for later consideration Stalin's demand for great quantities of German machinery to replace the Russian industry that the Nazis had destroyed. Without prejudice to later decisions about boundaries, the three also considered the partition of Germany, at the least a separation of Prussia from the rest of the nation and some form of special isolation and control for the industrial areas of the Saar and the Ruhr.

In the months immediately following the Teheran Conference, planning for the treatment of Germany fell to three major groups — two in London, one in Washington. In London, Ambassador John G. Winant joined representatives of the Soviet Union and the United Kingdom on the European Advisory Commission. Working without specific instruction from Washington, Winant had three influential assistants: George F. Kennan (until mid-1944), Philip E. Mosely, and E. F. Penrose, all of whom tempered their views toward Germany with an abiding suspicion of the Soviet Union. But the President's views and the preferences of the American Joint Chiefs of Staff contributed to the demarcations of occupation zones which the EAC approved in April 1944. Those lines established an eastern Russian zone as the EAC had originally envisaged it, consisting of about 40 per cent of the German territory of 1937 and about 36 per cent of the population, and including all of Berlin, though the city was to be jointly occupied by the three powers. An east-west line of latitude divided the rest of Germany into northern and southern zones. It remained unclear which of those zones would fall to the British, which to the Americans, but Roosevelt in mid-1944 much preferred the northern area. Fearing that France would succumb to a postwar revolution, the President wanted to stay out of the southern part of Germany, to which access was available only through France.

By July 1944, the European Advisory Commission had also adopted a draft of a surrender document. The document, while postponing questions of detail, provided for the disarming of Germany but left unsettled the question of the disposition of prisoners of war. It proclaimed the Allies as supreme political authorities in Germany and announced that they would impose "political, administrative, economic, financial, military and other requirements." Winant and his staff hoped that the surrender and occupation would leave behind for the long-range future a disarmed but unified Germany with a strong economy under democratic government.

Meanwhile, other plans had emanated from Supreme Headquarters, Allied Expeditionary Forces, where General Eisenhower presided. In April and May 1944, SHAEF received drafts of pre-surrender directives from the Combined Chiefs of Staff in

Washington. Those orders called for the arrest of high Nazi leaders and government officials, for the dissolution of the Nazi Party, for purging the German courts of Nazis, and for forbidding all political activity except by special permission of the Supreme Commander. They also directed Eisenhower to provide for the revival of German agriculture, to import food and other supplies so as to "prevent disease and unrest," to restore public utilities, and to operate coal mines and transportation facilities. On the basis of those provisions, Eisenhower's military government officers in June 1944, completed the draft of a "Handbook for Military Government in Germany." For the occupying armies in Germany, that volume set the task of assuring "that the machine works and works efficiently." The armies were to preserve the centralized German administrative system, and to retain and rehabilitate enough light and heavy industry to make Germany self-supporting and also to keep the whole European economy on "a reasonably even keel." Above all, SHAEF stressed the primacy of military considerations during the period of occupation. Since the War Department and the Army expected the German economy to be in a state of collapse, Eisenhower's planners also asserted the authority of the occupying forces over economic affairs.

Finally, American planners were at work in Washington in various committees of the State Department. In January 1944, Edward R. Stettinius, Jr., had succeeded Sumner Welles — who had resigned — as senior officer for postwar planning. Welles had favored a harsh peace, but Stettinius adopted the more generous views of his chief advisers. Foremost among them were Mosely and Leo Pasvolsky, a professional economist and valued counselor to Cordell Hull. In the spring of 1944, the Department's postwar committee, with Hull's approval, recommended against the partitioning of Germany and against a harsh peace, though it accepted the idea of zones of occupation. Further, it endorsed a statement on economic policy toward Germany by the interdepartmental Executive Committee on Economic Foreign Policy. That statement owed most of its content to Pasvolsky and most of its form to Dean Acheson. Harry White, who represented the Treasury on the interdepartmental committee, had been preoccupied with the Bretton Woods negotiations during most of the discussions of the memorandum, which was ready for circulation on August 4, 1944. The memorandum advocated a limited control of the German economy and the elimination of Germany's economic domination of Europe, but the eventual reabsorption of Germany into the world economy. It also called for short-term collections of reparations in kind, to be taken from current production rather than German capital equipment, and for maintenance of German production at a level sufficient to maintain a tolerable standard of living. The memorandum constituted one part of the State Department's emerging policy of a "stern peace with reconciliation."

At the end of July 1944, Morgenthau knew nothing about the State Department memoranda or about the planning for Germany that had gone on at Teheran and in London. Except in his discussions of occupation currency, he had given little thought to German questions. Still, he had distrusted the Germans since the time of the First World War, which he attributed to their aggression, and he never forgot the cruelty that he had personally observed on the Turkish front. He disliked German manners and abominated Prussian autocracy as much as he admired French civilization and applauded British democracy. The advent of Hitler and Nazism had confirmed those feelings, and Nazi policies repelled Morgenthau as they did all civilized men. Even before the Munich Conference of 1938, and certainly thereafter, he considered the elimination of Nazism the first requisite for a peaceful and democratic world. That belief hardened in 1943 with his intimate involvement, for the first time, in the fate of the European Jews. As a Jew himself, Morgenthau had naturally resented Nazi racial doctrines, but their sting, he often later recalled, dated from his horror when he began to investigate the whole hideous record of Nazi atrocities. It was then, in December 1943, as he indicated in a remark to his staff, that he applauded what seemed to him a "trend . . . for a much more aggressive approach towards our enemies."

The Germans, Morgenthau believed, would cultivate dreams

of world domination even in defeat. "Last night," he noted in his Diary on June 17, 1944, "I phoned Miss Tully and asked her to find out from the President whether it would be all right for me to say in my speech in Chicago* that if the Germans thought they were losing, there was danger of the German general staff's wanting to sue for peace while the fighting was still on French, Italian and Finnish soil, and to warn the American people against this. I would also say that in this way the Germans could save their Army and be ready for another war in the next generation." The next day both Roosevelt and Hull approved the proposed text. "The German war machine has plans for survival," Morgenthau said. "We can be sure of that. Such plans have worked before. . . . It is an easy guess that Germany may offer Hitler and the Nazi gang to bribe conditions out of us. We won't be bribed. Our terms are unconditional surrender."

It was not enough, in Morgenthau's view, to settle for the capture or the execution of Hitler and his aides, not enough even to liberate the nations the Germans had overrun and to occupy Germany itself. A lasting peace also required the education of the German people in the meaning and the ways of democracy — at best a long and laborious process, and the elimination from Germany of the industrial capacity for making war. Only under those conditions would Europe and the world be safe. Only those conditions would permit the early and complete withdrawal of American troops from Europe, a withdrawal that the American people were demanding and the President was expecting. But if Morgenthau had strong convictions about Germany, he had no specific recommendations until he learned that planners in Washington and London were charting courses that seemed to him to risk German resurgence.

* To sell war bonds.

2. Portentous Misgivings

The catalyst of Morgenthau's involvement in German planning
was the Acheson-Pasvolsky memorandum on economic policy.
"I was not in agreement with the recommendations . . . ,"
Harry White wrote, "and I felt that it was not in line with the
Secretary's views. Knowing that the Secretary was interested in
the subject and not wanting to take any action until he had had
an opportunity of going over the report, I instructed the Treasury delegates to reserve the Treasury's position." The Treasury
never approved the report, for Morgenthau reacted to it precisely as White thought he would.

The story really began, Morgenthau later wrote, on August 6,
1944, on "an airplane to Europe. I was making the trip primarily
to see how the Treasury's financial arrangements for the liberated areas of France were working out. . . . But as we were
swinging out over the Atlantic, one of my assistants* pulled out
of his briefcase a copy of a State Department memorandum on
reparations in Germany. I settled back to read it, first with interest, then with misgivings, finally with sharp disagreement." In
England, Morgenthau learned more from Colonel Bernard Bernstein, a former Treasury official who was then with the Civil
Affairs section of SHAEF. As White later put it: "Bernstein
described . . . the directives which were being prepared for the
occupation of Germany. The Secretary regarded them as reflecting the wrong policy decision. His later discussions of the
post-surrender terms followed from the necessity of taking a position." That was also Morgenthau's recollection. "When I
planned the European trip," he reflected, "I did not expect to
become involved in the question of the future of Germany. But
as a result of the trip, I found myself projected unexpectedly into

* White. Also on the trip were Fred B. Smith and Josiah E. DuBois.

the very center of the German discussions." At that center Morgenthau found not only the State Department's memorandum on economic policy but also the "Handbook for Military Government in Germany," and the policy papers of the European Advisory Commission, to all of which he took strong objection. And close to the center, in London, where German V-1 bombs were working their nightly havoc, and on the front in Normandy, where the battle for Europe raged, Morgenthau saw at first hand the ravages of the war the Nazis had begun. From Churchill and Sir John Anderson he heard again, with more force than ever before, the accounting of the material cost of the war to Great Britain, with its implications for American Lend-Lease during Stage II, while the conversations conducted by his subordinates about asylums for refugees reminded him continually of the face that Nazism had shown the world.

Firsthand impressions of the war, mingling with discussions of high policy, fed Morgenthau's interest in planning for Germany during his entire trip. As he told his staff after his return: "We started right in with General Eisenhower to find out where he stood on this business of how he is going to treat Germany when he first gets in. He was very positive that he was going to treat them rough. He was perfectly willing to let them stew in their own juice." According to the Secretary's later recollection, White noted that the Civil Affairs Division of SHAEF "would have a different job in Germany from its job in the liberated countries. The goal in the liberated countries was to build up the economy as quickly as possible; to repair transportation, to restore the necessary services of life, to improve the standard of living as fast as we could. Surely, my assistant said, this would not be our goal in Germany." Eisenhower replied: "I want to say that I am not interested in the German economy, and personally would not like to bolster it if that will make it easier for the Germans." Demands for a soft peace, Eisenhower continued, came from those who wanted to make Germany "a bulwark against Russia." Soviet strength was "fantastic," but the General thought the Russians would be busy for generations digesting what they had already swallowed. "I never saw Eisenhower in such good shape," Morgenthau reported. "He made the best impression he has ever made on me." *

In London Morgenthau spent two hours with Winston Churchill. "I got a great kick," the Secretary told his staff, "he took me through his own map room . . . which was quite a thrill. He is a great fellow." The Prime Minister, to Morgenthau's delight, showed great affection for Franklin Roosevelt. "Just to hear the President shout 'Hello'," Churchill said, "is like drinking a bottle of champagne." Churchill then, as Morgenthau recalled, "started off, bang, on how England was busted. . . . He and I got along very well. We put it right on the line. . . .

"The interesting thing with Churchill was — he said, well, he was practically seventy and it was time he made peace with his Maker, and as soon as the war was over he would resign and be the most unpopular man in England. . . . I got the impression he wanted the Germans treated in a stern manner."

On August 12, 1944, Morgenthau invited Ambassador Winant and several of his advisers on German questions to luncheon at the country house in Wiltshire where the Secretary was staying. After luncheon, according to the account of E. F. Penrose, one of Winant's group, discussion of plans for Germany "took place in bright August sunshine, on the wide lawn which surrounded the house. As we lounged on the grass Mr. Morgenthau in brief, simple terms expounded his views." Then Harry White, amplifying Morgenthau's statement, came as close as possible, in Penrose's opinion, to "clothing a bad thesis with an appearance of intellectual respectability." Germany, Morgenthau and White argued, should never again be in a position to wage war. To attain that objective, which would keep the peace, it might be necessary to reduce Germany to the status of a fifth-rate power. Philip Mosely, frankly hostile to that analysis,

---

* Eisenhower, in his own memoir, recalled expressing himself "roughly as follows: . . . The German people must not be allowed to escape a sense of guilt. . . . Prominent Nazis . . . must be . . . punished. . . . The German nation should be responsible for reparations. . . . The warmaking power of the country should be eliminated. . . ." His memoir notes no reference to Russia but asserts that he opposed Morgenthau's suggestion for flooding the mines in the Ruhr, though Morgenthau did not remember having made that suggestion at that time. Later, beyond any question, both White and Eisenhower opposed it.

said that any attempt to "smash" the German economy would drive the Germans to dependence on Russia, which would in turn expose all of Europe to Soviet control. For his part Winant, who agreed with Mosely, nevertheless confined his remarks to a description of the status of the European Advisory Commission. "It was not doing very much," Morgenthau later recalled, ". . . because it lacked clear authority and instructions." To get that authority and to block Morgenthau's purpose, Winant after this meeting, without the Secretary's knowledge, cabled Roosevelt for instructions compatible with EAC attitudes, but he did not receive them.

Before leaving England, Morgenthau saw Anthony Eden, the British Foreign Secretary. "Very much surprised," as Morgenthau put it, that Winant considered the EAC so powerless, Eden ". . . exclaimed that this had all been settled at Teheran. To prove his point he sent out for the minutes of the Teheran Conference.

"I was astonished to hear that the Big Three had already specifically instructed the EAC to study the problem of partitioning Germany. Stalin, determined that Germany should never again disturb the peace of Europe, strongly favored its dismemberment. Roosevelt backed him wholeheartedly, and Churchill reluctantly agreed that the European Advisory Commission consider the proposal.

"Eden and I were both amazed to learn that the EAC was cheerfully drawing its plans on the basis not of German dismemberment, but of German unity. Winant had been at Teheran. But having received no instructions from the State Department to proceed along the Teheran lines, he felt that they might not know of the Big Three decision and that it was not his business to inform his superiors on such matters."

Shaken by much he had learned, Morgenthau had been even more disturbed, he later wrote, by the sight of London — "that bombed city with its courageous people." On the eve of his departure he made his deepest convictions the theme of a broadcast to the English people:

"There can be no peace on earth — no security for any man,

woman or child — if aggressor nations like Germany and Japan retain any power to strike at their neighbors.

"It is not enough for us to say, 'we will disarm Germany and Japan and *hope* that they will learn to behave themselves as decent people.' Hoping is not enough."

Back in Washington on August 17, Morgenthau called early the next morning on Cordell Hull. Immediately after their conference he dictated his memory of it for his Diary:

I told him I had called on General Eisenhower and asked him how he felt about the way Germany should be treated the first few months after we entered Germany, and he said that his impression was that they should be treated sternly and that they should be allowed to stew in their own juice.

Then I told Hull that I had a talk with Churchill . . . and I got the impression he wanted the Germans treated in a stern manner. I then told him that I had done a lot of probing, and through talking with Winant and with the people who assist Winant, and also based on a memorandum . . . of Mr. Pasvolsky I found that from all appearances it seemed that the Germans were going to be treated in a manner so that they could be built up over a number of years to pay reparations, and that at the end of ten years, they would be prepared to wage a third war.

I also told Hull that . . . with Eden . . . I learned, by having Mr. Eden read from the minutes of the Teheran Conference, that during discussions about Poland the President switched the conversation to a discussion of Germany, and it was then and there decided * that Germany should be dismembered in either three or fifteen parts, and that a commission would be appointed to study this question. . . .

When I made this statement, Mr. Hull literally gasped and he said to me, "Henry, this is the first time I have ever heard this. . . . I have never been permitted to see the minutes of the Teheran Conference. . . . I have asked and I have not been allowed to see them, and what you have told me is the first time I have ever heard this." . . .

And I said, "Well, now Pasvolsky has made a study along quite contrary lines, and Winant has also made a study . . . along different lines." I said that when I was in Winant's office I didn't

---

* In fact Roosevelt and Stalin supported partition, Churchill did not, and the matter was discussed rather than decided at Teheran. It was also referred for study to the EAC.

think he was telling the truth because he first said he was making a report on reparations for Germany, but that about two weeks ago he began to make a new study which would take into consideration the dismemberment of Germany. I really don't think that anybody has made a study along the lines the President and Churchill decided on at Teheran.

When I first mentioned the European Advisory Committee, Hull said, "That has been a complete failure. The trouble is that Winant is trying to do two big jobs and he can't do them both." So I had to treat the next thing very carefully. I said, "I am not quite sure whether at Teheran Winant knew about the clause for the dismemberment of Germany or whether he didn't." I said he was a little vague about it, but Winant kept saying right along that he had no instructions. However, at one stage in the game Winant did say that the reason he was hesitating telling me all the facts about this Conference was that Mr. Hull had not seen the minutes. . . . He said that he was there, but it put him in a very embarrassing position because he didn't know how much to tell back home. . . .

The sum and substance of this is that here a meeting takes place sometime last November in Teheran where . . . Roosevelt, Churchill and Stalin, agree to the dismemberment of Germany, and all these people go ahead and make studies without taking that into consideration and without explicit instructions. It is like telling an architect to build a new house and not telling him where it should be built, how it should be built, or how many people it is to house.

Hull was quite upset, so I said to him, "You know, Cordell . . . I appreciate the fact that this isn't my responsibility, but I am doing this as an American citizen, and I am going to continue to do so, and I am going to stick my nose into it until I know it is all right. . . . If I find out anything I will come over and tell you about it." He said that was all right.

I said to Hull, "Where do you stand on this?" And he said, "You know the reason I got along so well with the Russians was because when I was in Moscow I told the Russians that I would hold a secret trial before which I would bring Hitler and his gang and Tojo and his gang, and I would shoot them all, and then I would let the world know about it a couple of days later." . . . I asked him what he was going to do about the state of Germany, and he said, "I don't have any chance to do anything. I am not told what is going on. . . . I am told that that is a military affair. . . . I am not even consulted." . . .

Then I went on and told him about the plans which the Army is making where we would go into the south of Germany and England in the north of Germany. That is contrary to the way the President wanted it, but the only way they could have carried out the President's wishes would have been to have the two armies cross each other, so the army decided to do it the other way. . . .

I also told Hull that Russia had kept completely aloof from the European Advisory Committee, and I told him the reason they were keeping out of it, in my opinion, was because they realized how the American and English delegates were proceeding on this matter, and they wanted no part of it.

From my talk with Hull, I am sure if Hull got a directive on the dismemberment of Germany he would go to town. My trip to Europe was many, many times worthwhile just for what I learned and what I told Hull, and we will see what happens when I see the President.

With Roosevelt on August 19, 1944, Morgenthau, according to his recollection right after their conversation, said: "Mr. President, here in the State Department . . . Pasvolsky has been making a study, but he didn't know about the Teheran Conference agreement." The Secretary then told Roosevelt about his conversation with Hull. "The President didn't like it," Morgenthau wrote, "but he didn't say anything. He looked very embarrassed, and I repeated it so that he would be sure to get it." Morgenthau also told Roosevelt about Winant and the work of his committee. Nobody, the Secretary said, "has been studying how to treat Germany roughly along the lines you wanted."

"Give me thirty minutes with Churchill and I can correct this," the President said. ". . . We have got to be tough with Germany and I mean the German people not just the Nazis. We either have to castrate the German people or you have got to treat them in such manner so they can't just go on reproducing people who want to continue the way they have in the past."

"Well, Mr. President," Morgenthau replied, "Nobody is considering the question along those lines. . . . In England they want to build up Germany so she can pay reparations."

"What do you want reparations for?" Roosevelt asked. Morgenthau, though he did not reply, opposed them.

As the Secretary put it, Roosevelt "left no doubt whatsoever in my mind that he personally wants to be tough with the Germans. He said, 'They have been tough with us.'"

Confident that the President shared his own opinions, aghast at the policies of EAC and the Army, Morgenthau soon after leaving the White House appointed a special committee of Harry White, John Pehle, and Ansel Luxford "to draft the Treasury's analysis of the German problem." That committee began at once, with strict attention to the Secretary's specific instructions, to define what became the Morgenthau Plan.

3. The Morgenthau Plan

Morgenthau dominated the work of the Treasury's committee on Germany. The members of that committee followed the Secretary's instructions to the letter even though they sometimes disagreed with him. Further, in the tradition of high departmental morale that had long existed, the committee presented a united front to others in Washington. And others took strong exception to the Treasury's position. In his Diary, the Secretary reported his conversation of August 23, 1944, with Henry Stimson and John McCloy:

> Stimson was . . . anxious to see me. I told him the whole story even including the part that Hull had never seen the minutes. . . . McCloy's interest is the immediate one — what is the Army going to do as soon as they go in there? Stimson's interest is the long-range one. . . . He is thinking along the lines that you have to have a long Armistice or a period of at least twenty years to police Germany while the present generation is in control and until a new generation grows up. He was also very much interested evidently in a proposal made by Jean Monnet to internationalize the Saar Basin and have joint control by some international body and permit the Germans to work there but not run it. They thought if we could control the Saar we could keep the Germans from going to war again. So I said, "Well, if you let the young children of

today be brought up by SS Troopers who are indoctrinated with Hitlerism, aren't you simply going to raise another generation of Germans who will want to wage war? . . . Don't you think the thing to do is to take a leaf from Hitler's book and completely remove these children from their parents and make them wards of the state, and have ex-US Army officers, English Army officers and Russian Army officers run these schools and have these children learn the true spirit of democracy?" . . .

I also gave him my idea of the possibility of removing all industry from Germany and simply reducing them to an agricultural population of small land-owners. He said that the trouble with that was that Germany was that kind of a nation back in 1860, but then she only had 40 million people. He said that you might have to take a lot of people out of Germany. So I said, "Well, that is not nearly as bad as sending them to gas chambers."

I got the impression that Stimson felt this was a very important subject . . . but he hasn't given too much thought to it. . . .

I then said that I thought a committee of Hull, himself and myself ought to draw up a memorandum for the President so that he will have it before he meets Churchill again. . . . I said, "I don't think Churchill is going to worry about it and the President hasn't time to think about it." . . . I asked him whether when he saw the President again he wouldn't suggest that to him, and he thought he would rather do it in a memorandum.

More than Morgenthau yet realized, Stimson opposed his ideas about the German economy. Accordingly the two secretaries were far apart about the "Handbook of Military Government" which SHAEF had prepared in London. To Roosevelt on August 25, 1944, Morgenthau took a memo on that handbook, which was designed to guide American and British military government officers. The memo quoted a number of excerpts which the Secretary found objectionable. "Your main and immediate task," one excerpt read, ". . . is to get things running, to pick up the pieces, to restore as quickly as possible the official functioning of the German civil government. . . . The first concern of military government will be to see that the machine works and works efficiently." Other excerpts called on the officers of military government to reorganize the German police so as to maintain law and order, to control German finances, to establish and maintain adequate standards of public health, to promote agriculture, to restore public utilities, to provide for the gradual rehabilitation of peacetime industry, to employ labor and prevent industrial unrest. The Allied officers were also to assist in the conversion of industrial plants to the production of consumer goods, and to reconstruct German foreign trade with priority for the needs of the United Nations. "The highly centralized German administrative system," the "Handbook" ordered, "is to be retained unless otherwise directed by higher authorities. . . . All existing German regulations and ordinances relating to . . . production, supply or distribution will remain in force unless specifically amended or abrogated. Except as otherwise indicated by circumstances or directed by higher authority, present German production and primary processing of fuels, ores and other raw materials will be maintained at present levels. . . . The food supply will be administered so as to provide, if possible . . . a diet on the basis of an overall average of 2000 calories per day. Members of the German forces will be rated as normal consumers. . . . Should the indigenous products of Germany be insufficient to provide such a basic ration, the balance will be made up by imports. . . . All possible steps will be taken to insure the utilization of German economic, material and industrial facilities to an extent necessary to provide such raw materials, goods, supplies and services as are required for military and essential civilian needs. . . . The main objective of Allied Military Government in the financial field is to take such temporary measures as will . . . minimize the potential financial disorder . . . that is likely to occur. . . . International boundaries will be deemed to be as they were on 31 December, 1937."

In his Diary Morgenthau described the President's reaction: "I called on the President this morning, and I really was shocked for the first time because he is a very sick man, and seems to have wasted away. . . . I . . . gave him my memorandum which he read very carefully, and he said to me, 'Well, you could read this thing two ways,' meaning that you could interpret it both hard or soft. So I said, 'Look, Mr. President, this is based on a handbook which we picked up in England and which I understand has not yet been approved, but lacking a directive from the top this is what is going to be used. . . . I told McCloy to tell Stimson that I was going to speak to you about it, but I understand you are seeing him* and I don't want to annoy him so I think maybe you'd better give me back the memorandum and the handbook,' but the President said, 'No, if you don't mind, I would like to keep it and read it tonight and then I will return it to you.' . . . I'm going to continue to feed the President suggestions, but it is quite obvious that he wants to keep me very much in the background, and wants to do it his own way as usual."

The President's "own way" appalled the War Department. After talking with Morgenthau on August 23, Stimson had prepared a memorandum that he delivered to the President at luncheon two days later. In conversation with Roosevelt, as in his memorandum, the Secretary of War opposed Morgenthau's position. To be sure, like Morgenthau, Stimson favored the reeducation of German children, the disarmament of Germany, and the punishment, after trial, of leading Nazis. But he objected to breaking Germany up into several small states and he proposed international control of the industries of the Ruhr and Saar. Dismemberment and deindustrialization, he told Roosevelt, would result in the starvation of thirty million people, a barbaric prospect.

Of the two Cabinet members, Morgenthau left the deeper impression on Roosevelt on August 25. After reading the Treasury memorandum on the "Handbook" that night, the President the next day sent Stimson a sharp letter. It quoted the excerpts Morgenthau had quoted, incorporated some of his phraseology, and carried the sting of Roosevelt's own prose:

> This so-called "Handbook" is pretty bad. I should like to know how it came to be written and who approved it down the line. If it has not been sent out as approved, all copies should be withdrawn and held until you get a chance to go over it.
>
> It gives me the impression that Germany is to be restored just as

* Later that morning.

much as the Netherlands or Belgium, and the people of Germany brought back as quickly as possible to their pre-war estate.

It is of the utmost importance that every person in Germany should realize that this time Germany is a defeated nation. I do not want them to starve to death, but, as an example, if they need food to keep body and soul together beyond what they have, they should be fed three times a day with soup from Army soup kitchens. That will keep them perfectly healthy and they will remember that experience all their lives. The fact that they are a defeated nation, collectively and individually, must be so impressed upon them that they will hesitate to start any new war. . . .

There exists a school of thought both in London and here which would, in effect, do for Germany what this Government did for its own citizens in 1933 when they were flat on their backs. I see no reason for starting a WPA, PWA or a CCC for Germany when we go in with our Army of Occupation.

Too many people here and in England hold to the view that the German people as a whole are not responsible for what has taken place — that only a few Nazi leaders are responsible. That unfortunately is not based on fact. The German people as a whole must have it driven home to them that the whole nation has been engaged in a lawless conspiracy against the decencies of modern civilization.

Please let me see the revision of this and also let me have this original copy back.

That revision would have to reflect the deliberations of the committee Roosevelt appointed at the suggestion of Stimson, who in turn was following a recommendation of Morgenthau. The two Secretaries and Hull, the President had directed at the Cabinet meeting on August 25, were to confer about the treatment of Germany. Roosevelt then sent the Treasury and State Departments copies of his note to Stimson about the "Handbook," surely with the purpose of guiding the interdepartmental discussions. Characteristically, Hull resented having to share command for policy with Morgenthau, whose opinions about the German economy he rejected, and with Stimson, whose interpretation of military and political necessities conflicted at various points with those of the Department of State. Here, too, according to Morgenthau's account of the Cabinet meeting: "The President was more firm about this opposite Hull than I've

ever seen him, and so was Stimson." The Treasury's intercession, Morgenthau felt, had accomplished his first purpose. "Mc-
Cloy can't — Stimson can't — wash their hands of the fact," the
Secretary told his staff, "that if we hadn't gone to Europe and
dug this stuff up, that 'Handbook' would have gone into effect."

Stimson was distressed less about the President's response to
the "Handbook" than about Morgenthau's point of view. In Sar-
anac, New York, over a long Labor Day weekend from August
26 through September 3, 1944, Stimson confided to his diary his
grave reservations about Morgenthau's "very bitter atmosphere
of personal resentment against the entire German people without
regard to individual guilt and I am very much afraid that it will
result in our taking mass vengeance . . . in the shape of clumsy
economic action. This in my opinion will be ineffective and will
inevitably produce a very dangerous reaction in Germany and
probably a new war."

Morgenthau, whose convictions were equal and opposite, also
left Washington for the Labor Day weekend. As he departed,
he instructed White and Pehle to devote their whole time to
their studies of Germany. "The President is hungry for this
stuff," he told them by telephone two days later. "This thing is
so much a . . . psychological matter, it's a question of how to
handle the Germans who have been inculcated with this fanati-
cism. . . . It's a question of attacking the German mind. . . . I
wouldn't be afraid to make the suggestion just as ruthless as is
necessary to accomplish the acts."

By telephone daily through the weekend Morgenthau reviewed the memorandum White and Pehle were drafting. Their
first efforts struck the Secretary as not tough enough. "I wish,"
he said on August 31, 1944, "that your men would attack the
problem from this angle, that they take the Ruhr and completely
put it out of business. . . . And also the Saar. Now, the reason
I said particularly the Ruhr, you can find out very easily what
their production of coal and steel and that sort of thing is, and
consider what it would do in the way of helping England and
Belgium if they stage a come-back because, after all, the Ruhr
— it was partly responsible for the great unemployment in Eng-

land, and one of our problems is to put England back on its feet. And both of these studies and all other studies that I've ever seen are contemplating keeping the Ruhr in existence. And I'd like to approach the thing from — just putting the whole Ruhr out of production. And also, as a separate thing, what would happen if we put the Saar out of production? . . .

"And . . . as I say, what competition the Ruhr gave to both the Belgium coal and steel and England coal and steel, and an estimate to guess how long it would take before Russia could be in production and that she could take care of customers — I mean, England, Belgium and Russia could take care of the customers that Germany used to have — with coal and steel."

"This Ruhr," White objected, "is the most difficult problem. You see . . . crushing it as you say presents us with about fifteen million out of eighteen million people who . . . will have absolutely nothing to do, and . . . some of the boys feel . . . that we'd never get away with it politically. . . . That's the problem with the Ruhr. If you internationalize it, it has other problems. You can't give it to France; it's too big. You can't give it to Belgium and Holland; it will swallow Belgium and Holland. It's . . . the most difficult problem and, we'll . . . work along the lines that you're suggesting. I think that the question of how it will help Britain and France . . . will be a good selling argument, but it certainly oughtn't to be the decisive consideration. . . . But we'll investigate it."

"I can tell you this," Morgenthau replied, "that if the Ruhr was put out of business, the coal mines and steel mines of England would flourish for many years." When White continued to express doubts, the Secretary said categorically that "the Ruhr ought to be put out of business." Further, in answer to White's question of what to do with the Germans in the area who would lack employment, Morgenthau proposed "an international T.V.A." manned by "a couple of million Germans" at work on reclamation and hydroelectric projects all over the world.

While redrafting proceeded at the Treasury, Morgenthau on September 2, 1944, gave the President the preliminary version of the Treasury's memorandum on Germany. They met, as they often had before, in the handsome, spacious family house that Morgenthau had rebuilt on his farm in Fishkill, New York. It was a peaceful setting, with the great trees in their late summer glory and the nearby orchards laden with the apple crop. Both men relaxed in that stately but pastoral environment. The Secretary's Diary entry for the day recounted their conversation:

> The President and Mrs. Roosevelt came to tea this afternoon, and stayed about an hour and a quarter. Fully an hour of the time we used to discuss the German situation. I gave him the memorandum of the outline of suggestions plus a map. The President said, "I wonder if you have the three things in it that I am interested in." . . . I explained to the President this was preliminary and had not yet been circulated fully in the Treasury, and that my own criticism of it was that it didn't go nearly far enough.
>
> The President read this memorandum very carefully, and as soon as he got to the map he said, "This isn't what we agreed to at Teheran or since then," and he started to talk about Poland. I said, "Mr. President, we have been working wholly within the Treasury, and we just don't know what anybody else has been doing for you. . . . This is approximately correct except that, as I remember it, from the Kiel Canal north toward Denmark they made that an international zone, and they made the Saar district an international zone." He was keenly interested in the memorandum and read it very slowly and very carefully. When he got through, he told me about the three things he wanted, and I think that his thinking is along these lines — Germany should be allowed no aircraft of any kind, not even a glider, and that Germany should be served from the air by other countries. The second was that nobody should be allowed to wear a uniform, and there was no marching, that would do more to teach the Germans than anything else that they had been defeated. So I said, "That's very interesting . . . but I don't think it goes nearly far enough. . . . Where this memorandum falls down, as far as I am concerned, is that the heart of the German war machine is the Ruhr, and I would like to see the Ruhr dismantled, and the machinery given to those countries that might need it. . . . I realize that this would put eighteen or twenty million people out of work, but if we make an international zone of it it is just time before Germany will attempt an Anschluss. . . . This will have a tremendous effect on England and Belgium, and ought to guarantee their prosperity for the next twenty years because their principal competition for their

coal and steel came from the Ruhr, and this ought to go a long way towards solving the economic future of England."

Well, the President liked all of this, and I said, "Then the other problem which this memorandum doesn't touch on is the mentality of the German between the ages of 20 and 40 . . . who have been inculcated with Nazism. . . . I am convinced that you could change them, and you may even have to transplant them out of Germany to some place in Central Africa where you can do some big TVA project. . . . The other big problem is what to do with the children of these people so that they will get the right kind of education."

The President listened very closely and seemed to be in complete sympathy with what I was saying. I don't think he had done any thinking along these lines. He did interrupt me to say, "You know you will have to create entirely new textbooks for the Germans," and I said that I realized that. . . .

Towards the end of the conversation, I said to the President, "How did you ever appoint Robert Murphy as political advisor to Eisenhower?" . . . Then the President went into a long discussion about . . . how he had directed the business with Darlan and how he had saved 10,000 lives of American soldiers. . . . He got quite excited about it as Mrs. Roosevelt pushed him on this. So I said, "Mr. President, why not let bygones be bygones? . . . I don't want to discuss what has gone in the past, but why pick Robert Murphy for this job? In the minds of the people it connoted Darlan and everything that goes with it." . . .

During my discussion with the President on Robert Murphy, Mrs. Roosevelt said that with the attitude of the Pope, she thought it was a mistake to send a Catholic to Germany, and the President came to the Pope's defense particularly in regard to this last speech the Pope made on private property. He said the Pope had always been for private property, and was against Communism. His arguments weren't very reassuring or convincing. . . .

I felt it had been distinctly worthwhile to see Mrs. Roosevelt because I never knew just how she might feel towards treating the Germans so harshly. She had been slightly pacifist before the war and I thought she might think we should go a little easy on the Germans, but she doesn't.

Again at the Treasury on September 4, Morgenthau instructed White to include in the memorandum on Germany the President's wishes forbidding the Germans aircraft, uniforms and

marching. The Secretary also said that Roosevelt was in accord
with his idea for the Ruhr. "I think that somebody is going to be
confronted," White protested, "with what to do with fifteen
million people." The President, Morgenthau replied, would feed
them from the Army's soup kitchens. Pehle asked how long that
would last, and Morgenthau said Roosevelt would not worry
about that, but Pehle predicted that "he is not going to be able to
sell that kind of program." White then, as he had before, proposed an alternative "of making the Ruhr an industrial area under
international control which will produce reparations for twenty
years."

"Harry," Morgenthau said, "you can't sell it to me at all. . . .
You just can't sell it to me, because you have it there only so
many years and you have an Anschluss and the Germans go in
and take it. The only thing you can sell me, or I will have any
part of, is the complete shut-down of the Ruhr. . . . Just strip
it. I don't care what happens to the population. . . . I would
take every mine, every mill and factory and wreck it. . . .
Steel, coal, everything. Just close it down. . . . I am for destroying it first and we will worry about the population second.

"That is the place where war can spring from, and that is the
place that closed down the steel mills in Birmingham, the coal
mines in England, that caused the misery and the low standards
of living in England. . . . It is the competition. . . . I would
close down those things tight. There is nothing left. . . . I
want to see as good a job done as I can on the war criminals, but
over and above that, my interest is the future. . . . Looking to
the future peace of this world . . . and the only way I know is
to shut that thing down.

"I don't know how much the Saar has or how much their
production is; if necessary, shut that down or give it to France.
But certainly if that area [the Ruhr] is . . . stripped of its machinery, the mines flooded — dynamited — wrecked — it would
make them impotent to wage future wars. . . .

"Now, as soon as you start arguing with me, and I begin to
give way, let this in or that in, or let that area or that population
continue their skills, they will do just what they do in the hills of

Pennsylvania — they will mine bootleg coal. . . . A fellow will have a coal mine in his basement, and those fellows are so clever and such devils that before you know it they have got a marching army. . . .

"I am not going to budge an inch. . . . Sure it is a terrific problem. Let the Germans solve it. Why the hell should I worry about what happens to their people? . . .

"It seems a terrific task; it seems inhuman; it seems cruel. We didn't ask for this war; we didn't put millions of people through gas chambers, we didn't do any of these things. They have asked for it.

"Now, what I say is, for the future of my children and grand-children I don't want these beasts to wage war. I don't know any other way than to go to the heart of the thing, which is the Ruhr, and I am not going to be budged. I can be overruled by the President, but nobody else is going to overrule me."

The destruction of the Ruhr, Morgenthau admitted, would impose some sacrifices on Great Britain and the United States, at the least reduce export markets, but that seemed to him a small price. He had already told the President, he went on, that the preliminary memorandum had not gone far enough. He wanted army engineers to go "into every steel mill, in every coal mine, every chemical plant, every synthetic gas business, . . . and put dynamite in and open the water valves and flood and dynamite." And as Morgenthau interpreted the President, "he is willing to go as far as I am, or he is willing to go farther than I am. . . . The man is hungry, crazy to get some stuff to work with. When he saw what we were talking about he said, . . . 'It will be tough sledding with Churchill.'

"But he is very, very anxious to get something down in black and white on this thing. . . . You put your Ruhr under lock and key and make it a ghost area, the Germans cannot wage war with what they have left."

Adamant though the Secretary clearly was, his subordinates continued to try to persuade him to soften his views. White suggested permitting the Ruhr to produce coal so as to alleviate the "terrific coal shortage" that Western Europe and Great Britain would face after the end of hostilities. "To answer," Morgenthau said, "as to letting them produce coal, that doesn't answer what I have in mind. . . . I am not going to give in while I have got breath. . . . I want to make Germany so impotent that she cannot forge the tools of war."

That statement ended the argument within the Treasury. The destruction of the Ruhr formed the core of Morgenthau's plan for Germany. The plan itself, Morgenthau believed on September 4, 1944, would win Roosevelt's full support. It would also, he was sure, contribute to the awakening of prosperity in England; to the relief of Russian fears of German resurgence, and therefore to Russian-American friendship; to the elimination of Germany as a threat to the world, and therefore to a lasting peace. And by nightfall of September 4 his staff, their objections vetoed, had completed the draft which was to remain for Morgenthau the essential statement of his ideas. Its form that day was identical with the form he later published in facsimile in his book of 1945, *Germany Is Our Problem.*

Entitled "Program to Prevent Germany from Starting a World War III," the Morgenthau Plan began by calling for "the complete demilitarization of Germany in the shortest possible period of time after surrender. This means completely disarming the German Army and people (including the removal or destruction of all war material), the total destruction of the whole German armament industry, and the removal or destruction of other key industries which are basic to military strength." With regard to geography, the plan proposed giving Poland that part of East Prussia which did not go to the Soviet Union, and also the southern portion of Silesia. France was to get the Saar and adjacent territories bounded by the Rhine and Moselle rivers. And an International Zone was to contain the Ruhr and its surrounding territory. The remaining part of Germany "should be divided into two autonomous, independent states . . . the South German state comprising Bavaria, Wurttemberg, Baden and some smaller areas and . . . a North German state comprising a large part of the old state of Prussia, Saxony, Thuringia and smaller states." There was to be a customs union between the

South German country and Austria, which was to be restored to her pre-1938 borders.

The plan next discussed the Ruhr, including the Rhineland, the Kiel Canal, and all German territory north of that canal: "Here lies the heart of German industrial power. This area should not only be stripped of all . . . existing industries but so weakened and controlled that it cannot in the foreseeable future become an industrial area." To that end, if possible within six months after the end of the fighting, "all industrial plants and equipment not destroyed by military action shall be completely dismantled and transported to Allied Nations as restitution. All equipment shall be removed from the mines and the mines closed."

The Morgenthau Plan went on to hold that "reparations, in the form of future payments and deliveries, should not be demanded," though it did make provisions for restitution and some reparations through the transfer of existing German resources and territories, including forced German labor outside of Germany and the confiscation of German assets outside of Germany.

Within Germany, "all schools and universities will be closed until an Allied Commission of Education has formulated an effective reorganization program. It is contemplated that it may require a considerable period of time before any institutions of higher education are reopened. Meanwhile the education of German students in foreign universities will not be prohibited. Elementary schools will be reopened as quickly as appropriate teachers and textbooks are available.

"All German radio stations and newspapers, magazines, weeklies, etc. shall be discontinued until adequate controls are established and an appropriate program formulated."

Taking a strong stand for the dismemberment of Germany, the Morgenthau Plan contemplated the military occupation as a step toward an eventual partitioning of the country. On that account, military authorities were to dismiss all policy-making officials of the German government and deal instead with local governments. Those governments were in time to organize federal governments both in North Germany and South Germany.

"The sole purpose of the military in control of the German economy," the Morgenthau Plan continued in direct contrast to the "Handbook," "shall be to facilitate military operations and military occupation. The Allied Military Government shall not assume responsibility for such economic problems as price controls, rationing, unemployment, production, reconstruction, distribution, consumption, housing, or transportation, or take any measures designed to maintain or strengthen the German economy, except those which are essential to military operations. The responsibility for sustaining the German economy and people rests with the German people with such facilities as may be available under the circumstances."

For a period of at least twenty years after the surrender of Germany, the United Nations was to maintain controls over foreign trade and capital imports. Those controls were to prevent the establishment or expansion of key industries "basic to the German military potential." They were also to break up all large estates and divide them "among the peasants, and the system of primogeniture and entail should be abolished."

The Morgenthau Plan, after noting the need for a program for the punishment of war crimes, proceeded to incorporate Roosevelt's particular suggestions: "No German shall be permitted to wear . . . any military uniform or any uniform of any quasi-military organization . . . no military parades shall be permitted . . . and all military bands shall be disbanded . . . all aircraft . . . will be confiscated for later disposition." No German was to be allowed to "operate or to help operate any aircraft, including those owned by foreign interests."

"Although the United States would have full military and civilian representation on whatever international commission or commissions may be established for the execution of the whole German program," the Morgenthau Plan concluded, "the primary responsibility for the policing of Germany and for civil administration in Germany should be assumed by the military forces of Germany's continental neighbors. Specifically, these should include Russian, French, Polish, Czech, Greek, Yugoslav, Norwegian, Dutch and Belgian soldiers." And in its last sentence, the Morgenthau Plan stated categorically what the President expected the American people to demand: "Under this program United States troops could be withdrawn within a relatively short time."

The Secretary had now to attempt to make his program the policy of the United States.

4. Discord in Washington

At a dinner at his home on September 4, 1944, with Henry Stimson, John McCloy, and Harry White, Morgenthau unveiled his newly completed plan for Germany. "With temperateness and good will," which Morgenthau returned in kind, Stimson immediately attacked the economic features of the plan. Stimson expanded his argument at a meeting the next day of the Cabinet committee on Germany, of which Roosevelt had made Harry Hopkins chairman. Immediately after the meeting Morgenthau described it to his staff:

> Stimson is opposed to making Germany a barren farm country. I gathered he wanted an international Ruhr and Saar and let them continue to produce. . . . More and more Stimson came out very emphatically, very very positively, that he didn't want any production stopped. He said it was an unnatural thing to do, it ran in the face of the economy. . . . And more and more it developed that Hull did want to take very drastic steps.* . . . Stimson kept making these speeches about why we must keep up production in Germany. . . . Nothing we told them last night made any impression. . . . In the beginning Hopkins stated both sides of the issue . . . but as Hull more and more made himself felt — Hopkins finally said to Stimson that he disagreed with him in his conclusions. So Stimson said, "This is just fighting brutality with brutality."
>
> So Hopkins said to him, "Well, look, do you mean to say that

* Stimson in his diary called Hull "as bitter as Morgenthau."

if we stopped all production of steel in Germany that that would be a brutal thing to do?" . . .

I came away with a very clear picture that Hull . . . is approaching this thing with the same viewpoint that I have. . . . He said . . . : "This Nazism is down in the German People a thousand miles deep and you have just got to uproot it, and you can't do it by just shooting a few people." . . .

Stimson didn't even seem to like that and he went into a long legal discussion of how you would have to have legal proceedings before you shot the people. . . . Well, Hull doesn't want to wait; he just wants to shoot them all at dawn.

The three Cabinet members could agree only to submit separate memoranda to Roosevelt and to see him together the next afternoon at four. "That was most encouraging," Morgenthau told Hopkins over the telephone. " . . . I wanted to get up and kiss Cordell."

"You probably knew," Hopkins replied, ". . . what you were going to get from the other fellow [Stimson]. My God! He was terrible. . . . Henry, . . . it hurts him so to think of the nonuse of property. . . . He's grown up in that school so long that property . . . becomes so sacred. . . . Do you think he disagrees with us so sharply? . . . I think it's fruitless to talk with him any more. . . . And . . . I feel confident . . . about where the President is going to land."

So did Morgenthau, who believed that Roosevelt would blow up if Stimson were to say to him, as he had to the others, that "kindness and Christianity" would have to play a part in the reconstruction of Germany. What Stimson really wanted, Morgenthau suggested to Hopkins, was for Germany to serve as a buffer to the Soviet Union. Here Morgenthau misread the Secretary of War, for Stimson was less worried about the implications of the Morgenthau Plan for Russia than about its implications for the future economy of Europe and ultimate rehabilitation of Germany. Yet if Morgenthau had understood Stimson exactly, he would have opposed him nonetheless.

Politely but vehemently, Stimson attacked the Morgenthau Plan in his memorandum for Roosevelt:

I cannot conceive of such a proposition being either possible or effective, and I can see enormous general evils coming from an attempt to so treat it. During the past eighty years of European history this portion* of Germany was one of the most important sources of the raw materials upon which the industrial and economic livelihood of Europe was based. Upon the production which came from the raw materials of this region during those years, the commerce of Europe was very largely predicated. Upon that production Germany became the largest sources of supply to no less than ten European countries. . . . The production of these materials from this region could not be sealed up and obliterated . . . without manifestly causing a great dislocation to the trade upon which Europe has lived. . . .

I cannot treat as realistic the suggestion that such an area in the present economic condition of the world can be turned into a . . . "ghost territory." . . .

I can conceive of endeavoring to meet the misuse which Germany has recently made of this production by wise systems of control or trusteeship or even transfers of ownership to other nations. But I cannot conceive of turning such a gift of nature into a dust heap.

War is destruction. This war more than any previous war has caused gigantic destruction. The need for the recuperative benefits of productivity is more evident now than ever before. . . . Moreover speed of reconstruction is of great importance if we hope to avoid dangerous convulsions in Europe.

We contemplate the transfer from Germany of ownership of East Prussia, Upper Silesia, Alsace and Lorraine (each of them except the first containing raw materials of importance) together with the imposition of general economic controls. We are also considering the wisdom of a possible partition of Germany into north and south sections, as well as the creation of an internationalized state in the Ruhr. With such precautions, or indeed with only some of them, it certainly should not be necessary for us to obliterate all industrial productivity in the Ruhr area. . . .

Nor can I agree that it should be one of our purposes to hold the German population "to a subsistence level" if this means the edge of poverty. This would mean condemning the German people to a condition of servitude in which, no matter how hard or how effectively a man worked, he could not materially increase his economic condition in the world. Such a program would . . . create tensions and resentments far outweighing any immediate ad-

* The Ruhr and Saar.

vantage of security and would tend to obscure the guilt of the
Nazis and the viciousness of their doctrines and their acts.

By such economic mistakes I cannot but feel that you would also
be poisoning the springs out of which we hope that the future
peace of the world can be maintained.*

At the White House late in the afternoon of September 6,
1944, the two Secretaries repeated their opposing arguments
about the Saar and Ruhr, with Hopkins supporting Morgenthau's position and Hull, in contrast to his behavior on the previous day, moving closer to Stimson's side. It was a "very unsatisfactory meeting," Morgenthau told his staff:

> Stimson started off right away . . . and when Stimson got
> through the President took the same position I have been taking,
> on the Ruhr; namely, that the English would have the advantage of
> the steel business if the Ruhr were closed. . . .
>
> But the President kept saying, "Well, you can do this economic
> thing in six months — a year; there is no particular hurry." I tried
> to explain to him what that was. . . . Then the President went
> into something quite new. He said he was thinking of Dutchess
> County and how it was back in 1810, and how the people lived in
> home-spun wool. He went back to when he was a boy. . . . That
> there is no reason why Germany couldn't go back to 1810, where
> they would be perfectly comfortable but wouldn't have any lux-
> ury. . . . He expounded on that at great length. . . .
>
> What seemed to be in the President's mind was that while he
> wouldn't touch the steel mills right away — he would leave them
> there and sort of decide gradually what would happen to them —
> he had the idea that this thing was good for England, but he didn't
> have the whole picture.
>
> Hopkins, on the other hand, made a very forceful argument
> against there being any steel mills at all, or any other war fac-
> tories. . . .
>
> The unfortunate thing is that the President gave us barely a half
> hour. . . . He certainly gave aid and comfort to Stimson.
>
> On the other hand, when they got on this question of Germany,
> on trade and her position, he turned to Hull and said, "Now, of
> course, Mr. Hull, you and I together, for the last fifteen years,
> have stood for increased trade, and increased prosperity and peace

* Though Morgenthau did not know it, General George Marshall fully agreed
with Stimson.

and . . . I am sure you agree with me that we have got to do that in Germany," and Hull didn't answer him. . . .

But the sad part about this thing is . . . although I pointed out to the President that he had to do this thing right away . . . he just won't give you time enough to talk the thing out. I mean, this thing is a matter of hours. . . . I said, "This is the directive which is enforced by the Combined Chiefs of Staff, on which this Handbook is based, and this directive is still in existence."

But the next day Morgenthau took heart from Roosevelt's attitude. "I saw the President," the Secretary noted in his Diary, "and before I could say anything, he said, 'Don't be discouraged about yesterday's meeting. . . . The whole question seems to be about closing down the plants, and we have got to do the thing gradually.'

"But the amazing thing was that he should have greeted me the way he did because he must have realized the way I felt and this was most encouraging."

So was a conversation with Cordell Hull on September 8, 1944, which Morgenthau reported in his Diary:

I found him looking very tired and very badly. . . . Hull said that the President had asked him to go to Quebec,* but he told him he couldn't go because he had been working so hard on this South American thing . . . that he was exhausted.

I told him that I was discouraged after the meeting with the President because he seemed to be influenced by Stimson, and Hull just brushed Stimson aside and said that the President wasn't going to listen to Stimson and that I should forget about it. . . .

He said that there were inter-departmental committees on this German business set up in Europe, and they should make a report. . . . I said, "The trouble is, Cordell, the President has never given a directive on how he feels Germany should be treated. . . . The first thing we know we will be in Germany and we will have no policy." He said, "Well, you heard the President say he wants to put the Germans on a soup kitchen diet and Stimson wants to give them luxuries." I said, "I know but I still say the President has got to give out a directive on how to treat Germany." . . . I said

* For Roosevelt's pending conference with Churchill.

that during the next three months the thing in Germany will have to be settled. . . .

Hull said he hoped that the President wouldn't take up the question of the partition of Germany and the economic future of Germany at all at Quebec and just confine the conference to military matters. He said that Russia wouldn't be at the conference and it might get them upset if the matter was discussed. . . . I said . . . that I thought we ought to try to get the President . . . to decide on some kind of statement which would clarify his position in regard to Germany, and Hull thought that we might do that.

Whatever Hull's preferences, the President, Morgenthau believed, would discuss German questions with Churchill at Quebec. So, too, the issues of Lend-Lease during Stage II were bound to arise at their meeting. The Secretary therefore had his staff prepare a set of memoranda — a "Black Book," he called it — on German and British problems. One of them simply restated the Morgenthau Plan. Another contended that "the British could supply all the coal for coking purposes if we lose the coal mines in the Ruhr." Still another held that "the statement that a healthy European economy is dependent upon German industry was never true, nor will it be true in the future. Therefore the treatment to be accorded to Germany should be decided upon without reference to the economic consequences upon the rest of Europe. At the worst, these economic consequences will involve relatively minor disadvantages. . . . At best . . . they will speed up the industrial development of Europe outside of Germany. But any disadvantages will be more than offset by real gains to the political objectives and economic interests of the United Nations as a whole." His staff, Morgenthau said, had done "a perfectly amazingly good job. . . . I should think it would be very useful to the President at Quebec. . . . It is very, very necessary. And out of this thing, what I am hoping is, there will come a directive from the President as to his policy."

At the White House on September 9, 1944, Morgenthau, Stimson, and Hull delivered the papers presenting their several cases for the treatment of Germany. According to Morgenthau's report:

Hopkins brought up the question of partition, and . . . the President . . . said that he is in favor of dividing Germany into three parts. . . . During the discussion Stimson said that we must get along with Russia.

The President kept looking through the book* and wanted to know whether I had the part put in about uniforms and marching, and I said that it was there. The President read out loud . . . "It is a fallacy that Europe needs a strong industrial Germany." The President said, "That is the first time I have seen this stated." He says that everybody seems to disagree on that point, but he said, "I agree with this idea. . . . Furthermore, I believe in an agricultural Germany." (I evidently made a real impression on the President the time he came to my house, and the more I talk to him the more I find that he seems to be coming around to our viewpoint.) . . .

The President put up this question, "Supposing the Russians want to insist on reparations, and the English and the United States don't want any, what happens then?" So I spoke up and said, "Well, my experience with the Russians at Bretton Woods was that they were very intelligent and reasonable, and I think that if the matter is put to them about reparations, that there is a good chance of their going on with us, providing we offer something in lieu thereof."

As a result of this conference, I am very much encouraged and if I could only have a chance to talk to the President alone I think I could get somewhere.

I kept saying, "Don't you want this committee to draft for you a suggestion for the American policy toward Germany?" I said it a couple of times and got nowhere and then Hull said that he had sent some paper on the economic future of Germany to Stimson, and he had not heard from Stimson. Stimson said he didn't know what he was talking about.

Hull just won't get in on the discussion, and just what his game is I don't know. As I came in, the President was asking Hull whether he didn't want to come to Quebec, and Hull said he was too tired. At the beginning of the discussion the President said, "Well, I think there will be two things brought up in Quebec. One is the military and the other is the monetary because Churchill keeps saying he is broke. . . . If they bring up the financial situation, I will want Henry to come up to Quebec." This is the second time he has said that.

---

* The Treasury's set of memoranda.

But Morgenthau was nevertheless surprised by the telegram that reached him on September 12, 1944: "Please be in Quebec by Thursday, 14 September, noon. Roosevelt." The Secretary had never before attended one of the top-level Anglo-American conferences. Now, with Hull absent by his own choice, and with Hopkins temporarily in some disfavor with the President, Morgenthau had his first chance to observe, even to participate in, negotiations between the President and the Prime Minister. In part, those negotiations would pertain to the problems of financing Lend-Lease that fell regularly within the Treasury's domain.

5. Octagon*

His first evening in Quebec Morgenthau attended a state dinner where the President asked him to explain the Treasury's proposals for Germany. As the Secretary wrote in a reminiscing article several years later, "I had barely got under way before low mutters and baleful looks indicated that the Prime Minister was not the most enthusiastic member of my audience. . . . I have never seen him more irascible and vitriolic than he was that night. . . . After I finished my piece he turned loose on me the full flood of his rhetoric, sarcasm and violence. He looked on the Treasury Plan, he said, as he would on chaining himself to a dead German.

"He was slumped in his chair, his language biting, his flow incessant, his manner merciless. I have never had such a verbal lashing in my life.

"The President sat by, saying very little. This was part of his way of managing Churchill. He let the Prime Minister wear himself out attacking me; he used me, so to speak, to draw the venom. Then, when the time came, he could move in with his superb and infectious humor and compose the situation. But I

* For details of the negotiations at the OCTAGON Conference at Quebec about Lend-Lease, see the previous chapter.

went unhappily to bed just the same and spent a sleepless night."

The next morning Lord Cherwell cheered Morgenthau. Churchill's attitude the previous night, Cherwell said, had surprised him; the Prime Minister had not altogether understood what Morgenthau was driving at. Cherwell himself, in contrast, seemed to agree with the Morgenthau Plan, which he and the Secretary discussed prior to their meeting at noon that day with Roosevelt, Churchill, and Eden. Morgenthau described that noon conference in his Diary only a few hours after it ended:

Churchill, turning to Lord Cherwell and myself, said, "Where are the minutes on this matter of the Ruhr?" Then according to our agreement we said that we didn't have them. The reason we didn't have them was because I felt, when I read the minutes which Lord Cherwell had written, that it presented much too weak a case, and I thought that we could get Churchill to go much further. He seemed quite put out that we didn't have the minutes of the previous meeting, and the President said the reason we didn't have them was because Henry interspersed the previous discussion with too many dirty jokes, and that sort of broke the ice. So Churchill broke in and said, "Well, I'll restate it," which he did, and he did it very forcefully and very clearly. Then he suggested that Lord Cherwell and I withdraw and try to do a job on dictating it, which we did. It only took us a few minutes, and we came back up to the room where they were meeting and just calmly walked in. When Churchill read our very short memorandum, he said, "No, this isn't what I want." Then he started to talk and dictate to us, and I said, "I don't know what the rules of the game are, but is there any reason why we can't have a stenographer present? Then you could dictate directly to her." He said, "By all means" and Cherwell went out and got Churchill's secretary and she came in and he began to dictate to her. He dictated the memorandum, which finally stood just the way he dictated it. He dictates extremely well because he is accustomed to doing it when he is writing his books.

While Churchill was dictating, he used the memorandum which I had dictated as a sort of a text.

Roosevelt's important contribution, while Churchill was dictating, was that when he got talking about the metallurgical, chemical and electrical industries, Roosevelt had him insert the very important words "in Germany." What Roosevelt meant — because it came up later — that he didn't have in mind just the Ruhr and the Saar, but he had in mind entire Germany and that the matter we were talking about, namely, the ease with which metallurgical, chemical and electrical industries in Germany can be converted from peace to war, does not only apply to the Ruhr and the Saar, but the whole of Germany, which of course is terribly important.

When Churchill got through, Eden seemed quite shocked at what he heard, and he turned to Churchill and said, "You can't do this. After all, you and I publicly have said quite the opposite. Furthermore, we have a lot of things in the works in London which are quite different." Then Churchill and Eden seemed to have quite a bit of argument about it. Roosevelt took no part in it, and I took a small part and kept throwing things in. Churchill's main argument was what this meant in the way of trade; they would get the export trade of Germany. So Eden said, "How do you know what it is or where it is?" and Churchill answered him quite testily, "Well, we will get it wherever it is." I was quite amazed and shocked at Eden's attitude; in fact, it was so different from the way he talked when we were in London. Finally Churchill said, "Now I hope, Anthony, you're not going to do anything about this with the War Cabinet if you see a chance to present it. . . . After all, the future of my people is at stake, and I when I have to choose between my people and the German people, I am going to choose my people." Churchill got quite nasty with Eden and I understand from the President that all the rest of the day Eden was not at all helpful. The President was quite disappointed.

Of course the fact that Churchill has dictated this himself strengthens the whole matter tremendously. Naturally, I am terrifically happy over it as we got just what we started out to get.

So Morgenthau had, for Churchill's dictated memorandum, dated September 15, 1944, and initialed by the President and the Prime Minister, expressed a stern view toward Germany:

"At the conference between the President and the Prime Minister upon the best measures to prevent renewed rearmament by Germany, it was felt that an essential feature was the future disposition of the Ruhr and the Saar.

"The ease with which the metallurgical, chemical and electrical industries in Germany can be converted from peace to war has already been impressed upon us by bitter experience. It must also be remembered that the Germans have devastated a large portion of the industries of Russia and of other neighboring Allies, and it is only in accordance with justice that these injured countries should be entitled to remove the machinery they require in order to repair the losses they have suffered. The industries referred to in the Ruhr and in the Saar would therefore be necessarily put out of action and closed down. It was felt that the two districts should be put under somebody under the world organization which would supervise the dismantling of these industries and make sure that they were not started up again by some subterfuge.

"The program for eliminating the war-making industries in the Ruhr and in the Saar is looking forward to converting Germany into a country primarily agricultural and pastoral in its character."

At Roosevelt's invitation, Morgenthau returned for an evening conference that day. According to the Secretary's account in his Diary immediately thereafter:

"I got in about 6:00 and stayed until after 7:30. I tried several times to get up to go because I thought the President wanted to rest, but he evidently just wanted to sit and talk. We haven't had a talk like this since almost going back to the time when he was governor. He was completely relaxed, and the conversation was entirely on the week's work.

"While I was waiting for the President . . . I was sitting there talking with Grace Tully and Admiral Leahy. . . . He said that they had only settled that afternoon what part of Germany the English would go into, and what part the USA would go into. In the morning when I arrived at 12:00 the President was sitting alone in his room with three different colored pencils and a map of Europe, and he then and there sketched out where he wanted to go and where he wanted the English to go. . . . He had before him a map of the Combined Chiefs of Staff, which he said was terrible. According to Admiral Leahy, this afternoon the President showed Churchill his map and got what he wanted. . . . Leahy . . . was very happy because he said that the English were going to occupy the Ruhr and the Saar and they would have to carry this thing out.*

"Late in the afternoon in my discussion with the President, to

---

* The United States would occupy the southern zone, contrary to Roosevelt's earlier preferences at Teheran.

my surprise he told me that Leahy had been favorable to my plan. The President said that he had withheld bringing up this question of where our armies should go because he wanted to get Churchill in a good humor and wanted everything else settled.

"The President was very relaxed and not at all tired. I asked him what he meant about the suggestion of having the United Nations meet at the end of October,* and he said he felt it had taken much too long to bring up the League of Nations after World War I, and he wanted to do this in October. So I said, 'Well, it makes good window dressing for the campaign,' and he said, 'Yes.' "

Back in Washington, Morgenthau told his staff that "the thing up at Quebec . . . was unbelievably good. . . . As far as I went personally, it was the high spot of my whole career in the Government. . . . And the thing that attracted Churchill the most was a suggestion that they would get the German export business that is the bait that he bit and swallowed and got hooked so deep that he couldn't . . . cough it up. Of course, the parallel all through this was the so-called Phase II — Lend-Lease — . . . which was agreed to. . . .† I can't over-emphasize how helpful Lord Cherwell was because he would advise me how to handle Churchill. . . . Roosevelt was very firm through the whole thing, and I imagine the reason he sent for me was he had tried this [the Morgenthau Plan] out on Churchill and got nowhere. He then cabled me to come on up."

Herbert Gaston observed that the Quebec memorandum "goes beyond what you proposed making it primarily agricultural and pastoral." Morgenthau said that had been his intention from the time that he had visited England, but the word "pastoral" — "that was Churchill."

Harry White, who had accompanied Morgenthau to Quebec, suggested a month later that Churchill had accepted the Morgenthau Plan as a quid pro quo for American assurances about Stage II of Lend-Lease. Churchill, White recalled, had had difficulty persuading Roosevelt to sign the Lend-Lease document. "What

---

* Later postponed six months.
† See Chapter XX, above.

do you want me to do," Churchill asked at one point, "stand up and beg like Fala?" But Roosevelt had agreed to the document after Churchill's oral consent to Morgenthau's proposals for Germany.

Morgenthau thought White's memory was wrong. At dinner, the Secretary recalled, Churchill had indeed opposed the German plan, but "the next morning he came around, but Mr. Roosevelt wouldn't discuss the Lend-Lease thing until the second morning." The Prime Minister, Morgenthau had reported within a few days of the Quebec meeting, "agreed to the policy on Germany prior to the final drafting" of the memo on Lend-Lease. Still, White believed that in the minds of the British, the German and the Lend-Lease matters were tied together.

Morgenthau recognized then and later that the two questions had had some bearing upon each other at Quebec, but he never thought that he and Churchill had struck a bargain in any direct sense. Further, during the autumn of 1944 he continued to advocate American assistance to Great Britain during Stage II even though Churchill in that time backed away from the agreement on Germany. The Prime Minister then responded both to his own second thoughts and to the pressure on him from Eden, from others in his Cabinet, and from the Parliament. During the same period, Morgenthau was fighting to prevent similar pressures from influencing Roosevelt.

XXII

THE PROBLEM OF GERMANY

1944—1945

THE QUEBEC MEMORANDUM on Germany settled less than Morgenthau at first believed. As he discovered, the language of the agreement needed interpretation. The provision for closing down the industry of the Saar and Ruhr did not necessarily demand the degree of destruction of mines and other installations that Morgenthau had contemplated in earlier comments to his staff. A country "primarily agricultural and pastoral" might remain secondarily industrial. There was no indication of the amount of deindustrialization that Roosevelt and Churchill had in mind. Further, their memorandum did not indicate precisely what territory Germany was to include, whether or in what manner Germany was to be partitioned permanently, if at all, and how those and other objectives were to be reached. Most immediately, the President had yet to approve any directive for the American occupation of Germany, and primary responsibility for the drafting of such a directive still lay with the War Department, just as the State Department retained a primary voice in the formulation of American policy for the period after the occupation. Roosevelt had given Morgenthau and the Treasury a place on the committee concerned with those questions, but in spite of his success at Quebec, the Secretary had by no means committed either Hull or Stimson to his program.

1. Retreat from OCTAGON

Morgenthau reported to the Secretaries of State and War on September 20, 1944. "He did it marvelously," Stimson noted in his Diary, "and without rubbing it in, but it was the narration of a pretty heavy defeat for everything that we had fought for." Where Stimson was saddened, Hull was disgruntled because in his absence Roosevelt had made foreign policy at Quebec. Both, moreover, were resolved to fight to overturn the Quebec memorandum.

That fight entailed a direct confrontation between Morgenthau and Stimson. In his earlier memoranda to the President, the Secretary of War had attacked the Morgenthau Plan for being vengeful toward the Germans and dangerous for the economy of Europe. Morgenthau replied to those criticisms in a memorandum for Roosevelt of September 20, 1944. Stimson's suggestion for leaving the German economy virtually intact, Morgenthau argued, "would permit Germany within a period of fifteen to twenty-five years to become so strong economically, and as a consequence politically and militarily, that she could again be instrumental in bringing to these nations of good will even greater death, horror and destruction than she has caused in this war. It was this same attitude of appeasement that was so fruitful in helping Germany plunge the world into the present war."

Stimson, as Morgenthau interpreted him, labored under misconceptions about the Treasury's program. The Treasury's objective was not punitive; rather, "its purpose is highly humanitarian. . . . The motivating factor is the welfare of human beings throughout the world." Regardless of the nature of the program for Germany, the German people would have a hard time during the several years after their defeat. The very fact of defeat would result in intense suffering. But after a transition of five or ten years, the Treasury program, Morgenthau maintained, would permit the Germans to adjust to a fuller life. More important, outside of Germany the welfare of some two billion people was at stake. During the war Germany had caused the death of more human beings than there were within her own borders, and in another war she would destroy still more if she were permitted to rebuild her army. "The more effective it is in preventing World War III," Morgenthau said of his plan, "the more humanitarian it will be." The Morgenthau Plan, he went on, would not arrest Germany's economic development. Rather, it would channel that development along lines fruitful for peacetime pursuits. The energies that Germans had previously devoted to war would be devoted to social services. Accordingly, there was no need to presume that the Morgenthau Plan would give rise to suffering or bitterness beyond that inherent in defeat itself.

Morgenthau did not write about one foundation for his convictions. His profession, he frequently said, was that of an apple farmer. He had always loved life on the land. More than that, he believed that those engaged in agriculture achieved a contentment that managers and workers in industry could only rarely and incompletely enjoy. He was a Jeffersonian, a devotee of agricultural society as the nearest equivalent to an Eden on earth, as the garden in which men cultivated not only the land but also their souls, from which they reaped their understanding of each other, of community, of human dignity and democratic behavior. In a pastoral country, then, the German people would not only lack the means to embark again on a mission of conquest; they would also find the means to reconstruct themselves. By contrast, Stimson's vision of postwar Germany struck Morgenthau both as menacing to the world and as preventing the reformation of the German spirit.

For his part, Stimson could see the Morgenthau Plan only as a function of Jewish vengeance. Yet there were eminent Christian men, like James B. Conant, who in 1944 supported the plan, and eminent, influential Jews, like Felix Frankfurter, who opposed it. Neither Stimson nor Morgenthau understood the motives of the other, perhaps largely because both were so confident of their own integrity and so zealous in their quest for the allegiance of the President.

Roosevelt, close to Morgenthau at Quebec, soon returned to the ambiguous position he had struck before the Secretary's trip to England. Churchill's change of heart surely influenced the President, as possibly also did the continuing Russian demand for reparations out of current production, which the Morgenthau Plan forbade. Doubtless, too, Stimson's arguments made some mark. But the precipitating factor in the President's new caution about German policy was the public reaction to a series of leaks that divulged the contents of the Morgenthau Plan and of the Quebec Agreement, still officially secret.

In the Washington *Post* on September 21, 1944, Drew Pearson reported on the rift within the Cabinet about the "Handbook" for Germany. His column, based on an unauthorized but informed account, referred to the blistering letter that Roosevelt had written Stimson about that "Handbook." Arthur Krock published a similar story in the *New York Times* on September 22. The next day the *Wall Street Journal* described the main details of the Morgenthau Plan, noting that it was not yet official policy and that there was considerable opposition to it within the Cabinet. On September 24, John Hightower wrote further on the same subject for the Washington *Evening Star* in the first of three articles that provided a remarkably accurate narrative of much of the debate within the Cabinet since Morgenthau's return from England. And Krock on September 29 wrote about the "value of publicity" in a column that announced that the President had returned the responsibility for planning for Germany to the Department of State. Adverse reactions to the Morgenthau Plan, Krock judged, had influenced the President, as had the propaganda of high-ranking Nazis who were spurring the Germans to renewed resistance to the Allied troops by warning them of the Quebec program for the Reich.

Krock's conclusions were only partly true. Goebbels had attacked the Morgenthau Plan on the German radio and in the German press, but the Office of Strategic Services doubted that propaganda any longer made a difference within Germany. Rather, the state of the battle for Europe, and in particular the attenuation of Allied lines of supply just at the time when the

Germans were mounting a counteroffensive, explained the growing difficulties on the Western Front. But some American newspapers had criticized the Morgenthau Plan severely, and while
others had endorsed it, the criticism troubled Roosevelt during
the early weeks of his campaign for a fourth term. Further, his
opponent, Governor Thomas Dewey of New York, not only
attacked the Morgenthau Plan but also blamed it for the intensity of the fighting near the German border.

Morgenthau worried about the effects of the publicity on
Roosevelt. With the President characteristically shy of any unnecessary controversy during a campaign, with the Republicans
condemning the Morgenthau Plan, the Secretary knew, as he put
it to his staff, that he would have to lie low until the election was
over. "This isn't the first time that I have been the whipping boy
for the President," he said, "and I have taken it on taxes again
and again. . . . So don't worry; I can take it. . . . I have not
yet had any indication from the President that he had changed. I
don't agree . . . that he is going to change."

But for the time being, Roosevelt was also not going to associate himself with the Morgenthau Plan. The President dissolved
the Cabinet committee on German policy. At his press conference on September 29, he denied flatly that there had been a
breach within the Cabinet about Germany. In the course of the
denial, he made public a letter he had written Leo Crowley, the
head of the Foreign Economic Administration, instructing him
to work out an economic policy for Germany. On the same day
Roosevelt privately instructed the State Department alone to
"study and report upon the problem" of Germany, and he told
Hull that "no one wants 'complete eradication of German industrial productive capacity in the Ruhr and Saar.'" Further, the
President sent a memorandum to the Secretaries of State, War,
and Treasury that suggested a division of functions in planning
for Germany which restricted the Treasury to questions of
finance.

The President had already told Stimson, according to Stimson's report in his diary, that he did not really intend to make
Germany a purely agricultural country. His motive, Roosevelt

said, was to help pull England out of its postwar depression. Later he said as much to Hull, too. On October 3, 1944, again according to Stimson's diary entry, Roosevelt "grinned and looked naughty and said 'Henry Morgenthau pulled a boner' or an equivalent expression, and said that we really were not apart on that; that he has no intention of turning Germany into an agrarian state and that all he wanted was to save a portion of the proceeds of the Rhur for use by Great Britain which was 'broke.' . . . He got so affirmative to this effect that I warned him that the paper which Churchill had drawn and which he had initialed did contain the proposition of converting Germany 'into a country primarily agricultural and pastoral in its character,' and I read him three sentences. . . . He was frankly staggered by this and said he had no idea how he could have initialed this. . . .

"I told him that in my opinion the most serious danger of the situation was the getting abroad the idea of vengeance instead of preventive punishment and it was the language in the Treasury paper which had alarmed me on this subject. . . . I said throughout the war his leadership had been on a high moral plane. . . . Now during the post-war adjustment 'you must not poison this position.' "

The leaks and the responses to them made a substantial change in the balance of influence within the Cabinet. On the basis of Roosevelt's instructions of September 29, Hull presented a revised State Department plan for Germany that called for postponing a decision about the partition of the country and for destroying only those factories "incapable of conversion to peaceful purposes." While the President replied only indirectly to those proposals, noting that he disliked making "detailed plans for a country which we do not yet occupy," he made no mention whatsoever of the Morgenthau Plan or of its terms in his carefully moderate comments about Germany in a speech of October 21 before the Foreign Policy Association in New York. At that time it no longer seemed, as it had in September, that Germany was about to surrender, and Roosevelt apparently intended to postpone final decisions about German policy for weeks or even months. The President's mood, on the whole encouraging to Hull, weakened without eliminating the influence of the Treasury on the ongoing drafting of a military directive for the occupation of Germany, JCS 1067. All in all, by election day Morgenthau had lost most of the ground he had gained just before and during OCTAGON.

On November 7, with Roosevelt's reelection accomplished, he hoped soon to recoup. But the Treasury influenced the drafting of JCS 1067 primarily in its section on financial matters. To be sure, Morgenthau successfully demanded that McCloy restore to JCS 1067 a sentence stating that "it may generally be assumed in the absence of evidence to the contrary" that any German holding even minor positions in government was a Nazi or Nazi sympathizer. That sentence, as Mortenthau read it, put the burden of proof on the Germans rather than on American military officers. Beyond that Colonel Bernstein, who advanced Morgenthau's views, saw to it that the Treasury's draft of the Financial Directive made explicit the responsibility of the Germans for taxation and public finance. He and others in the Treasury also wrote into the directive orders to the zonal commander, subject only to a veto by the Allied Control Council, that forbade him to establish any general rate of exchange between the Reichsmark and the dollar and other currencies, except for use in the payment of troops and for military accounting. Further, without his specific authorization, no government or private bank or agency could issue bank notes or currency. He could require German authorities to make available Reichsmarks or bank credits free of cost and in amounts sufficient to meet all expenses of the forces of occupation, including the costs of Allied Military Government. He was to prohibit or regulate dealings in private or public securities and real estate and other property. He was to close stock exchanges and insurance companies and similar institutions until he had completed the de-nazification of their personnel. He was to prohibit the payment of military pensions or other emoluments to former members of the Nazi Party or its affiliates. He was to prohibit or regulate all dealings in gold, silver, foreign exchange, and all foreign financial and trade transactions of any kind. He was forbidden to authorize any outlay of German foreign exchange assets for imports, and forbidden to make credits available to the Reichsbank or any other public or private bank or institution except on an emergency basis.

With the completion of the draft of the Financial Directive, Morgenthau felt that he had, for the time being, done all he could to mold occupation policy. After January 1945, he left further negotiations about that subject largely to his subordinates. His own interests, even before that date, had come to focus again on long-range policy for Germany, especially on the State Department's emerging proposals.

2. *To Yalta and Beyond*

During the late fall of 1944, the State Department strengthened its voice in the making of German policy. A new State-War-Navy Coordinating Committee facilitated the cooperation of Cabinet officers of moderate opinions — Stimson, Stettinius, and Secretary of the Navy James Forrestal, who was to announce his disapproval of the "enslavement" of Germans and of the industrial devastation of their country. Charles E. Bohlen, for whom Harry Hopkins arranged an appointment as liaison officer between the State Department and the President, brought intellectual vigor, broad experience with Soviet affairs, and a suspicion of Soviet motives to the preparation of memoranda on Germany. Perhaps most important, the President's apparent indecision encouraged State Department officers to press their objections to the Morgenthau Plan.

They did so emphatically in a draft statement on economic policy submitted to Roosevelt on November 10, 1944. The paper asserted that both Great Britain and the Soviet Union intended to retain much of the existing organization, structure, and

productivity of the German economy. That purpose, the argument continued, would not threaten Britain's export markets. A
conflicting American purpose, however, would endanger tripartite cooperation, while any "sweeping deindustrialization" would
undermine international security programs in Europe. It would
be essential, the State Department concluded, for the occupying
powers to guide the German economy away from autarky but
also to prevent "development of a chaotically unmanageable
economic situation."

Morgenthau's contrasting opinions won timely support on
November 13, 1944, from the Senate Subcommittee on War
Mobilization, of which Harley M. Kilgore of West Virginia was
chairman. "A real disarmament program," the Kilgore Committee then reported, "requires not only the dismantling of all direct
munitions industries but also the dismantling and removal to the
devastated areas of Europe of the primarily indirect munitions industries including the metallurgical and chemical industries."
The report impressed Roosevelt. "Yesterday the President said
that since the Kilgore Report came out," Morgenthau told his
staff on November 16, "as far as he is concerned, what the
public thinks now he doesn't care. He thinks the Kilgore
Report was so wonderful." Roosevelt also told Morgenthau to
examine the draft paper on the German economy which the
State Department had sent to the White House. "I didn't know
anything about it," Morgenthau told Stettinius on November 16,
"but he brought it up and said that this was in the works and he
wanted my advice and wanted me to go over it. . . . Since the
Kilgore Committee and the publicity they got, his attitude on
this whole business is just like lifting a cloud."

Roosevelt's invitation to Morgenthau to review economic policy probably surprised Stettinius, who had gathered from the
President earlier in the day that the draft paper met his general
approval. Now, with the Treasury again a factor, the State Department modified its position. Its "Summary . . . Views on
Economic Treatment of Germany," dated November 22, 1944,
also reflected the President's statement, reported by Stettinius,
that "he was still in a tough mood and . . . is determined to be

tough with Germany." The "Summary . . . Views" called for a "rock-bottom standard of living for the Germans," for transfer of industrial equipment as reparations "limited only by necessity for maintaining a minimum German economy," for the conversion of that economy to peacetime production, for the elimination of those identified with Nazism from high industrial positions, but also for the operation of the economy "as nearly as possible as a unit." There was no mention of deindustralization, and there was a strong reminder of the importance of Germany in the long run to the economic interdependence of the European nations. The two departments were still far apart.*

Nevertheless, Morgenthau liked Stettinius, who had been acting as Secretary of State for several months. Hull, ill and bitter, had deferred resigning only to avoid embarrassing the President before the election. When at last Hull left, Morgenthau supported Stettinius for the vacant office.

In preparation for a meeting with Stettinius at the White House on January 10, 1945, Morgenthau had his staff draw up a memorandum reviewing his position on Germany:

> The more I think of this problem, and the more I read and hear discussions of it, the clearer it seems to me that the real motive of most of those who oppose a weak Germany is not any actual disagreement on these three points. On the contrary, it is simply an expression of fear of Russia and communism. It is the twenty-year-old idea of a "bulwark against Bolshevism" — which was one of the factors which brought this present war down on us. Because the people who hold this view are unwilling (for reasons which, no doubt, they regard as statesmanlike) to come out in the open and lay the real issue on the table, all sorts of smoke screens are thrown up to support the proposition that Germany must be rebuilt. Examples are:
>
> A. The fallacy that Europe needs a strong industrial Germany.
>
> B. The contention that recurring reparations (which would require immediate reconstruction of the German economy) are necessary so that Germany may be made to pay for the destruction she has caused.

* The November 22 draft became part of the material included within the pouch the State Department prepared for Roosevelt to take to Yalta, see below, this section.

C. The naive belief that the removal or destruction of all German war materials and the German armament industry would in itself prevent Germany from waging another war.

D. The illogical assumption that a soft peace would facilitate the growth of democracy in Germany.

E. The fallacy that making Germany a predominately agricultural country, with light industries but no heavy industries, would mean starving Germans. . . .

This thing needs to be dragged out into the open. I feel so deeply about it that I speak strongly. If we don't face it I am just as sure as I can be that we are going to let a lot of hollow and hypocritical propaganda lead us into recreating a strong Germany and making a foe of Russia. I shudder for the sake of our children to think of what will follow.

There is nothing that I can think of that can do more at this moment to engender trust or distrust between the United States and Russia than the position this Government takes on the German problem.

On reflection, the Secretary decided not to submit that statement. As he put it to his staff on returning from the White House: "I decided before I went over not to give him the German thing. The President was very tired . . . and I am awfully glad I did not. We will put this in the . . . pouch. It will be much better. He will be at Hyde Park."

If the Secretary's tactics were subdued, his purpose was not. Prior to a scheduled meeting with the representatives of the State Department, his staff tried to get him to soften his views. "We all feel," White said on January 17, "that it would be easier and helpful if you would in your discussions leave yourself a little vague in the treatment of the coal mines. . . . We think that one of the strongest objections of the other side will be centered on the closing of the coal mines and the elimination of the industry, and they'd pick on that one point and assume that that is indicative or illustrative of your entire program." As he had before, so again Morgenthau said: "I am not going to change on that. There is no use pounding me on it."

With Stettinius and a number of his subordinates, Morgenthau later that day reaffirmed his dedication to his plan for Germany, his belief that that plan would abet the economic recovery of Great Britain, and his hope for a genuine friendship with Russia, to be cemented at the outset by a $10 billion American credit. The meeting proceeded in good temper, but the two departments had reached an impasse on German policy.

The Treasury was at odds, though less bitterly, with the conclusions of the Foreign Economic Administration, to which Roosevelt had referred the question of the German economy. The FEA report to the President of January 10, 1945, urged the control rather than the destruction of German industry. It recommended only that "economic and industrial disarmament" which would do "a minimum of damage to the economic fabric of Europe," but it approved the elimination of some German industries, particularly "any substantial war potential in the aircraft industry." On the matter of the Ruhr, it suggested only further study.

But at the end of January 1945, Morgenthau had yielded in his views toward Germany neither to his colleagues in the Cabinet nor to the arguments of his subordinates. So also, he had conceded nothing to the objections of Churchill, Eden, and Sir John Anderson. Nor was he moved by Russian plans. In conversation with Herbert Gaston, Vladimir Pravdin, a Washington correspondent for TASS, held that the real solution to the German problem was socialism. "They would have large scale industry," Gaston reported to Morgenthau, "operated by the government and would give the Allies a dominating position in directing the industries for years to come." That solution did not satisfy the Secretary, for it left the heavy industry intact, and he feared a renaissance as much in the Russian zone of occupation under socialism as in the British or the American zones under capitalism. In January as in September, for the future containment of Germany, he trusted only the Morgenthau Plan.

But in January Roosevelt was even more reluctant to settle the long-range future of Germany than he had been in October. After his reelection, the President had continued to postpone decision while his subordinates wrangled. Morgenthau's criticisms accompanied the State Department papers that the President took to Yalta, but on his way to that rendezvous, Roosevelt, obviously more tired than he had ever been before, gave no attention whatsoever to the documents in his pouch. And at Yalta, the President approached the German problem in the context of a multiplicity of issues about which the United States, Great Britain, and the Soviet Union disagreed.

In his characteristic way, Roosevelt at Yalta tried to plaster over differences by directing deliberations toward general policies on which the Allies could agree. The President also made some concessions to the Soviet Union, concessions in any event implicit in the military positions and potentialities of the various armies, in return for Russian cooperation on issues important to the United States, including the prosecution of the war against Japan and the establishment of the United Nations. In the circumstances, the Yalta agreements on Germany bore the marks of British, Russian, and American preferences.

Most of the discussion about Germany at Yalta fell to the three foreign ministers, Stettinius, Eden, and Molotov. Their decisions, which their chiefs approved, assigned to the United States, the United Kingdom, and the Soviet Union "supreme authority with respect to Germany." In the exercise of that authority, the three nations were to "take such steps, including the complete disarmament, demilitarization and the dismemberment of Germany as they deem requisite for future peace and security." The ambiguous last phrase, which Eden demanded, left undetermined, subject to future interpretations of the rquirements of peace, the very issues the article raised. Similarly, a long debate among the Big Three about reparations ended inconclusively. They agreed to refer the matter to a three-power commission to meet in Moscow, but the instructions to that group stated that "the Soviet Union and the United States believed that the Reparations Commission should take as a basis of discussion the figure of reparations as 20 billion dollars and fifty per cent of these should go to the Soviet Union." That phraseology left open the question of what proportion of reparations should come from current production. The Soviet figure, however, was so large that current production would have to supply some part of it, contrary to the provisions on reparations in the Morgenthau Plan.

Other agreements on Germany were of less interest to Morgenthau. The Big Three turned over the question of major war criminals to the foreign ministers "for report in due course." Reluctantly, Stalin agreed to permitting France a zone of occupation in Germany which was to be carved out of the area previously assigned to Great Britain and the United States. The French were also to join the other three powers in the Central Control Council in Berlin. There was no agreement about the western boundary of Poland or about the ultimate disposition of the Ruhr and Saar.

On February 12, 1945, Roosevelt, Churchill, and Stalin published an official communiqué about Germany. "It is our inflexible purpose to destroy German militarism and Nazism," they said, "and to insure that Germany will never again be able to disturb the peace of the world. We are determined to disarm and disband all German armed forces; break up for all time the German General Staff . . . remove or destroy all German military equipment; eliminate or control all German industry that could be used for military production; bring all war criminals to just and swift punishment and exact reparation in kind for the destruction wrought by the Germans; wipe out the Nazi party, Nazi laws, organizations and institutions, remove all Nazi and militarist influences from public office and from the cultural and economic life of the German people; and take in harmony such other measures in Germany as may be necessary to the future peace and safety of the world. It is not our purpose to destroy the people of Germany, but only when Nazism and militarism have been extirpated will there be hope for a decent life for Germans, and a place for them in the community of nations."

In Washington again on February 28, 1945, Roosevelt commissioned Stettinius to carry out the political understandings of the Yalta Conference. The assignment of that task to Stettinius, as well as the implications of the public communiqué from Yalta (the detailed agreements were still secret), seemed to Morgenthau to guarantee dominance to the State Department in further planning for Germany. Yet he was not ready to leave the field of controversy, and Roosevelt was not ready to reach any final decisions. The debate about Germany had only entered a new phase.

3. *Two Black Weeks*

"I am anxious to see," Roosevelt wrote Morgenthau and Stimson on March 12, 1945, "that the decisions we reached at the Crimea Conference should . . . be carried forward as expeditiously as possible in conjunction with our Allies. I have, therefore, charged the Secretary of State with the responsibility for implementing the Crimea decisions exclusive . . . of those dealing with purely military matters. . . . Mr. Stettinius will . . . wish to tell you personally of those decisions . . . which are of interest to you in connection with your duties."

"Delighted to cooperate with Mr. Stettinius," as he replied to Roosevelt on March 14, Morgenthau was shaken by the report he received the next day from John J. McCloy. As the Secretary recorded in his Diary:

"McCloy called me up this morning in great excitement and came over to see me. He had gotten a copy of the document on reparations which was agreed to at Yalta, which he feels is terrible, and then another document which he had gotten somehow on the sly which had been prepared in the State Department, and agreed to . . . by the President yesterday. This is a substitute for 1067, and, according to McCloy sets up complete authority for central control of Germany. . . . One of the reasons McCloy was so excited was that . . . Stettinius told the President that the War Department had seen this and agreed to this, which was untrue. . . . Nobody in the War Department had seen it and McCloy feels it's up to Stettinius to tell this to the President. . . .

"It is quite evident that he wanted me to go to this meeting
. . . with Stettinius and raise hell. Well, I am not going to do
it . . . ; it's up to Stimson to take the lead on this thing."

The State Department paper to which McCloy had referred
was a "Draft Directive for the Treatment of Germany," dated
March 10, 1945, which the President had initialed without consulting either the Treasury or War Department. That paper,
following the State Department's interpretations of the Yalta decisions, departed from the thrust of JCS 1067 and from what
Morgenthau later construed to be the meaning of the Yalta
agreements on Germany. The "Draft Directive" did not call for
the dismemberment of Germany. According to its terms, the
inter-Allied control machinery for Germany was to take the
place and assume the functions of the central government of
Germany, and the authority of the Control Council was to be
paramount throughout the Reich. The zones of occupation
would be areas for the enforcement of the Council's decisions
rather than regions in which the zone commanders possessed
much autonomous power. While the "Draft Directive" generally satisfied Morgenthau in its remarks about denazification, its
sections on the German economy did not provide for the destruction of a significant proportion of Germany's heavy industry. Rather, they instructed Allied Military Government to provide "a minimum standard of living for the German people,"
including food, shelter, and medical supplies. The Allies were to
meet the requirements of the occupation forces and of the German people before directing any excess goods and services to restitution and reparations payments. The proposed schedule for
the delivery of reparations permitted Germany to discharge its
obligations within ten years, and the volume and character of
German reparations were to be defined so as to reduce Germany's relative predominance in the capital goods industries and
so as to strengthen and develop those industries in other European countries. Though the memorandum forbade the production or the maintenance of facilities for the manufacture of
aircraft, synthetic oil, synthetic rubber, and light metals, it recommended restraining rather than removing the metals, machin-

ery, and chemical industries, and it ordered the facilitation of German production of coal and light consumer goods.

Besides initialing the directive, Roosevelt, at the State Department's suggestion, on March 15 appointed an Informal Policy Committee on Germany, which Washington quickly called IPCOG. Assistant Secretary of State William L. Clayton held the chairmanship of that committee, on which the other members were John J. McCloy, Harry White, Ralph A. Bard, the Under Secretary of the Navy, and W. H. Fowler of the Foreign Economic Administration. As Morgenthau's representative, White of course examined the "Draft Directive" of March 10, and his description of its contents prompted Morgenthau to "take the lead" he had wanted to relinquish to Stimson in attacking it.

Stimson had seen the President, McCloy reported on March 17, 1945, and told him that he did not want to reinvolve himself in the German issue. He would therefore henceforth interest himself only in seeing that the administration of Germany was militarily possible. Roosevelt, according to McCloy, had then told Stimson not to pay much attention to the State Department's "Draft Directive." Consequently, McCloy was arranging for the War Department to restudy JCS 1067 in the light of the Yalta decisions. The question of how far the occupation authorities went on economic controls was not of interest to the military, McCloy said, but the military did care about being able to carry out effectively whatever program was defined. McCloy promised to examine whatever the Treasury prepared. "This business is all pretty delicate," he said, "because of the relations with the State Department, but I think that now, that in the light of the fact that they went off on a frolic of their own . . . that . . . we've got a right to sulk on it."

"We've got a right to talk," Morgenthau said. ". . . It's damnable, an outrage."

In order to exercise that right, Morgenthau instructed his staff to prepare for his signature a memorandum criticizing the "Draft Directive," especially for its incompatibility with the Yalta agreements and for its economic policy. He was encouraged by his luncheon conversation on March 19 with the Soviet ambassador. As the Secretary put it in his Diary:

"He told me that at Yalta the Russians and the US Government agreed in connection with reparations that the Germans should pay $20 billion over a term of years in kind. I questioned him very closely whether they intended to build up German industries so that they could pay reparations and he said definitely not. . . . I said, 'If Germany needed electric power to produce reparations, would you want us to send electrical machinery into Germany in order to build her power plant?' And he said, 'No.'

"On dismemberment . . . he said that it was agreed that they would dismember Germany, and again England said she hadn't had time to study it. I said that there were some people . . . who believed that in running Germany during the occupational period all occupational zones should be treated alike, and that we should establish a strong central authority. He said, 'What's the use of doing that? If we start to dismember Germany, we might as well start right.' "

Interpreting those remarks to indicate full support of the Morgenthau Plan, the Secretary that afternoon told Harry White to sharpen the tone of the Treasury memo criticizing the "Draft Directive" and to indicate that the Treasury assumed Germany was to be dismembered.

With only insignificant changes from the Secretary's instructions, and with some help with phraseology from McCloy, White on March 20, 1945, produced a memorandum for the State Department and one for the President, both of which Morgenthau signed. "On the basis of decisions made at Yalta of which I have been informed," the memorandum for Stettinius read, "it seems clear that the directive has adopted certain definite views on the most fundamental issues involved in the treatment of Germany, which views are not required by or even implied in the Yalta decisions. I understand that these views were advanced prior to Yalta within the State Department; they are completely opposed to the Treasury's views on these issues; are contrary in major respects to decisions made by this government prior to Yalta; and are opposed in their most important implications to the views which I understood the President holds on Germany." The memo went on then to urge the administrative decentralization rather than integration of Germany, and the elimination of German heavy industry. The industrial provisions in the State Department directive, the Treasury memo held, were "contrary to the Quebec Agreement." Further, the Treasury maintained that "the Yalta decisions clearly did not contemplate that the collection of reparations requires the Allies to take steps designed to rehabilitate and strengthen the German economy." If any decision had been reached to dismember Germany, the memo went on, "or if there is a likelihood that such a decision will be reached, then the directive will . . . undermine this basic policy."

Morgenthau's March 20 memorandum for Roosevelt on the "Draft Directive" restated the Treasury's familiar position on Germany:

> From many conversations that I have had with you, as to how to deal with a defeated Germany, I am confident that this Directive goes absolutely contrary to your views. I would like to call your attention to some of the fundamental points contained in the March 10 directive which seem to me to be contrary to the views you hold and the views that were contained in JCS 1067 which I understand you collaborated on.
>
> (1) *Decentralization of Germany* — it required the Control Council to "utilize centralized instrumentalities for the execution and implementation of its policies to the maximum extent possible" and requires that for this purpose "central German agencies . . . shall be revived or replaced as rapidly as possible."
>
> (2) *Elimination of German Heavy Industry* — it allows Germany to maintain "metal, machinery and chemical industries" with controls on exports; and forbids "aircraft, synthetic oil, synthetic rubber and light metals" industries.
>
> (3) *Control of German Internal Economy* — it states that "a substantial degree of centralized financial and economic control is essential" and requires the Allies to "direct, control and administer" the German economy in order to collect reparations and for other purposes. It requires the Control Council to formulate policies governing "public finance," "prices and wages," "rationing," "international commerce," etc.
>
> Carrying out the above directions would build up a strong cen-

tral German Government and maintain and even strengthen the German economy. You, of course, would know whether or not it was decided at Yalta to move in that direction.

I strongly urge that the directive of March 10 be redrafted in accordance with the three principles indicated below which, in my opinion, reflect your views.

1. We should avoid assuming responsibility for the functioning of the internal German economy and its economic controls. The maintenance and rehabilitation of the German economy is a German problem and should not be undertaken by us in order to collect reparations or for any other reason except the security of the occupying forces.

2. We should aim at the greatest possible contraction of German heavy industry as well as the elimination of her war potential. The occupying forces should accept no responsibility for providing the German people with food and supplies beyond preventing starvation, disease, and such unrest as might interfere with the purposes of the occupation.

3. During the period of military occupation policies in the separate zones should be coordinated through the Control Council, but the actual administration of affairs in Germany should be directed toward the decentralization of the political structure.

McCloy agreed with Morgenthau that the three policies recommended to Roosevelt would clear up the basic confusion. But he reminded Morgenthau of Stimson's opposition to the Quebec Agreement, and he warned Morgenthau, who was about to have luncheon with the President, against getting Roosevelt's signature before the War and State Departments had had a full hearing.

"The President's thought was this," Morgenthau told Undersecretary of State Joseph Grew immediately after luncheon on March 20, "that he'd like something along the lines which I prepared as a draft, if we could come to an agreement. He wants to withdraw this memorandum that he and Ed signed as of March 10 . . . and he wants us to come to an agreement as to what we do from here on. . . . The thought is that this committee of Clayton, White and McCloy should prepare something to take the place of this March 10th memorandum; he had absolutely no recollection of having seen it or signed it."

"Amazing," Grew replied.

Though he did not say so to Grew, Morgenthau was "very low." He was disturbed alike by the President's obviously bad health and by the constant presence in Roosevelt's company of Anna and John Boettiger.* To McCloy that afternoon Morgenthau said:

"This is sort of embarrassing, but, everything is embarrassing. . . . I gave the President the documents we prepared. . . . He read them very carefully. . . . He was in thorough agreement. . . . Boettiger . . . was there . . . to keep me from making my case. Now the thing that Boettiger is talking about so earnestly is that we must regulate prices, we must tell the Germans how much they eat . . . we must tell them how much coal they mine, and all the rest of it. . . . I told Boettiger in front of the President that I had spent four hours with you and Hilldring, . . . and that Hilldring said that . . . as a professional soldier that he was satisfied with 1067 . . . and that General Eisenhower was satisfied. . . . Well, Boettiger kept saying that people down the line didn't understand it, and it wasn't workable, and Winant wouldn't accept it. . . . So we got all kind of mixed up. . . . But the thing ended this way: . . . Boettiger wanted the President to call the three Cabinet members together. And I said, 'No, we have a committee' . . . and this committee should go to work and make recommendations to the three Cabinet members, and then from that to the President. . . . And I told him I didn't want to pull on him what the State Department pulled on us. He [Roosevelt] was perfectly ready to sign that document. . . . I didn't ask him. . . . I stuck by my guns . . . and I did accomplish this — that March 10th is to be cancelled and something new in its place."

Morgenthau had also talked with Roosevelt specifically about German coal production. The President, according to the Secretary's report to McCloy, admitted he had not given that question much thought. He was also, as was Morgenthau, aware that Europe would need some coal from Germany, but again like Morgenthau, he did not want the occupation authorities supervising

* Roosevelt's daughter and her husband.

mining. As the Secretary recalled Roosevelt's statement for Mc-
Cloy, the President had said: "All right, I'll appoint a committee
of three German businessmen to run the coal mines, and we'll
supervise them in Washington. If they don't get out the coal
. . . we'll shoot them."

The Informal Policy Committee on Germany met on March
21, 1945, to begin to formulate a substitute paper for the abandoned "Draft Directive" of March 10. At that meeting Will
Clayton attempted to have IPCOG produce only an interpretation of the directive of March 10, but McCloy demanded a re-
placement. Most of the discussion centered on the Army's insistence on flexibility in military government. On practically every
point the State Department gave way. Only in the last ten minutes of the meeting did the group consider economic matters, too
late for useful discussion.

The next afternoon, McCloy stopped at the Treasury on his
way to the White House. There had been a meeting, he told
Morgenthau, between him and Clayton from which the State
Department had definitely excluded the Treasury. There Mc-
Cloy had seen a State Department paper replying to the Treasury memoranda of March 20. The paper, McCloy thought, was
wholly unfair to the Treasury. The document emerging from
IPCOG, furthermore, reflecting the influence of Will Clayton
and others in the State Department, would come down strongly
in favor of centralization in Germany.

Morgenthau had come to expect from the State Department
the furtive treatment he was receiving. Still later in the afternoon of March 22, 1945, Joseph Grew telephoned to say he was
sending over the State Department's answer to the Treasury
"which I think is going to be good to be used to bring our ideas
together." But while that paper was on its way, Grew went to
the White House to urge Roosevelt to approve the IPCOG
paper advocating centralization in Germany. Morgenthau
would probably never have known what Grew said to the President had not McCloy, who was there at Roosevelt's request, related the story. On his return from the White House, McCloy
on the telephone to Morgenthau said that Roosevelt started out

with the statement that he "thought he had been sold a bill of goods. . . . That is what he said — that there were many elements in this thing that he didn't like. . . . That rather backed the people [from the State Department] off a bit. . . . Then he [Roosevelt] said that he thought there was a little too much emphasis on centralization . . . that it was pitched that way, and that he agreed, however, that there had to be some controls from above on what he called . . . the public services. By that he meant telephones, transportation, and the services necessary to carry those out. . . .

"And the President talked about his experiences in Germany as a boy. Then he went from that into how he would run the thing if he were running it."

"Did he talk about a committee of three," Morgenthau asked.

"Yes," McCloy replied. ". . . A committee of three, and if they didn't behave, he'd take them out and shoot them in the morning.

"Then he said, 'In short, I would say that you have to have these controls, to some extent, but that you should exert them to the minimum extent possible in order to carry out the objectives of your occupation.' . . . He wanted a political decentralization, and . . . he wanted as much economic decentralization as possible, but with the recognition that there would be some necessity for some central administration, but what he kept coming back to were public services. . . . Clayton spoke about the chaotic conditions — the necessity for some controls if we were going to . . . make anything out of this affair at all. . . . Clayton said that he wanted to point out that there would be a very large measure of central administration. . . . The President said maybe so; he said he didn't know. He thought you would have to go in and take a look and see. . . . Then there was a lot of conversation. . . . Then Grew said, 'Well, then I think . . . we're very close. We think . . . you agree generally with the paper that Mr. Stettinius submitted to you.' "

"My God," Morgenthau interrupted.

"And the President said," McCloy continued, " 'Why, yes, I guess so.' Then he caught himself. And he said, 'Oh, you mean the March 10 paper? . . . No, that will have to be rewritten.' "

"Oh," Morgenthau interpolated, "wonderful."

"Yeah," McCloy said. "Then Mr. Clayton said, 'Well, I wonder whether it's desirable to rewrite that. Hadn't we better try a new shot at it? . . . This . . . paper which was prepared at the State Department this morning, Mr. President, . . . I think you will agree with that.' He [Roosevelt] said, 'Well, let me think about it a little bit,' and that was about all he said. . . . Then we adjourned . . . and it was at that point that Grew decided that he thought he had better cancel his appointment with you, because he didn't know just where he did stand . . . and see if we couldn't get together and redraft something that would be suitable in the light of that conversation. But the general tone that the President took was definitely one in which he didn't agree with the strong emphasis upon centralization that runs throughout March 10th."

"I'm a new man," Morgenthau said.

"I would gather," McCloy pointed out, as their conversation continued, "that the President is trying to take the view that there was more control than you would do . . . but a long way off from the tone that the State Department was taking."

"Well," Morgenthau replied, "I don't think that we are apart at all because the control that you people explained to me would take place when General Eisenhower went there. . . . But that's a long way from saying how many grams of food and what price and all the rest of the stuff. I mean that it is one thing to have communications and a railroad, and it is something else to have an OPA."

McCloy wanted Morgenthau to labor under no misunderstanding. The Secretary's statement had reminded him of still other remarks of the President. As McCloy reported it, Roosevelt at one point had said: "I don't want you to eliminate German industry — not at all. . . . I want you to change the character of it, but I don't want you to eliminate it. I'm not for throwing salt into the mines and doing all those things. . . . I want to have German industry maintained to the fullest extent necessary to maintain the Germans so that we don't have the

burden of taking care of them. I think that means a very substantial degree of preservation of the German industry, but I am
very leery of their exports."

In spite of that added information, Morgenthau, as he said, was
"very happy," and particularly grateful to McCloy. "It may
sound silly," the Secretary told McCloy as their conversation
ended, "to say thank you because when I'm treated squarely it is
so unusual that I have to say thank you. . . . It has happened so
rarely in Washington . . . it is something unusual and I do say
thank you. . . . It's a pleasant surprise."

Will Clayton, also tired of intrigue, took the IPCOG directive
on Germany to the Treasury on March 23, 1945, where he, Morgenthau, McCloy, and a group of their subordinates quickly
agreed to endorse, with small revisions, a new War Department
paper, "Summary of U.S. Initial Post-Defeat Policy Relating to
Germany." McCloy had designed that paper to bring the departments together and to incorporate the President's opinions.
Later in the day Roosevelt approved it: "O.K. F.D.R., supersed-
ing the memo of March 10, 1945." Morgenthau, McCloy, and
Clayton also signed it.

"The authority of the Control Council to formulate policy,"
the March 23 memo read, "with respect to matters affecting
Germany as a whole shall be paramount, and its agreed policy
shall be carried out in each zone by the zone commander. In the
absence of such agreed policies, and in matters exclusively affecting his own zone, the zone commander will exercise his authority
in accordance with directives received from his own government."

Going on, the memo reflected what Roosevelt had told Grew
and McCloy on March 22. "The administration of affairs in
Germany," it stated, "should be directed toward the decentralization of the political structure and the development of local responsibility. The German economy shall also be decentralized,
except that to the minimum extent required for carrying out the
purposes set forth herein, the Control Council may permit or
establish central control of . . . essential national public services such as railroads, communications and power; . . . finance

and foreign affairs, and . . . production and distribution of essential commodities."

The memo then continued, rather in the vein of the Morgenthau Plan:

> Controls may be imposed upon the German economy only as may be necessary . . . to carry out programs of industrial disarmament and demilitarization, reparations, and of relief for liberated areas as prescribed by appropriate higher authority and . . . to assure the production and maintenance of goods and services required to meet the needs of the occupying forces and displaced persons in Germany, and essential to prevent starvation or such disease or civil unrest as would endanger the occupying forces. No action shall be taken, in execution of the reparations program or otherwise, which would tend to support basic living standards of Germany on a higher level than that existing in any one of the neighboring United Nations. All economic and financial international transactions, including exports and imports, shall be controlled with the aim of preventing Germany from developing a war potential. . . . Recurrent reparations should not . . . require the rehabilitation or development of German heavy industry and should not foster the dependence of other countries upon the German economy.
>
> In the imposition and maintenance of economic controls, German authorities will to the fullest extent practicable be ordered to proclaim and assume administration of such controls. Thus it should be brought home to the German people that responsibility for the administration of such controls and for any breakdown in those controls, will rest with themselves and their own authorities.

Morgenthau was pleased, too, by provisions relating to the dissolution of the Nazi Party and its affiliated organizations, to the elimination of Nazi and militarist doctrines from German education, and to the repeal of laws of the Hitler regime relating to race, creed, and public opinion. He could see his influence also in the demand that "all members of the Nazi Party who had been more than nominal participants in its activities . . . will be removed from public office and from positions of responsibility in private enterprise." The memo provided further for the arrest and trial of Nazi leaders, for a suitable program of restitution, and for the demobilization of the German army and general staff.

Though the March 23 memorandum preserved much of the Morgenthau Plan, Henry Stimson judged it a "fairly good paper." He and McCloy applauded the initiative left with the zone commanders and the references to considerable centralized economic control. Morgenthau, for his part, accepted that degree of centralization. The March 23 memo, he told his staff, was "the first step toward a kind of peace which I think will last. . . . The fact that they have got this thing out and we got them to . . . change it completely was a very satisfactory thing. . . . We have got a good tough document with decentralization responsibility on the Germans. . . .

"I have never been under such pressure in my life to give way on principles, and I didn't. . . . We stand for something worthwhile. . . . It was one of the most important conferences that I have ever participated in, and it is very encouraging that we had the President to back us up. . . . They tried to get him to change, and they couldn't — the State Department crowd. Sooner or later the President just has to clean his house."

"It's a very good job," McCloy told Morgenthau. "Good progress, great thing, and the Treasury should be given credit for it."

"I'm happier," Morgenthau replied, "than I've been since March 10th."

4. *The Last Evening*

The President had been clear in mind but exhausted in body during his conferences of March 22 and 23. Indeed, he had seemed old and ill since his return from Yalta. As he prepared to leave Washington for a long rest in Warm Springs, Georgia, Morgenthau asked his consent for the project on which some of the Secretary's staff had been working, the publication of a book on Germany written to persuade its readers to support the Morgenthau Plan.

"Since you are going away for a time," Morgenthau wrote Roosevelt on March 23, "and events are moving fast, I should like your permission before you go to get some facts on the German economy ready for publication in book form* when Germany falls.

"The people of this country are going to need information of this nature if they are to understand our policy.

"With your approval, I want to get to work on this at once. It will take several months to get the material ready."

Through Mrs. Roosevelt, the President inquired "why a book now?" When she explained that the Secretary would withhold publication until the war in Europe was over, Roosevelt said: "That's all right. Let him go ahead and make the study." But on reflection, Roosevelt on March 28 asked Morgenthau to delay: "The plan you outlined . . . is laudable in purpose, but I find it difficult to know just what to say. The people of the country are going to need information on the German economy.

"The spirit of the Nation must be given articulate expression. But it's not so easy to say when the Nation will or can speak. Timing will be of the very essence. We must all remember Job's lament that his enemy had not written a book.

"Anyway, we'll have to keep thinking about it."

During the next fortnight, Morgenthau had little chance to think about the book or anything else relating to Germany or other public affairs. His subordinates, to be sure, worked along with their counterparts from the State and War Departments on evolving drafts of JCS 1067, and worked also on plans for the Moscow conference on reparations. But the Secretary had to leave Washington for Florida where his wife Elinor was in the hospital suffering from what he described as "heart trouble." Distraught, he hoped to refurbish his spirits and to explain the

---

* *Germany Is Our Problem* was published in the fall of 1945 by Harper, after Morgenthau had left office, and at a time when American public opinion was moving away from his point of view. Most reviews of the book took positions close to Stimson's.

purpose of his book during the evening he spent at Warm Springs on April 11, 1945, at Roosevelt's invitation. For his Diary, before he went to bed that night, Morgenthau dictated a long account of his visit:

Around 7:30 P.M. Eastern War Time, I called on the President. He had been out for a two-hour drive. When I came in, he was sitting in a chair with his feet up on a very large footstool with a card table drawn up over his legs. He was mixing cocktails.

I was terribly shocked when I saw him, and I found that he had aged terrifically and looked very haggard. His hands shook so that he started to knock the glasses over, and I had to hold each glass as he poured out the cocktail. He had a jar of Russian caviar, and I asked him whether he wanted some. They had eggs and onions to go with it, and I said, "If I remember correctly, Mr. President, you like it plain," and he said, "That's right," so I fixed him some. I noticed that he took two cocktails and then seemed to feel a little bit better. I found his memory bad, and he was constantly confusing names. He hasn't weighed himself so he didn't know whether he had gained weight or not. I have never seen him have so much difficulty transferring himself from his wheelchair to a regular chair, and I was in agony watching him.

I brought him a box of candy, and I said, "That's for the ladies of your house." He said, "Why the ladies? I would like it," and he seemed very much pleased, and after supper he took some.

At supper, the President sat at one end of the table and I sat at the other. There were two ladies on each side. . . . We had veal and noodles for dinner, and then a marvelous chocolate waffle with whipped cream and chocolate sauce, which the President seemed to enjoy very much. . . .

Just before supper, I went into the President's own bedroom and bathroom, and they seemed exactly the same as they had been years ago when I spent several nights at the cottage.

During supper we joked about the early Valkill furniture* with which the cottage is decorated. I carried on a conversation at my end of the table, and the President's hearing seemed so bad that it didn't disturb him. . . .

The President said he would be in Washington on the 19th and up until noon on the 20th.† At first I said that I wouldn't be there, and then I said I would stay until he left and that seemed to please

* Which Mrs. Roosevelt was having manufactured at Hyde Park.
† Before departing for the United Nations Conference in San Francisco.

him. He said, "I have been offered a beautiful apartment by a lady in the top floor of some hotel [in San Francisco], but I am not taking it. I am going there on my train, and at three o'clock in the afternoon I will appear on the stage in my wheelchair, and I will make the speech." Then he made a grimace and clapped his hands and said, "And then they will applaud me, and I will leave and go back on my train, go down to Los Angeles and dump my daughter-in-law, and I will be back in Hyde Park on May first."

Early in the evening he had been very solicitous about Mrs. Morgenthau and he let it slip that he was in touch with some heart doctor — I think he said at the Presbyterian Hospital in New York. . . .

When the President and I started to talk, I said, "Mr. President, I am doing a lot of things in regard to Germany and I want you to know about it. We are having a lot of troubles, and I don't want to be doing these things if it isn't agreeable to you." He didn't say anything, so I went on and said, "You know what happened on that March 10th memorandum on Germany." The President said, "Oh, wasn't that terrible? I had to rewrite the whole thing." So I said, "Yes, it was pretty bad. . . . A lot of the things I am doing really should be done by Leo Crowley and the Foreign Economic Warfare, but the War Department seems to want to work with me."

I told the President that Clay* had called on me and I had asked him what he was going to do about Robert Murphy, and he said that he realized that was one of his headaches. The President said, "Well, what's the matter with Murphy?" And I said . . . 'Murphy was too anxious to collaborate.' †

The President said, "Well, what have you got on your mind?" I said, "In order to break the State Department crowd . . . just the way you broke the crowd of Admirals when you were Assistant Secretary of the Navy, my suggestion is that you make Claude Bowers‡ political adviser to Eisenhower . . ." The President thought that it was a wonderful idea, and so that he wouldn't forget it, I made him write it down. . . .

I then got on to the question of my writing a book, and I showed the President the photostat of the letter he had written to me. . . . The President said, "Where did you get that from? I

---

* General Lucius Clay, who was to be in charge of the American military occupation in Germany.
† With Darlan and the Vichy regime.
‡ Bowers, a perfervid liberal and Democrat, then Ambassador to Chile, in 1932 keynoter of the Democratic National Convention; also a sprightly historian whose biases always showed.

have never seen it before." So I said, "Well, the reason I am bringing it to your attention is because I want to know what it means." He said, "I don't know what it means. . . . Somebody told me you wanted to get a book out right away, and I thought it was a mistake." I said, "No, what I want is to get out a textbook after V-E Day. For example, I would like to write a chapter on how 60 million Germans can feed themselves." He said, "I said they could." . . . I told him that when the book has written I wanted to show it to him, and that I hoped he would write the preface. I told the President that if he didn't write the preface I would like to have Stettinius do it. He said, "I think that's fine. You go ahead and do it. I think it is a grand idea. . . . I have a lot of ideas of my own. I would like to put something in there about my conversations with Dr. Schacht." Then he went on and told me the story about how Dr. Schacht came over here and wept on his desk about his poor country. He said that Schacht came over three or four times saying that the Germans were going broke and they never did. This is a story that I have heard the President tell about three different times, but he seems to enjoy telling it. . . .

I said to the President, "General Hilldring couldn't get in on this reparations matter, and he called me up and asked me to arrange it for him, and I did arrange it. . . . McCloy is away you know." Then the President said, "McCloy is all right now, but he was all wrong about De Gaulle, but I explained things to him and now he has been loyal to me." I said, "I am glad you feel that way." . . . I was glad to hear the President say that because I think some people around town have been trying to poison him against McCloy. . . .

I asked the President if he wanted me to interest myself in the future treatment of Germany. He didn't answer me directly. I said, "Look, Mr. President, I am going to fight hard, and this is what I am fighting for. . . . A weak economy for Germany means that she will be weak politically, and she won't be able to make another war. . . . I have been strong for winning the war, and I want to help win the peace." The President said, "Henry, I am with you 100 per cent." I said, "You may hear things because I am going to fight for this," and he made no comment, but I certainly put him on notice as to what I was going to do. I repeated it two or three times. . . .

I had just about concluded my conversation when the four ladies came in. I asked whether I could use the telephone. . . . Then I came back and said good-bye to the President and his company, and when I left them they were sitting around laughing and chatting, and I must say the President seemed to be happy and enjoying himself.

The next morning he died.

Americans mourned Roosevelt. The faces that lined the streets along the route of his cortege revealed a sorrow greater than any the nation had known since Lincoln's death. The world mourned him, too, and rightly so. Particularly for those who had known him well, nothing ever replaced Roosevelt's spirit, Roosevelt's leadership, Roosevelt's very presence.

For Henry Morgenthau, Jr., the President's death was a catastrophe. He had lost his sponsor, his chief, his closest friend. For years he felt the shock of personal deprivation. From the first, as he suspected immediately, he faced also the lesser loss of the support without which he could no longer effectively pursue his public purposes, his plan for Germany not the least. The evening of April 11 was, in a special sense, the last evening of Morgenthau's public career, as well as the last evening of Franklin Roosevelt's life. After April 11, there remained for Morgenthau as a public figure only a tense and trying epilogue.

XXIII

EPILOGUE: HARRY S TRUMAN
APRIL–JULY 1945

MORGENTHAU, like the others in Roosevelt's Cabinet, scarcely knew Harry S Truman. Like them, too, he could not foresee what his relationship with the new President would be. The Secretary's entire public career had hinged on his friendship with Franklin Roosevelt. Now, bereft by Roosevelt's death, weary after twelve years in Washington, upset by the continuing illness of his wife, Morgenthau hoped to remain in office only until the war in Europe ended and only in order to advance the programs he had nurtured for international monetary cooperation, for economic aid to Great Britain, and for the occupation of Germany. For the months ahead, as in the years behind, he could succeed only if he had the support of the President.

1. President Truman

In his Diary Morgenthau recorded his first conversations with and impressions of President Truman. Immediately after Roosevelt's death on April 12, Truman summoned the Cabinet. "I want every one of you to stay and carry on, and I want to do everything just the way President Roosevelt wanted it," he said. "Nobody said anything," Morgenthau recollected later that day, "so I nodded to Stettinius to say something, and he did. He simply said that we would all be back of him. Then I spoke up and said, 'Mr. Truman, I will do all I can to help, but I want you to be free to call on anyone else in my place.' Then Wickard said that I had expressed his sentiments also."

Two days later Morgenthau called on the President at nine in the morning. As the Secretary recalled that meeting: "He didn't keep me waiting a minute. I went in, and he started to tell me how badly he felt and he said, 'I think I admired Mr. Roosevelt as much as you did.' I said, 'I don't think that's possible. . . . Mr. President, I am ready to help, but I want you to feel that your hands are untied as far as I am concerned.' . . . Then I said, 'I would like to talk to you sometime about Germany. I have some very definite ideas, and I would like to explain them to you and explain the Morgenthau Plan.' He said, 'I would like to know about it.' . . . Truman has a mind of his own. As he took me to the door, he said, 'Now I want you to stay with me,' and I said, 'I will stay just as long as I think I can serve you.' He said, 'When the time comes that you can't, you will hear from me first direct.'

"The man has a lot of nervous energy, and seems to be inclined to make very quick decisions. He was most courteous with me, and made a good impression, but, after all, he is a politician, and what is going on in his head time only will tell."

Time found Morgenthau and Truman of a single mind about aid for China. The Secretary discovered in mid-May that his subordinates had been denying the Chinese gold requested as part of the American obligation under the credit of 1942. "These people own this gold," Morgenthau reminded his assistants. ". . . I think that the Treasury up to this time, has been correct. And I certainly am part and parcel of this policy of slowing down the shipment of gold just as much as we could, because it wasn't good for them, and looking forward to the day they really need the money. And it's there. . . . We have two targets. One is we have to first defeat Japan, and the other target is to liberate China. . . . The Chinese are beginning to fight now. That seems to be fairly well substantiated, and there's a determination to fight, and if we can get these people to fight . . . that means saving lives, many lives, and it's a very expensive investment. . . . I suddenly made up my mind that this was all wrong, . . . particularly when I see that my written word and the promise of Franklin Roosevelt is at stake. . . . There is my written word you can have $200 million worth of gold. . . . That influences me greatly. . . . I don't think we have a leg to stand on. Even if the Chinese weren't fighting . . . they could have this."

On May 16, 1945, T. V. Soong called at the Treasury. "I had a chance to talk this morning with President Truman," Morgenthau said, ". . . and he told me that you had told him that mistakes had been made in the past with regard to the handling of this gold and that you assured him in the future that these mistakes would be corrected.

"I am just back . . . and I would like to write you a letter pointing out the mistakes we think have been made. . . . So there will be no future misunderstanding . . . also pointing out in this letter the steps that we hope will be taken to correct them, we are writing this letter and the rest is up to you. We recognize that the United States Government had made this commitment and we are prepared to carry it out. . . .

"I am pointing out that how you use this gold will have great influence on any future assistance which this government may or may not be prepared to make. . . . We'll be influenced by what you do about the suggestions which I have made about a fund."

Morgenthau's letter of May 16 did just what he had said it would. He also persuaded Joseph Grew, the acting Secretary of State, to send him a letter expressing State Department support for Treasury policy. As for President Truman, who Morgenthau consulted about both the gold and a proposed shipment of cotton which others in Washington opposed, as the Secretary noted in his Diary on May 23, 1945: "I talked to him about cotton for China, and I told him how slow everybody was. . . . He pounded the desk and said, 'What the hell is the matter with these people? Don't they know we have a war on our hands?' "

By early June, at Morgenthau's direction, the gold was on its way to China. The Secretary had been able also to procure trucks and textiles for the Chinese because Truman had given him direct support. He had already discovered how difficult it was to accomplish anything when the President was hostile.

The end of the war in Europe gave a new urgency to Great Britain's economic problems. With the Allied victory in Germany, Lend-Lease entered Stage II, for which Morgenthau had made plans with his American and British colleagues in the months immediately after the Quebec Conference. But Stage II was commencing in May 1945, instead of in January, as Roosevelt and Churchill had hoped it might when they met at Quebec. By May, the American Joint Chiefs of Staff considered the military requirements for Stage II significantly changed from their estimates of five months earlier. The army now held that strategic plans necessitated a reduction in Lend-Lease shipments to Great Britain previously contemplated. Morgenthau agreed that military considerations would govern the allocations of weapons and civilian supplies, but he also felt that the United States had incurred a moral commitment to assist the United Kingdom during Stage II, particularly to help England ease restrictions on civilian consumption and begin to reconvert to a peacetime economy. Further, the Secretary knew that the British were disturbed about their prospects during Stage III, the period to follow the defeat of Japan. As J. M. Keynes had put it, there was need for some new "brain wave" to inspire a plan for American assistance to Great Britain. Pending that "brain wave," the British were deliberately holding back in making or disclosing their plans for postwar economic policy in Europe, for those plans would depend heavily upon the willingness of the United States to strengthen British finances.

While convinced that American contributions toward British prosperity constituted one essential of a stable peace, Morgenthau recognized, as he told President Truman, that the entire Lend-Lease program had to be surveyed and overhauled as soon as possible. For reasons of his own, Truman agreed. As he later recalled, he doubted that Congress would continue Lend-Lease once the fighting was over. Without consulting the Treasury, the President on V-E Day, May 8, 1945, accepted the advice of Leo Crowley of the Foreign Economic Administration and Acting Secretary of State Joseph C. Grew, and signed an order which Roosevelt had approved. It authorized FEA and the State Department "to take joint action to cut back the volume of Lend-Lease supplies." Interpreting the order literally, Crowley immediately "placed an embargo on all shipments to Russia and to other European nations." Soviet protests quickly persuaded Truman to rescind the order, but the British had suffered even more than the Russians. For the benefit of both Allies, the President on May 23 "explained that the order . . . was intended to be not so much a cancellation of shipments as a gradual readjustment to conditions following the collapse of Germany. . . . All allocations provided for by treaty or protocol would be delivered and . . . every commitment would be filled."

Yet Truman chose not to have Morgenthau interpret the commitment to Great Britain, though in the weeks after Quebec the Secretary had been responsible for defining it. "I don't want to give them everything they ask for," Truman told Morgenthau on May 23. "I never have," Morgenthau replied; "in fact, they have complained about it." Morgenthau suggested that a committee representing the Treasury, State Department, and Foreign Economic Administration review Lend-Lease policy for Stage II. Truman agreed to study that suggestion, but he soon rejected it.

While the President was ruminating, Chancellor of the Exchequer Sir John Anderson, in a cable to Morgenthau, expressed his fear that the forthcoming Lend-Lease appropriation would not cover British needs during Stage II. The War Department, Anderson noted, had already indicated to British representatives that the United States was not bound by the principles of the agreement of the previous fall. Morgenthau, who disagreed with that interpetation, could do nothing about it. As he told his staff on May 28, the President had yet to decide who was to handle

Lend-Lease negotiations with the British: "It's a nice mix-up."

The confusion distressed Winston Churchill. "When I met President Roosevelt in Quebec," Churchill cabled Truman on May 28, ". . . we both initialed an agreement about Lend-Lease after the defeat of Germany. In accordance with that agreement a detailed plan was worked out. . . . I now hear that your War Department has told our people in Washington that they are expecting so large a cut in their . . . appropriation for the US Air Corps that supplies to us must be drastically curtailed below the schedule of our requirements as agreed last autumn. These requirements were, of course, subject to subsequent modification in the light of changes in the strategical situation. I am hopeful that our requirements . . . can now be reduced, but the details of the reduction depend upon discussions between our respective Chiefs of Staff, which will not have been completed before 31 May. Meanwhile I hope that your people can be told that the principles your predecessor and I agreed on at Quebec will stand."

Informed of the general content of Churchill's cable, Morgenthau replied that the fault was not his, though he was often blamed. Now he would not intrude without a direct invitation from Truman. "I am waiting for the President," he said on May 29, 1945, "to tell me whether he wants me in on it. . . . I want it in writing and I want it made public. . . . Churchill gets on the floor in Parliament and thanks Lord Keynes for the wonderful job he did, and I never get a line. I'm not going to take it. I was willing to take it from Roosevelt because I was his friend, but I want a little more now."

Truman turned not to Morgenthau but to Judge Fred Vinson, his close friend and now the head of the Office of War Mobilization and Reconversion. During the first week of June, Vinson consulted representatives of the State and War Departments, the Foreign Economic Administration, and the Treasury. They proceeded on the basis of principles entirely different from those established at Quebec. Angry, Morgenthau argued that Truman should tell Churchill that the United States expected to carry out the Quebec agreement on Lend-Lease "just the way I expect you

to carry out other agreements which were made at Quebec." *
The President should say, in effect, that "what you and Mr.
Roosevelt agreed on, bingo, I carry out."

But when the Secretary approached Truman about Stage II,
the President said emphatically: "I am going to take care of
that personally." The State Department, with White House approval, assumed control of planning for Stage III. Morgenthau
felt left out. Even more, he resented what appeared to him to
be the drift of Anglo-American politics in Europe, especially in
Germany.

2. Demise of the Morgenthau Plan

His policies for Germany, Morgenthau liked to believe, had had
the support of Franklin Roosevelt. That support, if ambiguous
at times, had been exhibited, as the Secretary saw it, during his
conversation with Roosevelt the night before he died, and in the
late President's apparent sympathy for the Treasury's suggestions for revising JCS 1067. Truman's position was less clear.
While in his early weeks in office the new President listened cor-
dially to Morgenthau's comments about Germany, he tended to
rely on the State Department and the War Department for
counsel about matters diplomatic or military, and German questions fell primarily into those categories. According to his later
recollections, Truman from the first shared Stimson's views
about Germany, but at the time he did not so inform Morgenthau. Further, the President feigned indecision about the appointment of a new Secretary of State, though he had decided to
replace Stettinius with Jimmy Byrnes, to whom Morgenthau was
openly antagonistic. Early in May, as the war in Germany
reached its end, so did the guarded truce between Truman and
Morgenthau.

* Including, presumably, the agreement on Germany.

"The President asked me to stay after Cabinet," Morgenthau recorded in his Diary on May 4, "and he handed me this chapter [of the book on Germany] . . . and he said that he had read it twice, and for two hours last night he couldn't sleep because he was worrying about it. He said . . . 'I read over the Yalta Agreement again, and Churchill, Stalin and I have to agree on a plan. . . . It's up to me. . . . You have to give me time. . . . I wish you wouldn't do anything about it,' so I said, 'All right. I really have only two aims in life — the first one is to win the war and then to help to win the peace, and . . . I will abide by your request.' "

On May 9 Morgenthau resumed the conversation. As he put it in his Diary, "I got on the Plan for Germany, and I said, 'Mr. President, I realize you don't want me to publish this thing . . . but I have accepted your decision.' He said, '. . . I have got to see Stalin and Churchill, and when I do I want all the bargaining power — all the cards in my hand, and the plan on Germany is one of them. I don't want to play my hand before I see them. . . . I am studying this myself.' . . .

"I said, 'I got the impression you liked my plan,' and he said, 'Yes, by and large, I am for it.' So I said, 'Well, here is the part on agriculture.' I went over the charts with him, and he was amazed when I showed him that Germany was fourth in production on the various important food items. . . . He was very anxious to have this chapter, and he said he would read it and study it. . . .

"I went away with the distinct feeling that the man likes me and has confidence in me."

But painfully, little by little, Morgenthau came to see his distance from the President. In the last week in May 1945, the Secretary criticized the plans formulated by Supreme Court Justice Robert Jackson for the trial of German war criminals. Morgenthau felt that Jackson, absorbed in the niceties of legal procedure, would unduly prolong the work of the Allied tribunal and delay indefinitely any convictions. As Morgenthau put it to French Foreign Minister Bidault on May 22: "The thing that worried me was this Crime Commission. . . . The way the matter was drawn up, I doubted if they could get around to trying these various organizations like the Gestapo and the SS, and getting a conviction before Christmas. . . . By that time all of these organizations would have gone underground and they would have a hard time finding them. . . . I finally said . . . 'My motives are not revenge but one hundred years of peace in Europe.' " To Truman on May 23, 1945, Morgenthau made the same point. The President disagreed. Jackson, he said, would do a good job; as for himself, Truman said: "I don't want to do it the way the English want it without a trial. . . . Even the Russians want to give them a trial."

Bothered by that reply, Morgenthau was even more anxious about the gossip predicting the appointment of Jimmy Byrnes as Secretary of State. On June 1 he asked Truman whether the rumors were true. "I can't get along with him," Morgenthau said, adding that Byrnes was not a good team man and was not expert on foreign affairs. Truman answered by describing his difficulties in completing arrangements for the conference at Potsdam where he was to meet with Stalin and Churchill. "You don't know how difficult the thing has been for me," the President said. "Everybody around here that should know anything about foreign affairs is out." Further, the Democratic leaders considered it dangerous to have Stettinius next in line for succession to the Presidency. They wanted a better party man as Secretary of State, and although they did not insist on Byrnes, Truman was "studying the situation." The gossip about Byrnes, Morgenthau could conclude privately, was not without foundation.

There was nothing evasive about Truman's next refusal of a request by Morgenthau. In mid-June, at the instigation of Jean Monnet and René Pleven, the French Government invited Morgenthau to open an exhibit of War bonds in Paris early in July. "I only want to go," Morgenthau told Acting Secretary of State Joseph Grew, "if it is completely agreeable to the President and the State Department. . . . I'm going to ask the President if I go . . . to let me go up into the Ruhr and the Saar and see what is going on." On June 13, 1945, Morgenthau discussed the proposed trip with Truman. "I saw the President," the Secretary noted in his Diary,

> . . . and asked him if he had received the invitation for me to go to France. He said he had. . . . The President seemed very much distracted and fidgety, and sort of jumped around the room and paced up and down. He said, "I just haven't had time to think this thing through." I said, "Well, the French feel that it would help to teach democracy to their people, and that is important to them." He kept saying, "Just let me read the thing. I want to take it home and read it. I want to think it through." I said, "I have talked to Mr. Grew about it, and they approve." He said, "I know but I have certain things in mind." I asked him if he were going to Paris, and he said, "No."
>
> All I can say is that there is a definite block in his brain on this thing. . . . I said to the President, "I certainly don't want to go without your blessing," and he said, "I don't want you to go without it, and if you do go you will go with my entire blessing." I said, "I think my going could supplement your going," which didn't make any hit at all. . . .
>
> Finally, the President said, "When I make up my mind, I will put all my cards on the table," and I said, "I certainly expect you to do that."

By June 18, 1945, the President had made up his mind. As Morgenthau reported that day in his Diary:

> I had been prepared to make a little speech to him to the effect that my going to France wasn't a matter of life and death. . . . As soon as I came in, the President opened up right on me very direct, and said, "I have been thinking about your going to France . . . and I don't want you to go. I want you to stay here. I don't want you and myself over there at the same time. When I come back you can go any place, any where you want to in September. . . . I won't go to France, I will leave that to you. . . . I have got to work out with Stalin and Churchill a plan for Germany," and I don't know just how he put it, but the idea he conveyed to me was he didn't want me messing around over there at the same time because it might make it difficult for him. I said, "Mr. President, that's all right with me." . . .
>
> During this discussion, he said that he felt like a brother toward me, and he wished I would feel that way towards him, and I said

that I would like to. I said, "Mr. President, about my own affairs you have been wonderful, and you have made my position much easier." He said, "I want to do that. I like to do that." He said that if the time ever comes that we can't get along we will separate company, and I said, "That suits me." He treated me more on a man-to-man equal basis today than he ever had before. He made one remark that didn't make sense. He said, "I have no ambitions, there is nothing I want." I would like to remind him about that two years from now when he begins to run for reelection. I said, "Well, I certainly haven't anything I want except to serve you."

At the end of June the Secretary learned that the President, worried about coal supplies in Europe, had overruled the Treasury's recommendations about German mining. Jean Monnet, Morgenthau recorded in his Diary, had reported that Truman was sending a cable "which is going to set up the production of coal in the Saar and the Ruhr. . . . What they need is another million tons of coal per month which would give a half a ton of coal to every family in France. . . . I certainly want to be informed about what is going on."

That was not to be the case. Early in July Truman joked with Henry Stimson about Roosevelt's reliance on Morgenthau at Quebec. Morgenthau and Baruch, the President said, were alike; "they couldn't keep from meddling in" German questions. It was not they, but Stimson, that Truman wanted at his side at the Potsdam Conference.

On July 5, 1945, Morgenthau sat in his office with Dan Bell and Herbert Gaston, those old reliables who had been with him longer than had any others on the Treasury staff; Henrietta Klotz, his private secretary and friend for more than twenty years; and Edward Greenbaum, his family lawyer and close personal friend for some three decades. They were the first to learn about the Secretary's meeting with Truman, just ended:

I called on the President and said, "Look, Mr. President, the last time I was here you said you felt like a brother to me, and I would like to reciprocate that feeling. . . . I would like to reciprocate that feeling and have an official family talk. . . . You are leaving, and there is all this gossip which has been increasing more and more about my being through, and I would like to raise the question with you before you leave because I am assuming a great responsibility while you are away." He interrupted me and said, "Oh, I am going to say that you are the man in charge* while I am gone." I went right on though and said, "Well, I would like to know whether you want me to stay until V-J Day." He said, "Well, I don't know. I may want a new Secretary of the Treasury." I said, "Well, Mr. President, if you have any doubts in your mind after my record of twelve years here, and after several months with you and when I have given you my loyal support, you ought to know your mind now, and if you don't know it, I want to get out now."

"Well," he said, "let me think this thing over." I said, "Mr. President, from several remarks you have dropped you must have something in your mind. Either you want me or you don't, and you know it now." He said, "I can't make up my mind." I said, "Well, Mr. President, I am going to write you a letter of resignation. . . . Would you like me to stay while you are abroad or would you like to have it take effect immediately?" He said, "I would like you to stay while I am abroad." I said, "Well, I will write you a letter. Do you want me to put in a draft of an answer for you?" And he said, "Yes."

I said, "Do you want me to break in Vinson as my successor while you are gone?" And he said, "Oh, Vinson is going with me on account of Lend-Lease."

He said that he would say publicly that I was staying and I told him that I believed him but unfortunately the public didn't. I told him I was willing to stay until after he came back and he said, "You are rushing it." He repeated that several times. Then I said, "Well, if you don't give it out tonight I will be forced to give it out tomorrow, and I wouldn't like to do that while you are on the high seas," so he said that he would do it tonight.

He said several times . . . that he wanted to think this over, and I said, "Either you want me to stay until V-J Day or you don't. . . . After all, Mr. President, I don't think it is conceited to say that I am at least as good or better as some of the five new people you appointed in the Cabinet, and on some of them I think you definitely made a mistake." He said, "Well, this makes me feel very badly," and I said, "Well, don't feel badly." . . .

I found him very weak and indecisive, but I sensed definitely that he had it in mind that I was on the way out, but he wanted to

* Since there was no Vice President and the new Secretary of State, Byrnes, would be at Potsdam with the President.

choose the time, and I am very glad that my intuition was correct and that I picked the time rather than having him pick the time.

I said to him, "It is unfortunate that you haven't taken anybody from the Treasury with you because we have information nobody else has," and he made no comment. Then I asked him whether he would like to have the Morgenthau Plan with him and he said "Oh, I have read it, and I know everything that is in it, and I think it is very good." Then I said, "Well, once I am a private citizen, you won't have any objection to my giving it out?" And he said, "Oh, no, I am in complete accord with that."

Later on July 5 Morgenthau gave a similar report about his meeting with Truman to others on his staff. "I feel sorry," the Secretary then said, "only on account of the great disturbance it will cause you people, rather than it will cause me, because the disturbance caused me happened when Mr. Roosevelt died; that is when I was disturbed. This doesn't disturb me now. In fact, I am beginning to feel kind of good. . . .

"Nobody, especially after being Secretary of the Treasury for twelve years . . . can take that, and I don't see why I should have to. . . . I couldn't hold my head up and have this man say to me he was uncertain about me. After all, I didn't ask him to appoint me for the next three and one-half years as Secretary of the Treasury. I would have liked to have stayed but I didn't say that to him. I would like to have stayed until the war was won, but I didn't say that to him. . . . It has been a good twelve years, and we've worked hard."

Morgenthau's letter of resignation, dated that same day, July 5, 1945, revealed none of his tension.

The Secretary wrote Truman:

When Franklin D. Roosevelt came to Washington, he asked me to come with him, stating that when he was through we would go back to Dutchess County together. For twelve of the most eventful years in American history I was associated with him, actively participating in meeting the important problems confronting the country both before and during the war.

Immediately after President Roosevelt's death I told you how I felt, and stated that I wanted you to know that your hands were untied as far as I was concerned. You were good enough to say that you needed my help and urged me to remain.

Since then, with your support, I have completed many of the most urgent tasks that were then pending. As I told you this morning, I feel the time has now come when I can appropriately be released from my responsibilities. Accordingly, I now tender my resignation as Secretary of the Treasury. My preference was to have this resignation effective immediately, but since you stated this morning that you wish me to remain until you return from Europe I will, of course, comply with your wishes.

Permit me to express my appreciation of the fine support you have given me since you became President.

I most fervently hope for the great success of your Administration in solving the difficult problems which lie ahead.

Truman's reply, which the President had agreed would accompany the resignation, was drafted in the Treasury and carried the same date. It said that the President was sorry to learn of Morgenthau's decision but grateful that the Secretary would remain in office until the end of the Potsdam Conference. The letter remarked on Morgenthau's long and efficient service in peace and war, and mentioned particularly his work in the formulation and administration of the Federal tax programs which had raised unprecedented revenues, the Treasury's war bond campaign and other financial activities, the Treasury's close cooperation with Allied governments during the war, and Morgenthau's advocacy of the agreements reached at Bretton Woods.

On July 6, the very day of the President's departure from Washington, Truman announced his intention to appoint Fred Vinson to succeed Morgenthau, and when the Secretary called to congratulate him, he learned that Vinson, contrary to Truman's earlier statement, was remaining in Washington while the President went to Europe. Morgenthau therefore saw no reason why he should continue as Secretary of the Treasury. Neither, as it developed, did Truman, who sent Judge Rosenman, one of his special assistants, to urge Morgenthau to depart at once.

What Truman had in mind was to have Vinson in Washington as the senior Cabinet officer during the Potsdam Conference. Aware of this, Morgenthau, who wanted to get out of an uncomfortable situation, prepared another letter to the President along with two replies for Truman to use if he wished. Rosenman had suggested that Truman might want to appoint Morgenthau governor of the International Bank or Director of the International Monetary Fund. The President did not. He merely accepted the immediate resignation that the Secretary cabled him.

It was the last official word that Morgenthau received from the White House. He did not really want a position with the Fund or the Bank, but he would like to have been asked. He later remembered resenting the way Truman had handled the resignation, just as Truman recalled his impatience with Morgenthau. But on Morgenthau's part resentment quickly disappeared. Indeed, in retrospect the four months he spent in Truman's Cabinet seemed to the Secretary trivial, anticlimatic. In office and out, Morgenthau thought of the President of the United States as Franklin Roosevelt. The twelve eventful years, the twelve good years, had ended when Roosevelt died. Roosevelt had made possible Morgenthau's participation in those years, Morgenthau's contributions to the New Deal and to the war. Roosevelt had imbued those years.

The Secretary's last annual report emphasized the policies naturally related to the Treasury — policies pertaining to taxation, finance, and the domestic and international management of money. Those were important, of course, but in looking back over the whole record, Morgenthau twenty years later cared much more about what he had accomplished for the least privileged Americans, the beneficiaries of New Deal housing, relief, and farm loan policies. So it was that in memory the sharp differences he had had with Henry Wallace and Harry Hopkins seemed less important than their common concern and common effort, under Roosevelt, to lift the distress of the bankrupt farmer and unemployed laborer. So it was that Morgenthau always rather enjoyed recalling the ways in which Hopkins, after spending too fast, had made him the cooperative victim in the "squeeze plays" that produced new funds to provide more help for men and women needing it. "I took a lot from Hopkins," Morgenthau said in one moment of reflection, "with cherries, too, and Franklin didn't help any; Franklin would never call a proper conference on unemployment, though I begged him to a dozen times. Harry had a tough job, and Harry down at the bottom was all right; he was a New Dealer and so was I and there weren't many of us and we didn't get much thanks."

So, too, Morgenthau liked to remember his struggles to discipline the great corporations, especially those engaged in banking and finance. "They were selfish," he said. "They put themselves above the interests of the people and the interests of the country. . . . The only flag they followed was their own gain. Franklin and I moved the money capital from London and Wall Street to Washington, and they hated us for it, and I'm proud of it. Business should make profits, and government should be glad when business does, and that's why I was for a balanced budget no matter what the economists had to say, but the budget wasn't the important issue. The important issue was who governs, and the New Deal made the government govern American banking and monetary affairs, and I'm proud of my part in bringing that about."

Even more, Morgenthau drew retrospective satisfaction from his role in assisting the victims of Nazi aggression, in preparing the United States for war, and in assisting the prosecution of the war. "If Hitler had won," he said, "there wouldn't be any democracy anywhere, here or in England or in Europe. We were all too weak; we were all too slow to wake up. And then we had to move fast, and the United States had to supply all the armies that fought the Axis. It was unbelievable. I don't know how we did it. I don't think we'll ever have time enough to do it again. But we did do it. And Franklin gave me a chance to do a lot of it, to stick my neck out and be the whipping boy if I failed. And we got the airplanes produced, and the goods to Churchill, and Lend-Lease; and none of them, not the English or the Russians or the Chinese could have fought without us, and we didn't get much thanks after it was over. But it was worth it, more than worth it. We've got problems now [1965] but none of them is as bad as the Nazi threat. I had an opportunity, thanks to Franklin, to help beat back that threat, and it was the greatest thing in my life. Sure, we made mistakes, but the greatest mistake would have been to lose, and we won, and I don't need any decorations, any orders of the garter or the red star, because we did win, and if we hadn't, there wouldn't be anything worthwhile left. I was lucky. Franklin gave me the chance to help in the most important job this country's had to do in this century — beating the Nazis, demolishing Nazism."

His record in office, the Secretary often said, could speak for itself. He had kept the evidence, his Diary. He was prepared to "let the chips fall where they may." He knew what his critics thought — that he had been too orthodox in fiscal policy, that some of his subordinates had been communists, that he had been too harsh toward Germany. He disagreed. He also thought his critics missed the major points — the central significance of the New Deal's large domestic policies, and of victory in the second World War.

When he left office, Morgenthau stood fast to the root ideals of his early manhood. The source of the good life, he believed, was the land. The purpose of the good life was helping those who needed help. The land and the people were the important things, the things he cared about. He did not think he knew the secrets of the universe, but he did think he knew good from evil, and he believed the land and people good.

He was a farmer, a reformer, a democrat, one of the children of American plenty whose spirits transcended the material advantages of their personal inheritances. With another man of wealth and independence and high purpose he tried, to the exhausting limits of his energy and determination, to make the world a better place in which all men could live a better life. In that, he felt, he had succeeded. More important, he knew he had tried without stint or let or compromise.

He knew Roosevelt had trusted him and that he had never breached that trust. The long, close, rewarding relationship with Franklin and Eleanor Roosevelt gave Elinor and Henry Morgenthau, both at the time and in the Secretary's recollection, a measure of satisfaction and comfort that no one could adequately describe, no one could overestimate. For Morgenthau, public life had been a long adventure in collaboration and friendship with the Roosevelts. He rejoiced in having had the chance for service, but still more, in having had the confidence and companionship of the President. For Morgenthau, when the scales were balanced, that mortal friendship, no matter what the other weights, was immortality enough.

A NOTE ON SOURCES

INDEX

A NOTE ON SOURCES

THE MORGENTHAU DIARIES, more than eight hundred bound volumes, are in the Franklin D. Roosevelt Library in Hyde Park, New York. They are not diaries in the ordinary meaning of the word, though they occasionally include reflective observations. Rather, the Morgenthau Diaries consist primarily of papers that crossed the Secretary's desk, letters and memoranda, incoming and outgoing; of verbatim transcripts of meetings held in his office; of stenographic transcripts or summaries of other meetings that he or his subordinates attended; and of verbatim transcripts of conversations he had on the telephone. The Diaries are supplemented by other of his papers, by scrapbooks, by transcripts of his press conferences, by personal diaries covering his years at Exeter and thereafter, his service in Albany and in the Farm Credit Administration, and certain of his meetings with the President. Besides those materials, I have consulted the Franklin D. Roosevelt Papers, the Harry Hopkins Papers, and some lesser collections at Hyde Park, as well as the Henry L. Stimson Papers in the Yale University Library. I have relied, too, on sundry newspapers and magazines, and much more on the often impressive works of historians of Roosevelt, the New Deal, and World War II, as well as memoirs of the New Dealers themselves. All those sources are cited extensively in the notes for the three volumes: *From the Morgenthau Diaries: Years of Crisis, Years of Urgency, Years of War* (Boston, 1959, 1965, 1967).

This volume, as its table of contents indicates, follows the basic organization of its three predecessors, though whole chapters and whole sections of chapters of the previous work are here omitted, and others without exception are condensed. Still, the reader of this volume who wants to find the origin of a particular quotation or statement can do so by consulting first the text of the three-volume work and then the notes on the text. Accordingly, this volume includes no notes or bibliography.

Elsewhere I have indicated my gratitude to various colleagues who advised me in my work, but here I want to acknowledge again my special debt to Herman Kahn, Elizabeth Drewry and the staff of the Franklin D. Roosevelt Library; to Arthur Schlesinger, Jr., and Craig Wylie; and, for their support in time, funds or facilities, to the Aspen Institute for Humanistic Studies, the Massachusetts Institute of Technology, the Social Science Research Council, and Yale University. Individuals or corporations, they should not be held responsible for any aspect of this book but only for their generosity to me. Most important, there would have been no book without the goodwill of Henry Morgenthau, Jr., and his family.

INDEX

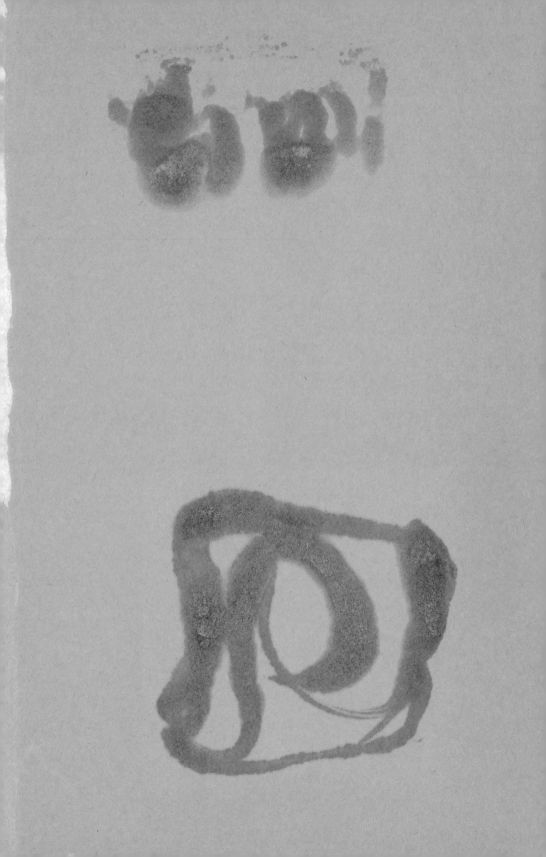

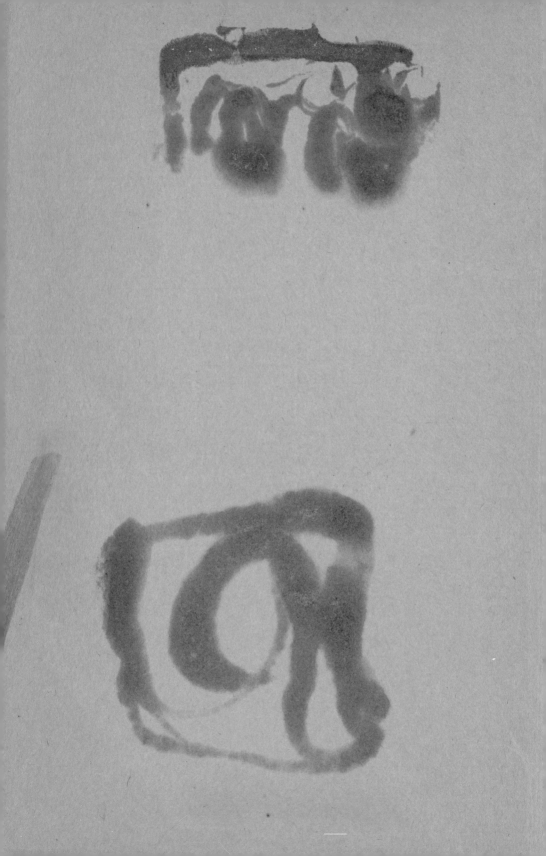